Encyclopedia of the Underground Railroad

Encyclopedia of the Underground Railroad

J. Blaine Hudson

McFarland & Company, Inc., Publishers
Jefferson, North Carolina, and London

Library of Congress Cataloguing-in-Publication Data

Hudson, J. Blaine.
Encyclopedia of the underground railroad / J. Blaine Hudson.
p.   cm.
Includes bibliographical references and index.

ISBN-13: 978-0-7864-2459-7
(illustrated case binding : 50# alkaline paper) ∞

1. Underground railroad — Encyclopedias.
2. Fugitive slaves — United States — History — Encyclopedias.
3. Slavery — United States — History — Encyclopedias.
I. Title
E450H855   2006   973.7'115 — dc22   2005037582

British Library cataloguing data are available

Manufactured in the United States of America

*McFarland & Company, Inc., Publishers
Box 611, Jefferson, North Carolina 28640
www.mcfarlandpub.com*

To my family,
lost and found, living and dead

Contents

Introduction

Throughout the African diaspora, persons of African birth or ancestry challenged the practice of slave trade and the institution of slavery. However, while the determination to regain or achieve freedom was a constant, the strategies employed were highly adaptive to — and the likelihood that those strategies would be successful was highly dependent on — the specific realities of enslavement in a given time and place.

In the Caribbean and Latin America, enslaved Africans greatly outnumbered whites, and the weight of superior numbers often compensated for decisive European advantages in weaponry. Not surprisingly, large-scale revolts and, where geography permitted, the formation of autonomous "maroon" settlements in remote areas were relatively common. In contrast, Africans enslaved in colonial America and later the antebellum United States, except in rare cases, were themselves a numerical minority. Being outnumbered and outgunned, they could not overcome the power of whites through violent means. Being defined as property, they had no standing under American law and could not free themselves legally. Thus, in the United States, two strategies proved most effective in challenging slavery:

• the antislavery or abolitionist movement, i.e., the political struggle against the "peculiar institution" that brought together whites opposed to slavery and free people of color working to liberate their kinsmen; and

• running away from slavery, i.e., crossing the political and geographic boundary between slave and free territory was, despite the obvious risks, a more practical and effective strategy of resistance.

The first strategy embodied the efforts of those who were not enslaved to free those who were. The second embodied the efforts of those who were enslaved to free themselves. The history of fugitive slaves and the Underground Railroad weaves together these two historical narratives.

The first Africans were brought to colonial America in August 1619, and slave escapes were recorded as early as the 1640s. With slavery legal in all British North American colonies, freedom seekers from the Carolinas and later Georgia tended to flee "south" instead of "north" in hopes of finding freedom in Spanish Florida. Runaways from Virginia tended to flee "north" or "west" to the often friendly Native American societies living beyond the frontier. In most regions, flight to the swamps, the mountains or simply the backcountry — and the consequent formation of maroon settlements — was not uncommon. As a result, by the 1700s, fugitive slave notices became a standard feature in early American newspapers. Further, by employing this established strategy of resistance in the confusion of the American Revolution, an estimated 100,000 African Americans escaped from bondage, fleeing to Canada, or to the

Spanish or French colonies, or forming short-lived maroon colonies in Georgia, North Carolina, New York, New Jersey and Virginia.

The division of the United States into free and slave zones in the generation following independence created a border within the country and the need to define the legal meaning of that border as it related to fugitive slaves. As a consequence, Article IV, section 2.3 of the U.S. Constitution makes a crucial distinction between fugitives from justice and fugitive slaves—specifically, that a fugitive slave retained slave status even in free territory and was subject to recapture by his or her owner. To enforce this provision, the Second Congress passed "An act respecting fugitives from justice, and persons escaping from the service of their masters" on February 12, 1793, authorizing the arrest or seizure of fugitives and empowered "any magistrate of a county, city or town" to rule on the matter. Still, however precise its language and however severe its penalties for those who assisted freedom seekers, the law did little or nothing to deter escape attempts by freedom seekers themselves.

As individuals, fugitive slaves were a unique subset of the total population of enslaved African Americans. According to Franklin and Schweninger (1999) and Hudson (2002), freedom seekers were predominantly young and male and more likely to be racially mixed than African Americans in the aggregate. Fugitive slaves escaped in reaction to or to avoid brutality, sexual exploitation, separation from family — and in response to broken promises, or simply because freedom beckoned. They escaped alone or in small groups, with women and children more likely to flee in the 1850s than before — and, in most cases, with little or no assistance. Slave escapes occurred more frequently on the weekends and, by the 1840s, in the cooler months. In planning their journeys, freedom seekers relied on

shreds of information gleaned from travel or travelers, from the "slave grapevine" and occasionally from friends of the fugitive operating covertly in the South. In preparation for flight, they hoarded or stole clothes, food, money and, if possible, weapons. In more elaborate escapes, fugitives often concocted deceptions and employed various disguises. Then they fled toward free territory, e.g., Pennsylvania, the Ohio River area, Mexico, or Native American territory, converging on towns and urban centers with significant black populations or cities farther north with significant antislavery factions.

From the Revolutionary period through the Civil War, slave escapes were more than a trickle, but less than a flood. While many escapes from the deep southern interior were acts of protest that did not have freedom as their ultimate goal, those that did followed certain broadly predictable and similar patterns. Of course, the first task faced by freedom seekers was escaping slave territory. In some cases, help could be found in the South itself. For example, there were counties in Mississippi where enslaved African Americans were two-thirds of the population, but other counties in which only one percent of the population was black. Similar demographic and political patterns could be founds in parts of the Carolinas, Georgia, Alabama, Tennessee, and Texas. The whites in these sections of the South were seldom friends to slaveholders and some were occasionally friends to African Americans seeking freedom through flight. Although distance to free soil was a formidable barrier to would-be fugitives, freedom seekers living near the Mississippi River or the Atlantic coast or the Gulf of Mexico did have slightly better odds if they could escape by sea. Of course, in Texas, freedom seekers could flee either to Mexico, the West or the North.

Freedom seekers from or passing through central Tennessee could escape overland, following (or shadowing) more or less the old buffalo traces and trails, and the newer roads that led from northern Tennessee through the Bowling Green, Kentucky, area, past Mammoth Cave and then to north central Kentucky. Alternatively, they could follow the unusual course of the Cumberland River — which loops from Kentucky through Tennessee, then back into Kentucky again, flowing into the Ohio River near Paducah. Fugitive slaves from or passing through the far eastern and far western sections of Tennessee could either follow the Appalachian Mountains and exit in eastern Kentucky or Ohio— or flee west to follow the routes leading from central Tennessee. In the West, escape by the Tennessee or Cumberland rivers into western Kentucky was an attractive prospect to many fugitives, as was escape by steamboat on the Mississippi River.

Escaping slave territory meant crossing a border within the United States. Consequently, the slave-side border states— particularly Missouri, Kentucky, Virginia and Maryland— and the free-side border states— particularly Iowa, Illinois, Indiana, Ohio and Pennsylvania — became a battleground in a decades-long "quiet insurrection" against slavery. Escape routes and corridors converged on crossing points in the borderland between slave and free territory, and then snaked through free territory toward numerous destinations where fugitive slaves could find safe haven or from which they could continue their journey out of the United States altogether.

The most heavily traveled escape routes east of the Appalachians were determined by demography and geography. Even after the emergence and expansion of the "Cotton Kingdom" shifted millions of enslaved African Americans to the Gulf States, large numbers remained in Maryland, Virginia and the Carolinas. Fugitive slaves from these states, who chose not to risk escape through the mountains, followed numerous routes through the East — often linking or leading to settlements of Quakers or concentrations of free people of color. For example, the border counties of Maryland, i.e., Frederick, Carroll, Washington, Hartford and Baltimore, were sources of disproportionately high numbers of fugitive slaves, both from those counties and as escape corridors for fugitives from Virginia and points farther south. With roughly 25,000 free people of color by the 1850s, Baltimore was a key "junction" at which fugitives could receive active or passive assistance — as was Washington, D.C.

Fugitive slaves crossing this border could press on to eastern Pennsylvania and then cross either into New Jersey or proceed to Philadelphia — then to New York City, then to New England and, perhaps, to Canada. Freedom seekers moving through central Pennsylvania could reach Susquehanna County, then move into central New York and then perhaps Canada. Other routes extended north on a fairly direct line to Albany, Rochester, Utica, Syracuse, Oswego and Niagara Falls.

Many of the most famous friends of the fugitive operated in this broad region, including Thomas Garrett, William Still, Harriett Tubman, David Ruggles, Jermain Loguen and Frederick Douglass.

For fugitive slaves seeking refuge in Canada, New England was usually off the beaten track. However, many freedom seekers found their way to New England, particularly before 1850, not as a detour on their journey to Canada, but as a place to live in comparative safety given the strong anti-slavery sentiment that prevailed in large sections of the region. Typically, freedom seekers who reached New England passed first through New York or Philadelphia and were often aided by the vigilance societies operating in those cities. Others arrived by ship from southern ports and entered through major port cities such as New Bedford, Massachusetts ("the fugitive's Gibraltar");

New Haven; Connecticut; Boston; and Portland, Maine.

The likelihood of pursuit and recapture diminished as fugitive slaves moved farther north. Under such conditions, the Underground Railroad seldom "ran underground" in these areas and, at least before 1850, friends of the fugitive operated through local vigilance societies and antislavery networks with a degree of openness impossible in the South, or the border regions or the "lower North." In the 1850s, these local societies orchestrated several highly publicized, although not always successful, rescues of fugitive slaves detained under the Fugitive Slave Act of 1850.

As Wilbur Siebert (1898) noted, more fugitive slaves escaped into the states of the Old Northwest than into any other region of the United States and most were funneled through Kentucky. To reach free territory, these freedom seekers faced several challenges: how to reach the Kentucky "borderland"; how to cross the Ohio River; and how to find sanctuary in the North or Canada. In Kentucky, slave escape routes led to 12 major Ohio River crossing points along the northern border of the state and spaced roughly 50 miles apart — from the Jackson Purchase region of Kentucky in the west to the Appalachians in the east, with major centers in the regions surrounding Louisville; Madison, Indiana; Cincinnati; and Maysville, Kentucky.

Once across the Ohio River, fugitive slaves faced new and still daunting challenges with important regional variations. For example, while extreme southern Illinois would seem a natural escape route for fugitives from far western Kentucky and western Tennessee, this section of Illinois had a reputation for intense hostility to African Americans and was home to relatively few free people of color. As a consequence, southern Illinois was not a particularly attractive escape route for Kentucky fugitives. However, fugitives from slavery in eastern Missouri had better options and several routes through central Illinois that converged ultimately at Chicago.

Several escape corridors traversed Indiana. One extended along the Wabash River in the west. Another extended from the Louisville region northward through central Indiana to Michigan. Still another coiled from the Cincinnati region northward along the eastern borders of the state. However, proslavery sentiment was strong in the southern sections of Indiana and the state became less hospitable to African Americans in general under the domination of the Know-Nothing Party in the 1850s.

Ohio brought together the three elements most attractive to fugitive slaves: the presence of free African American communities; the presence of antislavery whites; and reasonably direct routes from slave to free territory — eventually to Canada, if necessary. For this reason, much as the majority of fugitive slaves in the trans-Appalachian west escaped from or through Kentucky, the majority of these fugitives probably crossed into and passed through some part of Ohio as they continued their long journey to freedom. Well-used escape corridors evolved that connected key centers of antislavery activity, e.g., Cincinnati, Xenia, Columbus, Ashtabula, Sandusky, Cleveland and the Western Reserve (Oberlin). Fugitive slaves could find sanctuary at these and other smaller centers and many remained in Ohio — although, after 1850, freedom seekers were more apt to seek refuge in Canada by crossing Lake Erie or continuing to Detroit.

Not surprisingly, many of the most intrepid friends of the fugitive operated in the trans-Appalachian west, such as Elijah Anderson, Levi Coffin, George DeBaptiste, Calvin Fairbank, Chapman Harris, John Jones, Owen Lovejoy, John Parker, John Rankin, Delia Webster and many others.

Few states west of the Mississippi River were admitted to the Union before the Civil

War and, consequently, few were home either to meaningful numbers of enslaved African Americans or directly involved in the sectional divisions over slavery. Still, there was an African American presence and a connection to the history of freedom seekers. For example, Iowa, in particular, played a key role in the passage of fugitive slaves from Missouri and Kansas as settlement moved westward and the controversy over slavery erupted in Kansas after the passage of the Kansas-Nebraska Act in 1854. African Americans were among the famous trappers, e.g., James Beckworth and Jacob Dodson, and explorers, e.g., York, of the West. Many enslaved African Americans passed through the territories that would become Wyoming, Colorado, Montana, New Mexico and Arizona as they accompanied their owners westward. Many free African Americans migrated westward — and some fugitive slaves followed these wagon routes and trails as well. African Americans also ventured or fled into the mining camps of the West, particularly to California after the Mexican War, and several court cases in that state in the 1850s revolved around the fate of fugitive slaves.

While some fugitives from slavery in the United States sought freedom in the far West, Mexico or the Caribbean, most fled to and hoped to remain in the northern and midwestern states. As noted by Benjamin Quarles (1969), "to the great majority of footloose slaves, the region above the Ohio River had one irresistible attraction Mexico lacked — a substantial black population like themselves in language and outlook." This attraction outweighed the risk of recapture for most fugitive slaves. However, fugitive slaves could find freedom in the North, but never security. Thus, after the passage of the Fugitive Slave Act of 1850, Canada — which had been a long-distance option for freedom seekers for decades — became a much more attractive destination since it removed fugitives from the reach of U.S. law

and the machinations of slave-catchers. By 1850, an estimated 20,000 runaways had settled in Canada and double, perhaps triple, that number would cross the border in the decade before the Civil War.

Freedom seekers had much to gain but also much to lose. To the slave-holding South, each successful slave escape represented an economic loss and a political defeat. Consequently, slaveholders and their agents became increasingly vigilant and aggressive in the 1840s and 1850s. Patrols and other forms of surveillance became commonplace. The temptations created by sizable rewards for the apprehension of freedom seekers spawned a shadowy host of informants and slave catchers. Fugitive slaves who were apprehended faced gruesome punishments and the virtual certainty of being "sold down the river" to the deep southern interior from which the probability of escaping successfully was much lower.

Still, slave escapes did not diminish and, because the Fugitive Slave Act of 1793 was considered inadequate to stem the flow of fugitive slaves and to curb the activities of friends of the fugitive, the call for a stronger, enforceable law was a central slave state demand in the divisive sectional struggle that produced the Compromise of 1850. As a key element of the Compromise, the Fugitive Slave Act of 1850 criminalized active and passive assistance to fugitive slaves. However, in the end, the stronger law promoted what it sought to prevent, i.e., the law stimulated rather than stemmed the tide of slave escapes and, at the same time, deepened sectional divisions and forced friends of the fugitive to intensify and organize their efforts.

By the 1800s, most white Americans had come to expect flights from slavery as inevitable and, hence, predictable acts of resistance, realizing that some enslaved African Americans behaved more like captives than "slaves." Such resistance could not be prevented entirely despite the best efforts of slaveholders, but its effects, as noted, could be limited and controlled through the use of deterrents, careful policing and degree of regional mobilization. However, white Americans who opposed slavery posed a special and profoundly irksome problem in a nation where most whites either supported the "peculiar institution" or were willing to tolerate its existence. This problem became especially acute after the 1831 Nat Turner Revolt when a new and more militant antislavery movement coalesced in the North and Midwest. This new abolitionist movement demanded an immediate end to slavery and expressed the ideals and courage of the many men and women, black and white, who were not themselves enslaved but who chose to challenge the institution of slavery on moral or political grounds. For many, their opposition to slavery extended into the practical arena of assisting fugitive slaves.

By the 1840s, active sympathy for and assistance rendered to fugitive slaves came to be associated with the term "Underground," or "Underground Road," or "Underground Railroad," after the invention of the actual steel railroad — which was coined, according to legend, in roughly 1831 when Tice Davids escaped across the Ohio River at Maysville, Kentucky, and his owner was said to have exclaimed that Davids "must have gone off on an underground road." The term "Underground Railroad," however, has been used for generations without being defined clearly on the basis of historical evidence.

One might debate whether slave escapes were a trickle, a stream or a flood — but slave escapes were an undeniable fact of the colonial and antebellum periods. That some whites and some free African Americans sometimes assisted freedom seekers is also a fact. But do these two interrelated bodies of fact, taken together, "add up" to the existence of an Underground Railroad? In other words, whether there was a true

Underground Railroad raises a related, but different, set of questions. To elaborate, scholarly and popular accounts concerning the Underground Railroad have swung from one extreme interpretation to another over the past century. For example, early studies by William Still (1872), Levi Coffin (1876), and Wilbur Siebert (1898) were consistent with antebellum perceptions of an elaborate, organized and far-flung "conspiracy" to assist fugitive slaves— based and operating primarily in the North. Later scholars such as Gara (1961), to some extent Blockson (1994), and Franklin and Schweninger (1999) argued that such a conspiracy, if it existed at all, was loosely organized — and that the courage and initiative of fugitive slaves themselves, the dedication of free people of color and, finally, the involvement of a relatively small number of antislavery whites were its constitutive elements.

Under the most liberal interpretation, any assistance rendered to fugitive slaves, however random and even passive, constituted the "Underground Railroad." Under the most conservative, nothing short of a far-flung formal organization with a corporate structure would suffice.

The criterion that best fits the historical evidence is decidedly simple: The Underground Road or Railroad emerged when significant local and regional coordination of the efforts of friends of the fugitive was achieved. Deepening divisions over slavery in the late 1840s and through the 1850s were the catalyst that wove isolated local efforts into such a larger network in the border regions and the North. In other words, crossing this critical threshold transformed friends of the fugitive, collectively, into a more organized social movement. However, becoming better organized was not synonymous with becoming an organization, and this movement spawned more formal organizations only in a few sites such as Cincinnati and Philadelphia.

In other words, the Underground Railroad did not exist everywhere. However, by the 1850s, when wholly unaided escaped became more difficult, fugitive slaves in the West were drawn increasingly toward a network of crossroads and crossing points such as Louisville and Maysville, Kentucky; Madison, Indiana; and Cincinnati — and fugitive slaves escaping east of the Appalachians flowed through Pennsylvania to sanctuaries in the mid-Atlantic and New England states. This steady stream of fugitive slaves speaks volumes regarding how African Americans experienced and often responded to slavery. The fact that so many fugitives received some form of assistance also speaks volumes in support of the presence of the Underground Railroad in and near the borderland — at times as an organization, but always as a network, as a "conspiracy of conscience."

Free people of color, i.e., African Americans who were not enslaved, were the bedrock of this movement — the most numerous, reliable and least often acknowledged friends of the fugitive. To elaborate briefly, the number of free people of color grew steadily after the American Revolution as the northern states abolished slavery between 1777 and the 1820s and slavery was barred from the Northwest Territory (1787). For example, by 1800, the black American population had grown to slightly more than one million persons, 11 percent of whom were free. However, by 1830, the black population stood at more than 2,300,000 — 14 percent of whom were free.

Although an increasing number of African Americans were legally free, their status in American society was ambiguous at best. Because of intense racial antagonism, they were treated as outcasts throughout much of the North and West. However, the strength of this antagonism varied regionally and, in the "border and upper south," free people of color were tolerated, grudgingly, as an alien element.

Their presence was also tolerated in much of the "lower north," i.e., the southern sections of Iowa, Illinois, Indiana, Ohio, Pennsylvania and New Jersey, where the racial attitudes of whites were quite similar to those just south of the "border." Finally, in the "upper north" or "Greater New England" region, opposition to slavery was strongest and most uncompromising, and free people of color, although few in number and seldom welcomed enthusiastically, were accepted more readily and even protected.

Fugitive slaves had few reasons to trust their respective fates to whites, given the nature of the slave experience. On the other hand, fugitive slaves and free people of color were bound by race and often family relationships— and, much as freedom seekers often sought help from free African Americans, most free African Americans felt obligated to provide it. Thus, the Underground Railroad ran principally through free black communities and, in the memorable words of historian Benjamin Quarles (1969): "To a Negro abolitionist, few things could be so satisfying as helping a runaway." For this reason, the most effective white friends of the fugitive nearly always worked in collaboration with free people of color.

As friends of the fugitive intensified and organized their efforts in the 1840s and 1850s, Underground Railroad strategies and terminology became more standardized to facilitate communication within and between regions. For example, "assisting" or "enticing slaves to escape" or "harboring fugitive slaves" were the crimes committed typically by friends of the fugitive. The site at which such crimes were often committed was termed a "station" in Underground Railroad parlance. A "station" might be a house, a barn, a church or any structure wherein freedom seekers could find sanctuary and from which they would often be "conducted" (led or transported) to the next "station." The operator or "station-keeper" might be a free person of color or a white antislavery activist. Although most stations were temporary stops on the Underground Railroad, many free African American communities afforded fugitives the rare opportunity to "hide in plain view." In some cases, a free African American community or a community in which blacks and whites worked together was a "station" or junction of sorts—in essence, a cluster of individual stations—where many people were capable of making various arrangements for the short- or long-term concealment of fugitives.

After the passage of the 1850 Fugitive Slave Act, the South's determination to recapture fugitives and, if possible, punish their friends necessitated that those friends become far better organized. Routes of escape became more clearly defined. The means by which fugitives were aided on their journey became more systematic and routine—and, because working together for the benefit of freedom seekers also required effective, although secret, means of communication, a variety of code words and signals evolved. For example:

• Agents: persons who dispensed information, possibly coordinated the planning or plotted the course of an escape.

• Conductors: persons who transported or guided fugitives from slave territory, or across major bodies of water, or through hostile northern territory.

• Freedom Train: Underground Railroad network.

• Gospel Train: Underground Railroad network.

• Heaven: Canada, freedom.

• Packages (e.g., loads of potatoes, parcels, bundles of wool, bushels of wheat): codes for fugitive slaves.

• Preachers: leaders of or speakers for the Underground Railroad, or both.

• Promised Land: Canada, the North, freedom.

• Shepherds: escorts for fugitives, short distance conductors.

• Station Master: keeper of safe-house.

• Stockholder: donor of money, clothing, food, et al.

• "The wind blows from the South today": a warning that slave catchers may be near.

• "A friend with friends": password used to signal arrival of fugitives with Underground Railroad conductor or shepherd.

• "A friend of a friend sent me": identification used by a fugitive slave traveling between stations alone.

Still, it is important to remember that fugitive slaves were in the greatest danger—and most likely to be recaptured—in the South, where they had the least assistance and were forced to depend most on their own courage and good fortune. The danger was only slightly less in the borderland due to its proximity to slave territory, where the assistance of black and white friends of the fugitive could make a decisive difference. However, despite a number of highly publicized (and often highly politicized) fugitive slave rescue cases, the danger grew correspondingly less as freedom seekers moved farther North. As noted perceptively in the national historic site nomination materials for Rokeby House in Vermont:

> The popular conception of the UGRR ... is of brave, white abolitionists taking great risks to transport hotly pursued fugitives in deepest secrecy. As "agents" moved the "dusky strangers" along the "route" from "station" to "station," they were well concealed in secret hiding places ... Yet, the oral tradition of the UGRR ... is more melodrama than history. The key to the popular conception is pursuit. All of the conventions of the popular understanding—the need to operate clandestinely, to communicate in secret, to travel at night, and to create hiding places—arise from the assumption of hot pursuit by a determined, ruthless, and often armed slave catcher. While many fugitives were in precisely such danger in the first days and miles of their escapes, it diminished as they put more and more distance between themselves and the slave south.

Every antebellum state or territory in the United States, particularly those east of the Mississippi River, has at least one existing site that was associated with fugitive slaves or the Underground Railroad. It is important to note that these sites describe neither the routes followed by fugitive slaves nor the full extent of the Underground Railroad network in any given region. They reflect instead what is known of these journeys and the physical structures that have survived a century and a half after the last fugitive slave made his or her desperate break for freedom.

The final question is, fundamentally, one of numbers, and this question can be answered broadly by revisiting and reconstructing the available evidence — and, ultimately, by distinguishing between what evidence is and is not credible. For example, the 1850 and 1860 Census records listed only slightly more than 1,000 fugitive slaves (at large) nationally. However, these numbers are inaccurate for reasons rooted in the politics of the late antebellum period. On one hand, downplaying the number of slave escapes was reassuring to southerners since too many runaways were as unsettling and as intractable a public relations problem as too many mulattoes — and, in these census years, those who controlled the process of census data collection and reporting were decidedly sympathetic to the South. On the other hand, inflating the number of runaways (and thereby magnifying the role of the Underground Railroad) gave southern politicians an effective example of northern meddling in southern affairs and northern lack of respect for southern property rights. Thus, while the likelihood of significant under-counting is considerable, the question remains — by how much?

Oddly enough, the *Congressional Record* confirms some of the older primary sources. As Siebert noted (1898):

In August 1850, Atchison of Kentucky informed the Senate that "depredations to the amount of hundreds of thousands of dollars are committed upon the property of people of the border slave states annually." Pratt, of Maryland, said that not less than $80,000 worth of slaves was lost every year ... Mason, of Virginia, declared that the losses to his state ... were then in excess of $100,000 per year. Butler, of South Carolina, reckoned the annual loss of the southern section at $200,000.

These sources estimated that the South lost $30,000,000 in slave property "through the 100,000 slaves abducted from her" between 1810 and 1850. Perhaps, most telling of all, in the debates surrounding efforts to forestall secession in late 1860 and early 1861 — when southern representatives had nothing to gain from inflating such statistics — many northern states sought to mollify the South by promising to rescind their personal liberty laws and to make a more serious effort to enforce the Fugitive Slave Law of 1850. It was stated in these debates by "Polk, of Missouri," that Kentucky lost $200,000 in slave property annually. These estimates also correspond rather closely to those that can be extrapolated from newspapers, court records, private documents, and other primary sources pertaining to the work of various antislavery and vigilance groups.

Using these figures and using an average price of $300 per enslaved African American (derived from the same sources), the following estimates fit the available historical evidence reasonably well:

Estimated Rate of Slave Escapes, 1810–60

	East	West	Total
Number of Slave Escapes			
1810–1829	24,000	16,000	40,000
Escapes per Year	1,200	800	2,000
1830–1849	30,000	30,000	60,000
Escapes per Year	1,500	1,500	3,000
1850–1860	15,000	20,000	35,000
Escapes per Year	1,500	2,000	3,500
Total (1810–1860)	**69,000**	**66,000**	**135,000**

Note: Figures in the East are based on a reasonably constant flow of fugitives until the overall increase in escapes in the 1850s. Figures for the West reflect the shift of slave population to the Gulf States and the opening of the Texas "market" in the 1830s and 1840s.

The loss of fugitives—and population losses attributable to death and the transfer of significant slave property to the southern interior through domestic slave trade — was more than offset by natural population increase. Thus, it is clear that, while the institution of slavery was being weakened steadily by this slow bleeding, it was in no immediate danger of hemorrhaging to death. However, the economic loss to slaveholders was real and significant. And, perhaps most significant of all, the symbolic meaning of slave escapes in the context of late antebellum sectional divisions created a "multiplier effect," i.e., lending each escape a meaning that transcended numbers and even dollars alone. Because of this multiplier effect, the very human act of fleeing bondage and the very humane act of helping the oppressed challenged the legitimacy and helped erode the foundation of the institution of slavery

As was the case during the American Revolution, the turmoil created by the Civil War added significantly to these numbers. During the conflict, the boundary between slavery and freedom became "fluid" as the Union Army moved into and through Confederate territory and, by mid–1862, the early steps toward general emancipation nullified, for all practical purposes, the Fugitive Slave Act of 1850. Under these conditions, 500,000 or more enslaved African Americans emancipated themselves by the end of the war. Fugitive slaves became, first, refugees and then freedmen — and, later, as free men, many returned to the South wearing Union Army uniforms.

In conclusion, fugitive slaves and the Underground Railroad belong to the evermore distant American past. Yet, as indicated by congressional actions and National Park Service initiatives of the 1990s, the Underground Railroad remains a powerful symbol—a legend with an enduring hold on the American imagination. This legend has one dominant image: desperate and weary fugitive slaves receiving some sort of assistance from well-meaning whites, often Quakers such as Levi Coffin or Thomas Garrett, who followed the biblical injunction: "Thou shalt not deliver unto his master the servant which hath escaped unto thee; he shall dwell with thee ... in that place which he shall choose in one of thy gates where it liketh him best; thou shalt not oppress him" (Deut. 23: 15, 16).

Obviously, there were many such scenes, played out on thousands of occasions.

A history built around this legend is not inaccurate — only incomplete and subtly misleading. There are other images with as much historical validity, if not familiarity. Two are most representative of all: enslaved African Americans escaping alone; and enslaved African Americans being aided by other African Americans. These images embody the struggle against oppression, and their legacy is a powerful affirmation of the humanity and strength of African Americans faced with a type and degree of dehumanization unprecedented in American, if not global, history. This legacy is also a lesson, repeated often in American history, that African Americans and other oppressed people must first help themselves before they can expect any help from others—that constructive changes in racial conditions and race relations never occur until those "who suffer the wrong," in the haunting words of Frederick Douglass, act in their own interests.

Thus, for African Americans, the flight from slavery embodied a willingness to strive for freedom — even if the meaning of freedom was unknowable at first and even if the reality of freedom, in a racial state, proved disappointing at last. That freedom was circumscribed by racial hostility in the regions "north of slavery" did not move African Americans to despair, or to yearn for their old masters and the "security" of bondage. Rather, the vicissitudes of life in the free states and even Canada simply crystallized for freedom seekers a fundamental truth of which free African Americans were already aware: that ending slavery was only the first major battle in the long struggle for true freedom and equality.

Still, the more familiar image is a powerful affirmation of another equally important principle: the ideal of a multiracial democracy. From the time of the American Revolution, the progressive ideals on which this nation was founded have competed with the raw reality of a political economy dominated by one racial (and one gender and class) group. The white Americans who were "practical abolitionists," beyond believing that slavery was wrong or evil, actually helped real — not abstract — African Americans and risked much in the service of this higher ideal. This ideal of multiracial democracy remains the stated, but still unrealized, promise that the United States will become a nation in which racial, ethnic, gender and class differences "make no difference." The legacy of the white Underground Railroad workers is the concrete expression of this ideal in action. In this respect and because of its multiracial composition, the Underground Railroad stands even today as one of the great human rights movements in human history.

FURTHER READING

Blockson, Charles. *Hippocrene Guide to the Underground Railroad.* New York: Hippocrene Books, 1994.

Bordewich, Fergus M. *Bound for Canaan: The Underground Railroad and the War for the Soul of America.* New York: Amistad, 2005.

Buckmaster, Henrietta. *Let My People Go: The Story of the Underground Railroad and the Growth of the Abolition Movement.* Boston: Beacon Press, 1941.

Cockrum, Col. William M. *History of the Underground Railroad, As It Was Conducted by the Antislavery League.* 1915. Reprint, New York: Negro Universities Press, 1969.

Coffin, Levi. *Reminiscences of Levi Coffin.* New York: Augustus M. Kelley, 1876.

Drew, Benjamin. *The Refugee: Or the Narratives of Fugitive Slaves in Canada.* Boston: John P. Jewett, 1856.

Franklin, John H., and Schweninger, Loren. *Runaway Slaves: Rebels on the Plantation.* New York: Oxford University Press, 1999.

Gara, Larry. *The Liberty Line: The Legend of the Underground Railroad.* Lexington: University Press of Kentucky, 1961.

Haviland, Laura S. *A Woman's Life Work.* Cincinnati: Walden and Stowe, 1882.

Hudson, J. Blaine. *Fugitive Slaves and the Underground Railroad in the Kentucky Borderland.* Jefferson, NC: McFarland, 2002.

McDougall, Marion G. *Fugitive Slaves, 1619–1865.* 1891. Reprint, New York, Bergman Publishers, 1967.

Mitchell, William M. *The Under-Ground Railroad.* London: N.P., 1860.

National Historic Landmarks Survey. *Underground Railroad Resources in the United States.* Washington, D.C.: U. S. Department of the Interior, 1998.

Pettit, Eber M. *Sketches in the History of the Underground Railroad.* 1879. Reprint, Freeport, NY: Books for Libraries Press, 1971.

Quarles, Benjamin. *Black Abolitionists.* New York: Oxford University Press, 1969.

Ross, Alexander M. *Recollections and Experiences of an Abolitionist; From 1855 to 1865* Toronto: Rowsell & Hutchinson, 1875.

Siebert, Wilbur H. *The Underground Railroad from Slavery to Freedom.* 1898. Reprint, New York: Russell and Russell, 1967.

Smedley, R.C. *History of the Underground Railroad.* 1883. Reprint, New York: Arno Press, 1969.

Still, William. *The Underground Railroad.* 1872. Reprint, Chicago: Johnson, 1970.

Switala, William J. *Underground Railroad in Delaware, Maryland, and West Virginia.* Mechanicsburg, PA: Stackpole, 2004.

Switala, William J. *Underground Railroad in Pennsylvania.* Mechanicsburg, PA: Stackpole, 2001.

Wade, Richard C. *Slavery in the Cities: The South, 1820–1860.* New York: Oxford University Press, 1969.

Williams, George Washington. *History of the Negro Race in America.* 1883. Reprint, New York: Bergmann, 1968.

Winks, Robin W. *Blacks in Canada: A History.* New Haven, CT: Yale University Press, 1971.

A Guide for Readers

The *Encyclopedia of the Underground Railroad* is intended to serve as a reference work for students of fugitive slaves and the Underground Railroad and for members of the public desirous of learning more about these fascinating and complex historical topics. With that in mind, a brief guide to how the book might best be used, including a few notes on content and organization and some "how-to's," will be helpful.

First, the study of the Underground Railroad brings together three overlapping and, to varying degrees, interdependent "histories," specifically:

• Fugitive slaves or freedom seekers, i.e., the history of enslaved African Americans who fled bondage;

• The struggle against slavery and for full freedom and equality by free African Americans, the "Black Abolitionists" who were the bedrock of the Underground Railroad movement; and

• The American antislavery movement as it relates to those white "practical abolitionists" who assisted fugitive slaves directly and those who challenged the laws of slavery, particularly laws concerning fugitive slaves, by more indirect political means.

The book focuses principally on the people, ideas, events and places associated with these interrelated histories. In this respect, the book is neither an encyclopedia of colonial and antebellum African American history, nor an encyclopedia of slavery and

slave trade, nor an encyclopedia of the American antislavery movement, nor an encyclopedia of colonial and antebellum American history — although it does, and must, contain elements of each, and although it does, and must, establish the broader historical context necessary to understand each in relation to the others.

Second, the main body of the book consists of alphabetical entries. Every effort has been made to ensure that all important people, ideas, events and places associated with fugitive slaves and the Underground Railroad are included. Further, every effort has been made to ensure that each entry includes a summary of the relevant factual information, with at least one supporting historical reference. The only exceptions concern references to some site entries. Specifically, because so many sites have either been described in Professor Charles Blockson's *Hippocrene Guide to the Underground Railroad* (1994) or appear in various National Park Service listings, readers should assume that site entries without other specific references are documented in Blockson's work or can be found, where noted, in one of the appendixes.

Third, this encyclopedia is a work of history and, although a significant number of site entries are included, not a compendium of or guide to Underground Railroad sites. As a work of history, it relies on two types of historical evidence: primary sources, i.e., historical materials created at the time of or by those who lived during the period under study; and secondary sources, i.e., historical materials based on primary sources. Both draw heavily, directly and indirectly, on public records of various kinds, document collections, slave autobiographies and the memoirs of abolitionists, antebellum newspapers and the seminal works of early Underground Railroad scholars such as Wilbur Siebert. Where sufficient corroboration exists, this more formal evidentiary base is supplemented by oral traditions, family and community legends, and the findings of archaeologists.

Readers should note that, although the encyclopedia is comprehensive, it is not and cannot be exhaustive. Some potential entries were excluded or incorporated in other related entries since, in some instances, documentation was too limited or too suspect, or historical significance too slight. Beyond that, much remains unknown even in a field so long and well-researched. The author takes full responsibility for such choices and, of course, for his own limitations, and hopes that errors of fact and omission are few.

Fourth, organizing the book alphabet-ically simplifies the search for specific entries. However, presenting the many small pieces of an enormous historical puzzle in alphabetical order also works against achieving a coherent understanding of the larger puzzle and where the individual pieces fit. In hopes of bringing some order out of potential chaos:

• Most entries will contain at least one "pointer" (in **boldface**) to one or more related entries;

• As indicated in the table of contents, the book includes a chronology, a detailed index, several appendices, and a reasonably comprehensive, although still selected, bibliography;

• For readers interested in historical context, some extended entries have been included on several topics, e.g., the Colonial Period, Free People of Color, Fugitive Slaves, Routes of Escape, Slave Trade, Slavery, and Strategies for Escape.

Finally, beyond all scholarly and otherwise technical considerations, the *Encyclopedia of the Underground Railroad* will have value only to the extent that it is used — and the author hopes that it will not only be used, but enjoyed as well.

Timeline: Slavery and the Underground Railroad

1441
September. Portugal inaugurates European slave trade with West Africa. Trade remains small-scale since slave labor is more readily available in eastern European and central Asian markets.

1454
Ottoman conquest of Constantinople creates a barrier to western European access to the Slavic populations of eastern Europe and central Asia. Slave trade from Africa grows slightly.

1480
A few hundred Africans each year arrive in Portugal; some are resold to other European kingdoms.

1492
Christopher Columbus inaugurates European colonization of the Americas, intending initially to exploit Native Americans as slave labor. African servants, explorers and slaves later accompany the first Spanish and French expeditions.

1493
The pope divides the world into separate spheres open to colonization and exploitation by Spain and Portugal. North America and most of South America are assigned to Spain, except for the easternmost section of South America (which would become the Portuguese colony of Brazil). Portugal is assigned Africa and Asia. This agreement is ratified by treaty (Tordesillas) in 1494.

1501
King Ferdinand of Spain authorizes the transportation of "Ladinos," i.e., persons of African ancestry enslaved in Spain, to the New World Spanish colonies.

1517
Since Spain cannot exploit Africa, the Spanish crown issues the first of many licenses—the Asiento—to other European kingdoms to supply the Spanish colonies with enslaved Africans.

1520
The Native American population is dying rapidly—due primarily to disease. Enslaved Africans are imported in growing numbers to replace the lost Native American source of labor.

1522
First recorded African slave revolt on the island of Hispaniola.

1526
Lucas Vasquez de Allyon attempts to establish a Spanish colony with a group of Spanish settlers and enslaved Africans in what would become South Carolina. The Africans revolt and flee to neighboring Native Americans; the remaining Spanish colonists retreat to Hispaniola by the end of the year.

1530s
Beginning of sugar cane cultivation in Brazil.

1540
An estimated 10,000 Africans per year are arriving in the Americas—alive.

1581
Spanish residents of St. Augustine, Florida, import the first enslaved Africans to the North American mainland.

1619
First Africans arrive at Jamestown, established on the James River, Virginia, in 1607. Their status is similar, if not equivalent, to that of indentured servants, i.e., persons in temporary bondage. For the next two generations, white indentured servants are the principal labor force of British North America.

1641
An African servant, John Punch, and two white indentured servants of European descent are captured while attempting to run away. The European servants are punished by extending the term of their indenture by two years, but John Punch is sentenced to serve "in durante vita," i.e., for the rest of his life.

Massachusetts becomes the first British North American colony to legalize slavery.

1642
Virginia makes it illegal to help runaway slaves, punishable by fine of 20 pounds of tobacco for each night of assistance.

1650
Sugar cultivation spreads to the Caribbean; roughly 40,000 Africans per year are arriving in the Americas—alive.

1661–1700
A series of laws are passed, first in Virginia and then in other colonies, fully institutionalizing American slavery. "Slave codes" are also enacted, modeled on those of the Caribbean colonies, giving slave-owners and/or the state the power of life and death over enslaved African Americans.

1663
Major slave conspiracy in Gloucester County, Virginia, involving an alliance between black and white indentured servants.

1672
Virginia sets a bounty on the heads of escaped Africans who form maroon communities in and around the Great Dismal Swamp.

1676
Bacon's Rebellion in Virginia, after which enslaved Africans become the labor force of choice and white indentured servitude nearly disappears by 1700.

1680
To deter slave escapes, Massachusetts prohibits the captain of any "ship, sloop, ketch, or vessel" from allowing blacks on board without a permit.

1682
The precedent for using courts of oyer and terminer (Latin for "hear and decide") is established for enslaved Africans accused of crimes, including flight, i.e., no jury trials and no appeals.

1688
Pennsylvania Quakers sign the "Germantown Mennonite Resolution," the first protest against slavery in the American colonies.

1700
Samuel Sewall publishes *The Selling of Joseph*, the first attack on slavery in the New England colonies.

1705
Virginia laws allow slave-masters to "kill and destroy" runaways.

1712
Slave revolt in New York City; whites killed. Nineteen rebels are executed.

1722
South Carolina makes escaping from slavery a capital offense.

1735
South Carolina law mandates the death penalty for any fugitive slave who resists capture with a weapon of any kind.

1739
Stono Slave Revolt near Charleston, South Carolina. As many as 100 enslaved Africans steal weapons and flee toward freedom in Florida (then under Spanish rule). Crushed by the South Carolina militia, the revolt results in the deaths of 40 blacks and 20 whites. Still, at least a dozen rebels escape successfully.

1740
North Carolina makes it illegal to assist fugitive slaves.

1754

Quaker John Woolman publishes *Some Considerations on the Keeping of Negroes,* an anti-slavery tract.

1754–1763

French and Indian War. Numerous fugitive slaves flee to the Native Americans of the trans-Appalachian west.

1772

James Somerset Case, England. British judge rules that enslaved Africans brought into Britain, where slavery did not exist, were free.

1775

American Revolution begins. Anthony Benezet of Philadelphia founds the Pennsylvania Abolition Society to protect fugitive slaves and freed blacks unlawfully held in bondage. Benjamin Franklin becomes its president in 1787.

1776

Declaration of Independence. The Continental Congress asserts "that these United Colonies are, and of Right ought to be Free and Independent States."

1777

First Emancipation begins. Vermont amends its constitution to ban slavery. Over the next 25 years, other northern states emancipate their slaves and ban the institution: Pennsylvania, 1780; Massachusetts and New Hampshire, 1783; Connecticut and Rhode Island, 1784; New York, 1799; and New Jersey, 1804. Some of the state laws stipulate gradual emancipation, but, by the late 1820s, slavery no longer exists in the North.

1783

Treaty of Paris certifying American independence.

1784

Congress narrowly defeats Thomas Jefferson's proposal to bar slavery from new territories after 1800.

1787

The Northwest Ordinance prohibits slavery in the Northwest Territory (what later becomes the states of Ohio, Indiana, Illinois, Michigan, and Wisconsin). The ordinance, together with state emancipation laws, creates a free North. However, the U.S. Constitution includes Article IV, section 2.3, declaring that those enslaved in one section of the country remain legally bound if they escape into free territory. Ratified in 1789.

The Free African Society is organized in Philadelphia by Richard Allen and Absalom Jones—leading to the establishment of the African Methodist Episcopal church, the first African American religious denomination in the United States.

1790

United States treaty with the Creek Nation provides for the return of fugitive slaves who have fled to Native American territory.

First census; 757,208 African Americans (19.3 percent of the U.S. population); 59,557 are nominally free.

1793

To enforce Article IV, Section 2.3 of the U.S. Constitution, Congress passes the first Fugitive Slave Act, allowing slave-owners to cross state lines to recapture fugitive slaves.

1794

Eli Whitney patents the cotton gin, a machine that separates cotton seeds from cotton fiber. The invention turns cotton into the cash crop of the South—and creates a huge demand for slave labor.

Mother Bethel African Methodist Episcopal Church is established in Philadelphia, Pennsylvania, by the Reverend Richard Allen.

1798–1803

Series of court decisions effectively ends slavery in Canada.

1800

Gabriel (Prosser) slave revolt in Virginia. Nat Turner and John Brown are born; Denmark Vesey purchases his freedom with the proceeds of a lottery.

1804

Underground "Road" begins when General Thomas Boudes of Columbia, Pennsylvania, refuses to surrender a fugitive slave to authorities.

1808

January 1, United States bans international slave trade, although small-scale smuggling continues. Growing labor demand for cotton cultivation leads to a brisk and expanding internal or domestic slave trade that moves thousands of enslaved African Americans from the "upper" to the "lower" South each year.

1816–1817

Creation of the American Colonization Society — with the aim of protecting slavery by removing free people of color from the United States. Slave Trade Act passed by Congress in 1819 leads to the establishment of Liberia in 1822 as a site to which free African Americans could be sent.

1818

Seminole Wars begin in Florida as a result of fugitive slaves taking refuge with Seminole Indians.

As a response to the Fugitive Slave Act (1793), abolitionists use the Underground Railroad to assist slaves to escape into Ohio and Canada.

1820

Missouri Compromise divides the Louisiana Purchase into free and slave zones. Missouri is admitted to the Union as a slave state; Maine, as a free state. Slavery is forbidden in any subsequent territories north of latitude 36°30'.

1821

Kentucky representatives present a resolution to Congress protesting Canada's friendly reception of fugitive slaves.

1822

Denmark Vesey conspiracy in Charleston, South Carolina.

1826

Levi Coffin leaves North Carolina, settles in Newburyport, Indiana, and begins his long career as a friend of the fugitive. Moves to Cincinnati, Ohio, in 1847 and becomes known as "President of the Underground Railroad."

1829

Publication of David Walker's *Appeal,* incendiary call for resistance to slavery. Walker is found dead in Boston in 1830.

August. Free blacks attacked by white mobs in Cincinnati, Ohio. Many flee to Canada and establish the Wilberforce colony.

1830

September 30. The first Convention of Free People of Color meeting at Mother Bethel AME Church in Philadelphia signals the political maturity of free African Americans and represents an early precursor of the American civil rights movement.

1831

January. In Boston, William Lloyd Garrison founds the abolitionist newspaper *The Liberator,* signaling a dramatic shift in the antislavery movement. In the previous decades, the antislavery movement was centered in the South and favored a combination of compensated emancipation and colonization. However, in the 1830s, militant abolitionists demand an immediate end to slavery, which they consider a moral evil, without compensation to slave-owners.

August. Nat Turner, a literate enslaved African American preacher, leads a slave revolt in Virginia. He and his followers kill 57 whites; as many as 200 enslaved African Americans are executed in reprisal. The widespread fear of slave revolt, compounded by the rise of militant abolitionism, leads legislatures across the South to increase the harshness of slavery and to suppress expressions of antislavery sentiment through state and private censorship — and outright intimidation.

Convention of Free People of Color rejects colonization, i.e., migration to Africa, declaring "Here we were born and here we will die."

1832

New England Antislavery Society established.

In response to the Nat Turner Revolt, several slave states outlaw black preachers and exhorters and ban black religious services except in the presence of "certain discreet white men."

1833

William Lloyd Garrison joins Arthur and Lewis Tappan to establish the American Antislavery Society.

Riot in Detroit, Michigan, after African Americans rescue Thornton and Lucie Blackburn, two fugitive slaves from Kentucky.

1834

British Parliament abolishes slavery in the British Empire.

New York Vigilance Committee organized under the leadership of David Ruggles.

1836

In response to militant abolitionism, the U.S. House of Representatives passes a "gag rule" that bars discussion and congressional action on any antislavery resolutions or legislation. The "gag rule" is not overturned until 1845.

1837

Abolitionist editor Elijah P. Lovejoy murdered in Alton, Illinois, by a proslavery mob.

First Antislavery Convention of American Women meets in New York; ten percent of the members are African American.

1838

Black abolitionist Robert Purvis becomes chairman of the General Vigilance Committee of Philadelphia.

Frederick Douglass escapes from slavery in Maryland.

1839

Amistad, a Spanish slave-ship seized by Africans in a bloody revolt, is brought into Montauk, New York. Ultimately, the surviving Africans are freed and returned to Sierra Leone in 1842.

1841

Creole Affair. Enslaved African Americans revolt and divert the *Creole*— sailing from Virginia to New Orleans, to the Bahamas instead. The rebels are freed by a British court.

1842

In *Prigg v. Pennsylvania,* the U.S. Supreme Court upholds the Fugitive Slave Act of 1793. At the same time, the court declares that enforcement of the Fugitive Slave Act is a federal responsibility in which states are not compelled to participate. As a result, between 1842 and 1850, nine northern states pass new personal liberty laws that forbid state officials from cooperating in the return of alleged fugitive slaves and bar the use of state facilities for that purpose.

1843

Sojourner Truth leaves New York and begins her abolitionist pilgrimage.

Massachusetts and Vermont legislatures defy the Fugitive Slave Act—forbidding state officials from assisting in the recapture of fugitive slaves.

1845

Frederick Douglass publishes *Narrative of the Life of Frederick Douglass,* an account of his slave experience and escape to freedom.

1846–48

Mexican War. Defeated, Mexico surrenders most of the "West" to the United States, creating a divisive sectional struggle over the extension of slavery into these western territories.

1847

Frederick Douglass begins publishing *The North Star* in Rochester, New York.

1849

Harriet Tubman escapes from bondage. After fleeing slavery, Tubman returns south repeatedly to help rescue several hundred others.

1850

Compromise of 1850. In exchange for California's entering the Union as a free state, northern congressmen accept a harsher Fugitive Slave Act.

1852

Uncle Tom's Cabin published by Harriet Beecher Stowe. This novel, dramatizing the horrors of slavery, sells 300,000 copies within a year of publication and, as a consequence, the South suffers a public relations disaster from which it never entirely recovers. Years later, President Abraham Lincoln, on meeting Stowe, would remark, "So, you're the little lady who started this big war."

1854

Kansas-Nebraska Act essentially nullifies the Missouri Compromise of 1820 and allows residents of these new western territories to choose whether to allow slavery. Violent conflict erupts between free-state and proslavery factions in a dress-rehearsal for the Civil War.

1857

The U.S. Supreme Court rules in the *Dred Scott v. Sandford* case. In the majority opinion, Chief Justice Roger Taney holds that Scott is still a slave with no standing to sue; that black Americans (slave or free) are not citizens and do not have civil rights protected by the U.S. Constitution; and that neither the territorial government nor the federal government can exclude slavery from the U.S. territories, thus making the Northwest Ordinance and Missouri Compromise unconstitutional as they relate to slavery.

1859
October. John Brown, a radical white abolitionist and veteran of "Bleeding Kansas," attempts to capture the federal arsenal at Harpers Ferry, Virginia (now West Virginia) and foment a slave rebellion. Brown and his co-conspirators are unsuccessful. Brown and other survivors are executed, becoming martyrs to the antislavery cause.

1860
Abraham Lincoln of Illinois becomes the first Republican to win the United States presidency — on a platform opposed, not to slavery, but to the extension of slavery into the western territories.

South Carolina secedes from the Union on December 20. Most other slave states secede in the first months of 1861.

1861
April. Civil War begins. First Confiscation Act passed August 6 — responds to the first wave of slave escapes (i.e., acts of self-emancipation) from Confederate territory during the Civil War, defining enslaved African Americans who are captured or who reach Union lines on their own as "contraband of war."

1862
April 16: slavery abolished in the District of Columbia. June 19: slavery abolished in all U.S. territories. July 17: Second Confiscation Act passed by Congress; frees fugitive slaves who reach Union Army lines. September 22: President Abraham Lincoln issues the Emancipation Proclamation, which declares "all persons held as slaves within any state ... in re-

bellion against the United States shall be ... forever free." Lincoln, however, encourages freed African Americans to leave the United States.

1863
January 1. Emancipation Proclamation signed by President Lincoln. Decrees that all enslaved African Americans in Confederate territory are free, but does not apply to enslaved African Americans in the Union slave states — i.e., Delaware, Kentucky, Maryland, Missouri and, ultimately, West Virginia.

1864
June 28. Fugitive Slave Act repealed.

October. National African American Convention, chaired by Frederick Douglass, presses for voting and civil rights, and land redistribution as essential to fulfilling the full promise of emancipation.

1865
January. Land redistribution to freed African Americans begins — initiated by General William Tecumseh Sherman.

March. Bureau of Refugees, Freedmen and Abandoned Lands established by Congress. President Lincoln states support for limited black voting rights.

April. Civil War ends. Lincoln assassinated.

President Andrew Johnson begins the process of reversing President Lincoln's reconstruction policies. Begins pardoning former Confederates in May 1865. Orders an end to land redistribution in summer 1865. Allows "unreconstructed" Confederates to enact "Black Codes" to regulate newly freed African Americans — replacing the old "Slave Codes."

December 18. The Thirteenth Amendment to the United States Constitution is declared ratified. Slavery is forever outlawed.

The Encyclopedia

Abolitionist Movement

The Abolitionist (or Anti-Slavery) Movement was the political and moral struggle to end **slavery** in the United States. Flowing from the ideas of the Enlightenment, anti-slave trade and antislavery agitation emerged during the American Revolutionary period in the United States and parts of Europe. Because many of the founders of the United States grasped the paradox of espousing the value of freedom as a natural right and, at the same time, holding persons of African ancestry in bondage, this early antislavery movement contributed significantly to the "first emancipation," i.e., the end of slavery in the North and Old Northwest between 1777 and 1827. Organized antislavery groups emerged as well, e.g., the **Pennsylvania** Anti-slavery Society, whose members included Thomas Paine, Benjamin Franklin and the Marquis de LaFayette. However, by the early 1800s, antislavery sentiment in the United States grew increasingly conservative and gradualistic, and was often linked to "colonizationist" schemes to send free blacks to Africa or some other part of the world as a means of making the institution of slavery more secure.

Northern politicians did not challenge slavery in the southern states and remained largely silent and nonjudgmental when Virginia was threatened by the Gabriel and Sancho conspiracies of 1800 and 1802, respectively. By the time of the Denmark Vesey conspiracy in 1822 (Charleston, South Carolina), growing sectional divisions over the extension of slavery into the Louisiana Territory had already prompted the 1820 **Missouri Compromise**. Still, northerners sympathized, in general, when southerners were traumatized by Vesey's massive conspiracy. However, by the time Nat Turner's revolt swept through

The woodcut image of a supplicant male slave in chains appears on the 1837 broadside publication of John Greenleaf Whittier's antislavery poem, "Our Countrymen in Chains." The design was originally adopted as the seal of the Society for the Abolition of Slavery in England in the 1780s. (Library of Congress)

21

Southampton County, Virginia, in late August 1831, North and South had drifted further apart and a more militant antislavery movement extended no sympathy to the South — declaring, instead, that the South had, in essence, created its own problem.

The antislavery movement was driven by the ideals and courage of the many men and women, black and white, who chose to challenge slavery — a challenge that extended, for many of them, into the practical arena of assisting **fugitive slaves**. Among the better known white Abolitionists were William Lloyd **Garrison**, Harriett Beecher **Stowe**, Samuel J. **May**, Wendell **Phillips**, Benjamin **Lundy** and many, many others — including some, such as John **Brown**, Laura S. **Haviland**, the Reverend John **Rankin,** and Levi **Coffin**, who were committed to "practical abolitionism" as manifested by active involvement in the work of the Underground Railroad.

African Americans played a significant role in the political Abolitionist Movement — as orators, organizers and propagandists, e.g., Frederick **Douglass**, Sojourner **Truth**, Charles Lenox **Remond**, Samuel Ringgold **Ward**, William Wells **Brown** and many others. Not surprisingly, sympathy for fugitive slaves had deep roots and a long history among free African Americans who also played key roles as "practical abolitionists" — such as Harriett **Tubman**, Chapman **Harris**, John **Parker**, Jermain **Loguen**, David **Ruggles,** and many others.

Less known, perhaps, is the role — and the importance — of those who not only shared the progressive ideals of the movement, but who also helped to finance its organizations and operations. In this regard, persons such as Gerrit **Smith**, Arthur and Lewis **Tappan** — and African Americans such as Frances Ellen Watkins **Harper,** Robert **Purvis** and William **Whipper** — were among the better-known "financiers" of the abolitionist movement and, at times, the Underground Railroad.

FURTHER READING

Brooks, Elaine. "Massachusetts Anti-slavery Society." *Journal of Negro History* 30(1945): 311–332.
Bruns, Roger, ed. *Am I Not a Man and a Brother: The Anti-slavery Crusade of Revolutionary America, 1688–1788.* New York: R. R. Bowker, 1977.
Finnie, Gordon E. "The Antislavery Movement in the Upper South Before 1840." *Journal of Southern History* 35, no. 3(1969): 319–342.
Guy, Anita A. "The Maryland Abolition Society and the Promotion of the Ideals of the New Nation." *Maryland Historical Magazine* 84, no. 1(1989): 342–349.
Harlow, Ralph Volney. "The Rise and Fall of the Kansas Aid Movement." *American Historical Review* 41, no. 1(1935): 1–25.
Harrold, Stanley. "The Intersectional Relationship between Cassius M. Clay and the Garrisonian Abolitionists." *Civil War History* 35(1989): 101–119.
Hill, D.G. "The Negro as a Political and Social Issue in the Oregon Country." *Journal of Negro History* 33, no. 2(1948): 130–145.
Johannsen, Robert W. "The Secession Crisis and the Frontier: Washington Territory, 1860–1861." *Mississippi Valley Historical Review* 39, no. 3(1952): 415–440.
Litwack, Leon F. "The Abolitionist Dilemma: The Anti-Slavery Movement and the Northern Negro." *New England Quarterly* 34(1961): 50–73.
Pease, Jane H., and William H. Pease. "Ends, Means, and Attitudes: Black-White Conflict in the Antislavery Movement." *Civil War History* 18(1972): 117–128.
Quarles, Benjamin. *Black Abolitionists.* New York: Oxford University Press, 1969.
_____. "Sources of Abolitionist Income." *The Mississippi Valley Historical Review* 32(1945): 63–76.
Ranney, Joseph A. "Suffering the Agonies of Their Righteousness: The Rise and Fall of the States Rights Movement in Wisconsin, 1854–1861." *Wisconsin Magazine of History* 75, no. 2(1992).
Shriver, Edward O. "Antislavery: The Free Soil and Free Democratic Parties in Maine, 1848–1855." *New England Quarterly* 42, no. 1(1969): 82–94.
Stampp, Kenneth M. "The Fate of the Southern Anti-Slavery Movement." *Journal of Negro History* 28(1943): 10–22.
Stewart, James B. "The Aims and Impact of Garrisonian Abolitionism, 1840–1860." *Civil War History* 15, no. 3(1969): 197–209.
Towner, Lawrence W. "The Sewall-Saffin Dialogue on Slavery." *William and Mary Quarterly* 21(1964): 40–52.
Zorn, Roman J. "The New England Anti-Slavery Society: Pioneer Abolition Organization." *Journal of Negro History* 43(1957): 157–176.

African American National Historic Site

See Boston African American National Historic Site

African Diaspora

See Slave Trade; Slavery

African Episcopal Church (Edgar, Canada)

Underground Railroad site in Canada. In the early 1800s, a small African American community coalesced near Edgar in Canada's Ontario Province. Originally named "Oro," derived from the Rio del Oro (River of Gold) in West Africa, nearly 30 families of fugitive slaves made their homes there by 1828. In 1849, the African Episcopal Church was built as a unifying community institution. *See also* Underground Railroad, Sites of; and Appendixes 3 and 4.

African Meeting House (Boston, Massachusetts)

Underground Railroad site. Built in 1806 with funds raised by the formerly enslaved Cato Gardner, the African Meeting House served as one of several centers of antislavery activism in the African American community of **Boston**, Massachusetts. The congregation harbored **fugitive slaves** and the African Meeting House, known as the "Abolition Church," was the site at which William Lloyd **Garrison** and his associates founded the New England Anti-Slavery Society on December 16, 1832. *See also* Underground Railroad, Sites of; and Appendixes 3 and 4.

African Meeting House (Nantucket Island, Massachusetts)

Underground Railroad site. Built in 1820, the African Meeting House served as the centerpiece of "New Guinea," the African American community of Nantucket Island, Massachusetts. Black and white sailors working in the Nantucket whaling industry often assisted freedom seekers escaping by sea, and the meeting house often served as a place of refuge.

Also of historical interest, Frederick **Douglass** delivered his first public address there on August 12, 1841 — launching his illustrious career. *See also* Underground Railroad, Sites of; and Appendixes 3 and 4.

African Union Methodist Church (Oxford, Pennsylvania)

Underground Railroad site. Founded by African Americans in 1829, the African Union Methodist Church — also known as the "African Meeting House" — served as an important Underground Railroad station in Oxford, Pennsylvania. The church is now located on the campus of Lincoln University. *See also* Underground Railroad, Sites of; and Appendixes 3 and 4.

Agents

Agents were individuals who rendered direct assistance to **fugitive slaves**. Some provided information and were often termed "field agents." Others facilitated communication between friends of the fugitive along an escape route. Still others provided food or clothing. Although distinct from Underground Railroad conductors and stationkeepers, agents acted at great risk and were directly involved in the initial and often the later phases of many escapes.

FURTHER READING
Hudson, J. Blaine. *Fugitive Slaves and the Underground Railroad in the Kentucky Borderland*. Jefferson, NC: McFarland, 2002.

Allen, Richard (1760–1831)

Religious and antislavery leader. Richard Allen was born enslaved in **Philadelphia** on February 14, 1760, and with his family was sold as a child into slavery in Delaware. There, in 1780, he and his brother joined the Methodist Society and, with the permission of their owner, began attending classes sponsored by the society.

In 1783, Allen purchased his freedom (adopting the surname "Allen"), but soon thereafter was falsely accused of being a fugitive slave and imprisoned unjustly. Allen was fortunate to receive assistance from **Isaac Hopper**, who paid for his defense, and was soon released from custody.

Due to his strength of character and his religious training, Allen became a leader of African American Methodists in Philadelphia. In 1787, when he and other African Americans were denied the right to worship in the St. George Methodist Episcopal Church, Allen and his followers organized the African Methodist Episcopal (AME) Church. The congregation grew and, in 1794, he founded Bethel, the "Mother" church, Philadelphia. Allen continued to lead his congregation

Bishop Richard Allen, surrounded by other AME bishops, circa 1876. (Library of Congress)

while supporting himself as a shoemaker and, in 1816, after other AME churches sprouted in the emerging free African American communities in the North and the border states, Allen was consecrated the first bishop of the first independent black religious denomination in the United States— and a bulwark of the black Underground Railroad.

Between 1815 and 1830 Richard Allen was recognized as the most important leader of free people of color in the North. In 1817, his Bethel AME Church hosted the first mass meeting of African Americans to protest the American Colonization Society and, in 1830, issued the call for the First Convention of Free People of Color. Bishop Allen died in 1831. *See also* Appendixes 1 and 2.

FURTHER READING

George, Carol V. R. *Segregated Sabbaths: Richard Allen and the Emergence of Independent Black Churches, 1760–1840.* New York: Oxford University Press, 1973.

Nash, Gary B. "New Light on Richard Allen: The Early Years of Freedom." *William and Mary Quarterly* 46(1989): 332–340.

Allen B. Mayhew Cabin (Nebraska City, Nebraska)

Underground Railroad site. Allen B. Mayhew and his family were abolitionists who pioneered the settlement of Nebraska. With his father-in-law, Abraham Kagi, Mayhew built a log cabin home, now the oldest standing building in Nebraska, and farmed the surrounding land a few miles west of Nebraska City.

Given its strategic location and the politics of its owners, the Mayhew farm became an important Underground Railroad station for **fugitive slaves** fleeing bondage in Missouri en route to other stations in **Iowa**. Once there, fugitive slaves were concealed in the "Black Din," also known as "John Brown's Cave," which had a hidden entrance, ventilation and contained three chambers that could accommodate as many as 15 people.

In his efforts to assist freedom seekers, Mayhew worked closely with John Boulwar, who operated a ferry service used to transport fugitive slaves across the Missouri River.

See also Underground Railroad, Sites of; and Appendixes 3 and 4.

Alston, John (1794–1874)

Friend of the fugitive, John Alston, born in 1794, was a Quaker who assisted fugitive slaves in the 1840s and 1850s through the **Appoquinimink Friends Meeting House** near Odessa, Delaware. There he worked closely with his cousin and fellow Quaker, **John Hunn**, and **Samuel Burris**, a free African American Underground Railroad conductor who led fugitive slaves from Delaware and Maryland into Pennsylvania.

An 1841 entry in Alston's diary closes with, "O Lord ... enable me to keep my heart and house open to receive thy servants that they may rest in their travels that this house that thou has enabled me to build may be holy dictates unto thee of the pilgrim's rest." Alston was the treasurer of the Appoquinimink Meeting House and worked as caretaker of the building until his death in 1874.

FURTHER READING
Still, William. *The Underground Railroad.* 1872. Reprint, Chicago: Johnson, 1970.

AMA

See American Missionary Association

American Missionary Association (AMA)

The American Missionary Association (AMA) evolved from a committee organized in 1839 by abolitionists such as Lewis **Tappan** and Charles Finney to defend the Africans of the *Amistad* slave ship rebellion. The AMA itself was established formally in 1846 by the merger of this committee with two missionary societies formed, initially, to promote the colonization of free persons of color outside the United States. However, the AMA was clearly an antislavery organization and, of the 12 men who served on its first board, four were African Americans: Theodore S. Wright, **Samuel Ringgold Ward**, **James Pennington**, and **Charles Bennett Ray**. In later years Samuel E. Cornish, **Henry Highland Garnet**, Amos N. Freeman, and Sella Martin also served as officers.

During the Civil War, the AMA supported schools in the South for African Americans emancipated by the Union Army and those who emancipated themselves through flight. In the decades that followed, the AMA founded more than 500 schools for African Americans—schools that eventually became part of the public school systems of the South. The AMA made even more lasting contributions in the field of higher education, and 10 historically black or integrated institutions received AMA support: Atlanta University, **Berea College**, Dillard University, Fisk University, Hampton Institute (now Hampton University), Howard University, Houston-Tillotson College, Le Moyne College, Talladega College, and Tougaloo College.

FURTHER READING
Amistad Research Center. *American Missionary Association Archives.* Westport, CT: Greenwood Publishing Company, 1970.

American Revolution

The American Revolution and the consequent emergence of the United States as an independent nation had two principal causes. One was eminently practical: the desire of propertied and wealthy colonial Americans to be free of British interference and control. The other, however, was more philosophical, if not ideological — drawn from the seminal ideas of the Enlightenment or the Age of Reason. Embedded in these ideas and the writings of John Locke and Jean Jacques Rousseau was the assumption that there were certain natural rights shared by all people and that governments should exist to protect these rights by the consent of the governed.

Because freedom was foremost among these rights, the American Revolutionary period confronted American colonists with an inescapable paradox. On one hand, many of those who demanded freedom and fought for democracy were slaveholders with no intention of relinquishing their right to human property. Many wondered, as did British author Samuel Johnson: "How is it that we hear the loudest yelps for liberty among the drivers of Negroes?" On the other hand, many others found **slavery** fundamentally incompatible with Revolutionary philosophy and worked to abolish the institution itself. As John Jay noted: "To contend for liberty and to deny that blessing to others involves an inconsistency not to be excused." Thus, with respect to race, despite its many contradictions, the American Revolution brought the first, great liberal or progressive period in the history of the United States—and a time during which blacks and their supporters worked actively to end slavery.

For example, as the American colonists began to talk of independence in the 1760s, enslaved African Americans sensed an opportunity and took the initiative to petition for an end to slavery. In 1766, blacks in Massachusetts sued their master for trespass, thereby challenging the legality and morality of slavery. In May 1774, a "Petition of a Grate Number of Blacks" was sent to the governor of Massachusetts and, in 1775, groups of blacks and whites in Western Massachusetts joined forces to petition for the end of slavery.

Slavery was a powerful political issue as the coalition of rebellious colonies was formed. In this respect, it is important to remember that the founding fathers were divided over the issue of slavery — that for every slaveholder, e.g., George Washington and Thomas Jefferson, there were other equally significant founding fathers who opposed slavery, such as Benjamin Franklin, John Adams, Thomas Paine and James Otis. As evidence of these divisions, the First Continental Congress passed an agreement banning the importation of slaves after December 1, 1774. Further, the original draft of the Declaration of Independence (1776) contained a condemnation of slave trade, but that passage was dropped in order to placate slaveholders.

For African Americans during the Revolutionary period, the desire for freedom transcended political loyalties and blacks were active participants on both sides of the conflict. On March 5, 1770, Crispus **Attucks** (a 47-year-old fugitive slave) was killed in the Boston Massacre, a protest over British troops being quartered in Boston, and gained the distinction of being "the first to fall" in the Revolution. When hostilities began in April 1775, African Americans fought bravely in the battles of Lexington and Concord, and at Bunker Hill in June 1775. However, when George Washington, a Virginia slaveholder, assumed command of the Continental Army, he issued an order (July 9, 1775) forbidding the further

enlistment of blacks, slave or free. However, on November 12, 1775, Lord Dunmore (George Murray, the British Governor of Virginia) proclaimed that enslaved African Americans who chose to fight for the British would receive their freedom immediately — and, by promising freedom as a reward for military service, the British inadvertently helped to destabilize slavery in British North America. Lord Dunmore's strategy would be employed by Abraham Lincoln in the **Civil War** by using the Emancipation Proclamation to destabilize the Confederacy.

After Lord Dunmore's proclamation, Washington was forced to revise his policy and, by December 30, 1775, eased his ban on the enlistment of African Americans. Eventually, between 4,000 and 6,000 African Americans served in the Continental Army, most from the northern colonies and most in integrated units. African Americans also served in the Navy, most notably James Forten of Philadelphia — who later became a wealthy inventor, businessman, and antislavery leader. Besides Forten and Crispus Attucks, many other blacks distinguished themselves in the Revolutionary cause, including Peter Salem (who became a hero at the Battle of Bunker Hill); Salem Poor (hero at Bunker Hill as well); James Armistead who served as a spy for General Lafayette (1781) and was granted his freedom in 1786; and many others. Also, the famous Black Legion from Haiti (composed of free blacks brought by the French) saved an entire American army by covering its retreat at the siege of Savannah in 1778.

Still, the threat posed by the proclamation was felt most keenly in the southern colonies where enslaved African Americans were concentrated most heavily. Throughout the war, African Americans fled to the British lines. Many fought with the British and, when the British were defeated in 1781, many accompanied them on their retreat. For example, more than 3,000 African Americans left the United States with the British from New York, more than 5,000 from Savannah, and more than 6,000 from Charleston. Ironically, slavery would have ended sooner had the British put down the Revolution — since it ended, officially, in all British colonies by 1838.

More noteworthy than military service, although largely unknown, was the third strategy employed by African Americans seeking freedom during the Revolutionary period: running away from slavery. In other words, those who became fugitives chose to fight for freedom, not for either the British or the Americans— and it has been estimated that as many as 100,000 enslaved African Americans escaped during the American Revolution. With a total of little more than 500,000 blacks in British North America when hostilities commenced, this loss through escape represented as much as 20 percent of the black population. African Americans escaped to Canada, or to the Spanish or French Colonies. Some formed maroon societies and short-lived colonies in Georgia, North Carolina, New York, New Jersey and Virginia. In these unsettled conditions, conspiracies were frequent and there were also occasional revolts. As a consequence, the southern colonies devoted as much, if not more, of their manpower to policing enslaved African Americans and chasing fugitive slaves as to the Revolutionary cause.

The Revolution period, as noted, was a liberal, progressive period ideologically. However, the period during which the U.S. Constitution evolved witnessed a gradual shift toward more conservative policies. The northern states began passing laws for the gradual emancipation of the slaves, setting in motion the first emancipation, which resulted in the end of slavery in that region by the 1820s. Further, in 1787, the Northwest Ordinance prohibited slavery in the territories north of the Ohio River. However, deeper divisions surfaced when the Constitutional Convention met in the summer of 1787 to write a constitution that would supersede the weak Articles of Confederation. Slavery was at the heart of these divisions and the process of constitution-making was, ultimately, one of compromise between regions—foreshadowing the divisions, debates and compromises of 1820 and 1850, and the failure to achieve a workable compromise in 1860.

For example, southern delegates insisted on a constitution with provisions designed to protect property and institutionalize slavery and, in order to form a unified nation, the convention deferred to the wishes of these delegates. In the end, the constitution contained four specific provisions that protected the institution of slavery: Article I, Sec. 2. 3, the famous "Three-fifths Compromise"; Article I, Sec. 8.15, which permitted the use of the militia to suppress insurrections; Article I, Sec. 9. 1, which permitted international **slave trade** until 1808; and Article IV, Sec. 2.3, a fugitive slave provision (see **Somerset Case** and **Fugitive Slave Act of 1793**).

As with most progressive periods in history, the Revolutionary period was followed by one of reaction. The U.S. Constitution legalized and protected slavery. Still, the end of slavery had begun and African Americans had gained in status, stature and assertiveness— and had also gained many powerful white allies who opposed slavery.

FURTHER READING

Bailyn, Bernard. *The Ideological Origins of the American Revolution.* Cambridge, MA: Harvard University Press, 1967.
Knoblock, Glenn A. *"Strong and Brave Fellows": New Hampshire's Black Soldiers and Sailors of the American Revolution, 1775–1784.* Jefferson, NC: McFarland, 2003.
Nash, Gary B. *Race, Class, and Politics: Essays on American Colonial and Revolutionary Society.* Urbana, IL: University of Illinois Press, 1986.
Quarles, Benjamin. *The Negro in the American Revolution.* Chapel Hill, NC: University of North Carolina Press, 1961.
Waldstreicher, David. *Runaway America: Benjamin Franklin, Slavery, and the American Revolution.* New York: Hill and Wang, 2004.

Amherstburg, Canada

Located on the east bank of the Detroit River, Amherstburg in Ontario West, originally called Fort Malden, was one of the key points of entry for freedom seekers entering **Canada**. Many **fugitive slaves** reached the town by crossing the river from Detroit, making Detroit an important center of Underground Railroad operations and the point of convergence for escape routes snaking through **Indiana** and **Ohio**. Others crossed Lake Erie from Cleveland, Sandusky or Toledo, Ohio. By the mid–1850s, records indicate an average of 30 fugitives arrived per day. Many were destitute, and the **American Missionary Association**, particularly through the leadership of Isaac **Rice**, played an active role in providing food, clothing and shelter. As the black population increased, the more enterprising African Americans developed businesses, schools and churches—although most new arrivals and some less fortunate long-time residents remained indigent.

Many fugitive slaves were uncomfortable living so close to the United States, within comparatively easy reach of kidnappers. This led some to move farther into the interior of Ontario West, converging on towns such as London, Ingersoll, and Chatham.

FURTHER READING

Landon, Fred. "Amherstburg, Terminus of the Underground Railroad." *Journal of Negro History* 10(1925).

Amistad Affair (1839)

Famous slave ship revolt. In February 1839, Portuguese slave-traders acquired 53 Africans from Sierra Leone and smuggled

Joseph Cinquez (or "Cinque"), in an August 1839 portrait, led a revolt among African slaves aboard the Amistad. (Library of Congress)

them to Havana, Cuba, in violation of a host of treaties designed to regulate the African slave trade. In June 1839, the Africans were sold to two Spanish planters, Don Jose Ruiz and Don Pedro Montez, and then loaded aboard the Cuban schooner *Amistad* (Spanish for "friendship") for trans-shipment to a Caribbean sugar plantation.

On July 1, 1839, a 25-year-old African named Sengbe Pieh (or "Cinque" in Spanish) freed himself, released the other Africans and, together, they proceeded to kill most of the crew of the *Amistad*. The Africans then ordered the planters to sail to Africa. However, the planters deceived the Africans and, by appearing to sail east during the day and turning westward at night, followed a zig-zag course for 63 days that led into American waters. On August 24, 1839, the *Amistad* was seized off Montauk Point, Long Island, New York, and the Africans were charged with piracy and murder, and imprisoned in New Haven, Connecticut, as "salvage property."

The murder charges were dismissed, but the Africans remained in custody as the focus of the case turned to salvage claims and property rights—with the issue of slavery looming in the background. The Spanish planters (and the government of Spain) sought to re-claim their property. Still, other claims were advanced, based on the "law of salvage," that the monetary value of the Africans should be included in their share of value of the *Amistad*. Under strong diplomatic pressure from Spain, President Martin Van Buren favored extraditing the Africans to Cuba. In response, members of the Abolitionist Movement opposed extradition, hired a translator for the Africans and raised funds for their legal defense.

In September 1839, the Connecticut Federal District Court ruled that the Africans had been enslaved illegally and, therefore, were neither property nor liable for their acts in illegal bondage. After the circuit court upheld this decision, the case was appealed to the United States Supreme Court where, in January 1841, former President John Quincy Adams led the legal team representing the Africans. The Supreme Court called the case "peculiar and embarrassing" and decided in favor of the Africans. Thirty-five, including Cinque, were returned to their homeland on the ship

Gentleman. The others died at sea or in prison while awaiting trial.

FURTHER READING
Cable, Mary. *Black Odyssey: The Case of the Slave Ship Amistad.* New York: Viking Press, 1971.
Jones, Howard. *Mutiny on the Amistad: The Saga of a Slave Revolt and its Impact on American Abolition, Law, and Diplomacy.* New York: Oxford University Press, 1987.
Osagie, Iyunolu F. *The Amistad Revolt: Memory, Slavery, and the Politics of Identity in the United States and Sierra* Leone. Athens, GA: University of Georgia Press, 2000.
Owen, William A. *Black Mutiny: The Revolt on the Schooner Amistad.* Baltimore, MD: Black Classic Press, 1997.

Anderson, Bill

Fugitive slave. In 1839, men from Virginia attempted to gain legal custody of Bill Anderson, a fugitive slave from that state who was living in Marion County, Ohio, and return him to bondage. The Marion County court ruled that Anderson, known as "Black Bill," was a free man and ordered him released. However, the Virginians attempted to capture him again and, this time, local Quakers concealed him in the home of Reuben **Benedict** and assisted him in moving farther north to safety. *See also* Reuben Benedict House.

FURTHER READING
National Park Service. *Underground Railroad: Special Resource Study.* Washington, D.C.: U.S. Government Printing Office, 1995.

Anderson, Elijah

Friend of the fugitive. Elijah Anderson was one of the most important leaders of the Underground Railroad network in the **Madison**, Indiana area. Anderson was born in Fluvanna County, Virginia, and settled in Madison, **Indiana**, in 1837. Anderson was considered a "superintendent" of the Underground Railroad. As such, he established a key fugitive slave crossing at Carrollton in the 1840s at the mouth of the Kentucky River, and made numerous forays into Kentucky to organize and lead slave escapes—venturing as far south as Frankfort, Kentucky. After becoming a hunted man, Anderson moved for a time to Lawrenceburg, Indiana, and worked closely with the Ohio Underground Railroad network.

In 1857, Anderson was arrested in Carrollton and was acquitted, initially, since there was insufficient evidence to convict him of any crime related to **fugitive slaves**. However, he was soon arrested again and conveyed to Bedford in nearby Trimble County, Kentucky. This time, "his carpet bag was found to be filled with incendiary documents, proving that he had been engaged in running-off slaves in the neighborhood of Carrollton. The papers ... also implicated many distinguished northerners." (*The Provincial Freeman*, January 3, 1857, in Hudson, 2002: 150.) Anderson was convicted and sent to the Kentucky penitentiary at Frankfort. There, he died tragically—probably a victim of murder—in his cell on the day he was scheduled for release. His brother, William, founder of the African Methodist Episcopal Church in Madison, continued his work. *See also* Appendixes 1 and 2.

FURTHER READING
Coon, Diane P. *Southeastern Indiana's Underground Railroad Routes and* Operations. Indianapolis, IN: Indiana Department of Natural Resources, 2001.
Crenshaw, Gwendolyn J. *Bury Me in a Free Land: The Abolitionist Movement in Indiana, 1816–1865.* Indianapolis: Indiana Historical Bureau, 1993.
Hudson, J. Blaine. *Fugitive Slaves and the Underground Railroad in the Kentucky Borderland.* Jefferson, NC: McFarland, 2002.

Anderson, John

Fugitive slave. After the passage of the **Fugitive Slave Act of 1850**, the free states became increasingly unsafe as havens for **fugitive slaves**. At the same time, **Canada** was another nation — and, because Canadian law prohibited the extradition of freedom seekers, one that became increasingly attractive as an ultimate destination for runaways. Frustrated by the protection afforded by Canadian law, American slave-holders believed that establishing a legal precedent for the extradition of fugitive slaves would enhance significantly their ability to recover their lost human property. The 1860 Anderson case was an attempt to establish such a precedent.

John Anderson was enslaved in Howard County, Missouri. In 1853, his owner, Seneca Diggs, threatened to sell Anderson away from his wife and four children and, when Diggs attempted to seize Anderson and dispose of him to a waiting buyer, Anderson resisted. In the ensuing struggle, Anderson stabbed and mortally wounded Diggs. Anderson knew that killing his master was a death sentence and, in November 1853, fled Missouri and reached Detroit, from which he crossed to Chatham, Canada. There, he enlisted the assistance of Laura **Haviland**, then doing missionary work among fugitive slaves in Canada, who helped him inquire about the welfare of his family. Unfortunately, his inquiries alerted the Missouri authorities to his location and, beginning in late 1853, they began a determined campaign to lure him back onto American soil where he could be arrested.

In 1859, a Canadian judge arrested and jailed Anderson after learning that Anderson was an accused murderer and notified Diggs' friends in Missouri, who then applied to the U.S. government for extradition papers. On November 24, 1860, Anderson's case reached the Court of the Queen's Bench and, on December 15, 1860, the Court ruled (two to one) in favor of extraditing Anderson — prompting a loud public outcry and a mass protest meeting on December 19. Anderson's many supporters, including abolitionist Gerrit **Smith**, decided to appeal the case to English courts and obtained an order from the Court of Queen's Bench at Westminster to bring Anderson there. At the same time, the case was carried to the Court of Common Pleas in Toronto where, on February 16, 1861, Anderson was finally acquitted. Thus, on the eve of the **Civil War**—which would transform the fugitive slave question and, ultimately, make it moot — Canada remained a safe haven for fugitive slaves.

Further Reading
Landon, Fred. "The Anderson Fugitive Case." *Journal of Negro History* 7(1923): 233–242.

Anderson (Armstead), Rosetta

Fugitive slave. Rosetta Armstead was the central figure in an important slave rescue case. Armstead was the property of the Reverend Henry M. Dennison, an Episcopal clergyman who lived in **Louisville**, Kentucky. The young woman belonged originally to former President John Tyler, the father of Dennison's

recently deceased wife, and had been given by Tyler to the Dennisons. In March 1855, after his wife's death, Dennison asked Dr. Miller, "who was bound for Virginia, to take charge of Rosetta, whom he intended as a nurse for his little girl." (*The Louisville Courier,* March 15, 1855, in Hudson, 2002: 141.) The **Ohio River** was ice-locked and the doctor, being forced to travel by rail, was delayed at Columbus. While he was there,

> The news spread through our city that a slave was in our midst, and the Rev. Wm. B. Ferguson, a colored Baptist minister, made complaint before the Judge of Probate, and the Sheriff was dispatched at 12 o'clock on Saturday night, to take charge of the girl ... Dr. Miller stated to the Court his agency in the case, and asked, as a favor that the case might lie over until ... Mr. Dennison could reach here and he could take whatever measures he might deem advisable. But the girl declaring that she desired to remain in freedom in Ohio, and the legal question of the rights being conceded, she was, as a minor, permitted to choose a guardian. L. G. VanSlyke of this city, was selected ... and took charge of her person. [*The Louisville Courier,* March 15, 1855, in Hudson, 2002: 141–142.]

Additional details were presented in the *Ohio Columbian* and reprinted in the African American press, noting that "a colored man ... in the cars from Cincinnati ... fell into conversation with a colored girl ... and learnt from her that she was a slave on her way from Louisville, Ky., to Richmond, Va., in charge of a friend of her master." This unnamed gentleman "informed her that she had a right to her freedom." When so informed, "she manifested surprise ... and at once said she wished to be free." However, after having been "declared free" by the Ohio court, Rosetta — now surnamed "Anderson" in newspaper and court documents— was then "arrested by the U.S. Marshal to be tried by the U.S. Commissioner as a fugitive from slavery" under the provisions of the **Fugitive Slave Act of 1850.** The news report added "there were serious demonstrations on the part of the mob, white and black, to rescue her from the custody of the marshal, but the marshal was resolute and well sustained." (*The Louisville Courier,* March 31, 1855 and April 3, 1855, in Hudson, 2002: 142.) In April 1855, U.S. Commissioner Pendery ruled that

... the proof did not show her to be a fugitive from slavery; but that, on the contrary, she was brought into the State by the consent and at the instance of those who held her ... Being brought thus under the operation of Ohio law, without making an escape, she did not come within the provisions of the fugitive slave act. He also held that the alleged right of transit with slaves as property through the State did not exist. [*The Louisville Courier*, April 6, 1855, in Hudson, 2002: 142.]

Pendery ordered Anderson's release and her "discharge was followed by cheers of the crowd and ... a large number of persons went up and shook hands with her" and "the freed girl seemed much astonished at the greetings she met, and the congratulations she received on attaining the estate of a free woman." (*The Louisville Courier*, April 6, 1855, in Hudson, 2002: 142.) *See also* Fugitive Slaves; Kentucky; Ohio.

FURTHER READING

Hudson, J. Blaine. *Fugitive Slaves and the Underground Railroad in the Kentucky Borderland.* Jefferson, NC: McFarland, 2002.

Anderson, William J. (b. 1811)

Fugitive slave and later friend of the fugitive, William J. Anderson was born free in Hanover County, Virginia, in 1811 to a family headed by a veteran of the American Revolution. However, Anderson's father died and his mother, having no other means of support, hired him to a Virginia slaveholder who soon sold him into slavery despite his free status. In 1836, Anderson, who had learned secretly to read while serving in Virginia, forged a pass and escaped from slavery near Vicksburg, Mississippi, settling in **Madison, Indiana**.

Anderson prospered as a free man, owning three farms and operating businesses both in Madison and later in Indianapolis, Indiana. He also became a key member of the Madison Underground Railroad and, after obtaining a license to preach, became a circuit preacher and pastor of an African Methodist Episcopal Church in Madison.

FURTHER READING

Anderson, William J. *Life and Narrative of William J. Anderson, Twenty-four Years a Slave.* Chicago: Daily Tribune Book and Job Printing Office, 1857.

Anthony, Susan B. (1820–1906)

Leading women's rights crusader and New York friend of the fugitive. Susan B. Anthony was born on February 15, 1820, into a family divided between Baptist and liberal Quaker sympathies. She worked as a teacher for many years and, when she was 29 years old, joined the Daughters of Temperance. She soon became secretary of the organization and inaugurated her public career speaking against the evils of alcohol.

Disenchanted with Quaker divisions over the issue of slavery, Anthony joined the Unitarian Church of William Henry Channing. In 1848, through this new network of contacts, she was invited to attend the first Women's Rights Convention in Seneca Falls, New York, where she met Elizabeth Cady Stanton with whom she would share a close 50-year friendship. Anthony also met Frederick **Douglass**, who had moved to Rochester, and formed another life-long, although at times strained, friendship. Anthony became a stalwart crusader for women's rights and against slavery. Although she did not assist fugitive slaves directly, she did assist friends of the fugitive, most notably through her friendship with

An anti-slavery speech by Susan B. Anthony (Library of Congress)

Douglass and her willingness to house Harriett **Tubman**.

After the Civil War, Anthony remained actively engaged in the women's rights movement for decades. She died on March 13, 1906, at the age of 86. Just before her death, she remarked (holding up her hand and measuring a little space on one finger), "Just think of it, I have been striving for over sixty years for a little bit of justice no bigger than that, and yet I must die without obtaining it. Oh, it seems so cruel!"

FURTHER READING
Barry, Kathleen. *Susan B. Anthony: A Biography of a Singular Feminist.* New York: New York University Press, 1988.

Anti-Slavery Movement

See Abolitionist Movement

Appoquinimink Friends Meeting House (Odessa, Delaware)

Underground Railroad site recognized and documented by the National Park Service. *See also* Appendix 5.

Archy Case

Significant **California** fugitive slave rescue and legal case. In 1857, Archy Lee was brought to California by his owner, C.V. Stovall. Once in the new state, Lee asserted a claim to freedom on the grounds that California law prohibited slavery and, since slavery could not exist in the state, he became free when he reached free soil. Not surprisingly, Stovall contested Lee's claim in court and the California Supreme Court upheld his right to Lee as slave property. This decision provoked a strong reaction among black and white abolitionists in the state, particularly in San Francisco.

When Stovall attempted to return to the South with Lee, he mistakenly passed through San Francisco where antislavery forces had made elaborate preparations to free Lee. After several dramatic and confrontational events, Lee was declared free by federal officials.

FURTHER READING
Lapp, Rudolph M. "The Negro in Gold Rush California." *Journal of Negro History* 49, no. 2(1964): 81–98.

Asa Wing House (Parish, New York)

Underground Railroad site recognized and documented by the National Park Service. *See also* Appendix 5.

Ashley, James M. (b. 1823)

Friend of the fugitive. In the 1840s, James Ashley lived near Greenupsburg, **Kentucky**, and assisted **fugitive slaves** escaping from or through eastern Kentucky through the vicinity of Portsmouth, Ohio. In 1840, working with an elderly enslaved African American, he "rescued a group of five Negroes and took them across the river to a man named Goodrich, living just ... ten miles southeast of Portsmouth. A reward of $500 was offered for the recovery of the slaves. James strolled through Portsmouth to learn whether suspicions were afloat. Two local abolitionists knew what he had been doing. A merchant handed him a ten-dollar gold piece and said he might need it; an old Quaker gave him a hundred-dollar bill, with an approving look." (Siebert, 1895: 2.) Ashley continued his daring rescues until 1851, when he moved to Toledo. *See also* Quakers; and Appendixes 1 and 2.

FURTHER READING
Hudson, J. Blaine. *Fugitive Slaves and the Underground Railroad in the Kentucky Borderland.* Jefferson, NC: McFarland, 2002.

Attucks, Crispus (1723–1770)

Fugitive slave. Crispus Attucks, a fugitive slave and seaman, was killed by the British in March 1770 in what came to be called "the Boston Massacre." Attucks and other Bostonians were protesting the quartering of British troops in **Boston** when the troops opened fire. Attucks was mortally wounded and gained the distinction of being "the first to fall in the American Revolution." *See also* Fugitive Slaves.

FURTHER READING
Quarles, Benjamin. *The Negro in the American Revolution.* Chapel Hill: University of North Carolina Press, 1961.

Austin F. Williams House (Farmington, Connecticut)

Underground Railroad site recognized and documented by the National Park Service. *See also* Appendix 5.

Crispus Attucks (Library of Congress)

Barker, David, and Vania Barker

Friends of the fugitive. David and Vania Barker were **Quakers** living near Niagara Falls, New York. Barker used his large home to conceal **fugitive slaves** and often transported them himself by wagon to Niagara Falls. *See also* Appendixes 1 and 2.

Barney L. Ford Building (Denver, Colorado)

Underground Railroad site recognized and documented by the National Park Service. *See also* Appendix 5.

Bates, Polly Ann

Fugitive Slave. *See also* Bates and Small Fugitive Slave Rescue

Bates and Small Fugitive Slave Rescue

Fugitive slave rescue. On July 30, 1836, Polly Ann Bates and Eliza Small, **fugitive slaves** from Baltimore, Maryland, arrived in **Boston, Massachusetts,** by ship. While still in port, Matthew Turner, agent of a Baltimore

slaveholder, claimed the two women and, when one produced a certificate of freedom, Turner confiscated the document and refused to return it. He then procured a warrant for their arrest.

Word spread swiftly through the black and white antislavery community of Boston, and members of the abolitionist movement soon obtained a writ of habeas corpus from Chief Justice Lemuel Shaw. Turner's attorney argued for the return of the women under the provisions of the **Fugitive Slave Act of 1793.** Samuel Sewall, a young antislavery attorney, argued that the women were and should remain free.

Shaw ruled in favor of Bates and Small on narrow legal grounds and Turner then threatened to obtain a warrant and have the women arrested in open court. At this point, blacks and whites in the crowded courtroom threw the court officer to the floor and rushed Bates and Small to a waiting carriage. They escaped from Boston with a posse in hot pursuit.

A month later, a sailor from Baltimore, who claimed to be a relative of the owner of Bates and Small, entered Samuel Sewall's office and beat him with the butt of a horsewhip.

FURTHER READING
Anti-Slavery Collection, Boston Public Library.
Cumbler, John T. "To Do Battle for Justice and the Oppressed." Unpublished manuscript. Department of History, University of Louisville, 2004.
Levy, Leonard W. *The Law of the Commonwealth and Chief Justice Shaw.* Cambridge: Harvard University Press, 1957.

Battle Creek, Michigan

Underground Railroad junction. Located in central Michigan, Battle Creek, later better-known for cereal, was an important center of Underground Railroad activity in the 1840s and 1850s. Under the leadership of Erastus **Hussey** and others, friends of the fugitive assisted over one thousand **fugitive slaves** in the decades before the **Civil War.**

Sojourner **Truth** moved to the area in 1857 and, for 10 years, lived in the nearby village of Harmonia, a community of **Quakers** and Spiritualists a few miles west of Battle Creek. In 1867, she and her family moved into town, where she lived until her death in 1883. *See also* Underground Railroad, Sites of; and Appendixes 3 and 4.

Baxter, James

Friend of the fugitive in **Madison**, Indiana. *See also* Appendixes 1 and 2.

Beckley, Guy (d. 1847)

Friend of the fugitive in Ann Arbor, Michigan. *See also* **Guy Beckley House.**

Beecher, Henry Ward

Friend of the fugitive in Brooklyn, New York. *See also* **Plymouth Church of the Pilgrims.** *See also* Appendixes 1 and 2.

Bell, Charles

Friend of the fugitive in Brandenburg, **Kentucky**. *See also* Bell-Wright Affair. *See also* Appendixes 1 and 2.

Bell, David

Friend of the fugitive in Brandenburg, **Kentucky**. *See also* Bell-Wright Affair. *See also* Appendixes 1 and 2.

Bell-Wright Affair (1857)

On September 25, 1857, an enslaved African American named Charles escaped from his owner, Henry A. Ditto of Brandenburg, **Kentucky**. Charles received assistance from several men: David Bell, who owned and operated the Brandenburg ferry; Charlie Bell, his son and assistant; and Oswell Wright, a free person of color living in Corydon, **Indiana**. The Bell family migrated to Indiana in 1829 and moved from New Albany to Harrison County in 1839. The elder Bell was suspected of being an abolitionist, but never made any public declaration of such sentiments. Oswell Wright moved to Indiana from Maryland, probably in the 1820s as well, and found work in Corydon as a laborer.

Virtually nothing is known about Charles, but, when he decided to escape, he knew whom to contact. Once arrangements were finalized, the Bells ferried Charles across the **Ohio River** and, presumably, delivered him to Wright — who then conveyed Charles to Brownstown where other antislavery sympa-

thizers spirited him farther north. Charles vanishes from the formal history at this point.

Ditto and his slaveholding neighbors suspected that David and Charlie Bell had contrived to aid Charles. Their suspicions were strengthened by the testimony of C.E. Johnson, who claimed that he met Wright in Brownstown, befriended him and gained his confidence, and that Wright admitted his role in Charles' escape. Johnson then claimed to have insinuated himself into the company of the Bell family by posing as someone wishing to arrange for the escape of Charles' wife. Johnson later stated in court that

> ... he went to the house of the Bells, and after laying around for several days, drinking whisky and telling tales about running off Negroes, until he gained the confidence of the old man Bell, that he (Bell) confessed that he had assisted the boy Charles in getting off. He said he communicated these facts to Mr. Ditto, whereupon a posse of Kentuckians crossed the river and kidnapped and carried the two Bells across the river, together with the Negro Oswell, and lodged them in the Brandenburg jail. [*The Louisville Courier,* November 19, 1857, in Hudson, 2002: 149.]

The Bells and Wright were indicted subsequently for the crime of "assisting slaves to escape." All three languished in jail well into 1858 as the case was continued repeatedly. In the meantime, Bell's other sons, Horace and John, were called home from **California** to rescue their father and brother. The other Bells were well-equipped for such a task, particularly Horace — a colorful and adventuresome figure who had already survived William Walker's ill-fated attempt to seize Nicaragua in 1857 and who would later rise to the rank of major in the Union Army. In May 1858, Horace and John Bell executed a classic "jailbreak":

> ... on a day when many of the citizens of Brandenburg were away attending a picnic, they went to Brandenburg where they forced the jailor to open the doors and liberated their father and brother. The four ran quickly to their skiff and started to cross the river, but were soon discovered and pursued. Horace stood up in the boat with a revolver in each hand and by keeping up a rapid fire held the pursuers at bay until they reached the Indiana shore. [Saulman, 1999: 73.]

Oswell Wright was not rescued. Ultimately, he was tried, convicted and sentenced to five years in the Kentucky State Penitentiary. Interestingly, Wright was defended by Judge William A. Porter (1800–1884), one of the most prominent men in southern Indiana and a man also suspected of having aided an occasional fugitive. Wright survived his prison term and returned to Corydon, where he died — a local legend — in 1875.

As a postscript, Iris Cook of the Federal Writers' Project interviewed Mrs. Mattie Brown Smith in the mid–1930s, then a resident of New Albany. Smith's parents had been enslaved in Kentucky and Charles, the fugitive slave in the Bell-Wright affair, was her fraternal uncle, Charles Woodruff. From her knowledge of family and community oral traditions, Smith added crucial details to the published accounts that are remarkably consistent with those accounts (of which she was unaware). For example, she recounted that her uncle was a blacksmith hired out in Brandenburg who used contacts established through his work to arrange his escape. A white man "found out Uncle wanted to go across" and

> ... got in touch with a certain man who ferried slaves across the river ... an old white man named Charles Bell living in Harrison county, just below Corydon ... Mr. Bell had a skiff which he used to carry the slaves over ... and one dark night Uncle Charles got a few things together and he sneaked around and told his wife and children goodbye, and they went down to the Ohio River ... Bell took Uncle Charles across the river in a skiff, and on back through the woods on a mule to his house where he hid him a few weeks and then took him on up thru Corydon ... and he went up to Canada and got out to California. [Cook, 1936: 15–17.]

When the **Civil War** began, Smith indicated that Woodruff returned from California and joined the Union Army. *See also* Free People of Color; Fugitive Slaves.

FURTHER READING

Cook, Iris L., "Underground Railroad in Southern Indiana." Federal Writers' Project, unpublished notes, ca. 1936. Presented to the author by Ms. Cook's grandniece, 1999.

Hudson, J. Blaine. *Fugitive Slaves and the Underground Railroad in the Kentucky Borderland.* Jefferson, NC: McFarland, 2002.

Saulman, Earl O., "Blacks in Harrison County, Indiana." Unpublished manuscript, Corydon, Indiana, 1999.

Benedict, Reuben

Friend of the fugitive Reuben Benedict, his wife, Anna, and their 12 children migrated from New York to Morrow County, **Ohio** in 1812. The Benedict family became the nucleus of the first Quaker settlement in the region and their home served as a station on the Underground Railroad. As one example, in 1839, the Benedict home was a refuge for fugitive slave Bill **Anderson**. *See also* Quakers; Reuben Benedict House.

FURTHER READING

National Park Service. *Underground Railroad: Special Resource Study.* Washington, D.C.: U.S. Government Printing Office, 1995.

Berea College (Berea, Kentucky)

Anti-Slavery and Underground Railroad site. Berea College was founded in 1855 by the Reverend John G. Fee. Located on land given to Fee by **Kentucky** abolitionist Cassius Marcellus Clay, Berea was the only institution in a slave-holding state committed to educating both African Americans and whites. The college was also reputed to have served as an Underground Railroad station.

Hostile whites forced Berea to close after John **Brown**'s Raid in 1859, but the college reopened a multi-racial institution in 1865. Before African Americans were barred from attending Berea by the Kentucky General Assembly in 1904, Berea's African American graduates included Dr. Carter G. Woodson and James M. Bond, grandfather of activist Julian Bond.

FURTHER READING

Peck, Elisabeth S. *Berea's First Century, 1855–1955.* Lexington: University of Kentucky Press, 1955.

Pelton, Louise. *A Brief History of Berea College.* Berea, KY: N.p., 1963.

Sears, Richard D. *A Utopian Experiment in Kentucky: Integration and Social Equality at Berea, 1866–1904.* Westport, CT: Greenwood Press, 1996.

Bethel AME Church (Greenwich Township, New Jersey)

Underground Railroad site recognized and documented by the National Park Service. *See also* Appendix 5.

Bethel AME Church (Indianapolis, Indiana)

Underground Railroad site recognized and documented by the National Park Service. *See also* Appendix 5.

Bethel AME Church (Providence, Rhode Island)

Underground Railroad site. Bethel AME Church originated in 1795 as the African Freedmen's Society. The church was a well-known Underground Railroad station during the ante-bellum period. *See also* Underground Railroad, Sites of; and Appendixes 3 and 4.

Bethel AME Church (Reading, Pennsylvania)

Underground Railroad site recognized and documented by the National Park Service. *See also* Appendix 5.

Bibb, Henry (1815–1854)

Fugitive slave and friend of the fugitive. Henry Bibb, known as Walton to his owner, was born enslaved in 1815 in Shelby County near Louisville, **Kentucky**. In Bibb's words, he "was brought up in the Counties of Shelby, Henry, Oldham and Trimble. Or, more correctly speaking, in the above counties, I may safely say that I was flogged up" (Bibb, 1849). Bibb attempted his first escape in 1835, was caught and whipped, but soon escaped again and was caught and flogged yet once more, then returned to his increasingly exasperated owner.

Bibb's determination to escape subsided temporarily while he courted and subsequently "married" Malinda, a lovely young African American woman enslaved in Oldham County — the daughter of a free woman of color living in nearby Bedford, Kentucky. Fatherhood soon followed, but being a husband and father whose wife and child were the property of another man rekindled his longing for freedom, this time for himself and his family. Promising to return for them, Bibb escaped on Christmas day in 1837.

Bibb reached **Cincinnati** and, with the assistance of a free man of color and some local Abolitionists, moved north until he reached Perrysburgh, "where he found quite a

Engraved by P H Reason

Henry Bibb

Henry Bibb (Library of Congress)

settlement of free people of color, many of whom were fugitive slaves." (Bibb, 1849: 89.) Settling there, Bibb returned to Kentucky several times until, in 1839, after finally rescuing his family, he was caught and imprisoned in Louisville along with his wife and child. Eventually, the Bibb family was loaded aboard the steamboat *Water Witch* bound for Vicksburg and later New Orleans. Bibb's next year was filled with a succession of foiled escapes, brutal punishments and, ultimately, separation from his wife and daughter in 1840, when Malinda and their child were sold to gamblers and Bibb was sold to a Native American. Not surprisingly, in early 1841, Bibb escaped again across the prairie, reached the Mississippi River and traveled by steamboat to Portsmouth, **Ohio**. He would never see his wife and daughter again.

With no hope of recovering his family, Bibb turned his attention and devoted his considerable abilities to advancing the anti-slavery cause. He remarried in 1848 and, after becoming a noted Abolitionist lecturer, published *Narrative of the Life of Henry Bibb, An American Slave* in 1849. On January 1, 1851, with the assistance of his wife, Mary, Bibb established the first successful African American newspaper in **Canada** West, *Voice of the Fugitive*, and became both a true friend of his fellow fugitives and a tireless advocate of black self-help in Canada. Unfortunately, Bibb, died on August 1, 1854 at the age of 39.

While Bibb's newspaper became an important although short-lived publication, his *Narrative* developed a life of its own. Because his extraordinary courage and devotion to family strained credibility even among his friends, Bibb introduced his *Narrative* with a collection of documents intended to "establish the truth" of his account, among which was even a letter from the son of his former owner. As a result, although Bibb hoped to serve one purpose with his autobiography, he created an unusually reliable source for the study of **fugitive slaves** and friends of the fugitive.

Bibb's last glimpse of Kentucky as he beheld it on his final steamboat journey to freedom is a poignant evocation of the ambivalence so many fugitives felt toward a home that was never truly their home: "I was permitted by the smiles of good providence, once more to gaze on the green hill-tops and valleys of old Kentucky, the State of my nativity ... my very soul was pained to look upon the slaves in the fields ..."(Bibb, 1849: 150).

FURTHER READING

Bibb, Henry. *Narrative of the Life of Henry Bibb, An American Slave.* New York: Privately printed, 1849.

Cooper, Afua. "The Fluid Frontier: Blacks and the Detroit River Region, A Focus on Henry Bibb." *Canadian Review of American Studies* 30(2000): 129–149.

Kimmel, Janice M. "Break Your Chains and Fly for Freedom." *Michigan History Magazine* 80, no. 1(1996): 21–27.

Big Dipper

The Big Dipper, or Ursa Major (the Great Bear), is a northern circumpolar constellation used to locate Polaris, the **North Star** that served as a beacon and a guide to enslaved African Americans fleeing slave territory. The Big Dipper served this unique purpose because its brightest stars outline the shape of a vessel or bowl with a handle and the two bright stars in the front of the bowl point to the North Star. Even enslaved African American children were taught to use the Big Dipper as the most reliable means of locating true north.

In the African tradition, Ursa Major was known as the Drinking Gourd. Hence, the famous Underground Railroad song, "Follow the Drinking Gourd," developed as a code song for enslaved African Americans seeking to escape the Cotton Kingdom, particularly from Alabama and Georgia. *See also* Songs.

Bigelow, Jacob

Friend of the fugitive in **Washington, D.C.** *See also* Appendixes 1 and 2.

Black Seminoles

Fugitive slaves and **friends of the fugitive.** The history of Florida was heavily influenced by the evolution of an alliance between Africans and the Muscogulges, i.e., members of the Seminole nation. The Seminoles broke away from the Creek Nation, centered in Alabama, in the 1600s and migrated into Spanish territory in northern Florida.

As enslaved African Americans poured into the Carolinas, Florida became an attractive destination for fugitive slaves fleeing bondage in the rice and indigo plantations. This attraction was heightened by the Spanish promise of freedom to those fugitive slaves who reached Florida and pledged their loyalty to the Spanish colonial government. Thus, by the early 1700s, African Americans had become a significant minority in northern Florida and were central to the defense of the colony — e.g., in 1738, blacks founded Mose (Gracia Real de Santa Teresa de Mose, later know as **Fort Mose**) in Northeastern Florida. Further, by this time, many African Americans had blended —culturally and biologically — with the Seminoles, producing the Black Seminoles. In essence, the Spanish regarded the Black Seminoles and other African American freedom seekers in Florida as colonists, while the British regarded them as fugitive slaves or "maroons."

Because they were armed, dangerous and willing to defend their freedom, African Americans and Black Seminoles in Florida were a source of both consternation and fear to the American colonists. For example, alone or with the help of their Seminole allies, blacks raided plantations in Georgia and the Carolinas, carrying off arms and often other willing fugitives. Not surprisingly, the enslaved African Americans who joined in the Cato Rebellion in 1739 near Charleston, South Carolina, had, as their goal, escape to freedom in Florida.

When Britain gained control of Florida in 1763, as a consequence of the French and Indian War, many blacks fled to Cuba with the retreating Spanish. During the American Revolution, political instability along with the promise of freedom, made explicit in Lord Dunmore's Proclamation of November 1775, stimulated an extremely heavy flow of fugitive slaves from the southern U.S. colonies into Florida. After the Revolution, this attraction persisted because Florida became Spanish property again until 1819 — and, if the Seminoles and black maroons trusted the British less than the Spanish, they had reason to trust the United States even less than the British. Their fears were well-founded.

Negro Abraham.

Abraham was a fugitive slave who lived with the Seminoles. (Library of Congress)

The problem was simple. After the War of 1812, the great southern Native American nations (i.e., the Chickasaws, Cherokees, Choctaws, Creeks and Seminoles) blocked the expansion of cotton cultivation and slavery into the Gulf States— and Florida was the literal "wide open back door" of American slavery through which blacks pouring into the heart of the Cotton Kingdom could escape. Ultimately, by warfare and duplicity, the Native Americans were dispossessed by the Indian Removal Act (1830). However, the Seminoles, because of the Black Seminole and black maroon presence, posed a far more formidable problem than the other groups.

To remove this presence, the United States fought a series of bitter and costly wars in Florida against as many as 60,000 Seminoles and black maroons. In 1816, the First Seminole War began when American land and sea forces converged on Fort Negro on the Appalachiola River. Three hundred Black Seminoles defended the fort and the American attack had little initial effect until a cannon ball ignited a munitions dump, touching off massive explosions in the fort that lifted "smoke, flame, debris, and mangled bodies" into the air. (Wright, 1986: 199.) The fort was taken and its leaders executed. Many of the Black Seminoles escaped to other settlements, but the black settlement around Fort Negro which stretched for miles along the river was abandoned. In 1818, the United States Army constructed Fort Gadsden, adjoining the ruins of Fort Negro, to prevent the resurrection of that maroon community.

By the 1830s, a new generation of Black Seminole warrior leaders had emerged — most importantly, Osceola, part African himself, with an African wife; Wildcat; and the Black Seminole, John Horse. The Black Seminoles had retreated farther into the swamps and remote areas, and retained an antislavery philosophy that derived more from the philosophy of the American Revolution than from the views of William Lloyd **Garrison**. Tensions mounted in the aftermath of the 1831 Nat Turner Revolt as whites grew fearful of restive Indians and blacks. To force the Seminoles to comply with the Indian Removal Act (1830), Major Francis Langhorne Dade was dispatched from Tampa on December 23,

1835 to pacify the region around Fort King, about 100 miles north. Dade was accompanied by roughly 100 troops and, on December 29, 1835, was attacked and killed along with all of his men. Black Seminoles figured prominently in this attack that was coordinated with another foray led by Osceola that killed the Seminole Indian agent, Wiley Thompson, at Fort King.

The Second Seminole War continued until 1842, but the defeat of Major Dade as the last great victory for the Seminoles. In the end, the Black Seminoles — as with other Native American societies — were vastly outnumbered and, rather than suffering a decisive defeat, were simply worn down by attrition. In March 1837, the United States set the terms under which the Seminoles would be moved to Indiana Territory in Oklahoma. In December 1837, Osceola was captured, although under a flag of truce, and jailed in St. Augustine. Instead of being sent to Oklahoma, he and his family were sent to Charleston, where he died two months later. As conditions worsened, many Black Seminoles fled to the Caribbean after slavery was abolished on the British islands between 1834 and 1838. Still, Wildcat and John Horse fought on until October 1841, when they were sent to Oklahoma. Florida was finally pacified and became a state in 1845. A desultory Third Seminole War was fought in the mid–1850s, but had little effect on the small pockets of Seminoles and Black Seminoles who remained in the remote swamps of Florida.

The Second Seminole War cost over $40 million and as the most costly of all U.S. "Indian Wars"—something of a nineteenth-century Viet Nam War—largely because it was not an "Indian War" at all. As General Thomas Jessup stated in 1837: "This, you may be assured, is a Negro, not an Indian war, and if it be not speedily put down, the South will feel the effects of it on their slave population before the end of the next season." (Wright, 1986: 275.) Abolitionist Congressman Joshua **Giddings** also emphasized that race was the fundamental issue in the Seminole Wars in his book, *Exiles of Florida* (1858).

Many of the Black Seminoles who were "deported" to Oklahoma soon found their way into Mexico and later distinguished themselves as some of the most formidable warriors in America in the Civil War — and as forbearers of some of the members of the 9th and 10th Cavalries (i.e., the Buffalo Soldiers). *See also* Fugitive Slaves; Maroon Societies.

FURTHER READING

Deagan, Kathleen A., and MacMahon, Darcie. *Fort Mose: Colonial America's Black Fortress of Freedom.* Gainesville: University Press of Florida, 1995.

Katz, William Loren. *Black Indians: A Hidden Heritage.* New York: Atheneum, 1986.

Landers, Jane. "Gracia Real de Santa Teresa de Mose: A Free Black Town in Spanish Colonial Florida." *The American Historical Review* 95(1990): 9–30.

Lindsay, Arnettt G. "Diplomatic Relations Between the United States and Great Britain Bearing on the Return of Negro Slaves, 1783–1828." *Journal of Negro History* 4(1920): 391–419.

Porter, Kenneth Wiggins. "Negroes and the Seminole War, 1835–1842." *Journal of Southern History* 30(1964): 427–450.

Price, Richard, ed. *Maroon Societies: Rebel Slave Communities in the Americas.* Baltimore, MD: The Johns Hopkins University Press, 1996.

Twyman, Bruce E. *The Black Seminole Legacy and North American Politics, 1693–1845.* Washington, D.C.: Howard University Press, 1999.

Wright, J. Leitch, Jr. *Creeks and Seminoles: The Destruction and Regeneration of the Muscolgulge People.* Lincoln, NE: University of Nebraska Press, 1986.

Blackburn, Thornton (b. 1814), and Lucie Blackburn

Fugitive slaves and fugitive slave rescue case. Thornton and Lucy Blackburn were notable fugitives from **Louisville,** Kentucky in the early 1830s. Thornton Blackburn was born about 1814 in Maysville, **Kentucky**. He moved to Louisville with his owners in 1830 and escaped on July 3, 1831. In the fugitive slave advertisement placed after his flight, Blackburn was described as "about 5 feet, 9 or 10 inches high; stout made, and of a yellow complexion; light eyes, and of good address."

His wife, Lucie Blackburn —called "Ruth" or "Ruthie"— described herself as "a Creole from the West Indies." She was purchased by Virgil McKnight, president of the Bank of Kentucky, only a few weeks before she fled with her husband. Given McKnight's propensity to purchase enslaved African Americans in estate sales, and then sell them south, the real possibility that Lucy would be sold may have precipitated their flight.

The fugitive couple crossed the **Ohio River** to Jeffersonville, **Indiana**, and, posing as free people of color, boarded the steamboat, *Versailles*. Disembarking at **Cincinnati, Ohio**, they traveled to Sandusky, Ohio, by stagecoach and reached **Detroit** on July 18, 1831. The relative ease with which they escaped suggests that they had a sound plan, possibly contacts in Jeffersonville and **Cincinnati**—and that they had funds.

They remained in Detroit, living humbly but happily by all accounts, until discovered by a member of the Oldham family in 1833. They were arrested and jailed, and a trial ensued to determine whether or not the couple should be returned to bondage in Kentucky. The presiding judge ruled in favor of their owner(s). However, Detroit's free black community refused to accept this decision and "took matters into their own hands." First, Mrs. George French and Mrs. Madison Mason, wives of ministers of Detroit's Black Baptist Church were allowed to visit Lucie Blackburn. While unobserved, Mrs. French changed clothing with Lucie, who then escaped the jail in this disguise and was "spirited ... across the Detroit River and into Canada." (Smardz, 1999: 249–250.)

Not surprisingly, Lucie's escape tightened the restrictions on her husband. On June 17, when he was bound in chains for his long return journey to Kentucky, the black and now also many white citizens of Detroit became so incensed that 400 of them marched on the jail where he was held captive. They wrested Thornton from custody after beating the sheriff so severely that he died of his injuries a year later. Thornton was then placed in a wagon and a wild race began toward the Detroit River with a posse in hot pursuit. Thornton's entourage thought it best to abandon their wagon and hastened through the forest to the riverbank on foot. There, one of Thornton's eight rescuers sacrificed his gold watch to pay his passage across the river. The Blackburns settled eventually in Toronto and became pillars of the Canadian antislavery movement. *See also* Abolitionist Movement; Canada.

FURTHER READING
Smardz, Karolyn E. "There We Were in Darkness, Here We Are in Light: Kentucky Slaves and the Promised Land." In *The Buzzel About Kentuck: Settling the Promised Land*, edited by Craig Thompson Friend, 243–248. Lexington: University Press of Kentucky, 1999.

Bloodhounds

Using bloodhounds was such an effective and potentially deadly means of recapturing fugitive slaves that the animals were sometimes termed "Negro dogs." These hunting animals were specially trained to catch runaways by following the scent from a shoe or article of clothing, and trainers typically let young dogs track enslaved African Americans as practice. Ironically, although many different breeds were used for this purpose, the best-known dogs were the fierce bloodhounds imported from Cuba and specially bred by President Zachary Taylor, who owned a plantation in Louisiana.

Once on a scent trail, bloodhounds were relentless in their pursuit and, when they overtook or "treed" their quarry, would literally rip him or her apart if not restrained. If a fugitive slave was foolish or unfortunate, a slave hunt—like lynching in later years—could become a sport, with a mounted party of slave catchers and slave-holders following the hounds, who followed their prey. *See also* Fugitive Slaves; Patrols.

FURTHER READING
Franklin, John H., and Schweninger, Loren. *Runaway Slaves: Rebels on the Plantation.* New York: McGraw-Hill, 1999.

Booth, Griffith

Friend of the fugitive in **Madison, Indiana**. *See also* Underground Railroad, Sites of; and Appendixes 3 and 4.

Booth, Sherman

Friend of the fugitive in Wisconsin. *See also* Glover Case; and Underground Railroad, Sites of; and Appendixes 3 and 4.

Borderland

According to John **Parker,** the courageous African American Underground Railroad conductor operating out of Ripley, **Ohio,**

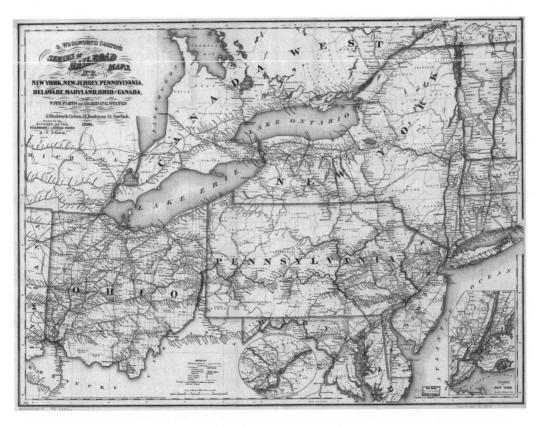

The Borderland (1860) (Library of Congress)

in the **1850s**, the "Borderland" was the "strip of land between northern and southern states ... between Kentucky and Ohio, with the Ohio River flowing between." Extending Parker's definition, the Borderland included the border slave states—i.e., Missouri (and Kansas), Kentucky, Virginia, Maryland, and Delaware — and the free states immediately to the North, i.e., Nebraska, **Iowa, Illinois, Indiana**, Ohio, **Pennsylvania**, and New Jersey.

In this region, **fugitive slaves** negotiated the perilous passage from slave to free territory. Also, in this region, free people of color were most numerous and conflicts between pro- and antislavery advocates were most intense on a practical, if not ideological, level. In this respect, the Borderland was the true battleground of the Underground Railroad. *See also* Kentucky; Ohio River.

FURTHER READING

Hudson, J. Blaine. *Fugitive Slaves and the Underground Railroad in the Kentucky Borderland.* Jefferson, NC: McFarland, 2002.

Sprague, Stuart S., ed. *His Promised Land: The Autobiography of John P. Parker, Former Slave and Conductor on the Underground Railroad.* New York: W. W. Norton, 1996.

Boston, Massachusetts

Underground Railroad junction. In 1629, the Reverend William Blackstone reached a stream known as Shawmet by the Algonquin inhabitants of the area. On September 17, 1630, John Winthrop and his Puritan settlers of the Massachusetts Bay Colony founded a permanent settlement at the site and named it Boston, after Winthrop's hometown in Lincolnshire, England.

Boston and its surrounding region grew and prospered through the 1700s, and maritime trade, including slave trade, developed into a major enterprise. Loyalty to the British crown began to weaken in the 1730s when the mother country began increasing taxes on American subjects to replenish the royal treasury. Soon, Boston became a center of colonial resistance and played a central role in the American Revolution and, when Massachusetts abolished slavery in 1783, a small free black community took root in Boston.

Massachusetts prospered in the early 19th century with improved roads, new canals, and the construction of railways, linking cities and towns, and Boston was a key beneficiary of this general prosperity, attracting numerous immigrants, especially from Ireland, beginning in the 1830s. During this period, Boston became a center of the American antislavery movement and an important sanctuary for **fugitive slaves**. The combined efforts of an active white antislavery community and a committed free black community made Boston one of the true havens for freedom seekers, many of whom settled there before the **Fugitive Slave Act of 1850** made it increasingly dangerous to remain in the United States. For related entries, see Anthony **Burns**, William Lloyd **Garrison**, Leonard A. **Grimes**, Lewis **Hayden**, Shadrach **Minkins**, Wendell **Phillips**, and Charles **Sumner**.

FURTHER READING
Hart, Albert Bushnell. *Commonwealth History of Massachusetts*. 1927. Reprint, New York: Russell & Russell, 1966.
Jacobs, Donald M., ed. *Courage and Conscience: Black and White Abolitionists in Boston*. Indianapolis, IN: Indiana University Press, 1993.
Winsor, Justin, ed. *The Memorial History of Boston, including Suffolk County, Massachusetts, 1630–1880*. Boston: N.p., 1880.

Boston African American National Historic Site

Underground Railroad site recognized and documented by the National Park Service. *See also* Appendix 5.

Boston Slave Riot

See Burns, Anthony

Boston Vigilance Committee

See Vigilance Committees

Boulwar, John

Friend of the fugitive in Nebraska City, Nebraska. *See also* Appendixes 1 and 2.

Bowditch, William Ingersoll

A friend of the fugitive, William Ingersoll Bowditch was a conveyancer with a home in Brookline, **Massachusetts** and an office in **Boston**. Between 1845 and 1867, he was a popular antislavery lecturer and member of the Boston Vigilance Committee. He also harbored fugitive slaves in his home and conducted them to neighboring stations.

Those to whom Bowditch gave refuge included William and Ellen **Craft** and the younger son of John **Brown** in flight from the authorities after his father's ill-fated attempt to seize the federal arsenal at **Harpers Ferry** in 1859. *See also* Bowditch House.

Bowditch House (Brookline, Massachusetts)

Underground Railroad site recognized and documented by the National Park Service. *See also* Appendix 5.

Bowen, Anthony

Friend of the fugitive in **Washington, D.C.** See also Appendixes 1 and 2.

Brent, Linda

See Jacobs, Harriet A.

Bridge Street AME Wesleyan Church (Brooklyn, New York)

Underground Railroad station. Bridge Street A. M. E. Wesleyan Church, in what is now the Bedford-Stuyvesant section of Brooklyn, New York, traces its origins to 1766, when a British officer conducted outdoor religious services there. African Americans and whites later worshipped together at the same location — but blacks broke away to form their own AME Wesleyan Church in 1818.

The oldest African American church in Brooklyn, Bridge Street AME became a sanctuary for hundreds of **fugitive slaves**. Bridge Street also contributed to the founding of **Wilberforce College** (now University) near **Xenia, Ohio**. *See also* Underground Railroad, Sites of; and Appendixes 3 and 4.

Bristol Hill Church (Fulton, New York)

Underground Railroad site recognized and documented by the National Park Service. *See also* Appendix 5.

British Fort (Franklin County, Florida)

Underground Railroad site recognized and documented by the National Park Service. *See also* Appendix 5.

British Methodist Episcopal Church (St. Catherine, Canada)

Underground Railroad site. Located in St. Catherine, Ontario, **Canada**, the British Methodist Episcopal Church was termed the proverbial "last stop" on the Underground Railroad. The church was founded in 1840 and, after the original structure was destroyed, was rebuilt in 1855. *See also* Underground Railroad, Sites of; and Appendixes 3 and 4.

Brown, Henry "Box" (b. 1815)

Fugitive slave. One of the most famous **fugitive slaves**— with one of the most memorable and unique modes of escape — was Henry Brown. Henry Brown was born en-slaved in 1815 in Louisa County, Virginia. By 1830, he was hired out to work in a Richmond, Virginia, tobacco factory and, as a highly regarded worker, was able to earn some wages. In the mid–1830s, he "married" abroad to a "slave washerwoman" named Nancy, i.e., Brown and his wife had different owners. Brown used his meager funds to pay Nancy's master for the time she spent caring for their three children. In 1848, Brown's wife and children were sold into North Carolina. Brown was said to have walked a few miles with them as their coffle moved south, but was not allowed to accompany them farther — and never saw them again. Devastated by this loss, Brown laid his plan to escape.

On March 29, 1849, Samuel A. Smith, a white Virginian, nailed Henry Brown in a wooden crate and shipped him by the Adams Express Company from Richmond, Virginia, to William H. Johnson, an abolitionist in Philadelphia. In 27 hours, Brown traveled 350 miles — all in danger and considerable discomfort since, at 5 feet 8 inches tall and 200

A somewhat comic yet sympathetic portrayal from a broadside shows Henry "Box" Brown emerging from a crate in the office of the Pennsylvania Anti-Slavery Society. Frederick Douglass, second from left, holds a claw hammer. (Library of Congress)

pounds, he was not a small man. When the crate arrived on March 30, 1849, it was delivered to the Philadelphia Vigilance Committee under the leadership of William **Still**. When the nervous abolitionists opened the box, Henry Brown "calmly emerged" and said, "How do you do, gentlemen?" And then fainted. He soon revived and proceeded to sing the 40th Psalm.

Once news of his escape spread, Henry "Box" Brown became an instant celebrity. He stayed briefly with abolitionists James and Lucretia Mott and then moved farther from slave territory to **Boston** and later **New Bedford, Massachusetts**. He became a popular lecturer on the antislavery lecture circuit, with an entertaining message and a good singing voice, and published the narrative of his life in 1850.

Brown's public visibility and determination to speak out against slavery made his freedom precarious. He narrowly escaped capture on August 30, 1850, and fled to England after the passage of the **Fugitive Slave Act of 1850** in September.

Incidentally, Samuel A. Smith, the white Virginian who "packed and mailed" Brown, was arrested and convicted in October 1849 for "boxing up" two other fugitives. Smith was imprisoned, suffered greatly, and was not released until June 18, 1856. Additionally, James Caesar Anthony Smith, a free person of color who also assisted Brown, was also arrested and, although he admitted to assisting fugitives since 1826, was not imprisoned. Apparently, James Smith had worked with an African American carpenter, John Mattauer, to build special escape trunks and crates.

While in England, Brown continued on the lecture (and singing) circuit until 1862. As was the case with many fugitive slaves, Brown returned eventually to anonymity as a free man and disappeared from the historical record in 1864. His date and place of death are unknown. *See also* "The Mirror of Slavery"; Vigilance Committees.

FURTHER READING
Brown, Henry. *Narrative of the Life of Henry "Box" Brown*, 1850.
Nichols, Charles H., ed. *Black Men in Chains: Narratives by Escaped Slaves*. New York: L. Hill, 1972.
Still, William Still. *The Underground Railroad*. 1872. Reprint, Chicago: Johnson, 1970.

Brown, James

Friend of the fugitive in **Wilberforce, Canada**. *See also* Appendixes 1 and 2.

Brown, John (1800–1859)

A militant white abolitionist and friend of the fugitive who became a martyr to the cause of freedom. John Brown was born in Torrington, Connecticut, on May 9, 1800. In 1820 he married Dianthe Lusk. Before she died in childbirth in 1832, their marriage produced seven children. In 1833, Brown married Mary Ann Day, of Meadville, Pennsylvania, and his second marriage produced 13 children, six of whom survived to adulthood.

Over the years, Brown engaged in a variety of occupations and became a strong proponent of direct and practical methods to oppose **slavery**. After the passage of the 1854 Kansas-Nebraska Act, Brown moved to Kansas

John Brown, 1859 (Library of Congress)

John Brown and other prisoners leave the engine room after being trapped in an 1859 engraving. (Library of Congress)

Territory with other antislavery settlers determined to prevent the territory from entering the Union as a slave state. When Lawrence, Kansas, a free-state stronghold, was destroyed by proslavery forces in 1856, John Brown, his four sons and a few others retaliated by killing five proslavery men living near Pottawatomie Creek on May 24, 1856. Afterward, Brown declared to his son, Jason: "I have only a short time to live — and only one death to die, and I will die fighting for this cause. There will be no peace in this land until slavery is done for." (Reynolds, 2005: 202.)

Proslavery forces retaliated and attacked Brown's small band at Osawatomie in August 1856, inflicting numerous casualties. Brown then left Kansas, conducting **fugitive slaves** from Missouri through **Iowa** on his journey east, and began to formulate plans for a much more ambitious assault on slavery.

As a man of action, Brown grew increasingly critical of the "milk and water" abolitionists and moved to **Canada** to recruit what amounted to a small paramilitary force from the large fugitive slave population resident there. Ultimately, he organized a band of 12 whites and 34 African Americans, raised a significant amount of money from American abolitionists, drew up a document titled the

"Provisional Constitution and Ordinances for the People of the United States"— and laid plans for the immediate emancipation of enslaved African Americans through violent means.

Brown's plan was ambitious but simple. He and his followers would attack a stronghold in slave territory near an area that would lend itself to the formation of what would be, essentially, a maroon colony. He would then seize weapons and liberate enslaved African Americans in the immediate area. Once established in a defensible position, his band would become a magnet and a refuge for other African Americans willing to flee and strike a blow against slavery. He then planned to organize a free black government — and attempted, unsuccessfully, to persuade Frederick **Douglass** to serve as "Provisional President." In other words, his actions would be tantamount to lighting a fuse that would either trigger a massive slave insurrection throughout the South or force the South to adopt emancipatory measures to stave off chaos.

In the summer of 1859, Brown moved 21 of his followers to the Kennedy Farm in Maryland (see **John Brown's Headquarters**) — on the Potomac River across from **Harpers Ferry**,

Virginia (now West Virginia). There they spent several weeks in training and final preparations. On October 16, 1859, Brown led fewer than 50 men, many of them African American, on a raid intent on capturing the federal arsenal at Harpers Ferry and seizing some local citizens as hostages. However, literally from the beginning of the raid, little proceeded as planned. Brown refused to seek refuge in the mountains and fortified himself in an engine house. Unable to attack, escape or retreat, he was eventually captured by a contingent of U.S. Marines commanded, ironically, by Colonel Robert E. Lee. Only one member of the band, an African American abolitionist named Osbourne Anderson, escaped Harpers Ferry and reached safety in Canada.

Brown was tried, convicted and sentenced to death by hanging. He was executed on December 2, 1859. His last statement, handed to a guard shortly before his execution, read simply: "I, John Brown, am now quite certain that the crimes of this guilty land will never be purged away but with blood."

John Brown's raid, although unsuccessful, terrified the South as had nothing since Nat Turner's Revolt in 1831. Still, the fear of a large-scale slave revolt was the nightmare with which southerners had lived for generations (note Thomas Jefferson's memorable image of slavery being like "holding a wolf by the ears"). However, the terror was magnified by the specter of a white man — and the prospect of other northern whites— willing to attack the South and lead a "servile insurrection." The entire region was placed on a semi-war footing. Rumors and threats of revolt were ubiquitous.

As Frederick Douglass wrote, posthumously, of Brown, "His zeal in the cause of freedom was infinitely superior to mine ... I could live for the slave; John Brown could die for him." *See also* Abolitionist Movement; John Brown's Cabin; John Brown's Farm and Gravesite; John Brown's House; John Brown, Jr.'s House.

FURTHER READING

DuBois, W. E. B. *John Brown*. Reprint, New York: International Publishers, 1962.

Geffert, Hannah N. "John Brown and His Black Allies: An Ignored Alliance." *The Pennsylvania Magazine of History and Biography* 126, no. 4(2002): 591–610.

Landon, Fred. "Canadian Negroes and the John Brown Raid." *Journal of Negro History* 6, no. 2(1921): 174–182.

McGlone, Robert E. "Rescripting a Troubled Past: John Brown's Family and the Harpers Ferry Conspiracy." *Journal of American History* 75, no. 4(1989): 1179–1200.

Oates, Stephen B. "John Brown and His Judges: A Critique of the Historical Literature." *Civil War History* 28, no. 1(1971): 5–24.

Reynolds, David S. *John Brown, Abolitionist*. New York: Knopf, 2005.

Villard, Oswald Garrison. *John Brown 1800–1859: A Biography Fifty Years After*. 1910. Reprint, Gloucester, MA: Peter Smith, 1965.

Brown, Moses (1738–1836)

Friend of the fugitive. Moses Brown was born in 1738 in Providence, Rhode Island. Brown belonged to a Quaker family that had prospered in the slave trade business and had used its wealth to establish Brown University. After a catastrophic loss of life in a 1765 revolt aboard one of his ships, Brown repudiated his involvement with slave trade and became a stalwart abolitionist. Brown's mansion in Providence became an important Underground Railroad station. *See also* Quakers; Underground Railroad, Sites of; Underground Railroad, Stations on; and Appendixes 1–4.

Brown, Thomas

Friend of the fugitive. Thomas Brown was one of the few Underground Railroad **agents** sufficiently daring to venture into the southern interior and assist **fugitive slaves**. Thomas Brown and his family moved from **Cincinnati, Ohio**, to Henderson County, **Kentucky**, in 1850. Employing subterfuge and disguises, Brown's wife operated a "millinery shop" and Brown peddled his wares from a small horse-drawn wagon. The wagon was "heavily curtained," ostensibly "to protect his goods from the weather." (Coleman, 1940: 215–216.) However, Brown used his peddling to canvass the area and identify enslaved African Americans interested in reaching free territory, dispensing information to prospective fugitives and often transporting them in his wagon. Unfortunately, after slave escapes escalated steeply in the surrounding counties, Brown was arrested in 1854 and sentenced to the Kentucky penitentiary in April 1855. *See also* Appendixes 1 and 2.

FURTHER READING
Coleman, J. Winston, Jr. *Slavery Times in Kentucky.* Chapel Hill, NC: The University of North Carolina Press, 1940.
Hudson, J. Blaine. *Fugitive Slaves and the Underground Railroad in the Kentucky Borderland.* Jefferson, NC: McFarland, 2002.

Brown, William Wells (c. 1814–1884)

Fugitive and friend of the fugitive. William Wells Brown was one of the most versatile and engaging **fugitive slaves**, who himself became an effective friend of the fugitive and an important author. Brown was born enslaved in Lexington, **Kentucky** about 1814, the son of an enslaved woman, Elizabeth, and a white male relative of his owner. He escaped from slavery in January 1834. Later in 1834, after settling in the North, Brown met and married Elizabeth Spooner, a free woman of color, with whom he had three daughters.

Between 1834 and 1836, Brown worked on a Lake Erie steamboat and assisted runaways crossing to **Canada**. After moving to Buffalo in 1836, he joined the Western New York Anti-Slavery Society and became an extremely popular and polished speaker. In 1843, Brown helped host the National Convention of Colored Citizens meeting in Buffalo and, through his antislavery work in general, became well-acquainted with and was highly regarded by the leading antislavery figures of the period, including Frederick **Douglass**, Charles Lenox **Remond**, and many others. In May 1847, he was retained as a lecturer and agent of the **Massachusetts** Anti-Slavery Society and also published the narrative of his life.

Working as an antislavery agent, Brown visited Haiti and Cuba to explore emigration possibilities, lived in England between 1849 and 1854 and, while he was there, British abolitionists purchased his freedom. Also, while abroad and adjusting to the dissolution of his marriage, Brown spoke widely and devoted considerable time to his creative writing. After returning to the United States, he published *Clotel: The President's Daughter* in 1854, the first novel published by an African American. Later he published *St. Domingo*, a travelogue, a play and a collection of antislavery songs. After the **Civil War**, Brown remained a prolific writer and published a three-volume history of African Americans and, in 1880, *My Southern Home: Or, the South and its People.* Brown lived in **Boston** until his death in 1884. *See also* Abolitionist Movement; and Appendixes 1 and 2.

FURTHER READING
Brown, William Wells. *The Narrative of William Wells Brown.* Boston: American Antislavery Society, 1847.
Coleman, Edward M. "William Wells Brown as an Historian." *Journal of Negro History* 31, no. 1(1946): 47–59.
Simmons, William J. *Men of Mark: Eminent, Progressive and Rising.* Cleveland, OH: George M. Rewell, 1887.

Buckout, Abram (1813–1884)

Friend of the fugitive in Oswego, New York. *See also* Buckout-Jones Building.

Buckout-Jones Building (Oswego, New York)

Underground Railroad site recognized and documented by the National Park Service. *See also* Appendix 5.

Burleigh, C.C. (1810–1878)

Friend of the fugitive. Charles Calistus Burleigh was born in Plainfield, Windham County, Connecticut, on November 3, 1810. His mother, Lydia Bradford Burleigh, was a descendant of Governor William Bradford of the Plymouth Colony. His father, Rinaldo Burleigh, graduated from Yale with a classical education. Burleigh was one of six sons and two daughters and, although he received some early schooling at Plainfield Academy, Burleigh's father was the source of much of his formative education.

Burleigh later studied law and was admitted to the bar in 1835. While pursuing his legal studies, he published an attack on the Connecticut "Black Law" directed against Prudence Crandall's attempt to educate black and white girls together. Burleigh's article impressed abolitionist Samuel J. **May** and, through May, Burleigh was offered the editorship of the *Unionist*, an antislavery paper financed by Arthur **Tappan** in 1833. Burleigh was instrumental in protecting William Lloyd

Garrison from a mob in Boston in October 1835, and soon became a regular contributor to the *Liberator*. In the late 1830s, Burleigh became one of the editors of the *Pennsylvania Freeman*, later the organ of the Eastern Pennsylvania Anti-Slavery Society.

Burleigh grew into a striking figure, tall and full-bearded, with a reputation as a great orator. Because of his gifts, his intelligence and the strength of his convictions, Burleigh served as a full-time antislavery lecturer for the American Anti-Slavery Society in the mid–1830s. On his travels, he met Gertrude Kimber and the two were married in 1842.

In his lectures, Burleigh defended **fugitive slaves** and cited slave escapes as irrefutable proof of the evils of slavery. Health problems curtailed his involvement in antislavery and broader reform work in the 1840s and 1850s. Burleigh died in Florence, Massachusetts, in 1878. *See also* Abolitionist Movement; and Appendixes 1 and 2.

FURTHER READING

Brown, Ira V. "An Anti-Slavery Agent: C. C. Burleigh in Pennsylvania, 1836–1837." *The Pennsylvania Magazine of History and Biography* 105, no. 1(1981): 66–84.

Galbreath, C. B. "Anti-Slavery Movement in Columbiana County." *Ohio State Archaeological and Historical Quarterly* 30: 389–91 (1921).

Burns, Anthony (ca. 1830–1862)

In 1854 Anthony Burns, a 24-year-old fugitive slave escaped from Charles F. Suttle of Virginia and stowed away on a vessel bound for **Boston**, Massachusetts. Burns found employment in a Boston clothing store, but, on May 24, 1854, he was arrested by a federal marshal under the provisions of the **Fugitive Slave Act of 1850** and held in a U.S. Court House. The Reverend Leonard A. **Grimes** was able to visit Burns and persuade him to contest his case.

In the meantime, news spread of Burns' arrest and, on May 25, a large public meeting was held at **Faneuil Hall** at which noted abolitionists such as Wendell **Phillips** and William Lloyd **Garrison** made emotional speeches. Now incensed, a large group led by the Reverend Thomas Higginson marched on the Boston Courthouse and attempted to free Burns by force. The group fought with a large

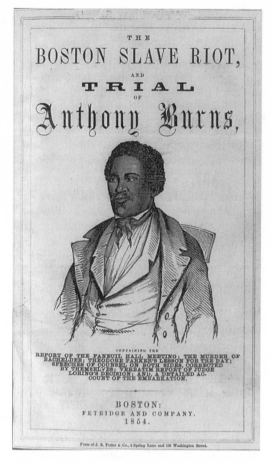

Anthony Burns (Library of Congress)

contingent of deputies and, in what was later known as "The Boston Slave Riot," one of the deputies, James Batchelder, was injured and later died. Burns, however, remained in custody.

Defeated but not deterred, Grimes and his congregation raised $1200 to purchase Burns' freedom, but their efforts were blocked by a U.S. attorney determined to enforce the Fugitive Slave Act in abolitionist Boston. Denied bail, trial by jury, the right of appeal, and the right to testify in his own behalf, Burns was escorted by federal troops and the Boston militia to a government vessel bound for Virginia and returned to his owner. He was then jailed in Richmond for five months.

Eventually, Grimes and his associates were successful in purchasing Burns' freedom. Burns returned to the North and toured briefly as an antislavery speaker. In 1860, he settled in St. Catherine's, Ontario, **Canada**, became a minister and died in 1862. *See also* Abolitionist Movement.

FURTHER READING

Bearse, Austin. *Reminiscences of Fugitive-Slave Law Days in Boston.* Boston: Warren Richardson, 1880.

The Boston Slave Riot, and Trial of Anthony Burns. Northbrooke, IL: Metro Books, 1972.

Maginnes, David R. "The Case of the Court House Rioters in the Rendition of the Fugitive Slave Anthony Burns, 1854." *Journal of Negro History* 56, no. 1(1971): 31–42.

Schwartz, Harold. "Fugitive Slave Days in Boston." *New England Quarterly* 27, no. 2(1954): 191–212.

Stevens, Charles Emery. *Anthony Burns: A History.* 1856. Reprint, New York: Arno Press, 1969.

Burris, Samuel (1808–1869)

A friend of the fugitive, Samuel Burris was born free in Willow Grove, Delaware, in 1808. As an adult, he relocated to the relative safety of **Philadelphia** and, in 1845, began working as a conductor on the Underground Railroad — venturing into slave territory to lead **fugitive slaves** to freedom. In this work, Burris collaborated closely with John **Hunn** and William **Still** to assist enslaved African Americans escaping from Delaware and Maryland.

Burris took unusual risks as a conductor on the Underground Railroad since, under **Pennsylvania** law, any free African American convicted of aiding escape of slaves could be sold into slavery. In June 1847, Burris ran afoul of this law when he was apprehended for assisting Maria Mathews' escape from bondage in Dover. He was jailed for nearly a year before being brought to trial, then was convicted and sentenced to be sold into slavery himself.

In September 1848, Burris was placed on the auction block in the center of Dover's town square, stripped nearly naked and forced to suffer the humiliation of inspection and appraisal for sale by prospective buyers. However, unknown to Burris, members of the Pennsylvania Anti-Slavery Society had organized a rescue and, when Burris was placed on the auction block, Isaac A. Flint, a member of the society posing as a slave trader, outbid the other traders present and "bought" Burris. Once a bill of sale had been executed, Flint

escorted the understandably relieved Burris back to Philadelphia.

Burris moved to California in 1852. During the **Civil War**, he raised money for freedmen's aid efforts in the South. Burris died in San Francisco in 1869. *See also* Appoquinimink Friends Meeting House.

FURTHER READING

Still, William. *The Underground Railroad.* 1872. Reprint, Chicago: Johnson, 1970.

Bushnell, Simeon

Friend of the fugitive in Oberlin, **Ohio**. *See also* Oberlin-Wellington Rescue. *See also* Appendixes 1 and 2.

Butler, Benjamin F. (1818–1893)

Friend of the fugitive and politician. Benjamin Franklin Butler was born in Deerfield, New Hampshire, on November 5, 1818. Butler graduated from Waterville College (now Colby College) in 1838 and was admitted to the Massachusetts bar in 1840. He was elected to the state legislature in 1853 and to the state senate in 1858, but was defeated in his run for governor in 1859. In 1861, Butler volunteered to serve the Union cause.

After Butler occupied Baltimore on 13 May 1861, he was promoted to the rank of major-general and ordered to assume command of **Fortress Monroe** in Virginia. Soon afterwards, runaways began to appear at the fort seeking protection, followed by slaveholders pressing for the return of their "property." Butler refused and declared that the **fugitive slaves** were "contraband of war" — thus coining this particular use of the term. Butler was also one of the few Union commanders who favored the recruitment of African American and, largely on his own authority, organized the First Regiment Louisiana Native Guards. In December 1864, he united 37 black regiments to form the Twenty-Fifth Corps.

Even more controversial than his policies at Fortress Monroe was his term as commander of the forces occupying New Orleans in 1862. There, he confiscated funds intended ostensibly for the Confederacy, executed a man for abusing an American flag and issued an order that the white women of New Orleans, if they persisted in insulting his soldiers, were to be treated as prostitutes. For these acts, southerners would remember Butler as the "Beast."

After the war, Butler joined the Republican Party and was elected to the 40th Congress. As a committed Radical Republican, Butler supported land redistribution to African American freedmen and was a sharp critic of President Andrew Johnson. In 1868, Butler was a leader in the unsuccessful attempt to impeach Johnson. Later, he was a leader in the effort to control the terrorist activities of the Ku Klux Klan and kindred groups in the South — an effort that culminated in the passage of the first Enforcement Act in 1871. Butler also played a leading role in securing the passage of the Civil Rights Act of 1875 — the last attempt by Radical Republicans to protect the rights of African Americans as Reconstruction drew to a close.

Butler grew disillusioned with the Republican Party and, after several unsuccessful campaigns, was elected governor of Massachusetts in 1882. He published his memoirs, *Autobiography and Personal Reminiscences*, in 1892, and died in **Washington, D.C.** on January 11, 1893. *See also* Appendixes 1 and 2.

FURTHER READING

Butler, Benjamin F. *Autobiography and Personal Reminiscences of Major-General Benj. F. Butler; Butler's book. By Benj. F. Butler. A Review of His Legal, Political, and Military Career.* Boston: A. M. Thayer, 1892.

Hearn, Chester G. *When the Devil Came Down to Dixie: Ben Butler in New Orleans.* Baton Rouge: Louisiana State University Press, 1997.

Westwood, Howard C. "Benjamin Butler's Enlistment of Black Troops in New Orleans in 1862." *Louisiana History* 26(1985): 5–22.

Buxton (Kent County, Ontario West, Canada)

Buxton, or the Elgin Settlement, was "in many respects the most important attempt made before the Civil War to found a Negro refugee colony in Canada." (Landon, 1918: 360.) The town, much like its origins, was unique, owing to the work of the Reverend William King. King immigrated to the United States from Ireland and became rector of a college in Louisiana. Through marriage, he became joint owner of 15 enslaved African

Americans. In 1848, when he was sent to **Canada** as a missionary, he took the enslaved African Americans with him and they became free upon crossing the border.

King then worked through the Presbyterian Church to establish a settlement for fugitive slaves in Kent County, Ontario. He was assisted by the Elgin Association, named in honor of the governor-general of Canada, in promoting his project "for the settlement and moral improvement of the colored population of Canada, for the purpose of purchasing crown or clergy reserve lands ... and settling the same with colored families resident in Canada." (Landon, 1918: 361.)

In 1849, the Elgin Association purchased 9,000 acres of densely forested land south of Chatham, within two miles of Lake Erie. The land was surveyed and divided into small farm plots of 50 acres each. "Colonists" could purchase up to 50 acres at $2.50 per acre, payable in 10 annual installments. To maintain ownership, "colonists" were required to clear heavy forest (with some trees up to four feet in diameter), build a house at least 18 by 24 feet, 12 feet high, and "with a stoop running the length of the front." (Landon, 1918: 363.)

By 1853, there were 520 inhabitants of Buxton, 500 acres had been cleared and 415 were under cultivation, and a school had been established. By 1857, there were 800 black settlers, 1,000 acres had been cleared, and significant quantities of wheat and corn were under cultivation. A sawmill, brickyard, blacksmith, carpenter shop, shoe shops and a grocery store had emerged, as had a number of churches and yet another school.

In 1864, Dr. Samuel R. Howe of the Freedmen's Inquiry Commission visited Buxton and stated in his report:

> Most interesting of all are the inhabitants. Twenty years ago most of them were slaves, who owned nothing, not even their own children. Now they own themselves; they own their houses and farms; and they have their wives and children about them ... The present condition of all these colonists as compared with their former one is remarkable ... This settlement is a perfect success. [Landon, 1918: 366.]

See also Fugitive Slaves; Underground Railroad, Sites of; and Appendixes 3 and 4.

FURTHER READING

Landon, Fred. "The Buxton Settlement in Canada." *Journal of Negro History* 3, no. 4(1918).

Winks, Robin W. *Blacks in Canada: A History*. New Haven, CT: 1971.

Cain, John

Friend of the fugitive in **Louisville, Kentucky.** *See also* Appendixes 1 and 2.

California

The African American presence in California dates to the early days of Spanish exploration and settlement. By the time California became the northern section of independent **Mexico**, Africans and persons of mixed ancestry were a sizable and stable minority of the population.

After becoming property of the United States as a result of the Mexican War (1846–1847), African Americans journeyed or were brought to California by various routes and in several statuses. For example, during the California Gold Rush, free people of color migrated in search of wealth and greater independence. **Fugitive slaves** sometimes fled to California, often masquerading as **free people of color.** Some enslaved African Americans were sent alone to California with the promise that they could purchase their freedom and that of their families with their share of earnings from prospecting or other work. Still, slave-owners brought other enslaved African Americans to California. Both groups of enslaved African Americans sometimes escaped en route or sought their freedom in the courts once there. Some traveled by wagon train. Others traveled or were brought by ship via Panama, then part of Colombia, where they also escaped en route at times.

By 1850, there were nearly 1,000 African Americans in California. The black population remained small, but increased rapidly to roughly 2,000 by 1852 and over 4,000 by 1860, representing a bit more than one percent of the state population. Also in 1860, about one-third of the black population, 1,176, lived in San Francisco; 468 African Americans lived in Sacramento; and another 87 lived in Los Angeles. Racial prejudice was strong among white American migrants to the state, but African Americans were attracted by the promise of relatively greater freedom and the possibility of acquiring wealth during the Gold Rush. Many achieved this goal and, by 1855, this small black population had amassed $2,375,000 in total assets and probably controlled more wealth, per capita, than African Americans in any other state. On this foundation, African Americans established schools and churches, and developed a strong and educated leadership group. One of the most significant early black leaders was J. B. Sanderson, a veteran of antislavery work with Frederick **Douglass** in the 1840s. Another was Mary Ellen **Pleasant**, who ventured west on the Gold Rush and became an entrepreneur in San Francisco.

Although slavery was prohibited, the language in California's 1849 constitution did not clarify the status of African Americans enslaved before that year or those brought into California from slave states in the East. As a result, during the **1850s**, distinguishing between African Americans who were legally free and those who were fugitive slaves became a bitterly divisive political issue. So many African Americans claimed their freedom that, by 1852, California passed its own Fugitive Slave Law — and many proslavery Californians began lobbying to detach southern California from the rest of the state and make slavery legal there. Even after the **"Frank"** Case of 1851, and not until the **Archy Case** was decided in 1857, was this issue finally settled and slavery was completely outlawed in the state.

Thus, California, although far removed from the bulk of the African American population, played a role in the history of fugitive slaves and the Underground Railroad — not only as an issue in the **Compromise of 1850**, but as a site of the struggle for freedom. *See also* Fugitive Slave Law of 1850; Mexico.

FURTHER READING

Beasley, Delilah L. "Slavery in California." *Journal of Negro History* 3, no. 1(1918): 33–44.

Blackburn, George M., and Sherman L. Ricards. "Unequal Opportunity on a Mining Frontier: The Role of Gender, Race and Birthplace." *Pacific Historical Review* 62(1993): 19–37.

Hudson, Lynn M. "A New Look, Or, 'I'm Not Mammy to Everybody in California': Mary Ellen Pleasant, a Black Entrepreneur." *Journal of the West* 32(1993): 35–40.

Lapp, Rudolph M. "The Negro in Gold Rush California." *The Journal of Negro History* 49, no. 2(1964): 81–98.

McAfee, Ward M. "California's House Divided." *Civil War History* 33(1987): 115–130.

Savage, W. Sherman. "The Negro in the Westward Movement." *Journal of Negro History* 25, no. 4(1940): 531–539.

Woolfolk, George R. "Turner's Safety Valve and Free Negro Westward Migration." *Pacific Northwest Quarterly* 56(1965): 125–130.

Callahan Expedition (1855)

Fugitive slaves from Texas fled routinely into northern **Mexico** to escape the reach of American authorities and were often protected, or at least not apprehended, by Mexican citizens and government officials. Angered by the loss of fugitive slaves, Texas slave-owners sent a representative to meet with Governor Santiago Vidaurri of Nuevo León y Coahuila in the summer of 1851. Governor Vidaurri refused to cooperate and then subsequently placed his military commanders along the Texas/Mexico border on alert in anticipation of an invasion. Vidaurri's fears proved well-founded.

On October 1, 1855, James Hughes Callahan and a party of 111 men invaded Mexico by crossing the Rio Grande near Piedras Negras, Coahuila. After a skirmish with a Mexican military detachment at the Río Escondido on October 3, Callahan retreated to and occupied Piedras Negras. He was pursued and, as the Mexican forces approached, ordered his men to burn the town to cover his retreat. The Callahan party finally reached safety on American soil on October 6, after American forces based at Fort Duncan covered his retreat across the Rio Grande.

Not until 1876 were 150 Mexican citizens awarded $50,000 in damages, based on the findings of a claims commission that began considering the case in 1868, resulting from Callahan's invasion of Mexico.

FURTHER READING
Savage, W. Sherman. "The Negro in the Westward Movement." *Journal of Negro History* 25, no. 4 (1940): 531–539.

Camp Nelson, Kentucky

An important Civil War sanctuary for fugitive slaves, Camp Nelson, located in Jessamine County, **Kentucky**, was the largest and most significant Union military encampment and hospital facility in the region, outside of **Louisville**, during the **Civil War**. For example, over the course of the war, nearly 80,000 troops were stationed at or used the camp.

Although significant in supplying Union Army operations in Tennessee and Virginia, Camp Nelson was even more important as one of the largest recruitment centers for African American troops. Eight regiments of U.S. Colored Troops were organized and three others were trained there, making Camp Nelson the third largest African American recruitment center in the nation. Many enslaved African Americans fled bondage to gain their freedom through enlistment in the Union Army, and brought their families to Camp Nelson in hopes that they, too, would be emancipated. The refugee camp established for these women and children became the town of Hall, Kentucky, after the Civil War.

FURTHER READING
Sears, Richard D. *Camp Nelson, Kentucky: A Civil War History.* Lexington, KY: University Press of Kentucky, 2002.

Camp Warren Levis (Godfrey, Illinois)

Underground Railroad site. Based on both historical evidence and oral tradition, Camp Warren Levis, at Rocky Fork in Godfrey, **Illinois** served as a destination and a refuge for **fugitive slaves** escaping Missouri as early as 1816. Fugitive slaves continued to escape to and through the area until **slavery** finally ended in Missouri in 1865.

This site has been designated part of the National Underground Railroad Network to Freedom.

FURTHER READING
National Park Service. *Researching and Interpreting the Underground Railroad.* Washington, D.C.: United States Government Printing Office, 1999.

Underground Railroad Special Resource Study. Washington, D.C.: United States Government Printing Office, 1995.

Campbell African Methodist Episcopal Church (Philadelphia, Pennsylvania)

Underground Railroad site. Founded by **Philadelphia** African Americans in 1817, the

Campbell African Methodist Episcopal Church served as a center of the Black Underground and as a station for **fugitive slaves** through much of the antebellum period. *See also* Underground Railroad, Sites of; and Appendixes 3 and 4.

Canada

Enslaved Africans were brought to Canada in the early seventeenth century and, by 1759, more than 1,000 were held in what was then New France. After the fall of New France to Britain in 1783, many British loyalists emigrated from the United States and brought their enslaved African Americans, with many settling **Nova Scotia**. Although Great Britain would not abolish **slavery** in its colonies until 1834, beginning in 1798, a series of court rulings— drawing on the precedent of the 1772 **Somerset Case**—effectively eroded the legal basis of slavery in Canada. On February 8, 1800, in the last of the suits, the Robin case, a Canadian fugitive slave was ordered released from confinement — which, in practical terms, ended slavery in Canada.

Some fugitives from slavery in the United States sought freedom in the far West, Mexico or the Caribbean, but most fled to and hoped to remain in the northern and Midwestern states. This attraction outweighed the risk of recapture for most fugitive slaves. However, **fugitive slaves** could find freedom in the North, but never security. Thus, after the passage of the **Fugitive Slave Act of 1850**, Canada — which had been a long-distance option for freedom seekers for decades— became a much more attractive destination since it removed fugitives from the reach of U.S. law and the machinations of slave-catchers. By 1850, an estimated 20,000 runaways had settled in Canada and double, perhaps triple, that number would cross the border in the decade before the **Civil War**.

The geography of Lower Canada determined the final stages of the journey of most African American freedom seekers and where black settlements would develop. Situated between Lake Huron and Lake Erie, north and west of New York, north of Ohio and east of Michigan, Ontario province was the section of Canada most readily accessible to fugitive slaves and thousands found their way there. As with Underground Railroad activity in the United States, it is impossible to determine

THE FUGITIVES ARE SAFE IN A FREE LAND.   Page 25.

Canada is shown as the Promised Land (Library of Congress)

how many cities, towns and villages became destinations through the organized Underground Railroad system. In 1829, free African Americans fleeing mob violence in **Cincinnati, Ohio** established the pioneer settlement at **Wilberforce** in 1829. In later years, however, Ontario was a prime regional destination. Harriet **Tubman** lived in St. Catherine between 1851 and 1858; smaller settlements such as Kingston, Prescott, Montreal, Stanstead and St. John in New Brunswick also attracted African Americans, as did Toronto, Queens Bush, Wellesley, Galt and Hamilton.

Many fugitive slaves reached Canada by crossing the Detroit River to Windsor, making **Detroit** an important center of Underground Railroad operations and the point of convergence for escape routes snaking through **Indiana** and **Ohio**. Others crossed Lake Erie from Cleveland, Sandusky or Toledo, Ohio. Other Underground Railroad routes converged on Milwaukee, Racine, South Port and Chicago. As one Canadian observer described, "Slaves cannot breathe in America; if their lungs receive our air, that moment they are free! They reach our country and their shackles fall."

To aid newly arrived freedom seekers, missions and schools were established, often funded and visited by both U.S. abolitionists and Canadian benefactors. Levi **Coffin**, William Beard, and John **Brown** all made journeys north to inspect progress. Coffin visited a mission in Amhertsburg, then known as Fort Malden, and was so impressed that he called the mission "the principal terminus of the Underground Railroad in the West." (Coffin, 1876: 250.)

Fugitive Aid societies also formed to help freedom seekers adapt to a new life by procuring lands and partially financing settlements. The largest of these colonies were **Amherstburg**, the **Dawn** Settlement at Dresden, the Elgin Settlement at **Buxton,** and the Refugees Home near Windsor. The communities never became what their promoters hoped. Dawn did not survive the **1850s**, but Buxton endured until after the **Civil War.**

Although Canada was free territory and a comparatively safe haven for fugitive slaves fortunate or intrepid enough to cross its borders, the attitude of most white Canadians was decidedly lukewarm toward the newcomers. Although Canadians did not attempt to expel black freedom seekers or permit their extradition, they did attempt to bar them from voting and exercising other civil rights.

With the coming of **Civil War** and Emancipation, most of the fugitive slaves who sought asylum in Canada returned to the United States. Those who remained, supplemented by immigrants from the British Caribbean colonies, became the nucleus of Canada's small Afro-Canadian population.

FURTHER READING

Baily, Marilyn. "From Cincinnati, Ohio to Wilberforce, Canada: A Note on Antebellum Colonization." *Journal of Negro History* 58(1973): 427–440.

Coffin, Levi. *Reminiscences of Levi Coffin.* New York: Augustus M. Kelley, 1876.

Grant, John N. "Black Immigrants to Nova Scotia." *Journal of Negro History* 58(1973): 253–270.

Hill, Daniel G. *The Freedom-seekers: Blacks in Early Canada.* Agincourt: Book Society of Canada, 1981.

Landon, Fred. "The Anderson Fugitive Case." *Journal of Negro History* 7(1923): 233–242.

Siebert, Wilbur H. *The Underground Railroad from Slavery to Freedom.* 1898. Reprint, New York: Russell and Russell, 1967.

Silverman, Jason H. *Unwelcome Guests: Canada West's Response to American Fugitive Slaves, 1800–1865.* Port Washington, NY: Associated Faculty Press, 1985.

Winks, Robin W. *Blacks in Canada: A History.* New Haven, CT: Yale University Press, 1971.

Cannon, Lucretia Hanley (Patty) (d. 1829)

Kidnapper. Lucretia Hanley (Patty) Cannon became notorious for her role in kidnapping African Americans and selling them into **slavery**. Cannon, described as a large woman who could fling a man to the ground by the hair, is believed to have moved to Maryland from **Canada** in 1802. Working from her base at Johnson's Crossroads in Dorchester County, Maryland, near the Delaware border, Cannon and her husband Joe Johnson operated a slave trade business. They would steal slaves or free blacks and sell them back down South to the plantation owners—a literal "Underground Railroad in reverse." Cannon and her associates preyed on African American children from **Philadelphia** and on

African Americans arriving by ship in **Philadel-phia** and Camden, New Jersey. Once unfortunate free blacks or fugitive slaves were snared, Cannon's agents used a system of station houses to move their prey from freedom to slavery.

As Blockson notes, "In her former home and tavern at Johnson's Crossroads was a blood stained oak door and wrought-iron rings on the walls where shackled African Americans awaited purchase and shipment to the Deep South." (Blockson, 1994: 30.) Cannon and her gang were soon implicated in over a dozen murders.

Cannon was arrested in 1829 and was taken to Georgetown, Delaware. She was charged with murder, to which she confessed, and was sentenced to death by hanging. She committed suicide the night before her execution using poison smuggled into the prison under her skirts. *See also* Underground Railroad, Sites of; and Appendixes 3 and 4.

FURTHER READING
Blockson, Charles. *Hippocrene Guide to the Underground Railroad*. New York: Hippocrene Books, 1994.

Carleton House (Littleton, New Hampshire)

Underground Railroad site. In 1837, Edmund Carleton, an attorney, quit the legal profession and founded the Littleton Anti-Slavery Society in Littleton, New Hampshire. He and his wife, Mary, also gave refuge to **fugitive slaves** in their home, and Carleton often conducted freedom seekers through his section of the state. *See also* Underground Railroad, Sites of; and Appendixes 3 and 4.

Carneal House (Covington, Kentucky)

Underground Railroad site. Built in 1815 and located on the Licking River, the Carneal House (or Rothier House) is the oldest home in Covington, **Kentucky**— across the **Ohio River** from **Cincinnati, Ohio**. A tunnel leads from the house to the Ohio River that, based on local references and legends, was used by **fugitive slaves**. *See also* Ohio; Underground Railroad, Sites of; and Appendixes 3 and 4.

FURTHER READING
Harris, Theodore H. "The Carneal House and the Underground Railroad: A Covington Family Es-capes from Slavery." *Northern Kentucky Heritage* 6(1999): 35–38.

Carr, John

Friend of the fugitive in **Madison, Indiana**. *See also* Appendixes 1 and 2.

Carter, John

Friend of the fugitive in **Madison, Indiana**. *See also* Appendixes 1 and 2.

Cartland Homestead (Lee, New Hampshire)

Underground Railroad site. The Cartland family belonged to the Society of Friends and was related to John Greenleaf **Whittier**. Located in Lee, New Hampshire, their homestead, built in 1745, was a haven for **fugitive slaves** who were hidden in a small room in the cellar. *See also* Quakers; Underground Railroad, Sites of; and Appendixes 3 and 4.

Cary, Mary Ann Shadd (1823–1893)

Friend of the fugitive. Mary Ann Shadd was born in Wilmington, Delaware, on October 9, 1823, one of seven children in a free African American family dedicated to the abolition of slavery. Her father, Abraham Shadd, operated a shoemaking business and was a prominent abolitionist, an agent for the *Liberator*, manager of the American Anti-Slavery Society, and friend of the fugitive. Since access to education was difficult in the slave state of Delaware, Shadd's family moved to West Chester, Pennsylvania, in 1833, where she studied at the Quaker-sponsored Price's Boarding School. After completing her education in 1839, she returned to Wilmington to conduct a private school for black children and continued teaching for the next 12 years in Wilmington, New York City, and Norristown, Pennsylvania.

In 1851, after the passage of the **Fugitive Slave Act of 1850**, Mary Ann Shadd, her brother, Isaac, and her father migrated to Windsor, Ontario, and began assisting fugitive slaves in **Canada**. In Windsor, she opened a school for blacks and began lecturing throughout the U.S. and Canada to encourage emigration to a nation where African Americans "could be free and prosper." Shadd believed strongly in self-reliance, in the liberating power of education and in pressing for the full integration of African Americans into Canadian life. This latter conviction brought her into direct conflict with Henry **Bibb**, fugitive slave from **Kentucky** and influential editor of *The Voice of the Fugitive* newspaper — who believed just as strongly in the need for fugitive slaves to form entirely segregated, autonomous settlements in Canada.

In 1853, Shadd and the noted black abolitionist, Samuel Ringgold **Ward**, founded the non-sectarian *Provincial Freedman* newspaper to express her point of view. Serving as editor from 1854 to 1857, she became the first woman of African ancestry in North America to edit a newspaper. In 1855, she was also the first African American woman to address a National Negro Convention and both impressed and developed friendships with leaders such as Frederick **Douglass**.

In 1856, Shadd married Thomas F. Cary of Toronto and the couple had two children. Although financial problems forced her to close the newspaper in 1858, her influence and reputation continued to grow, as did her fierce determination to oppose slavery. As one example:

> One Sunday a slave boy without hat, coat, or shoes who had thus far eluded his pursuers, was overtaken in Chatham and about to be carried off. Mrs. Cary tore the boy from the slave hunters, ran to the court-house and had the bell rung so violently that that whole town was soon aroused. Mrs. Cary with her commanding form, piercing eyes, and stirring voice soon had the people as indignant as herself — denouncing in no uncertain terms the outrage perpetrated under the British flag... [Brown, 1926: 94.]

After the death of her husband in 1860, Cary and her children returned to the United States, where she recruited black soldiers for the Union Army during the **Civil War** and taught in **Washington, D.C.** In 1869, Carey then entered the law school of the newly established Howard University and, when she earned her law degree in 1883, became the second African American woman in the United States — and one of the first American women of any race — to do so. Cary continued to write, lecture and teach, and worked with Susan B. **Anthony** and Elizabeth Cady Stanton in the women's movement in the period after Reconstruction. She died in 1893 in Washington, D.C. *See also* Fugitive Slaves; Quakers; and Appendixes 1 and 2.

FURTHER READING

Beardon, Jim, and Linda Jean Butler. *Shadd: The Life and Times of Mary Shadd Cary.* Toronto: NC Press Ltd., 1977.

Brown, Hallie Q. *Homespun Heroines and Other Women of Distinction.* Xenia, OH: Aldine, 1926.

Hill, Daniel G. *The Freedom-seekers: Blacks in Early Canada.* Agincourt: Book Society of Canada, 1981.

Olbey, Christian. "Unfolded Hands: Class Suicide and the Insurgent Intellectual Praxis of Mary Ann Shadd." *Canadian Review of American Studies* 30(2000): 151–174.

Rhodes, Jane. *Mary Ann Shadd Cary: The Black Press and Protest in the Nineteenth Century.* Bloomington, IN: Indiana University Press, 1998.

Winks, Robin W. *Blacks in Canada: A History* New Haven, CT: 1971.

Chace, Elizabeth Buffum (1806–1899)

Friend of the fugitive. Elizabeth Buffum was born in 1806 and was raised on her family's farm in Smithfield, Rhode Island. Although born into a Quaker family, she came to value independence and freedom of speech — and learned from her father, Arnold Buffum, a strong abhorrence of slavery. She received her formal education at village schools and, at 18, spent one year at the Quakers' Yearly Meeting Boarding School. In 1825, she and her family moved to Fall River, where she met and married Samuel Chace, whose family operated a cotton mill.

In the 1830s, Chace became a close associate of William Lloyd **Garrison** and an active participant in the antislavery movement. In 1835, she and her sisters founded the Fall River Female Anti-Slavery Society. Her house in Central Falls became an important Underground Railroad station. Chace also defended the rights of women and children working in her husband's factories. Unlike many white abolitionists, Chace and her sister, Lucy Buffum Lovell, were also proponents of racial equality. As an example, they invited "a few very respectable young colored women" to join the Fall River Female Anti-Slavery Society and were steadfast when many white members threatened to withdraw. (Chace, 1937: 119.)

Having fought to abolish **slavery** in the

years before the **Civil War**, Chace spearheaded the drive for women's suffrage in Rhode Island in the last decades of the nineteenth century. Her daughter, Lillie Chace Wyman (1847–1929), was also an advocate of racial equality and carried the legacy of the radical antislavery movement into the twentieth century. Chace died in 1899. At her death she was hailed as "the conscience of Rhode Island." *See also* Abolitionist Movement; Quakers; and Appendixes 1 and 2.

FURTHER READING
Chace, Elizabeth Buffum. *Two Quaker Sisters: From the Original Diaries of Elizabeth Buffum Chace and Lucy Buffum Lovell.* New York: Liveright Publishing Corporation, 1937.
Stevens, Elizabeth C. *Elizabeth Buffum Chace and Lillie Chace Wyman: A Century of Abolitionist, Suffragist and Workers' Rights Activism.* Jefferson, NC: McFarland, 2003.

Chamberlain Farm (Canterbury, New Hampshire)

Underground Railroad site. Located near Canterbury, New Hampshire, the farmstead of John Abbot Chamberlain was a sanctuary for **fugitive slaves**. *See also* Underground Railroad, Sites of; and Appendixes 3 and 4.

Chapman, William

Friend of the fugitive in **Washington, D.C.** *See also* Appendixes 1 and 2.

Charles B. Huber Homesite (Williamsburg, Ohio)

Charles Boerstler Huber (d. 1854) owned a tannery in Williamsburg, **Ohio**, and was the chief stationmaster of the Underground Railroad in his area. His home at 160 Gay Street was an active station at which Huber assisted as many as 500 freedom seekers in the decades before his death in 1854. Huber's nickname, "Boss," derived from his key role in managing the movement of **fugitive slaves** through Clermont County, Ohio.

This site has been designated part of the National Underground Railroad Network to Freedom.

FURTHER READING
National Park Service. *Researching and Interpreting the Underground Railroad.* Washington, D.C.: United States Government Printing Office, 1999.

National Park Service. *Underground Railroad Special Resource Study.* Washington, D.C.: United States Government Printing Office, 1995.

Charles Perry House (Westerly, Rhode Island)

Underground Railroad site. Charles Perry was one a few, embattled abolitionists in Westerly, Rhode Island. Perry concealed **fugitive slaves** in nearby stone huts with sod roofs. *See also* Underground Railroad, Sites of; and Appendixes 3 and 4.

Cheney, Moses

See Cheney House

Cheney, Oren Burbank

See Cheney House

Cheney House (Peterborough, New Hampshire)

Underground Railroad site. Several members of the Cheney family of Peterborough, New Hampshire, were staunch friends of the fugitive. From 1835 to 1845, the home of Deacon Moses Cheney served as a sanctuary for **fugitive slaves**. He, other family members and sympathetic neighbors also conducted freedom seekers through the area.

The Reverend Oren Burbank Cheney (1816–1903), son of Deacon Cheney, worked to assist fugitive slaves in his youth. He later became a Baptist minister and founded the Maine State Seminary in Lewiston, soon renamed Bates College, serving as president of the institution from 1857 to 1894. In this capacity, he opened the college to African American students. The Reverend Cheney also contributed to the establishment of Storer College for African Americans at **Harpers Ferry,** West Virginia. *See also* Underground Railroad, Sites of; and Appendixes 3 and 4.

Chester, Thomas Morris (1834–1892)

Friend of the fugitive and African American leader. Thomas Morris Chester was born in 1834 in Harrisburg, **Pennsylvania**. Chester's father was born in Haiti and his mother was a fugitive slave who escaped from Baltimore, Maryland, in 1825. In his youth, Chester assisted his parents and siblings in harboring **fugitive slaves** in their Harrisburg, Pennsylvania, restaurant.

Between January 1851 and January 1853, Chester attended Avery College at Allegheny City, Pennsylvania. He then sailed for Liberia in West Africa and attended the Alexandria High School, returning to the United States in December 1854. He next entered the junior class of the Thetford Academy in Vermont, graduating in 1856, after which he returned to Liberia and became director of a school, editor of the *Star of Liberia* newspaper and a correspondent for the *New York Herald.*

Chester recruited African American soldiers during the **Civil War** and, in 1864, the Philadelphia *Press* commissioned him to report on the activities of African American troops on the Virginia front, making Chester the only black Civil War correspondent for a major daily newspaper. In a particularly ironic moment, he even sat at the desk of Jefferson Davis and wrote dispatches describing the fall of Richmond, the Confederate capitol — recounting the exploits of African American soldiers in the last phase of the war. After the Emancipation Proclamation, Chester also assisted in recruiting African American troops in his home state and, later, raised money for the Freedmen's Bureau.

In 1867, Chester journeyed to England to study law and was "called to the English bar" in 1870. In July 1870, Avery College awarded him the degree of master of arts and, in March 1873, he was licensed to practice law in Louisiana. In 1875, Chester was appointed a district superintendent of education and granted the position of brigadier general of the Louisiana state militia. In 1878, he was appointed United States commissioner for the district of Louisiana.

A supporter of the Kansas Exodus movement of 1879, Chester was also the president of a short-lived railroad organized by African American investors. With the end of Reconstruction and the failure of the Exodusters, Chester returned to Pennsylvania and, on June 22, 1881, was admitted to practice in the Supreme Court of Pennsylvania. Thomas Chester died in 1892 in Harrisburg, ending his eventful and illustrious life. *See also* Appendixes 1 and 2.

FURTHER READING

Blackett, R. J. M., ed. *Thomas Morris Chester, Black Civil War Correspondent: His Dispatches from the Virginia Front.* New York: Da Capo, 1991.

Chicago, Illinois

Underground Railroad junction. *See also* Illinois; Jones, John; Lovejoy, Elijah; Lovejoy, Owen; Pinkerton, Alan.

Christiana Resistance or Christiana Massacre

The Christiana Massacre was a major act of defiance of the **Fugitive Slave Act of 1850.** On September 11, 1851, Maryland slaveholder Edward Gorsuch, his son and five others attempted to capture seven **fugitive slaves** being harbored by William Parker, a free person of color, in Christiana, Lancaster County, Pennsylvania. One of the fugitive slaves spied Gorsuch and his party as they lay in ambush near Parker's home and fled back to his house with the slave-catchers in pursuit. Parker and the fugitives barricaded themselves on the second floor of his home and Parker blew a horn from an upper window. Within an hour, between 30 and 40 free African Americans living in the area responded to this alarm and attempted en masse to prevent Gorsuch from capturing the freedom seekers. Most were armed, and Caster Hanway, a Quaker neighbor, tried to prevent the parties from resorting to violence. However, one of the fugitive slaves attempted to leave Parker's house and, when confronted, pushed Gorsuch aside. In a rage of embarrassment, Gorsuch and his son and nephew opened fire. The African Americans responded in kind. Gorsuch was killed, and his nephew and several African Americans were wounded. Parker and some of the fugitive slaves escaped to **Canada.**

A company of U.S. Marines joined U.S. Marshals in a house-to-house search of the neighborhood, and Hanway and 40 others (38 of whom were black) were charged with treason in trying to resist the Fugitive Slave Act. All were held in prison while their trials unfolded at Philadelphia's Independence Hall. Two fugitive slaves were among the prisoners and escaped before the trials. The rest, defended by a team of lawyers that included the famous abolitionist and U.S. Congressman, Thaddeus **Stevens**, were acquitted on December 11, 1854.

As an example of open defiance of the Fugitive Slave Act of 1850, the Christiana

In the Christiana Resistance, shown in this 1872 engraving, African-Americans fired on slave-catchers at the home of William Parker, near Christiana, Pennsylvania. (Library of Congress)

Resistance became a defining moment in the struggle against slavery—the "war before the war" in the **borderland**. *See also* Quakers.

FURTHER READING
Forbes, Ella. "By My Own Right Arm: Redemptive Violence and the 1851 Christiana, Pennsylvania Resistance." *Journal of Negro History* 83, no. 3(1998): 159–167.
Slaughter, Thomas P. *Bloody Dawn: The Christiana Riot and Racial Violence in the Antebellum North.* New York: Oxford University Press, 1991.
Still, William. *The Underground Railroad.* 1872. Reprint, Chicago: Johnson, 1970.

Cincinnati, Ohio

Underground Railroad center. As early as 1820, Cincinnati boasted an embryonic antislavery movement organized around a congregation of **Quakers** and a small African American community of 400 people. By 1829, the African American population increased to 2,258. The resulting heightened competition for jobs and living space triggered a race riot in 1829 that prompted an exodus of more than 1,000 African Americans who then formed the nucleus of **Wilberforce**, the first major black American settlement in **Canada**. This sobering event also led to the call for the first Convention of Free People of Color—which met in Philadelphia in September 1830 and inaugurated the first American civil rights movement.

Still, mob violence did not deter African American migration to Cincinnati and certainly did not stem the tide of **fugitive slaves**. As Siebert notes, "from far and near fugitive slaves entered the city" and "numerous fugitives crossed over from Covington and its vicinity." Once in Covington, "escaping slaves were harbored by Thomas Carneal in his mansion, which he erected in 1815." (Siebert, 1895: 2.) In 1848, Martin **Delany** visited Cincinnati seeking support for the antislavery movement (and subscribers to *The North Star*). He spoke to many groups, met many free blacks individually and had ample opportunities to observe their social world. Delany found most black Cincinnatians warmly receptive to his message, and noted "whenever our principles are fully made known, they meet with many who readily subscribe to them, practical antislavery being that which the people desire." However, Delany concluded that those strong sentiments required organization and direction, adding that "the harvest in the West is truly ready, but the laborers are few." Interestingly, Delany was most impressed with the African American "women of the west" and found them more strongly opposed to slavery than their counterparts in the "east." (*The North Star,* May 26, 1848 in Hudson, 2002: 121.) From Delany's description, a picture emerges of an African American community nearing political maturity, strongly antislavery and strongly profugitive slave — awaiting some catalyzing event(s) to force it toward greater organization and unity of purpose.

White abolitionists were quite active as well and played roles that are far better known historically. Among the best-known, Harriet Beecher **Stowe** harbored fugitives in her home from 1836 until she moved in 1850. By the 1840s, there were at least 30 rather visible Abolitionists in Cincinnati. Underground Railroad activity reached a new pitch of intensity when Levi **Coffin** and his family moved from the Richmond, Indiana, area to Cincinnati in April 1847. Coffin believed that more formal organization and management were needed since some of the older Abolitionists had either died or relocated and, in his view, only a few of the local African Americans such as Shelton **Morris** were "shrewd managers." As an immediate result, Coffin organized a vigilance committee that included blacks and whites and transformed his free labor store (that sold no slave-produced goods) at the corner of Sixth and Elm Streets into a way station for fugitives. Women were also involved in key roles through the Anti-Slavery Sewing Society. Coffin was soon considered the "president" and, by 1850, Cincinnati gained the distinction of being the "Grand Central Station" of the Underground Railroad. *See also* Carneal House; Kentucky; Harriet Beecher Stowe House (Cincinnati).

FURTHER READING
Coffin, Levi. *Reminiscences of Levi Coffin.* New York: Augustus M. Kelley, 1876.
Hudson, J. Blaine. *Fugitive Slaves and the Underground Railroad in the Kentucky Borderland.* Jefferson, NC: McFarland, 2002.

Middleton, Stephen. "The Fugitive Slave Crisis in Cincinnati, 1850–1860: Resistance, Enforcement, and Black Refugees." *Journal of Negro History* 72, no. 2(1987): 20–32.
Siebert, Wilbur H. "The Mysteries of Ohio's Underground Railroad." 1895. Draft manuscript, in the Wilbur Siebert Papers, The Ohio Underground Railroad, Box 116, Ohio Historical Society.
Woodson, Carter G. "The Negroes of Cincinnati Prior to the Civil War." *Journal of Negro History* 1(1916): 1–22.

Cinque, Joseph (or Sengbe Pieh)

See Amistad Affair

Civil War (1861–1865)

Both the volume and significance of slave escapes escalated dramatically with the coming of the Civil War. As with the American Revolution, the turmoil of war multiplied the opportunities for flight, and the progressive shift in federal policy in favor of general emancipation, for all practical purposes, nullified the **Fugitive Slave Act of 1850** by mid–1862. The boundary between **slavery** and freedom became fluid as the Union Army moved into and through Confederate territory.

The 1863 Emancipation Proclamation applied only to territory under Confederate control and did not apply to the Union slave states (Missouri, Maryland, **Kentucky**, Delaware and West Virginia). However, neither those sections of the Confederacy near Union lines nor the Union slave states could isolate themselves from the forces of history — and slavery began to collapse in these sections of the country despite bitter opposition from local slaveholders. African Americans contributed significantly to this collapse — not by adopting a new strategy to undermine slavery, but by expanding, opportunistically, the use of the old one. Thus, under these conditions, enslaved African Americans emancipated themselves in massive numbers (probably more than 500,000 by 1865) — and, in the crucible of Civil War, the flight of African Americans from slavery became a social revolution that unfolded against the backdrop of military conflict.

Parallel to the social and military struggle, there was a bitter struggle in the U.S. Congress over the fugitive slave issue. For example,

Slaves make a mass escape on Maryland's Eastern Shore during the Civil War as shown in this 1872 engraving. (Library of Congress)

Emancipation, by Thomas Nast, 1865 (Library of Congress)

This circa 1856 map shows the comparative area of the free and slave states and the territory open to slavery or freedom by the repeal of the Missouri Compromise. (Library of Congress)

early in the Civil War, Confederate use of enslaved African Americans as servants and laborers prompted the passage of the First Confiscation Act (signed by President Abraham Lincoln on August 6, 1861). This act, while intended to legalize the confiscation of "the property used for insurrectionary purposes," was also applied — albeit unevenly — to fugitive slaves, i.e., the "property" that was not necessarily captured, but that presented itself voluntarily to the Union Army.

Bills to repeal the Fugitive Slave Act of 1850 were debated throughout much of the war, beginning as early as July 1861. Typically, legislators from the Union slave states strongly opposed such measures and were able to prevent their enactment for several years. Still, Congress bowed gradually and grudgingly to

the tide of events unleashed by the war. Slavery in the District of Columbia was abolished on April 16, 1862. Slavery in U.S. territories was abolished June 19, 1862. Many of the issues related to the repeal of the Fugitive Slave Act found their way into the Second Confiscation Act (signed by President Lincoln on July 17, 1862), which stated specifically that "all slaves" that come to or come into Union hands "shall be deemed captives of war and shall be forever free, and not again held as slaves." And, although this act, much like the Emancipation Proclamation, did not apply to the Union slave states, it made them islands in an expanding sea of free states. Eventually, the Fugitive Slave Act itself became a dead letter and was repealed on June 28, 1864.

Thus, by the time slavery ended officially

in December 1865 (with the ratification of the Thirteenth Amendment), only a shadow of the former institution remained. Although long ignored by historians, the determination of African Americans to emancipate themselves was both a cause and an effect of making emancipation a war aim, a change that transformed African American runaways from fugitives into refugees, i.e., from property into persons. *See also* Fugitive Slaves.

FURTHER READING

Castel, Albert. "Civil War Kansas and the Negro." *Journal of Negro History* 51(1966): 125–138.

DuBois, W. E. B. *Black Reconstruction in America, 1860–1880.* 1935. Reprint, New York: Macmillan, 1992.

Hudson, J. Blaine. *Fugitive Slaves and the Underground Railroad in the Kentucky Borderland.* Jefferson, NC: McFarland, 2002.

McPherson, James M. *The Negro's Civil War.* New York: Ballantine Books, 1965.

Randall, James G. "Some Legal Aspects of the Confiscation Acts of the Civil War." *American Historical Review* 18, no. 1(1912): 79–96.

Schoonover, Thomas. "Misconstrued Mission: Expansionism and Black Colonization in Mexico and Central America during the Civil War." *Pacific Historical Review* 49(1980): 607–620.

Siebert, Wilbur H. The *Underground Railroad from Slavery to Freedom.* 1898. Reprint, New York: Russell and Russell, 1967.

Still, William. *The Underground Railroad.* 1872. Reprint, Chicago: Johnson, 1970.

Urwin, Gregory J. W. "'We Cannot Treat Negroes ... As Prisoners of War': Racial Atrocities and Reprisals in Civil War Arkansas." *Civil War History* 42(1996): 193–210.

Westwood, Howard C. "Benjamin Butler's Enlistment of Black Troops in New Orleans in 1862." *Louisiana History* 26(1985): 5–22.

Wilson, Henry. *History of the Anti-Slavery Measures of the Thirty-Seventh and Thirty-Eighth Congresses, 1861–64.* 1864. Reprint, New York: Negro Universities Press, 1964.

Clark, Starr (1793–1866)

An important friend of the fugitive, Starr Clark was born in Lee, **Massachusetts**, in 1793. In 1816, he and his wife, Harriett Loomis Clark, traveled by oxcart from Connecticut to Utica, New York. In 1832, the Clark family moved to Mexico, New York, where Clark prospered as a stove dealer and tin manufacturer — building a home east of his shop and store on Main Street.

Clark and his family were key figures in the antislavery movement in Mexico and operated an active Underground Railroad station in their home from the early 1830s until the Civil War. The Clark family welcomed and concealed **fugitive slaves** either in the Tin Shop, their own home, or in the homes of other antislavery families — and then arranged schedules and transportation for "the goods" (the code language often employed) to the next stations. Typically, fugitive slaves moved from Mexico either west to Oswego, or to Port Ontario, Cape Vincents, Sacketts Harbor, or points north.

On April 26, 1833, Harriet and Starr Clark joined the Mexico Presbyterian Church. However, in the 1840s, Clark was dismissed from the denomination because he advocated the ideal of Christian Union: He believed that all Christians should join together in one church. He then joined the local Methodist Church where his religious views and, quite possibly, his antislavery work, were not so controversial.

Clark died in 1866 and was remembered as "an active and influential citizen."

FURTHER READING

Wellman, Judith. *Grass Roots Reform in the Burned-Over District in Upstate New York: Religion, Abolitionism, and Democracy.* New York: Garland, 2000.

Clarke, Edwin W. (1801–1884)

A friend of the fugitive, Edwin W. Clarke was born September 10, 1801 in Pompey Hill, New York. The family, headed by Deodatus Clarke, a physician, and Nancy Dunham Clarke, moved to Oswego, New York, in 1807 and settled on a 250-acre farm east of the town. Clarke became an attorney and, in 1828, the first clerk of Oswego. In 1833, he married Charlotte Ambler (b. 1809) and the couple had six children.

Clarke also became an early, vocal and active abolitionist, serving as president of the Oswego County Anti-Slavery Society and raising funds for various antislavery groups. In 1840, Clarke supported the Liberty Party and campaigned for the release of James Seward, a free African American from Oswego County who had been captured and enslaved in Louisiana. In a letter to the *Oswego Palladium*,

Clarke declared that "the principles of slavery and liberty are never dormant, never stand still. They are at constant war, each striving for its own life, and conscious that it can exist only by the annihilation of the other."

Edwin W. Clarke was also a central figure in the Underground Railroad in Oswego and the surrounding region — working with his brother and sister-in-law (Sidney and Olive Jackson Clarke), who lived on a farm east of Oswego, to shelter and otherwise assist fugitive slaves. As an example, both Clarke families were involved in the famous rescue of **Jerry McHenry** in October 1851 and Clarke himself gave McHenry refuge for four days until a ship could be found to bear McHenry across Lake Ontario.

Clarke died in 1884 and was buried in Riverside Cemetery, Company Route 57; his grave marker reads: "Just, fearless, humane ... He gave the best of his years and powers to the relief of the oppressed and to the aid and succor of slaves escaping from bondage, having in all he did the effective sympathy and cooperation of his devoted wife." *See also* Edwin W. Clarke House.

FURTHER READING

Clarke, John Jackson. "Memories of the Anti-Slavery Movement and the Underground Railway." December 19, 1931. Clarke Papers. Oswego County Historical Society.

Wellman, Judith. *Grass Roots Reform in the Burned-Over District in Upstate New York: Religion, Abolitionism, and Democracy.* New York: Garland, 2000.

Clearfield Farm (Smyrna, Delaware)

Underground Railroad site. Clearfield farm is located in a sparsely populated section of Delaware and was a refuge for **fugitive slaves**. Constructed in about 1755, the house was expanded by Daniel Corbet in 1840 to include a crawl space in the attic and a cellar connected to the fireplace, both of which were hiding places for freedom seekers. Corbet worked closely with Thomas **Garrett** and Jonathan Hunn (see **Wild Cat Manor** and **Great Geneva**). *See also* Underground Railroad, Sites of; and Appendixes 3 and 4.

Clemens, James (1781–1870)

A friend of the fugitive, James Clemens, a free man of color, migrated from Virginia to Darke, County, **Ohio** in 1818. There, he became the first African American property owner of record in German township. Clemens was accompanied by his wife, Sofia, who was probably the daughter of Adam Sellers of Rockingham County, Virginia, Clemens' former owner.

Clemens' farm prospered and he became the founder of Longtown (Greenville settlement), one of Ohio's earliest black settlements, and was instrumental in starting the first school, the Wesleyan Church and a cemetery for the community. Clemens' home was also an Underground Railroad station, and members of his family were sometimes Underground Railroad conductors and later soldiers in the **Civil War**. *See also* Joseph and Sophia Clemens Farmstead.

FURTHER READING

National Park Service. *Underground Railroad: Special Resource Study.* Washington, D.C.: U.S. Government Printing Office, 1995.

Siebert, Wilbur H. *The Underground Railroad from Slavery to Freedom.* 1898. Reprint, New York: Russell and Russell, 1967.

Cleveland, Ohio

Underground Railroad junction. *See also* Oberlin-Wellington Rescue; Ohio; Underground Railroad, Sites of; and Appendixes 3 and 4.

Coffin, Levi (1798–1877)

Friend of the fugitive. Levi Coffin was born on October 28, 1798, near Greensboro, North Carolina. After a brief education at home, he taught school for several years. Coffin was a Quaker and, along with his cousin Vestal **Coffin**, attempted in 1821 to start a Sunday school for enslaved African Americans. Alarmed local slave-owners refused to allow their enslaved African Americans to attend and later forced the school to close.

As the laws and customs of North Carolina became increasingly restrictive, Coffin migrated north with other members of his family to the **Indiana** frontier. In 1826, he moved to Newburyport, Indiana, established a store and ventured into butchering pork and manufacturing linseed oil. Newburyport was also located on one of the main routes traveled by **fugitive slaves** making their way from or through **Kentucky** to sanctuary in the northern free states or **Canada**. Working with free people of color who settled nearby, Coffin soon became involved in helping the runaways.

Even as he prospered as a merchant, it has been estimated that as many as 3,000 fugitive slaves were harbored at his home on their long and perilous journey. His thriving business and importance in the community helped deflect opposition to his Underground Railroad activities from proslavery supporters and slave hunters in the area. Questioned about why he aided fugitive slaves, Coffin stated: "I am a firm believer in the doctrines and precepts of the gospel, which teaches us to do unto others as we would that they do unto us; and to feed the hungry, clothe the naked, etc.; but does not make any distinction of color." (Coffin, 1876: 592.)

In 1847, Coffin moved to **Cincinnati** and opened a wholesale warehouse that handled cotton goods, sugar, and spices produced by free labor. In Cincinnati, Coffin and his wife continued to help fugitive slaves and, drawing on contacts in Cincinnati's free black and white antislavery communities, created a well-organized Underground Railroad system that stretched tentacles throughout the Ohio Valley and the western trans-Appalachian borderland region. This organized network was chiefly responsible for Cincinnati gaining the distinction of being the "Grand Central Station" of the Underground Railroad.

Both during and after the **Civil War**, Coffin served as a leading figure in the Western Freedmen's Aid Society and, in only one year, raised more than $100,000 for the society in England and Europe. In 1867 he was a delegate to the International Anti-Slavery Conference in Paris and, in 1876, published his autobiography, *The Reminiscences of Levi Coffin.* Coffin died on September 16, 1877 in Cincinnati and is buried in Spring Grove Cemetery. *See also* Levi Coffin House; Quakers.

FURTHER READING

Coffin, Levi. *Reminiscences of Levi Coffin.* New York: Augustus M. Kelley, 1876.

Siebert, Wilbur H. "The Mysteries of Ohio's Underground Railroad." 1895, draft manuscript, in the Wilbur Siebert Papers, The Ohio Underground Railroad, Box 116, Ohio Historical Society.

Siebert, Wilbur H. *The Underground Railroad from Slavery to Freedom.* 1898. Reprint, New York: Russell and Russell, 1967.

Coffin, Vestal

Friend of the fugitive. As early as 1819, Vestal Coffin, a Quaker, organized an Underground Railroad network in Guilford, North Carolina, and the surrounding area. **Fugitive slaves** were hidden in homes, out buildings and nearby forests. Coffin's son, Addison, assisted in aiding freedom seekers on their northward journey — and Coffin's cousin, Levi **Coffin**, became one of the central figures in Underground Railroad history after moving first to Richmond, **Indiana** and, in 1847, to **Cincinnati**, Ohio. *See also* Ohio; Quakers; Underground Railroad, Sites of; and Appendixes 1–4.

Colonel William Hubbard House (Ashtabula, Ohio)

Underground Railroad site recognized and documented by the National Park Service. *See also* Appendix 5.

Colonial Period (1607–1776)

The political geography of the colonial period was extremely fluid and differed from that of the antebellum era in several crucial respects. Vast tracts of land were still occupied and controlled by Native American nations. Other sections of North America were claimed by other European powers, i.e., France and Spain. Slavery was legal in all British North American colonies (including Canada), so the distinction between "free" and "slave" states that would so divide the nation in the 1800s had not yet been created — and **fugitive slaves** operated in an historical context quite different from the decades immediately preceding the **Civil War**.

In colonial America, plantation systems emerged in the 1600s and 1700s in the Chesapeake Bay region — the tobacco growing sections of Virginia and Maryland — and in coastal sections of the Carolinas and Georgia, where rice and indigo were cultivated. The conditions of enslavement were most brutal and dehumanizing in these regions and, consequently, slave escapes were most frequent — with records dating to as early as 1640.

The table below, compiled from several sources in the research literature, provides a useful, objective baseline for understanding slave escapes in the colonial South:

Slave Escapes

	Males		Females	
	Escapes	%	Escapes	%
North Carolina	114	89.1	14	10.9
South Carolina	4,402	82.6	671	17.6
Virginia	1,138	89.0	141	11.0
Total	5,654	87.3	825	12.7

As noted in advertisements for the recovery of these freedom seekers, most North and South Carolina runaways were field hands (87.3 percent and 88.7 percent, respectively). However, in Virginia, 68.4 percent were field hands, while 14.8 percent were artisans, 7.5 percent were watermen and 7.8 percent were domestics.

It is important to note that **slave trade** from Africa and the Caribbean contributed significantly to the black population during the colonial period and, throughout, the proportion of the African American population that was African-born remained comparatively high. This pattern varied, however, from colony to colony. For example, as late as 1775, 49.1 percent of the adult black population of South Carolina was African-born, compared to roughly 33 percent of the adult black population in North Carolina and only 10 percent of the adult black population in Virginia. These patterns are important since African-born bondspersons were more likely to attempt escape than their American-born (Creole) counterparts; a third of Virginia runaways were African-born, as were more than half of North Carolina fugitive slaves.

In colonial America, the destinations pursued by fugitive slaves also differed rather dramatically from those pursued by runaways in the ante-bellum period. For example, runaways from South Carolina and later Georgia tended to flee south, seeking freedom in Spanish Florida. Runaways from slavery in Virginia tended to flee north or west to the frontier and often friendly Native Americans (consistent with the dictum that "the enemy of my enemy is my friend"). Given the greater distance between their place of enslavement and free territory, North Carolina fugitives had fewer options and often tended to remain hidden in the colony. Not surprising, in a more sparsely settled continent, flight to the swamps, the mountains or simply the "back country," and the consequent formation of maroon societies or colonies, was comparatively common.

FURTHER READING

Berlin, Ira, and Ronald Hoffman, eds. *Slavery and Freedom in the Age of Revolution.* Charlottesville: University Press of Virginia, 1983.

Bruns, Roger, ed. *Am I Not a Man and a Brother: The Anti-Slavery Crusade of Revolutionary America, 1688–1788.* New York: R. R. Bowker, 1977.

Chaplin, Joyce E. "Tidal Rice Cultivation and the Problem of Slavery in South Carolina and Georgia." *William and Mary Quarterly* 49(1992): 29–61.

Kay, Marvin L., and Lorin L. Cary. "Slave Runaways in Colonial North Carolina." *The North Carolina Historical Review* 63, no. 1 (1981).

Meadors, Daniel E. "South Carolina Fugitives as Viewed through Local Colonial Newspapers with Emphasis on Runaway Notices, 1732–1801." *Journal of Negro History* 59(1975): 288–319.

Mullin, Gerald W. *Flight and Rebellion: Slave Resistance in Eighteenth Century Virginia.* New York: Oxford University Press, 1972.

Wax, Darold D. "'The Great Risque We Run': The Aftermath of Slave Rebellion at Stono, South Carolina, 1739–1745." *Journal of Negro History* 67(1982): 136–147.

Colonization

Colonization refers to the organized attempt to return African Americans to Africa or to settle them in another part of the world outside the United States. At various times in American history, whites have advocated colonization as a solution to the problem of race. At other times, particularly when blacks felt most frustrated, betrayed, and victimized by American society (when freedom and equality seemed for away), blacks have advocated colonization as well.

The first proposal to remove blacks (primary free blacks) from the U.S. was advanced by the **Quakers** in 1714. In 1785, Quaker William Thornton proposed that a "commonwealth" be created in West Africa for free blacks and enslaved African Americans who would be freed only as a precondition for their removal. In 1790, Ferdinand Fairfax of Virginia asked the U.S. Congress to create a colony in Africa for free and freed blacks, and even Thomas Jefferson supported the general idea. After 1803, others, who felt that mass deportation would be too expensive, supported the use of a portion of the Louisiana Territory as a separate colony for blacks.

In 1802, after the Gabriel Revolt, the Virginia House of Delegates asked President Jefferson to create or obtain a colony for free blacks (who were considered a destabilizing force with respect to slavery). Given the influence of Toussaint L'Ouverture's revolution in Haiti, the Gabriel Revolt and the growing population of free blacks, these ideas were widely supported. Moreover, as early as 1786, England had begun deporting blacks living in England to Sierra Leone, and, in 1808, Sierra Leone was made a British Crown Colony, establishing a precedent.

Paul Cuffe (1759–1817), a wealthy African American ship-owner, grew frustrated with the conservative shift following the American Revolution and became a leading early black proponent of colonization. Cuffe sailed to England and Sierra Leone before the War of 1812 to organize a colonization effort, but died soon after the war before his plans could be realized.

After the War of 1812, the expansion of the **Cotton Kingdom** accelerated, and free people of color, who were considered a threat to the institution of **slavery**, were as much "in the way" as were Native Americans. Not surprisingly, much as a policy and strategy evolved for the removal of Native Americans from the South, colonization would be employed in an attempt to remove free people of color.

On December 21, 1816, a conference to develop a colonization plan convened in Washington, D.C., attended by key leaders of the young nation, including Henry Clay of Kentucky, Francis Scott Key (who wrote the lyrics to the "Star Spangled Banner"), General Andrew Jackson and many others. The conference enunciated the following principles: Free people of color would never be welcome in American society; returning free people of color to Africa was "morally right"; coloniza-

tion would rid the United States of a potentially dangerous element and spread "civilization" to Africa; the option of colonization would be limited to free people of color — and the question of abolishing slavery was not to be discussed. On December 28, 1816, based on these principles, The American Society for Colonizing Free People of Color of These United States, or the American Colonization Society, was established formally. Over the next decades, branches of the larger society were established in most southern states.

The society sent its first petition to Congress for the establishment of an African colony on January 14, 1817. Although early efforts met with resistance, the society was able to secure the passage of the Slave Trade Act on March 3, 1819, which authorized President James Monroe to return blacks to Africa and "provide for them in the West Coast of the continent." This act led to the establishment of Liberia — an American version of Sierra Leone. However, by 1830, only 1,420 African Americans had emigrated to Liberia and, by 1860, no more than 15,000 had been resettled in Africa. In essence, the American Colonization Society was often successful politically — every American president from Monroe to Lincoln endorsed its aims — but failed miserably to achieve its practical purpose. The reasons for this failure are many.

First, **slave trade** and slavery were profitable, but returning blacks to Africa was costly. Thus, if the government would not allocate funds for the deportation of free people of color, colonizationists could pursue their agenda only by using private means.

Second, white support for colonization was uneven. Although the society reflected the views of some wealthy, powerful, white southerners, many other slave-holding whites opposed it. Other whites, who considered colonization a humanitarian measure at first, often abandoned it in favor of militant abolitionism by the 1830s.

Third, and most important, African Americans were ambivalent regarding colonization at first and came to oppose it strongly in later years. The reasons were many, some obvious and others more subtle. Trust was a major barrier, since the whites who supported colonization were usually staunch supporters of slavery and, to many African Americans, efforts to remove free blacks from the United States were intended to benefit whites, not blacks. Further, by the early 1800s, many African Americans were one or more generations removed from Africa, with little or usually no clear idea regarding their or their ancestors' point of origin in Africa. In other words, African Americans neither rejected Africa nor abjured their African origins, but simply did not identify strongly with them. As free people of color began the slow process of institution building, the abolition of slavery and equal rights in this country became their primary concerns. For example, in 1830, when the first Convention of Free People of Color met in Philadelphia, led by Richard Allen and James Forten, the convention condemned colonization as "evil." Thus, while Paul Cuffe embodied pro-colonization sentiment, the views of Allen and Forten were more typical.

Still, the call for a "return to Africa" would echo, periodically, through black America in later years, particularly during periods of unusually poor race relations. Some of the most important leaders in African American history would endorse the idea of leaving the United States — but for their own reasons and on their own terms — as attested to by the movements initiated by Martin R. **Delany** in the 1850s, Bishop Henry McNeal Turner in the 1880s and 1890s, and Marcus Garvey in the 1920s. Moreover, different variations on this theme are common in contemporary black America, although "returning to Africa" is now most often an expression of cultural identification, political sympathy, academic interest and economic ties to the emerging nations of Africa.

FURTHER READING

Fox, Early Lee. *The American Colonization Society, 1817–1840*. Baltimore: The Johns Hopkins Press, 1919.

Franklin, John Hope, and Alfred A. Moss, Jr. *From Slavery to Freedom: A History of African Americans*. 8th ed. New York: McGraw-Hill, 2000.

Garrison, William Lloyd. *Thoughts on African Colonization*. 1832. Reprint, New York: Arno Press, 1968.

Compromise of 1850

The United States was founded as two nations under one government, one in which **slavery** was legal and the other in which slavery was not. The maintenance of a tenuous national unity necessitated the creation of a fragile political balance between these two regions.

Given the structure of the U.S. government, representation in the House of Representatives is based on population. Because an enslaved African American could only be counted as three-fifths of a person, based on the Three-fifths Compromise of the U.S. Constitution (Article 1, section 2.3), the free-states and their interests would come to dominate the lower chamber — particularly as waves of European immigrants poured into the North and West beginning in the 1840s. On the other hand, each state, regardless of population, had two seats in the U.S. Senate. Thus, maintaining a balance in the Senate could stalemate any free state attempts to pass legislation deemed injurious to slave state interests. However, this balance could be achieved only by, first, ensuring that there were as many free states as slave states — and, second, since the vice president of the United States serves as president of the U.S. Senate and can vote to break any tie votes in that chamber, by ensuring, insofar as possible, that the president of the United States (and, hence, the vice president) were sympathetic toward or, at minimum, not inclined to act against slavery.

Each time significant new territory was added to the United States, this sectional balance was threatened and a political crisis over slavery soon ensued, resulting in the negotiation of a new agreement to stave off disunion. For example, the question of how the Louisiana Purchase would be divided between freedom and slavery was resolved, ultimately, by the Missouri Compromise of 1820. After most of the western third of the country was acquired by virtue of the Mexican War (1846–1847), a similar crisis erupted when **California** pressed for admission to the Union in 1849 since, by the late 1840s, there were 15 free states and 15 slave states and California, if admitted, would create a free state majority and upset the sectional balance.

As the nation stood on the brink of disunion or civil war, Henry Clay, Daniel Webster and Stephen Douglas maneuvered, between January and September 1850, to engineer a compromise. By the summer of 1850, this package of legislation — the Compromise of 1850 — had been approved. Under the provisions of the compromise, California was admitted to the Union as a free state; New Mexico and **Utah** were organized as slave territories; Texas had its boundaries set; and slave trade was outlawed in Washington, D.C. In response to slave state demands, the **Fugitive Slave Act of 1850** was enacted.

The test of a good compromise is whether it gives all parties something they want or need, without requiring any party to relinquish anything it cannot do without. By that test, the Missouri Compromise, which endured for a generation, was a "good" compromise. By that same test, the Compromise of 1850 was a poor one. Rather than defusing sectional tensions, opposition to the Fugitive Slave Act and the turmoil provoked by slave state efforts to manufacture more slave states (e.g., the Kansas-Nebraska Act of 1854, and southern intrigues in Central America and the Caribbean) exacerbated those tensions. Ultimately, the nation moved from crisis to crisis through the decade of the **1850s** — with the issue of slavery at the heart of each.

FURTHER READING

Campbell, Stanley. *The Slave Catchers: Enforcement of the Fugitive Slave Law, 1850–1860.* Chapel Hill: University of North Carolina Press, 1968.

Lee, R. Alton. "Slavery and the Oregon Territorial Issue: Prelude to the Compromise of 1850." *Pacific Northwest Quarterly* 64(1973): 112–119.

Concord, Massachusetts

Underground Railroad center. Concord, **Massachusetts**, was home to some of the most influential thinkers and writers in nineteenth century America, including Ralph Waldo **Emerson,** Henry David **Thoreau**, Franklin S. Sanborn, and the family of Louisa May Alcott. Emerson is best known for his transcendentalist philosophy and Thoreau for his treatise on civil disobedience, his musings on Walden Pond and his influence on the intellectual and political development of Dr. Martin Luther King, Jr. In addition to their seminal contributions to American letters, both Emerson and Thoreau were staunch advocates of the antislavery cause, supporters of John **Brown** and harbored **fugitive slaves** in their

Concord homes. *See also* Underground Railroad, Sites of; and Appendixes 3 and 4.

Corbet, Daniel

See Clearfield Farm

The Cotton Kingdom (1790–1820)

The Industrial Revolution, beginning in the late 1700s, resulted in basic changes in both the economic and political organization of the major European societies and the United States. African Americans, the institution of **slavery** and the politics of the early United States were shaped definitively by the development of an immensely profitable, but highly exploitative, agricultural system that provided raw cotton for industrial textile production.

English inventors, by 1800, had devised the spinning and weaving machines necessary for the cheap manufacture of cotton textiles. The public demand for such goods was strong. However, it was necessary to separate cotton seeds from fiber before raw cotton was ready for the newly invented looms, and this process was slow and labor-intensive. In 1792, Georgia sponsored a commission to explore the feasibility of inventing a cotton gin and, in 1793, Eli Whitney (from New England) succeeded in devising such a machine. In the years following the invention of the cotton gin, the South underwent an economic revolution. One enslaved African American operating this new machine could clean as much cotton as 50 enslaved African Americans working solely by hand. Thus, with this invention, enslaved African Americans could be employed almost exclusively in cotton cultivation, which did not require a large capital investment, prompting many planters and small farmers to shift from rice, indigo or tobacco to cotton. And slavery, which seemed a dying institution in the 1780s, gained a renewed lease on life.

Before the War of 1812, cotton exports mounted rapidly and prices for "raw" cotton remained high. For example, cotton production rose from 6,000 bales in 1792 to 17,000 bales in 1795, to 73,000 bales in 1800, to 146,000 bales in 1805. Given this profit potential, some planters purchased more land and more slave labor — and large-scale cotton

cultivation drove the small yeomen farmers and planters to the economic margins. Within a few decades, the prosperity of the entire region, soon known as the "Cotton Kingdom," was bound inextricably to the cultivation of one crop and the many ancillary activities that supported such cultivation. Further, by the 1830s, cotton had become the chief export crop of the United States and a key source of wealth not only for southern planters, but for northern financial and mercantile interests as well.

The emergence of the Cotton Kingdom had several implications. First, cotton cultivation required vast quantities of land and labor. With respect to labor, the demand for enslaved African Americans increased significantly in the decades following the invention of the cotton gin, but, after international slave trade became illegal in 1808, this demand could be met, legally, only by "growing" the slave population within the United States and shifting enslaved African Americans to areas in which cotton could be grown profitably. Consequently, natural population growth among African Americans was encouraged strongly and, in rare cases, even "slave-breeding" was practiced — and a thriving internal or "domestic" slave trade developed.

Domestic slave traders could realize significant profits, often 30 to 50 percent, from this otherwise disreputable business. Slave trading centers emerged in many of the older and newer states: Baltimore, Maryland; Richmond, Virginia; Lexington, **Kentucky**; **Louisville**, Kentucky; Charleston, South Carolina; Montgomery, Alabama; Memphis, **Tennessee**; and New Orleans, Louisiana. Perhaps the most notorious market of all was based in Washington, D.C., where this seamy business was conducted within sight of the centers of the United States government.

With respect to land, cotton cultivation required a climate with a relatively long growing season and ample rainfall. Such conditions existed in South Carolina, Georgia and sections of North Carolina and Tennessee, but not in the Upper South and the early border states with their shorter growing seasons. On

the other hand, there were millions of acres of land between the Appalachian Mountains and the Mississippi River (south of Tennessee) that were quite suitable for cotton. This land was reserved, however, by various treaties for the "Five Civilized Indian Nations": the Creeks, Choctaws, Cherokees, Chickasaws and Seminoles. After the War of 1812, American settlers and American government policy began the long process of Native American "removal" from these lands and opening them to cotton cultivation, through the Creek War in 1817, the First Seminole War in 1818, the Indian Removal Act of 1830 (leading to the "Trail of Tears"), and the Second Seminole War of 1835–1842. As the Native Americans retreated, white settlers and enslaved African Americans poured into the Gulf States. Louisiana became a state in 1812, Mississippi in 1817, Alabama in 1819, and Texas and Florida in 1845. Domestic slave trade moved thousands of enslaved African Americans each year from the Upper South to these newly settled regions. Soon, so much arable land came under cotton cultivation that the South became increasingly unable to produce its own foodstuffs or industrial goods. For example, in 1806, South Carolina did not grow enough corn to feed its own population — while, in 1790, it could feed its people and export more than 100,000 bushels of corn to other states.

It is also important to note that the Cotton Kingdom emerged against the backdrop of the French Revolution and the Napoleonic Wars in Europe, the War of 1812 in North America — and black revolt and revolution throughout the Western Hemisphere. For example, in the 1790s, the Second Maroon War in Jamaica, efforts to suppress the Garifuna (or "Black Caribs") in the eastern Caribbean, the Gabriel Conspiracy in Virginia in 1800 and the Sancho Conspiracy in 1802 all spread lingering unrest and unease. Most significantly, the Haitian Revolution, under the leadership of Toussaint L'Ouverture, created the first independent black nation in the Americas by 1804. This singular event, along with prompting Napoleon to sell his now

Opposite: A man with a whip stands behind a line of slaves in the Cotton Kingdom in this 1834 engraving. (Library of Congress)

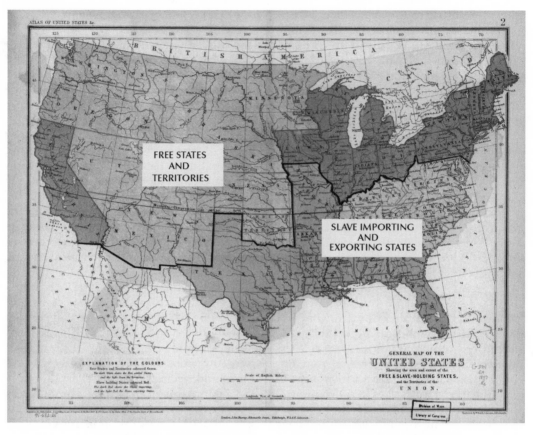

An 1857 map shows the free and slave-holding states. (Library of Congress)

"worthless" North American real estate to the United States in the Louisiana Purchase of 1803, also led to the end of international slave trade. Thus, as the Cotton Kingdom grew, southerners found themselves increasingly afraid of and dependent upon enslaved African American laborers — and, as the slave population expanded rapidly in the Gulf States, the institution of slavery grew more rigid, brutal and exploitative.

What the Industrial Revolution did for capitalism, the cotton culture did for the institution of slavery. Small to moderate-sized farms became plantations, and plantations became factory-like agricultural production operations — large, impersonal and exploitative. Cotton cultivation through the use of slave labor threatened all other forms of labor and economic activity in the South. Enslaved African Americans became one of the most rapidly growing segments of the southern population. For example, there were fewer than 700,000 enslaved African Americans in 1790, but more than 2,000,000 in 1830 — more than 600,000 of whom were concentrated in the Gulf States.

Land and slave-ownership became more concentrated and, although the majority of slave-owners were small farmers with slave-holdings of 20 or fewer persons, it is important to note that, by 1860, 75 percent of white southerners owned no slaves and had no clear economic interest in maintaining slavery. Nevertheless, slavery permeated the politics and economy of the South because most staple crops were produced on plantations where slave labor was employed, giving planters a disproportionate share of wealth and power. Despite this class division, most non-slave-owners aspired to become slave owners — and identified with the interests and prejudices of that class.

Slavery was fading from the North as it became more deeply entrenched in the South, and the two broad regions of the United States slowly drifted apart culturally, socially and economically. By 1820, these differences became a political fault line that precipitated, first, the **Missouri Compromise**, then the **Compromise of 1850** and, eventually, the **Civil War.**

FURTHER READING

Franklin, John Hope, and Alfred A. Moss, Jr. *From Slavery to Freedom: A History of African Americans*. 8th ed. New York: McGraw-Hill, 2000.

Huggins, Nathan I. *Black Odyssey: The African American Ordeal in Slavery*. New York: Vintage Books, 1990.

Cowles, Horace

Friend of the fugitive in **Farmington, Connecticut.** *See also* Appendixes 1 and 2.

Craft, William (1824–1900) and Ellen Craft (1826–1891)

Fugitive slaves. Disguises, ruses and subterfuge were common strategies employed by **fugitive slaves**. One of the more memorable examples, and one of the most spectacular, if not legendary, slave escapes in American history, was that of William and Ellen Craft, a young enslaved husband and wife from Georgia.

Ellen Craft was born in Clinton, Georgia, in 1826. With a biracial mother and white father, James Smith — an attorney, surveyor and Ellen's owner — Ellen was so fair complexioned that she appeared "near white." Ellen's resemblance to her white relatives prompted her owner/father's wife to "give Ellen" as a wedding present to her daughter in Macon, Georgia, in 1837. There, she met William Craft, born in 1824 in Macon, and the two married in 1846.

Using money William earned working as a hired mechanic, cabinet-maker and waiter at a local hotel, the young couple planned a daring escape. On December 21, 1848, William and Ellen Craft escaped from Macon and arrived in **Philadelphia** on Christmas Day. To execute their escape, Ellen posed as a sick young white man traveling north for medical treatment with his (her) servant, William. Ellen's face and right hand were bandaged, to limit her need to speak or write (both William and Ellen were then illiterate).

The two fugitives rode by train from Macon to Savannah, Georgia, then traveled by steamer to Charleston, South Carolina — where they lodged at the "best hotel" — then by another steamer to Wilmington, North Carolina, then by rail through Virginia, by another steamer to **Washington, D.C.,** then another train to Baltimore, Maryland and yet another to Philadelphia. Through the many stages of this complex and dangerous journey, William could "be himself" but Ellen had to act the part not only of someone of another race but someone of another gender as well.

Once in Philadelphia, the Crafts were befriended by William Wells **Brown** and William Lloyd **Garrison.** They soon moved to Boston, where they lived with Lewis **Hayden,** and became popular on the antislavery lecture circuit. With William recounting their adventure on stage, and with Ellen standing nearby, the Crafts thrilled audiences throughout the North.

Soon after the passage of the **Fugitive Slave Act of 1850,** Ellen Craft narrowly escaped an attempted kidnapping by slave-catchers in **Boston.** For their safety, the Crafts then fled to Maine, then **Canada** and eventually to England in November 1850. There, they had five children, acquired an education and became active in social reform activity. William even became an active member of the African Aid Society and established a school and a business in Dahomey, in West Africa, between 1863 and 1867.

In 1869, the Crafts returned to the United States with two of their children and settled, in 1870, near Ways Station, Georgia, where they purchased a farm and grew cotton and rice. The Crafts also attempted to establish the Woodville Industrial School. However, they were forced to close this institution when the local Ku Klux Klan burned their home and barn in the autumn of 1870. The Crafts remained, although in reduced circumstances. Ellen died in 1891 and was buried, at her request, under her favorite tree. After her death, William moved to Charleston, South Carolina, where he died in 1900.

FURTHER READING

Craft, William, and Ellen Craft. *Running a Thousand Miles for Freedom*. 1860. Reprint, New York: Arno Press, 1969.

Still, William. *The Underground Railroad*. 1872. Reprint, Chicago: Johnson, 1970.

Crenshaw, John Hart (d. 1871)

Kidnapper. Like Patty **Cannon**, John Crenshaw kidnapped free persons of color and captured fugitive slaves in **Illinois**, and sold them into **slavery**.

Although Illinois was a free territory and later a free state, slavery continued to exist there in various forms, such as indenture contracts, until the 1840s. **Free people of color** were especially vulnerable to kidnapping and, while the Illinois Black Code of 1819 imposed a $1,000 fine on anyone convicted on this crime, African Americans could not testify on their own behalf—thus rendering the law essentially useless.

Crenshaw operated at Shawneetown in the far southern section of Illinois—close to both Missouri and **Kentucky**. His career as a kidnapper was long, lucrative and blood-stained. As early as 1825, Crenshaw, John Forrester and Preston W. Davis were indicted for kidnapping. Available documents indicate that a "prominent resident of Shawneetown, Mr. John C ... kept the slaves in a cave on the Wabash River near his home." (Harris, 1904: 55.) No such cave exists on the Wabash in Gallatin County, but one could be found only a few miles from Crenshaw's home and his salt works on the Saline River.

Free blacks continued to disappear and fugitive slaves were often decoyed and intercepted in their flight by the false promise of assistance and sanctuary. By 1830, Crenshaw's wealth had increased and he owned a steam mill near Equality and three of the nine salt works in the area. In 1833, he began building **Hickory Hill**, a three-story home later known as the **Old Slave House**. There, Crenshaw imprisoned and, according to some accounts, tortured the unfortunate African Americans he was able to capture, pending their sale "south." Crenshaw kept his victims in the attic and was reputed even to keep "stud slaves" for "slave breeding" purposes. Crenshaw also gave enslaved or stolen African Americans as "gifts," then would steal and resell them back into slavery.

One of the most dramatic and well-documented examples of the latter practice concerned the 1842 kidnapping of Maria Adams and her children, given as gifts to Crenshaw's own daughter and son-in-law in 1837, whom Crenshaw later abducted and sold to a slave trader named Lewis Kuykendall. Crenshaw was acquitted on a technicality since, while it was known he had kidnapped Maria and her children, the prosecutor could not prove that the victims had been taken from the state.

Crenshaw was connected with several other kidnappings in the 1840s, but, by the **1850s**, became more involved in farming his thousands of acres of land. Still, as Muscrave concludes: "John Hart Crenshaw ... was a slave-holder of indentured servants, but was at least twice indicted as a kidnapper of free blacks. In effect, Crenshaw was a conductor of an Underground Railroad that operated in reverse, from north to south, from freedom to slavery."

FURTHER READING

Blockson, Charles L. *Hippocrene Guide to the Underground Railroad*. New York: Hippocrene Books, 1994.

Dean, Terry. "Present Owners of Crenshaw House Look to State for Funding." *Daily Egyptian* (Southern Illinois University at Carbondale), February 29, 2000.

Harris, N. Dwight. *The History of Negro Servitude in Illinois and of the Slavery Agitation in that State 1719 to 1864*. Chicago: A. C. McClurg, 1904.

Musgrave, Jon. "History Comes out of Hiding atop Hickory Hill." *Springhouse Magazine*, 1996.

Creole Affair (1841)

Slave-ship revolt. In the autumn of 1841, the slave-ship *Creole* sailed from Virginia with a cargo of 135 enslaved African Americans, 19 white crew members and other passengers bound for the southern market in Louisiana. After 11 days at sea, 19 enslaved African Americans seized the ship, killing at least one of the crew, and forced the *Creole* into the British port of Nassau in the Bahamas—becoming **fugitive slaves** in the process. There, the *Creole* was seized by the British military and the "mutineers" were arrested. When black Bahamians became aware of these events, they surrounded the ship with as many as 50 boats and freed the remaining captives. After considerable diplomatic pyrotechnics, the British officially freed the enslaved African Americans.

In the furor that ensued, Daniel Webster, secretary of state, indicated that the American government would demand indemnification — i.e., some form of restitution—from the British for the slave-owners who had "lost their property." Coming so closely on the heels of the *Amistad* case, the position of the government outraged members of the antislavery movement. On March 21, 1842, Congressman Joshua R. **Giddings** of **Ohio** introduced a series of resolutions declaring that

> ... as slavery was an abridgment of a natural right, it had no force beyond the territorial jurisdiction that created it; that when an American vessel was not in the waters of any state it was under the jurisdiction of the United States alone, which had no authority to hold slaves; and that the mutineers of the Creole had only resumed their natural right to liberty, and any attempt to re-enslave them would be unconstitutional and dishonorable. [Jervey and Huber, 1980: 206.]

These resolutions created a furor in their own right and the House voted to censure Giddings. Giddings resigned and was reelected by his Ohio constituents. The fugitive slaves remained free. However, more than a decade later, Britain ruled that Bahamian officials had acted improperly and, in 1855, the American owners of the "*Creole* mutineers" were awarded $110,330 in compensation.

FURTHER READING
Jervey, Edward D., and C. Harold Huber. "The Creole Affair." *The Journal of Negro History* 65(1980): 196–209.
Jones, Howard. "The Peculiar Institution and National Honor: The Case of the Creole Slave Revolt." *Civil War History* 21(1975): 28–50.

Crosby, William

Friend of the fugitive in **Madison, Indiana.** *See also* Appendixes 1 and 2.

Crosswhite, Adam (b. c. 1799)

Fugitive slave. *See also* Crosswhite Affair.

Crosswhite Affair (1843–1847)

The 1847 Crosswhite Affair was a dramatic fugitive slave rescue that intensified the debate leading to the passage of the **Fugitive Slave Act of 1850.** The sequence of events leading to the rescue itself began in 1843, when 44-year-old Adam Crosswhite learned that his owner, Frank Giltner, planned to sell Crosswhite's children. Unwilling to permit the destruction of his family, Crosswhite, his wife, Sarah, and their four children escaped from Giltner's plantation in Carroll County, **Kentucky,** and continued northward until they reached Marshall, Michigan, near Battle Creek and its strong antislavery forces led by Erastus **Hussey.** Crosswhite found work, purchased a cabin and soon a fifth child was born.

Determined to recover his lost property, Giltner hired Francis Troutman, a young attorney, to track the fugitives. Troutman's efforts proved futile until December, 1846, when he located the Crosswhite family and proceeded to notify Giltner and the local authorities in Marshall. In late January, 1847, Giltner's son, David, along with Franklin Ford and John S. Lee, joined Troutman in Marshall and, in the early morning of January 27, 1847, they and Harvey Dixon, a deputy sheriff, descended on Crosswhite's cabin and attempted to arrest the family. Crosswhite held the party at bay and raised an alarm — according to some accounts, by firing a warning shot as a prearranged signal. His neighbors heard the shot and soon the Kentuckians were surrounded by an angry crowd of several hundred blacks and whites—including community leaders such as Charles T. Gorham, a banker, George Ingersoll, Jarvis Hurd, O.C. Comstock Jr., Asa B. Cook and John M. Easterly.

Troutman demanded the names of Crosswhite's defenders and many identified themselves—and Gorham even demanded that his name be recorded in capital letters. Finally, Dixon, sensing the volatility of the situation, arrested and jailed the Kentuckians for assault, battery and housebreaking. A trial ensued over the next two days before Randall Hobart, a justice of the peace with antislavery sympathies. By the time the Kentucky party posted bond, the Crosswhites had been spirited out of Marshall in a cart and transported by rail from Jackson to Detroit, and then to **Canada.**

Incensed over his treatment in Michigan, Troutman returned to Kentucky and, with Giltner, began a two-pronged campaign to punish those who defended Crosswhite. First, they pressed for and secured a resolution from the Kentucky General Assembly demanding redress from the Michigan citizens involved in the rescue. Next, they prepared a report summarizing their version of the Crosswhite affair and submitted it to the United States Senate on December 20, 1847. This report, calling for a stronger fugitive slave law, would be cited by Senator Henry Clay in the debates leading to the **Compromise of 1850**.

At the same time, Giltner filed suit against Gorham and several other leaders of the Marshall "mob" for the value of his "lost slave property." The suit was heard in Detroit federal circuit court by U.S. Supreme Court Justice John McLean, a former Kentuckian. McLean ruled in Giltner's favor and levied fines against those who defended Crosswhite. The Crosswhite Affair, arguably the defining moment in Michigan's Underground Railroad history, is commemorated by a plaque on a boulder at the site of the Crosswhite cabin. *See also* Fugitive Slaves.

FURTHER READING
Blockson, Charles L. *Hippocrene Guide to the Underground Railroad.* New York: Hippocrene Books, 1994.
Sherwood, John C. "One Flame in the Inferno: The Legend of Marshall's Crosswhite Affair." *Michigan History* 73(1989): 41–47.

Cunningham, James

Friend of the fugitive in **Louisville, Kentucky**. *See also* Appendixes 1 and 2.

Daniel Howell Hise House (Salem, Ohio)

An important Underground Railroad station, the Daniel Howell **Hise** House was located in the industrial Quaker community of Salem. Daniel Howell Hise (b. 1813), a noted abolitionist, purchased this one-and-a-half story Gothic Revival farmhouse in the late **1850s**, after which he effected renovations that added hidden rooms under the house and in an accompanying barn. There, Hise and his wife, Margaret, assisted **fugitive slaves** and hosted antislavery meetings.

The Daniel Howell Hise House is located at 1100 Franklin Ave., in Salem, **Ohio**, and has been designated a stop on "The Underground Railroad Travel Itinerary" by the National Park Service, United States Department of the Interior.

See also Quakers; Underground Railroad, Sites of.

FURTHER READING
National Park Service. *Underground Railroad: Special Resource Study.* Washington, D.C.: U.S. Government Printing Office, 1995.

Davids, Tice

Fugitive slave. Legend holds that the term "Underground Road" or "Underground Railroad" originated in roughly 1831 when Tice Davids, an enslaved African American, escaped across the **Ohio River** at Maysville, **Kentucky**. Pursued by his owner, Davids reached the river bank and seemed simply to disappear. The owner was said to have exclaimed that Davids "must have gone off on an underground road" or, in other versions, "the damned abolitionists must have an underground road." (Gara, 1961: 174.) *See also* Fugitive Slaves.

FURTHER READING
Coffin, Levi. *Reminiscences of Levi Coffin.* New York: Augustus M. Kelley, 1876.
Gara, Larry. *The Liberty Line: The Legend of the Underground Railroad.* Lexington: University Press of Kentucky, 1961.
Siebert, Wilbur H. *The Underground Railroad from Slavery to Freedom.* 1898. Reprint, New York: Russell and Russell, 1967.

Dawn, Ontario West, Canada

A major Canadian destination of **fugitive slaves**. The Dawn settlement was established in the 1840s and funded by abolitionists and philanthropic groups. In this respect, while organized to assist fugitive slaves, Dawn — much like **Buxton**— was also an experiment designed to test whether the courage demonstrated by fugitive slaves in their flight from slavery indicated their ability to function as free and self-sufficient citizens. Dawn attracted some 500 African American settlers to its 1,500 acres situated near Dresden. Its chief attraction, aside from the assistance and comfort of a shared community, was the promise of education in its manual labor school. *See also* Abolitionist Movement; Canada.

FURTHER READING
Winks, Robin W. *Blacks in Canada: A History.* New Haven, CT: 1971.

DeBaptiste, George (c. 1815–1875)

Friend of the fugitive. Born free in Virginia about 1815, George DeBaptiste arrived in **Madison, Indiana** in 1838 and was hired, in 1840, as the personal attendant of William Henry Harrison. In this capacity, he served as a steward in the White House during Harrison's brief term as president of the United States.

DeBaptiste opened a barbershop after returning to Madison and became actively involved in aiding fugitives, also venturing across the **Ohio River** into **Kentucky** to conduct some runaways to freedom. In fact, his barbershop became the "nerve center" of the Madison Underground Railroad — much as was probably the case with Washington **Spradling**'s barbershop in nearby **Louisville, Kentucky**. After repeated proslavery attacks, DeBaptiste relocated to **Detroit**, Michigan, in 1846. There, he prospered in business and became a leader in the Detroit black community while continuing to work with the Underground Railroad. DeBaptiste died in 1875. *See also* Fugitive Slaves; and Appendixes 1 and 2.

FURTHER READING

Crenshaw, Gwendolyn J. *Bury Me in a Free Land: The Abolitionist Movement in Indiana, 1816–1865.* Indianapolis: Indiana Historical Bureau, 1993.

Howard-Filler, Saralee R. "Detroit's Underground Railroad and the Museum of African American History." *Michigan History* 71(1987): 28–29.

Hudson, J. Blaine. *Fugitive Slaves and the Underground Railroad in the Kentucky Borderland.* Jefferson, NC: McFarland, 2002.

Delany, Martin Robison (1812–1885)

African American leader and friend of the fugitive. Martin Robinson Delany was born enslaved in Charleston, Virginia, on May 6, 1812. He was taught to read, illegally,

Parade and portraits of black life, illustrating the rights granted by the Fifteenth Amendment, from an 1870 lithograph. (Library of Congress)

by his mother and became conscious and proud as a child of his royal African ancestry. In 1823, Delany's father purchased the family's freedom and, by 1831, Delany found his way to Pittsburgh, Pennsylvania. There, he attended the Bethel Church School and worked for Dr. Andrew McDowell as an assistant. There, also, Delany became a committed black abolitionist and an active friend of **fugitive slaves**, using his home as a sanctuary for freedom seekers.

In 1843, Delany married Catherine Richards and began publishing *The Mystery,* an antislavery newspaper. In 1847, he joined Frederick **Douglass** briefly as co-editor of the *North Star.* His collaboration with Douglass was short-lived since the two differed over ideology and strategy — and, perhaps, more fundamentally, in temperament. For example, Douglass once observed "I thank God for making me a man, but Delany thanks him for making him a *black* man." Between 1849 and 1852, Delany also attended Harvard Medical School and later established a medical practice in Pittsburgh.

Angered and disillusioned by the **Compromise of 1850**, Delany became an articulate and forceful advocate of colonization — on terms advantageous to African Americans— and would later be considered the "father of Black Nationalism." Delany himself moved to Chatham, Ontario, in the **1850s** and organized emigrationist conventions in both the United States and Canada. While living in **Canada**, Delany also consulted with John **Brown** as Brown organized his ill-fated raid on **Harpers Ferry**. Some of Delany's associates accompanied Brown on the raid.

In 1852, he published the *Destiny of the Colored People in the United States* and, in 1859, led an expedition to explore the Niger River Delta area in West Africa as a possible location for the settlement of African Americans in Africa. Despite his pride in his own African ancestry, Delany had a rather negative view of the Africa of his time. As noted by Moses:

> On arriving in Nigeria, Delany discovered that those blacks with whom he felt the strongest sense of comradeship were not the most independent African leaders. In fact the friendly relations that Delany established with Africans were

> with the urbanized creoles and puppet chiefs ... He was appalled by the ... customs of the unchristian populations, for he considered Protestantism to be the most advanced stage of civilization. [Moses, 1978: 36.]

During the **Civil War**, Delany abandoned his emigration project and returned to the United States. He recruited black soldiers for the Union Army and, in 1865, was awarded the rank of major, becoming the first senior African American commissioned officer in the Army. After the war, Delany worked for the Freedmen's Bureau. However, as Reconstruction was undermined by white southern resistance, Delany attempted to resurrect his colonization project and became an active supporter of the Liberian Exodus Joint Stock Exchange Company. His efforts met with only limited success. Despite his seminal contributions to the struggle for African American freedom, Martin Robinson Delany died in relative obscurity in Wilberforce, **Ohio**, on January 24, 1885. *See also* Appendixes 1 and 2.

FURTHER READING

Delany, Martin Robison. *The Condition, Elevation, Emigration and Destiny of the Colored People of the United States, Politically Considered.* Philadelphia: Martin R. Delany, 1852.

Levine, Robert S. *Martin Delany, Frederick Douglass, and the Politics of Representative Identity.* Chapel Hill: University of North Carolina Press, 1997.

Moses, Wilson Jeremiah. *The Golden Age of Black Nationalism, 1850–1925.* New York: Oxford University Press, 1978.

Ullman, Victor. *Martin R. Delany: The Beginnings of Black Nationalism.* Boston: Beacon Press, 1971.

Detroit, Michigan

Underground Railroad junction. *See also* Blackburn, Thornton and Blackburn; DeBaptiste, George; Jewish Friends of the Fugitive, William Webb House.

Dickson, Moses (1824–1901)

Abolitionist and friend of the fugitive. Moses Dickson was born free in **Cincinnati, Ohio**, on April 5, 1824. Before the **Civil War**, Dickson worked as a barber on the steamboats that plied the Ohio and Mississippi Rivers and witnessed the horrors of **slavery** first-hand. In 1846, Dickson and 11 African Americans from St. Louis organized the Twelve Knights of Tabor (also known as the Knights of Liberty), a black secret society committed to the struggle against slavery. Through the Knights, Dickson and his associates assisted hundreds of **fugitive slaves** from their base in St. Louis.

With the coming of Civil War, Dickson enlisted in the Union Army and, after his discharge, devoted the remainder of his life to racial uplift causes and projects. He was ordained as a minister of the African Methodist Episcopal Church and preached at several churches in the St. Louis area. He became an active Republican and a member of the Equal Rights League, and was one of the founders of Lincoln Institute, which evolved into Lincoln University in Jefferson City, Missouri. He organized the International Order of Twelve Knights and Daughters of Tabor (an African American philanthropic organization) in 1872. In the late 1870s, Dickson served as president of the Refugee Relief Board in St. Louis and assisted as many as 16,000 African American "Exodusters" bound for Kansas.

After a distinguished career of service, Moses Dickson died on November 28, 1901. *See also* Abolitionist Movement; Underground Railroad, Sites of; and Appendixes 1–4.

Ditcher (Dicher), James (Jack)

Friend of the fugitive. Jack Ditcher lived in Lawrence County in southeastern Ohio and was one of the most effective and colorful African American Underground Railroad leaders in the region. Known as the "Red Fox" of the Underground, even his closest associates marveled at his courage and the risks he took in assisting **fugitive slaves** crossing into **Ohio** from eastern **Kentucky**— many of whom had escaped through the Appalachians. *See also* Appendixes 1 and 2.

FURTHER READING
Siebert, Wilbur H. *The Underground Railroad from Slavery to Freedom.* 1898. Reprint, New York: Russell and Russell, 1967.

Douglas, H. Ford (1831–1865)

Fugitive slave and antislavery leader. Hezekiah Ford Douglas was born in Virginia in 1831. His father, William, was white and his mother, Mary, was enslaved. Douglas escaped from bondage when he was 15 and

reached Cleveland, **Ohio**. There, he became a barber and acquired a formal education. By 1850, Douglas had gained recognition for his unusual gifts as an orator and his advocacy of the emigration of African Americans from the United States.

Douglas became active in the black convention movement in Ohio and, in 1854, addressed the Emigration Convention in Cleveland. In 1856, he moved to Chicago and operated an American office of the *Provincial Freeman,* the Canadian-based African American newspaper controlled by Mary Ann Shadd **Cary**. He soon moved to **Canada** and supported Cary's position that African Americans should integrate into Canadian society as thoroughly as possible. Returning to the United States in 1858, he remained a popular and active speaker, often sharing the stage with Frederick **Douglass**.

Douglas abandoned his emigrationist stance when the **Civil War** commenced and, on July 26, 1862, enlisted in the **Illinois** Infantry Volunteers— becoming one of the few African Americans to join a majority white regiment and, when promoted to captain in 1863, one of fewer than 30 black commissioned officers. In September 1863, Douglas contracted malaria on military duty in Vicksburg, Mississippi. His health gradually deteriorated and, after being mustered out of the army in July 1865, Douglas died on November 11, 1865 in Leavenworth, Kansas. *See also* Abolitionist Movement.

FURTHER READING
Harris, Robert L., Jr. "H. Ford Douglas: Afro-American Antislavery Emigrationist." *Journal of Negro History* 62(1977): 217–234.

Douglass, Frederick Augustus Bailey (1817–1895)

Fugitive slave; friend of the fugitive; "Tribune of his people." Perhaps the greatest American of the nineteenth century and, arguably, the most significant of all African Americans, Frederick Augustus Bailey was born enslaved on or about February 14, 1817, near the Chesapeake Bay in Maryland. He did not know his father and his contact with his mother was infrequent before her death when he was eight years old. An attractive and intellectually precocious child, Bailey was able to acquire the rudiments of literacy from the white children of his owner's large and wealthy extended family.

Building on this foundation, Bailey continued his education independently and in secret. However, the more he learned, the more constraining and unnatural the world of slavery became to him and, as an adolescent, he began to dream of freedom. After narrowly avoiding death for an aborted escape, Bailey succeeded in reaching New York City in 1838, was given asylum by David **Ruggles**, then moved to **New Bedford, Massachusetts**. He changed his name to "Douglass," after a character in *Ivanhoe*, and married Anna, a free woman of color from Baltimore, who followed him to New York.

By the time Frederick Douglass escaped from **slavery**, the militant **Abolitionist Movement** was well-established. Thus, on August 12, 1841, when Douglass rose at an antislavery meeting to tell his story, he did not invent a movement — rather he joined a movement of free blacks and sympathetic whites that had existed for some time. Through the 1840s, Douglass grew in stature both as a man and as a public figure. Apart from his natural charisma, imposing physique and unforgettable voice (called "the Golden Trombone"),

Frederick Douglass (**Library of Congress**)

it was Douglass' message that gave his speeches both historical and literary value. Simply put, Douglass advocated the immediate and total abolition of slavery, opposed any distinctions based on race — and was pragmatic enough to realize that racial and gender equality had to be reflected both in American law and in the distribution of national wealth and power.

Douglass lectured unceasingly throughout the North and Midwest, often in defiance of violent proslavery mobs. He published the first version of his autobiography in 1845 and, having thus identified himself as a fugitive slave, was advised to leave the United States to avoid capture and re-enslavement. For the next two years, he toured much of Europe, lectured often in the British Isles, and was able to purchase his legal freedom with funds raised by European antislavery sympathizers. After returning to the United States, he founded *The North Star,* his antislavery newspaper, in 1847, and edited a series of such publications over the next 20 years.

Frederick Douglass represented in his person the most telling refutation of American racial mythology, and was perhaps the most brilliant orator in American history. As an example, his "Fifth of July" speech, delivered on July 5, 1852, is generally considered the greatest antislavery speech of all time. In this speech, Douglass stressed the irony of asking an escaped slave to celebrate the independence of a nation that held millions of his people in bondage — declaring, "What, to the American slave, is your Fourth of July?" — and then proceeded to defend the U.S. Constitution as a flawed, but perfectible, document, one that could be amended to abolish slavery and to protect the rights of blacks. As he warmed to his task, his eloquence became prophetic:

> There is consolation in the thought that America is young. Great streams are not easily turned from channels worn deep in the course of ages. They may sometimes rise in quiet and stately majesty, and inundate the land ... They may also rise in wrath and fury, and bear away, on their angry waves, the accumulated wealth of years of toil and hardship. They, however, gradually flow back to the same old channel, and flow on as serenely as ever. But, while the river may not be turned aside, it may dry up, and leave nothing behind but the withered branch, and the

unsightly rock, to howl in the abyss-sweeping wind, the sad tale of departed glory. As with rivers so with nations... [Douglass, 1852 in Anderson, 1996: 110].

Throughout this period, Douglass never ceased to speak and act against slavery. He worked with the Underground Railroad and harbored **fugitive slaves** in his home in Rochester, New York. He was a strong and consistent supporter of women's rights—even attending the Seneca Falls Convention in 1849. He befriended John **Brown** and flirted with the notion of joining Brown's ill-fated attack on **Harpers Ferry** in 1859.

In perhaps his finest hour, Douglass brought unceasing public pressure to bear on Abraham Lincoln to transform the **Civil War** from a war to restore the Union into a war to end slavery ("No war but an abolition war! No peace but an abolition peace!"), and to allow blacks to fight for their freedom in the Union Army—as did his four sons. During the tumultuous years of Reconstruction, when the United States had and lost the opportunity to institutionalize racial equality, Douglass was a tireless champion of land redistribution, full political empowerment and equal rights for all African Americans. His was often a solitary and controversial voice. But, in the truest sense, the emancipation of enslaved African Americans and the Fifteenth Amendment, which gave blacks the right to vote in 1870, are monuments to the work of Frederick Douglass.

Over the course of his long life, Douglass remained true to his fundamental principles and struggled to apply them to ever-changing conditions. He served in a series of federal posts and, in the 1880s, served briefly as the American ambassador to Haiti. Most importantly, he served as the acknowledged leader of black America and became the prototype for black leaders in the generations that followed. Perhaps, Douglass never stood taller than at the end of his life, when blacks were being terrorized and segregation from the "cradle to the grave" was being institutionalized, and few (black or white) had the courage to speak out. Frederick Douglass rose defiantly in **Washington, D.C.**, on January 9, 1894, and delivered his last great speech, "The Lessons of the Hour." This long and complex speech on the "race problem" of his time ended with the simple and summative injunction: "Let the nation try justice and the problem will be solved."

On February 20, 1895, Frederick Douglass died suddenly after attending a women's rights rally in Washington, D.C. *See also* Frederick Douglass National Historic Site; and Appendixes 1 and 2.

FURTHER READING
Anderson, William L., ed. *The Oxford Frederick Douglass Reader.* New York: Oxford University Press, 1996.
Blight, David W. "Frederick Douglass and the American Apocalypse." *Civil War History* 31, no. 4(1985): 309–328.
Hudson, J. Blaine. "Frederick Douglass and W. E. B. DuBois: The Lessons of the Past." Lecture presented at the First Unitarian Church, Louisville, KY, February 24, 1991.
Pease, Jane H., and William H. Pease. "Ends, Means, and Attitudes: Black-White Conflict in the Antislavery Movement." *Civil War History* 18(1972): 117–128.
Schor, Joel. "The Rivalry between Frederick Douglass and Henry Highland Garnet." *Journal of Negro History* 64, no. 1(1979): 30–38.
White, Richard H. "The Spirit of Hate and Frederick Douglass." *Civil War History* 46, no. 1(2000): 41–49.

Downing, George T. (1819–1903)

Friend of the fugitive. George T. Downing was born in New York in 1819. He learned the restaurant business from his father—the proprietor of a popular New York restaurant and oyster house. At his father's restaurant, Downing met and was influenced by the leaders of the antislavery movement who were among his father's patrons—and joined the movement at a very early age.

Downing moved to Newport, Rhode Island, in the mid–1840s and soon prospered in business himself, becoming one of the wealthiest and most highly respected African Americans in the United States. Downing contributed funds to the antislavery movement and his home served as an Underground Railroad station. He numbered Frederick **Douglass** and Charles **Sumner** among his close friends and once refused to shake hands with President Millard Fillmore because "he was unwilling to touch the hand that had signed the Fugitive Slave Law of 1850."

After the Civil War, Downing worked to desegregate the Newport schools and was a long-time supporter of the equal rights movement in Rhode Island. Interestingly, for a decade, Downing operated the dining room of U.S. House of Representatives in **Washington, D.C.**—which increased his wealth and afforded him an opportunity to lobby his patrons. Downing died in 1903. *See also* Fugitive Slave Law of 1850; and Appendixes 1 and 2.

FURTHER READING
Youngken, Richard C. *African Americans in Newport: An Introduction to the Heritage of African Americans in Newport; Rhode Island 1700–1945.* Providence: Rhode Island Historical Preservation & Heritage Commission, 1995.

Doyle, Edward James "Patrick"

Friend of the fugitive. Edward James "Patrick" Doyle, a young Irish immigrant, was at the center of one of the largest mass slave escapes ever recorded in the United States. However, for a variety of reasons, Doyle cannot be considered a typical friend of the fugitive — or, at least, not without some lingering doubts as to his motives.

On Sunday, August 5, 1848, Doyle led a band of some 40 to 75 **fugitive slaves**, "for the most part trusted house servants of Lexington's most socially prominent families, on a march to the Ohio River." Doyle was a student at Centre College in Danville, **Kentucky**, and most of the fugitives escaped from nearby Fayette County. Early reports spread alarm that the fugitives were "firing pistols, whooping and singing songs and ditties." Such a massive escape bordered on insurrection, and "the entire Bluegrass, with threats of summary violence, turned out to apprehend the fugitives." Hundreds of whites "scoured the countryside" and eventually overtook and captured Doyle and the runaways in a Bracken County, Kentucky, hemp field only 15 miles south of the **Ohio River**. (Pritchard, 1999: 3–5.)

Commencing August 30, more than 40 fugitives were tried for insurrection in the Bracken Circuit Court. Three of the runaways from Fayette County — Shadrack, Harry and Prestley — were convicted and condemned to death. Doyle was tried in Fayette Circuit Court beginning on September 27, 1848. Not

surprisingly, he was found guilty on October 9 and sentenced to 20 years in the Kentucky penitentiary. Interestingly, prison records describe this daring interloper as a rather small and unprepossessing man, 22 years old, five feet two inches tall, weighing only 128 pounds.

Assessing Doyle's role in Kentucky history is complicated by two facts. First, a week previous to leading the mass escape, Doyle himself had escaped from jail in Louisville "where he was confined for attempting to sell several free Negroes whom he had induced to accompany him from Cincinnati." Initial testimony taken in the case suggested that Doyle offered his services for a fee, as much as $20 per fugitive.

Whether or not Doyle's motives were pure, the African Americans who followed him on that desperate dash to the Ohio River had freedom as their clear and unambiguous goal. The failure of Doyle's enterprise fell most heavily and tragically upon them. Some may have escaped in the confusion that surrounded their pursuit. Most were captured and, of these, some were sold down the river. Three others were accused and convicted of the capital crime of insurrection — since escaping from slavery was not, in itself, a crime — and were executed. Edward J. Doyle died in prison. *See also* Appendixes 1 and 2.

FURTHER READING
Coleman, J. Winston, Jr. *Slavery Times in Kentucky.* Chapel Hill, NC: University of North Carolina Press, 1940.
Pritchard, James M. "Into the Fiery Furnace: Anti-Slavery Prisoners in the Kentucky State Penitentiary, 1844–1870." Paper presented at the Kentucky Underground Railroad Symposium, Maysville, Kentucky, June 1999.

Drapetomania

To account for the many unassisted slave escapes, defenders of **slavery** defined a new category of mental illness known as drapetomania, or the "flight from home madness." Explaining why African Americans would flee bondage posed a rather thorny problem for those who defended slavery in that each freedom seeker was, to some extent, a living refutation of the racial stereotypes used to justify slavery itself. These runaways were clearly not happy and content with bondage, did not "love" their masters, and did have intellect and character. However, if the facts could not be denied, slave-holders—and more than a few later historians—could still interpret and distort those facts within the limits of prevailing racial myths and stereotypes. For example, slave escapes could be blamed on nefarious white abolitionists who spirited away ignorant slaves—an interpretation that was useful, although inadequate to explain the many unassisted escapes.

In the end, those who defended slavery as a "positive good" (and not a necessary evil), were compelled to invent this rather bizarre new category of mental illness, "drapetomania," to account for **fugitive slaves** acting clearly on their own initiative. As noted by Thomas and Sillen:

> The black man, it was repeatedly claimed, was uniquely fitted for bondage by his primitive psychological organization. For him, mental health was contentment with his subservient lot, while protest was an infallible symptom of derangement. Thus, a well-known physician of the antebellum South, Dr. Samuel Cartwright of Louisiana, had a psychiatric explanation for runaway slaves. He diagnosed their malady as drapetomania, literally the flight-from-home madness. [Thomas and Sillen, 1972: 16–17.]

See also Abolitionist Movement.

FURTHER READING
Thomas, Alexander, and Samuel Sillen. *Racism and Psychiatry.* New York: Citadel Press, 1972.

Drayton, Daniel (b. 1802)

Friend of the fugitive and captain of the *Pearl.* Daniel Drayton was born in 1802, in Cumberland County, New Jersey, near Delaware Bay. His mother, who died when he was young, was a "zealous member of the Methodist church." (Drayton, 1854: 1.) His father was a farmer and apprenticed Drayton to a shoemaker. However, Drayton disliked the business of shoe-making and chose instead to "follow the water." (Drayton, 1854: 8.) He signed on board a sloop and quickly "rose from cook to captain in the woodcarrying business from the Maurice River to Philadelphia" and then "in the coastal traffic from Philadelphia southward." (Paynter, 1916: 245.)

In 1847, he sailed his ship, the *Pearl,* into the harbor of **Washington, D.C.**, to unload

Captain Daniel Drayton (Library of Congress)

oysters. While the ship was at the dock, an African American man asked him to take a woman and her five children north. She had freed herself through self-purchase, but her owner had taken her money and then reneged on his promise to emancipate her—vowing instead to sell her farther south. Captain Drayton agreed and successfully completed the first of many trips with **fugitive slaves** aboard.

In 1848, 76 enslaved African Americans fled to Drayton's ship while their owners were involved in festivities elsewhere in Washington. Drayton set sail at midnight before the fugitives' absence was detected. However, he encountered foul weather about 150 miles from Washington and the consequent delay gave pursuing slave-owners time to overtake the *Pearl* and force it back to port.

Drayton and his crew were indicted and jailed for four years before winning a pardon from President Millard Fillmore. The fugitive slaves were sold and resold, shipped and sent to parts unknown.

After his release, Drayton wrote his memoirs and noted simply:

> I knew it was asserted in the Declaration of Independence that all men are born free and equal, and I had read in the Bible that God had made of one flesh all the nations of the earth. I had found

out, by intercourse with the negroes, that they had the same desires, wishes and hopes as myself. I knew very well that I should not like to be a slave even to the best of masters, and still less to such sort of masters as the greater part of the slaves seemed to have ... for the life of me, I could not perceive why the gold rule of doing to others as you would wish them to do to you did not apply in this case. [Drayton, 1854: 21.]

See also Appendixes 1 and 2.

FURTHER READING

Drayton, Daniel. *Personal Memoir of Daniel Drayton, for Four Years and Four Months a Prisoner (for charity's sake) in Washington Jail, Including a Narrative of the Voyage and Capture of the Schooner Pearl.* Boston: B. Marsh, 1854.

Paynter, John N. "The Fugitives of the Pearl." *Journal of Negro History* 1, no. 3(1916): 243–264.

Rohrs, Richard C. "Antislavery Politics and the Pearl Incident of 1848." *The Historian* 56, no. 4(1994): 711–724.

Dred Scott v. Sandford (1857)

Landmark 1857 U.S. Supreme Court decision bearing on **slavery** and freedom. As sectional divisions deepened in the **1850s**, the U.S. Supreme Court was drawn into the mounting controversy over slavery in the case of Dred Scott v. Sandford, which concerned, among other issues, the interpretation the fugitive slave clause of the U.S. Constitution.

Dred Scott, originally an enslaved African American called "Sam," was purchased in St. Louis in 1832 or 1833 by John Emerson. When Emerson became an army surgeon, he took Scott with him into free territory, north of the 1820 Missouri Compromise line. There, Scott lived essentially as a free man, married and had a family. When Emerson died in 1846, Scott sought to purchase his legal freedom and that of his family. However, Emerson's wife, and later her heirs, refused. With the help of an attorney with antislavery sympathies, Scott sued for his freedom and his case ultimately reached the U.S. Supreme Court in February 1856.

In 1857, the court ruled that Scott was not a citizen of Missouri — and that African Americans were never intended to be citizens, adding, in the words of Chief Justice Roger B. Taney, that African Americans "had no rights which whites were bound to respect." Hence, he had no legal standing and could not sue.

The court further reaffirmed the fugitive slave clause of the U.S. Constitution and declared that Congress did not have the authority to outlaw slavery in U.S. territories—as it had done in the 1820 Missouri Compromise.

In this respect, although *Dred Scott v. Sandford* was not a fugitive slave case, per se, the court ruled against Scott as though he was a fugitive slave. Ironically, however, while seeming to strengthen the legal position of the South, the Dred Scott decision so inflamed public opinion in the North that it broadened the base of the movement opposed to the extension of slavery and strengthened the determination of abolitionists and friends of the fugitive to oppose slavery by legal and illegal means. As such, the decision was a major step toward **Civil War**. *See also* Abolitionist Movement; Fugitive Slaves.

FURTHER READING

Fehrenbacher, Don E. *The Dred Scott Case: Its Significance in American Law and Politics.* New York: Oxford University Press, 2001.

Gordon-Reed, Annette, ed. *Race on Trial: Law and Justice in American History.* New York: Oxford University Press, 2002.

Hodder, F. H. "Some Phases of the Dred Scott Case." *Mississippi Valley Historical Review* 16, no. 1(1929): 3–22.

Kutler, Stanley I., ed. *The Supreme Court and the Constitution: Readings in American Constitutional History.* New York: W. W. Norton, 1989.

Wiecek, William M. "Slavery and Abolition Before the United States Supreme Court, 1820–1860." *The Journal of American History* 65(1978): 34–59.

Durkee, Chauncey

Fugitive slave. *See also* Eells, Richard.

Dyer, Edward Galusha

Friend of the fugitive in Wisconsin. *See also* Quarreles, Caroline. *See also* Appendixes 1 and 2.

Edgewater (Haddonfield, New Jersey)

Underground Railroad station. Edgewater was constructed in 1748 near Haddonfield, New Jersey. In the 1800s, Thomas and Josiah Evans hid **fugitive slaves** in the attic before transporting them to nearby Mount Holly. *See also* Underground Railroad, Sites of; and Appendixes 3 and 4.

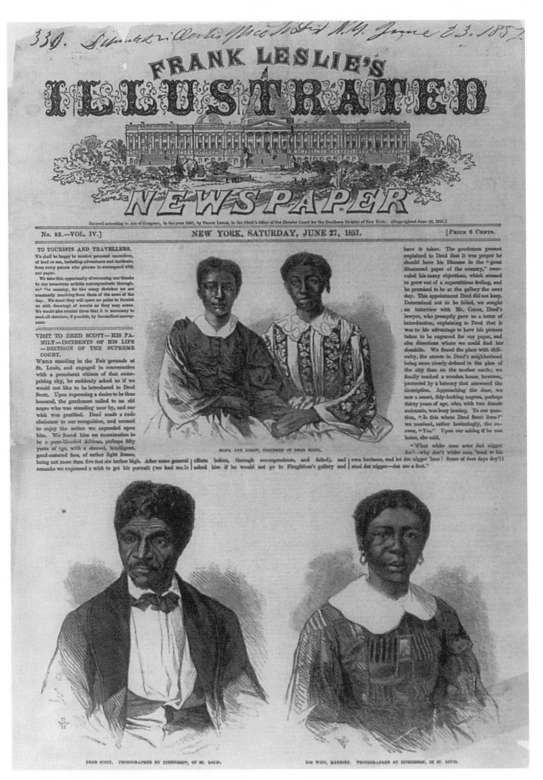

Dred Scott and his children, Eliza and Lizzie, and his wife, Harriet, in an 1857 engraving (Library of Congress)

Edgewood Farm (Kennett Square, Pennsylvania)

Underground Railroad site. Edgewood was the farm and home of John and Hannah Cox, well-known abolitionists. Located near Kennett Square, **Pennsylvania**, Edgewood was an important Underground Railroad station. *See also* Underground Railroad, Sites of; and Appendixes 3 and 4.

Edwards, John B. (1802–1895)

A friend of the fugitive, John B. Edwards was born on May 23, 1802 in Monmouth County, New Jersey. In 1807, his family moved to Lyons, New York, and, as a young adult, he became first a laborer, then a sub-contractor, and finally a superintendent on the Erie Canal. In 1824, Edwards moved to Oswego, New York, to supervise construction of a hydraulic canal there and later built and maintained docks and piers. He became a leading citizen, holding many public offices, and was active in the Methodist Church. In 1826, Edwards married Lydia M. Hall (1806–1856) and the couple had four children.

Between 1831 and 1874, Edwards also managed the harbor and real estate investments of his friend, the famous and wealthy abolitionist, Gerrit **Smith**—and the extant correspondence between the two is a remarkably rich source of documentation for Edwards' involvement in assisting **fugitive slaves**.

As examples, on July 17, 1847, Edwards observed that "Nine poor fugitives from slavery's prison left this port last evening for **Canada**. They were I am told in much fear that pursuers were after them. They said that they left in a company of 100 and that about 60 of their number were captured before they got out of the slave states." On April 29, 1852, he reported that "the Fugitive Slave Dorsey came to me today with your letter. I have put him aboard of a vessel bound for Canada and gave him a $1.00." On March 19, 1860, Edwards explained that "the young colored man that was at your house last week arrived at my house last evening. I shall keep him a few days to recuperate."

After Lydia Edwards' death on January 20, 1856, Edwards married Julia M. Imlay. He died on November 5, 1895. *See also* **John B. and Lydia Edwards House.**

FURTHER READING
Gionta, Mary Ann. "John B. Edwards." Papers. Special Collections, Penfield Library, Oswego, New York. Includes list of Edwards' correspondence with Gerrit Smith in Smith Papers, Syracuse University.
Wellman, Judith. *Grass Roots Reform in the Burned-Over District in Upstate New York: Religion, Abolitionism, and Democracy.* New York: Garland, 2000.

Edwin W. Clarke House (Oswego, New York)

Underground Railroad site recognized and documented by the National Park Service. *See also* Appendix 5.

Eells, Richard

Friend of the fugitive. Dr. Richard Eells was a leader of the antislavery movement in Illinois and his home in Quincy, **Illinois** was an important Underground Railroad station. In 1842, Dr. Eells was arrested and convicted of **harboring** and otherwise assisting a fugitive slave, Chauncey Durkee, from Missouri. He was ordered to pay a $400 fine and appealed, ultimately to the U.S. Supreme Court — which upheld the lower court ruling in 1852. *See also* Underground Railroad, Sites of; and Appendixes 3 and 4.

The 1850s

The 1850s was a decade of mounting conflict and deepening divisions between North and South. Beginning with the debates that produced the **Compromise of 1850** and the **Fugitive Slave Act of 1850**, the decade of the 1850s moved from one crisis to another — with **slavery** at the heart of each. The publication of **Uncle Tom's Cabin** in 1852 challenged the southern view of both slavery and the character of African Americans, and created a public relations disaster from which the South would never recover entirely. The furor precipitated by the Kansas-Nebraska Act (1854) and its explicit nullification of the 1820 **Missouri Compromise** offered the South the hope that the political balance upset by the territorial acquisitions of the Mexican War might be restored by the creation of new slave states.

However, the determination of the South to extend slavery was matched by the determination of the North (and, now, the West) to limit its "extension"—as evidenced by the political shifts that undermined the Whig Party and created the Republican Party in the mid–1850s. New crises soon followed—"Bleeding Kansas," the 1857 Dred Scott case (see **Dred Scott v. Sandford),** and John **Brown**'s raid in 1859—eventually bringing Abraham Lincoln to the presidency of a "house divided against itself" in 1860 and culminating in **Civil War** in 1861.

Those wishing, as Lincoln did, only to limit slavery to the existing slave states were hardly abolitionists. Yet, to southern politicians, particularly from the deep southern interior, opposition to the extension of slavery was synonymous with opposition to slavery itself. From their perspective, if slavery could not grow, it would die — or be destroyed at the whim of a new American majority. Because this new majority was created by industrialization, European immigration, urbanization in the Northeast and Midwest, and the drive to settle the Great Plains and the West — its needs and worldview, and the attendant forces of change and modernization swelling its numbers were only beginning to manifest themselves. In other words, although still profitable and deeply embedded in the lifeways of the South, slavery was becoming as obsolete in the industrializing United States as it had become in the British Empire, where it was abolished in 1838.

Still, the institution of slavery could be only so strong and only so secure in such a divided nation. Along the many borders between free and slave territory, where the structure of slavery was weakest and most porous, slave escapes became more, rather than less, frequent. Conspiracy scares became routine and, beyond the efforts of enslaved African Americans, this "quiet" but not always bloodless "insurrection" was complemented, aided and abetted by a broad conspiracy of conscience on the part of free African Americans and white antislavery activists throughout the region. The Underground Railroad emerged as an organized expression and instrument of that conspiracy.

FURTHER READING
Harlow, Ralph Volney. "The Rise and Fall of the Kansas Aid Movement." *American Historical Review* 41, no. 1(1935): 1–25.
Hudson, J. Blaine. *Fugitive Slaves and the Underground Railroad in the Kentucky Borderland.* Jefferson, NC: McFarland, 2002.
Siebert, Wilbur H. *The Underground Railroad from Slavery to Freedom.* 1898. Reprint, New York: Russell and Russell, 1967.
Wish, Harvey. "The Slave Insurrection Panic of 1856." *Journal of Southern History* 5(1939): 206–222.

Eleutherian College (Lancaster, Indiana)

Underground Railroad site recognized and documented by the National Park Service. *See also* Appendix 5.

Emerson, Ralph Waldo (1803–1882)

Philosopher, abolitionist and friend of the fugitive. Emerson, whose original profession was as a Unitarian minister, left the ministry to pursue a career in writing and public speaking. He became one of America's best-known philosophers and best loved nineteenth-century figures. Emerson also operated a station on the Underground Railroad in his **Concord, Massachusetts** home. *See also* Abolitionist Movement.

FURTHER READING
Bode, Carl. *Ralph Waldo Emerson: A Profile.* New York: Hill and Wang, 1968.
Fields, Peter S. *Ralph Waldo Emerson: The Making of a Democratic Intellectual.* Lanham, MD: Rowman and Littlefield, 2002.

Engineer

In Underground Railroad terminology, an "engineer" was a friend of the fugitive who was responsible for the actual transportation of **fugitive slaves** from one station to another. For example, if fugitive slaves were being moved secretly by wagon or carriage, the "driver" of the conveyance was an "engineer."

Enticing

Enticing was the legal term referring to the act of facilitating the escape of an enslaved African American. The use of "enticing" implied that, apart from enslaved African Americans whose escapes were presumably a manifestation of mental illness, others—who were supposedly content with bondage—could nonetheless be "led astray" by nefarious outsiders. In other words, had there been no enticement, there would have been no escapes. The available records suggest, however, that enslaved African Americans required little or no enticement, but did seek, value, and use information and other forms of assistance in planning and executing escapes. *See also* Drapetomania; Fugitive Slaves; Harboring.

Episcopal Parish House (Gardiner, Maine)

Underground Railroad site. The pastor and congregation of the Episcopal Parish House assisted **fugitive slaves** who reached this far northern region. The Parish House had several hidden rooms or chambers that could be easily defended against the encroachments of **slave catchers**. *See also* Underground Railroad, Sites of; and Appendixes 3 and 4.

Escape Routes

See Routes of Escape

Evans, George

Friend of the fugitive in **Madison, Indiana**. *See also* Appendixes 1 and 2.

Evans, Henry

Friend of the fugitive in Oberlin, **Ohio**. *See also* Wilson Bruce Evans House and Oberlin-Wellington Rescue.

Evans, Wilson Bruce

Friend of the fugitive in Oberlin, **Ohio**. *See also* Wilson Bruce Evans House and Oberlin-Wellington Rescue. *See also* Appendixes 1 and 2.

Fairbank, The Reverend Calvin (1816–1898)

Friend of the fugitive. Calvin Fairbank was born in New York in 1816, became a Methodist minister, later studied at **Oberlin College** and, by 1844, had gained extensive experience "in the business of rescuing slaves" (Fairbank, 1890: 5–7.) In that same year, Fairbank traveled to Lexington, **Kentucky** to res-

cue the family of Gilson Berry, a fugitive slave with whom Fairbank became acquainted at Oberlin. Around the first of September, he sought assistance from Delia **Webster**, a New England-born teacher working in a Lexington school for young women, after depleting his limited funds in the futile search for Berry's family. Webster introduced Fairbank to Lewis **Hayden**, an enslaved waiter at the Phoenix Hotel who wished to escape with his wife and child. Hayden was hired out and working toward self-purchase, and used his earnings to support Fairbank in Lexington and to finance their escape.

On Saturday, September 28, 1844, Lexington was crowded as the fall horse racing meet was nearing its close. At roughly five o'clock that evening, Fairbank called for Webster in a hired carriage, then continued north, picking up Hayden, his wife Harriet and their son, Jo. The party then drove north along the Lexington-Maysville road and reached Washington in Mason County by four o'clock in the morning of September 29, 1844. Later that day, they drove the four additional miles to Maysville. James Helm ferried them across the **Ohio River** and they were delivered to the Reverend John **Rankin** and his famous hilltop Underground Railroad station in Ripley, **Ohio**. The Hayden family was then spirited north.

By the time Webster and Fairbank returned to Kentucky, news of the slave escape had already spread as far as Maysville. Suspicion soon fell on the two northerners and both were arrested en route to Lexington. The two were indicted in the Fayette Circuit Court for the crime of "aiding and enticing slaves to leave their owners"—and news of the incident and its principal figures spread across the nation. The two were tried separately and both were found guilty. Fairbank was convicted and sentenced to five years in the state penitentiary. He served at hard labor until pardoned by Governor John Crittenden on August 28, 1849—after, it was rumored, $600 was paid to Hayden's owner.

After his release, Fairbank spoke frequently to antislavery groups in many northern cities and corresponded with the editors of the antislavery press. He also resumed his one-man Underground Railroad crusade and "on November 9, 1851, he was arrested in Jeffersonville, **Indiana**, on a charge of having stolen Tamar, a twenty-two year-old mulatto girl — doomed to be sold at auction by her master in Louisville." (Coleman, 1943: 138.) Fairbank's arrest was publicized widely and, on learning of it, Frederick **Douglass** expressed deep apprehension that "the evidence may be against him" and "he will be made to suffer the extreme penalty of Slave Laws of Kentucky." (*Frederick Douglass Paper,* November 27, 1851 in Hudson, 2002: 135.)

Fairbank was convicted and sentenced this time to 15 years in the Kentucky penitentiary. Fairbank survived the long nightmare of prison and was released on April 15, 1864 — and, in his autobiography, recounted that he suffered more than 3,000 lashes under the brutal regime of the Kentucky penitentiary.

He married soon after and, following a stirring round of speeches in which he described his experiences — one of which was even attended by President Abraham Lincoln and most of his cabinet — Fairbank settled down in New England and sank ultimately into relative obscurity. Years later, Fairbank published his autobiography, but was deeply disappointed at its reception. His great sacrifice seemed wholly forgotten. He died in 1898, and his grave remained unmarked for many years. *See also* Fugitive Slaves; and Appendixes 1 and 2.

FURTHER READING

Coleman, J. Winston, Jr. "Delia Webster and Calvin Fairbank — Underground Railroad Agents." *Filson Club History Quarterly* 17, no. 3 (1943): 129–142.

Fairbank, Calvin. *The Reverend Calvin Fairbank during Slavery Times.* Chicago: Patriotic, 1890.

Hudson, J. Blaine. *Fugitive Slaves and the Underground Railroad in the Kentucky Borderland.* Jefferson, NC: McFarland, 2002.

"Faithful Groomsman"

See Signals

Fanueil Hall (Boston, Massachusetts)

Center of antislavery and Underground Railroad activism in the city of **Boston**. Built by Peter Fanueil in the 1760s, who accrued great wealth in the African slave trade, the original Fanueil Hall was a given as a gift to the city of Boston. The hall was destroyed by fire, rebuilt and, in the 1840s, served as a focal point of the Boston antislavery movement. There, the great figures of the movement spoke and the commanding issues of the day were debated. *See also* Abolitionist Movement; Underground Railroad, Sites of; and Appendixes 3 and 4.

Farmington, Connecticut

Underground Railroad junction. Farmington, Connecticut is located alongside fugitive slave escape routes in the vicinity of Hartford and New Haven. Because of its location, the town was home to several prominent friends of the fugitive — including the homes of Horace Cowles, Lyman Hurlburt, Elijah Lewis, Timothy Wadsworth and Austin F. Williams — whose homes and churches served as Underground Railroad stations. *See also* Underground Railroad, Sites of; and Appendixes 1–4.

Farwell Mansion (Vassalboro Township, Maine)

Underground Railroad site. Built in 1842, the Farwell Mansion is located near Vassalboro Township, Maine. Ironically, the original owner, Captain Ebenezer Farwell, was a slave-trader who died on a voyage to Africa. After Farwell's death, his home was purchased by Israel Weeks, who worked to free enslaved African Americans rather than to enslave more of their African kinsmen. *See also* Underground Railroad, Sites of; and Appendixes 3 and 4.

Fee, John Gregg (1816–1901)

Friend of the fugitive, noted **Kentucky** abolitionist, and founder of **Berea College**. John Gregg Fee was born September 9, 1816 to a slaveholding family in Bracken County, Kentucky. He earned his B.A. at Augusta College, near Augusta, Kentucky, and, after two years (1842–44) at Lane Theological Seminary in **Cincinnati**, he became a convert to the abolitionist cause. For this life choice, Fee was disowned and disinherited by his parents.

Fee next joined the **American Missionary Association** and allied himself with Cassius Clay, the colorful Kentucky proponent of gradual emancipation. In 1854, Fee settled at

Berea, in southern Madison County, Kentucky, on 10 acres given as a gift by Clay. Although Clay was an abolitionist by Kentucky standards, his support for colonization and gradual emancipation were decidedly conservative views in the context of the national movement. Fee, on the other hand, although operating in a slave state, was a legitimate and fairly radical abolitionist. Not surprisingly, this alliance did not survive long and ended in a dispute over the **Fugitive Slave Act of 1850**. Between 1855 and 1857, Fee organized an abolitionist school that would later become Berea College.

Although driven from Kentucky in December 1859 by local slaveholders after John **Brown**'s Raid on **Harpers Ferry**, he returned in 1863 and resumed his missionary and educational work at Berea. In July 1864, Fee coordinated similar efforts at Camp Nelson, south of Lexington, Kentucky, for African American soldiers and refugees. Fee spent the remainder of his life in Berea as pastor of the church and a trustee of the college. He published his autobiography in 1891 and died in 1901. *See also* Abolitionist Movement; and Appendixes 1 and 2.

FURTHER READING

Howard, Victor B. *The Evangelical War against Slavery and Caste: The Life and Times of John G. Fee.* Selinsgrove, PA: Susquehanna University Press, 1996.

Lucas, Marion B. *A History of Blacks in Kentucky.* Vol. 1 of *From Slavery to Segregation, 1760–1891.* Frankfort: Kentucky Historical Society, 1992.

Sears, Richard D. *A Utopian Experiment in Kentucky: Integration and Social Equality at Berea, 1866–1904.* Westport, CT: Greenwood Press, 1996.

Felicity Wesleyan Church (Felicity, Ohio)

Underground Railroad site recognized and documented by the National Park Service. *See also* Appendix 5.

Ferguson, Joseph

Friend of the fugitive in **Detroit, Michigan**. *See also* Finney House. *See also* Appendixes 1 and 2.

Finney, Seymour

Friend of the fugitive. *See also* Finney House; and Appendixes 1 and 2.

Finney House (Detroit, Michigan)

Underground Railroad site. In 1834, Seymour Finney moved from New York to Detroit, Michigan, and, in 1846, erected the Finney House and barn in downtown Detroit. A tailor by profession, Finney became a hotel-keeper and, in 1850, purchased a site on which the Finney Hotel would stand. A staunch abolitionist, Finney assisted **fugitive slaves** passing through Detroit en route to **Canada** and coordinated his efforts with local friends of the fugitive such as George **DeBaptiste**, William Lambert, William Webb, Joseph Ferguson, William Monroe and John Richards. The Finney House and barn served as sanctuaries for freedom seekers awaiting transportation across the Detroit River and was considered the "last stop" on the Underground Railroad in the Detroit area. *See also* Underground Railroad, Sites of; William Webb House; and Appendixes 3 and 4.

First African Baptist Church (Savannah, Georgia)

Underground Railroad site. Founded in 1775 at Savannah, Georgia, the First African Baptist Church is the oldest African American congregation in the United States. Members of the congregation harbored **fugitive slaves** who fled through underground passageways in Savannah. The current church edifice, constructed in 1859, incorporated a four-foot wide tunnel beneath the church floor. *See also* Underground Railroad, Sites of; and Appendixes 3 and 4.

First Baptist Church (Chatham, Ontario, Canada)

Underground Railroad site. Founded in 1841, the First Baptist Church of Chatham in Ontario Province, **Canada**, was a fugitive slave destination and a center of antislavery activism. In 1858, John **Brown** held a convention in Chatham and, assisted by Mary Ann Shadd **Cary**, used the First Baptist Church to draft his Provisional Constitution of the People of the United States—the blue-print for the revolutionary government that would emerge in the Appalachian region following his planned insurrection at **Harpers Ferry**. *See also* Underground Railroad, Sites of; and Appendixes 3 and 4.

First Congregational Church (Detroit, Michigan)

Underground Railroad site. In 1844, the First Congregational Society was organized in **Detroit, Michigan**. The congregation soon outgrew its first church building and, in 1854, constructed a larger structure. **Fugitive slaves** were hidden in the church and assisted by its members. *See also* Underground Railroad, Sites of; and Appendixes 3 and 4.

Florida

See Black Seminoles

Ford, Barney Launcelot (1822–1902)

Fugitive slave and friend of the fugitive, Barney Launcelot Ford was born enslaved on January 22, 1822 in Stafford, Virginia. He was "sold South" as a child and raised in bondage on a South Carolina plantation. As a young adult, Ford escaped and reached safety in Chicago. There, he became involved in the antislavery movement after meeting Henry O. Wagoner, an active member of the Underground Railroad. Ford later married Wagoner's sister-in-law, Julia.

In 1860, Ford and his family moved to Colorado. Ford purchased land on Blake Street in Denver and built a small building there only to have it destroyed by fire the following year. He rebuilt the current brick building in which was located a restaurant, bar, barbershop and hair salon. From this initial business venture, Ford expanded his commercial holdings and became the first African American in Colorado to amass significant wealth.

Ford played an important role in the campaign for the admission of Colorado to the Union as a free state. A member of the Republican Party, he was the first African American to be nominated to the Territorial Legislature. He died in 1902. *See also* Barney L. Ford Building.

Forks of the Road Slave Market Terminus (Natchez, Mississippi)

Underground Railroad site recognized and documented by the National Park Service. *See also* Appendix 5.

Fort Donelson National Battlefield (Dover, Tennessee)

Underground Railroad site recognized and documented by the National Park Service. *See also* Appendix 5.

Fort Mose (St. John's County, Florida)

Underground Railroad site recognized and documented by the National Park Service. *See also* Appendix 5.

Fort Pulaski (Georgia)

Underground Railroad site recognized and documented by the National Park Service. *See also* Appendix 5.

Fortress Monroe (Virginia)

Fortress Monroe, guarding the entrance to the Chesapeake Bay, was one of four Union forts in Confederate territory that remained in Union hands throughout the Civil War. Early in the war, while under the command of General Benjamin F. **Butler**, Fortress Monroe became a refuge for **fugitive slaves**.

As Captain C. B. Wilder stated to the American Freedmen's Inquiry Commission in May 1863:

> Some 10,000 have come under our control, to be fed in part, and clothed in part, but I cannot speak accurately in regard to the number. This is the rendezvous. They come here from all about, from Richmond and 200 miles off in North Carolina. There was one gang that started from Richmond 23 strong and only 3 got through ... As I was saying they do not feel afraid now. The white people have nearly all gone, the blood hounds are not there now to hunt them and they are not afraid, before they were afraid to stir ..."We are not afraid of being carried back" a great many have told us and "if we are, we can get away again."

See also Underground Railroad, Sites of; and Appendixes 3 and 4.

FURTHER READING

Butler, Benjamin F. *Autobiography and Personal Reminiscences of Major-General Benj. F. Butler; Butler's book. By Benj. F. Butler. A Review of His Legal, Political, and Military Career.* Boston: A. M. Thayer, 1892.

Foster, Abigail "Abby" Kelley (1810–1887)

Famous friend of the fugitive, abolitionist and advocate of women's rights, Abigail "Abby" Kelley was born in 1810 to a Quaker family near Amherst, Massachusetts. An early convert to the antislavery cause, she began her personal crusade against **slavery** in 1837 when she heard William Lloyd **Garrison** speak. She joined the Female Anti-Slavery Society while working as a teacher in Lynn, Massachusetts, started raising money and taking petitions door to door for the group.

Kelley, also known as a "fiery little Irish Quaker," was one of the first female lecturers before sexually-mixed audiences and was often greeted with extreme hostility and derision, even from fellow abolitionists. However, prominent abolitionist Theodore Dwight **Weld** appreciated both her courage and her talents, and invited her to join the speaking circuit. She accepted in 1839 and promptly sparked a division between the American Anti-Slavery Society, led by Garrison, and the American and Foreign Anti-Slavery Society, led by Lewis **Tappan**, over the role of women in the movement.

In the 1840s she moved to the Western Reserve in Ohio and founded the Western Antislavery Society. In 1845, Kelley began publishing the *Anti-Slavery Bugle* and also married fellow abolitionist Stephen Symonds Foster. The couple had one daughter, Alla. After returning to Massachusetts in 1847, they remained active in the abolitionist movement and, on occasion, gave sanctuary to **fugitive slaves** in their Worcester, Massachusetts home—**Liberty Farm**.

In her later years, she devoted herself to the cause of women's rights. Kelley died in 1887.

See also Abolitionist Movement; Quakers; Underground Railroad, Sites of; and Appendixes 3 and 4.

FURTHER READING
Buckmaster, Henrietta. *Let My People Go: The Story of the Underground Railroad and the Growth of the Abolition Movement.* Boston: Beacon Press, 1941.

Foster, Amanda (b. 1806)

A friend of the fugitive, Amanda Foster was born free in New York in 1806. As an adult, she worked as a nurse for Arkansas Governor Conway and, on at least one occasion, used her "free papers" to assist a young fugitive slave woman escape from bondage in Arkansas. Foster returned to New York in 1837 and established a confectionary business in Tarrytown. There, she met and married Henry Foster around 1845.

In 1860, Foster founded what would evolve into the Foster Memorial AME Zion Church. Foster and other members of the congregation assisted **fugitive slaves** who settled in or passed through Tarrytown en route to **Canada**.

See also Foster Memorial AME Zion Church.

Foster, Stephen Symonds

Friend of the fugitive in Worcester, **Massachusetts**. *See also* Liberty Farm. *See also* Appendixes 1 and 2.

Foster Memorial AME Zion Church (Tarrytown, New York)

Underground Railroad site recognized and documented by the National Park Service. *See also* Appendix 5.

"Frank" Case (1850)

California fugitive slave case. In 1850, Frank, an enslaved African American from Missouri, was taken west to California's gold fields by his owner, a Mr. Calloway. Frank soon escaped and found refuge among free African Americans in San Francisco. Two months later, Frank's owner, Calloway, located him and had him imprisoned under the provisions of the **Fugitive Slave Act of 1850**. African Americans and whites committed to the antislavery cause protested Frank's imprisonment and pending rendition to Missouri, and retained legal counsel on his behalf.

The case was tried before Judge Roderick Morrison, who ruled that Calloway had produced no evidence to prove his legal ownership of Frank. Morrison added that, even if such ownership could be proven, the Fugitive Slave Act did not apply because Frank escaped from Calloway after reaching California and not across state lines. Ironically, Frank's own admission that he was, in fact, the "property" of Calloway was ruled inadmissible since, by California law, African Americans could not testify in court. Despite objections by Calloway's attorney, Frank was ruled a free man. The "Frank" Case was one of the most controversial trials in early California history and a unifying force in the evolution of the African American community of San Francisco.

FURTHER READING

Beasley, Delilah L. "Slavery in California." *Journal of Negro History* 3, no. 1(1918): 33–44.
Lapp, Rudolph M. "The Negro in Gold Rush California." *Journal of Negro History* 49, no. 2(1964): 81–98.
Savage, W. Sherman. "The Negro in the Westward Movement." *Journal of Negro History* 25, no. 4(1940): 531–539.

Frederick Douglass National Historic Site (Washington, D.C.)

Underground Railroad site recognized and documented by the National Park Service. *See also* Appendix 5.

Free People of Color

African Americans who were not enslaved were the most numerous and reliable friends of the fugitive. After the **American Revolution**, the northern states, where **slavery** had shallow roots, began the "first emancipation"—the abolition of slavery in New England and the mid–Atlantic states between 1777 and the 1820s. At the same time, the more southerly states, while contemplating the end of slavery in the 1780s, became its hostage after the invention of the cotton gin revitalized the peculiar institution. Both the enslaved and free African American populations grew dramatically thereafter. For example, by 1800, the black American population had grown to slightly more than one million persons, 11 percent of whom were free. However, by 1830, the black population stood at more than 2,300,000—14 percent of whom were free.

Although an increasing number of African Americans were legally free, their status in American society was ambiguous at best. Because of intense racial antagonism, they were treated as outcasts throughout much of the North and West. However, the strength of this antagonism varied regionally. States in the southern interior or "**Cotton Kingdom**" were dependent upon and committed uncompromisingly to slavery, with no place for free people of color. In the border states and upper south, slavery existed but climatic conditions did not permit cotton cultivation. There, free people of color were tolerated, grudgingly, as an alien element.

The "lower north" ran through the southern halves of **Iowa, Illinois, Indiana, Ohio, Pennsylvania** and New Jersey. Slavery ended in these states after the American Revolution and free people of color were numerous, but the racial attitudes of whites were quite similar to those just south of the "border." Finally, in the "upper north" or Greater New England region, opposition to slavery was strongest and most uncompromising, and free people of color, although few in number and seldom welcomed enthusiastically, were more widely accepted.

Given this framework, as slavery ended in the North, the border states and the lower North (and the new territories in the Old Northwest and the Louisiana Purchase) feared the prospect of becoming havens to the burgeoning free black population. As a result, efforts to prevent the migration of free people of color into the border states and lower North began as early as 1793, and a variety of strategies were employed to limit their rights and, most importantly, to prevent their numbers from growing larger. Frequent mob violence against free people of color was another factor that often reduced the struggle for equal black citizenship to a desperate search for a safe place to live — ideally, a place that promised the possibility of land ownership, work for decent wages or the opportunity to practice a trade. The combined effects of these factors scattered free African Americans throughout the border states and the North in towns, cities and rural enclaves where opportunities were greatest and resistance was least. The characteristics that made such communities attractive to free people of color made them attractive as well to **fugitive slaves**—both as places of sanctuary and sources of aid.

The Underground Railroad ran principally through free black communities and, in the memorable words of historian Benjamin Quarles: "To a Negro abolitionist, few things could be so satisfying as helping a runaway." *See also* Fugitive Slaves; and Appendixes 1 and 2.

FURTHER READING

Bolster, W. Jeffrey. "To Feel Like a Man: Black Seamen in the Northern States, 1800–1860." *Journal of American History* 76, no. 4(1990): 1173–1199.

Curry, Leonard P. *The Free Black in Urban America, 1800–1850.* Chicago: University of Chicago Press, 1981.

Griffler, Keith P. *Front Line of Freedom: African Americans and the Forging of the Underground Railroad in the Ohio Valley.* Lexington, KY: University Press of Kentucky, 2004.

Hudson, J. Blaine. *Fugitive Slaves and the Underground Railroad in the Kentucky Borderland.* Jefferson, NC: McFarland, 2002.

Jackson, Luther P. "Free Negroes of Petersburgh, Virginia." *Journal of Negro History* 41, no. 3(1927): 365–388.

Litwack, Leon F. "The Abolitionist Dilemma: The Anti-Slavery Movement and the Northern Negro." *New England Quarterly* 34(1961): 50–73.

Perlman, Daniel. "Organizations of the Free Negro in New York City, 1800–1860." *Journal of Negro History* 56, no. 3(1971): 181–197.

Sumler-Lewis, Janice. "The Forten-Purvis Women of Philadelphia and the American Anti-Slavery Crusade." *Journal of Negro History* 66, no. 4(1982): 281–288.

Winch, Julie. "Philadelphia and the Other Underground Railroad." *The Pennsylvania Magazine of History and Biography* 111, no. 1(1987): 3–25.

Free Presbyterian Church (Darlington, Pennsylvania)

Underground Railroad site. Formed in 1847 in response to the Presbyterian denominational split over **slavery**, the Free Presbyterian Church became a major Underground Railroad station in Darlington, **Pennsylvania**. Led by the Reverend Arthur B. Bradford, the congregation not only protested the **Fugitive Slave Act of 1850**, but worked actively to assist **fugitive slaves**— using not only the church itself but the homes of many members of the congregation, including the Reverend Bradford, as sanctuaries. *See also* Underground Railroad, Sites of; and Appendixes 3 and 4.

Free State Capitol (Topeka, Kansas)

An important antislavery site and part of the National Underground Railroad Network to Freedom, Constitution Hall was a two-story building, with a basement. Construction began in April 1855, and the building soon became the official headquarters for the Topeka Movement, the antislavery opposition to the forces working to legalize **slavery** in Kansas Territory after the passage of the 1854 Kansas Nebraska Act.

As the only substantial structure in the young town, Constitution Hall became the center of early Topeka's political, economic and social life — and a haven for **fugitive slaves** when hostilities escalated between the pro- and antislavery forces seeking to control the territory. As such, Constitution Hall housed a local newspaper, the *Tribune*. John H. Kagi, who died at **Harpers Ferry** with John **Brown**, was one of the reporters. Joseph Miller, a key agent for the Topeka Underground Railroad, lived and had a tin shop in the basement. The Reverend Lewis Bodwell, a Congregational Church minister and an Underground Railroad conductor, used the building as well.

The Free State Capitol building of Kansas (1864–1870) encapsulated old Constitution Hall and expanded it by extensions on each end. The building was the seat of state government until after the **Civil War**, when funds were appropriated to construct a more prestigious building.

FURTHER READING

National Park Service. *Researching and Interpreting the Underground Railroad.* Washington, D.C.: United States Government Printing Office, 1999.

National Park Service. *Underground Railroad Special Resource Study.* Washington, D.C.: United States Government Printing Office, 1995.

Freedom Seekers

See Fugitive Slaves

Friends of the Fugitive

Individuals or groups who aided **fugitive slaves**, whether such aid was rendered randomly, as a loosely organized conspiracy of conscience or through organized bodies more often associated with the Underground Railroad. *See also* Routes of Escape; and Appendixes 1 and 2.

Friends, Society of

See Quakers

The author confined in the pillory.

Jonathan Walker in a stockade, in an 1845 engraving (Library of Congress

Fugitive Slave Act of 1793

With the abolition of **slavery** in Vermont in 1777, the northern states began a half-century long process of ending the institution. As this "first emancipation" moved forward during and in the immediate aftermath of the **American Revolution**, the founders of the United States were compelled to address several legal and political problems inherent in a nation in which slavery was legal in some states and not in others. One of the most troublesome concerned the status of African Americans— enslaved in a state or territory that recognized and protected slavery legally — who were taken or fled into a state or territory that did not.

The 1772 **Somerset Case** established the principle under British law that a person enslaved in a British slave colony became free upon entering England itself where slavery was illegal. To ensure that this precedent did not apply in American law, Article IV, section 2.3 of the U.S. Constitution makes a crucial distinction between fugitives from justice and **fugitive slaves**, as noted in the relevant parts cited below:

A Person charged in any State with Treason, Felony, or other Crime, who shall flee from Justice, and be found in another State, shall on Demand of the executive Authority of the State from which he fled, be delivered up, to be removed to the State having Jurisdiction of the Crime.

No Person held to Service or Labour in one State, under the Laws thereof, escaping into another, shall, in Consequence of any Law or Regulation therein, be discharged from such Service or Labour, but shall be delivered up on Claim of the Party to whom such Service or Labour may be due.

To effect this provision, the Second Congress passed "An act respecting fugitives from justice, and persons escaping from the service of their masters" on February 12, 1793, with the following operative sections:

Article 4: For the better security of the peace and friendship now entered into by the contracting parties, against all infractions of the same, by the citizens of either party, to the prejudice of the other, neither party shall proceed to the infliction of punishments on the citizens of the other, otherwise than by securing the offender, or offenders, by imprisonment, or any other competent means, till a fair and impartial trial can be had by judges or juries of both parties, as near as can be, to the laws, customs, and usage's of the contracting parties, and natural justice: the mode of such trials to be hereafter fixed by the wise men of the United States, in congress assembled, with the assistance of such deputies of the Delaware nation, as may be appointed to act in concert with them in adjusting this matter to their mutual liking. And it is further agreed between the parties aforesaid, that neither shall entertain, or give countenance to, the enemies of the other, or protect, in their respective states, criminal fugitives, servants, or slaves, but the same to apprehend and secure, and deliver to the state or states, to which such enemies, criminals, servants, or slaves, respectively below [sic-belong].

The act authorized the arrest or seizure of fugitives and empowered "any magistrate of a county, city or town" to rule on the matter. The act further established a fine of $500 against any person who aided a fugitive.

Serious flaws in the law became evident before 1800 and, by the 1830s, the act proved inadequate to stem the rising tide of slave escapes and to control the actions of friends of the fugitive. As sectional tensions mounted during the 1840s, slaveholders grew increasingly insistent on the need for a stronger law. This need to deter slave escapes and Underground Railroad activity carried sufficient weight to prompt the adoption of a stronger law as a key component of the **Compromise of 1850**. See also **Fugitive Slave Act of 1850**.

FURTHER READING

Campbell, Stanley W. *The Slave Catchers: Enforcement of the Fugitive Slave Law, 1850–1860.* Chapel Hill: University of North Carolina Press, 1968.

David, C. W. A. "The Fugitive Slave Law of 1793 and Its Antecedents." *Journal of Negro History* 8, no. 1(1924): 18–25.

Finkelman, Paul. "The Kidnapping of John Davis and the Adoption of the Fugitive Slave Law of 1793." *Journal of Southern History* 56, no. 3(1990): 397–422.

Fugitive Slave Act of 1850

By the 1840s, the work of the Underground Railroad and the broader activities of the **Abolitionist Movement** embodied, to the slave states, the determination of some free state factions to destroy **slavery** and, hence, the way of life of the **Cotton Kingdom**— and the willingness of most free state citizens at least to tolerate the activities of the more radical minority. Because the **Fugitive Slave Act of 1793** was inadequate to control slave escapes and **friends of the fugitive**, the need for a stronger, enforceable law was a central slave state demand in the political wrangling that produced the **Compromise of 1850**.

On September 18, 1850, Congress passed "An Act to amend, and supplementary to, the Act entitled An Act respecting Fugitives from Justice, and Persons escaping from the Service of their Masters," approved February twelfth, one thousand seven hundred and ninety-three." **Sections 1, 2, 3** of the new fugitive slave Act concern the formal provisions for appointing commissioners "authorized and required to exercise and discharge all the powers and duties conferred by this act." **Section 4** gives the appointed commissioners "authority to take and remove such fugitives from service or labor ... to the State or Territory from which such persons may have escaped or fled."

Section 5 specifies the penalties for failure to comply with warrants issued under the provisions of the act. For example, "should any marshal or deputy marshal refuse to serve such warrant, or other process, when tendered, or to use all proper means diligently to execute the same, he shall, on conviction thereof, be fined in the sum of one thousand dollars." Furthermore, should an arrested fugitive manage to escape from custody, the marshal or deputy would be liable to prosecution, and could be sued for "the full value of the service or labor of said fugitive in the State, Territory or District whence he escaped." Commissioners were also empowered "to summon and call to their aid bystanders," and "all good citizens are hereby commanded to aid and assist in the prompt and efficient execution of this law, whenever their services may be required." Any failure to comply with such a summons would be a violation of the law.

Section 6 added " ... That when a person held to service or labor in any State or Territory of the United States, has heretofore or shall hereafter escape into another State or Territory of the United States, the person or persons to whom such labor or service may be due ... may pursue and reclaim such fugitive person, either by procuring a warrant from some one of the courts, judges or commissioners aforesaid ... or by seizing and arresting such fugitive, where the same can be done

Holy Bible.
Thou shalt not deliver unto the master his servant which has escaped from his master unto thee. He shall dwell with thee. Even among you in that place which he shall choose in one of thy gates where it liketh him best. Thou shalt not oppress him.
Deut XXIII.16.

Effects of the Fugitive-Slave-Law.

Declaration of independence.
We hold that all men are created equal, that they are endowed by their Creator with certain unalienable rights, that among these are life, liberty and the pursuit of happiness.

In this 1850 condemnation of the Fugitive Slave Act, four black men, possibly freedmen, are ambushed by a posse of six armed whites in a cornfield. (Library of Congress)

without process, and by taking, or causing such person to be taken, forthwith before such court, judge, or commissioner ... and upon satisfactory proof being made ... to use such reasonable force and restraint as may be necessary, under the circumstances of the case, to take and remove such fugitive person back to the State or Territory whence he or she may have escaped as aforesaid. In no trial or hearing under this act shall the testimony of such alleged fugitive be admitted in evidence."

Section 7 declared " ... That any person who shall knowingly and willingly obstruct, hinder, or prevent such claimant ... from arresting such a fugitive from service or labor, either with or without process as aforesaid, or shall rescue, or attempt to rescue, such fugitive from service or labor, from the custody of such claimant ... or shall aid, abet, or assist such person ... to escape from such claimant ... or shall harbor or conceal such fugitive, so as to prevent the discovery and arrest of such

person, after notice or knowledge of the fact that such person was a fugitive from service or labor as aforesaid, shall, for either of said offences, be subject to a fine not exceeding one thousand dollars, and imprisonment not exceeding six months ... and shall moreover forfeit and pay, by way of civil damages to the party injured by such illegal conduct, the sum of one thousand dollars for each fugitive so lost as aforesaid, to be recovered by action of debt."

Section 8 deals with the payments to be made to various officials for their part in the arrest, custody and delivery of a fugitive to his or her claimant. In effect, the financial incentives authorized under this clause turned the pursuit of escaped slaves into a species of bounty-hunting: The marshals, their deputies, and the clerks of the said District and Territorial courts, shall be paid for their services ... and in all cases where the proceedings are before a commissioner, he shall be entitled to a

PRACTICAL ILLUSTRATION OF THE FUGITIVE SLAVE LAW.

An 1851 satire on the antagonism between Northern abolitionists and Secretary of State Daniel Webster and other supporters of enforcement of the Fugitive Slave Act of 1850. (Library of Congress)

fee of ten dollars ... The person or persons authorized to execute the process ... shall also be entitled to a fee of five dollars each for each person he or they may arrest and take before any such commissioner.

Section 9 stipulates that if the claimant suspects an attempt will be made to rescue the fugitive by force, then the arresting officer is required "to retain such fugitive in his custody, and to remove him to the State whence he fled, and there to deliver him to said claimant."

The Fugitive Slave Act of 1850 was effective, but only within extremely narrow limits. Of the thousands of enslaved African Americans who fled slavery in the 1850s, only 191 were claimed in federal court under the provisions of the law. The law was enforced in 157, or 82.3 percent of these cases, but only 83 freedom seekers were eventually remanded to the custody of their owners. However, the impact of the law must be weighed against two other critical factors: first, the law stimulated rather than stemmed the tide of slave escapes; second, it deepened sectional divisions.

The most fundamental problem with the law was that it could not be enforced without the cooperation of the North, i.e., without a broad consensus among residents of the free states in support of its enforcement. By the 1850s, such a consensus did not exist and, in fact, public opinion swung decisively against slavery as the decade unfolded. Hence, in most cases, slave-holders and their agents met active opposition, at worst, or passive indifference at best. The Fugitive Slave Act was repealed on June 28, 1864. *See also* Fugitive Slaves.

FURTHER READING
Campbell, Stanley W. *The Slave Catchers: Enforcement of the Fugitive Slave Law, 1850–1860.* Chapel Hill: University of North Carolina Press, 1968.
Gara, Larry. "The Fugitive Slave Law: A Double Paradox." *Civil War History* 10(1964): 229–240.

Fugitive Slave Advertisements

Fugitive slave advertisements developed their characteristic form in the early newspapers of slaveholding colonies east of the Appalachians. Over time, stock engravings of runaway males and females developed to draw the attention of readers.

Typically, the reward offered for the return of the fugitive was highlighted, usually increasing as the fugitive fled farther from his or her place of enslavement. The name and residence of the slaveholder, and the date of the escape would be noted. Then followed the body of the advertisement in which the slaveholder or his or her agent provided information intended to help identify and locate the fugitive. Such information included the name of the runaway and other names by which he or she might be known, and a physical description usually noting approximate age, color, weight, height, clothing, identifying marks, scars or physical defects.

Many advertisements mentioned character or personality traits or unusual skills or abilities. Some also mentioned the presumed escape motive, possible destinations and whether the fugitive was thought to have received any assistance — and, occasionally, from whom. By the **1850s**, similar information could be found in editorials and news articles.

Given the nature of American **slavery**, enslaved African Americans usually existed only as property in public records and are lost in general anonymity as individuals. Consequently, apart from their obvious purpose, fugitive slave advertisements are also one of the best and least used primary sources for documenting the lives of **fugitive slaves** as human beings.

FURTHER READING

Franklin, John H., and Loren Schweninger. *Runaway Slaves: Rebels on the Plantation.* New York: McGraw-Hill, 1999.

Hudson, J. Blaine. *Fugitive Slaves and the Underground Railroad in the Kentucky Borderland.* Jefferson, NC: McFarland, 2002.

Meadors, Daniel E. "South Carolina Fugitives as Viewed through Local Colonial Newspapers with Emphasis on Runaway Notices, 1732–1801." *Journal of Negro History* 59(1975): 288–319.

Waldstreicher, David. "Reading the Runaways: Self-Fashioning, Print Culture, and Confidence in Slavery in the Eighteenth Century Mid-Atlantic." *William and Mary Quarterly* 56(1999): 243–272.

Fugitive Slave Rescues

Friends of the fugitive in many free state communities often attempted to rescue **fugitive slaves** seized by their owners or their owner agents before the freedom seekers could be remanded to the custody of their owners. Fugitive slave rescues were often dramatic, usually successful, and served as effective means of defying the federal fugitive slave laws. *See also* Anderson (Armstead), Rosetta; Archy Case; Blackburn, Thornton and Blackburn, Lucie; Burns, Anthony; "Christiana Resistance" or "Christiana Massacre"; Crosswhite Affair; Fugitive Slave Act of 1850; Fugitive Slave Act of 1793; Glover Case; Henry, William "Jerry"; Minkins, Shadrach; Nalle, Charles; Oberlin-Wellington Rescue; Sims, Thomas.

Fugitive Slaves

African Americans who escaped from slavery; runaways; freedom seekers.

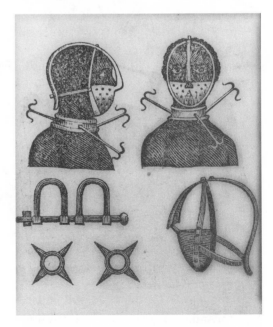

Instruments of punishment and restraint included the iron mask, collar, leg shackles and spurs, as shown in this 1807 woodcut. (Library of Congress)

A bust of Anthony Burns is surrounded by scenes from his life in this 1855 engraving. (Library of Congress)

Furber-Harris House
(Canaan, New Hampshire)

An Underground Railroad site. The Furber-Harris House was home to James Furber and his son-in-law, James Harris. From 1830 until the **Civil War**, the house served as a sanctuary to **fugitive slaves** passing through New Hampshire. *See also* Underground Railroad, Sites of; and Appendixes 3 and 4.

Garner, Margaret (1833–1858)

Fugitive slave. Of all the African Americans who escaped from **slavery** in **Kentucky**, perhaps the most tragic and haunting figure was a young woman called "Peggy" by her owner, who is better known as Margaret Garner. For a few months in the winter of 1856, she stood at the center of a series of events that riveted the attention of the nation. Margaret Garner also personified, in the extreme, the types of impossible choices often forced upon African Americans by an institution as unnatural as American slavery.

Margaret Garner was born enslaved on June 4, 1833, at the Maplewood plantation, near **Cincinnati, Ohio** in Boone County, Kentucky. She and Maplewood were the property of John P. Gaines, a comparatively prosperous farmer and hog-producer. In 1849, 16-year-old Margaret "married abroad" to 15-year-old Robert Garner, the property of James Marshall, who owned a neighboring farm. By autumn 1849, Margaret was pregnant. At roughly the same time, John Gaines was offered the post of governor of the Oregon Territory by President Zachary Taylor, under whom he had served during the Mexican War. Gaines "immediately accepted and almost as quickly arranged a sale of Maplewood and its slaves to his brother, Archibald, still a plantation owner in Arkansas." (Weisenburger, 1998: 34.)

With this change in ownership, Margaret's life became considerably more difficult and uncertain. Her oldest child, Thomas, was born in 1850. Another, Samuel, was born in 1852, then Mary in 1854, then Priscilla (or Cilla) in 1855 and, by early 1856, Margaret was

Margaret Garner, "The Modern Medea," with her four children, two of whom she killed so they would not have to endure slavery, and the men who pursued her, seen in an 1867 engraving. (Library of Congress)

again pregnant. How Margaret, Robert and the children were described in subsequent records raises troubling questions regarding Margaret's "role" at Maplewood under its "new management"—and suggests the strong probability that she was abused sexually. Although no conclusive evidence exists, it is possible that Robert Garner, who was hired out miles away through most of their "marriage," was not the biological father of Samuel and probable that he was not the biological father of Mary and Cilla. Further, if he was not the biological father of the younger children, it is quite possible that he was not the father of the child with whom Margaret was pregnant when the family escaped.

The winter of 1856 was one of the coldest ever recorded in Kentucky and a season during which numerous large-scale slave escapes (or "stampedes") occurred along the length of the frozen **Ohio River**. On Sunday night, January 27, 1856, the Garner family, including Robert's parents, and several other fugitives escaped in a stolen sleigh and fled along the Lexington-Covington Turnpike. They reached Covington at roughly 3:00 A.M. and then crossed the ice-bound river to Cincinnati. Their initial destination was the home of Elijah Kite, a free person of color living in Cincinnati who happened to be Margaret's cousin.

The party reached Kite's house at roughly 6:00 A.M. Kite then departed for Levi **Coffin's** house three miles away, where Coffin advised him to move the Garners immediately. Unfortunately, Kite delayed (causing Robert Garner to suspect him of betrayal) and, before the fugitives could be shifted to a safer location, Gaines, Marshall and several deputy marshals descended on Kite's cabin. Hundreds of neighboring whites and free people of color surrounded the posse. Robert Garner, who was armed, fired on Gaines and the others, wounding one man. In response, the posse "used chunks of firewood to smash the door and shuttered window" and soon overpowered and subdued Garner. (*Louisville Courier*, January 30, 1856 in Hudson, 2002: 145.) However, when Gaines and the others burst into the interior of the cabin, they were greeted by the following sight, as described in the initial report of the case:

In one corner of the room was a negro child bleeding to death ... Scarcely was this fact noticed when a scream issuing from an adjoining room threw their attention thither. A glance into the apartment revealed a negro woman holding in her hand a knife literally dripping with gore over the heads of two little negro children ... The negress avowed herself the mother of the children, and said that she had killed one and would like to kill the three others rather than see them again reduced to slavery. [*Louisville Courier*, January 30, 1856 in Hudson, 2002: 145.]

The stark image of Margaret Garner's tragic moment of determined madness would be immortalized in antebellum poetry and prose, and in Thomas S. Noble's 1867 painting, "The Modern Medea" (alluding to the mythical Carthaginian queen who murdered her children after being abandoned by Jason of the famed Argonauts) and more than a century later in Toni Morrison's prize-winning novel, *Beloved*.

Margaret and Robert Garner were taken into custody and jailed. Gaines and Marshall pressed for the return of their human property. However, John Joliffe, a member of the antislavery movement in Cincinnati, stepped forward as the Garners' attorney—and both the free black and antislavery white communities rallied around the fugitives throughout the ensuing trial. Testimony continued until February 13, and Commissioner John L. Pendery rejected Joliffe's argument and ordered "...that the parties named ... be delivered into the custody and possession of the claimant, Archibald K. Gaines." (*The Provincial Freeman*, March 15, 1856 in Hudson, 2002: 146.) On March 2, Margaret Garner and family were remanded to the custody of their owner, conveyed across the Ohio River, and greeted by "a large crowd ... which expressed its pleasure at the termination of the long proceedings ... with triumphant shouts." (*Louisville Courier*, March 3, 1856 in Hudson, 2002: 146.) After the fugitives were safe in jail, "the crowd moved off to the Magnolia Hotel, where several toasts were given." (*Louisville Courier*, March 3, 1856 in Hudson, 2002: 146.)

Even before returning to Kentucky with the Garners, Gaines contacted his brother, Benjamin—a plantation owner in Arkansas—and arranged to sell the family south. After returning briefly to Maplewood, Gaines moved the Garner family to **Louisville** by train and, on March 7, they departed for Arkansas on the steamboat *Henry Lewis.* However, in the vicinity of Owensboro, the *Henry Lewis* collided with another steamboat, the *Edward Howard*. The Garners, chained in steerage, were freed as the steamer broke apart and began to sink. This steamboat accident afforded Margaret Garner an opportunity to "save" another of her children from a life of slavery by casting her recently delivered infant into the river.

The party was soon placed aboard another southbound steamboat, the *Hungarian,* and reached Gaine's Landing on March 10, 1858. Because of political complications in Kentucky, Gaines was forced to bring Margaret back to Covington on March 31—placing her, technically, within the reach of **Ohio** authorities should they wish to requisition her for trial. However, Gaines was careful to suppress virtually all knowledge of her return to Kentucky and, on April 11, she was transported again to Louisville and then returned to Arkansas.

At that point, Margaret Garner was swallowed whole by the anonymity of American slavery. All that is known of her fate was disclosed in an 1870 interview with her husband, Robert — who restored her briefly to personhood. He related that Margaret contracted typhoid fever and died in Arkansas, probably in the autumn of 1858. He also reported that her last words were for him to "...never marry again in slavery, but to live in hope of freedom...." (Weisenburger, 1998: 278–279.)

FURTHER READING
Hudson, J. Blaine. *Fugitive Slaves and the Underground Railroad in the Kentucky Borderland.* Jefferson, NC: McFarland, 2002.
Weisenburger, Steven. *Modern Medea: A Family Story of Slavery and Child-Murder from the Old South.* New York: Hill and Wang, 1998.
Yanuck, Julius. "The Garner Fugitive Slave Case." *Mississippi Valley Historical Review* 40, no. 1(1953): 47–66.

Garnet, Henry Highland (1815–1882)

Fugitive slave, clergyman, and antislavery leader. Born enslaved in 1815, Henry Highland Garnet escaped from **slavery** in Maryland in 1824. Upon reaching New York,

Garnet attended the New York African Free School along with famous classmates Alexander Crummell and Ira Aldridge. He was ordained a Presbyterian minister and, by the late 1830s, became associated with the American Anti-Slavery Society.

As an antislavery activist, Garnet espoused a nationalistic vision of black liberation that, even allowing for the support of white abolitionists, emphasized the necessity of African American leadership in the struggle for freedom and civil rights. Garnet would declare, "They are our allies— Ours is the battle." Inspired by David Walker's *Appeal* (1829), he shocked his audience at the 1843 National Convention of Free People of Color by counseling insurrection, stating to enslaved African Americans: "You had better all die — die immediately than live lives as slaves and entail wretchedness upon your posterity ... Where is the blood of your fathers? Has it run out of your veins? Awake, awake, millions of voices are calling you. Your dead fathers speak to you from their graves." (Brewer, 1928: 44.)

The convention repudiated Garnet's stance and, shorn of supporters, he gradually turned more to religion. During the next two decades, Garnet served as pastor in a number of Presbyterian churches while espousing emigration to Liberia. Still a prominent abolitionist, he lectured in England and Scotland, and traveled to Jamaica in 1852 to work as a missionary. Several years later he returned to the United States and, during the **Civil War,** worked with freedmen and black refugees in **Washington, D.C.** In 1881, Garnet was appointed minister to Liberia, but died in 1882, two months after his arrival. *See also* Abolitionist Movement.

FURTHER READING
Brewer, W. B. "Henry Highland Garnet." *Journal of Negro History* 13, no. 1(1928): 36–52.
Schor, Joel. *Henry Highland Garnet: A Voice of Black Radicalism in the Nineteenth Century.* Westport, CT: Greenwood Press, 1977.
Schor, Joel. "The Rivalry between Frederick Douglass and Henry Highland Garnet." *Journal of Negro History* 64, no. 1 (1979): 30–38.
Simmons, William J. *Men of Mark: Eminent, Progressive and Rising.* Cleveland, OH: George M. Rewell, 1887.

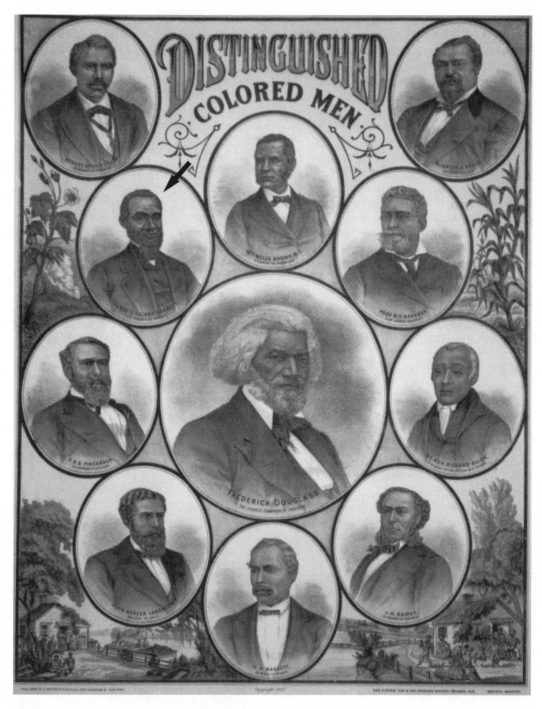

Henry Highland Garnet (*at arrow*). And Frederick Douglass (*center*), with Robert Brown Elliott (*top left*), Blanche K. Bruce (*top right*). *Clockwise from top center of circle*: William Wells Brown, R.T. Greener, the Right Reverend Richard Allen, J.H. Rainey, E.D. Bassett, John Mercer Langston, P.B.S. Pinchback, and Garnet. (Library of Congress)

Garrett, Thomas (1789–1871)

Friend of the fugitive. Thomas Garrett was born to Quaker parents on August 21, 1789 in Delaware County, Pennsylvania. As an adult, Garrett operated a successful tool-making and ironworks business. However, he was far better known for his antislavery work, his simple faith and his firm belief in the equality of all people.

As early as 1814, a black woman working for his family was kidnapped. Garrett pursued the kidnappers, overtook them near the Navy Yard in **Philadelphia** and recovered the woman. According to William **Still**, from this moment, Garrett "never failed to assist any fugitive from slavery on the way to freedom." (Still, 1872: 649.) Although hated by many of his neighbors and watched closely by the police, Garrett's personal courage and powerful physique intimidated his enemies. He often confronted slave-catchers directly, freely admitting that he had assisted or was harboring a fugitive, but refusing to divulge any meaningful information or to allow the slave-catchers entry to his home. In the late 1840s and **1850s**, he worked closely with William Still, head of the Vigilance Committee in Philadelphia, to channel fugitives from Delaware and Maryland into Philadelphia. Further, Harriett **Tubman** often hid with Garrett on her many journeys to conduct fugitives from Maryland into free territory.

In 1846, Garrett was sued by the owners of several fugitives he assisted in escaping from New Castle, Maryland. Garrett was convicted when the suit reached the U.S. Circuit Court in 1848. Defiant and bankrupt, he promised "to redouble his exertions." (Still, 1872: 650.) Although 60 years old, he started a new business, prospered and continued assisting fugitives. Ironically, the trial enhanced his reputation and increased the number of fugitives seeking his help, so much so that he built an additional story on one of his buildings. Garrett estimated that he assisted over two thousand freedom seekers after he began keeping records—and many more before. When he died on January 24, 1871, he was widely honored for his courage and commitment by both African Americans and whites. *See also* Abolitionist Movement; and Appendixes 1 and 2.

Thomas Garrett (Library of Congress)

FURTHER READING
Kashatus, William C. "Two Stationmasters on the Underground Railroad: A Tale of Black and White." *Pennsylvania Heritage* 27(2001): 4–11.
Still, William. *The Underground Railroad*. 1872. Reprint, Chicago: Johnson, 1970.
Switala, William J. *Underground Railroad in Delaware, Maryland, and West Virginia.* Mechanicsburg, PA: Stackpole Books, 2004.
_____. *Underground Railroad in Pennsylvania*. Mechanicsburg, PA: Stackpole Books, 2001.

Garrison, William Lloyd (1805–1879)

Abolitionist and friend of the fugitive. The son of a merchant sailing master, William Lloyd Garrison was born in Newburyport, Massachusetts, in 1805. In 1808, Garrison's father deserted the family, leaving them virtually penniless and forcing Garrison to work selling homemade molasses candy and delivering wood.

Garrison was apprenticed as a printer and began work in 1818 for the *Newburyport Herald* as a writer and editor. When he was 25, Garrison became associated with the American Colonization Society. However, by 1828, once he realized that the goal of the society was the removal of free blacks as a strategy to preserve and protect the institution of **slavery**, he converted to "the cause of the slave"—

largely through the influence of Benjamin **Lundy**.

A devoutly religious Baptist, Garrison denounced slaveholding as an abomination and demanded immediate, unqualified and uncompensated emancipation. After being jailed for libeling a slave trader, Garrison published the first issue of the *Liberator,* his legendary antislavery journal, in Boston on January 1, 1831, and issued the famous declaration: "I do not wish to think, or speak, or write, with moderation ... I am in earnest — I will not equivocate — I will not excuse — I will not retreat a single inch — AND I WILL BE HEARD." (*The Liberator,* January 1, 1831.)

Garrison founded the New England Anti-Slavery Society in 1832 and was one of the founders of the American Anti-Slavery Society in 1833. His approach emphasized nonviolence and "moral suasion" and, unlike many abolitionists, also stressed the equality of whites and African Americans. By the mid–1830s, Garrison gained a reputation for his scathingly denunciatory style and moral absolutism. He and his coworkers became the target of violence and political repression as mobs routinely attacked abolitionist meetings and President Andrew Jackson's administration did nothing when southerners removed antislavery materials from the federal mails.

In the late 1830s, as the issue of slavery's westward expansion divided the nation's politicians, the American Anti-Slavery Society split over issues raised by Garrison's uncompromising principles and leadership style. Many abolitionists objected to his growing advocacy of women's rights, Christian nonresistance, and a theology of Christian perfectionism. He, in turn, rejected the ideas put forward by many of his opponents that women should not be given political equality within the movement and that abolitionists should become active in electoral politics. Two new organizations emerged from this rift: the Liberty Party, a political organization; and the American and Foreign Anti-Slavery Society, which did not admit women. Further, in 1851, Frederick **Douglass**, Garrison's one-time protégé, stated his belief that the Constitution could be used as a weapon against slavery, and Garrison, feeling betrayed, attacked Douglass through his paper. The two

William Lloyd Garrison (Library of Congress)

would never reconcile their differences entirely.

As leader of an unpopular minority of agitators, Garrison's measurable impact on national politics was negligible in the 1840s and **1850s,** but his image as the living personification of abolitionism remained imposing. Ironically, when the **Civil War** began, Garrison was soon hailed in the North as a prophet whose warnings had been confirmed by the course of events.

Garrison continued to publish the *Liberator* until the ratification of the Thirteenth Amendment in December 1865 brought the complete abolition of slavery in the United States — remaining steadfast at his task over 35 years and 1,820 issues. He then resigned from the American Anti-Slavery Society and declared that his work was done. The society carried on until 1870 under the leadership of Wendell **Phillips.** Garrison died in **Boston** in 1879. *See also* Abolitionist Movement; William Lloyd Garrison House.

FURTHER READING
Jacobs, Donald M. "William Lloyd Garrison's *Liberator* and Boston's Blacks, 1830–1865." *New England Quarterly* 44(1971): 259–277.
Stewart, James B. "The Aims and Impact of Gar-

risonian Abolitionism, 1840–1860." *Civil War History* 15, no. 3 (1969): 197–209.

Still, William. *The Underground Railroad.* 1872. Reprint, Chicago: Johnson, 1970.

Zorn, Roman J. "The New England Anti-Slavery Society: Pioneer Abolition Organization." *Journal of Negro History* 43(1957): 157–176.

Geneva College (Northwood, Ohio)

Underground Railroad site. Geneva College was established in 1848 by the Reformed and United Presbyterian Church. Located originally Northwood, **Ohio**, near the Miami River, the college offered sanctuary to **fugitive slaves** in the many caves nearby. The college moved to Beaver Falls, Pennsylvania, in 1880. *See also* Underground Railroad, Sites of; and Appendixes 3 and 4.

George B. Hitchcock House (Lewis, Iowa)

Underground Railroad site recognized and documented by the National Park Service. *See also* Appendix 5.

Georgia Sea Islands

See Sea Islands, Sites of; and Appendixes 3 and 4.

Gerrit Smith Estate (Peterboro, New York)

Gerrit **Smith** (1797–1874) was a wealthy and influential abolitionist, and his estate in Peterboro, New York, was an important antislavery and Underground Railroad site. Smith made his home on the estate and, from his land office, constructed by his father, Peter Smith, in 1804, managed his family's extensive land holdings in New York. Both a businessman and a philanthropist, Smith sold 140,000 acres of farm land in western New York for one dollar per acre to three thousand poor African Americans between 1846 and 1850. Many of these black settlers were **fugitive slaves** assisted to freedom by Smith and other practical abolitionists with whom he made common cause.

The Gerrit Smith Estate and Land Office are located in Peterboro, New York, at the corner of Nelson and Main Streets, and are stops on the Underground Railroad Travel Itinerary developed by the National Park Service of the United States Department of the Interior.

See also Underground Railroad, Sites of.

FURTHER READING
National Park Service. *Underground Railroad: Special Resource Study.* Washington, D.C.: U.S. Government Printing Office, 1995.

Gibbons, Daniel

Friend of the fugitive in Lancaster County, **Pennsylvania**. *See also* Wright's Ferry Mansion. *See also* Appendixes 1 and 2.

Gibbons, Hannah

Friend of the fugitive in Lancaster County, **Pennsylvania**. *See also* Wright's Ferry Mansion. *See also* Appendixes 1 and 2.

Gibbs, Mifflin Wistar (1823–1915)

Friend of the fugitive. Mifflin Wistar Gibbs was born on April 17, 1823 in **Philadelphia, Pennsylvania**. The son of free African American parents with strong antislavery sympathies, the young Gibbs worked with William **Still** to assist **fugitive slaves**. Gibbs participated in the convention movement in Philadelphia and, although self-educated, once accompanied Frederick **Douglass** on a speaking tour in western New York.

When gold was discovered in **California**, Gibbs headed west. Although he never reached the gold fields, he became wealthy selling men's clothing and boots in San Francisco. Gibbs then established the first African American newspaper in San Francisco, the *Mirror of the Times.* However, when he became frustrated by racial discrimination in California, the discovery of gold in British Columbia drew him farther north. There, he opened a new store in Victoria, continued to prosper and was elected to represent a wealthy district in the Common Council of Victoria. Getting a taste for politics, Gibbs read law with an attorney in British Columbia, then, at forty-seven years of age, traveled east in 1870 to enroll in the law department of **Oberlin College**. While at Oberlin, he met and married Mariah A. Alexander of **Kentucky**, with whom he had four children.

Never one to remain too long in one place, Gibbs was persuaded to move to Arkansas by two prominent African Americans, Richard A. Dawson and J. H. Johnson. Gibbs arrived in Little Rock (Pulaski County), Arkansas, in early 1872 and was admitted to the Arkansas bar later that same year. Although he practiced law with a succession of partners, Gibbs was first and foremost a politician and, soon after moving to Arkansas, was appointed attorney for Pulaski County, and then was elected municipal judge of the city of Little Rock in 1873. Between 1877 and 1886, Gibbs also served as register of the United States Land Office for the Little Rock District of Arkansas and, in 1889, was appointed receiver of public moneys at Little Rock Land District, a position he held until 1897.

Gibbs used these positions and his growing influence to promote land ownership by African Americans and to support local and national civil rights efforts. He served as a member of the board of visitors of the Little Rock school system in the 1880s, and was active in Booker T. Washington's National Negro Business League. In 1897, Gibbs was appointed American consul to Madagascar. After he resigned as consul in 1901, he returned to Little Rock where he managed his business interests and remained active in the Republican Party. In 1903, Gibbs founded the Capitol City Savings Bank, the second African American-owned bank in Arkansas. Gibbs died in Little Rock in 1915. *See also* Appendixes 1 and 2.

FURTHER READING
Gibbs, Mifflin Wistar. *Shadow and Light: An Autobiography.* 1902. Reprint, New York: Arno Press, 1968.
Stanley, Jerry. *Hurry Freedom: African Americans in Gold Rush California.* New York: Crown Publishers, 2000.

Giddings, Joshua Reed (1795–1864)

Abolitionist, legislator, and friend of the fugitive. Joshua Giddings was born in Athens, Bradford County, **Pennsylvania**, on October 6, 1795. He moved with his family, first, to Canandaigua, New York, and, in 1806, to Ashtabula County, **Ohio**, where he worked on his father's farm and acquired an intermittent and uneven education.

In 1812, Giddings enlisted in the Army and saw action on the peninsula north of Sandusky Bay against Native Americans allied with the British. After the war, he taught school and studied law, and was admitted to the bar in 1820. In 1826, he was elected to the

Ohio legislature, but chose to serve only one term. In 1838, he returned to politics and was elected to the U.S. House of Representatives and soon became a prominent advocate of the abolition of **slavery** and the domestic **slave trade**.

On February 9, 1841, Giddings delivered a famous speech on the Second Seminole War — in which he argued that the war was being waged solely to enslave the black maroons of Florida, who were allied with the Seminoles. He elaborated his argument in the *Exiles of Florida* (1858).

Giddings was censured in 1842 for defending the "mutineers" in the **Creole** Affair. He then resigned from Congress in protest and appealed directly to his constituents, who re-elected him by a large majority. On returning to Congress, Giddings continued his campaign against slavery and expressed his strong opposition to the **Fugitive Slave Act of 1850** and the other measures of the **Compromise of 1850**. In 1856, and again in 1858, Giddings collapsed while addressing the House and chose not to seek re-election in 1858. Still, in 1861, President Abraham Lincoln appointed him United States consul-general in **Canada**. Giddings died in Montreal, Canada, on May 27, 1864. *See also* Abolitionist Movement; Black Seminoles; Maroon Societies; and Appendixes 1 and 2.

FURTHER READING
Ludlum, Robert P. "Joshua R. Giddings, Radical." *The Mississippi Valley Historical Review* 23(1936): 49–60.
Stewart, James B. *Joshua R. Giddings and the Tactics of Radical Politics.* Cleveland: Press of Case Western Reserve University, 1970.

Glover, John

Fugitive slave. *See also* Glover Case.

Glover Case (1854)

A famous fugitive slave rescue and legal case in Wisconsin. John Glover escaped from **slavery** in Missouri in 1852 and settled in Racine, Wisconsin. In early 1854, Benjamin Garland journeyed to Wisconsin to reclaim Glover. Garland obtained a writ for Glover's arrest under the **Fugitive Slave Act of 1850** and, on March 11, 1854, Glover was taken into custody.

By 1850, the two largest segments of the population of Wisconsin were migrants from New England and immigrants from the various German states. Both groups fiercely opposed slavery; thus, opposition to the Fugitive Slave Act was strong, consistent and broadly based, perhaps more than in any other state. Consequently, when the abolitionist community of Milwaukee learned of Glover's arrest, more than five thousand people converged on Racine determined to protest Glover's incarceration and to free him, if possible. After several hours of angry speeches, the crowd stormed the jail and freed Glover.

The antislavery faction was led by Sherman Booth, born in Connecticut in 1812 and involved in the **abolitionist movement** in New England. Booth moved to Wisconsin in 1848 and opened a newspaper, *The Free Democrat*, which became the leading antislavery organ in the state. He and other leaders of the Glover rescue were arrested. However, on May 22, 1854, Justice Abraham D. Smith of the Wisconsin Supreme Court ordered their release on the grounds that the Fugitive Slave Act was unconstitutional. The U.S. Supreme Court reversed Smith's ruling in 1859.

FURTHER READING
Ranney, Joseph A. "Suffering the Agonies of Their Righteousness: The Rise and Fall of the States Rights Movement in Wisconsin, 1854–1861." *Wisconsin Magazine of History* 75, no. 2(1992).

Goodnow, Lyman

Friend of the fugitive in Wisconsin. *See also* Quarreles, Caroline; and Appendixes 1 and 2.

Goodrich, Joseph (1800–1867)

An important friend of the fugitive, Joseph Goodrich was born in Hancock, **Massachusetts**, in 1800 to a family active in the Seventh Day Baptist Church, a denomination that officially denounced **slavery** in several resolutions. In 1819, he married Nancy Maxon and, in 1821, the couple moved to Alfred, Allegheny County, New York. There, he and his growing family remained until 1838, when he organized a party of fellow Seventh Day Baptists who migrated to the Wisconsin frontier hoping to claim unsettled land. The group built a log cabin and surveyed the land for the town that would become Milton.

Although few **fugitive slaves** passed through Wisconsin, there were sufficient numbers to occupy the attention of both local abolitionists and the local authorities. Milton, located near the Rock River, a tributary of the Mississippi River, was a key point on the route for fugitive slaves escaping to the communities along Lake Michigan. In 1844, Goodrich built the **Milton House**, a home and stagecoach inn and, as a man with strong antislavery sentiments, used the house as a refuge for fugitive slaves. Freedom seekers were given safe haven in the basement, entering through the cabin to the rear of the inn and then through a trap door in the cabin's floor to the dirt tunnel that led to the basement of the inn. There, the fugitives could eat and rest in preparation for the next stage of their journey — and, if an alarm was sounded, they could hide in or escape through the tunnel. *See also* Appendixes 1 and 2.

FURTHER READING
Clark, James I. *Wisconsin Defies the Fugitive Slave Law.* Madison, WI: State Historical Society of Wisconsin, 1955.

Goodridge, William C. (1805–1873)

Friend of the fugitive. William C. Goodridge was born free in Baltimore, Maryland, in 1805. His father was probably the white physician who owned his enslaved African American mother.

When he was six years old, Goodridge was apprenticed to the Reverend William Dunn's tannery in York, **Pennsylvania**. He left York in 1821, soon married (Emily) and began working as a barber. In 1823, Goodridge returned to York and opened his own barbershop on Centre Square in 1824, soon achieving great success with customers of both races. Due to his business acumen, he expanded his interests and soon became a wealthy man. By 1845, he owned a confectionery, bought and sold animal hides to tanneries, started York's first newspaper distribution business, owned a dozen buildings and built a five-story structure called Centre Hall. Goodridge next invested in the railroad business, founding the Goodridge Reliance Line, with 13 railroad cars serving 20 Pennsylvania communities. By the

1850s, his net worth probably exceeded $50,000.

Goodridge was willing to risk his fortune and his freedom to assist freedom seekers fleeing northward through eastern Pennsylvania. Despite being under constant surveillance by slave-catchers and local authorities, he concealed **fugitive slaves** either in a straw-lined trench under a building behind his home at 123 East Philadelphia Street or, alternatively, in a small secret room at the rear of his basement. Goodridge also used his railroad to transport fugitive slaves to Columbia or as far as **Philadelphia.**

Goodridge and his family moved to Minnesota in 1863. He died in Minneapolis in 1873. *See also* Underground Railroad, Sites of; and Appendixes 1–4.

Goodwin, Abigail, and Elizabeth Goodwin

Friends of the fugitive. Quaker sisters, Abigail and Elizabeth Goodwin, became active in assisting **fugitive slaves** through Salem, New Jersey, as early as 1836. Abigail, in particular, donated and raised money to support Underground Railroad activity in her area. *See also* Appendixes 1 and 2.

FURTHER READING
Still, William. *The Underground Railroad.* 1872. Reprint, Chicago: Johnson, 1970.

Grant, Tudor

Friend of the fugitive in Oswego, New York. *See also* Buckout-Jones Building.

Grau Mill (Illinois)

Underground Railroad site. The Grau Mill stands on a former stagecoach road from Quincy to Chicago, **Illinois**. There and at his home, Miller F. Grau, a German immigrant strongly opposed to **slavery**, gave refuge to **fugitive slaves**. *See also* Underground Railroad, Sites of; and Appendixes 3 and 4.

Gray, Jim

Fugitive slave and fugitive slave rescue case. *See also* John Hossack House.

Great Dismal Swamp

See Maroon Societies

Great Geneva (Dover, Delaware)

Underground Railroad site. Jonathan Hunn, a Quaker residing in Dover, worked closely with Thomas **Garrett** and Daniel Corbet to assist **fugitive slaves** in the 1840s and **1850s**. His home, Great Geneva, was a key sanctuary for freedom seekers and was among the many stations used by Harriett **Tubman** as she conducted runaways from Maryland to free territory. *See also* Clearfield Farm; Quakers; Underground Railroad, Sites of; and Appendixes 3 and 4.

FURTHER READING
Blockson, Charles L. *Hippocrene Guide to the Underground Railroad.* New York: Hippocrene Books, 1994.
Still, William. *The Underground Railroad.* 1872. Reprint, Chicago: Johnson, 1970.

Grimes, Jonathan (1802–1875)

A friend of the fugitive, Dr. Jonathan Grimes was born into a Quaker family in Morris County, New Jersey, on June 3, 1802 and, in 1828, moved to nearby Passaic County to practice medicine. In 1832, Grimes returned to the family homestead in Morris County. There, he assisted **fugitive slaves** and maintained an Underground Railroad station after moving to the nearby community of Boonton. There, he worked closely with Baxter Sayre of Madison.

Grimes was once arrested for harboring a freedom seeker and was frequently harassed by his proslavery neighbors. Grimes died in 1875.

See also Grimes Homestead.

FURTHER READING
National Park Service. *Researching and Interpreting the Underground Railroad.* Washington, D.C.: United States Government Printing Office, 1999.
National Park Service. *Underground Railroad Special Resource Study.* Washington, D.C.: United States Government Printing Office, 1995.

Grimes, Leonard A. (1815–1873)

Friend of the fugitive. Leonard A. Grimes was born of free African American parents in Leesburg, Virginia in 1815. As a young man, Grimes became one of the principal Underground Railroad agents operating in **Washington, D.C.** Working as a hackman, Grimes purchased several horses and carriages which he used in his business to transport **fugitive slaves** clandestinely through the Washington, D.C., area.

In October 1839, Grimes was arrested for assisting a woman named Patty and her six children escape from **slavery** in Loudoun County, Virginia. The case against Grimes was circumstantial, but he was convicted, assessed a $100 fine and served two years in prison in Richmond, Virginia.

After his release, Grimes and his family moved first to **New Bedford** and then **Boston, Massachusetts**, where he became pastor of the Twelfth Street Baptist Church, the "Fugitive Slave Church." There, he continued his Underground Railroad and abolitionist activities—and played a key role in the attempt to rescue Anthony **Burns**, a member of his congregation. After this effort proved unavailing and Burns was returned to slavery, Grimes raised money to purchase Burns' freedom in 1855. Grimes died in 1873. *See also* Appendixes 1 and 2.

FURTHER READING
Blockson, Charles L. *Hippocrene Guide to the Underground Railroad*. New York: Hippocrene Books, 1994.
Simmons, William J. *Men of Mark: Eminent, Progressive and Rising*. Cleveland, OH: George M. Rewell, 1887.

Grimes Homestead (Mountain Lakes, New Jersey)

Underground Railroad site recognized and documented by the National Park Service. *See also* Appendix 5.

Grinnell, Josiah Bushnell (1821–1891)

Abolitionist, politician, and friend of the fugitive. Josiah Bushnell Grinnell was born on December 22, 1821 in New Haven, Addison County, Vermont. As a boy, he attended the common schools in New Haven and, later, Oneida Institute where pursued classical studies. Grinnell graduated from Auburn Theological Seminary in 1847, and was ordained a Congregational minister. He had started his ministry in **Washington, D.C.** and **New York City**—preaching abolition as much as religion — before moving to **Iowa** in 1853. There, he founded the town of Grinnell in Poweshiek County, established the town's first Congrega-

tional Church and served as its first minister. Later, he founded Iowa College, eventually renamed Grinnell University, and served the institution in various capacities over the years.

Grinnell was instrumental in turning the town that bears his name into an important center of Underground Railroad activity. In March 1859, he aided John **Brown**, the militant abolitionist leader, who had used Iowa as a staging point for his battle with pro slavery forces in "Bleeding Kansas." After Brown's failed raid on **Harpers Ferry** in October 1859, Grinnell was the target of considerable criticism for his support of Brown, but never apologized for or regretted his actions.

While serving in the Iowa Senate from 1856 to 1860, Grinnell pursued the study of law and was admitted to the bar in 1858, shifting the focus of his efforts from the ministry to politics and the practice of law. He was selected as a delegate to the Republican National Convention in 1860 and served in the U.S. House of Representatives from 1863 through 1867. Once in Washington, Grinnell was passionate on the subject of racial equality and, in one angry speech, insulted a Democratic congressman from **Kentucky**. The next day, Grinnell was assaulted on the steps of the Capitol by the congressman and his friends. Still, Grinnell was not intimidated, and continued his strident support for the policies of Radical Reconstruction.

Grinnell left Congress and returned to Iowa, where he resumed the practice of law and pursued his new interest in building railroads. He became director of the Rock Island Railroad and later receiver of the Iowa Central Railroad. Grinnell died in Grinnell, Iowa, on March 31, 1891. *See also* Abolitionist Movement; and Appendixes 1 and 2.

FURTHER READING
Dykstra, Robert R. *Bright Radical Star: Black Freedom and White Supremacy on the Hawkeye Frontier*. Cambridge, MA: Harvard University Press, 1993.
Payne, Charles E. *Josiah Bushnell Grinnell*. Iowa City: State Historical Society of Iowa, 1938.

Guy Beckley House (Ann Arbor, Michigan)

Underground Railroad site recognized and documented by the National Park Service. *See also* Appendix 5.

Haines, Jonathan Ridgeway (d. 1899)

Friend of the fugitive in Alliance, **Ohio**. *See also* Jonathan Ridgeway Haines House (Alliance, Ohio).

Hamilton and Rhoda Littlefield House (Oswego, New York)

Underground Railroad site recognized and documented by the National Park Service. *See also* Appendix 5.

Hanby, Benjamin R. (1833–1867)

Friend of the fugitive and composer. Son of the abolitionist minister and friend of the fugitive, William **Hanby**, Benjamin Russell Hanby was born in 1833 in Westerville, **Ohio**, and grew to adulthood in an active Underground Railroad station. While known for his work as a practical abolitionist and as a minister, he is much better known as a composer.

One of his songs, "Up on the Housetop," is still sung during the Christmas season. Another song that was extremely popular in the antebellum period was "Darling Nelly Gray," composed in 1856, which was inspired by the story of a fugitive slave, Joseph Selby, who was given sanctuary by Hanby's family. Selby hoped that, after reaching Canada, he could return and rescue his sweetheart, Nelly Gray. The lyrics can be found in the Appendix 7. *See also* Underground Railroad, Sites of; and Appendixes 3 and 4.

FURTHER READING
Boni, Margaret Bradford, ed. *The Fireside Book of Favorite American Songs.* New York: Simon and Schuster, 1952.
Lowder, Jerry E. "Benjamin Russell Hanby, Ohio Composer-Educator, 1833–1867: His Contributions to Early Music Education." PhD dissertation, The Ohio State University, 1987.

Hanby, William (1808–1880)

Friend of the fugitive. William Hanby was born in **Pennsylvania** in 1808 and migrated to **Ohio** as a young man, finding work as a saddler. Hanby boarded with Samuel Miller, a devout member of the United Brethren, and was not only converted to that faith but married Miller's daughter, Anne (1807–1879) and became a minister.

In 1837, Hanby became a publishing agent and then editor of the church newspaper, *Religious Telescope,* which gave him a platform from which to advocate abolition. He was elected bishop in 1845 and, in 1847, co-founded Otterbein College. In 1854, the Hanby family purchased a home, Hanby House, in Westerville, Ohio, that became an important Underground Railroad station. **Fugitive slaves** were often hidden in Hanby's barn and then led through an alley to another nearby station. One of Hanby's most reliable assistants was his eldest son, Benjamin R. **Hanby**, the famous composer. *See also* Underground Railroad, Sites of; and Appendixes 1–4.

Hanby House

Underground Railroad site in **Ohio**. *See also* Hanby, Benjamin R.; Hanby, William; Underground Railroad, Sites of; and Appendixes 3 and 4.

Hanover, John T.

Friend of the fugitive. In 1851, "a man named Hansen" made the southern **Indiana** farm of Colonel James W. Cockrum "his headquarters" and remained with Cockrum "for more than five years." Hansen posed as "a representative of a **Philadelphia** real estate firm" with an "interest in natural history." Colonel Cockrum's youngest son, William, ran errands for Hansen and eventually became his confidante "and to this personal acquaintance Indiana is indebted for the most explicit account of the work of the Underground Railroad." According to William Cockrum, Hansen was actually John T. Hanover,

...an agent of the Anti-Slavery League, and the superintendent of its work in Indiana. The organization was extensively controlled by men of ability and well supplied with funds ... There were as many as fifty educated and intelligent young and middle-aged men on duty from some ways above Pittsburgh, Pennsylvania, along down the Ohio, both sides of it to the Mississippi River. These men had different occupations. Some were book agents ... some were singing teachers, school teachers, writing teachers, map makers carrying surveying and drafting outfits for that purpose; some were real Yankee peddlers; some were naturalists and geologists.... [Dunn: 152–153.]

Hansen established and "staffed" 12 major **Ohio River** crossing points along the northern border of **Kentucky**. These crossing points were spaced roughly 50 miles apart — from the Jackson Purchase in the west to the Virginia border in the east. *See also* Fugitive Slaves; and Appendixes 1 and 2.

FURTHER READING
Cockrum, Col. William M. *History of the Underground Railroad, As It Was Conducted by the Anti-Slavery League*. 1915. Reprint, New York: Negro Universities Press, 1969.
Dunn, Jacob P. "Indiana and Indianans." Indiana Underground Railroad, Vol.1, Box 79, Wilbur H. Siebert Papers. Ohio Historical Society.

Hanway, Caster

See Christiana Resistance or Christiana Massacre

Harboring

Whether in private urban residences, rural farmhouses, barns, and other outbuildings, or even in caves and other natural hiding places, **fugitive slaves** sought and were sometimes given sanctuary by sympathetic whites and African Americans. Rendering this particular type of aid was deemed the crime of "harboring fugitive slaves," and complemented that of **enticing** or assisting runaway slaves to escape.

FURTHER READING
Hudson, J. Blaine. *Fugitive Slaves and the Underground Railroad in the Kentucky Borderland*. Jefferson, NC: McFarland, 2002.

Harper, Frances Ellen Watkins (1825–1911)

Frances Ellen Watkins Harper was a famous African American author, activist and friend of the fugitive. The types of assistance furnished to **fugitive slaves** by agents of the Underground Railroad included food, clothing, shelter, transportation and even legal aid. Contemporary students of this historical period sometimes forget that such assistance was often costly. Consequently, those who helped to finance the Underground Railroad played an important although less visible role — and, because only those with financial means could provide significant financial assistance, those who supported the Underground Railroad were often among the most affluent and successful men and women, black and white, of

Frances Ellen Watkins Harper, 1898 (Library of Congress)

the time. One of the most noteworthy was Frances Ellen Watkins Harper.

Frances Ellen Watkins was born free in Baltimore, Maryland, in 1825. An only child who was orphaned at three years of age, Watkins was raised by her uncle, William Watkins, an AME minister. Because her uncle was founder of the Watkins Academy, an early opponent of colonization and one of the most important influences on the young William Lloyd **Garrison**, Frances grew to young womanhood in a household with impeccable antislavery credentials.

Frances Watkins was educated in the classics at the Watkins Academy and later learned the trades of seamstress and nurse. However, she exhibited great literary talent and, in 1846, published *Forest Leaves*, her first volume of poetry. In 1851, she left Baltimore to become an instructor at Union Seminary, a school for African Americans near Columbus, **Ohio**, established by the AME Church in 1847. After a brief initial stay in Ohio, she moved to York, **Pennsylvania**, in 1852 and became actively involved in assisting fugitive slaves — living in **Philadelphia** with William **Still**, head of the vigilance committee in Philadelphia, and his family. In 1854, she published

Poems on Miscellaneous Subjects, reprinted five times in 20 editions between 1854 and 1871, and earned the reputation of being the most popular black poet before Paul Laurence Dunbar. With this reputation, she also became a popular antislavery lecturer — known for her cultivated message and powerful voice — and worked for both the Maine and later the Pennsylvania Anti-Slavery Societies. Watkins donated most of the royalties from her books to finance the Underground Railroad operation in eastern Pennsylvania under Still's direction.

On November 22, 1860, she married Fenton Harper in **Cincinnati**, Ohio. She then invested her savings in a farm near Columbus and settled down to raise her child and stepchildren. However, Fenton Harper died in May 1864 and, to her surprise and chagrin, was found to be deep in debt. Frances Harper lost all her financial assets in settling his affairs. With the assistance of William Still, she returned to the speaking circuit as an advocate of both black and women's rights. In the bitter dispute between African Americans and the leaders of the Women's Movement over black voting rights, Harper sided strongly with Frederick **Douglass**— emphasizing the urgency of enfranchising African Americans even if the franchise was not granted to women immediately.

Harper toured the South during Reconstruction and worked to promote the adjustment of newly emancipated African Americans to freedom. As an account of her experiences, she published *Sketches of Southern Life* (1887), still regarded as the "most accurate description of black life in the South" during this period. (Bacon, 1989: 38.) Still later, she published a novel, *Iola Leroy* (1892), which celebrated independent black womanhood and black identity. Remaining an activist in her old age, she contributed to the founding of the National Association of Colored Women. Harper died in Philadelphia in 1911. *See also* Vigilance Committees; and Appendixes 1 and 2.

FURTHER READING
Bacon, Margaret Hope. "One Great Bundle of Humanity: Frances Ellen Watkins Harper." *Pennsylvania Magazine of History and Biography* 113, no. 1(1989).
Still, William. *The Underground Railroad.* 1872. Reprint, Chicago: Johnson, 1970.

Harpers Ferry, West Virginia

Underground Railroad site recognized and documented by the National Park Service. *See also* Appendix 5.

Harriet Beecher Stowe House (Brunswick, Maine)

Underground Railroad site recognized and documented by the National Park Service. *See also* Appendix 5.

Harriet Beecher Stowe House (Cincinnati, Ohio)

Underground Railroad site recognized and documented by the National Park Service. *See also* Appendix 5.

Harriet Tubman Home (Auburn, New York)

Underground Railroad site recognized and documented by the National Park Service. *See also* Appendix 5.

Harris, Catherine (1809–1902)

Friend of the fugitive. Catherine Harris was born on June 10, 1809, in Meadville, Pennsylvania, to a free black father and white mother. In 1828, she married and moved to Buffalo, New York. Her husband soon died, leaving her with one daughter and, in 1831, she and her daughter migrated to Jamestown, New York — becoming the first African American residents of the town.

In 1835, she married John Harris (d. 1852) and moved into a house on Spring Street that she would occupy for the next 70 years. Other African Americans migrated to the area, settled near Harris and, by the late 1840s, a small neighborhood had evolved that local whites called "Africa." The Jamestown AME Zion Church and Blackwell Chapel emerged as key community institutions— and Harris's home and those of her neighbors became important sanctuaries for **fugitive slaves**. *See also* Appendixes 1 and 2.

FURTHER READING
Blockson, Charles L. *Hippocrene Guide to the Underground Railroad.* New York: Hippocrene Books, 1994.
Lockwood, C. R. "Africa." Interview with Catherine Harris, Jamestown *Evening Journal,* May 3, 1902.

Cook and Coppock are hanged in Charlestown, West Virginia, Dec. 17, 1859. (Library of Congress)

Harris, Chapman (1802–1890)

Friend of the fugitive. Chapman Harris was probably the most colorful and heroic African American friend of the fugitive in the **Madison, Indiana** area — perhaps along the entire **Ohio River** border. Born in Virginia in about 1802, he arrived in Madison in 1837 and, in 1841, married 20-year-old Patsy Ann, formerly enslaved in Shelby County, **Kentucky**. As a major Underground Railroad operative, Harris was a prime target of the white mob violence that drove George **DeBaptiste** and John Lott from Madison in the late 1840s. However, Harris remained and, in 1849, organized the Second Baptist Church (later St. Paul's Baptist Church). While preaching the Gospel, he and his sons assumed the major responsibility in his region for transporting **fugitive slaves** across the Ohio River.

Along with being a minister, Harris was also a skilled blacksmith and applied his trade to fashion a unique and memorable signaling system — he hung an anvil in a tree and struck it to alert fugitive slaves hiding on the Kentucky side of the Ohio River that he and his sons planned to make a crossing. He and his associates were deadly serious about their work. As one example, when John Simmons, another African American, divulged crucial and incriminating information regarding Underground Railroad operations in the area, Harris "led a group of men who nearly whipped Simmons to death. Apparently, the only thing that saved the informant's life was that he bit part of Harris' lip off." (Crenshaw, 1993: 31.) Harris was arrested, tried, convicted and fined for this beating.

He was arrested again in **Louisville,** Kentucky, largely by chance, in November 1856. The records of his brief day in court provide both a description and an indication of how dangerous both he and the Madison area were perceived in Louisville. Harris was bound for Charleston, but when strong winds blew his steamboat to the Louisville shore,

Chapman Harris, a huge free Negro, black as the ace of spades, was found in this city — by Officer Ray ... He arrested him, and, on searching him, he was found to be armed with a deadly bowie knife, a pistol, Lucifer matches and powder and ball in abundance. The fellow is a preacher from some where back of Madison, Ind., where he is said to be an active member of the Freedom Party. [*Louisville Courier*, November 25,1856 in Hudson, 2002: 151.]

Although setting foot in Louisville was no crime, Harris was nonetheless "held to bail in the amount of $200" and ordered to leave the state.

One of the most tantalizing — although insufficiently corroborated — associations in Harris's long career involved the militant white abolitionist, John **Brown**. According to local sources, in the summer of 1859, a secret meeting was held behind Harris's cabin between Brown and more than a dozen African Americans from the Trimble County area. At this meeting, the African Americans present shared with Brown their plans for an insurrection in Trimble and the surrounding area. Such a plan was not as outlandish and implausible as it might seem — given the repeated rumors of large-scale conspiracies that swept the South in the **1850s** and the nearby Henry County, Kentucky, "Negro Plot" of 1854 (a conspiracy of several enslaved African Americans to murder the Herndon family and possibly others). Brown persuaded them to postpone their uprising until the larger revolt — that Brown would attempt to initiate at **Harpers Ferry** in October of that same year — began. Whether this meeting ever occurred is problematic. However, documents captured after the Harpers Ferry raid were sufficiently alarming to prompt federal authorities to issue a warning to the governor of Kentucky. Harris died in 1902. *See also* Appendixes 1 and 2.

FURTHER READING

Coon, Diane P. *Southeastern Indiana's Underground Railroad Routes and Operations*. Indianapolis, IN: Indiana Department of Natural Resources, 2001.

Crenshaw, Gwendolyn J. *Bury Me in a Free Land: The Abolitionist Movement in Indiana, 1816–1865*. Indianapolis: Indiana Historical Bureau, 1993.

Hudson, J. Blaine. *Fugitive Slaves and the Underground Railroad in the Kentucky Borderland*. Jefferson, NC: McFarland, 2002.

Harris, Eliza

Fugitive slave. While accounts of slave escapes are strewn throughout antebellum historical sources, few have been immortalized in significant works of American literature. One of the rare exceptions concerns Eliza Harris, a famous fugitive whose daring escape from bondage in **Kentucky** was central to *Uncle Tom's Cabin* (1852) — so much so that she is often presumed to be a fictional character and that separating the person from the character is difficult.

Eliza Harris was enslaved in the region surrounding Maysville, Kentucky, in about 1830. According to Harriet Beecher **Stowe** and the Reverend John **Rankin**, she bore three children, two of whom died in infancy. She was strongly attached to her remaining child, a two-year old son. When Harris learned that her owner planned to sell her son, she fled Kentucky immediately although it was winter and there was no time for planning or other preparations. Upon reaching the **Ohio River**, she found the ice broken and, having no other means of crossing to free territory, she jumped onto the ice with her child. By crawling, jumping and lifting herself and her child from one cake of ice to another she finally reached the **Ohio** side of the river.

Harris was then guided to nearby Ripley, Ohio, and the home of the Reverend Rankin. After she and her son recovered from their ordeal, she was conveyed to **Cincinnati** and then to the home of Levi **Coffin** in Newport, **Indiana**, where she remained for the next two weeks. With Coffin's assistance, she was transported next to Underground Railroad stations in Cabin Creek, near Georgetown in Randolph County (Indiana); to Pennville in Jay County; to Greenville, Ohio; to Sandusky — and then Chatham, **Canada**.

Interestingly, John Rankin, Jr., who worked for many years with his father and brothers to assist **fugitive slaves**, remembered a slightly different and, perhaps, more human Eliza Harris. According the younger Rankin, Eliza escaped with her youngest child and her husband. She then returned and rescued her other children — who had not been sold, but who remained in slavery in Kentucky. Rankin, Jr. also remembered her as a strong and stout woman, rather than a "delicate quadroon."

Although little else is known of Harris's life after slavery, what is known suggests that her story, unlike so many others, had a comparatively happy ending. In 1854, Levi Coffin, his wife and daughter visited some of the African American settlements in Canada West and encountered many of the thousands of fugitives they had assisted over the previous 30 years. At one meeting, "...a woman came up to Mrs. Coffin, seized her hand and exclaimed, 'How are you, Aunt Katie? God bless you!' Mrs. Coffin did not recognize her at first, then found it was Eliza Harris, whom she had befriended at her home in Newport years ago ... The Coffins visited Eliza in her home and found her comfortable and contented."

See also Underground Railroad, Stations on.

FURTHER READING
Coffin, Levi. *Reminiscences of Levi Coffin.* New York: Augustus M. Kelley, 1876.
Griffler, Keith. "Beyond the Quest for the 'Real Eliza Harris': Fugitive Slave Women in the Ohio Valley." *Ohio Valley History* 3(2003): 3–16.
Hudson, J. Blaine. *Fugitive Slaves and the Underground Railroad in the Kentucky Borderland.* Jefferson, NC: McFarland, 2002.
Stowe, Harriet Beecher. *Uncle Tom's Cabin.* 1852. Reprint, New York: Modern Library, 1996.

Haviland, Laura S. (1808–1898)

Abolitionist and friend of the fugitive. Laura Smith was born December 20, 1808, in Kitley Township, Ontario, **Canada**, the daughter of the Reverend Daniel Smith and Sene Blancher Smith, staunch members of the Society of Friends. She married Charles Haviland, Jr. on November 3, 1825 in Niagara County, New York, and lived for a time in nearby Royalton Township. In September 1829, she and her husband moved to Michigan Territory and settled in Raisin near her parents. Haviland's two oldest children were born before her move to Michigan; the younger six were all born on the Michigan frontier.

Drawn to antislavery work, Haviland grew too radical for the **Quakers** in the area and soon withdrew from the Society of Friends. After becoming Wesleyan Methodists, Laura and Charles set up the first Underground Railroad station in Michigan in 1834. In 1837 she established the Raisin Institute, one of the first manual labor schools in the United States open to African Americans. Both the institute, which continued its operations until 1864, and her home became havens to fugitive slaves, and she assisted over one hundred freedom seekers during her time in Raisin.

In 1845, Haviland's mother, father, husband and two daughters all died in an erysipelas epidemic. She responded to this unimaginable tragedy by devoting the remainder of her life entirely to the service of others. She assisted Levi **Coffin** with his Underground Railroad work in **Cincinnati** in the **1850s**, and even paid a memorable visit to the Reverend Calvin **Fairbank** in a **Louisville** jail after his arrest for assisting a fugitive slave in 1853. During the **Civil War**, Haviland worked as a hospital inspector and became a key figure in the Freedmen's Aid movement. After the Civil War, she was instrumental in helping to relocate freedmen to Kansas. Haviland died in April 1898, in Grand Rapids, Michigan. *See also* Abolitionist Movement; and Appendixes 1 and 2.

FURTHER READING
Haviland, Laura S. *A Woman's Life Work: Labors and Experiences of Laura S. Haviland.* Chicago: Publishing Association of Friends, 1889.

Hayden, Lewis (1811–1889)

Fugitive slave and friend of the fugitive. Lewis Hayden, the head of the family assisted to freedom by Delia **Webster** and Calvin **Fairbank**, was born enslaved in Lexington, **Kentucky**, in 1811, "a slave upon a plantation, brought up under the humiliating influences of the slave driver's lash." (Strangis, 1999: 1.) His mother was beaten into insanity for rejecting the sexual advances of her owner and Hayden himself was sold away from his family and passed through a series of owners over several decades. Not surprisingly, Hayden's experiences with Kentucky **slavery** left him an implacable foe of the institution.

Hayden "married" Esther Harvey, who was the property of a different owner, in the 1830s. After she bore a son, her owner's business failed and Esther and her child were sold to Henry Clay. Clay soon sold them and Hayden never saw them again. Hayden then "married" Harriet Bell, who already had a four-year-old son. By 1844, Hayden, who was then working as a waiter at the Phoenix Hotel, came to fear that he would be sold away. Since he had lost one family, it was not difficult to persuade him to attempt a group escape.

Hayden was already acquainted with Webster and confided his desire to escape to her. Webster put Hayden in contact with Calvin Fairbank, who then traveled to Ripley and arranged an escape with the Reverend John **Rankin**. On September 28, 1844, the Hayden family set out for free territory in a rented carriage accompanied by Webster, Fairbank and another fugitive. The party reached Ripley and moved four miles north to a farm at Red Oak, **Ohio**, where Fairbank bid them farewell. Fairbank and Webster were apprehended on their return to Lexington, but the Hayden family remained free.

Hayden settled, initially, in **Canada** West, but moved to Detroit in 1845 and then to **Boston** in 1846. There, he remained and became a staunch antislavery leader—famous (or infamous) in the **1850s** for his active opposition to and refusal to obey the **Fugitive Slave Act of 1850**. For example, Hayden defended William and Ellen **Craft**, the young southern couple who escaped slavery by Ellen posing as a sick white man and William posing as "his" servant. He led the rescue of Shadrack, in which the antislavery community of Boston fought to prevent the return of a fugitive slave to his owner. Hayden later assisted in recruiting African Americans for service in the **Civil War** and remained a highly and widely respected black leader until his death in 1889.

Frederick **Douglass** became well acquainted with Hayden in the 1850s and described him as "the Kentucky fugitive who has with him all that is noble and gallant of his native state, and has left behind him the last vestige of slavery." For his role in the Shadrach rescue, Douglass deemed Hayden a "warm hearted, fearless man" who, along with his wife, would stand with his "suffering people" to the last. (Frederick Douglass Paper, August 26, 1853 in Hudson, 2002: 136.) *See also* Appendixes 1 and 2.

FURTHER READING

Hudson, J. Blaine. *Fugitive Slaves and the Underground Railroad in the Kentucky Borderland.* Jefferson, NC: McFarland, 2002.

Robboy, Stanley J., and Anita W. Robboy. "Lewis Hayden: From Fugitive Slave to Statesman." *New England Quarterly* 46(1973): 591–613.

Schwartz, Harold. "Fugitive Slave Days in Boston." *New England Quarterly* 27, no. 2(1954): 191–212.

Strangis, Joel. *Lewis Hayden and the War Against Slavery.* North Haven, CT: Linnet Books, 1999.

Hayes, William (d. 1849)

Friend of the fugitive. William Hayes moved to the **Illinois** frontier from New York in 1832, settling first in Peoria and eventually in Randolph County in the southwestern section of the state. Hayes worked as a dairy farmer and small-scale land speculator. As a Covenanter, Hayes was committed to the antislavery cause. His home became an Underground Railroad station and Hayes himself conducted **fugitive slaves** on numerous occasions.

Largely unknown, except for an occasional court record when Hayes was accused of **enticing** or **harboring**, his role as an active friend of the fugitive is documented copiously by letters, dating from the early 1820s to the time of his death in 1849, describing his activities in detail. These letters were hidden in a desk owned by his descendants and treasured as a family heirloom — and not discovered until 1989. *See also* Underground Railroad, Stations on; Appendixes 1 and 2.

FURTHER READING

Pirtle, Carol. "A Flight to Freedom: A True Story of the Underground Railroad in Illinois." *Ohio Valley History* 3(2003).

Haynes, James

Friend of the fugitive in Randolph County, **Illinois**. *See also* Louisville, Kentucky; and Appendixes 1 and 2.

Henderson, Richard (b. 1801)

Fugitive and friend of the fugitive. Richard Henderson was born enslaved in Hagerstown, Maryland. In 1816, he escaped from slavery with his sister and two brothers. His sister contracted pneumonia and died, but the brothers reached safety in Meadville, **Pennsylvania**.

Henderson later became a barber and was believed to have assisted as many as five hundred **fugitive slaves**. He counted John **Brown** among his friends and was considered one of the most effective friends of the fugitive in northwestern Pennsylvania. *See also* Underground Railroad, Sites of; and Appendixes 3 and 4.

Henderson Lewelling House (Salem, Iowa)

Underground Railroad site recognized and documented by the National Park Service. *See also* Appendix 5.

Henry, William "Jerry"

Fugitive slave. William "Jerry" Henry escaped from **slavery** in Marion County, near Hannibal, Missouri, and arrived in Syracuse, New York, in the late 1840s, where he found work in a barrel shop. Widely known to be a fugitive slave, Henry was seized by federal marshals on October 1, 1851.

At the time, Syracuse was hosting a convention of the Liberty Party and some historians believe the arrest was timed to embarrass the abolitionists—who viewed Syracuse as an unassailable refuge for **fugitive slaves**. In the background loomed the figures of Daniel Webster, the U.S. secretary of state who had warned Syracuse residents that helping runaway slaves was an act of treason—and, of course, President Millard Fillmore, the Cayuga County, New York native who signed the **Fugitive Slave Act of 1850**.

When news of the arrest reached the convention, the abolitionists rushed to the office of U.S. Commissioner Joseph Sabine, where Henry was being held. After a large crowd gathered around the commissioner's office, Henry made a desperate escape attempt, diving down the stairs and into the street, and racing along the Erie Canal. Unfortunately, he was overtaken and recaptured on a bridge over the canal "and after a stiff fight the battered and disheveled prisoner was returned to the commissioner's office. (Quarles, 1969: 210.)

Henry was moved to the office of the police justice and, again, a large crowd gathered, this time with some people throwing stones and breaking windows. At this point, a group of leading abolitionists—including the great black abolitionist the Reverend Jermain **Loguen**, himself a former fugitive slave; famed lawyer Gerrit **Smith**, one of the richest men in the state; and Samuel J. **May**, an activist Unitarian minister, met at a nearby doctor's office to plan their next move. Determined to send a message to the nation that the Fugitive Slave Act would not apply in Syracuse, they rejoined the crowd—now armed with clubs and axes—in Clinton Square at about 8:00 P.M. Around 8:30 P.M., a battering ram appeared and a marshal fired into the crowd, injuring one man. As the crowd grew larger, louder and angrier, the sheriff from Missouri released the shackled Henry.

Henry was then placed in a buggy and driven away on a journey with several stops. In 1894 Susan Watkins, who was 16 years old at the time, recalled that she and her family removed Henry's shackles and dressed him in women's clothing to disguise him. Henry finally found shelter in the home of Caleb Davis, spent four days recuperating and then was hidden in a covered wagon and driven north. He eventually reached Kingston, Ontario, found work and married, but died of tuberculosis two years later.

Thirteen men were indicted in the uprising—nine whites and four blacks. Only one, a black man named Enoch Reed, was convicted. Two of the men who captured Henry were also arrested for kidnapping a citizen of Syracuse. Neither was convicted. *See also* Canada.

FURTHER READING

Quarles, Benjamin. *Black Abolitionists*. New York: Oxford University Press, 1969.

Roach, Monique P. "The Rescue of William 'Jerry' Henry: Antislavery and Racism in the Burned-over District." *New York History* 82, no. 3(2001): 135–154.

Henson, Josiah (1789–1883)

Fugitive slave and friend of the fugitive. Josiah Henson was born enslaved in Charles County, Maryland, on June 15, 1789. Henson was one of six children. Henson's father beat the overseer of their plantation after the overseer assaulted Henson's mother, and was then brutally beaten and maimed himself, after which he was sold into Alabama.

With his father gone, Henson's mother returned to the plantation of her owner, Dr. Josiah McPherson, after whom Josiah Henson was named. Under the influence of his devoutly Christian mother, Henson developed both intellectually and spiritually into an upright man and became a respected plantation manager and minister.

Henson had an opportunity to escape **slavery** in April 1825 when he conveyed 18 other enslaved African Americans by river from Maryland to Davies County, **Kentucky.** A black man conveying other enslaved African Americans to another place of enslavement was a novel, if not unsettling, sight and, stopping near **Cincinnati,** Ohio, Henson was pressed by many free people of color to escape from slavery. Henson demurred, thinking more at the time of freedom through self-purchase than by flight, but in later years recalled:

> Under the influence of these impressions, and seeing that the allurements of the crowd were producing a manifest effect, I sternly assumed the captain, and ordered the boat to be pushed off into the stream. A shower of curses followed me from the shore; but the Negroes under me, accustomed to obey, and, alas! too degraded and ignorant of the advantages of liberty to know what they were forfeiting, offered no resistance to my command ... Often since that day has my soul been pierced with bitter anguish at the thought of having been thus instrumental in consigning to the infernal bondage of slavery so many of my fellow-beings ... Having experienced myself the sweetness of liberty, and knowing too well the after misery of a great majority of them, my infatuation has seemed to me an unpardonable sin. But I console myself with the thought that I acted according to my best light, though the light that was in me was darkness. [Hartgrove, 1918: 4–5.]

Henson remained in Kentucky for three years. However, in 1828, by now a minister recognized by the Methodist Episcopal Church, he was assisted by a white Methodist preacher in devising a plan to gain his freedom. On his return to Maryland, Henson raised funds for self-purchase — and was particularly successful at the Methodist Conference in Chillicothe, **Ohio.** In 1830, only after his owner reneged on a self-purchase agreement did Henson finally escape to Upper **Canada** with his wife and four children.

According to his autobiography, he ventured secretly into Kentucky twice to lead other enslaved African Americans to freedom, and even as an aging man was an occasional conductor on the Underground Railroad. However, he became far better known as the model for the character Uncle Tom in Harriett Beecher **Stowe's** *Uncle Tom's Cabin.* Before he died in 1883, he visited England, was presented to Queen Victoria and spoke to large crowds anxious to hear "the original Uncle Tom." *See also* Appendixes 1 and 2.

FURTHER READING
Hartgrove, W. B. "The Story of Josiah Henson." *Journal of Negro History* 3(1918): 1–21.
Henson, Josiah. *Truth Is Stranger than Fiction. Father Henson's Story of His Own Life.* Boston: J.P. Jewett, 1858.

Hickory Hill (Junction, Illinois)

Underground Railroad site 28 miles from Mount Vernon, **Indiana**, and about 10 miles from **Kentucky**. Also known as the **Old Slave House** and the Crenshaw House, Hickory Hill was the site of a station on the Underground Railroad that operated in reverse. There, John **Crenshaw** kidnapped free persons of color and captured **fugitive slaves**, and sold them into **slavery**. *See also* Free People of Color; Underground Railroad, Sites of; and Appendixes 3 and 4.

Higginson, The Reverend Thomas

See Burns, Anthony

Hillyer, Elisha

Friend of the fugitive in **Louisville, Kentucky**. *See also* Appendixes 1 and 2.

Hise, Daniel Howell (b. 1813)

An important abolitionist and friend of the fugitive, Daniel Howell Hise was born in 1813 in the Quaker community of Salem, **Ohio**. In the 1840s, he became actively involved in the **abolitionist movement** and both he and his wife, Margaret, were members of the Western Anti-Slavery Society located in Salem.

Hise purchased a home in the late **1850s** that served as a station on the Underground

Railroad in Salem. Hise hosted frequent anti-slavery meetings and his antislavery convictions were so strong that he even helped erect a monument to Edwin Coppock, executed for his participation in John **Brown**'s Raid on **Harpers Ferry** in 1859.

See also Fugitive Slaves; Daniel Howell Hise House; Quakers; Underground Railroad, Sites of.

Hitchcock, George B. (1812–1872)

A key friend of the fugitive in the early West, George B. Hitchcock was born in **Massachusetts** in 1812. Hitchcock studied for the ministry, was ordained by the Congregational Church in 1844, and then traveled for several years as a circuit preacher along the western **Iowa** frontier.

In the mid–**1850s**, Hitchcock settled in Lewis, Iowa, and built a log cabin where he lived until the completion of his stone house around 1856. This house served as an Underground Railroad station for freedom seekers escaping from Missouri and Kansas. After the Civil War, Hitchcock moved first to Missouri and then to Kansas to work with African American freedmen. He died in 1872. *See also* George B. Hitchcock House; Underground Railroad, Sites of.

Holmes, Robin, and Polly Holmes

Fugitive slaves. In 1845, Nathaniel Ford journeyed to Oregon, accompanied by Robin Holmes, probably a free man of color, and Polly, an enslaved African American woman. Holmes and Polly married and had several children, all of whom were claimed as Ford's property.

In 1853, Robin and Polly Holmes attempted to leave Ford. When Ford threatened to deny them their children, Robin Holmes filed a writ of *habeus corpus* to obtain their custody. Judge George Williams ordered Ford to bring the children to court and show cause for their detention.

When the Holmes case came to trial in the summer of 1853, Judge Williams ruled that slavery did not exist under Oregon law when Robin and Polly Holmes entered the territory and that they, and their children, were free. This interpretation of the law and the U.S. Constitution would soon be challenged in the 1857 Dred Scott Decision. *See also* Dred Scott v. Sandford; Free People of Color; Underground Railroad, Sites of; and Appendixes 3 and 4.

Honeycomb AME Church (Lima, Pennsylvania)

Underground Railroad site. Founded in 1852 and located in the small African American community of Lima, the Honeycomb AME Church served as an Underground Railroad station in the late antebellum period. *See also* Underground Railroad, Sites of; Underground Railroad, Stations on; and Appendixes 3 and 4.

Hopper, Isaac T. (1771–1852)

Friend of the fugitive. Born in Gloucester County, New Jersey, on December 3, 1771, Isaac T. Hopper learned the tailor's trade from an uncle in **Philadelphia**. As a boy, he joined the **Quakers** and, by 1787, was assisting **fugitive slaves**. Later, Hopper became an active

Isaac Hopper, 1853 engraving (Library of Congress)

member of the Pennsylvania Abolition Society and gained a reputation for his willingness to defend the rights of African Americans—both those who were free and those who were fugitive slaves.

As an example, Hopper aided the Reverend Richard **Allen**, founder of the African Methodist Episcopal Church and one of the most influential figures in African American history, when Allen was falsely arrested in Philadelphia as a fugitive slave. Hopper paid for Allen's defense and, after a short trial, Allen was released.

Hopper was also one of the founders of a society for the employment of the poor and an overseer of the Benezet School for black children, and taught free blacks himself without compensation. In 1829, he moved to New York to manage a bookstore established by his fellow Quakers. A poor man with a large family, Hopper's home was nonetheless a station on the Underground Railroad.

Hopper died in **New York City** on May 7, 1852. *See also* Underground Railroad, Sites of; and Appendixes 1–4.

Horse, John

Friend of the fugitive in Florida. *See also* Black Seminoles; and Appendixes 1 and 2.

Hossack, John (1806–1891)

An abolitionist and friend of the fugitive, John Hossack was born in Scotland on December 6, 1806. He moved to **Canada** in 1818 and worked in his uncle's confectionery in Quebec. Once an adult, he opened his own business and, in 1833, married Martha Lens. Hossack next became employed in public works and for several years was a contractor on the "Long Soo" canal on the St. Lawrence River. In 1838, he moved to Chicago and secured contracts for the construction of the Illinois and Michigan canal. When work on the canal ceased and his funds were exhausted, Hossack opened a prairie farm in Cook county, near a fine grove, afterwards known as Hossack's Grove.

Hossack was fearless and outspoken in his opposition to **slavery**, and his farm became a haven for **fugitive slaves**. In 1849, he moved to Ottawa, **Illinois**, and opened a lumber business, shortly afterwards adding the business of buying and shipping grain to Chicago. In 1854, he erected a mansion that was used as an Underground Railroad station, and it was not unusual for Hossack to accommodate five to 10 fugitive slaves at any given time.

On September 4, 1859, Jim Grey, one of three slaves who had escaped from Richard Phillips, a planter living near Madrid, Missouri, was captured in Union County and imprisoned under the state law. Grey was rescued by local abolitionists—with Hossack being among their leaders. For this act, Hossack and several others were indicted by the federal grand jury and all but two were jailed in Chicago. They refused to post bail, but most were released a few days later on their own recognizance. John Hossack and Dr. Stout were convicted and sentenced to pay a $100 fine and to 10 days in prison. Hossack proceeded to deliver a bold antislavery address that became so widely known that he was later "feasted and banqueted" by the mayor of Chicago and nominated for governor of Illinois on the Abolition ticket.

Hossack continued to prosper in the grain and lumber business in Ottawa until 1873, when he became totally blind and retired from active life. He died on November 8, 1891.

FURTHER READING
"In Memoriam: John Hossack, Deceased November 8, 1891." *The Republican Times* (Ottawa, Illinois), 1892.

House of Many Stairs (Pennsdale, Pennsylvania)

Underground Railroad site. The House of Many Stairs was once known as Bull's Tavern, and served as an antebellum stage-coach stop and inn. Although only a two-story house, the building had seven staircases—with five steps leading into and out of each room. Edward Morris, the operator of the tavern, used this unique architectural feature to conceal **fugitive slaves** from their pursuers. *See also* Underground Railroad, Sites of; and Appendixes 3 and 4.

Houston, Thomas Jefferson (b. 1829)

Fugitive slave and friend of the fugitive. Thomas Jefferson Hunn was born enslaved on

August 10, 1829 in **Kentucky**. Later sold into Missouri, Hunn finally escaped after repeated attempts and settled in Springfield, **Illinois**, changing his name from Hunn to Houston. Houston used his home in Springfield as a station on the Underground Railroad and ventured into slave territory on several occasions to free members of his family. He also helped found the **Zion Baptist Missionary Church**.

Charles Hamilton Houston, architect of the NAACP legal strategy that culminated in the 1954 *Brown v. Topeka Board of Education* decision, is one of Houston's descendants. *See also* Underground Railroad, Sites of; Underground Railroad, Stations on; and Appendixes 1–4.

Hoyt, Benjamin

Friend of the fugitive in **Madison, Indiana**. *See also* Appendixes 1 and 2.

Hubbard, William

Friend of the fugitive in Ashtabula, **Ohio**. *See also* Colonel William Hubbard House. *See also* Appendixes 1 and 2.

Huber, Charles B. "Boss" (d. 1854)

Friend of the fugitive in Williamsburg, **Ohio**. *See also* Charles B. Huber Homesite.

Huckleberry Finn

Classic and controversial novel by Mark Twain (Samuel J. Clemens, 1835–1910). In October 1851, a dramatic fugitive slave rescue in Syracuse, New York — known as the Jerry Rescue (*see* **Henry, William "Jerry"**) — electrified the nation. Among those touched by it was writer Samuel Clemens, later known as Mark Twain, who visited Syracuse in 1853 and remarked in a letter to his mother, "...when I saw the Court House in Syracuse, it called to mind the time when it was surrounded with chains and companies of soldiers to prevent the rescue ... by the infernal abolitionists."

As the years passed, Clemens' views, so typical of "an ignorant white boy who was raised in a slave state," evolved as he wrestled with the questions inherent in the Jerry Rescue. Some of this change is reflected in *Huckleberry Finn,* written in 1884.

Ernest Hemingway considered *The Adventures of Huckleberry Finn* the source of all American literature. To Twain's critics, the novel is patently racist because the word "nigger" appears throughout. On the other hand, Twain's defenders argue that since the book is set in the South 20 years before the **Civil War**, the use of the term is authentic, although offensive, and that, oddly enough, the book itself is about nothing less than freedom and the quest for freedom. At its heart, *Huckleberry Finn* is the story of a fugitive slave, Jim, who risks his life to win his freedom and be reunited with his family, and a white boy, Huckleberry Finn, who becomes his friend and ultimately helps him escape.

Because of his upbringing, Huck believes that **slavery** is simply part of the natural order, yet, as the saga unfolds, he too wrestles with his conscience — and, when faced with the crucial moment of decision, he decides he will be damned rather than betray his black friend. Similarly, Jim, as Twain presents him, is no "Black Sambo." Rather, he is the moral center of the book, a man of courage and nobility, who risks his freedom and his life for the sake of his friend Huck.

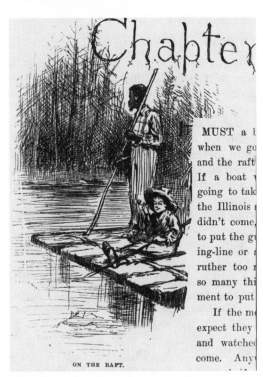

Huckleberry Finn and Jim on a raft in *Huckleberry Finn,* 1885. (Library of Congress)

African Americans have long held conflicting opinions about the book. Notwithstanding contemporary critics, Booker T. Washington once noted how Twain "succeeded in making his readers feel a genuine respect for Jim," and added that Twain, in creating Jim's character, had "exhibited his sympathy and interest in the masses of the negro people." (Fishkin, 1993: 105.) More recently, the great black novelist Ralph Ellison noted how Twain allowed Jim's "dignity and human capacity" to emerge in the novel — noting that "Huckleberry Finn knew, as did Mark Twain, that Jim was not only a slave but a human being [and] a symbol of humanity ... and in freeing Jim, Huck makes a bid to free himself of the conventionalized evil taken for civilization," i.e., slavery and racism. (Ellison, 1964: 50.)

FURTHER READING

Chadwick-Joshua, Jocelyn. *The Jim Dilemma: Reading Race in Huckleberry Finn.* Jackson: University Press of Mississippi, 1998.

Ellison, Ralph. *Shadow and Act.* New York: Random House, 1964.

Fishkin, Shelley Fisher. *Was Huck Black? Mark Twain and African American Voices.* New York: Oxford University Press, 1993.

Hudson, John W.

Friend of the fugitive. John Hudson, a free person of color, lived in Sardinia, **Ohio**, a small settlement 25 miles north of the Maysville, **Kentucky**, and Ripley, Ohio, fugitive slave crossing. Working directly or indirectly with the Reverend John **Rankin** and John **Parker**, Hudson was a key Underground Railroad conductor between 1834 and the **Civil War**. Described as "a powerful man with courage," he routinely traveled "on foot, horseback or by wagon" to assist fugitives and was paid wages by white abolitionists. *See also* Abolitionist Movement; and Appendixes 1 and 2.

FURTHER READING

Hudson, J. Blaine. *Fugitive Slaves and the Underground Railroad in the Kentucky Borderland.* Jefferson, NC: McFarland, 2002.

Hunn, John (1818–1894)

A friend of the fugitive, John Hunn was a Quaker, born in 1818, who assisted **fugitive slaves** in the 1840s and **1850s** through the Ap-

poquinimink Friends Meeting House near Odessa, Delaware. There he worked closely with fellow Quaker **John Alston**, and **Samuel Burris**, a free African American Underground Railroad conductor who led fugitive slaves from Delaware and Maryland into **Pennsylvania**.

In 1847, Hunn's neighbors reported his clandestine activities to the local authorities and he was sued by the owners of several fugitive slaves. Hunn was fined $2,500 and was forced to sell his farm, but continued his antislavery work thereafter. *See also* Appendixes 1 and 2.

FURTHER READING

Still, William. *The Underground Railroad.* 1872. Reprint, Chicago: Johnson, 1970.

Hunn, Jonathan

Friend of the fugitive in Dover, Delaware. *See also* Great Geneva; Wildcat Manor; and Appendixes 1 and 2.

Hurlburt, Lyman

Friend of the fugitive in Farmington, Connecticut. *See also* Appendixes 1 and 2.

Hussey, Erastus (b. 1800)

Friend of the fugitive. Erastus Hussey migrated to Michigan from New York in 1824 and purchased land in Wayne County. In 1839, he and his wife, Sarah, purchased a building in Battle Creek, Michigan, as a dry goods store and residence. As a Quaker, Hussey was committed to the antislavery cause and, by 1840, his home became a focal point of Underground Railroad operations in Battle Creek. There, he coordinated his efforts with other **friends of the fugitive**, including fugitive slave Samuel Strauther, who settled in Battle Creek after escaping **slavery**. Hussey served in the state legislature in the **1850s** as a member of the Free Soil Party and, on July 6, 1854, attended the convention in Jackson, Michigan, at which the Republican Party was founded.

When interviewed in 1885, Hussey described the Underground Railroad routes beginning in Cass County and running through central Michigan, with stations spaced 12 to 15 miles apart. He noted that, after 1855, **fugitive**

slaves tended to choose shorter routes through **Ohio**. Describing his own work, he stated "I have fed and given protection to over 1,000 fugitives, and assisted them on to Canada." When asked if any stationmasters received any compensation, Hussey answered simply, "No ... We were working for humanity." *See also* Canada; Quakers; and Appendixes 1 and 2.

FURTHER READING
"Battle Creek Remembers the Underground Railroad." *Michigan History Magazine* 78(1994): 40–41.

Hyde, Udney

Friend of the fugitive in Mechanicsburg, **Ohio**. *See also* White, Addison; and Appendixes 1 and 2.

Illinois

Illinois was part of the Northwest Territory in which **slavery** was prohibited under the provisions of the 1787 Northwest Ordinance. The southern section of the territory was bounded by two slave states— Missouri and **Kentucky**— and was settled earliest and largely by settlers with southern origins who brought their slaveholding proclivities to the Western frontier after the War of 1812. Through their influence, although slavery was illegal, long-term indenture arrangements were used as a quasi-legal form of slavery until the 1840s.

In contrast to the populations of **Indiana** and **Ohio**, Illinois had relatively few residents in 1850 and, in many respects, was only emerging from its frontier period. Of its 851,470 persons, only 5,436 (0.64 percent) were African Americans who, other than a few concentrations, were scattered very thinly across the state.

After 1820, the proslavery element in southern Illinois was joined by a new wave of settlers from the East with decidedly antislavery views. These newcomers "were quite willing to assist a slave escaping from bondage" and, by 1837, some loosely organized assistance was available to **fugitive slaves**. (Spicer, 1925: 8.)

Only a few Illinois counties were home to a sufficient number of **free people of color** to constitute small and marginal communities.

While extreme southern Illinois would seem a natural escape route for fugitives from the Jackson Purchase region of far western Kentucky and from **Tennessee**, this section of the state also had a reputation for intense hostility to African Americans and was home to relatively few free people of color; this region held many dangers and little help. As a consequence, Illinois was not a particularly attractive escape route for Kentucky fugitives. However, fugitives from slavery in eastern Missouri had better options—central Illinois, **Iowa** or one of the major rivers.

Three major fugitive slave escape routes extended across Illinois. One began at Chester, another at Alton and the other at Quincy. These served fugitives crossing Illinois's much longer Mississippi River border with Missouri, and all converged ultimately at Chicago. The third route from far western Kentucky contributed far fewer fugitives. This section of Illinois was simply smaller both in area and in African American population— and movement eastward by land or river to Indiana or Ohio was more attractive. Still, the flow of fugitive slaves from Kentucky into Illinois was not altogether insignificant. These runaways used two lesser known branch routes. The first led from Cairo northward to Springfield. The second and probably more important one followed the course of the Wabash River into Indiana. *See also* Underground Railroad, Sites of; and Appendixes 3 and 4.

FURTHER READING
Hudson, J. Blaine. *Fugitive Slaves and the Underground Railroad in the Kentucky Borderland.* Jefferson, NC: McFarland, 2002.
Mahoney, Olivia. "Black Abolitionists." *Chicago History* 20(1991): 22–37.
Spicer, Carl L. "The Underground Railroad in Southern Illinois," the Underground Railroad in Illinois, 1925. Wilbur H. Siebert Papers, Vol.1, Box 71, Ohio Historical Society.

Indiana

In the 1700s, enslaved African Americans were found in colonial French settlements such as Vincennes, in what would become Indiana. After the French and Indian War (1754–1763), the British gained control of the territory, but did little to dislodge the French settlers therein or to disturb the much larger Native American population. In 1779, when General George Rogers Clark captured Vincennes, the entire Northwest Territory — the future states of Indiana, **Illinois, Ohio,** Michigan and Wisconsin — became first the property of Virginia and, after 1783, the property of the newly fledged United States.

In 1787, the Northwest Ordinance (Article IV) outlawed **slavery** in this vast region — ensuring that, since slavery had already taken root in **Kentucky,** the **Ohio River** would become the boundary between free and slave territory in the early West. Despite this legal prohibition, most African Americans in Indiana remained enslaved through the territorial period. This seeming contradiction was permitted under a rather creative interpretation of Article IV that limited its application to African Americans brought into the territory

Frederick Douglass resists an Indiana mob. (Library of Congress)

and exempted those already there. Only Indiana's admission to the Union in 1816 finally ended all forms of legal servitude.

During the territorial and early statehood periods, Indiana was settled primarily along the Ohio and Wabash Rivers. Most early settlements were in the southern section of the state and, not surprisingly, white southerners were most numerous among these early pioneers—bringing with them servitude of one sort or another and their southern racial attitudes. In later years, the central and more northerly Indiana counties were settled predominantly by northerners or European immigrants—creating, in essence, two distinct zones in the state with respect to racial attitudes.

With generally hostile territory on both sides of the Ohio River, the location of **friends of the fugitive** was critically important to **fugitive slaves** moving into and through this region. One set of potential friends comprised southern whites who objected to slavery and moved to Indiana precisely because it was free territory—some emancipating their enslaved African Americans and others even transporting them to Indiana as well. These early antislavery families, of which **Quakers** represented a prominent sub-set, settled primarily in the eastern section of the state.

Equally, if not more, important were black Americans themselves. However inhospitable, Indiana was still a free state and, as such, was attractive to the hard-pressed free black population. By 1820, 1,420 African Americans, one percent of Indiana's 146,758 people, claimed residence in the state—increasing to 11,428 in 1860 (0.9 percent of the total state population). Although African Americans living in Indiana were only a small percentage of the state's population, their sheer numbers were far greater than those recorded for Illinois and sufficient to create several small, identifiable communities primarily in the southern sections of the state, such as Evansville, Corydon, New Albany and Jeffersonville (opposite **Louisville**), and **Madison**. Each of these small communities had its own unique character and some were major border crossing, harboring and transfer points for fugitive slaves from and passing through Kentucky.

Before 1850, Indiana's black population included a great many fugitive slaves and many others merely "passed through" Indiana en route to another free state or **Canada**. However, after the passage of the **Fugitive Slave Act of 1850** and the adoption of the 1851 Indiana Constitution, both fugitive slaves and **free people of color** living in Indiana became far more vulnerable to harassment and sometimes kidnapping—particularly those living unprotected along the Ohio River within easy reach of kidnappers and slave-catchers.

As escape became more difficult after 1850, assistance grew correspondingly in importance. In such fluid circumstances, these settlements along the border and throughout the "lower north" became the superstructure for a more sophisticated network of escape routes:

> The first ... was a continuation of the routes from Cincinnati and Lawrenceburg which converged in Wayne County. Thence a main line ran north through Winchester, Portland, Decatur, Fort Wayne, and Auburn into Michigan. The second main line originated from three branches which crossed the Ohio River at Madison, New Albany, and the vicinity of Leavenworth. These converged near Columbus and passed north through Indianapolis, Westfield, Logansport, Plymouth, and South Bend. The third main route crossed the Ohio at Evansville and followed the Wabash River through Terre Haute and then up to Lafayette. [Thornbrough, 1957: 40–41.]

See also Underground Railroad, Sites of; and Appendixes 3 and 4.

FURTHER READING

Crenshaw, Gwendolyn J. *Bury Me in a Free Land: The Abolitionist Movement in Indiana, 1816–1865.* Indianapolis: Indiana Historical Bureau, 1993.

Hudson, J. Blaine. *Fugitive Slaves and the Underground Railroad in the Kentucky Borderland.* Jefferson, NC: McFarland, 2002.

Thornbrough, Emma L. *The Negro in Indiana before 1900.* Bloomington: Indiana University Press, 1957.

Iowa

As a free state bordering the slave territories of Missouri and later Nebraska, Iowa was a seldom acknowledged but important border state. Even before settlement of the territory commenced in 1833, "some fugitives from slave states escaped to Indian communities where they were usually warmly received and often intermarried with the Indians." (Hill, 1982: 290.) The African American population of Iowa was small, with 188 African Americans in 1840, 333 in 1850 and 1,069 by 1860. However, because Iowa was settled largely by northern whites, this comparatively small number of African Americans and a strong faction of antislavery whites made Iowa a land of refuge for **fugitive slaves**.

After 1840, fugitive slaves from Missouri often passed through the southern section of the state on routes that ran northeast to Des Moines, then Grinnell and ultimately to Chicago. Well-documented Underground Railroad stations could be found at Croton, Bloomfield, Lancaster, **Cincinnati**, Farmington and Salem at which fugitive slaves could find a measure of protection from Missouri **slave catchers**. Other freedom seekers remained in Iowa and found work in the lead mines and sawmills of the early settlements, particularly those with **Quakers** nearby, in such areas as Henry and Jefferson Counties. Soon, small free black communities coalesced in DuBuque, Muscatine, and other towns as yet other sources of refuge and assistance for freedom seekers. *See also* Underground Railroad, Sites of; and Appendixes 3 and 4.

FURTHER READING
Dykstra, Robert R. *Bright Radical Star: Black Freedom and White Supremacy on the Hawkeye Frontier.* Cambridge, MA: Harvard University Press, 1993.
Hill, James L. "Migration of Blacks to Iowa, 1820–1960." *Journal of Negro History* 66, no. 4(1982): 289–303.

Jackson, Francis

Friend of the fugitive in Newton, **Massachusetts**. *See also* Jackson Homestead; and Appendixes 1 and 2.

Jackson, William (1783–1855)

A friend of the fugitive, William Jackson was born in Newton, **Massachusetts**, in 1783 and, as an adult, established a soap and candle factory on his family homestead. As a committed **abolitionist**, Jackson used his home as an Underground Railroad station and was assisted by his wife, Mary Bennett Jackson, and their three daughters. Jackson also worked closely with **William Bowditch** of Brookline to move fugitive slaves toward refuge in Canada.

Jackson died in 1855, but his family continued to assist **fugitive slaves** and was active in the freedmen's aid movement during and after the Civil War.

See also Jackson Homestead; Underground Railroad, Sites of; and Appendixes 3 and 4.

FURTHER READING
Siebert, Wilbur H. *The Underground Railroad from Slavery to Freedom.* 1898. Reprint, New York: Russell and Russell, 1967.

Jackson Homestead (Newton, Massachusetts)

Underground Railroad site recognized and documented by the National Park Service. *See also* Appendix 5.

Jacobs, Harriet A. (1813–1897)

Fugitive slave. Harriet Ann Jacobs was born enslaved in 1813 in Edenton, North Carolina. Although in bondage, she passed a placid childhood living with her free grandmother. "[We] lived together in a comfortable home," she wrote in her autobiography, *Incidents in the Life of a Slave Girl* (1861) "and, though we were all slaves, I was so fondly shielded that I never dreamed that I was a piece of merchandise." She even found happiness after her mother's death, when she moved into the home of her mother's owner, who taught Jacobs to read and sew. However, this kind owner died when Jacobs was 11 years old and Jacobs was "inherited" by three-year-old Mary Matilda Norcom. Once in the Norcom household, her young owner's father, Dr. James Norcom, became Jacobs' constant tormentor.

When Jacobs turned 15, Norcom began a relentless campaign of sexual advances. Jacobs rejected him repeatedly but, as time passed, his tactics became increasingly aggressive and, to hide his intentions from his suspicious wife, Norcom even built a cottage for Jacobs a few miles from town. To thwart Norcom's designs, Jacobs conceived a desperate strategy and cultivated a relationship with an unmarried lawyer, Samuel Tredwell Sawyer. From this liaison, Jacobs gave birth to two children,

Joseph and Louisa, in 1829 and 1833 respectively. When Jacobs learned that Norcom planned to sell her children or "send them to the fields," she escaped in June 1835 — but, having devised an unusual strategy, did not travel far.

With Jacobs gone, Norcom agreed to sell her children to Sawyer, who sent them to live with Jacobs' grandmother, Molly Horniblow. Consequently, Jacobs, instead of seeking freedom in the North, hid in a crawlspace above her grandmother's porch for seven years, emerging only for brief periods at night for exercise, and watching her children grow through a peephole.

In 1842, Jacobs made her escape to true freedom, sailing first to **Philadelphia** and then traveling by train to **New York City**, where she was reunited with her daughter who had preceded her. Jacobs later moved to Rochester, New York, to be close to her brother, also a fugitive slave, and became involved with the abolitionists associated with Frederick **Douglass'** paper, the *North Star*. In the following years, she would move back to New York, flee to **Massachusetts** to avoid Dr. Norcom, and finally become legally free after a friend arranged her purchase.

After much persuasion, Jacobs published her autobiography in 1861. Lydia Maria Child wrote the preface and, in the first edition, was listed as editor while Jacobs is referenced by the pseudonym, Linda Brent. The power of Jacobs' experience is undeniable as she writes:

> You never knew what is was like to be a slave; to be entirely unprotected by law or custom; to have the laws reduce you to the condition of a chattel, entirely subject to the will of another. You never exhausted your ingenuity in avoiding the snares, and eluding the power of a hated tyrant; you never shuddered at the sound of his footsteps, and trembled within hearing of his voice.

Jacobs was actively involved with the **abolitionist movement** before the onset of the **Civil War**. During the war she used her celebrity to raise money for black refugees and, after the war, she worked to improve the conditions of black freedmen. She died on March 7, 1897, in **Washington, D.C.**

FURTHER READING
Jacobs, Harriet. *Incidents in the Life of a Slave Girl, Written by Herself*. Boston: Privately printed, 1861.

James, The Reverend Thomas

Friend of the fugitive in Rochester, New York, and **Louisville, Kentucky**. *See also* St. James AME Church; and Appendixes 1 and 2.

James and Sophia Clemens Farmstead (Greenville, Ohio)

Underground Railroad site recognized and documented by the National Park Service. *See also* Appendix 5.

Jerry Rescue

See Henry, William "Jerry"

Jeter, William

Friend of the fugitive in **Louisville, Kentucky**. *See also* Appendixes 1 and 2.

Jewish Friends of the Fugitive

There were comparatively few Jews in the antebellum United States— and only a handful figure in the history of **slavery** or the struggle against it. However, one of the few documented examples of Jewish involvement in the antislavery movement and the Underground Railroad centers around the Jewish community of **Detroit, Michigan**.

Based on research conducted under the auspices of Detroit Temple Beth El, a number of Jewish Detroiters with Underground Railroad ties have been identified including Emil Heineman, Mark Sloman, and Rabbi Leibman Adler. These individuals drew inspiration from the memory of Jewish bondage in Egypt and compared fugitive slaves to the Hebrews fleeing Egypt.

FURTHER READING
Luckerman, Sharon. "Detroit Jews Broke the Law to Help Slaves Escape." *Detroit Jewish News Online* http://jnonline./upsoftware.com.

John B. and Lydia Edwards House (Oswego, New York)

Underground Railroad site recognized and documented by the National Park Service. *See also* Appendix 5.

John Brown, Jr.'s House (Ashtabula County, Ohio)

This Underground Railroad site, located in Ashtabula County, **Ohio**, the home of John

Brown, Jr., was an important staging point for the activities of his militant abolitionist father, John **Brown.** *See also* John Brown's Cabin; John Brown's Farm and Gravesite; John Brown's Headquarters; John Brown's House; Underground Railroad, Sites of; and Appendixes 3 and 4.

John Brown's Cabin (Osawatomie, Kansas)

Underground Railroad site recognized and documented by the National Park Service. *See also* Appendix 5.

John Brown's Cave

See Allen B. Mayhew Cabin; Underground Railroad, Sites of; and Appendixes 3 and 4.

John Brown's Farm and Gravesite (Lake Placid, New York)

Underground Railroad site recognized and documented by the National Park Service. *See also* Appendix 5.

John Brown's Headquarters (Samples Manor, Maryland)

Underground Railroad site recognized and documented by the National Park Service. *See also* Appendix 5.

John Brown's House (Chambersburg, Pennsylvania)

During the summer of 1859, John **Brown** (1800–1859) occupied an upstairs bedroom in this house in Chambersburg, **Pennsylvania,** now a stop on the Underground Railroad Travel Itinerary of the National Park Service. There, he refined his plan and stockpiled weapons for the attack on the federal arsenal at **Harpers** Ferry that he would lead on October 16, 1859.

While in Chambersburg, Brown posed as Dr. Isaac Smith, an iron mine developer who was scouting the area. He purchased tools and weapons from local businesses and stored them in the nearby Oak and Cauffman Warehouse on North Main Street. Brown then transported these tools and weapons to the Kennedy Farm, located in Samples Manor, Maryland. While residing in Chambersburg,

Brown also met with several abolitionist leaders, including Frederick **Douglass.** The citizens of Chambersburg did not realize that Brown had been their erstwhile neighbor until after news spread of the raid on Harpers Ferry.

See also John Brown's Cabin; John Brown's Farm and Gravesite; John Brown's Headquarters; John Brown, Jr.'s House; Underground Railroad, Sites of; and Appendixes 3 and 4.

John Freeman Walls Cabin (Puce, Ontario, Canada)

Underground Railroad site. The land in Puce, Ontario, on which the John Freeman Walls Cabin still stands was acquired in 1798 by the Sinclair family. The head of the family, Sir John Graves Sinclair, proposed the bill that led to the abolition of **slavery** in **Canada** west, prompting the migration of over one thousand **fugitive slaves** to Ontario province.

John Freeman Walls joined this migration when he escaped from slavery in Rockingham County, North Carolina — fleeing to Canada with his wife and children. In 1846, he purchased land and built a log cabin on a foundation of four rocks. There Walls and his family aided fugitive slaves who had survived the harrowing journey to freedom in Canada. Given its location, Walls' cabin became an end terminus of the Underground Railroad. *See also* Underground Railroad, Sites of; and Appendixes 3 and 4.

John Greenleaf Whittier House (Danvers, Massachusetts)

Underground Railroad site. John Greenleaf **Whittier,** the poet laureate of New England and one the most famous American poets of his time, lived near Danvers, **Massachusetts,** for 56 years. He not only wrote most of his poetry in his home, Oak Knoll, but sheltered **fugitive slaves** there as well. *See also* Underground Railroad, Sites of; and Appendixes 3 and 4.

John Hossack House (Ottawa, Illinois)

Underground Railroad site recognized and documented by the National Park Service. *See also* Appendix 5.

John Parker House (Ripley, Ohio)

Underground Railroad site recognized and documented by the National Park Service. *See also* Appendix 5.

John Rankin House (Ripley, Ohio)

Underground Railroad site recognized and documented by the National Park Service. *See also* Appendix 5.

Johnson, Elizabeth

Friend of the fugitive in **Philadelphia, Pennsylvania**. *See also* Johnson House; and Appendixes 1 and 2.

Johnson, Ellwood

Friend of the fugitive in **Philadelphia, Pennsylvania**. *See also* Johnson House; and Appendixes 1 and 2.

Johnson, Israel

Friend of the fugitive in **Philadelphia, Pennsylvania**. *See also* Johnson House; and Appendixes 1 and 2.

Johnson, Nathan (d. 1880) and Mary Johnson (d. 1871)

Friends of the fugitive, Nathan and Mary (Polly) Johnson were **free people of color** who lived in **New Bedford, Massachusetts** in the decades before the Civil War. The Johnsons married in New Bedford in 1819 and worked as servants to a wealthy Quaker family that helped them purchase a block of properties including their longtime home and the neighboring old Friends meetinghouse beginning in the mid–1820s.

Nathan Johnson was a noted social activist, belonged to several African American abolitionist organizations and worked with local Quaker abolitionist leaders in New Bedford. He was a delegate to the annual convention of free people of color from 1832 to 1835, and was elected the president of the 1847 National Convention of Colored People in Troy, New York. The Johnson home was a station on the Underground Railroad and is noted as the first residence of Frederick **Douglass** after his escape from **slavery** in 1838 — the only one of Douglass' three homes in New Bedford still standing today.

Nathan Johnson lost his small fortune in the 1840s and, along with many other young men of New Bedford, migrated to **California** in 1849 in search of gold and, perhaps, freedom of a different kind. Mary Johnson remained in New Bedford, with power of attorney to manage the couple's remaining properties. A provision in her will allowed Nathan a yearly stipend "provided he comes home to New Bedford within two years from the date of my decease." After she died on November 19, 1871, Nathan Johnson did return and lived in the family home, in reduced circumstances, until his death in 1880.

FURTHER READING
Da Silva, Janine. "Nathan and Mary (Polly) Johnson House 21 Seventh Street New Bedford, Massachusetts: Conservation Assessment." New Bedford, MA: New Bedford Historical Society, 1999.
Grover, Kathryn. *The Fugitive's Gibraltar: Escaping Slaves and Abolitionism in New Bedford, Massachusetts*. Amherst: University of Massachusetts Press, 2001.

Johnson, Rowland

Friend of the fugitive in **Philadelphia, Pennsylvania**. *See also* Johnson House; and Appendixes 1 and 2.

Johnson, Sarah

Friend of the fugitive in **Philadelphia, Pennsylvania**. *See also* Johnson House; and Appendixes 1 and 2.

Johnson, William H.

Friend of the fugitive in Richmond, Virginia. *See also* Henry "Box" Brown; and Appendixes 1 and 2.

Johnson House (Philadelphia, Pennsylvania)

Underground Railroad site recognized and documented by the National Park Service. *See also* Appendix 5.

Jonathan Ridgeway Haines House (Alliance, Ohio)

An Underground Railroad site and home of Jonathan Ridgeway Haines (d. 1899) and Sarah Grant Haines (d. 1903), who were Quaker farmers near Alliance. Haines declared himself an active abolitionist as early as

1842 and, in the **1850s**, his home served as an Underground Railroad station in eastern **Ohio**. As recounted by Erma Grant Pluchel in 1936:

> Many a fugitive slave was assisted to escape by Ridgeway Haines, his home being a station between Salem, Ohio, Marlboro and Limaville, O.... Many a night he stood guard gun in hand, taking care of the poor slaves he was harboring in the little attic room over his kitchen. His son, John C. or "Tump" as he was known, a boy of twelve also stood guard & helped to drive the slaves to the next station under cover of darkness. [Pluchel, 1936.]

Haines was a personal friend of and worked closely with Daniel Howell **Hise**, another Underground Railroad conductor whose journal is one of the most enduring records of mid–19th century Ohio. Haines died in 1899; his wife died in 1903. *See also* Quakers.

FURTHER READING
Pluchel, Erma Grant. Letter to Alliance Carnegie Library from Mrs. George Grant Pluchel, 1936, Rodman Public Library Collection, Alliance, Ohio.
Siebert, Wilbur H. *The Mysteries of Ohio's Underground Railroads.* Columbus, Ohio: The Ohio State University, 1951.

Jones, John (b. 1816)

Abolitionist and friend of the fugitive. John Jones was born a free person of color in 1816 in Green City, North Carolina. He migrated first to Memphis, **Tennessee**, and then, in 1845, to Chicago, **Illinois**. There, he opened a tailoring shop at 119 Dearborn Street and prospered, becoming eventually the wealthiest and most influential African American in Illinois. Jones, much like Washington **Spradling** of **Louisville**, used his wealth and influence to work for the freedom of his people.

As his fortune grew, Jones and his wife, Mary, purchased a large home and used it, as well as his business office, as a sanctuary for **fugitive slaves**. The Jones home was also a favorite meeting place for local and national antislavery leaders, including Alan **Pinkerton**, Frederick **Douglass**, and John **Brown**. When John Brown arrived in Chicago with 11 fugitive slaves in the late **1850s**, he was met by the famous detective Pinkerton, who later directed

him to John Jones. Writing from Chicago, Jones described the sentiments of African Americans in Illinois in the early 1850s and stated that "there are a few lingering skeletons lurking about through" the conservative southern part of the state, but that "they will be swallowed ... in the great Anti-Slavery flood which is now sweeping over the mighty West." He added that "the Underground Railroad is doing a fair business this season. We received eleven passengers last night ... and there were others on the road ... We will take care of them, and see that they are snugly shipped to Queen Victoria's land." (*Frederick Douglass Paper,* November 18, 1853 in Hudson, 2002: 106.)

Jones was willing to use as well as break the law. He led the successful struggle to repeal the Illinois Black Laws by speaking, writing, organizing blacks and whites, and lobbying the state legislature. Jones was also twice elected Cook County Commissioner between 1872 and 1875, and fought to eliminate school segregation in Chicago. Following his death, the *Chicago Tribune* reported that he had been the most prominent black citizen in the city. *See also* Free People of Color; and Appendixes 1 and 2.

FURTHER READING
Butler, Dominique. "John Jones." *Illinois History* 1996.
Hudson, J. Blaine. Fugitive *Slaves and the Underground Railroad in the Kentucky Borderland.* Jefferson, NC: McFarland, 2002.
Mahoney, Olivia. "Black Abolitionists." *Chicago History* 20(1991): 22–37.
Siebert, Wilbur H. *The Underground Railroad from Slavery to Freedom.* 1898. Reprint, New York: Russell and Russell, 1967.

Jordan, James Cunningham (b. 1813)

A friend of the fugitive, James Cunningham Jordan was born in Greenbrier County, Virginia, in 1813 to John and Agnes Cunningham Jordan. As a young man, Jordan had pursued **fugitive slaves**, but was sickened by the task. As an adult, he migrated west to the Iowa frontier, began raising and selling livestock, and later turned his attention to real estate and promoting railroad development. Jordan became director of the State Bank branch in Des Moines and, in 1854, was elected to the Iowa Senate to represent Valley Junction (now West Des Moines).

Jordan was a committed abolitionist and "chief conductor" for the Underground Railroad in Polk County. In this capacity, Jordan determined where fugitives would be hidden and when it was safe to move them to the next station. John **Brown** and his associates used Jordan's home to facilitate the flight of freedom seekers from Missouri, stopping there with 12 fugitive slaves on February 17, 1859, after raids at several Missouri farms that resulted in the death of one white farmer and hot pursuit by the Missouri authorities.

See also Jordan House.

Jordan House (West Des Moines, Iowa)

Underground Railroad site recognized and documented by the National Park Service. *See also* Appendix 5.

Joseph and Sophia Clemens Farmstead (Greenville, Ohio)

Underground Railroad site recognized and documented by the National Park Service.

Joshua Giddings' Law Office (Jefferson, Ohio)

Underground Railroad site. The small law office of Joshua **Giddings** (1795–1864), radical abolitionist congressman and friend of the fugitive, was built in 1823. Giddings shared the office with his law partner and fellow antislavery congressman, Benjamin Wade.

Working with his son, Grotium, Giddings used the office to shelter freedom seekers. *See also* Ohio; Underground Railroad, Sites of; and Appendixes 1–4.

FURTHER READING
Blockson, Charles L. *Hippocrene Guide to the Underground Railroad.* New York: Hippocrene Books, 1994.

Kennedy Farmhouse

See John Brown's Headquarters

Kentucky

Kentucky developed as a predominantly agricultural state with enslaved African Americans concentrated primarily in rural areas. By 1800, there were 220,955 people in Kentucky, 41,084 of whom were African American — with only a handful living in early Kentucky towns. Even Lexington, "the Athens of the West," boasted only 1,795 African Americans, followed by Frankfort (638), Washington (570), Paris (377) and **Louisville** (359).

The lives of African Americans in Kentucky were shaped both by the broadly generalizable constraints of American **slavery** and by conditions unique to the state. For example, the invention of the cotton gin made cotton cultivation immensely profitable and breathed new life into slavery. However, Kentucky's temperate climate and comparatively short growing season were not conducive to cotton monoculture. While tobacco and hemp cultivation depended heavily on slave labor, neither produced the large plantations and large slave-holdings that became common in the Gulf States after the War of 1812. As a result, fewer Kentucky families owned smaller units of slave property than did their counterparts in neighboring states.

Black population as a percentage of total state population peaked at 24.7 percent (170,130 of 687,917) in 1830 and declined to 20.4 percent by 1860 (236,167 of 1,155,684). While this percentage representation far exceeded that of African Americans in the free states, where black population was usually well below five percent of the state totals, it also fell far short of the percentage representation of African Americans in the mid-to-deep southern interior where African Americans — in the cases of Louisiana, Mississippi and South Carolina — equaled or exceeded whites numerically.

The institutionalization of slavery in Kentucky before 1800 was accompanied by a significant increase in both the demand for and the average price of enslaved African Americans — first in the state and, after 1815, in the cotton-growing states to the south. These factors ultimately produced a thriving inter-regional domestic slave trade and gave Kentucky the reputation of being a slave trading (if not slave breeding) state.

As slave population and cotton cultivation shifted steadily to the southwest after 1815, Kentucky also became central to the history of slave escapes by virtue of its place in the physical and political geography of the young United States.

A useful and fascinating account of the human and physical geography of the region was provided by Paul Wilhelm, Duke of Wurttemburg, who toured parts of the early United States between 1822 and 1824, journeying up the Mississippi and then the **Ohio Rivers** as far as Louisville. Wilhelm was intrigued by Louisville, where "for the first time we were in the vicinity of a U.S. town of size where the area could really be called populated." In contrast to Louisville, Lexington — Kentucky's first true urban area — was landlocked for all practical purposes. Its proximity to the many trails by which the early overland pioneers entered the state contributed to its singular importance in the late 1700s and early 1800s. However, both the expansion of settlement into the regions north of the Ohio River and the expansion of the "**cotton kingdom**" into the Gulf States to the south made proximity to the Ohio River far more important — and Lexington's location became increasingly disadvantageous relative to that of Louisville. As an outlet for slave-produced agricultural commodities and the center of Kentucky's domestic slave trade, Lexington and its surrounding area were also more deeply rooted in the economy and culture of the Kentucky Bluegrass, an economy and a culture similar to those of central **Tennessee**. Louisville, on the other hand, was already developing its paradoxical blend of southern culture and northern economic structure.

Enslaved African Americans comprised roughly half of the population of Lexington and Fayette County. In Lexington in the **1850s**, "there were blacks everywhere, engaged in a great variety of tasks." Clearly, enslaved African Americans in Louisville and countless other Kentucky towns performed the same tasks. The difference, where Louisville and Lexington were concerned, was one in both degree and kind. In essence, slavery and its traditions were far more central to daily life and life-ways in Lexington. This difference had two consequences of crucial importance with respect to Lexington's role in the history of **fugitive slaves** and the Underground Railroad. First, the slave system, with the use of police in the city and patrols in the countryside, was somewhat more rigid than in Louisville. Second, free African Americans in Lexington were too few, with too many restrictions and too few outlets to evolve into the type of self-conscious and organized community found in Louisville and **Cincinnati**. The slave system was stronger and the black community was weaker and more marginal, and Lexington was roughly 65 miles from free territory.

When enslaved African Americans acted on their desire for freedom, the factor of distance in relation to the political geography of the United States and the physical geography of Kentucky became critically important. As Lucas noted:

> Though generally poor roads made travel difficult, fewer than a hundred miles separated the state's largest centers of slave population from free soil, with no location more than two hundred miles from the Ohio River. Lexington, the heart of the Bluegrass and the region with the largest slave population, was about sixty-five miles from the Ohio River via either Louisville or Maysville. Covington, on the Ohio River across from Cincinnati, the city with the largest black population in Ohio, lay seventy-nine miles directly north of Lexington. The heavily slave populated counties of western Kentucky were even closer to the Ohio River. [Lucas, 1992: 61.]

Given these relative distances, the distribution of African Americans in Kentucky and the origins of the majority of fugitives, the broad **routes of escape** they followed and their most likely sources of aid were anything but random.

Free people of color were one such source of possible assistance. Although Kentucky was a slave state, the number of free people of color living there was nearly equal to the total black population of **Indiana**. In 1850, for example, there were 10,011 free people of color (4.5 percent of the total black population) in Kentucky compared to 11,262 African Americans in all of Indiana. However, as with enslaved African Americans, free people of color were not distributed evenly across the commonwealth. Some free people of color were concentrated in or near many of the same centers of slave population in the Bluegrass and western Kentucky. Still, there were fairly significant clusters outside those regions — and counties within those regions that held few, if any, free people of color. In general, free people of color were found more often in small communities in or near Kentucky towns and cities, giving this segment of the African American population a more decidedly urban character — even in Appalachia.

Thus, Kentucky was not only the origin of a significant number of fugitive slaves, but became a key region through which fugitive slaves from farther south were obliged to travel. *See also* Underground Railroad, Sites of; and Appendixes 3 and 4.

FURTHER READING
Baptist, Edward E. "'Cuffy,' 'Fancy Maids,' and 'One-Eyed Men': Rape, Commodification and the Domestic Slave Trade in the United States." *The American Historical Review* 106 (2001): 1619–1650.
Hudson, J. Blaine. Fugitive *Slaves and the Underground Railroad in the Kentucky Borderland.* Jefferson, NC: McFarland, 2002.
Lucas, Marion B. *A History of Blacks in Kentucky.* Vol. 1 of *From Slavery to Segregation, 1760–1891.* Frankfort: Kentucky Historical Society, 1992.
Wilhelm, Paul, Duke of Wurttemburg. *Travels in North America, 1822–1824.* 1824. Reprint, Norman, OK: University of Oklahoma, 1973.

Kimzey Crossing/Locust Hill (Tamaroa, Illinois)

Underground Railroad site recognized and documented by the National Park Service. *See also* Appendix 5.

King, The Reverend William

See Buxton

Knight, John

Friend of the fugitive in **Louisville, Kentucky.** *See also* Appendixes 1 and 2.

Knights of Liberty

Friends of the fugitive. *See also* Dickson, Moses; and Appendixes 1 and 2.

Lambert, William

Friend of the fugitive in **Detroit, Michigan.** *See also* Finney House; and Appendixes 1 and 2.

Lane, Lunsford (b. c. 1803)

Abolitionist. Lunsford Lane was born enslaved in North Carolina around 1803. Lane purchased his freedom, began working in the tobacco trade and accumulating funds with which to purchase the freedom of his wife and six children. Lane was forced to leave North Carolina and moved to **Massachusetts**, where he appealed to for help in freeing his family. In 1842, he returned to Raleigh to purchase his family, was arrested and barely avoided being lynched before finally completing the transaction. Once settled in Massachusetts, Lane became an active and committed abolitionist and, in 1842, published an account of his experiences. *See also* Abolitionist Movement.

FURTHER READING
Lane, Lunsford. *The Narrative of Lunsford Lane, Formerly of Raleigh, N.C. Embracing an Account of His Early Life, the Redemption by Purchase of Himself and Family from Slavery, and His Banishment from the Place of His Birth for the Crime of Wearing a Colored Skin.* Boston: J.G. Torrey, 1842.
Saxage, W. Sherman. "The Influence of John Chavis and Lunsford Lane on the History of North Carolina." *Journal of Negro History* 25(1940): 20–24.

Langley, Loudon S.

Friend of the fugitive. Loudon S. Langley was a free African American who lived in Hinesburg, Vermont, in the **1850s**. Langley assisted **fugitive slaves** and, after the Emancipation Proclamation was signed, enlisted in 54th **Massachusetts** infantry and served until the end of the **Civil War**. *See also* Underground Railroad, Sites of; and Appendixes 1–4.

Langston, John Mercer (1829–1897)

Friend of the fugitive, attorney, and politician. John Mercer Langston was born free in 1829 in Louisa County, Virginia, the youngest of four children. His father, Ralph Quarles, was a wealthy white planter; his mother, Lucy Langston, was a free woman of color. Although the causes of death were unrelated, both of Langston's parents died in 1834, leaving him a substantial inheritance.

Langston and his siblings then moved to Chillicothe, **Ohio**, where they lived under the care of William Gooch, a friend of Quarles. However, when Gooch moved to Missouri in 1838, Langston and his brothers moved to

Cincinnati, Ohio. At 14 years of age, Langston enrolled in the Preparatory Department of **Oberlin College** and graduated from the Collegiate Department in 1849. Langston enrolled in the graduate program in theology at Oberlin in preparation for later legal study. He earned his master's degree, but was denied entry to law school. Determined to become an attorney, Langston found an alternative route — and read law under Philemon Bliss of Elyria. Langston became the first black lawyer in Ohio when he passed the bar in 1854. Langston met and married Caroline Wall at Oberlin, settled in Brownhelm, Ohio, and opened a law practice. In 1855, he became the nation's first black elected public official when he was elected town clerk of Brownhelm.

During these formative years, Langston committed himself to the antislavery cause. In 1848, at the invitation of Frederick **Douglass**, Langston spoke in favor of assisting fugitive slaves at the National Black Convention in Cleveland — and, during his 15-year stay at Oberlin, assisted fugitive slaves himself on numerous occasions. Working with his brothers, Gideon and Charles, Langston organized antislavery societies at both the state and local level, and also spoke in favor of women's rights and temperance. In the tumult of the **1850s**, Langston's views grew more radical and more fluid. He advocated, then later repudiated, colonization. Langston advocated armed struggle and had contact with John **Brown**, but did not join him. He also became a staunch supporter of the Republican Party.

With the onset of **Civil War**, Langston was chief recruiter for the Union Army in the West and helped organize the Massachusetts 54th, the nation's first African American regiment, and the Massachusetts 55th and the 5th Ohio. In 1864, Langston crusaded for black suffrage in Ohio, Kansas, and Missouri. In the next years, as educational inspector for the Freedman's Bureau, he traveled throughout the South advocating educational opportunity, political equality and economic justice.

In 1868, Langston founded what became the law school at Howard University, and served as its first dean. Although appointed acting president of Howard in 1872, his efforts to become president in 1875 failed (Howard would not appoint its first black president until 1927). Langston next served a consul general to Haiti for eight years and, on returning to the United States in 1885, became president of Virginia Normal and Collegiate Institute (now Virginia State University). In 1888, Langston was elected to the U.S. Congress, the first African American elected from Virginia — although his election was contested and he could only serve six months of his term before losing his seat. Langston retired in 1894 and published his autobiography, *From the Virginia Plantation to the National Capital.* He died in **Washington, D.C.,** on November 15, 1897. *See also* Free People of Color; and Appendixes 1 and 2.

FURTHER READING

Bracey, John H., August Meier, and Elliott Rudwick. *Blacks in the Abolitionist Movement.* Belmont, CA: Wadsworth, 1971.

Cheek, William F. "John Mercer Langston: Black Protest Leader and Abolitionist." *Civil War History* 16(1970): 101–120.

_____, and Aimee Lee Cheek. *John Mercer Langston and the Fight for Black Freedom 1829–1865.* Urbana: University of Illinois Press, 1989.

Langston, John Mercer. *From the Virginia plantation to the national capitol, or, The first and only Negro representative in Congress from the Old Dominion.* Hartford, CT: American, 1894.

Latimer, George W. (b. 1819)

George Latimer was a fugitive slave and centerpiece of an important fugitive slave rescue. On October 4, 1842, Latimer and his pregnant wife, Rebecca, escaped from **slavery** in Norfolk, Virginia, and fled north by ship to **Boston, Massachusetts.** Four days later, Latimer was discovered by William R. Carpenter, a former employee of Latimer's owner, James B. Gray. Carpenter immediately contacted Gray and, on October 18, 1842, Latimer was arrested on a warrant issued at Gray's request under the provisions of the **Fugitive Slave Act of 1793.** Boston's active and multiracial antislavery community was incensed, and hundreds gathered at the courthouse in protest. To prevent Latimer's rescue by the angry crowd, local authorities imprisoned him in a strongly fortified jail.

Chief Justice Lemuel Shaw refused to issue a writ of habeas corpus and a rescue attempt failed, ending in the arrest of eight

African Americans. In the meantime, William Ingersoll **Bowditch**, Samuel Sewall, Francis Jackson, Wendell **Phillips** and the young Frederick **Douglass** organized a protest meeting at **Faneuil Hall** on October 30. Fearing that Latimer would eventually be rescued, Gray offered to sell Latimer for $400 and, despite deep misgivings over their complicity with slavery, Bowditch and his associates raised the necessary funds and freed Latimer legally on November 18, 1842.

The Latimer case spurred a petition campaign that amassed over 65,000 signatures and led, in 1843, to the strengthening of Massachusetts' personal liberty law. Under the revised statute, state officials and jails could not be used in the apprehension or rendition of **fugitive slaves**. Connecticut and Vermont soon adopted similar laws.

Fearing his re-enslavement, George Latimer later went into hiding, at great hardship to his family. His son Lewis Latimer (1848–1928) drafted the drawings for Alexander Graham Bell's patent application for the telephone. *See also* Personal Liberty Laws.

FURTHER READING

Fouche, Rayvon. *Black Inventors in the Age of Segregation: Granville T. Woods, Lewis H. Latimer and Shelby J. Davidson.* Baltimore: Johns Hopkins University Press, 2003.
"The Two Autobiographical Fragments of George W. Latimer." *Journal of Afro-American Historical and Genealogical Society* No. 1(Summer 1980).

Leavitt Thaxter Pease Homesite (Williamsburg, Ohio)

Underground Railroad site recognized and documented by the National Park Service. *See also* Appendix 5.

Lee, Archy

Fugitive slave. *See also* Archy Case.

LeMoyne, Francis Julius (1798–1879)

Pennsylvania friend of the fugitive. Francis Julius LeMoyne (1798–1879) was the son and grandson of French physicians through his father and a Scottish-Irish immigrant mother. After his parents married in 1797, they moved to Washington County in southwestern Pennsylvania, where the elder

LeMoyne practiced medicine and built a house on Maiden Street in 1812.

After graduating from Washington College, the younger LeMoyne worked on his father's farm and apprenticed as a physician, then studied medicine formally at Jefferson Medical College in **Philadelphia**. In 1823, he married Madelaine Romaine Bureau, the daughter of a French émigré settled at Gallipolis. The couple had three sons and five daughters, and eventually moved into the family home.

LeMoyne joined the antislavery movement in 1834, serving as president of the Washington County Anti-Slavery Society from 1835 until 1837, when he became a regional agent of the American Anti-Slavery Society. During this period, his Maiden Street home became a depot for antislavery literature, which was then distributed throughout the Ohio Valley. As evidence of LeMoyne's stature, he corresponded regularly with Gerrit **Smith** and Lewis **Tappan**, and was nominated by the Liberty Party as its first candidate for vice-president in 1840 (declining the nomination) and ran as its candidate for governor in 1841, 1844, and 1847, and as candidate for Congress in 1843.

In the mid–**1850s**, poor health made the active practice of medicine difficult and LeMoyne devoted most of his time to scientific farming, introducing improved strains of cattle, sheep, and horses to the county. After the **Civil War**, he gave the **American Missionary Association** $20,000 toward the endowment of a school for freedmen in Memphis, **Tennessee**. Until his death, he used his wealth and talent to support progressive causes. LeMoyne died in 1879. *See also* LeMoyne House; and Appendixes 1 and 2.

FURTHER READING

Bell, Raymond M. "Washington County, Pennsylvania, in the Eighteenth Century Anti-Slavery Movement." *Western Pennsylvania Historical Magazine* 25(1942): 125–142.
Blockson, Charles. *The Underground Railroad.* New York: Prentice Hall, 1987.
"Freedom Seekers: Underground Railroad Travelled through Valley." *Monongahela Valley Review* (February 1993): 8–9.
McCulloch, Margaret C. *Fearless Advocate of the Right: The Life of Francis Julius LeMoyne, M.D., 1798–1879.* Boston: Christopher Publishing House, 1941.

Turner, Edward R. "The Abolition of Slavery in Pennsylvania." *Pennsylvania Magazine of History and Biography* 36 (1912): 129–142.

LeMoyne House (Washington, Pennsylvania)

Underground Railroad site recognized and documented by the National Park Service. *See also* Appendix 5.

Levi Coffin House (Fountain City, Indiana)

Underground Railroad site recognized and documented by the National Park Service. *See also* Appendix 5.

Lewelling, Henderson (1809–1883)

An important friend of the fugitive, Henderson Lewelling was born into a Quaker family in Randolph County, North Carolina, on April 23, 1809. Lewelling moved with his family to Henry County, **Indiana**, in the early 1820s and married in 1830. In 1837, he moved to Salem, **Iowa**, the first Quaker community established in Iowa two years earlier.

Lewelling and his brothers planted the first fruit trees in Iowa — 35 varieties of apples, pears, cherries, peaches, plums, and small fruits. Lewelling was an active abolitionist, and his home served as an Underground Railroad station. Further, in 1843, he and other members of the Salem Monthly Meeting broke with more conservative **Quakers**, who did not believe in assisting **fugitive slaves**, to form the Abolition Friends Monthly Meeting.

In 1847, Lewelling moved to Oregon and, in 1853, to **California** — establishing fruit nurseries in both states and founding the community of Fruitvale in California. For his pioneering efforts, Lewelling is considered the father of the Pacific fruit industry. He died in Oakland, California, in 1883.

FURTHER READING
Dykstra, Robert R. *Bright Radical Star: Black Freedom and White Supremacy on the Hawkeye Frontier.* Cambridge, MA: Harvard University, 1993.

Lewelling House (Salem, Iowa)

Underground Railroad site recognized and documented by the National Park Service. *See also* Appendix 5.

Lewis, Elijah

Friend of the fugitive in **Farmington, Connecticut**. *See also* Appendixes 1 and 2.

The Liberator

See Garrison, William Lloyd

Liberty Farm (Worcester, Massachusetts)

Underground Railroad site recognized and documented by the National Park Service. *See also* Appendix 5.

Linn House (Bellefonte, Pennsylvania)

An Underground Railroad site located in the African American community of antebellum Bellefonte, the Linn House and the AME Church nearby served as hiding places for **fugitive slaves**. *See also* Pennsylvania; Underground Railroad, Sites of; and Appendixes 3 and 4.

Little Africa (Mercersburg, Pennsylvania)

Underground Railroad site. "Little Africa" refers to the African American community of antebellum Mercersburg, **Pennsylvania**. Concentrated along Fayette Street, many of the African American residents were **fugitive slaves** and the small community contained several homes and a church, Bethel African Methodist Episcopal, used to harbor freedom seekers. *See also* Harboring; Underground Railroad, Sites of; and Appendixes 3 and 4.

Loguen, Jermain W. (1814–1872)

Fugitive slave and friend of the fugitive. Jermain W. Loguen was born enslaved in **Tennessee** in about 1814. He escaped from bondage in 1834, spent a few years in St. Catherine's, Ontario, **Canada** and then settled in Rochester, New York, in 1837. There, he attended the Oneida Institute and was ordained as an AME minister.

He pastored churches in Bath and Ithaca before settling permanently in Syracuse in 1847. Along with his roles as an AME minister, teacher and antislavery lecturer, Loguen was a key figure in Underground Railroad operations in western New York. His home contained secret accommodations for fugitive slaves and Loguen and his family alone assisted an estimated 1,500 freedom seekers. Loguen was also involved centrally in the "Jerry Rescue" of 1851.

In 1840, Loguen married Caroline Storum of Bustin, New York. The two had six children. One daughter, Amelia, married Frederick **Douglass'** son, Lewis, in 1869. Another daughter, Sarah, became possibly the first black woman physician in the United States. Loguen died in 1872. *See also* Henry, William "Jerry," and Appendixes 1 and 2.

FURTHER READING
Siebert, Wilbur H. *The Underground Railroad from Slavery to Freedom.* 1898. Reprint, New York: Russell and Russell, 1967.
Still, William. *The Underground Railroad.* 1872. Reprint, Chicago: Johnson, 1970.

Long, John C.

Friend of the fugitive in **Louisville, Kentucky.** *See also* Appendixes 1 and 2.

Lott, John

Friend of the fugitive in **Madison, Indiana.** *See also* Appendixes 1 and 2.

Louisville, Kentucky

Underground Railroad junction. For reasons as much geographic as demographic, the role of Louisville was critical both to the flight of **fugitive slaves** and to the work of friends of the fugitive in the trans-Appalachian west. As William Cockrum concluded on the basis of his own experience:

> There were probably more negroes crossed over the Ohio river and two or three places in front of Louisville than any place else from the mouth of the Wabash to **Cincinnati.** The reason for this was that the three good sized cities at the Falls furnished a good hiding place for runaways among the colored people. Those crossing at these places were all conveyed to Wayne county, **Indiana,** and thence on to the Lake.

Growth in the free African American population, coupled with the presence of smaller but relatively stable free black communities in the Indiana towns facing Louisville across the **Ohio River** made the Louisville area a major refuge and crossing point for fugitive slaves. For example, in 1860, in addition to 1,917 free blacks in Louisville, there were 757 African Americans in Floyd County (New Albany) and another 520 in Clark County (Jeffersonville and Clarksville). However, free people of color were an anomaly, people who were black but not enslaved in a slaveholding city. Given such a hostile environment, the evolution of a cohesive community required wise leadership, and two individuals figured prominently in the community formation process— Shelton **Morris** and Washington **Spradling,** Sr. African American churches were products of this transformation and means of moving it forward. Among the most notable of the early African American churches was **Quinn Chapel AME Church,** "the Abolition Church," established by local **free people of color** in 1838.

These same community leaders and unifying community institutions figured prominently in the work of assisting fugitive slaves. Morris, before moving to Cincinnati in 1841, and Spradling for several decades, were central figures in the local Underground Railroad network. Based on court records alone, a great many others in the Louisville region were deeply involved as well and were convicted of violating the law for helping fugitive slaves. A few of these friends of the fugitive, black and white, included: John Cain, James Cunningham, Elisha Hillyer, William Jeter, John Knight, John C. Long, J. R. Sprinkle, William Tatum, and Ed Williams.

In such a densely populated urban area, fugitive slaves could only cross the Ohio River at certain spots and under certain conditions. For example, neither the wharf areas of Louisville, nor Shippingport and Portland (small towns at the eastern and western "ends" of the canal eventually annexed by Louisville), nor the Portland Canal around the Falls of the Ohio (completed in 1830) were advantageous locations. Crossings from downtown Louisville to Jeffersonville were often attempted, but only by the use of deception and disguise. East of Louisville, clandestine crossings were possible at or near the numerous ferries and small settlements such as Charleston (Indiana) and Westport (**Kentucky**) that dotted the Ohio riverbank for roughly 50 miles to **Madison, Indiana.** These crossings were used, but not in an organized fashion.

Notwithstanding these, the most important and best documented crossing point in the greater Louisville area was the **Portland Crossing Point** located west of Portland — leading from Louisville across the Ohio River to New Albany. Using this crossing point required considerable planning and coordination. After negotiating a river crossing, fugitives could follow several routes leading from New Albany or Jeffersonville to Salem, or an alternative station, and then northward.

Pamela Peters' research on the Underground Railroad in New Albany and southern Indiana yields important corroborative insights, one of which concerns the relationship between the Underground Railroad and the actual railroad in the **1850s**. In September 1855, this relationship stirred up considerable controversy in Louisville when one of the conductors on the New Albany and Salem Railroad, a Mr. James Haynes (or Hines), was accused of "endeavoring to assist in the escape of a runaway slave." Officials of the New Albany and Salem Railroad assured irate Louisvillians that "employees of the N. A. & S. R. will not be permitted to aid runaway negroes to escape." By the 1850s, between one and two fugitive slaves escaped from or through the Louisville area each day. *See also* Underground Railroad, Sites of; and Appendixes 3 and 4.

FURTHER READING

Gibson, William H., Sr. *Historical Sketches of the Progress of the Colored Race in Louisville, Kentucky.* Louisville: N. p., 1897.

Hudson, J. Blaine. "Crossing the Dark Line: Fugitive Slaves and the Underground Railroad in Louisville and North Central Kentucky." *Filson History Quarterly* 75(2001): 33–84.

Peters, Pamela. *The Underground Railroad in Floyd County, Indiana.* Jefferson, NC: McFarland, 2001.

Van Metre, Beulah. "The Underground Railroad Near Charlestown." Federal Writers' Project, unpublished notes, ca. 1936. Presented to the author by Ms. Iris L. Cook's grandniece, 1999.

Lovejoy, Elijah P. (1802–1837)

Friend of the fugitive and martyr to the antislavery cause. Elijah Parish Lovejoy was born in Albion, Maine, on November 9, 1802. After graduating from Waterville College (now Colby College) in 1826, he migrated to St. Louis to work as a teacher.

In 1831, Lovejoy studied at Princeton Theological Seminary, was ordained by the Presbytery of St. Louis in 1834, and was elected its moderator in 1835. Returning to St. Louis, he pastored the Des Peres Presbyterian Church, published a religious newspaper, *The St. Louis Observer,* and began to advocate the abolition of **slavery** vocally and visibly — in a slave state. After witnessing an enslaved African American, Francis J. McIntosh, being burned at the stake, he wrote a series of uncompromising editorials that aroused great anger. Soon thereafter, his printing press was destroyed by a mob in July 1836.

Lovejoy then moved to Alton, **Illinois**, became the stated clerk of the Presbytery in 1837 and the first pastor of the College Avenue Presbyterian Church. He continued his antislavery work, founded another news outlet, *The Alton Observer,* and helped with the organization of the Anti-Slavery Society of Illinois. His views and his conduct, again, provoked anger and outrage — and his neighbors destroyed three more printing presses in succession, casting them into the Mississippi River. Still, Lovejoy continued his crusade.

Elijah Lovejoy (Library of Congress)

On November 7, 1837, while attempting to defend and install yet another printing press, Lovejoy was killed by a blast from a double-barreled shotgun in a struggle with a proslavery mob. Lovejoy became a martyr, eulogized by men of the stature of Wendell **Phillips** who stated, many years after the murder, that: "I can never forget the quick sharp agony of that hour which brought us news of Lovejoy's death ... The gun fired at Lovejoy was like that of Sumter — it scattered a world of dreams." (Dillon, 1961: 178.) In retrospect, Lovejoy's death marked a turning point in the Abolitionist Movement, shifting the central focus of the movement from moral suasion, which had come to seem unavailing, to more direct action against slavery — including aid to fugitive slaves.

He was buried on his 35th birthday, November 9, 1837. *See also* Abolitionist Movement; Lovejoy, Owen; Owen Lovejoy House; and Appendixes 1 and 2.

FURTHER READING

Dillon, Merton-Lynn. *Elijah P. Lovejoy, Abolitionist Editor.* Westport, CT: Greenwood Press, 1961.

Finnie, Gordon E. "The Antislavery Movement in the Upper South Before 1840." *Journal of Southern History* 35, no. 3(1969): 319–342.

Gill, John. *Tide without Turning: Elijah P. Lovejoy and Freedom of the Press.* Boston: Starr-King Press, 1958.

Lovejoy, Owen (1811–1864)

Friend of the fugitive. Owen Lovejoy was born in Albion, Maine, on January 6, 1811. The son of a Congregational minister, he graduated from Bowdoin College in 1832. Lovejoy then studied, but never practiced, law.

In 1836, he was ordained and later accepted the pastorate of the Congregational Church in Princeton, **Illinois.** Lovejoy was as staunch an opponent of **slavery** as his brother, Elijah **Lovejoy,** the crusading abolitionist editor of the *Alton Observer* who was murdered by a proslavery mob on November 7, 1837. At his brother's funeral, Lovejoy vowed never to "forsake the cause sprinkled with his brother's blood." (Moore and Moore, 2004: xix.) He kept his vow, in part, by assisting **fugitive slaves.**

Lovejoy was a member of the Liberty Party and was elected to the Illinois House of Representatives in 1854. He also developed a friendship with Abraham Lincoln, although Lincoln considered Lovejoy's views too radical. After joining the new Republican Party, Lovejoy was elected to the U.S. Congress in 1856 and soon gained a reputation for his aggressive antislavery oratory.

During the 1840s and **1850s,** Lovejoy used his home to harbor fugitive slaves and faced prosecution several times. Lovejoy's role was so widely known that the fugitive slave escape route through Princeton was called the "Lovejoy Line." Lovejoy himself took great pride in his work as an Underground Railroad station keeper and admitted it publicly to taunt defenders of slavery. Most notably, in an 1859 speech on the floor of the U.S. Congress, he stated boldly: "Owen Lovejoy ... aids every fugitive that comes to his door and asks it. Proclaim it then from the housetops. Write it on every leaf that trembles in the forest, make it blaze from the sun at high noon ... I bid you defiance in the name of my God!" (Moore and Moore, 2004: 178.)

In 1860, he campaigned vigorously for Lincoln and argued strongly for emancipation and the enlistment of African Americans in the Union Army during the **Civil War.** Although frustrated by Lincoln's initial unwillingness to act on these issues, Lovejoy nonetheless moderated his criticism of the beleaguered president, stating in a speech delivered on June 12, 1862: "If he does not drive as fast as I would, he is on the right road, and it is only a question of time." (Moore and Moore, 2004: 346.) Owen Lovejoy died in Brooklyn, New York, on March 25, 1864. *See also* Abolitionist Movement; Owen Lovejoy House; Underground Railroad, Stations on; and Appendixes 1 and 2.

FURTHER READING

Blockson, Charles L. *Hippocrene Guide to the Underground Railroad.* New York: Hippocrene Books, 1994.

Moore, William F., and Jane A. Moore, eds. *His Brother's Blood: Speeches and Writings, 1838–64, of Owen Lovejoy.* Urbana, IL: University of Illinois Press, 2004.

"The Underground Railroad." In the *Historical Encyclopedia of Illinois.* Illinois Historical Society, 1901.

Lovell, Lucy Buffum

Friend of the fugitive in Rhode Island. *See also* Chace, Elizabeth Buffum; and Appendixes 1 and 2.

Lundy, Benjamin (1789–1839)

Friend of the fugitive and philanthropist. Benjamin Lundy was born on January 4, 1789 at Hardwick, Warren County, New Jersey. Born into a Quaker family, he worked on his father's farm, attending school for only brief periods and, from 1808 to 1812, lived at Wheeling, Virginia (now West Virginia), where he served an apprenticeship to a saddler.

In Wheeling, Lundy was exposed firsthand to the evils of **slavery** and the **slave trade**—and determined to devote his life to antislavery work. In 1815, while living at Saint Clairsville, **Ohio**, he founded the Union Humane Society and, within a few months, had attracted more than 500 members. For a short time, he assisted Charles Osborne in editing the *Philanthropist*. In 1821 he founded, at **Mount Pleasant, Ohio**, an antislavery paper, the *Genius of Universal Emancipation*—first as a monthly and later a weekly, published successively in Ohio, **Tennessee**, Maryland, the District of Columbia and **Pennsylvania**. He was bitterly denounced by slaveholders and, in January 1827, was assaulted and seriously injured by a slave-trader, Austin Woolfolk. Between September 1829 and March 1830, William Lloyd **Garrison** assisted Lundy in the editorship of the paper.

Lundy visited Haiti in 1825 and 1829, the Wilberforce colony in **Canada** in 1830, 1831, 1832 and 1833 — and even **Texas**, before its annexation by the United States— as prospective sites for the settlement of both emancipated African Americans and **fugitive slaves**. Between 1836 and 1838, Lundy founded and edited a new antislavery weekly, *The National Enquirer,* which eventually became *The Pennsylvania Freeman.* In 1839, Lundy moved to **Illinois** and revived the *Genius of Universal Emancipation,* which he published until his death on August 22, 1839. *See also* Wilberforce, Canada; and Appendixes 1 and 2.

FURTHER READING

Dillon, Merton L. *Benjamin Lundy and the Struggle for Negro Freedom.* Urbana: University of Illinois Press, 1966.

Finnie, Gordon E. "The Antislavery Movement in the Upper South Before 1840." *Journal of Southern History* 35, no. 3(1969): 319–342.

Lusk, Dr. Mary

See Portland Crossing Point

"Lying Out"

See Temporary Escapes

Madison, Indiana

Underground Railroad center. The fugitive slave escape corridor leading through Trimble and Carroll Counties in **Kentucky** to **Ohio River** crossing points in the vicinity of Madison, Indiana, was one of the most active and well-known in the trans-Appalachian west. By the 1820s, a number of free African Americans in the Madison area had begun assisting **fugitive slaves**. In these early years, "George Evans, Joe O'Neil, John Carter were the early leaders" and "from Graysville, Fountain Thurman and William Crosby provided leadership," while "at Greenbrier Jim Hackney was the acknowledged activist." (Coon, 1998: 8.)

John **Lott** was an early African American leader in the struggle against **slavery**. Lott was born in **Pennsylvania** and worked on the river before settling "in the beautiful, hilly country at Madison, Indiana." He, Chapman **Harris** and George Anderson were "powerful mates" in organizing the black Underground Railroad network in the area. However, in 1846, when proslavery whites attempted to drive African Americans from the Madison area, Lott followed the Underground Railroad himself and moved his wife and three children to Chatham, **Canada** West. (Horton, 1986: 1) Other African American Underground Railroad workers in the region included George **DeBaptiste** and Griffith Booth.

The Madison area also stands out as home to the most visible and consistently active group of antislavery whites at any point on the **Indiana** side of the river. This presence in Madison and its surrounding area had a long history. As early as 1809, Benjamin Whitson (1761–1829), a Methodist minister, moved to Madison from North Carolina, via Kentucky, and expressed open opposition to slavery. Others followed, including "James and

Daniel Nelson, from Vermont, who settled in Lancaster Township in 1820; the Hoyt and Tibbets families ... and Thomas and Lewis Hicklin." The Hicklin brothers were also ministers. Thomas was particularly zealous and, before moving from Kentucky, "there was a reward of $100 offered for him dead or alive, on account of his antislavery work." Lewis was centrally involved in organizing "the first antislavery meeting" at nearby Nells Creek in 1839. (Crenshaw, 1993: 31.)

Amelia Hoyt was the daughter of Benjamin Hoyt, an especially active member of this society. As an elderly woman, she recounted its work with fugitive slaves and recalled how her father and his comrades often left "their comfortable homes at dead of night to help the poor slave on toward the **North Star**, and to treat him as a man and a brother." (Anti-Slavery History of Jefferson County, 1998: 4.) When interviewed in 1880, Hoyt described an especially memorable incident that involved **Louisville** and Madison in the 1840s:

A slaveholding family from the far south was accustomed to spending the summer north — at Louisville ... They brought a trusted man-servant along. He overheard it said on one occasion: "This is our last visit." To himself, he said: "This is my last opportunity to escape." When the time came for the family to return home he was told to load their goods onto a waiting boat. He did so, but before the family appeared he walked down to the water, took a canoe fastened there, and paddled up the river. On a Saturday evening, he entered the town of Madison and enquired for a respectable colored family with whom he might spend the Sabbath, and was directed to the home of DeBaptiste. [Anti-Slavery History of Jefferson County, 1998: 11.]

DeBaptiste delivered the fugitive to Hoyt's father, who assisted him on his northward journey. As this incident suggests, at least by the 1840s, white antislavery activists began to support the work of and coordinate their efforts with local **free people of color**. For example, during this period, John Sering "opened the Clifty Falls route for fugitive slaves," a "rugged ravine and series of waterfalls ... located just a mile and a half west of Madison." Much like Mammoth Cave in south central Kentucky, "Clifty Falls provided a measure of cover for runaway slaves for some years." (Anti-Slavery History of Jefferson County, 1998: 13.)

Other activist whites included John C. Todd, Jacob Wagner, John Carr, Will Ryker, James Stewart and James Baxter. Nearby, the Nell's Creek Anti-Slavery Society, organized as noted in 1839, had 70 members by 1850. Through antislavery Baptist churches, some of its members contributed funds to **Eleutherian College** at Lancaster, Indiana — one of the few institutions in the antebellum United States committed to educating both blacks and whites.

FURTHER READING

Anti-Slavery History of Jefferson County. Madison, IN: Jefferson County Historical Society, 1998.
Coon, Diane P. "Reconstructing the Underground Railroad Crossings at Madison, Indiana," unpublished manuscript, 1998.
Coon, Diane P. *Southeastern Indiana's Underground Railroad Routes and Operations.* Indiana Department of Natural Resources, 2001.
Crenshaw, Gwendolyn J. *Bury Me in a Free Land: The Abolitionist Movement in Indiana, 1816–1865.* Indianapolis: Indiana Historical Bureau, 1993.
Horton, Colonel John Benjamin. *Old War Horse of Kentucky: The Life and Achievements of Albert Ernest Meyzeek.* Louisville: J. Benjamin Horton and Associates, 1986.
Hudson, J. Blaine. *Fugitive Slaves and the Underground Railroad in the Kentucky Borderland.* Jefferson, NC: McFarland, 2002.
Thornbrough, Emma L. *The Negro in Indiana before 1900.* Bloomington: Indiana University Press, 1957.

Maggie Bluecoat

See Palm, Margaret "Mag"

"The Man with the Branded Hand"

See Walker, Jonathan

Marks, Matthias

See Portland Crossing Point

Maroon Societies

From the earliest days of European colonization, regions beyond the boundaries of European settlement served as destinations for fugitive African slaves and a refuge wherein African-style societies, usually termed "maroon societies" or colonies (from the Spanish, "Cimarron," meaning "runaway"), were often established. Maroon societies were common in Central and South America (e.g., in Surinam, in Venezuela, in

Brazil) and on the larger Caribbean islands (e.g., Jamaica) and formed occasionally in North America as well.

Because **Native Americans**, often in pitifully reduced numbers, also dwelled beyond the frontiers of European settlement, the survival of runaway Africans often depended on whether they received a friendly reception from the nearby Native American societies. True to the old maxim, "the enemy of my enemy is my friend," Native Americans more often than not welcomed runaway Africans throughout the Americas—and some fascinating alliances emerged over the first two centuries and more of European colonization.

Fugitive slaves formed long-lived maroon settlements in the Louisiana bayous and the Great Dismal Swamp of Virginia and North Carolina. By far the most important North American maroon society was founded in northern and central Florida, where runaway Africans and Seminoles combined to produce a multiracial "state." The Seminoles and **Black Seminoles** began flocking to Spanish Florida before 1600 and, after the Carolina colony was founded in 1663 and began promoting the large scale importation of Africans, the flow of escaped slaves escalated and a complex society, blended through intermarriage, developed. Eventually, the United States would wage three costly and largely secret wars—the First (1816–1818), Second (1835–1842) and Third (1855) Seminole Wars— to remove this African/Native American presence. *See also* Slave Trade; Slavery.

FURTHER READING

Aptheker, Herbert. "Maroons within the present limits of the United States." *Journal of Negro History* 22(1939): 167–184.

Cobley, Alan G., and Alvin Thompson. *The African-Caribbean Connection: Historical and Cultural Perspectives*. Bridgetown, Barbados: University of the West Indies, 1990.

Forbes, J. D. *Africans and Native Americans: The Language of Race and the Evolution of Red-Black Peoples*. Urbana: University of Illinois Press, 1993.

Klein, Herbert S. *African Slavery in Latin America and the Caribbean*. New York: Oxford University Press, 1986.

Leaming, Hugo P. *Hidden Americans: Maroons of Virginia and the Carolinas*. New York: Garland, 1995.

Porter, K. W. "Relations between Negroes and Indians within the Present Limits of the United States." *Journal of Negro History* 16(1932): 287–367.

Price, Richard, ed. *Maroon Societies: Rebel Slave Communities in the Americas*. Baltimore, MD: Johns Hopkins University Press, 1996.

Wright, J. Leicht. *Creeks and Seminoles: The Destruction and Regeneration of the Muscogulge People*. Lincoln, NE: University of Nebraska Press, 1986.

Marrs, Elijah P. (1840–1910)

Fugitive slave. Elijah P. Marrs was born enslaved near Simpsonville, **Kentucky**, in January 1840, the son of a free man of color, Andrew Marrs, and an enslaved African American woman, Frances Marrs. Marrs learned secretly to read and write by age 11.

Marrs decided to flee **slavery** during the chaos of the **Civil War** in Kentucky. He persuaded 27 other men to join him and, on September 26, 1864, reached the Union Army recruiting office in nearby **Louisville, Kentucky**. Marrs enlisted in the U.S. Colored Troops, became a quartermaster and later commanded men in military actions near Bowling Green, Glasgow, Mumfordville and Elizabethtown, Kentucky.

After the war, Marrs was active in Republican Party politics and played a major role in education and religion in north central Kentucky. In 1866, he returned to his hometown, opened a school and became a teacher. In 1875, he was elected to serve as "messenger" to the General Association of Kentucky Baptists and, in 1879, helped found the Kentucky Normal and Theological Institute—which evolved into, first, Simmons University and, today, Simmons Bible College in Louisville. In 1880, he became pastor of Beargrass Baptist Church and, in 1881, became pastor of St. John Baptist Church in Louisville. Marrs died in Louisville on August 30, 1910. *See also* Fugitive Slaves.

FURTHER READING

Marrs, Elijah P. *History of the Reverend Elijah P. Marrs*. 1895.

Simmons, William J. *Men of Mark: Eminent, Progressive and Rising*. Cleveland, OH: George M. Rewell, 1887.

Mary Ann Shadd Cary House (Washington, D.C.)

Underground Railroad site recognized and documented by the National Park Service. *See also* Appendix 5.

Mary Meachum Freedom Crossing (St. Louis, Missouri)

Underground Railroad site recognized and documented by the National Park Service. *See also* Appendix 5.

Massachusetts

The history of Europeans in Massachusetts dates to 1620 when the Pilgrims, a group of English religious dissenters, first landed at Plymouth. Known initially as the Plymouth Colony, the early settlement flourished under the leadership of William Bradford. In 1629, the colony was renamed the Massachusetts Bay Colony and soon became the destination of many Puritans fleeing England in order to practice their religion without interference or persecution.

The colony expanded through warfare against the numerous **Native American** societies in the surrounding region and legalized **slavery** in 1641, bringing moderate numbers of enslaved African Americans into **Boston** and many of the smaller port and farming communities. Citizenship in Massachusetts was restricted to church members until 1664 and "dissidents" such as Anne Hutchinson and Roger Williams were banished. The early history of the colony was also shaped by a preoccupation with witchcraft and heresy, as exemplified in the Salem Witch Trials of 1692.

Massachusetts and many of its leading citizens played a prominent role in the **American Revolution**, e.g., the Boston Massacre on March 5, 1770, the Boston Tea Party on December 16, 1773, the "midnight ride" of Paul Revere on April 18, 1775, and the Battle of Bunker Hill in June 1775 at Charlestown. Early antislavery sentiment was strong as well and Massachusetts abolished slavery in 1783, one of key events that triggered the "first emancipation."

During the antebellum period, Massachusetts played two critical roles in the struggle against slavery. First, Massachusetts— and **Boston** in particular — were home to many of the most militant **abolitionists**, black and white. Second, although off the beaten track for fugitive slaves, Massachusetts communities such as Boston and **New Bedford** gained a well-deserved reputation as ports of entry for **fugitive slaves** escaping by sea and, even more importantly, for their determination to protect fugitive slaves from recapture. Once freedom seekers reached Massachusetts, some chose to remain in the state indefinitely, while others chose to follow the Connecticut River (through the Connecticut River Valley) northward in hopes of reaching **Canada**. *See also* Attucks, Crispus; Fugitive Slave Rescues.

FURTHER READING
Hart, Albert Bushnell. *Commonwealth History of Massachusetts.* 1927. Reprint, New York: Russell & Russell, 1966.
Siebert, Wilbur H. *The Underground Railroad from Slavery to Freedom.* 1898. Reprint, New York: Russell and Russell, 1967.
Siebert, Wilbur H. "The Underground Railroad in Massachusetts." *The New England Quarterly* 9(1936): 447–467.

Mattauer, John

Friend of the fugitive in Richmond, Virginia. *See also* Brown, Henry "Box"; and Appendixes 1 and 2.

Maulsby House (Plymouth Meeting, Pennsylvania)

Underground Railroad site. As early as 1820, Samuel Maulsby was an outspoken opponent of **slavery** and his large stone home served as a station on the Underground Railroad. *See also* Pennsylvania; Underground Railroad, Sites of; and Appendixes 3 and 4.

May, Samuel J. (1797–1871)

Friend of the fugitive. Samuel Joseph May, uncle of writer Louisa May Alcott, was born in 1797. May graduated from Harvard College and Cambridge Divinity School and spent most of his adult career as a minister in the Unitarian Church. While a minister in Brooklyn, Connecticut, he met Lucretia Flagge Coffin and the two married in 1825. After leaving Brooklyn, May also served as principal of the Normal School for Female Teachers in Lexington, **Massachusetts**. He then became minister of the Unitarian Church in Syracuse, New York, where he remained until his death.

May was a founding member of the American Antislavery Society. In this capacity, he organized numerous antislavery meetings, delivered frequent speeches and lectures, and occupied a broad range of leadership roles. May worked closely with the African American minister of the Syracuse AME Zion Church, the Reverend Jermain W. **Loguen**, to assist **fugitive slaves**—and used his home as an Underground Railroad station.

In 1846, May actively opposed the Mexican War and, in October 1851, he was a key figure in the famous Jerry Rescue in Syracuse. On the eve of John Brown's execution in December 1859, May organized a gathering in Brown's honor and, despite his deep ambivalence regarding the use of violent means in the struggle against slavery, stated simply: "The day has come; it is slavery or liberty. Compromises are at an end." (Yacovone, 1991: 166–167.) May viewed the destruction and bloodshed of the **Civil War** as a judgment on both the North and the South for participating in the sin of **slavery**. After emancipation, May raised money for freedmen's schools and other forms of assistance to ease the transition of formerly enslaved African Americans to freedom. May left the active ministry in 1868 and began living with his daughter, Charlotte May Wilkinson. He died in Syracuse on July 1, 1871. *See also* Henry, William "Jerry"; and Appendixes 1 and 2.

Samuel J. May (Library of Congress)

FURTHER READING
May, Samuel J. *Some Recollections of Our Anti-Slavery Conflict.* 1869. Reprint, New York: Arno Press, 1968.
Yacovone, Donald. *Samuel Joseph May and the Dilemmas of the Liberal Persuasion, 1797–1871.* Philadelphia: Temple University Press, 1991.

McClew, Charles, and Libby McClew

Friend of the fugitive. *See also* Murphy Orchards.

McKim, James Miller (1810–1874)

Friend of the fugitive. James Miller McKim was born in Carlisle, **Pennsylvania**, on November 14, 1810. He studied at Dickinson and Princeton colleges, and was ordained pastor of a Presbyterian church at Womelsdorf, Pennsylvania, in 1835.

Already an abolitionist, McKim helped found the American Anti-Slavery Society and, in October 1836, resigned the pulpit to become a full-time antislavery lecturer. He spoke throughout Pennsylvania — often at great personal risk and, in 1840, became the publishing agent of the Pennsylvania Anti-Slavery Society. McKim worked closely with William **Still** and the Underground Railroad operation in **Philadelphia**.

During the **Civil War**, he helped organize the freedmen's aid movement in 1862 and was a strong advocate of the enlistment of African American troops. McKim died in West Orange, New Jersey, on June 13, 1874. *See also* Underground Railroad, Sites of; and Appendixes 1–4.

FURTHER READING
Still, William. *The Underground Railroad.* 1872. Reprint, Chicago: Johnson, 1970.

Meachum, Mary

Friend of the fugitive in St. Louis, Missouri. *See also* Mary Meachum Freedom Crossing (St. Louis, Missouri); and Appendix 5.

Metropolitan AME Church (Washington, D.C.)

An important Underground Railroad station, Metropolitan AME Church was established in 1822 by disaffected African Americans who withdrew from a predominantly white church. Local oral tradition holds that fugitive slaves were harbored in the original church itself. Located at 1518 M Street, NW, the present church edifice was completed in 1886 and was the site of Frederick **Douglass**' funeral in 1895. *See also* Underground Railroad, Sites of; Underground Railroad, Stations on; Washington, D.C.; and Appendixes 3 and 4.

Mexico

Fugitive slave destination. The African **slave trade** delivered more than 200,000 Africans to Mexico over roughly 300 years, beginning as early as 1520. As in the rest of the Americas, African labor was vital to the Spanish colonies, and enslaved Africans were employed in the silver mines of Zacatecas, Taxco, Guanajuato, and Pachuca, on the sugar plantations in the Valle de Orizaba, on cattle ranches and in textile factories in Mexico City and Oaxaca.

Wherever **slavery** existed, Africans created adaptive networks that allowed them to cope, preserve something of their culture and resist bondage. For example, the first docu-

mented slave rebellion in Mexico occurred in 1537. Subsequent rebellions often involved **Native Americans** and mestizos (persons of mixed Native American ancestry) as allies. In addition, freedom seekers escaped into remote areas to establish maroon settlements known as "palenques," e.g., in the mountains near Veracruz under the leadership of Yagna. In the early 1800s, Native Americans, mestizos and mulattos were leaders in the struggle for Mexican independence, e.g., Jose' Maria Morelos y Parvon and Vicente Guerrero, later the second president of Mexico and the man who officially abolished slavery in 1822.

After the abolition of slavery, Mexico became a haven for fugitives from slavery in the United States, particularly in the Southwest. For example, in the summer of 1850, the Mascogos (the Seminoles and **Black Seminoles** from Florida) left the United States for the Mexican border state of Coahuila, founding the town of El Nacimiento, where many of their descendents remain today. *See also* Callahan Expedition; Routes of Escape; Texas;

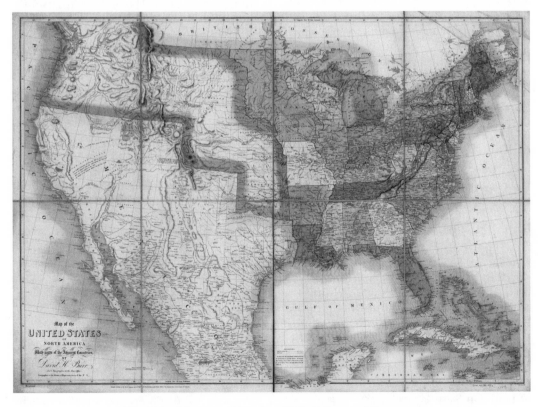

The United States and Mexico, 1839. (Library of Congress)

Underground Railroad, Sites of; and Appendixes 3 and 4.

FURTHER READING

Schoonover, Thomas. "Misconstrued Mission: Expansionism and Black Colonization in Mexico and Central America during the Civil War." *Pacific Historical Review* 49(1980): 607–620.

Zelinsky, Wilbur. "The Historical Geography of the Negro Population of Latin America." *Journal of Negro History* 34(1949): 153–221.

Michigan Avenue Baptist Church (Buffalo, New York)

An important Underground Railroad station, the Michigan Avenue Baptist Church is best known for its association with William Wells **Brown**. *See also* Underground Railroad, Sites of; Underground Railroad, Stations on; and Appendixes 3 and 4.

Miller, Jonathan P.

Friend of the fugitive. Colonel Jonathan P. Miller was a prominent attorney and legislator in antebellum Vermont. Miller used his home at Montpelier as an Underground Railroad station and **fugitive slaves**, according to the recollections of Miller's daughter, Mrs. Abijiah Keith, often arrived and departed by stagecoach. In 1836, Miller defended antislavery lecturer the Reverend Samuel J. **May**, facing down an angry proslavery crowd at the Montpelier State House to protect May and then escorting him to safety. *See also* Appendixes 1 and 2.

Milton House (Milton, Wisconsin)

Underground Railroad site recognized and documented by the National Park Service. *See also* Appendix 5.

Minkins, Shadrach

Fugitive slave and famous fugitive slave rescue case. Shadrach Minkins was born enslaved in Norfolk, Virginia, and, after having been sold several times, became the property of John DeBree. Minkins escaped and reached **Boston** in 1850, where he found work as a waiter at the Taft's Cornhill Coffee House. DeBree traced Minkins and presented proof of ownership to the Boston federal court under the provisions of the **Fugitive Slave Act of 1850**. On Saturday, February 15, 1851, two federal officers posing as customers seized Minkins and imprisoned him in a nearby courthouse pending a hearing.

Boston attorneys Robert Morris, Richard Henry Dana, Jr., Ellis Gray Loring, and Samuel E. Sewall offered their services as Minkins' counsel and petitioned for a writ of *habeas corpus* to secure his release. However, Lemuel Shaw, chief justice of the Supreme Judicial Court of **Massachusetts**, refused to consider their petition.

Boston was home to a small free black community and was a center of antislavery activity. As the first test of the Fugitive Slave Act of 1850, Minkins' arrest "in their own backyard" outraged both groups. As news of the arrest spread, a crowd of angry African Americans and white abolitionists converged on the courthouse, overcame armed guards and forced their way into the courtroom itself. In the struggle that ensued, the crowd rescued Minkins, spirited him from the courtroom and hid him temporarily in Beacon Hill. The entire event, from Minkins' arrest to his rescue, occurred over a period of only three hours. Then, Lewis **Hayden**, John J. Smith, and other members of Boston's free black community helped Minkins escape from Massachusetts altogether.

In the aftermath, nine abolitionists, including Lewis Hayden and the African American attorney Robert Morris were indicted. Charges against some were soon dismissed. Hayden and Morris were tried, but each was acquitted. Minkins was conducted to Watertown, then Cambridge and eventually found his way to Quebec Province, **Canada**. He married, raised a family and became a central figure in a small community populated largely by **fugitive slaves**.

As the first fugitive slave arrested under the Fugitive Slave Act of 1850, the mass defiance of the act embodied in the Shadrach Minkins rescue was termed, by some, as the first battle in the "war before the (Civil) war." *See also* Fugitive Slave Rescues.

FURTHER READING

Bearse, Austin. *Reminiscences of Fugitive-Slave Law Days in Boston*. Boston: Warren Richardson, 1880.

Collison, Gary. "This Flagitious Offense: Daniel Webster and the Shadrach Rescue Cases, 1851–1852." *New England Quarterly* 68, no. 4(1995).

Collison, Gary Lee. *Shadrach Minkins: From Fugitive Slave to Citizen.* Cambridge, MA: Harvard University Press, 1997.

The Mirror of Slavery

After escaping from **slavery** in a crate shipped from Richmond, Virginia, to **Philadelphia, Pennsylvania**, Henry "Box" **Brown** became a popular antislavery lecturer. To strengthen his public presentation, Brown borrowed $150 from abolitionist Gerrit **Smith** and engaged Josiah Wolcott to design and paint a panorama of African and African American history, *The Mirror of Slavery*. The *Mirror* began with sections on "the African **slave trade**," "the Nubian family in freedom," "the seizure of slaves" and extended to scenes of slavery — and black resistance — in the United States. Brown also commissioned Benjamin F. Roberts, a black printer from **Boston** (and plaintiff in the 1849 *Roberts v. Boston* school segregation case), to write an accompanying text, "The Condition of the Colored People in the United States."

The *Mirror* was first displayed on April 19, 1850, in Washington Hall in Boston for an adult admission fee of 25 cents and remained on exhibit for several months. After fleeing the United States in October 1850, Brown toured with the *Mirror* in England through the spring of 1851.

FURTHER READING
Brown, Henry. *Narrative of the Life of Henry "Box" Brown.* 1850.
Nichols, Charles H., ed. *Black Men in Chains: Narratives by Escaped Slaves.* New York: L. Hill, 1972.

Mississippi

As cotton cultivation expanded into the Gulf States after the War of 1812, the number of enslaved African Americans in Mississippi (statehood in 1817) increased rapidly. By 1860, more than half of the state population (55.3 percent) was black and virtually all African Americans in the state were enslaved.

Given the harsh conditions of **slavery**, particularly in the cotton belt, the large black population was restive. Escapes and revolts were common — although the probability of success of either strategy was low. As an early example, in 1800, the territorial governor requested additional weapons after the Gabriel

Revolt in Virginia. As another, in July 1835, an attempted insurrection in Madison County was foiled — resulting in the execution of 21 conspirators. Interestingly, six of those executed were white. Following this pattern, one white man and a number of blacks were executed after another conspiracy was squelched in July 1841. Rumors of larger scale uprisings were rife through the 1840s and **1850s**, culminating in a probable Christmas revolt near Canton.

The involvement of whites in these conspiracies and in assisting **fugitive slaves** reflects Mississippi's unusual demography. Specifically, while African Americans were 50 to 65 percent of the population in the cotton belt, there were counties in northeastern and southern Mississippi where the black population was less than one percent. In these nonslaveholding sections of the state, there were a great many whites who were no friends to slaveholders — and a few, apparently, who were friends to enslaved African Americans. *See also* Underground Railroad, Sites of; and Appendixes 3 and 4.

FURTHER READING
McKibben, Davidson B. "Negro Slave Insurrections in Mississippi." *Journal of Negro History* 34, no. 1(1949): 73–94.

The Missouri Compromise

By 1820, westward expansion and the spread of cotton cultivation in the Gulf States had deepened sectional divisions between the slave-holding and non-slave-holding states. A political balance had evolved, based on the very structure of the United States government, that served to "manage" these divisions.

The "formula" was simple, in principle. Under the U.S. Constitution, seats in the House of Representatives were apportioned on the basis of population and, because, enslaved African Americans were only counted as "three-fifths of a person," the slave-holding states could not expect to control the House. However, seats in the U.S. Senate were apportioned on the basis of two seats per state, regardless of population. Thus, if the number of slave states and free states remained equal — and the president and vice-president (who, as president of the Senate, could break any tie votes) were sympathetic to slavery —

any legislation that might harm slave-holding interests could be blocked.

The early settlement of the Louisiana Territory, acquired in 1803, threatened to upset this balance — specifically, over the issue of admitting Missouri to the Union as a slave state. **Slavery** existed in the Missouri territory, but, beginning in 1818, an effort was made to exclude slavery from the territory as a condition of statehood. When a bill was introduced in 1820 to allow Missouri to enter the Union as a state, Representative James Tallmadge (New York) proposed an amendment that would prohibit the further introduction of enslaved African Americans into Missouri and the gradual emancipation of those already there. Southern reaction was immediate, strong and negative, and many southerners threatened disunion if Tallmadge did not back down. In a December 10, 1819 letter to fellow former president, John Adams, Thomas Jefferson (d. 1826) stated that the issue was as terrifying as "a fire bell in the night." (Malone, 1981: 329.)

In the end, Henry Clay of **Kentucky**, a slave-holding member of the House, engineered a compromise: Missouri would be admitted as a slave state; Maine, formerly part of **Massachusetts**, would be admitted as a free state; and the remainder of the Louisiana Territory would be divided into areas open to slavery and areas closed to it — using latitude 36° 30 minutes N (the southern boundary of Missouri and Kentucky) as the dividing line. These key provisions were accepted and Missouri was admitted to the Union in 1821, and disunion was averted — for a generation.

Viewed somewhat differently, the Missouri Compromise also reflected unwillingness on the part of most northerners to risk civil war or disunion over the issue of slavery, but, at the same time, the determination of the South to fight, if necessary, for the preservation of its "peculiar institution."

FURTHER READING

Fehrenbacher, Don Edward. *The South and the Three Sectional Crises.* Baton Rouge, LA: Louisiana State University Press, 1980.

Franklin, John Hope, and Alfred A. Moss, Jr. *From Slavery to Freedom: A History of African Americans.* 8th ed. New York: McGraw-Hill, 2000.

Malone, Dumas. *Jefferson and His Time, Volume Six: The Sage of Monticello.* Boston: Little, Brown, 1981.

Monroe, William

Friend of the fugitive in **Detroit, Michigan.** *See also* Finney House; and Appendixes 1 and 2.

Morehead, Henry

Fugitive slave. In one of the most poignant slave escape accounts, a fugitive slave family, determined not to risk betrayal by asking for any assistance, made a courageous dash for freedom in 1854 and was rescued, ultimately, by **friends of the fugitive.** The husband, Henry Morehead, was interviewed in **Canada** in 1856, indicating that he had been "born and bred a slave" in **Louisville, Kentucky,** but that:

> I left **slavery** a little more than a year ago. I brought my wife and three children with me, and had not enough to bring us through ... I left because they were about selling my wife and children to the South. I would rather have followed them to the grave, than to see them go down ... so I took them and started for Canada. I was pursued — my owners watched for me in a free State, but, to their sad disappointment, I took another road. A hundred miles further on, I saw my advertisements again offering $500 for me and my family ... I was longer on the road than I should have been without my burden: one child was nine months old, one two years old and one four. The weather was cold and my feet were frostbitten, as I gave my wife my socks to pull on over her shoes. With all the sufferings of the frost and the fatigues of travel, it was not so bad as the effects of slavery. [Drew, 1856: 180–181.]

Although Morehead eventually "took the Underground Railroad" to complete his journey to Canada, his escape was unaided until its final phases — a testament to his courage and that of his family.

FURTHER READING

Drew, Benjamin. *The Refugee: Or the Narratives of Fugitive Slaves in Canada.* Boston: John P. Jewett and Company, 1856.

Hudson, J. Blaine. *Fugitive Slaves and the Underground Railroad in the Kentucky Borderland.* Jefferson, NC: McFarland, 2002.

Morris, Shelton (1806–1889)

Friend of the fugitive. Shelton Morris was an important friend of the fugitive in both **Louisville, Kentucky** and **Cincinnati, Ohio.**

Morris was born in 1806 and, along with his family, was freed by the will of Richard Morris of Louisa County, Virginia, in 1820. After the death of his mother, Morris, as the eldest of the six children, assumed responsibility for his younger brothers and invested his small inheritance in his barbershop, a bathhouse, and in real estate. Significantly, when Morris married Evalina Spradling in 1828, he also established an alliance with her brother, Washington **Spradling**, his partner as architect of Louisville's free black community.

Like Spradling, he loaned money to enslaved African Americans to facilitate their efforts at self-purchase — often purchasing and then emancipating them himself. Morris was also deeply involved in regional work of assisting **fugitive slaves**. For example, Morris's wife died in 1841 and he soon moved to Cincinnati, **Ohio**, after "being accused of voting for Gen. Harrison for President," since voting was an illegal act for a free person of color in Kentucky. (Gibson, 1897: 28.) In Cincinnati, he went into business with Michael Clark, the first husband of his sister, Eliza, and the African American son of Louisville's William Clark (of the Lewis and Clark Expedition), working as a barber in Cincinnati and on the steamboats that plied the Ohio and Mississippi Rivers.

Both he and his oldest son, Horace, were active in the antislavery movement and in the Underground Railroad in Cincinnati. There, he worked closely with Levi **Coffin** in the **1850s**, and was considered by Coffin to be the most "careful operator" in Cincinnati's African American community. Morris died at Wilberforce, Ohio, in 1889. *See also* Appendixes 1 and 2.

FURTHER READING

Graham, Ruth Morris. *The Saga of the Morris Family.* Columbus, GA: Brentwood Christian Communications, 1984.

Hudson, J. Blaine. "Crossing the Dark Line: Fugitive Slaves and The Underground Railroad in Louisville and North Central Kentucky." *The Filson History Quarterly* 75, no. 1(2001): 33–84.

Lucas, Ernestine G. *Wider Windows to the Past: African American History from a Family Perspective.* Decorah, IA: Anundsen, 1995.

Moses Sawyer House (Weare, New Hampshire)

Moses Sawyer was a committed abolitionist and friend of the fugitive. His home in Weare, New Hampshire, was an Underground Railroad station and possibly where Frederick **Douglass** began writing the first version of his autobiography. *See also* Underground Railroad, Sites of; and Appendixes 1–4.

Mother African Union Protestant Church (Wilmington, Delaware)

The Mother African Union Protestant Church was established in 1813 and served as a major Underground Railroad station under the able leadership of the Reverend Peter Spencer. The church still stands on French Street, between Eighth and Ninth Streets, in Wilmington. The Reverend Spencer is buried nearby. *See also* Underground Railroad, Sites of; and Appendixes 3 and 4.

Mother Zion AME Church (New York City)

Founded in 1800, Mother Zion AME Church is the oldest African American church in New York State. Under the leadership of the Rev. James Varick, Mother Zion was a bulwark of the abolition movement and significant station on the Underground Railroad. The original church was located on Leonard Street, but later moved to Harlem. *See also* Underground Railroad, Sites of; and Appendixes 3 and 4.

Motivations for Escape

Slave escapes were motivated by factors intrinsic to the lives and circumstances of fugitives themselves. In some cases, escapes were prompted by a discernible "trigger event." For example, the motives cited most frequently by **fugitive slaves** were physical or sexual mistreatment or the threat thereof, sale or the threat thereof, or broken promises (for example, if a slave-holder reneged on a promise to permit self-purchase). The threat of sale, with its impact on families, was particularly powerful in slave-trading states such as Missouri, **Kentucky**, Maryland and Virginia. In other cases, escapes seem to have been motivated only by the simple desire for freedom and, at times, pure opportunism.

A slave father is sold away from his family in this 1860 lithograph. (Library of Congress)

Runaway slaves would jeopardize their freedom to be near or seek to free loved ones. Although enslaved African Americans could not marry legally, they were often permitted to marry in plantation ceremonies that included rituals such as "jumping the broom" or even in church ceremonies as Christianity became more common among African Americans. Fear for the fate of one's children, even those unborn, seems to have prompted many escapes involving enslaved African American women. However, even with considerable assistance, slave escapes were dangerous and physically demanding for African American men; thus, given the risks of flight, escapes by pregnant women or women with children seemed particularly desperate and suggested either the operation of some powerful trigger-

ing event — or, perhaps, the expectation of significant assistance along the escape route that offset the impracticalities of flight. *See also* Drapetomania; Enticing; Harboring.

FURTHER READING

Hudson, J. Blaine. *Fugitive Slaves and the Underground Railroad in the Kentucky Borderland.* Jefferson, NC: McFarland, 2002.

Siebert, Wilbur H. *The Underground Railroad from Slavery to Freedom.* 1898. Reprint, New York: Russell and Russell, 1967.

Still, William. *The Underground Railroad.* 1872. Reprint, Chicago: Johnson, 1970.

Mott, Peter (c. 1807–1881)

A friend of the fugitive, Peter Mott was born free around 1810 in Delaware and moved to New Jersey as a young man. On November

2, 1833, he married Elizabeth Ann Thomas from Virginia and later became an African Methodist Episcopal minister.

The Motts settled in a free black community known as Snow Hill that later merged with a neighboring settlement called Free Haven, developed in 1840 by Ralph Smith, a white abolitionist who was the first secretary of the Philadelphia Vigilance Committee. As such, the small community grew as a result of the abolition of **slavery** in New Jersey and the migration of **free people of color**, like Peter Mott, from nearby slave states. In 1845, Mott purchased land in Free Haven, New Jersey, on which he built his two-story home in 1845.

Given its proximity to slave territory, Lawnside became a center of Underground Railroad activity — and Mott, as a community leader, played a central role in assisting **fugitive slaves**. He also became minister of Snow Hill Church, known today as **Mount Pisgah AME Church**, and founded its Sunday School in 1847. *See also* Peter Mott House; Vigilance Committees.

Mount Gilead AME Church (Buckingham Mountain, Pennsylvania)

Built in 1835 near Buckingham Mountain, the Mount Gilead African Methodist Episcopal Church was the last Underground Railroad station leading to the Delaware River and thence to New Jersey. Mount Gilead was founded by "Big Ben" Jones, himself a fugitive slave — six feet 10 inches tall. *See also* Pennsylvania; Underground Railroad, Sites of; and Appendixes 3 and 4.

Mount Pisgah AME Church (Lawnside, New Jersey)

Mount Pisgah AME church was founded in 1792 in the African American community of Lawnside (then known as Free Haven) in Camden County, New Jersey. The church was an important stop on the Underground Railroad and the home church of the Still family — including William **Still**, the great friend of the fugitive based in **Philadelphia**. *See also* Underground Railroad, Sites of; and Appendixes 3 and 4.

Mount Pleasant, Ohio

Underground Railroad site recognized and documented by the National Park Service. *See also* Appendix 5.

Mount Zion AME Church (Woolwich Township, New Jersey)

Underground Railroad site recognized and documented by the National Park Service. *See also* Appendix 5.

Mount Zion United AME Church (Washington, D.C.)

An important Underground Railroad station. Mt. Zion United AME Church had perhaps the oldest African American congregation in **Washington, D.C.** According to legend, **fugitive slaves** were concealed in a burial vault in the church cemetery. *See also* Underground Railroad, Sites of; and Appendixes 3 and 4.

Murphy Orchards (Burt, New York)

Underground Railroad site recognized and documented by the National Park Service. *See also* Appendix 5.

Murray, Samuel

A friend of the fugitive, Samuel Murray was a free African American shoemaker in Reading, **Pennsylvania**. In 1837, Murray, who also owned 13 local properties, used his holdings as collateral to finance the construction of the **Bethel AME Church** in Reading. Murray became the first pastor of Bethel AME — and he and his congregation provided refuge for **fugitive slaves** in the decades before the **Civil War**. *See also* Underground Railroad, Sites of.

FURTHER READING
National Park Service. *Underground Railroad: Special Resource Study.* Washington, D.C.: U.S. Government Printing Office, 1995.

Nalle, Charles (b. 1821)

Fugitive slave; fugitive slave rescue. Charles Nalle was born enslaved in 1821 in Stevensberg, Virginia. When he was 16, Nalle and other members of his family were sold to Blucher Hansborough, the son of a Virginia planter, who may also have been Nalle's younger half-brother. A few years later, financial reverses prompted Hansborough to consider selling some or all of his slave property. Faced with the prospect of sale, Nalle and another enslaved African American, Jim Banks, made their break for freedom in October 1858 and reached the Troy, New York, area — a seemingly safe haven with an active vigilance committee and a small but significant community of African Americans.

Nalle found work and lodged with the family of William Henry, a black grocer who was also a member of the vigilance committee. Deeply concerned about the family he left behind, but unable to read and write, Nalle asked an unemployed lawyer, Horace Averill, to help him compose letters that might free his family in Virginia. However, instead of helping Nalle, Averill betrayed him.

On April 27, 1860, Nalle was arrested by U.S. Deputy Marshall John W. Holmes on behalf of Henry Wale, a slave catcher from Stevensberg, Virginia. As word spread, a crowd soon gathered outside the U.S. commissioner's office, eager for an opportunity to rescue Nalle. Purely by coincidence, Harriett **Tubman**, the redoubtable "Moses of her people," was in Troy at the time, en route to an antislavery meeting in **Boston**. Once informed of Nalle's plight, Tubman hastened to the commissioner's office, forced her way through the excited crowd and rushed up the stairs to the room where Nalle was held. When the officers tried to remove Nalle,

> Tubman seized one and pulled him down, then another and tore him away from the man; and keeping her arms about the slave, cried to her friends: "Drag us out! Drag him to the river! Drown him! But don't let them have him!" They were knocked down together, and while down, she tore off her sunbonnet and tied it on the head of the fugitive. When he rose, only his head could be seen, and amid the surging mass of people the slave was no longer recognized, while the master appeared like the slave. Again and again they were knocked down, the poor slave utterly helpless, with his manacled wrists streaming with blood. Harriet's outer clothes were torn from her, and even her stout shoes were pulled from her feet. Yet she never relinquished her hold of the man, till she had dragged him to the river.... [Bradford, 1993: 1223–123.]

One African American was killed in the struggle and Tubman herself was injured. Nalle, however, escaped to Niskayuna, where he stayed in a secret location until it was regarded as safe for his return to Troy. He moved to Washington, D.C. in 1867.

FURTHER READING
Bradford, Sarah H. *Harriet Tubman: The Moses of Her People.* Bedford, MA: Applewood Books, 1993.

Nason House (Augusta, Maine)

The Nason family was committed to the antislavery cause and their home in Augusta served as a refuge for **fugitive slaves** bound for eastern **Canada**. The house had a hidden room behind a bookcase large enough to conceal two fugitive slaves; it led to a cellar and eventually to the outside. *See also* Underground Railroad, Sites of; and Appendixes 3 and 4.

Nathan and Mary (Polly) Johnson House (New Bedford, Massachusetts)

Underground Railroad site recognized and documented by the National Park Service. *See also* Appendix 5.

Nathan Thomas House (Schoolcraft, Michigan)

Built in 1835, the home and medical office of Dr. Nathan **Thomas** served as a station on the Underground Railroad. **Fugitive slaves** who found their way to the Thomas home were particularly fortunate since they could receive medical care as well as other forms of aid. *See also* Underground Railroad, Sites of; and Appendixes 3 and 4.

National Underground Railroad Freedom Center

The National Underground Railroad Freedom Center was proposed in 1994 and incorporated formally in 1995. The center, as stated in its mission, "...brings to life the inspiring, heroic stories of courage, cooperation and perseverance in the pursuit of freedom, especially from Underground Railroad history. We provide forums for inclusive dialogue, and encourage every individual to take a journey that advances freedom and personal growth."

The center was designed by Walter Blackburn of Blackburn Architects, Indianapolis, Indiana. Construction began on June 17, 2002; after roughly $100 million was raised, the center opened on August 23, 2004 in downtown **Cincinnati, Ohio**. At its opening, the center stood as a three-pavilion, 158,000 square-foot structure, organized around historical exhibits, artifacts, galleries and interactive learning stations. Dr. Spencer Crew was executive director and CEO, and Ed Rigaud was president; the staff included over ninety persons. The center also sponsors the Freedom Stations network of researchers and educators across the United States.

For further information, the National Underground Railroad Freedom Center can be contacted at 513–333–7500.

FURTHER READING
National Underground Railroad Freedom Center. Press release, August 2004.

National Underground Railroad Network to Freedom

See Appendix 5

Native Americans

In colonial America, many **fugitive slaves** escaped across the frontier into Native American territory. Acting consistent with the dictum that "the enemy of my enemy is my friend," Native Americans usually welcomed fugitive slaves in this early period. For example, in Spanish and, later, British, Florida, African Americans fleeing **slavery** in the Carolinas were granted freedom by the Spanish, helped defend the colony at fortifications such as **Fort Mose**, and forged a racially blended society with the Seminoles. In **Kentucky** and the Ohio Territory, the early white pioneers often found African Americans, such as Pompey, the "Black Shawnee," living among the Native Americans of the trans-Appalachian west.

Between the 1780s and 1840, as American settlement spread westward and the Native Americans east of the Mississippi River were systematically dispossessed, white Americans used their growing power to drive a wedge between the other two races. For example, seven of the eight treaties negotiated with major Native American societies between 1784 and 1786 contained clauses for the return of "Negroes and other property" as a condition attached to achieving peace or retaining territory. As cotton cultivation spread into the Gulf States after 1800, Native Americans such as the Cherokee and Chickasaw were also encouraged to become slave-holders to improve their relations with whites.

The passage of the Indian Removal Act in 1830 brought the relocation of the "five civilized Indian nations" (the Choctaw, Chickasaw, Creek, Cherokee and Seminole) from east to west of the Mississippi River by the early 1840s. As the frontier moved ever westward, escaping to the Native Americans became a less promising option than simply escaping across the border between the free and slave states or between the United States and **Canada** or **Mexico**.

Ultimately, the long-standing alliance between blacks and Native Americans could not withstand the growing power of the expanding United States that, first, pressed Native Americans to adopt slavery and, after the **Civil War**, employed black soldiers— the famous Buffalo Soldiers— to complete the conquest of the Native Americans of the Great Plains and the Southwest. *See also* Black Seminoles; Maroon Societies.

FURTHER READING
Jeltz, Wyatt F. "The Relations of Negroes and Choctaw and Chickasaw Indians." *Journal of Negro History* 33 (1948): 24–37.
Katz, William Loren. *Black Indians: A Hidden Heritage.* New York: Atheneum, 1986.
Willis, William S. "Divide and Rule: Red, White, and Black in the Southeast." *Journal of Negro History* 48(1963): 157–176.

"Negro Dogs"

See Bloodhounds

Negro Fort

See Black Seminoles; British Fort; Underground Railroad, Sites of; and Appendixes 3 and 4.

Nell, William Cooper (1816–1874)

Friend of the fugitive and abolitionist. William Cooper Nell was born in **Boston** in 1816. His father was William Guion Nell, a tailor from Charleston, South Carolina, and a friend and colleague of David Walker. At the age of 13, Nell entered the Abiel Smith School and won awards for academic achievement.

In the early 1830s, Nell worked for William Lloyd **Garrison** as an errand boy and was apprenticed as a printer for *The Liberator*. In 1840, Nell submitted a petition, with over two thousand signatures, to the **Massachusetts** Legislature demanding school integration. After the 1849 Roberts v. Boston ruling upheld segregation in the city's public education system, Nell launched a dogged campaign that resulted in the integration of Boston schools in 1855. More broadly, Nell opposed all separate black institutions, including churches, which brought him into conflict with other African American leaders of his time.

Nell championed the antislavery cause with the same skill and determination with which he worked to expand the civil rights of **free people of color**. In 1842, he was a founding member of the New England Freedom Association, an organization committed to assisting **fugitive slaves**. In 1847, despite his disagreement with other black abolitionists over integration, he nonetheless helped Frederick **Douglass** launch the *North Star* and, in 1851, assisted the rescue of Shadrach **Minkins**. Significantly, also in 1851, he published *Services of Colored Americans in the Wars of 1776 and 1812*, and, in 1855, *The Colored Patriots of the American Revolution*, giving him the distinction of being the first African American historian.

In 1861, Nell was appointed a clerk in the United States postal department, becoming the first African American to hold a federal government position. He died on May 25, 1874 in Boston. *See also* Abolitionist Movement; and Appendixes 1 and 2.

FURTHER READING
Horton, James, and Lois E. Horton. *Black Bostonians: Family Life and Struggle in the Antebellum North*. New York: Holmes & Meier, 1999.
Jacobs, Donald M., ed. Courage *and Conscience: Black and White Abolitionists in Boston*. Indianapolis, IN: Indiana University Press, 1993.
Smith, Earl. "William Cooper Nell on the Fugitive Slave Act of 1850." *Journal of Negro History* 66(1981): 37–40.
Smith, Robert P. "William Cooper Nell, Crusading Black Abolitionist." *Journal of Negro History* 55(1970): 182–199.

Nemacolin Castle (Brownsville, Pennsylvania)

Underground Railroad site. In 1786, Jacob Bowman built the stone structure known as Nemacolin Castle as a residence and trading post in Brownsville. Enlarged in 1847, Bowman's home was used to harbor **fugitive slaves** passing through the town. *See also* Pennsylvania; Underground Railroad, Sites of; and Appendixes 3 and 4.

New Bedford, Massachusetts

Underground Railroad center. New Bedford was an important sanctuary for **fugitive slaves**. As a key New England seaport, it was home to African American and white seamen who assisted fugitive slaves and served as a refuge for freedom seekers as well. Known as the "Fugitive's Gibraltar," the antislavery community of New Bedford prided itself on its determination to protect the fugitive slaves living in their midst — and, between 1790 and 1860, hundreds of fugitive slaves found refuge there.

Among them were Henry "Box" **Brown** and Frederick **Douglass.** Douglass lived for several years in the protective environs of New Bedford after his escape from **slavery** in 1838 and adapted to life as a free man before beginning his public career. *See also* Underground Railroad, Sites of; and Appendixes 3 and 4.

FURTHER READING
Grover, Kathryn. *The Fugitive's Gibraltar: Escaping Slaves and Abolitionism in New Bedford, Massachusetts*. Amherst: University of Massachusetts Press, 2001.

New England

See Routes of Escape

New York City

Underground Railroad junction. New York City was a center of the antislavery movement and an important sanctuary for **fugitive slaves**. The combined efforts of an active white antislavery community and a committed free black community made New York a haven for freedom seekers bound for New England or **Canada**. *See also* Ruggles, David; Underground Railroad, Sites of; and Appendixes 3 and 4.

Newspapers, Antebellum African American

Antebellum African American newspapers are a major primary source for the study of **fugitive slaves** and the Underground Railroad. Black newspapers were not numerous during the ante-bellum period, but those that were established focused on national rather than local issues and represent extremely valuable sources regarding fugitive slaves and the antislavery movement. The first, *Freedom's Journal,* began publication in **New York City** on March 16, 1827 under the joint editorship of John B. Russworm and Samuel E. Cornish. An important but short-lived effort, its last issue appeared on October 9, 1829 after Russworm immigrated to Liberia. Cornish later joined the editorship of *The Weekly Advocate* in January 1837, which became *The Colored American* in March 1837. Martin R. **Delany**, sometimes considered the first black nationalist, founded and edited the *Mystery* in Pittsburgh from 1843 to 1847. Moreover, as the black population in **Canada** increased, other black newspapers were established there, most important among them the *Provincial Freeman* by Mary Ann Shadd **Cary** and Samuel Ringgold Ward and the *Voice of the Fugitive* by Henry **Bibb**. Frederick **Douglass**, the most important black abolitionist, was also the most important black newspaper editor and publisher. His first publication, *The North Star,* appeared on November 1, 1847 in Rochester, New York — with Martin Delany as co-editor until May 1848. In 1851, *The North Star* merged with the *Liberty Party Paper* and was renamed the *Frederick Douglass Paper.* See the bibliography for a complete listing of ante-bellum black newspapers.

FURTHER READING
Wolseley, Roland E. *The Black Press, U.S.A.* Ames, IA: Iowa State University Press, 1991.

Niagara Frontier Bible Church (Lewiston, New York)

Underground Railroad site. A converted monastery, the Niagara Frontier Bible Church was a sanctuary for **fugitive slaves** awaiting transport — or an opportunity to swim — across the Niagara River to **Canada**. *See also* Underground Railroad, Sites of; and Appendixes 3 and 4.

North Star

Much as **fugitive slaves** used natural escape routes and sanctuaries, they also used natural and celestial objects as beacons on their journey to freedom. Fugitive slaves seeking liberty in the free states or **Canada** learned to follow the North Star, Polaris. As a result, Polaris became both a symbol of freedom and a guide-star to free territory.

In astronomical terms, Polaris, or Alpha Ursae Minoris, is a star near the north celestial pole. It is a hot, blue supergiant more than 400 light years distant from Earth, with a visual magnitude of 1.97 and a luminosity roughly 2400 times that of the sun — technically, a variable star whose luminosity varies by 0.15 magnitude every four days.

Because Polaris is so near the north celestial pole, it appears neither to rise nor set in the northern sky and always marks the direction north. Visually, however, Polaris is a rather ordinary, second magnitude star of moderate brightness in a constellation of dim stars to the naked eye, Ursa Minor (the Little Bear) or, in the United States, the Little Dipper. Thus, to find north it was first necessary to find the North Star and another, more famous star formation assisted fugitives in achieving this end. This constellation was known as the Big Dipper, or Ursa Major (the Great Bear). *See also* Routes of Escape.

FURTHER READING
Siebert, Wilbur H. *The Underground Railroad from Slavery to Freedom.* 1898. Reprint, New York: Russell and Russell, 1967.
Still, William. *The Underground Railroad.* 1872. Reprint, Chicago: Johnson, 1970.

Northup, Solomon (b. 1808)

Solomon Northup was born free in New York in 1808. In 1829, he married Anne Hampton and lived in Saratoga, New York, for a time where he worked in hotels and played the violin at night. While visiting **Washington, D.C.**, in 1841, Northup was captured by kidnappers and sold into **slavery** in Louisiana.

Northup became the property of Edwin Epps, a harsh owner, and became a common slave laborer. Eventually, Northup was able to get word to his wife with the assistance of a sympathetic white man who worked as free laborer on the same plantation. Anne Northup then petitioned the governor of New York. Northup regained his freedom in 1853 and recounted his ordeal in his autobiography, *Twelve Years a Slave*.

FURTHER READING
Northup, Solomon. *Twelve Years a Slave: Narrative of Solomon Northup, a Citizen of New-York, Kidnapped in Washington City in 1841, and Rescued in 1853.* Auburn, NY: Derby and Miller, 1853.

Nova Scotia

Underground Railroad destination in **Canada**. Between 1783 and 1785, in the immediate aftermath of the **American Revolution**, more than three thousand African Americans migrated to Nova Scotia in Upper Canada. These "Black Loyalists" formed several communities, such as Birchtown and Tracadie, in the late 1700s and early 1800s. In the 1790s, following the Second Maroon War in Jamaica, 600 Jamaica maroons were deported to Nova Scotia. Beginning during the War of 1812,

these settlements also served at times as destinations for **fugitive slaves** whose flight by sea or land brought them to Nova Scotia. *See also* Maroon Societies.

FURTHER READING
Grant, John N. "Black Immigrants to Nova Scotia." *Journal of Negro History* 58(1973): 253–270.

Oakdale (Chadds Ford, Pennsylvania)

Underground Railroad site recognized and documented by the National Park Service. *See also* Appendix 5.

Oberlin College (Oberlin, Ohio)

In 1833, the Oberlin Collegiate Institute opened at Oberlin, **Ohio**, and became Oberlin College in 1850. One of the first colleges to have interracial and coeducational classes, Oberlin College was also a center of abolitionism and a station on the Underground Railroad. *See also* Oberlin-Wellington Rescue.

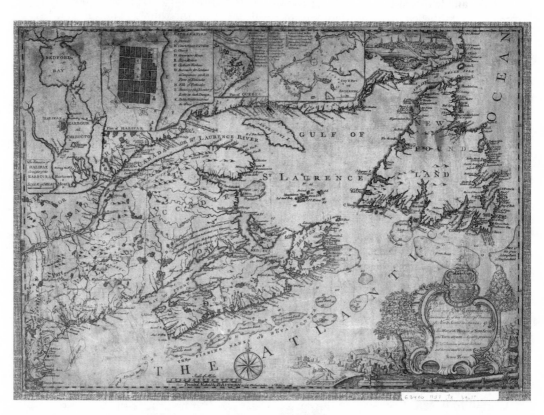

Canada's Maritime Provinces, 1776. (Library of Congress)

FURTHER READING

Fletcher, Robert S. "The Government of the Oberlin Colony." *The Mississippi Valley Historical Review* 20 (1933): 179–190.

Fletcher, Robert S. *A History of Oberlin College from Its Foundation through the Civil War.* Oberlin, OH: Oberlin College, 1943.

Oberlin-Wellington Rescue (1858)

The last significant fugitive slave rescue case of the **1850s**. In September 1858, John, who fled John G. Bacon of Mason County, **Kentucky**, was discovered at Wellington, **Ohio**. Ironically, John was identified accidentally by a slave-catcher, Anderson D. Jennings, who had traveled to nearby Oberlin, Ohio, in search of another fugitive. In hopes of profiting from this accident, Jennings contacted Bacon and was given authorization to act as Bacon's agent under the provisions of the **Fugitive Slave Act of 1850**.

Jennings obtained a warrant for John's arrest and, after decoying John out of town, captured and imprisoned him in a tavern in Wellington to await the arrival of a train for Columbus, Ohio. When the residents of Oberlin, a staunch antislavery stronghold, learned that John had been kidnapped, many armed themselves and hastened the nine miles to Wellington, where they freed John by force and spirited him to **Canada** in a wagon.

As with other noted fugitive slave rescue cases of the later 1850s, John's escape was, perhaps, less dramatic than the events triggered by his rescue. Such blatant and open defiance of federal law embarrassed the federal government, and the federal grand jury in Cleveland moved quickly to indict 37 persons for violating the Fugitive Slave Act. Those indicted included Charles Mercer **Langston**, one of the most important young black leaders of his generation; Simeon Bushnell, a store clerk who drove the escape wagon; the Reverend Henry Peck, a faculty member at **Oberlin College**; and the Reverend James M. Fitch, a missionary.

Some of the accused posted bonds in December. Others remained in jail under protest until the trials began in April 1859. The letter of the law was clear and each defendant was convicted, fined and sentenced to a short term in jail. However, the defendants maneuvered the court into trying each of them individu-ally, with a new jury, which slowed the proceedings and kept the pubic issue alive. Finally, a compromise was reached by which all charges were dropped. The rescuers were hailed as heroes when they returned to Oberlin.

FURTHER READING

Blue, Frederick J. "Oberlin's James Monroe: Forgotten Abolitionist." *Civil War History* 35(1989): 285–301.

May, Samuel J. *The Fugitive Slave Law and Its Victims.* New York: American Anti-Slavery Society, 1861.

Ohio

The antislavery movement was both more visible and more formidable in Ohio than in any "western" state. Free black settlements were not necessarily more numerous along the **Ohio River** border than was the case in **Indiana**, but were scattered more generally and in greater numbers as one moved through the central section of the state. Organized white antislavery activity was also spread more generally from the counties bordering Virginia (now West Virginia) and **Kentucky** to the major Lake Erie crossings from northern Ohio to **Canada** West — specifically, Toledo, Sandusky, Cleveland, and Ashtabula.

As a result, Ohio brought together the three elements most attractive to **fugitive slaves**: the presence of free African American communities; the presence of antislavery whites; and reasonably direct routes from slave to free territory — eventually to Canada, if necessary. For this reason, much as the majority of fugitive slaves in the trans-Appalachian west escaped from or through Kentucky, the majority of these fugitives probably crossed into and passed through some part of Ohio as they continued their long journey to freedom.

African Americans represented only 1.28 percent of the total population of Ohio in 1850. Most lived in the southwestern and south central sections of the state, with smaller numbers in a few clusters along the Ohio border with Virginia, **Pennsylvania** and Lake Erie. Ohio African Americans also tended to live in small rural settlements or urban neighborhoods in those counties in which black population was concentrated.

Of course, the attractions of Ohio, from the perspective of both **free people of color** and fugitive slaves, were not altogether relative. True, Ohio did not welcome African Americans and was only somewhat less hostile to their presence than were neighboring states. Mob violence against African Americans erupted repeatedly during the antebellum period, most notably in **Cincinnati** in August 1829 and September 1841. Further, in the words of Frederick **Douglass**, the "wicked and shameful" Ohio Black Laws exemplified this hostility as well. Still, the Black Laws were seldom enforced and there was a crucial loophole for fugitives created by law and by an 1841 decision of the Ohio Supreme Court. Specifically, "...if the owner of a slave brings him into the State or permits him to come, although it should be only for the purpose of visiting, or to pass through the State, the slave, in either case, the moment he touches the soil of Ohio, becomes a free man." This "personal liberty" provision did not exist under the laws of either **Illinois** or Indiana. Under these conditions, important Underground Railroad networks developed in Cincinnati, Ripley, Columbus, Xenia and the towns of northern Ohio. *See also* Personal Liberty Laws; Routes of Escape; Underground Railroad, Sites of; and Appendixes 3 and 4.

FURTHER READING

Hudson, J. Blaine. *Fugitive Slaves and the Underground Railroad in the Kentucky Borderland.* Jefferson, NC: McFarland, 2002.

Preston, E. Delorus. "The Underground Railroad in Northwest Ohio." *Journal of Negro History* 17, no. 4(1932): 409–436.

Preston, Emmett D. "The Fugitive Slave Acts in Ohio." *Journal of Negro History* 28(1943): 422–477.

Ohio River

The Ohio River was the great boundary between slave and free territory in the trans-Appalachian west and was known as the "Great River" to the Native Americans, and sometimes "River Jordan" or the "Dark Line" by **fugitive slaves** and **friends of the fugitive**.

The Ohio River drains an area the size of France, flowing from the Appalachians to the Mississippi River over the 981 miles between Pittsburgh, **Pennsylvania**, and Cairo, **Illinois**,

with the land elevation dropping from 710 to 250 feet above sea level. More than 600 of these miles form the northern border of **Kentucky**. This vast river system, with its major tributaries and countless smaller creeks and rivers, is now regulated by an extensive system of dams and locks, but the Ohio River of the antebellum years was a "turbulent, free-flowing and obstructed stream ... littered with snags and strewn with boulders, its flow broken by sand bars, rock ripples, and falls, especially the Falls of the Ohio where it dropped twenty-five feet over a two-mile stretch of limestone" at **Louisville, Kentucky**. (Johnson, in Reid, 1991: 180.)

Fugitive slaves escaping from or through Kentucky could not reach free territory without crossing the Ohio River and, because no bridges were built until after the **Civil War**, the river could only be crossed by boat (skiff, ferry or steamboat), on foot (if frozen) or by swimming. For fugitive slaves and those who assisted them, the nature of the "Great River" and its conditions at a given time and place were crucial factors. A flooded river was a problem. A river of low to average depth was not. Extreme cold, despite its other inconveniences, changed the elemental property of the river altogether and made it possible simply to run across. In any case, fugitive African Americans and those who assisted them were quite literally at the mercy of the Ohio River of their time.

FURTHER READING

Hudson, J. Blaine. *Fugitive Slaves and the Underground Railroad in the Kentucky Borderland.* Jefferson, NC: McFarland, 2002.

Johnson, Leland R. "Engineering the Ohio." In Robert L. Reid, ed., *Always a River: The Ohio River and the American Experience.* Bloomington, IN: Indiana University Press, 1991: 180–209.

Old Slave House (Junction, Illinois)

An unusual Underground Railroad site, the Old Slave House in Junction, **Illinois**, is 28 miles from Mount Vernon, **Indiana**, and about 10 miles from **Kentucky**. Also known as **Hickory Hill** and the Crenshaw House, the Old Slave House was the site of a station on the Underground Railroad that operated in reverse. There, John **Crenshaw** kidnapped **free people of color** and captured fugitives—

and sold them into **slavery**. *See also* Underground Railroad, Sites of; and Appendixes 3 and 4.

O'Neil, Joseph

Friend of the fugitive in **Madison, Indiana**. *See also* Appendixes 1 and 2.

Orchard Street Church (Baltimore, Maryland)

An important Underground Railroad station, the Orchard Street AME Church was built in Baltimore in the 1840s by free and enslaved African Americans. According to local oral tradition, the church served as a station on the Underground Railroad network in the region. Several churches were built on the original site and, in the 1970s, a tunnel was discovered beneath the church. Located at 512 Orchard Street, the church building still stands and is headquarters of the Baltimore Urban League and home to an African American museum.

In the ante-bellum period, William Watkins, one of the leaders of Baltimore's black underground, was closely associated with the Orchard Street church. His niece, Frances Ellen Watkins **Harper**, was born in Baltimore and would later become a famous poet, friend of the fugitive and a major figure in African American history. *See also* Underground Railroad, Sites of; and Appendixes 3 and 4.

Osceola

Friend of the fugitive in Florida. *See also* Black Seminoles; and Appendixes 1 and 2.

Oswego Market House (Oswego, New York)

Underground Railroad site recognized and documented by the National Park Service. *See also* Appendix 5.

Owen Lovejoy House (Princeton, Illinois)

Underground Railroad site recognized and documented by the National Park Service. *See also* Appendix 5.

Painter, H. F.

Friend of the Fugitive. H.F. Painter moved to Clarksville, **Tennessee**, in August 1852 and established himself as a chair maker. After accumulating debts, he moved to Nashville in December 1852 and his actual purpose in Tennessee was revealed.

A February 1853 article reprinted from the *Clarksville Jeffersonian* provides insight into his machinations and strategies of friends of the fugitive operating in the South:

> Since his departure revelations have been made by negroes here and in Robertson county, which prove that he had been tampering with the slave population. He promised a number of slaves safe passage to the free-States, upon the payment to him of twenty dollars, and authorized the same proposition to be made to the entire slave population ... Quite a gang of the negroes assembled in Robertson county during the holidays awaiting his return ... A vile attempt has been made upon the life of a respectable lady, masters have been robbed, and a rebellious spirit aroused in the hearts of the negroes by his villainy, and it behooves all good citizens to exert themselves to bring him to justice. [Louisville Journal, February 2, 1853, in Hudson, 2002: 102.]

Painter's actions were fairly consistent with those ascribed to Underground Railroad operatives in slave territory. The reaction of his neighbors was typical as well. *See also* Appendixes 1 and 2.

FURTHER READING
Hudson, J. Blaine. *Fugitive Slaves and the Underground Railroad in the Kentucky Borderland.* Jefferson, NC: McFarland, 2002.

Palm, Margaret "Mag" (b. c. 1836)

Friend of the fugitive. Margaret Palm was born around 1836 and lived with her family in Gettysburg, **Pennsylvania**. As an adult, she was sometimes called "Mag" Palm, but was better known as "Maggie Bluecoat." This colorful sobriquet referred to the sky-blue officer's uniform from the War of 1812 that she wore when assisting **fugitive slaves**. Working closely with the Dobbin family, her success in assisting freedom seekers made her notorious and also made her a prime target of Maryland kidnappers who hoped to capture and enslave her. In one local legend, Mag, herself a "powerful woman," was attacked and bound by a group of such nefarious characters, but escaped by biting off the thumb of one of her assailants. *See also* Appendixes 1 and 2.

Parker, John (1827–1900)

Friend of the fugitive. John Parker was born enslaved in Norfolk, Virginia, in 1827. As a child, he was sold and forced to march south to Mobile, Alabama. After failing in an escape attempt in about 1843, Parker, to prevent being sold farther south, persuaded a local widow to purchase him for $1800. Having already developed skills as a foundry worker, Parker repaid his benefactor and gained his freedom, legally, in 1845.

Parker migrated to Jeffersonville, **Indiana**, and found work as a molder. He soon moved to neighboring New Albany, then to **Cincinnati**, Ohio, and, eventually, to Ripley, **Ohio,** in the late 1840s. Ripley offered a unique combination of opportunities that appealed strongly to Parker — the opportunity to practice his trade in a foundry and the opportunity to aid **fugitive slaves**.

Parker became principally responsible for conveying fugitives across the **Ohio River,** working in what he termed "the **borderland**" between slave and free territory. He estimated that he rowed an average of roughly one fugitive per week across the river and delivered another 300 or more to the Union Army during the **Civil War**. Working at night and with confederates living in or near Maysville, **Kentucky,** Parker transported his charges to the Ohio shore and delivered them into the hands of men such as the Reverend John **Rankin**, who then arranged for the fugitives to be spirited northward. Parker indicated that he maintained "an accurate list of the names, dates, and original homes of his passengers" until after the passage of the **Compromise of 1850** when he, like many of his far-flung comrades, destroyed all potentially incriminating evidence.

His long residence at Ripley and his extensive and varied experiences with runaways provided invaluable insights into the land, the character of fugitives and their benefactors, and how fugitives moved through Kentucky and across the Ohio River. In his own words,

When I first began my work among the slaves, all northern Kentucky was still covered with virgin forest ... with many trails and few roads. But the prime bluegrass regions were thickly settled and rich with money and slaves. As the settlers began to build their cabins and make their clearings, the forest gradually disappeared. The increased population made it more difficult for the fugitive to pass through the country successfully ... Another disadvantage was the gradual reduction in the number of slaves in the Borderland. This was due to two causes: so many slaves ran away, their owners, fearful of loss, sold the slaves down the river. As the fugitive depended entirely on his own race for assistance, this removal of his own people increased his difficulties ... But these obstacles did not deter those slaves who were intelligent and determined to break away from their bondage. The early fall was the time most of them selected to strike out for themselves ... Frequently, they told me that they would wait weeks, after they had decided to run away, waiting for the corn to ripen ... Men and women whom I helped on their way came from **Tennessee**, requiring weeks to make the journey, sleeping under trees in the daytime and slowly picking their dangerous way at night ... As a matter of fact, they became backwoodsmen, following the **north star**, or even mountains, to reach their destination. These long-distance travelers were usually people strong physically, as well as people of character, and were resourceful when confronted with trouble ... The riff-raff runaways came from the Borderland, where it was comparatively easy to get away and they were not tested by repeated risks.... [Sprague, 1996: 8–9.]

By his own testimony, Parker rowed many fugitives across the Ohio River who escaped through the Appalachians—from western Virginia, eastern Tennessee, northern Georgia and even the upland Carolinas— and emerged in eastern Kentucky or eastern Ohio. Clearly, even a generation later, Parker considered the fugitives, not those who helped them — including himself — as the true heroes. As the evidence suggests, this perspective reflected more than the humility of a truly heroic man, but an honest appraisal from someone who understood and respected fugitive slaves as people.

After the Civil War, Parker opened his own foundry and became "one of only fifty-five African Americans to receive patents before 1901" when he invented his own unique tobacco press. (Sprague, 1996: 137–138.) Parker prospered for a time, but his business eventually failed. Still, despite the ebb and flow of his economic fortunes, Parker's family thrived and, at the time of his death in 1900, his three daughters and two sons were all educated and solidly middle-class. *See also* John Parker House; Appendixes 1 and 2.

FURTHER READING

Sprague, Stuart S., ed. *His Promised Land: The Autobiography of John P. Parker, Former Slave and Conductor on the Underground Railroad.* New York: W. W. Norton, 1996.

Parker, William

See Christiana Resistance or Christiana Massacre

Patrols

Slave-holders could not prevent slave escapes, but could take steps to deter them or, if deterrence failed, to recapture runaways as soon after their flight — and as close to "home" — as possible. Beginning in the 1700s, the creation of a network of local patrols in slave territory served both purposes.

Patrols were composed of local residents, from two to more than a dozen men. Some operated as loosely organized bands, while others were structured along the lines of militia or police units. In many areas, police forces even evolved from the "watch," i.e., individuals or small groups appointed to "patrol" potentially rebellious or escape-prone slave populations. Operating usually at night, when escapes were most frequent, or in response to special alerts, these patrols roamed the countryside and monitored the perimeters of towns. In the deep South, where slave escapes were more often temporary, patrols also mounted forays into known hiding places or maroon encampments from which **fugitive slaves** often staged raids for food or other goods.

Although serving with a local patrol was often a rite of passage for young white southerners, these patrols, however colorful, were seldom effective. As slave narratives and even the records of slave-holders attest, most freedom seekers could elude the typical patrol rather easily. *See also* Bloodhounds; Slave Catchers; Temporary Escapes.

FURTHER READING

Franklin, John H., and Loren Schweninger. *Runaway Slaves: Rebels on the Plantation.* New York: McGraw-Hill, 1999.

Hudson, J. Blaine. *Fugitive Slaves and the Underground Railroad in the Kentucky Borderland.* Jefferson, NC: McFarland, 2002.

Siebert, Wilbur H. *The Underground Railroad from Slavery to Freedom.* 1898. Reprint, New York: Russell and Russell, 1967.

Paxton, James

Friend of the fugitive in Washington, **Kentucky**. *See also* Paxton Inn; and Appendixes 1 and 2.

Paxton Inn (Washington, Kentucky)

An Underground Railroad site. The Paxton Inn is located immediately to the south of the important **Ohio River** crossing point from Maysville, **Kentucky**, to Ripley, **Ohio**. James Paxton, an attorney and abolitionist, used his inn as an Underground Railroad station, before relocating to Ohio. *See also* Underground Railroad, Sites of; and Appendixes 3 and 4.

Payne, Daniel Alexander (1811–1893)

African American religious leader and friend of the fugitive. Daniel Alexander Payne was born in Charleston, South Carolina, on February 24, 1811 to free African American parents, London and Martha Payne. Payne attended a private school in Charleston, South Carolina, and, in 1835, moved to **Pennsylvania** to attend Gettysburg Seminary.

Payne was ordained an elder in the Lutheran Church in 1837 and was admitted to the **Philadelphia** Annual Conference in 1842. In 1843, he shifted to the African American controlled African Methodist Episcopal Church. As member of the new denomination, Payne pastored churches in **Washington, D.C.**, New York and Baltimore, was elected the historiographer in 1848, then bishop at the General Conference in **New York City** on May 7, 1852 — thus becoming the sixth bishop of the African Methodist Episcopal Church and the first to have formal theological training.

During his long tenure, Payne founded **Wilberforce College** near **Xenia, Ohio,** in 1856 and became the first African American college president in the United States. Both at the many churches he pastored and at Wilberforce, Payne was closely associated with the work of assisting **fugitive slaves**. In this work, he was aided by his wife, Eliza Morris Clark Payne, sister of Shelton **Morris.**

Payne was an important author and his

most significant publication, *History of the African Methodist Episcopal Church,* is still considered the most authoritative source of the early history of the denomination. Bishop Daniel Alexander Payne died on November 2, 1893. *See also* Appendixes 1 and 2.

FURTHER READING

Payne, Daniel A. *History of the African Methodist Episcopal Church.* Nashville, TN: Publishing House of the *AME* Sunday School Union, 1891.

_____. *Recollections of Seventy Years.* Nashville, TN: Publishing House of the *AME* Sunday School Union, 1888.

Simmons, William J. *Men of Mark: Eminent, Progressive and Rising.* Cleveland, OH: George M. Rewell, 1887.

Pearl

See Drayton, Daniel

Pearson, Benjamin

Friend of the fugitive in Keosauqua, **Iowa**. *See also* Pearson House; and Appendixes 1 and 2.

Pearson House (Keosauqua, Iowa)

Built in the 1840s by Benjamin F. Pearson, this large Georgian home served as an important Underground Railroad station in **Iowa**. To hide **fugitive slaves**, the house had inner and outer cellars, and a room hidden by a trapdoor concealed by a rug. *See also* Underground Railroad, Sites of; and Appendixes 3 and 4.

Pease, Leavitt Thaxter

Friend of the fugitive in Williamsburg, **Ohio**. *See also* **Leavitt Thaxter Pease Homesite**.

Peck, The Reverend Henry

Friend of the fugitive in Oberlin, **Ohio**. *See also* Oberlin-Wellington Rescue; and Appendixes 1 and 2.

Pennington, James W.C. (c. 1807–1870)

Fugitive slave and antislavery leader. Dr. James William Charles Pennington was born Jim Pembroke, enslaved in Maryland. As a boy, he was apprenticed to a stonemason and then to a blacksmith. In 1827, when he was 20 years old, conflicts between his parents and their owner, along with brutal treatment, prompted him to escape. He was apprehended, only to escape again — this time reaching **Pennsylvania**. His journey was hair-raising, as **slave catchers** apprehended and held him for a time, though he managed a second escape.

In 1828, Pennington moved to New York, where he resumed his trade as a blacksmith. He joined the campaign against **slavery** and, during this period, became friends with William Lloyd **Garrison**. He continued with his education and worked as a schoolteacher in Newtown, Long Island, before becoming pastor of the Temple Street Congregational Church. In 1831, he had achieved sufficient stature that he was chosen as a delegate to the first annual Convention of Free Colored Persons.

From 1834 to 1838, Pennington, then the first black pastor of New Haven's Dixwell Avenue Church, tried in vain to gain admission to Yale in hopes of receiving a formal ministerial license, but was able only to audit courses. For four years, he contended against this handicap to complete the requirements for licensure as a Congregational minister.

He later published his own life as a slave narrative, *The Fugitive Blacksmith,* in 1859, and became one of America's most renowned antislavery spokesmen. On a visit to England, Pennington was offered an honorary doctorate of divinity, but refused, saying: "No, gentlemen, I have too much respect for the degree to run the risk of seeing it placed upon the auction block; for it is possible, on my return to America, that I might be seized...." (Bragg, 1925: 104–105.) James Pennington remained active in religious, educational and racial uplift work until his death in 1870.

FURTHER READING

Bethel, Elizabeth R. *The Roots of African American Identity: Memory and History in Antebellum Free Communities.* New York: St. Martin's Press, 1997.

Bragg, the Reverend George F. *Men of Maryland.* Baltimore: Church Advocate Press, 1925.

Quarles, Benjamin. *Black Abolitionists.* New York: Oxford University Press, 1969.

Simmons, William J. *Men of Mark: Eminent, Progressive and Rising.* Cleveland, OH: George M. Rewell, 1887.

Pennock, Abraham L. (1786–1868)

Friend of the fugitive. Abraham Liddon Pennock, Sr., was born in **Philadelphia**, Pennsylvania, on August 7, 1786. Pennock prospered as a dry goods merchant, and later in the wire business. In 1840, he retired and moved to Haverford and then Upper Darby Township where he managed him numerous estates.

Pennock gained a reputation for the strength and consistency of his opposition to **slavery**, e.g., he refused to use any products of slave labor in his business or personal life. Pennock was also an active member of the **Pennsylvania** Anti-Slavery Society and used his home — Hoodland — in Upper Darby Township as an Underground Railroad station. Pennock died on May 12, 1868. *See also* Underground Railroad, Sites of; and Appendixes 1–4.

Pennsylvania

Pennsylvania originated as the colony of New Sweden in 1637 when the Swedes founded the first permanent settlement at what later became Wilmington, Delaware. In 1643, Johan Printz, Swedish governor of the young colony, established his capital on Tinicum Island within the current boundaries of the state. In 1655, Dutch Governor Peter Stuyvesant of New Netherlands seized New Sweden, but Dutch control proved even more short-lived than that of Sweden and, in 1664, the English seized all Dutch possessions in North America.

Much of early Pennsylvania history revolves around William Penn. Penn was born in London on October 24, 1644, the son of Admiral Sir William Penn, and despite his wealth and education, joined the Society of Friends, or **Quakers** — then a persecuted sect. As a means of settling a large debt, Penn asked King Charles II to grant him land in the territory between Lord Baltimore's province of Maryland and the Duke of York's province of New York. Penn's petition was granted and the king signed the Charter of Pennsylvania (Latin for "Penn's woods or forest") on March 4, 1681, naming the new colony in honor of William Penn's father. In 1682, the Duke of York deeded to Penn his claim to the three lower counties on the Delaware, which now compose the state of Delaware.

Penn and his heirs, consistent with their Quaker principles, neither granted nor settled any land in Pennsylvania without first purchasing it from the Native Americans of the region. By 1789, all Native American claims had been purchased or otherwise signed away — and those Native Americans who had survived disease and warfare migrated westward. Further, despite Quaker opposition to **slavery**, about 4,000 enslaved African Americans were resident in Pennsylvania by 1730 and this number increased to roughly 10,000 by 1790. However, as a result of the Pennsylvania Gradual Abolition Act of 1780, the first such statute in the United States, nearly 6,300 were already free. As the number of **free people of color** increased, institution and community building became possible.

By 1776, the Province of Pennsylvania had become the third largest English colony in America and **Philadelphia** had become the second largest English-speaking city in the world (next to London). The **American Revolution** had urban origins and Philadelphia was a center of revolutionary agitation and ferment — and, after war, the site of the Constitutional Convention in 1787.

In the antebellum period, the tradition of Quaker opposition to slavery and Pennsylvania's location as the most important border state east of the Appalachians made the state a key battleground in the struggle against slavery. Both antislavery and proslavery sentiments were strong. **Fugitive slaves** passed and were often assisted through many sections of the state en route to New England or New York, or **Canada** — following overland routes or using the major waterways: the Allegheny, Susquehanna, Delaware and Ohio Rivers. The state outlawed the use of its jails to detain fugitive African Americans in 1847 and one of the defining acts of resistance to the **Fugitive Slave Act of 1850** occurred in Christiana in 1851.

Numerous citizens aided fugitive slaves. Thomas **Garrett** and Harriett **Tubman** operated in the region. William **Still** managed the work of the vigilance committee in Philadelphia. Women such as Anna Dickinson, Lucretia Mott, Ann Preston and Jane **Swisshelm** also played prominent roles. *See also* Allen, Richard; and Christiana Resistance.

FURTHER READING

Dunaway, Wayland Fuller. *A History of Pennsylvania.* Englewood Cliffs, NJ: Prentice-Hall, 1948.
Klein, Philip Shriver. *A History of Pennsylvania.* University Park, PA: Pennsylvania State University Press, 1980.
Siebert, Wilbur H. *The Underground Railroad from Slavery to Freedom.* 1898. Reprint, New York: Russell and Russell, 1967.
Waldstreicher, David. *Runaway America: Benjamin Franklin, Slavery, and the American Revolution.* New York: Hill and Wang, 2004.

Pennypacker, Elijah Funk (1802–1888)

An abolitionist and friend of the fugitive, Elijah Funk Pennypacker was born in Chester County, **Pennsylvania**, on November 20, 1802. He was educated in the private schools in Burlington, New Jersey, taught there, and subsequently engaged in land surveying in Phoenixville, Pennsylvania. Pennypacker then became interested in real estate, was elected to the Pennsylvania legislature in 1831 and served as chairman of its committee on banks, and became a strong proponent of public education.

In 1841, Pennypacker joined the Society of Friends and devoted himself thereafter to the abolition movement, becoming president of the local antislavery society, and the Chester county and Pennsylvania state societies. He also became a key manager of the Underground Railroad and his home, **White Horse Farm**, served as a sanctuary for hundreds of **fugitive slaves**. Pennypacker personally transported many of these freedom seekers from his home to Norristown and other points to the north and east, and was reputed never to have lost anyone in his care.

In later years, Pennypacker held many important business posts and remained involved in Pennsylvania politics. Upon learning of Pennypacker's death on January 4, 1888, abolitionist poet, **John Greenleaf Whittier,** wrote that Pennypacker was "tall as Saul of old — the bosom friend of Thad Stevens." (Whittier to Elizabeth Neall Gray, January 12, 1888.)

See also Quakers; Underground Railroad, Sites of; White Horse Farm; and Appendixes 3 and 4.

FURTHER READING

Pickard, John B., ed. *The Letters of John Greenleaf Whittier, Vol. III: 1861–1892.* Cambridge: Harvard University Press, 1975.
Still, William. *The Underground Railroad.* 1872. Reprint, Chicago: Johnson, 1970.

Perry, Charles

Friend of the fugitive in Westerly, Rhode Island. *See also* Charles Perry House; and Appendixes 1 and 2.

Personal Liberty Laws

State laws that protected the rights of **fugitive slaves,** even declaring enslaved African Americans free upon reaching free soil, and often protected **free people of color** against kidnapping. In 1842, the U.S. Supreme Court ruling in *Prigg v. Pennsylvania* upheld the constitutionality of the **Fugitive Slave Act of 1793.** However, although the ruling upheld the act, it also defined its limits and revealed several points of vulnerability, the most important of which was the lack of any legal obligation on the part of "northerners" to render active assistance to "southerners" seeking to recover fugitive slaves.

In response, several northern states passed laws that "forbade state officers from performing their duties" under the 1793 Act: **Massachusetts** (1843); Vermont (1843); Connecticut (1844); New Hampshire (1846); **Pennsylvania** (1847); and Rhode Island (1848). These laws rendered the Fugitive Slave Act unenforceable and were viewed by the South not only as acts of northern defiance but as clear evidence that northerners had no intention of respecting southern "property rights." As sectional conflict deepened after the Mexican War, the need for a stronger fugitive slave law that corrected these deficiencies played a major role in shaping the **Compromise of 1850.**

The **Fugitive Slave Act of 1850** imposed a positive obligation on northerners to assist in the apprehension of fugitive slaves. However, even without loopholes in the law, and threats from President Millard Fillmore, a number of northern states determined simply to defy the new law. Although Vermont passed a new personal liberty law in 1850, the most active defiance of the federal law occurred after the passage of the Kansas-

Nebraska Act in May 1854 — and the intense reaction against this attempt to extend **slavery** into the western territories. In 1854, in the **Glover Case,** the Wisconsin Supreme Court declared the Fugitive Slave Act unconstitutional and freed Sherman Booth, the Milwaukee abolitionist jailed for helping rescue Glover. Connecticut, Rhode Island and Vermont passed new **personal liberty laws** in 1854. Michigan, Maine, and Massachusetts passed similar legislation in 1855.

The 1857 ***Dred Scott v. Sandford*** decision brought a new and equally intense reaction. New Hampshire passed a version of its personal liberty law in 1857 that contained a "sojourner clause," declaring that any enslaved African Americans brought into the state by southern travelers would be considered free. Maine also passed a new law and **Ohio** adopted a personal liberty statute, although the measure was repealed the next year. These laws differed in their details, but were broadly similar. At their core was the straightforward prohibition against the use of state officials and state facilities in fugitive slave cases.

FURTHER READING

Finkelman, Paul. "Prigg v. Pennsylvania and the Northern State Courts: Anti-Slavery Use of a Pro-Slavery Decision." *Civil War History* 25, no. 1(1979): 5–35.

Nogee, Joseph. "The Prigg Case and Fugitive Slavery, 1842–1850." *The Journal of Negro History* 39, no. 3(1954).

Ranney, Joseph A. "Suffering the Agonies of Their Righteousness: The Rise and Fall of the States Rights Movement in Wisconsin, 1854–1861." *Wisconsin Magazine of History* 75, no. 2(1992).

Rosenberg, Norman L. "Personal Liberty Laws and Sectional Crisis: 1850–1861." *Civil War History* 18(1971): 25–44.

Peter Mott House (Lawnside, New Jersey)

Underground Railroad site recognized and documented by the National Park Service. *See also* Appendix 5.

Philadelphia, Pennsylvania

Underground Railroad junction. In March 1681, William Penn (an active Quaker) received the title to **Pennsylvania** in a land grant from King Charles II of England. Penn assigned a commission to select a location with suitable water frontage on the Delaware River and established the city of Philadelphia on this site in October 1682.

Philadelphia was designated the capital of the colony of Pennsylvania in March 1683. In the next decade, the city expanded rapidly and flourished, with the population growing from a few hundred to 7,000 by the time the city was incorporated in 1701. Most early settlers were **Quakers,** but, as Philadelphia grew into a trading, manufacturing and maritime center, German, Scottish, and Irish immigrants soon arrived. By 1776, Philadelphia had become the largest English-speaking city in the world next to London.

Philadelphia played a significant role in the struggle for American independence. By 1774, the city had become the military, economic, and political center of the American colonies. The First Continental Congress convened at Carpenters' Hall in 1774. Congress adopted the Declaration of Independence on July 4, 1776 at Independence Hall. In 1787, the Constitution of the United States was drafted at the State House.

During the antebellum period, Philadelphia became a center of antislavery movement and an important sanctuary for **fugitive slaves.** The combined efforts of an active white antislavery community and a committed free black community made Philadelphia a haven for freedom seekers bound for New England or **Canada.** *See also* Brown, Henry "Box"; Free People of Color; Garrett, Thomas; Harper, Frances Ellen Watkins; Still, William; Tubman, Harriett; and Appendixes 3 and 4.

FURTHER READING

Hendrick, George, and Willene Hendrick, eds. *Fleeing for Freedom: Stories of the Underground Railroad / As told by Levi Coffin and William Still.* Chicago: Ivan R. Dee, c2004.

Lapsansky, Emma Jones. "Feminism, Freedom, and Community: Charlotte Forten and Women Activists in Nineteenth-Century Philadelphia." *Pennsylvania Magazine of History and Biography* 113, no. 1(1989): 3–19.

Nash, Gary B. *First City: Philadelphia and the Forging of Historical Memory.* Philadelphia: University of Pennsylvania Press, 2002.

_____. *Forging Freedom: The Formation of Philadel-*

phia's Black Community, 1720–1840. Cambridge, MA: Harvard University Press, 1988.

Scharf, J. Thomas and Thompson Westcott. *History of Philadelphia, 1609–1884.* Philadelphia: L. H. Everts, 1884.

Switala, William J. *Underground Railroad in Pennsylvania.* Mechanicsburg, PA: Stackpole Books, 2001.

Walther, Rudolph. *Happenings in ye Olde Philadelphia 1680–1900.* Philadelphia: Walther Printing House, 1825.

Philbrick, Samuel

Friend of the fugitive in Brookline, **Massachusetts.** *See also* **Tappan-Philbrick House.**

Phillips, Wendell (1811–1884)

Friend of the fugitive. Wendell Phillips was born in **Boston, Massachusetts** on November 29, 1811. He earned a law degree from Harvard in 1833 and was admitted to the bar in 1834, but, being independently wealthy, soon abandoned his law practice to devote his life to a number of progressive causes, principally the abolition of **slavery.**

His eloquent speech (1837) in **Faneuil Hall** on the assassination of the abolitionist editor Elijah P. **Lovejoy** established him as an orator of the first rank and began his long and distinguished career as a lecturer. Phillips worked closely with William Lloyd **Garrison** and contributed frequently to the *Liberator.* He opposed the **Fugitive Slave Act of 1850** and used his legal training to represent **fugitive slaves** in court.

After the **Civil War,** Phillips contended that the nation owed formerly enslaved African Americans not merely their freedom, but land, education, and full civil rights as well. In later years, Phillips' social vision grew more radical, with interesting similarities to that of Karl Marx, e.g., he praised the 1871 Paris Commune and Russian nihilism. Phillips died in Boston on February 2, 1884. *See also* Appendixes 1 and 2.

FURTHER READING

Marcus, Robert D. "Wendell Phillips and American Institutions." *Journal of American History* 56, no. 1(1969): 41–58.

Stewart, James B. *Wendell Phillips, Liberty's Hero.* Baton Rouge: Louisiana State University Press, 1986.

Wendell Phillips (Library of Congress)

Pine Forge (Pennsylvania)

Built in the 1700s by Thomas Rutter, an abolitionist and ironmaster, the ironworks at Pine Forge, Pennsylvania offered both employment to free African Americans and refuge to **fugitive slaves.** Rutter's descendants concealed freedom seekers in tunnels under the Pine Forge manor house. *See also* Underground Railroad, Sites of; and Appendixes 3 and 4.

Pinkerton, Alan (1819–1884)

Friend of the fugitive. Alan Pinkerton was born in Glasgow, Scotland, in 1819, the son of a policeman crippled in a riot. He was trained as a cooper and emigrated to the United States in 1842, possibly fleeing the law. Pinkerton moved west to **Illinois** and, taking up his father's profession, became a deputy sheriff, first, of Dundee, Illinois, and, then of Chicago.

In 1852, he formed an elite group of detectives and specialized for a time in solving railway robberies. Pinkerton was appointed chief of Union Intelligence during the **Civil War** and, after the war, his agency and his fame grew as he opened numerous branch offices throughout the United States.

Ironically, as a literal legend in the annals of law enforcement, Pinkerton was nonetheless willing to break the law in the service of a higher cause. As a committed abolitionist, he assisted **fugitive slaves** in Chicago for many years, coordinating his efforts with those of John **Jones**, African American leader of the Underground Railroad in the city. For example, when John **Brown** arrived in Chicago with 11 slaves in the late **1850s,** Pinkerton met them, fed them in his home and escorted them to Jones. Pinkerton died in 1884 and is buried in the same cemetery as Jones and other abolitionists of that generation. *See also* Abolitionist Movement; and Appendixes 1 and 2.

FURTHER READING
Butler, Dominique. "John Jones." *Illinois History,* 1996.
Voss, Frederick, and James Barber. *We Never Sleep: The First Fifty Years of the Pinkertons.* Washington, D.C.: Smithsonian Institution Press, 1981.

Pleasant, Mary Ellen (c. 1814–1904)

A friend of the fugitive in the far West. The circumstances of the early life of Mary Ellen Pleasant are largely unknown. Available sources indicate that she was born enslaved in about 1814 near Augusta, Georgia, and, after being hired out, was freed at nine years old by a sympathetic planter. She left the South and reached Nantucket, lodged with **Quakers** and worked as a clerk in a general store. In 1841, she moved to **Boston** and worked as a tailor's assistant and church soloist.

Pleasant married James W. Smith and worked with him to assist **fugitive slaves.** When her husband died in the mid–1840s, she inherited moderate wealth. Pleasant continued her work as an Underground Railroad agent, but, by 1852, fled to **California** to escape those who wished to punish her for aiding fugitive slaves— eventually reaching San Francisco.

Pleasant supported the antislavery movement financially and, according to some accounts, this support even extended to backing John **Brown**'s Raid. Her boardinghouse in San Francisco also gave refuge to Archy Lee, a central figure in California's most celebrated fugitive slave case. After the **Civil War,** Pleasant became the "Mother of Civil Rights" in California. She helped shape early San Francisco, covertly amassing a small fortune and fighting tirelessly for rights and economic opportunities for African Americans and women. For example, in 1866, she sued a San Francisco trolley car company for repeatedly refusing to stop when she hailed their cars.

Pleasant died in San Francisco in January 1904. *See also* Archy Case.

FURTHER READING
Beasley, Delilah H. *The Negro Trailblazers of California.* Times Mirror Printing and Binding House, 1919.
Billington, Monroe Lee, and Roger D. Hardaway. *African Americans on the Western Frontier.* Niwot, CO: University of Colorado Press, 1998.
Katz, William Loren. *Black Women of the Old West.* New York: Atheneum, 1995.

Plymouth Church of the Pilgrims (Brooklyn, New York)

An antislavery site and a stop on the Underground Railroad Travel Itinerary of the National Park Service, the Plymouth Church of the Pilgrims became famous as a center of religious antislavery sentiment in the decade before the **Civil War.** Under the leadership of the Reverend Henry Ward Beecher — the brother of Harriet Beecher **Stowe,** author of ***Uncle Tom's Cabin,*** and son of Lyman Beecher, a well-known clergyman of liberal views— a congregation as large as 2,500 people crowded the plain brick building each week to hear Beecher and other antislavery orators. William Lloyd **Garrison,** Wendell **Phillips,** Charles **Sumner,** and John Greenleaf **Whittier** were among those who spoke from the pulpit.

In the **1850s,** Beecher preached opposition to the **Fugitive Slave Act of 1850** and encouraged his congregation to become active in the Underground Railroad. He even "auctioned" several enslaved African Americans from his pulpit as a means of securing their legal freedom and, at the same time, dramatizing the inhumanity of **slavery.**

See also Abolitionist Movement; Underground Railroad, Sites of; and Appendixes 3 and 4.

FURTHER READING
National Park Service. *Underground Railroad: Special Resource Study*. Washington, D.C.: U.S. Government Printing Office, 1995.

Polaris

See North Star

Polly Brandish House (West Upton, Massachusetts)

Polly Dean Brandish and her husband, Harvey, were important Underground Railroad station-keepers in West Upton. Their home on North Main Street had a secret stairway to an attic where **fugitive slaves** were concealed. *See also* Massachusetts; Underground Railroad, Sites of; and Appendixes 3 and 4.

Portland Crossing Point (Louisville, Kentucky)

The most important crossing point in the greater **Louisville, Kentucky** area was located west of Portland, a small town that became a Louisville neighborhood — leading from Louisville across the **Ohio River** to New Albany, **Indiana**. Using this crossing point required considerable planning and coordination. Supplies and a hack had to be obtained. Arrangements with someone in New Albany were necessary as were communications between parties on both sides of the river throughout the enterprise. **Fugitive slaves** had to arrange to reach a certain point, "below the lower ferry," on a certain day, at a certain time. Someone from New Albany had to secure a skiff and cross the river on the same day, at the same time — and, presumably, someone was waiting to receive and conceal the fugitives in New Albany, and then "pass them on" to the north or east.

The origins of the systematic use of this crossing point date to the **1850s**, although unassisted crossings were reported in earlier years. As an example, Henry Webb of New Albany was told by his father, who was born enslaved in the Louisville area, that a major fugitive slave route ran through Louisville and New Albany. Webb, when interviewed by the Federal Writers' Project, stated simply that:

> ... runaway Negroes used to come across the Ohio River from Portland ... Plans for escapes were hatched in a colored Masonic Lodge,

located in Portland. The Negroes would cross the river in a skiff, manned by fishermen (supposedly) and if the coast was not clear on this side they would go up the river for a short distance ... Many that crossed hid with friends in the hills back of New Albany and then after all danger was past made their way north by way of Salem. [Rawick, 1972: 232.]

After negotiating a river crossing, fugitives could follow several routes leading from New Albany or Jeffersonville to Salem, or an alternative "station," and then northward.

> One of the most notable routes was that which was conducted by **Quakers** and Covenanters and a few other abolitionists through Harrison and Washington Counties ... One of the most remarkable leaders in the business was "Little Jimmie" Trueblood, ably assisted by his wife. He was only five feet two inches tall and never over 110 pounds, and his wife was also very small ... Many of the fugitives came by way of New Albany, but more by way of Harrison County, the main line running through Palmyra and the vicinity of Salem and thence north to Sparkville and Bloomington. This was known as the "west line," and was the most used ... Besides "Little Jimmie" Trueblood, others believed to have been leaders along the route were Thomas H. Trueblood, a Quaker; Matthias Marks, Isaiah Reed and Dr. Mary Lusk. [Cook, 1936: 11–13.]

See also Underground Railroad, Sites of; and Appendixes 3 and 4.

FURTHER READING
Cook, Iris L. "Underground Railroad in Southern Indiana." Federal Writers' Project, unpublished notes, ca. 1936. Presented to the author by Ms. Cook's grandniece, 1999.
Hudson, J. Blaine. Fugitive *Slaves and the Underground Railroad in the Kentucky Borderland*. Jefferson, NC: McFarland, 2002.
Peters, Pamela R. *The Underground Railroad in Floyd County, Indiana*. Jefferson, NC: McFarland, 2001.
Rawick, George P., Ed. "Indiana and Ohio Narratives." In *The American Slave: A Composite Autobiography, Supplement*, Series 1, Vol. 5. Westport, CT: Greenwood, 1972.

President Street Station/ Baltimore Civil War Museum (Baltimore, Maryland)

Part of the National Underground Railroad Network to Freedom, the President Street Station and office of the **Philadelphia**, Wilmington & Baltimore Railroad, was built in 1838 and often used by **fugitive slaves**. The original transportation office and depot were razed in 1850 when the President Street Station was constructed. *See also* Underground Railroad, Sites of; and Appendixes 3 and 4.

FURTHER READING
National Park Service. *Researching and Interpreting the Underground Railroad.* Washington, D.C.: United States Government Printing Office, 1999.
National Park Service. *Underground Railroad Special Resource Study.* Washington, D.C.: United States Government Printing Office, 1995.

Prigg v. Pennsylvania (1842)

A significant legal case that weakened the **Fugitive Slave Act of 1793**. In 1832, Margaret Morgan, an enslaved African American woman, moved from Maryland to **Pennsylvania** with her husband, a free man of color. Morgan had lived as a free woman before relocating to Pennsylvania, but had never been emancipated formally.

In 1837, Morgan's owner, living in Baltimore, Maryland, dispatched her agent/attorney, Edward Prigg, to recapture Morgan as a fugitive slave. Prigg obtained a warrant from the justice of the peace in Morgan's county of residence under an 1826 Pennsylvania law and seized Morgan. However, when the county judge refused to remand Morgan to Prigg's custody, Prigg simply took Morgan involuntarily back to Maryland. Prigg was then charged with kidnapping under the same 1826 law and the case eventually reached the U.S. Supreme Court.

The issues before the court were both legally complex and politically sensitive. While the 1793 Fugitive Slave Act allowed slave-holders or their agents to pursue and apprehend runaways in free territory and prescribed penalties for those who harbored or otherwise assisted fugitives, the law did not require that "northerners" do anything to assist slave-holders or their agents in their efforts. As the numbers of **fugitive slaves** increased, and as efforts to assist them became more systematic through the early Underground Railroad, this fundamental defect of the law became obvious and correcting it became a central preoccupation of those determined to protect **slavery**. Thus, attempts were made to pass a stronger law in 1796, 1801, 1817

and 1822. To complicate matters further, a number of northern states passed **personal liberty laws** in the 1820s and 1830s to protect fugitives who reached free soil or other laws to prevent the kidnapping of **free people of color**.

In 1842, against this backdrop, the U.S. Supreme Court ruled in favor of Prigg, upholding the constitutionality of the 1793 act and any state laws derived from it. The court reaffirmed the penalties for assisting fugitive slaves, but left open the question of whether citizens in the free states and territories were under any obligation to assist in the recovery of those freedom seekers. Thus, while seemingly a victory for slave-holders, the ruling had several unintended consequences—the most important of which was defining the limits of the 1793 Fugitive Slave Act and establishing that northerners could not obstruct but were under no obligation to assist slaveholders and their agents.

Using this ruling as a framework, several northern states passed new or amended existing personal liberty laws to include language that actually prevented state officers from performing their duties under the 1793 act. As a result, Prigg v. Pennsylvania made the 1793 act essentially unenforceable, led to an increase in the number of fugitive slaves and made their recovery increasingly difficult, prompting the demand for the stronger fugitive slave law that was enacted as part of the **Compromise of 1850**. *See also* Fugitive Slave Act of 1850.

FURTHER READING
Finkelman, Paul. "Prigg v. Pennsylvania and the Northern State Courts: Anti-Slavery Use of a Pro-Slavery Decision." *Civil War History* 25, no. 1(1979): 5–35.
Nogee, Joseph. "The Prigg Case and Fugitive Slavery, 1842–1850." *The Journal of Negro History* 39, no. 3(1954).
Wiecek, William M. "Slavery and Abolition Before the United States Supreme Court, 1820–1860." *The Journal of American History* 65(1978): 34–59.

Promised Land

"Promised land" is a term used for free territory, whether in the free states of the North or **Canada**.

Purvis, Robert (1810–1898)

Abolitionist and friend of the fugitive. Robert Purvis was born in Charleston, South Carolina, on August 4, 1810, as the second of three sons of a white cotton merchant and a free woman of color. At the age of nine, his father sent the family to **Philadelphia**. There, Purvis enrolled in the Clarkson School, sponsored by the **Pennsylvania** Abolition Society, and later attended Amherst College in **Massachusetts**.

Purvis inherited significant wealth when his father died and, with his great business acumen, prospered in his own right — becoming one of the wealthiest African Americans in the United States. In 1831, he married Harriet Forten, the daughter of James Forten, another successful African American entrepreneur and antislavery leader. In 1833, he joined William Lloyd **Garrison's** American Anti-Slavery Society and traveled to Europe to speak against slavery. Purvis was also a key supporter of the Philadelphia vigilance committee and operated a "safe house" of his own for **fugitive slaves**.

Purvis was a strong proponent of emancipation during the **Civil War**, but, doubting President Andrew Johnson's intentions, rejected an offer to head the Freedmen's Bureau at war's end. Because of Johnson's approach to Reconstruction, Purvis grew disillusioned with the Republican Party. Further, in the 1870s, he was criticized by many African Americans for opposing the Fifteenth Amendment on the grounds that the franchise was not extended to women. Purvis died in Philadelphia in April 1898. *See also* Robert Purvis House; Appendixes 1 and 2.

FURTHER READING
Bacon, Margaret Hope. "The Double Curse of Sex and Color: Robert Purvis and Human Rights." *The Pennsylvania Magazine of History and Biography* 121(1997): 53–75.
Still, William. *The Underground Railroad*. 1872. Reprint, Chicago: Johnson, 1970.

Quakers

Although some Quakers were slaveowners, other members of the Society of Friends were among the most consistently active sources of aid to freedom seekers. Quakers permitted African Americans to attend religious meetings and provided some informal schooling to blacks as early as the 1680s, and issued the first American resolution opposing **slavery** in 1688. As slavery ended in the North and old Northwest after the **American Revolution**, **fugitive slaves** found refuge with and assistance from Quakers in **Pennsylvania** and many sections of the South, including North Carolina.

As cotton monoculture and slavery became deeply rooted in the South after 1800, many Quakers migrated from the South — often emancipating any enslaved African Americans in their possession and often bringing those African Americans with them. Not surprisingly, rural Quaker settlements and free black communities were often near each other, and this combination of free African Americans and sympathetic whites attracted numerous **fugitive slaves**.

Among the most noteworthy Quakers were Levi **Coffin**, reputed "president of the Underground Railroad" in Richmond, **Indiana**, and later **Cincinnati**, and Thomas **Garrett**, heroic friend of the fugitive in Pennsylvania. There were, however, many others.

FURTHER READING
Siebert, Wilbur H. *The Underground Railroad from Slavery to Freedom*. 1898. Reprint, New York: Russell and Russell, 1967.
Still, William. *The Underground Railroad*. 1872. Reprint, Chicago: Johnson, 1970.

Quarreles, Caroline (b. c. 1826)

Fugitive slave. In the spring of 1842, 16-year-old Caroline Quarreles (or Quarles) asked permission from her owner to visit a friend, probably stole some money, bundled her clothes together and escaped from **slavery** in St. Louis, Missouri. Quarreles used her extremely fair complexion as a disguise and traveled by steamboat to Alton, **Illinois**. From Alton, on the advice of an African American who suspected she was a fugitive slave, she boarded a stagecoach for Milwaukee, Wisconsin.

Quarreles was pursued and eventually discovered in Milwaukee. With the assistance of local **friends of the fugitive**, most notably H. N. Wells and Asahel Finch, she was taken across the Milwaukee River and eventually to Spring Prairie near Burlington. There, she was entrusted to the abolitionist Lyman Goodnow, who transported her to Burlington and Dr. Edward G. Dyer. Dr. Dyer had a reputation of being an outspoken abolitionist, a station master and financial supporter of the Underground Railroad. In August 1842, Dr. Dyer dispatched Quarreles, still in the care of Goodnow, in a wagon pulled by a borrowed horse, with a pillowcase filled with food and $20. Dr. Dyer also gave the pair a list of trusted people and blanket letter of introduction to any "freedom minded" person who might give them aid on their journey.

So provisioned, Goodnow and Quarreles crossed into Illinois and, five weeks later, reached Detroit, Michigan. Quarreles then crossed the Detroit River into **Canada** and safety. Once in Canada, Quarreles later married Allen Watkins, a fugitive slave from **Kentucky**. The Quarreles escape was the first instance of a fugitive slave being assisted from Wisconsin into Canada. After this daring escape, Dr. Dyer named the street in front of his house, "Liberty Avenue." *See also* Underground Railroad, Sites of; and Appendixes 3 and 4.

Quilts

See Signals

Quindaro (Kansas)

Underground Railroad site in Kansas. Established in 1857, Quindaro was a Wyandot settlement in Kansas named for Nancy Quindaro Brown, daughter of the Wyandot Chief, Adam Brown. The term "Quindaro" itself means "a bundle of sticks," or "in union there is strength," and, in keeping with that meaning, the settlement was founded as a "freeport" through which antislavery immigrants could enter and leave the territory in relative safety.

Quindaro combined the land of 13 Wyandot families and, by 1858, had a population of 608 people. Ultimately, it would boast a sawmill, large hotel, large docking and shipping facilities, over 100 buildings, businesses, and even a daily newspaper, *The Chindowan*. Given the presence of numerous **friends of the fugitive**, Quindaro also became an important Underground Railroad center. Today, Quindaro is one of the richest archaeological sites in the Midwest, and the Wyandot Nation is working to preserve the town site and ruins. *See also* Underground Railroad, Sites of; and Appendixes 3 and 4.

Quinn, William Paul (1788–1873)

Friend of the fugitive. William Paul Quinn, the fourth bishop of the African Methodist Episcopal Church, was born on April 10, 1788. Quinn was present at the organization of the African Methodist Episcopal Church in 1816 and was ordained an AME deacon in 1818 and an elder in 1838.

Quinn pastored numerous churches in New Jersey, **Pennsylvania**, and **Illinois**, and spearheaded the "Western Mission" of organizing AME churches in the trans-Appalachian West, e.g., in Missouri and Kentucky. In recognition of his efforts, the General Conference of the AME Church, meeting at Pittsburgh, elected him bishop on May 19, 1844. He became the senior bishop of the African Methodist Episcopal Church on May 9, 1849, after the death of Bishop Morris Brown, and remained the senior bishop for the remainder of his life. Besides being a religious leader, Quinn assisted **fugitive slaves** and presided over an independent African American religious denomination that prided itself on its opposition to **slavery**. Quinn died in Richmond, **Indiana**, on February 3, 1873. *See also* Underground Railroad, Sites of; and Appendixes 1–4.

Quinn Chapel AME Church (Louisville, Kentucky)

Founded by local **free people of color** in 1838, Quinn Chapel AME was the most notable and most politically active of the early African American churches in **Louisville, Kentucky**. As William Gibson noted, "it was considered by the community as an abolition church," but "the idea of an abolition church established in this city among the slaves could not be tolerated by some slaveholders; hence they forbade their slaves visiting that Free Negro Church." (Gibson, 1897: 11–12.)

Quinn Chapel was a linchpin of organized AME activity along the **Ohio River** border. As such, it was connected closely to other small AME congregations in southern **Indiana** and **Ohio**—and to the "Quaker friends of Indiana" who "gave liberally" to assist in the construction of a new church edifice in 1854. In essence, Quinn Chapel, probably more than any of the other seven antebellum black churches in Louisville, was part of the network associated with Underground Railroad activity in north central **Kentucky**. *See also* Underground Railroad, Sites of; and Appendixes 3 and 4.

FURTHER READING

Gibson, William H., Sr. *Historical Sketches of the Progress of the Colored Race in Louisville, Kentucky.* Louisville: N. p., 1897.

Hudson, J. Blaine. "Crossing the Dark Line: Fugitive Slaves and the Underground Railroad in Louisville and North Central Kentucky." *The Filson History Quarterly* 75, no. 1(2001): 33–84.

Rankin, The Rev. John (1793–1886)

Friend of the fugitive. The Reverend John Rankin, a Presbyterian minister and abolitionist, was born in 1793, migrated to **Kentucky** in 1821, and served as pastor of the Presbyterian Church in Ripley, **Ohio**, from 1822 to 1866. In 1828, Rankin and his family moved from their first home near the **Ohio River** to a new brick house on what came to be called Liberty Hill overlooking Ripley. The house, with its windows ablaze with light, was a beacon to and haven for fugitives—and Rankin and his associates were chiefly responsible for conveying runaways delivered to them by men such as John **Parker** from southern into central Ohio. One of Rankin's sons, when interviewed by Wilbur Siebert in the 1890s, stated that his family "lodged and forwarded not less than 2,000 slaves ... not losing one." (Sprague, 1996: 12.)

A significant body of evidence attests to Rankin's steadfastness and commitment over more than three decades. William Lloyd **Garrison**, the great New England abolitionist, described himself as Rankin's "disciple and humble co-worker in the cause of emancipation." After Rankin's death, Siebert observed: "John Rankin did more to propagate practical abolition in Ohio than any other citizen of the State. No other house along Ohio's riverfront was so well situated, or so admirably staffed, to be both magnet and beacon for liberty-loving slaves." (Siebert, 1895: 2–3.)

As another indication of Rankin's stature, he and his family were on friendly terms with the Beecher family. Both belonged to the same religious denomination and shared the same commitment to abolition. Through this rela-

tionship, Harriet Beecher **Stowe** became acquainted with most of the real-life characters that formed the basis for *Uncle Tom's Cabin*. Rankin died in 1886. *See also* John Rankin House; Appendixes 1 and 2.

FURTHER READING

Hagedorn, Anne. *Beyond the River: The Untold Story of the Heroes of the Underground Railroad.* New York: Simon and Schuster, 2002.

Hudson, J. Blaine. *Fugitive Slaves and the Underground Railroad in the Kentucky Borderland.* Jefferson, NC: McFarland, 2002.

Siebert, Wilbur H. "The Mysteries of Ohio's Underground Railroad." 1895. Draft manuscript, in the Wilbur Siebert Papers, The Ohio Underground Railroad, Box 116, Ohio Historical Society.

Siebert, Wilbur H. *The Underground Railroad from Slavery to Freedom.* 1898. Reprint, New York: Russell and Russell, 1967.

Sprague, Stuart S., ed. *His Promised Land: The Autobiography of John P. Parker, Former Slave and Conductor on the Underground Railroad.* New York: W. W. Norton, 1996.

Ray, Charles Bennett (1807–1886)

Abolitionist, editor, and friend of the fugitive. Charles Bennett Ray was born free on December 25, 1807 in Falmouth, **Massachusetts**. As a boy, he attended school in Falmouth and later studied theology at Wesleyan University in Middletown, Connecticut.

Ray was ordained a Congregational minister and eventually pastored the Bethesda Congregational Church in **New York City** for 20 years. However, he is best known for his multi-faceted involvement in the antislavery movement. Ray joined the American Anti-Slavery Society in 1833 and was an active participant in the African American convention movement. He assisted **fugitive slaves**, served as editor of *The Colored American* from 1839 to 1842, and later figured prominently in efforts to free the Weems family in 1855. Ray died on August 15, 1886. *See also* Abolitionist Movement; Weems, Ann Maria; and Appendixes 1 and 2.

FURTHER READING

Work, M. N. "The Life of Charles B. Ray." *Journal of Negro History* 4(1919): 361–371.

Reed, Isaiah

See Portland Crossing Point

Remond, Charles Lenox (1810–1878)

African American antislavery leader. Charles Lenox Remond was born free in Salem, **Massachusetts**, in 1810. An outstanding orator, he joined the American Anti-Slavery Society and, in 1838, became its first African American lecturer.

Remond spoke at public meetings in Massachusetts, Rhode Island, Maine, New York, and **Pennsylvania**. In 1840, he delivered antislavery lectures throughout Europe and attended the World's Anti-Slavery Convention in London, England.

During the **Civil War**, Remond recruited African American soldiers for the Union Army in Massachusetts. Later, he worked as a street light inspector and a clerk in the **Boston** Customs House. Charles Lenox Remond died in Massachusetts in 1878. *See also* Appendixes 1 and 2.

FURTHER READING
Quarles, Benjamin. *Black Abolitionists.* New York: Oxford University Press, 1969.

Reuben Benedict House (Peru Township, Ohio)

Underground Railroad site recognized and documented by the National Park Service. *See also* Appendix 5.

Revels, Hiram Rhoades (1827–1901)

Friend of the fugitive and the first African American elected to the United States Senate. Hiram R. Revels was born on September 1, 1822 to free African American parents in Fayetteville, North Carolina. As a boy, Revels was educated in **Indiana** and **Illinois** and, in 1845, was ordained a minister in the African Methodist Episcopal Church. Revels traveled as a circuit preacher through the Midwest and border slave states working with AME congregations well-known for their involvement in Underground Railroad. Eventually, he settled in Baltimore, Maryland, pastoring a church and administering a school for African American children.

In 1861, Revels organized two volunteer black regiments for service in the Union Army and, in 1863, joined the Army himself as chaplain to an African American regiment stationed in **Mississippi.** After the war Revels settled in Natchez, Mississippi, as pastor of a large black congregation. In 1868, the military governor appointed him an alderman and, in 1869, Revels was elected to the state senate. Although black and a Republican, Revels advocated moderation toward members of the former Confederacy and, in January 1870, was elected to the U.S. Senate to serve out the unexpired term of the former Confederate president, Jefferson Davis—becoming the first African American to serve in this capacity. While in office, he pressed for non-segregated schools and public transportation.

After leaving the Senate, Revels became president of Alcorn Agricultural and Mechanical College near Lorman, Mississippi. He was dismissed from this position in 1874, but returned as president in 1876, ironically, with the support of the Democratic "redeemer" government that had overthrown Reconstruction in Mississippi. Revels remained president of Alcorn until his retirement. He died on January 16, 1901 at Aberdeen, Mississippi. *See also* Appendixes 1 and 2.

FURTHER READING
Thompson, Julius Eric. *Hiram R. Revels, 1827–1901: A Biography.* New York: Arno Press, 1982.

Rice, Isaac (1793–1866)

Friend of the fugitive. Isaac Rice was born free in 1793, moved to Newport, Rhode Island, as a child and spent the remainder of his life there. Rice worked as a gardener for the governor of Rhode Island and became one of the most prominent African Americans in the state. His home was an important station on the Underground Railroad and was visited at various times by Frederick **Douglass** and Sojourner **Truth**. *See also* Underground Railroad, Sites of; and Appendixes 1–4.

Richards, John

Friend of the fugitive in **Detroit, Michigan**. *See also* Finney House; and Appendixes 1 and 2.

Risks of Escape

Although some aid was often crucial, there were serious risks associated with seeking and accepting such assistance. Sizable rewards for **fugitive slaves** made slave-catching a dirty but profitable business—and at times even other African Americans would facilitate the capture of fugitives for this reason. Even otherwise innocent **free people of color** were vulnerable to kidnappers who would sell them into **slavery** or **slave catchers** who would claim them (falsely) as fugitives. *See also* Motivations for Escape; Routes of Escape.

FURTHER READING

Hudson, J. Blaine. *Fugitive Slaves and the Underground Railroad in the Kentucky Borderland.* Jefferson, NC: McFarland, 2002.

Siebert, Wilbur H. *The Underground Railroad from Slavery to Freedom.* 1898. Reprint, New York: Russell and Russell, 1967.

"River Jordan"

See Ohio River

Robert Purvis House (Philadelphia, Pennsylvania)

Located at 1601 Mt. Vernon Street in **Philadelphia**, the home of Robert **Purvis**, African American friend of the fugitive, served as an Underground Railroad station and a center of antislavery activity. *See also* Underground Railroad, Sites of; and Appendixes 1–4.

Robinson, Rowland Thomas (1796–1879)

Friend of the fugitive. Son of staunch Quaker abolitionists, Rowland Thomas Robinson grew to adulthood in Vermont and became a strong supporter of William Lloyd **Garrison**. Working with his neighbors and friends, Robinson also played an active role in assisting **fugitive slaves** in their efforts to settle in or move through Vermont.

The number of fugitive slaves assisted by Robinson was comparatively small, but his home, Rokeby House, survives and has been designated an historic site by the National Register. Not only has Robinson's home survived the ravages of time, but the importance of this site is more than complemented by a remarkable collection of primary source documents. These documents, the Rokeby Collection, include more than ten thousand items: letters, account books, diaries, newspapers (with a complete run of Garrison's *The Liberator*), pamphlets, and other records dating to the late 18th century. The letters from

the 1830 to 1860 period are filled with references to the antislavery movement — and, in several cases, describe the operations of the Underground Railroad in Vermont in great detail. Most importantly, these primary source documents indicate how neighbors and friends, mostly **Quakers**, created an informal network before 1850 that functioned largely "above ground."

As a fitting tribute, William Lloyd Garrison wrote Robinson in July 1878 as follows:

> I always placed you high on my list of friends and co-laborers the most esteemed and the truest; and it affords me the greatest satisfaction to know that you have been preserved to hear the ringing of the jubilee bell, and to witness all those marvelous changes which have taken place in our land within less than a score of years. (William Lloyd Garrison to Rowland Thomas Robinson, July 11, 1878, Robinson Family Letters, Rokeby Collection, Sheldon Museum, Middlebury, Vermont.)

See also Abolitionist Movement; Rokeby; and Appendixes 1 and 2.

FURTHER READING

Garrison, William Lloyd to Rowland Thomas Robinson, July 11, 1878, Robinson Family Letters, Rokeby Collection, Sheldon Museum, Middlebury, Vermont.

Siebert, Wilbur H. *Vermont's Anti-Slavery and Underground Railroad Record.* New York: Negro University Press, 1969.

Zirblis, Raymond Paul. *Friends of Freedom: The Vermont Underground Railroad Survey Report.* Montpelier: Vermont Department of State Buildings, Vermont Division for Historic Preservation, 1996.

Rokeby (Ferrisburg, Vermont)

Underground Railroad site recognized and documented by the National Park Service. *See also* Appendix 5.

Roots, B. G.

Friend of the fugitive in Tamaroa, Illinois. *See also* **Kimzey Crossing/Locust Hill.**

Ross, Alexander M. (1832–1897)

Friend of the fugitive. Dr. Alexander Milton Ross was born on December 13, 1832, in Hastings, Belleville, Upper **Canada**. Ross gained an international reputation as an ornithologist and, in the **1850s**, used his profession — and his professional stature — to travel through the South. There, as one of the few **friends of the fugitive** willing to operate in slave territory, Ross held secret meetings with enslaved African Americans desirous of escaping from bondage and helped organize hundreds of escapes. In 1875, he chronicled his exploits in the classic, *Recollections and Experiences of an Abolitionist: From 1855 to 1865*. Ross married Hester Harrington in 1857 and died on October 27, 1897, in Detroit. *See also* Appendixes 1 and 2.

FURTHER READING
Ross, Alexander M. *Recollections and Experiences of an Abolitionist: From 1855 to 1865*. Toronto: Rowsell and Hutchison, 1875.

Ross, Jacob

A fugitive slave and later friend of the fugitive, Jacob Ross fled **slavery** in Virginia and settled in the African American community of Reading, **Pennsylvania**. In 1837, he contributed to the establishment of the **Bethel AME Church (Reading, Pennsylvania)**, and worked with other members of the congregation to assist **fugitive slaves** escaping northward. *See also* Underground Railroad, Sites of.

FURTHER READING
National Park Service. *Underground Railroad: Special Resource Study*. Washington, D.C.: U.S. Government Printing Office, 1995.

Rothier House

See Carneal House

Routes of Escape

Fugitive slaves did not follow well-marked and well-defined "roads" or "lines," contrary to what much of the more highly romanticized Underground Railroad literature suggests. However, the paths chosen and followed by freedom seekers were not altogether random — and were shaped by a host of human and geographic factors, most of which varied over time. In this respect, it is more accurate to think of broadly defined escape routes and corridors, rather than of fixed lines of escape.

As the United States expanded westward in the early 1800s, four broad zones of **slavery** and, hence, of fugitive slave activity, emerged —

each with its characteristic patterns, challenges, possibilities and limitations:

(1) the region east of the Appalachians, with escape routes leading to the mid-Atlantic and New England states or, ultimately, to eastern **Canada**;

(2) the region west of the Appalachians along the **Ohio River**, with escape routes leading to the Midwestern free territories or states or, ultimately, to western Canada (across from Detroit or Cleveland);

(3) the west side of the Mississippi River, with escape routes leading sometimes into the Ohio River border region or farther west or into **Mexico**; and

(4) the southern interior in which most escapes were temporary acts of resistance, still with some escape routes leading to the eastern or western border zones — or farther south to Florida or the Caribbean in the early years.

Given the location of the vast majority of enslaved African Americans, the border zones immediately east and west of the Appalachians witnessed the heaviest fugitive slave traffic for several simple reasons. Fugitive slaves escaped most often from those regions in which the enslaved African American population was concentrated most heavily. Escape routes and corridors connected these areas of enslaved black population and crossing points in the extended **borderland** between free and slave territory. Thus, the obvious necessity of quitting slave territory made the slave-side border states — particularly **Kentucky**, Virginia and Maryland — and the free-side border states — particularly **Illinois, Indiana, Ohio** and **Pennsylvania** — the literal arena in which a decades-long "quiet insurrection" unfolded. Secondarily, escape routes and corridors connected these crossing points with communities on free soil, sufficiently distant from the Borderland, in which fugitive slaves could find safe haven or from which they could continue their journey out of the United States altogether.

How fugitive slaves crossed into and moved through free soil is documented far more reliably than how and by what routes they moved through slave territory. Even the men and women who assisted fugitive slaves north of the Ohio River in the west and the Pennsylvania border in the east had little knowledge of how those runaways reached the border or free states.

For generations, conventional scholarly and popular wisdom held that fugitives "usually kept to the woods and fields" and that "few if any land routes ... could be traced in the South." (Purtee, 1932: 32.) However, an examination of source materials created primarily by fugitive slaves themselves suggests that this generalization is far too broad and that there were important exceptions.

The heaviest concentrations of enslaved African Americans were in sections of the United States where plantation systems developed and flourished. In colonial America, such systems first emerged in the tobacco growing regions of Virginia and Maryland, and in the rice growing regions of the coastal Carolinas and Georgia. While enslaved African Americans remained numerous in these regions after the **American Revolution**, the invention of the cotton gin in the 1790s and the later expansion of the **Cotton Kingdom** shifted black population dramatically to the southwest after 1800. Thus, as black population increased through the ante-bellum period, it became increasingly concentrated in the Cotton Belt bordering the Gulf of Mexico.

Since the most reliable sources of assistance for fugitive slaves were **free people of color**, understanding fugitive slave escape routes also requires that one understand the geographic distribution of free African Americans in the South. Specifically, as cotton cultivation became more deeply entrenched in vast sections of the deep South, free people of color were subjected to legal restrictions of increasing severity and, in many states, laws were passed after the 1831 Nat Turner Revolt with the intent of driving free blacks out of these states altogether. Ultimately, the free black population became increasingly concentrated in the major urban centers of the South, such as Richmond, Savannah, Charleston, New Orleans, Nashville, **Louisville**, Baltimore and **Washington, D.C.** As in the border states and the North, fugitive slaves could blend into the black populations of these cities and towns for short periods of time, and could expect assistance as well.

The location and activities of white friends of the fugitive must be understood in two contexts. First, in the decades before the **Civil War**, sectional divisions, fugitive slaves, fear of large-scale slave revolt and growing economic dependence on slavery produced a literal siege mentality in the South. Speech or conduct that expressed the slightest reservations about the legitimacy of slavery was suppressed, often violently. Thus, whites who chose to assist fugitive slaves had to operate "deep" underground — and their activities can more often be inferred than documented with precision. As Siebert observed:

> There were friends of the discontented slave in the South ... although it cannot be said that these were sufficient in number or so situated as to maintain regular lines of escape northward. Doubtless many acts of kindness to slaves were performed by individual southerners, but those were not, in most cases, known as the acts of persons cooperating to help the slave from point to point until freedom and safety could be reached. [Siebert, 1898: 116.]

For example, there were counties in **Mississippi** where enslaved African Americans were two-thirds of the population, but other counties in which only one of one hundred persons were black. Similar demographic and political patterns could be founds in parts of the Carolinas, Georgia, Alabama, **Tennessee**, and **Texas**. The whites in these sections of the South were seldom friends to slaveholders and some, apparently, were even friends to African Americans — including those seeking freedom through flight. Distance to free soil was a formidable barrier to would-be fugitives from the southern interior, but freedom seekers living near the Mississippi River or the Atlantic coast or the Gulf of Mexico did have slightly better odds if they could escape by sea. Of course, in Texas, freedom seekers could flee either to Mexico, the west or the north. As enslaved African Americans flowed into Texas in the 1840s, the number of fugitive slaves increased proportionately. Texas newspaper editor John S. Ford claimed that 4,000 African Americans left Texas in 1855 alone, though this estimate cannot be substantiated.

Given their unusual east-west configuration, both Tennessee and Kentucky figured prominently in slave escapes west of the Appalachians and in escapes from the east that used mountain routes. Geographically, antebellum Tennessee was divided into three sections, each with its distinctive economic and slave-holding pattern. Eastern Tennessee belonged to the Appalachian upland. Central Tennessee was fertile and, with its luxuriant bluegrass, resembled central Kentucky. The western section of the state was added in 1818 when Andrew Jackson consummated the Chickasaw Purchase and brought the territory between the Tennessee and Mississippi Rivers into the state. African Americans were concentrated in the western and central regions of Tennessee, with some pockets of population concentration in the eastern valleys. Central Tennessee formed the northern border of Alabama and western Tennessee bore the same relation to northern Mississippi. Consequently, fugitives escaping overland from these cotton-growing states were funneled through central and western Tennessee, then through Kentucky, to free territory.

Fugitives from or passing through central Tennessee had two alternative routes in a broad and general sense. They could escape overland, following (or shadowing) more or less the old traces and trails, and the newer roads that led from northern Tennessee through the Bowling Green, Kentucky, area, past Mammoth Cave and then to north central Kentucky. Alternatively, they could follow the unusual course of the Cumberland River, which loops from Kentucky through Tennessee, then back into Kentucky again, flowing eventually into the Ohio River.

Fugitives from or passing through the far eastern and far western sections of Tennessee had fewer options. Eastern Tennessee was situated in the Appalachian region and its valleys, and fugitives could either follow the mountains and exit in eastern Kentucky or Ohio, or flee west to follow the routes leading from central Tennessee. In the west, escape by the Tennessee or Cumberland Rivers into western Kentucky was an attractive prospect to many fugitives, as was escape by steamboat on the Mississippi River. Many of these fugitives passed through the Jackson Purchase area of Kentucky.

These far eastern and far western routes had some advantages. In the west, the key advantages were proximity to the Mississippi River and, even more fundamentally, to free territory. In the east, a corridor of small free black communities led into and through the more protected terrain of the mountains—a more difficult journey, but one with natural barriers as potential allies.

The most heavily traveled escape routes east of the Appalachians were determined by demography and geography. Even after the emergence and expansion of the Cotton Kingdom shifted millions of enslaved African Americans to the Gulf States, large numbers remained in Maryland, Virginia and the Carolinas. Fugitive slaves from these states, who chose not to risk escape through the mountains, followed numerous routes through the east, often linking or leading to settlements of **Quakers** or Covenanters, and concentrations of free people of color.

As in other regions, distance from free territory was a critical determinant of the likelihood of a successful escape attempt: The odds favored fugitives who had less distance to travel through slave territory. Consequently, in the east, the border counties of Maryland (Frederick, Carroll, Washington, Hartford and Baltimore), were sources of a disproportionately high number of fugitive slaves, both from those counties and as escape corridors for fugitives from Virginia and points farther south. With roughly 25,000 free people of color by the **1850s**, Baltimore was a key junction at which fugitives could receive active or passive assistance.

Fugitives crossing this border could then press on for Adams, Chester, Delaware, Lancaster and York counties in Pennsylvania, all with concentrations of Quakers and other antislavery whites. Depending on the county, freedom seekers could then cross either into New Jersey or proceed to **Philadelphia**—then to New York, on to New England and, perhaps, to Canada. Fugitives moving through central Pennsylvania could reach Susquehanna county and then move into central New York at Peterboro, the home of abolitionist Gerrit **Smith**, and then perhaps to Canada. Many of the most famous **friends of the fugitive** operated in this region, e.g., Thomas **Garrett**, William **Still**, and Harriett **Tubman**, to name only a few.

Some of the earliest Underground Railroad literature identified four principle fugitive slave escape routes across New York. One originated in Washington, D.C., and extended north on a fairly direct line to Albany, New York. According to Frederick **Douglass**, another passed through Philadelphia, then **New York City**, then Albany and, eventually, Rochester. Others extended across Pennsylvania into central New York. There were also lateral and alternative routes from Utica to Syracuse to Oswego or Niagara Falls. Some of the key African American operatives were William Still in Philadelphia, David **Ruggles** in New York City, Stephan Myers in Albany, Jermain **Loguen** in Syracuse, and Frederick Douglass in Rochester.

For fugitive slaves seeking refuge in Canada, New England was usually out of the usual way. However, many freedom seekers found their way to the New England states, particularly before 1850, not only as a detour on their journey to Canada, but as a place to live in comparative safety given the comparatively strong antislavery sentiment that prevailed in large sections of the region. Many fugitives who reached New England passed first through New York or Philadelphia — and were often aided by the vigilance societies operating in those cities. Others escaped by ship (usually as stowaways or in disguise) from southern ports and entered through major port cities such as **New Bedford, Massachusetts** ("the fugitive's Gibraltar"); New Haven, Connecticut; **Boston**; and Portland, Maine.

In New Bedford, there were even boarding houses available to fugitive slaves, and local blacks and white willing to assist in arranging for the employment of runaways. Schools were established and the town prided itself on its untarnished record of protecting fugitive slaves who reached and lived within its limits.

From New Haven, an escape route wound through the Connecticut River valley to Canada. A number of routes through Vermont (e.g., through Burlington) were important as well. Boston was an important destination and sanctuary, with active black and white antislavery communities led by men such as former Kentucky fugitive Lewis **Hayden**. From Boston, many fugitive slaves were spirited along the Atlantic coast to Maine and then to New Brunswick and Lower Canada, or

through New Hampshire to Maine and then Canada. Most fugitives who reached Maine traveled either by these routes or by ship from the South. A few continued their flight by ship even as far as Europe; fugitive slaves from Kentucky were found begging in the streets of London, England, in the 1850s.

Still, the likelihood of pursuit and recapture diminished as fugitive slaves moved farther northward. Under such conditions, the Underground Railroad seldom "ran underground" in these areas and, at least before 1850, friends of the fugitive could operate through local antislavery networks with a degree of openness impossible in the South, or the borderland states or "lower North."

The flow of fugitives was probably heavier west of the Appalachians by the late antebellum period and Underground Railroad work was probably more widespread, although not as widely known. However, before discussing the region between the Appalachians and Mississippi River, it is important to remember that more westerly free states such as **Iowa** were also border states. Iowa, in particular, played a major role in the passage of fugitive slaves from Missouri and Kansas as settlement moved westward and the controversy over slavery erupted in Kansas after the passage of the Kansas-Nebraska Act in 1854.

Many states in the far West did not enter the Union until well after the Civil War and, consequently, were neither home to meaningful numbers of enslaved African Americans nor directly involved in the sectional divisions over slavery. Still, there was an African American presence and a connection to the history of freedom seekers. African Americans were among the famous trappers (James Beckworth and Jacob Dodson) and explorers (York), of the West. Many enslaved African Americans passed through the territories that would become Wyoming, Colorado, Montana, New Mexico and Arizona as they accompanied their owners westward. Many free African Americans migrated westward — and some fugitive slaves followed these wagon routes and trails as well.

African Americans also ventured or fled into the mining camps of the West, particularly to **California** after the Mexican War, and several court cases in that state in the 1850s revolved around the fate of fugitive slaves.

Runaway slaves sometimes traveled the roads that evolved from old Buffalo traces and Native American trails, particularly through sparsely populated areas where they could travel unobserved. More often, these routes could be followed on foot from a safe distance. However, while long-distance travel relied on long-distance routes, there were numerous local trails forged by smaller animals—"deer and varmint" paths, "ghost roads" through forests and over hills that could be extremely useful to fugitives as means of avoiding patrols, and circumventing unwelcoming towns and more densely settled areas.

As Wilbur Siebert observed, far more fugitive slaves escaped into the states of the Old Northwest than into any other region of the United States. African Americans escaping from slavery in the trans-Appalachian west — the region bounded by the Appalachian Mountains in the east and the Mississippi River in the west — were funneled most often through Kentucky. To reach free territory, these freedom seekers faced several challenges: how to reach the Kentucky Borderland; how to cross the Ohio River; and how to find safe haven in the North or Canada. In Kentucky, slave escape routes led to 12 major Ohio River crossing points along the northern border of the state. These crossing-points were spaced roughly 50 miles apart, from the Jackson Purchase region of Kentucky in the west to the Appalachians in the east.

There were five major crossing points in the western third of the state, all leading eventually to Lake Michigan:

(1) through far western Kentucky, i.e., through Cairo, Illinois, and Paducah, Kentucky, to the east;

(2) through Posey County in southwest Indiana, then north along the Wabash River;

(3) through Evansville, Indiana, with its free black community;

(4) through Warrick County, Indiana, and then north through Oakland City to Petersburg, Indiana; and

(5) between Owensboro, Kentucky, and Rockport, Indiana.

In the middle third of Kentucky, between Meade County and Carroll County, there were three crossing points around Louisville, through which a substantial number of fugitives escaped in the decades before the Civil War. Typically, these crossing points and those to the east led ultimately through Indiana or western Ohio to Lake Erie:

(1) Leavenworth, Indiana, leading toward Corydon, Indiana.

(2) the Louisville region, including New Albany, Jeffersonville and Clarksville, Indiana.

(3) **Madison, Indiana**; Trimble and Carroll Counties, Kentucky.

In the eastern third of Kentucky, there were four crossing points, the latter two of great consequence:

(1) the **Cincinnati**, Ohio and Covington, Kentucky area, the "Grand Central Station" of the Underground Railroad;

(2) the Maysville, Kentucky, and Ripley, Ohio areas;

(3) the Portsmouth, Ohio area, leading toward Chillicothe and then central Ohio; and

(4) near the Kentucky/Virginia/Ohio border in the Appalachians, leading through eastern or central Ohio.

Moving northward, three major escape routes then extended across Illinois. One began at Chester, another at Alton and the other at Quincy. These served fugitive slaves crossing Illinois's much longer Mississippi River border with Missouri, and all converged ultimately at Chicago. The third route from far western Kentucky contributed far fewer fugitives. This section of Illinois was smaller both in area and in African American population and was strongly proslavery—and movement eastward by land or river to Indiana or Ohio was more attractive. Still, the flow of fugitive slaves from Kentucky into Illinois was not altogether insignificant. These runaways used two lesser branch routes. The first led from Cairo northward to Springfield. The second and probably more important followed the course of the Wabash River into Indiana.

Before 1850, many fugitive slaves "passed through" Indiana en route to another free state or Canada, while others settled in the state and blended into existing African American settlements near or along the Ohio River. As escape became more difficult after 1850, assistance grew correspondingly in importance.

In such fluid circumstances, these settlements along the border and throughout the "lower North" became the superstructure for a more sophisticated network of escape routes, as noted by Siebert:

> The first ... was a continuation of the routes from Cincinnati and Lawrenceburg which converged in Wayne County. Thence a main line ran north through Winchester, Portland, Decatur, Fort Wayne, and Auburn into Michigan. The second main line originated from three branches that crossed the Ohio River at Madison, New Albany, and the vicinity of Leavenworth. These converged near Columbus and passed north through Indianapolis, Westfield, Logansport, Plymouth, and South Bend. The third main route crossed the Ohio at Evansville and followed the Wabash River through Terre Haute and then up to Lafayette. [Siebert, 1898: 137–138.]

With Evansville to the west, on the Indiana side of the Ohio, and Henderson to the east, on the Kentucky side, the first crossing point from Kentucky to southwestern Indiana was especially appealing to fugitives from western Kentucky wishing to avoid southern Illinois— and those from western Kentucky and Tennessee following the Cumberland or Tennessee Rivers.

The fugitive slave crossing points in Meade County, Kentucky, represented the western limit of the Louisville region. These crossings were near the towns of Brandenburg on the Kentucky side of the river and Leavenworth on the Indiana side. Given its location between Owensboro and Louisville, the Meade County crossing served as an alternative slave escape route for African Americans fleeing from the Bluegrass region and from far western Kentucky. This escape route led next to Corydon and then converged at Columbus with branch routes leading from Louisville and Madison.

For reasons as much geographic as demographic, the role of Louisville was critical both to the passage of fugitive slaves and to the work of friends of the fugitive in the trans-Appalachian west. As William Cockrum concluded on the basis of his own experience:

> There were probably more negroes crossed over the Ohio river and two or three places in front of Louisville than any place else from the mouth of the Wabash to Cincinnati. The reason for this was that the three good sized cities at the Falls furnished a good hiding place for runaways among the colored people. Those crossing at these places were all conveyed to Wayne county, Indiana, and thence on to the Lake. [Cockrum, 1915: 21.]

The most important crossing point in the greater Louisville area — the **Portland Crossing Point**— was located west of the Portland neighborhood; it led from Louisville across the Ohio River to New Albany, Indiana.

To the east of Louisville, the fugitive slave escape corridor leading through Trimble and Carroll counties in Kentucky to Ohio River crossing points in the vicinity of Madison, Indiana, was one of the most active and well-known in the region, and also channeled fugitive slaves toward Columbus, Indiana, where it converged with those branch routes from the west. As the origin of numerous fugitives associated with this crossing suggests, the location of this route roughly midway between Louisville and Cincinnati made it an oft-traveled alternative route for fugitives escaping from or through the central Bluegrass.

From the standpoint of fugitive slaves, the role of Ohio was comparable in importance to that of Kentucky. According to Siebert, "Ohio was the foremost state in the abolition business, being peculiarly located for this purpose," with "thirteen ports of entry on the Ohio River" and "a network of from 2800 to 3000 miles of road throughout the state." This complex network of routes extended toward "five termini or ports of embarkation on Lake Erie." (Siebert, 1894.)

Five Ohio counties shared an Ohio River border with Kentucky: Hamilton, Clermont, Brown, Adams and Lawrence (from west to east). A number of southern antislavery families and free people of color settled in Hamilton and Clermont counties before 1810. Already predisposed to aiding fugitives, their presence attracted and they often assisted thousands of runaways who passed through the region before 1830. Brown and Hamilton Counties, in particular, were known as bastions of antislavery sentiment along the river. Much like the crossings and routes from Kentucky to southern Indiana, the major Ohio crossings had an underlying structure:

> At the western edge of the state the routes originated at Cincinnati or North Bend, fifteen or

twenty miles down the river, whence the fugitives were practically always taken to College Hill (now a part of Cincinnati), where Lane Seminary was located. From College Hill the principal routes went either northwest through Hamilton ... to Richmond or Newport, Indiana, both Quaker towns, or northeastward through either Wilmington or Xenia to Springfield and thence to Bellfontaine, Kenton, Tiffin and Sandusky. From Xenia a second set of routes reached Mechanicsburg, Marysville ... passing on to Sandusky ... Cleveland or some other lake port. [Purtee, 1932: 36.]

African Americans often lived along Underground Railroad lines that branched in several directions from Cincinnati. One route stretched north through Preble and Darke Counties — with a branch-line that crossed into Indiana through "a colored settlement in Israel Township, where Nathan Brown, Ebenezer Elliott and others had stations." Another western route passed through West Fork, "a damned abolition hole," then north to Dunlap "... a Negro settlement from which Hansel and Wade Roberts passed them to Hamilton." In eastern Cincinnati, the "Old Stone Jug Tavern" was used to hide "hundreds of liberty-seekers." Other routes from Cincinnati were "the Miami Canal, completed to Toledo in 1842, and the Cleveland, Columbus and Cincinnati Railroad, which was running through trains by March 1851." As in Indiana, "these new means of transportation were promptly utilized by leading abolitionists of Cincinnati and towns along the way." (Siebert, 1895: 6–8.)

In Clermont County, Ohio, immediately east of Hamilton County (and Cincinnati), a similar network existed — adapted to the realities of a less populous and more rural area. To the east, the same escape routes leading from crossings into Clermont, Brown and Adams Counties merged at Wilmington or **Xenia** with the branch lines leading northeasterly from Cincinnati. However, "the important gateway of Ripley sent its fugitives straight northward to Wilmington, or over to the line into Adams County, where they were taken along the Maysville-Chillicothe pike (Zane's trace)." (Everts, 1880: 441–442.)

The fugitive slave escape route leading from Lexington and the densely populated central Bluegrass region to Maysville was one of the earliest and most heavily traveled in Kentucky and was mentioned frequently in fugitive slave notices and articles. Ripley, Ohio, stood opposite and a few miles to the west of Maysville and, much like Madison, Indiana, was home to numerous antislavery whites who had "chosen or been forced to leave the South." By 1840, more than 300 whites belonged to the Ripley Abolition Society led by men such as "U.S. Senator Alexander Campbell (Ohio's first Abolitionist), Theodore Collins, Tom Collins, Eli Collins, Tom McCague, Dr. Beasley, Reverend James Gilliland." Ripley was also home to two black settlements established before 1820. To the north, there were many friends of the fugitive in towns such as Red Oak, "where Reverend James Gilliland and his congregation formed the core of the largest concentration of Underground Railroad conductors in Ohio." (Purtee, 1932: 37.) These antislavery activists were surrounded by adamantly proslavery neighbors on both sides of the Ohio River. Transcending the importance of this antislavery infrastructure were the roles and work of a few extraordinary individuals — one white, the aforementioned Reverend John **Rankin** (1793–1886), and two black, John **Parker** (1827–1900) and John **Hudson**.

The Ohio counties bordering the eastern and more mountainous sections of Kentucky witnessed the crossing of fugitives from Kentucky and some, as noted previously, who followed routes from the southern interior through the Appalachians. The Scioto River bisects Scioto County and flows into the Ohio at Portsmouth. The earliest records of slave escapes from Kentucky into this region of southern Ohio date to 1820. However, the Borderland in Scioto County was unusually hostile. Portsmouth was a strong proslavery center and, by 1830, had driven out most of the hundred or more African Americans once resident there. Still, fugitives escaped through this region and often found assistance from white Underground Railroad workers such as James M. **Ashley**.

Also drawing fugitives from eastern Kentucky and the Appalachian escape routes, Lawrence County witnessed a moderate but steady flow of runaways beginning in the 1830s, if not earlier. Ironton was founded in

1840 at what was already a principal crossing point. There, Joseph H. Creighton, a Methodist minister, and John Peters "befriended fugitive slaves, who came across in skiffs and joe boats." (Siebert, 1895: 1.) Lawrence County was also home to one of the most effective and colorful African American Underground Railroad leaders, Jack **Ditcher** (or Dicher), the legendary "Red Fox" of the Underground.

From this point, another route branched northeast, through a chain of stations operated by black and white agents to the Poke Patch Colored Settlement in Gallia County along the Ohio/Virginia border. Given this location, Poke Patch was a crossroads for fugitives bound north from both Kentucky and Virginia. Friends of the fugitive were committed and well organized, even holding a "convention of the colored citizens of Gallia County in 1851" at which they articulated, among other resolutions, their sympathy with fugitive slaves. (Frederick Douglass Paper, January 1, 1852 in Hudson, 2002: 126.)

In general, fugitives crossing from Kentucky into Scioto and Lawrence Counties followed routes through southeastern Ohio — perhaps the most important of which passed first through Chillicothe — that converged ultimately at Columbus in central Ohio.

Finally, escape routes on the Underground Railroad were not limited to trails and roads, but also included oceans, rivers, streams and man-made waterways such as canals. The Ohio River was, perhaps, the most important waterway and water boundary, but there were many other important water routes from slave to free territory. For example, many freedom seekers used the Mississippi and Missouri Rivers. Others used the Gulf of Mexico. Still others used the Monongahela River to reach Pittsburgh, Pennsylvania, while others crossed the Delaware and Chesapeake Bay to reach Delaware County, Pennsylvania. The Great Lakes and the Detroit and Niagara Rivers were means by which freedom seekers entered Canada. Whether a water route might figure in an escape — and which body or bodies of water might be involved — depended on the region of the country from which the fugitive escaped and the region of the country, or Canada or Mexico, the fugitive was attempting to reach.

Skiffs, rafts and other small vessels were sometimes hidden by friends of the fugitive — or stolen by fugitive slaves themselves — along the inland and coastal water routes, such as the major crossing points along the Ohio River. Conductors such as John Parker of Ripley, Ohio, ferried hundreds of fugitives from the Kentucky shore to free territory. Fugitive slaves who reached towns bordering Lake Erie found ship captains willing to transport them to Canada, which led to many such vessels being termed "abolition boats." Philo Carpenter of Chicago arranged passage for more than 200 freedom seekers. In Maryland, sympathetic captains transported fugitive slaves from the ports of Annapolis and Baltimore. Others crossed Chesapeake Bay on small boats bound for the Susquehanna River and Underground Railroad stations in Pennsylvania.

Some vessels and ships that engaged in trade along the East Coast also became involved, sometimes inadvertently in the case of stowaways, in transporting fugitive slaves from southern seaports to the North. A notable example was Captain Daniel **Drayton** of the *Pearl*, who transported runaways down the Potomac River, to Chesapeake Bay, then to the Delaware River and into New Jersey. To discourage abolitionist sailors from assisting fugitive slaves, many southern states passed laws to penalize ship captains and steam boat owners for harboring fugitives — and, first, to quarantine black sailors when in port, or, in the later antebellum period, to require that they carry passports.

Once again, rather than the fixed and well-defined "lines" described by Siebert and others, fugitive slave escape routes were more akin to broad corridors. Points of origin and destinations at various stages of the journey to freedom changed over time — as did the simplest and safest route(s) between the two. What did not change over time was the determination of freedom seekers to reach free and safe haven, by whatever route.

FURTHER READING

Addington, Wendell G. "Slave Insurrections in Texas." *Journal of Negro History* 35, no. 4(1950): 408–434.

Berlin, Ira, and Ronald Hoffman, eds. *Slavery and Freedom in the Age of Revolution.* Charlottesville: University Press of Virginia, 1983.

Blackburn, George M., and Sherman L. Ricards. "Unequal Opportunity on a Mining Frontier: The Role of Gender, Race and Birthplace." *Pacific Historical Review* 62(1993): 19–37.

Blassingame, John W. *Slave Testimony: Two Centuries of Letters, Speeches, Interviews and Autobiography.* Baton Rouge: Louisiana State University Press, 1977.

Bolster, W. Jeffrey. *Black Jacks: African American Seamen in the Age of Sail.* Cambridge: Harvard University Press, 1997.

Cockrum, Col. William M. *History of the Underground Railroad, As It Was Conducted by the Anti-Slavery League.* 1915. Reprint, New York: Negro Universities Press, 1969.

Coffin, Levi. *Reminiscences of Levi Coffin.* New York: Augustus M. Kelley, 1876.

Dykstra, Robert R. *Bright Radical Star: Black Freedom and White Supremacy on the Hawkeye Frontier.* Cambridge, MA: Harvard University, 1993.

Everts, Louis H. *History of Clermont County* (Philadelphia, 1880) in the Wilbur Siebert Papers, The Ohio Underground Railroad, Vol. XII, Box 112, Ohio Historical Society: 441–442.

Farr, Joseph. "Joseph Farr Remembers the Underground Railroad in St. Paul." *Minnesota History* 57(2000): 123–129. Reprint of 1895 article in the *St. Paul Pioneer Press.*

Franklin, John H., and Loren Schweninger. *Runaway Slaves: Rebels on the Plantation.* New York: Oxford, 1999.

Hill, James L. "Migration of Blacks to Iowa, 1820–1960." *Journal of Negro History* 66, no. 4(1982): 289–303.

Hudson, J. Blaine. *Fugitive Slaves and the Underground Railroad in the Kentucky Borderland.* Jefferson, NC: McFarland, 2002.

Kay, Marvin L., and Lorin L. Cary. "Slave Runaways in Colonial North Carolina." *The North Carolina Historical Review* 63, no. 1(1981).

Mullin, Gerald W. *Flight and Rebellion: Slave Resistance in Eighteenth Century Virginia.* New York: Oxford University Press, 1972.

Purtee, Edward O. "The Underground Railroad from Southwestern Ohio to Lake Erie." Unpublished Ph.D. dissertation, Ohio State University, 1932, in Wilbur H. Siebert Papers, Underground Railroad in Ohio, Vol. XII, Box 112, Ohio Historical Society.

Savage, W. Sherman. "The Negro in the Westward Movement." *Journal of Negro History* 25, no. 4(1940): 531–539.

Siebert, Wilbur H. "The Mysteries of Ohio's Underground Railroad." 1895. Draft manuscript, in the Wilbur Siebert Papers, The Ohio Underground Railroad, Box 116, Ohio Historical Society.

Siebert, Wilbur H. *The Underground Railroad from Slavery to Freedom.* 1898. Reprint, New York: Russell and Russell, 1967.

_____. "Underground Railroad: How Slaves in Early Days were Piloted to Canada." *The Ohio Journal,* November 14, 1894, in the Wilbur Siebert Papers, The Ohio Underground Railroad, Box 105, Ohio Historical Society.

_____. *Vermont's Anti-Slavery and Underground Railroad Record.* New York: Negro Universities Press, 1937.

Strother, Horatio T. *The Underground Railroad in Connecticut.* Middletown, CT: Wesleyan University Press, 1962.

Switala, William J. *Underground Railroad in Delaware, Maryland, and West Virginia.* Mechanicsburg, PA: Stackpole Books, 2004.

_____. *Underground Railroad in Pennsylvania.* Mechanicsburg, PA: Stackpole Books, 2001.

Ruggles, David (1810–1849)

Friend of the fugitive. David Ruggles was born free on March 15, 1810, in Norwich, Connecticut, the eldest of five children. He received his early education at the Sabbath School for the Poor in Norwich and, at age 17, moved to **New York City** as the last vestiges of **slavery** were finally ending in the state. Between 1829 and 1833, Ruggles operated a grocery store and, having become increasingly involved in the antislavery movement, became a traveling agent for *The Emancipator* and gained a reputation as a passionate and effective antislavery lecturer.

In 1834, Ruggles opened a bookstore in New York City, possibly the first African American-owned bookstore in the United States. He also operated a lending library and published pamphlets arguing strongly against the colonizationist movement. In September 1835, his bookstore was destroyed by fire and he moved from antislavery agitation to "practical abolitionism" when, on November 20, 1835, he was elected secretary of the Friends of Human Rights— otherwise known as the New York Committee of Vigilance.

The Committee of Vigilance positioned itself to assist all **fugitive slaves** passing through the region who sought or were directed to it for help. In its first year of operations, Ruggles and his associates assisted 335 fugitive slaves. During his active career, Ruggles probably assisted at least one thousand fugitives himself. Many were sheltered in his home for varying periods. The most famous of them was Frederick **Douglass** after his escape from slavery in Maryland in September

1838. In fact, when Anna Murray joined Douglass in New York, the two were married in Ruggles' home by the Reverend James W.C. **Pennington**. Ruggles also assisted Douglass in relocating to **New Bedford, Massachusetts**.

In 1838, Ruggles was arrested and jailed for harboring Thomas Hughes, a fugitive slave from Arkansas, and, although he was neither tried nor convicted, was not freed until November 1839. His health suffered and, among other maladies, his sight began to fail. To compound his problems, Ruggles also became embroiled in a complex lawsuit filed against him by Samuel Cornish over a letter published in the *Colored American*. The letter concerned a case of alleged slave trading, which resulted in a suit against Cornish, for which Cornish blamed Ruggles. Although Ruggles was exonerated, the lawsuit ruined both him and the Committee of Vigilance financially — and compromised his reputation. At the end of January 1839, Ruggles resigned his post as secretary of the committee and, by 1842, found himself almost completely blind and destitute.

Lydia Maria Child learned of his condition and helped him move to Northampton, Massachusetts — an Underground Railroad station headed by Basil Dorsey, a fugitive once assisted by Ruggles. There, Ruggles resumed his antislavery work and, more significantly, was introduced to hydrotherapy (the "water cure") that restored his health and sight to some degree. Having taken the cure, Ruggles learned its methods and techniques and became a practitioner. Beginning in 1846, Ruggles purchased over 100 acres and erected several well-appointed buildings for "Dr. Ruggles' Water-Cure Establishment." Unfortunately, as his prosperity and fame were growing, Ruggles died on December 26, 1849.

Years later, Frederick Douglass would describe Ruggles as "... a whole-souled man, fully imbued with a love of his afflicted and hunted people ... This brave and devoted man suffered much from the persecutions common to all who have been prominent benefactors." (Porter, 1943: 32–33.) *See also* Vigilance Committees; and Appendixes 1 and 2.

FURTHER READING
Perlman, Daniel. "Organizations of the Free Negro in New York City, 1800–1860." *Journal of Negro History* 56, no. 3(1971): 181–197.

Porter, Dorothy B. "David Ruggles: An Apostle of Human Rights." *Journal of Negro History* 38, no. 1(1943): 23–50.

Rush R. Sloane House (Sandusky, Ohio)

Underground Railroad site recognized and documented by the National Park Service. *See also* Appendix 5.

Rutter, Thomas

Friend of the fugitive in **Pine Forge, Pennsylvania**. *See also* Appendixes 1 and 2.

Ryker, Will

Friend of the fugitive in **Madison, Indiana**. *See also* Appendixes 1 and 2.

St. James AME Church (Ithaca, New York)

Underground Railroad site recognized and documented by the National Park Service. *See also* Appendix 5.

St. John's AME Church (Niagara Falls, New York)

Underground Railroad station. St. John's A. M. E. Church was the first black church founded in Niagara County, New York, and remains located today in the heart of Niagara Falls' African American community. In the antebellum period, St. John's, like many structures in Niagara County, was a key station on the Underground Railroad. *See also* Underground Railroad, Sites of; and Appendixes 3 and 4.

Samuel and Sally Wilson House (Cincinnati, Ohio)

Underground Railroad site recognized and documented by the National Park Service. *See also* Appendix 5.

Sanderson, J. B.

Friend of the fugitive in San Francisco, **California**. *See also* Appendixes 1 and 2.

Sandwich First Baptist Church (Canada)

Underground Railroad site. In 1844, **fugitive slaves** built the First Baptist Church at

Sandwich, near **Amherstburg**. The church was constructed of bricks made with clay from the Detroit River, and was one of many fugitive slave destinations in Ontario. *See also* Canada; Underground Railroad, Sites of; and Appendixes 3 and 4.

Sawyer, Moses

Friend of the fugitive in Weare, New Hampshire. *See also* Moses Sawyer House; and Appendixes 1 and 2.

Schuylkill Friends Meetinghouse (Phoenixville, Pennsylvania)

Underground Railroad site. The Schuylkill Meetinghouse was a small Quaker meetinghouse in Phoenixville, **Pennsylvania**. The meetinghouse served as a sanctuary for **fugitive slaves** and hosted frequent antislavery meetings. *See also* Quakers; Underground Railroad, Sites of; and Appendixes 3 and 4.

Sea Islands

Underground Railroad sites. The islands of the coast of South Carolina, Georgia, and North Florida embody a fascinating historical and cultural link between Africa and the United States. Africans enslaved on these islands during the antebellum period lived and worked in relative isolation, and, in many cases, had more contact with Native Americans than with whites and other enslaved African Americans. This isolation permitted the preservation of linguistic and cultural practices and traditions, usually termed Gullah or Geechee, that are more distinctly African — and influenced strongly by the cultures of the principal areas of Nigeria (e.g., the homelands of the Yoruba and Ibo people) exploited by British and American slave traders in the eighteenth and early nineteenth centuries.

The Sea Islands also served as a temporary and, at times, permanent destination for **fugitive slaves** escaping from regions of the deeper South. For these freedom seekers, the distance to free territory made a successful escape difficult, if not improbable. Escape by small boat to a refuge on one of the Sea Islands was often an attractive alternative. *See also* Underground Railroad, Sites of; and Appendixes 3 and 4.

FURTHER READING
Blockson, Charles L. *Hippocrene Guide to the Underground Railroad*. New York: Hippocrene Books, 1994.
Branch, Muriel Miller. *The Water Brought Us: The Story of the Gullah-Speaking People*. New York: Cobblehill Books/Dutton, 1995.
Crum, Mason. *Gullah: Negro Life in the Carolina Sea Islands*. New York: Negro Universities Press, 1968.
Goodwine, Margaretta L., ed. *The Legacy of Ibo Landing: Gullah Roots of African American Culture*. Atlanta: Clarity Press, 1998.

Second Baptist Church (Detroit, Michigan)

Underground Railroad site. In 1836, the Second Baptist Church was founded by 13 African Americans and became home to the first African American congregation in Michigan. Located on Monroe Street in Detroit, Michigan, the church assisted an estimated five thousand **fugitive slaves** in the quarter century before the **Civil War**, particularly under the leadership of the Reverend George **DeBaptiste** in the late 1840s and **1850s**. Frederick **Douglass** spoke in the Second Baptist Church in 1859. *See also* Underground Railroad, Sites of; and Appendixes 3 and 4.

Seminole Wars

See Black Seminoles

Seminoles

See Black Seminoles

Sering, John

Friend of the fugitive in **Madison, Indiana**. *See also* Appendixes 1 and 2.

Shadd, Mary Ann

See Cary, Mary Anne Shadd

Shadrach Rescue

See Minkins, Shadrach

Signals

In regions with well-established free African American communities and Underground Railroad networks, rudimentary systems of signals and passwords developed by which **fugitive slaves** and **friends of the fugitive** could recognize one another. The list is long indeed; among the most important were the following:

- songs;
- dances, particularly the African "Bamboula" in New Orleans;
- bird calls;
- a certain sequence of knocks on a door or window;
- lamps or candles in windows;
- coded messages sent by regular mail (in which fugitives were referred to as "packages";
- being sent from one place to another;
- Masonic signs and cabalistic symbols; secret hand-shakes or hand-signs;
- coins emblazoned with antislavery sentiments (such as "Am I Not a Man and a Brother" or "Am I Not a Woman and a Sister");
- ribbons tied to trees;
- broken branches; and
- hitching posts or "faithful" or "slave groomsmen."

All of these devices were used in some way, but the available evidence suggests that their uses were local, situation-specific and limited. Indeed, the only essential requirement of any signaling system was that the signals were understandable to all parties to an escape and not easily recognizable by others.

Even more sophisticated signaling systems are cited in the secondary literature. For example, Dobard and Tobin contend that quilts using certain African-derived symbols were employed in the Carolinas to help fugitives choose the time, route and destination of their escape. Some of the issues in the controversy over the possible role of quilts in the Underground Railroad are summarized by Xenia E. Cord in *Underground Railroad Quilts — Another View* (2004):

> Occasionally a theory is presented that offers an engaging view of the American past; the theory may not have substance and may not be documentable in any scholarly way, but it provides a vehicle through which we believe we can understand our past. This is the case with studies that supposedly reveal hidden codes or messages in quilts ... The theory hangs from a slender thread, a single story narrated by an African American woman in Charleston, SC, whose business was selling quilts in a local marketplace ... No surviving quilts supporting the theory have been found...

Although not precisely what Dobard and Tobin had in mind, the **Jordan House** in West Des Moines, **Iowa** does provide a rare example of the use of quilts as an Underground Railroad signaling system. Specifically, a quilt hanging outside the home of James Cunningham **Jordan** with a small black square woven into its design signified that it was safe for fugitives to seek refuge there. However, a square of a different color signified danger and that the fugitive should seek refuge elsewhere. *See also* Songs.

FURTHER READING

Cord, Xenia E. *Underground Railroad Quilts — Another View. American Quilt Study Group*, 2004.

Franklin, John H. and Loren Schweninger. *Runaway Slaves: Rebels on the Plantation*. New York: Oxford, 1999.

Siebert, Wilbur H. *The Underground Railroad from Slavery to Freedom*. 1898. Reprint, New York: Russell and Russell, 1967.

Tobin, Jacqueline L., and Raymond G. Dobard. *Hidden in Plain View: A Secret Story of Quilts and the Underground Railroad*. New York: Doubleday, 1999.

Sims, Marcus

A friend of the fugitive, Marcus Sims was a free African American who migrated from Virginia to Williamsburg, **Ohio**. Sims worked at a tannery owned by Underground Railroad stationmaster, Charles B. **Huber**. Working with Huber in a rather different capacity, Sims was an "**engineer**" on the Underground Railroad, i.e., the wagon-master who actually transported freedom seekers delivered to Huber's care from Williamsburg to stations in nearby Brown or Clinton Counties. *See also* Charles B. Huber Homesite.

Sims, Thomas (b. 1828)

Fugitive slave and fugitive slave rescue case. In February 1851, 23-year-old Thomas Sims escaped from **slavery** in Savannah, Georgia, and made his way by ship to **Boston, Massachusetts**. After Sims' whereabouts were discovered through a letter to his wife, his owner initiated steps to recover him under the provisions of the **Fugitive Slave Act of 1850**.

On April 3, 1851, Sims was seized and imprisoned as a fugitive slave. Legal efforts to free him proved unavailing. In an effort to free

Sims illegally, the Reverend Leonard **Grimes** hatched a plan to place a mattress under Sims' jail window — out of which Sims would jump and then flee to safety. However, this gambit was anticipated and Boston authorities barred the windows before Sims could jump to freedom. In addition, the memory of the Shadrach **Minkins** rescue only a few months before was fresh on the minds of local authorities — and, taking special precautions against another successful act of mass defiance of the Fugitive Slave Act of 1850, they placed a heavy chain around the building and more than 100 officers stood guard.

On April 13, Sims was marched to the Boston Wharf, surrounded by 300 policemen and followed by 100 abolitionists. Sims, his face streaked with tears, walked up the gangplank and vanished again into the anonymity of **slavery**.

Sims' rendition stiffened the resolve of Boston's antislavery community not to allow the recapture of **fugitive slaves** in the future and swelled the ranks of the local vigilance society. As for Sims himself, he escaped from slavery again during the **Civil War** and eventually found his way back to Boston. In 1877, former U. S. Marshall Charles Devens — ironically, the man who had prosecuted Sims in 1851 — repaid him with a job at the Massachusetts Department of Justice. *See also* Abolitionist Movement; Vigilance Committees; and Appendixes 1 and 2.

FURTHER READING

Bearse, Austin. *Reminiscences of Fugitive-Slave Law Days in Boston.* Boston: Warren Richardson, 1880.
Levy, Leonard W. "Sims' Case: The Fugitive Slave Law in Boston in 1851." *Journal of Negro History* 35(1950): 39–74.
Quarles, Benjamin. *Black Abolitionists.* New York: Da Capo, 1969.

Sites of the Underground Railroad

See Underground Railroad, Sites of

Slave Autobiographies

Slave autobiographies, usually termed "slave narratives," were personal accounts of life in bondage and represent both a significant genre of antislavery literature and key primary sources for the study of the antebellum African American experience.

Beginning in 1745, over 300 slave autobiographies were published and can be grouped into two broad categories: ante-bellum narratives, i.e., the autobiographies of formerly enslaved African Americans written before the **Civil War**; and post-bellum narratives, i.e., the autobiographies of formerly enslaved African Americans written after the Civil War. Because ante-bellum slave narratives were often authored by **fugitive slaves**, these documents also provide invaluable sources for the study of slave escapes and the Underground Railroad.

Slave narratives were immensely popular with the public and, by giving northerners their closest look at **slavery**, provided a factual counter-weight to the idyllic pictures of slavery described by slaveholders. By their very existence, the narratives demonstrated that African Americans were people with mastery of language and the ability to write their own personal stories. The narratives told of the horrors of family separation, the sexual abuse of black women, and the unceasing work regimen and inhuman workload of slavery. They told of free blacks being kidnapped and sold into slavery. They described the frequency and brutality of flogging, other forms of violence and sexual exploitation, and the severe living conditions of slave life. They also told exciting tales of escape, heroism, betrayal and tragedy. The narratives also gave northerners a window into life in enslaved communities: describing the love among family members; the respect for elders; bonds of friendship; and forms of cultural expression such as music, folktales and religion.

Of the hundreds of ante-bellum slave narratives, among the most influential were Frederick **Douglass**'s *Narrative of the Life of Frederick Douglass,* which sold 30,000 copies between 1845 and 1860; William Wells **Brown**'s *Narrative,* which went through four editions in its first year; and Solomon **Northup**'s *Twelve Years a Slave,* which sold 27,000 copies during its first two years in print. Many narratives were translated into other languages and sold well abroad, particularly in Europe.

From 1936 to 1938, over 2,300 formerly enslaved African Americans were interviewed by writers and journalists employed by the Works Progress Administration in what came to be known as the American Slave Biography Project. This special category of post-bellum narratives is an excellent complement to the autobiographies noted above.

(See Appendix 6 for a bibliography of slave autobiographies.)

FURTHER READING

Rawick, George P., ed. *The American Slave: A Composite Autobiography.* 16 vols. Westport, CT: Greenwood Publishing Company, 1972.

Slave Catchers

The determination of slaveholders to recover **fugitive slaves** spawned a unique and shadowy class of bounty hunters. Known as slave catchers or slave hunters, these bounty hunters would pursue and apprehend freedom seekers in return for a monetary reward. Although some amateurs viewed slave catching as an occasional adventure, it became a serious profession for others because, since local **patrols** were rarely effective in capturing runaways, they could offer slaveholders a valuable service.

While Underground Railroad lore is filled with vivid and dramatic accounts of slave catchers, often accompanied by slave-holders, doggedly pursuing fugitive slaves into their hiding places in the North, most slave catchers actually operated in slave territory. In the deep southern interior, escapes aiming at free soil were not, perhaps, as common as **temporary escapes** to southern cities or towns, to avoid certain punishment, or to protest work or other conditions of enslavement. Consequently, slave catchers could be reasonably effective when fugitive slaves were not necessarily "freedom seekers" and were lurking relatively near their place of enslavement — particularly if the slave catcher was familiar with the countryside, nearby towns or cities, or river systems. And their effectiveness could be enhanced significantly by the use of specially trained "Negro dogs," e.g., **bloodhounds**.

Some slave catchers worked for the posted reward independent of any agreement with a slaveholder. Others contracted with slaveholders and charged by the day or the mile, or both. However, once fugitive slaves reached free territory, the significantly greater cost and lower probability of recovery made

Slaves try to resist slave catchers in this 1872 engraving of the 1853 capture of Robert Jackson. (Library of Congress)

A BOLD STROKE FOR FREEDOM.

Freedom seekers resist slave-catchers in this 1872 engraving. (Library of Congress)

hiring slave catchers an expensive proposition for most slaveholders. Ironically, available records suggest that most runaways recaptured in the North were apprehended by northerners, if they were recaptured at all.

FURTHER READING

Franklin, John H., and Loren Schweninger. *Runaway Slaves: Rebels on the Plantation.* New York: McGraw-Hill, 1999.

Hudson, J. Blaine. *Fugitive Slaves and the Underground Railroad in the Kentucky Borderland.* Jefferson, NC: McFarland, 2002.

Siebert, Wilbur H. *The Underground Railroad from Slavery to Freedom.* 1898. Reprint, New York: Russell and Russell, 1967.

Slave Hunters

See Slave Catchers

Slave Narratives

See Slave Autobiographies

Slave Patrols

See Patrols

Slave Trade

One cannot understand what motivated enslaved African Americans to flee **slavery** at the risk of their lives without understanding the nature of the institution from which they fled. And one cannot understand the nature of slavery in the North American British colonies or, later, the United States, without first understanding the forces and processes that shaped the institution and drove the forced migration of millions of Africans to the Americas.

By the time Jamestown was settled in 1607, the forced migration (i.e., slave trade) of Africans to the Americas had been underway for more than a century—and the forced migration of Africans to Europe had been in progress for more than 160 years. This traffic in human beings began as a trickle in September 1441, when Antam Goncalves, a young Portuguese captain who was a retainer of Prince Henry the Navigator, kidnapped nine Africans near the Rio del Oro along the West

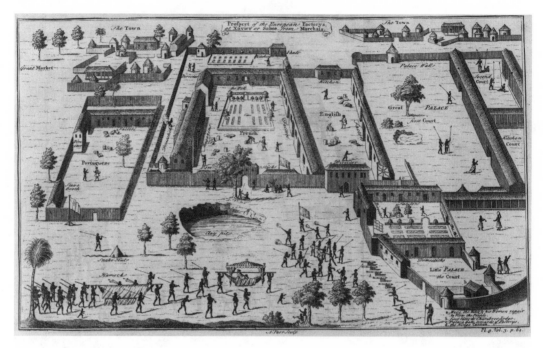

Slave trade compounds in what is now Nigeria, shown in a 1746 engraving. (Library of Congress)

African coast. With the blessing of the Portuguese king and the pope, comparatively small numbers of Africans began to appear in Portugal, some of whom were re-sold into Spain, southern France and the various city-states occupying the Italian peninsula. After the Ottoman conquest of Constantinople (1453) cut-off easy western European access to the slave-hunting grounds in eastern Europe and central Asia, Africa became the principle alternative source of bound labor and the flow of Africans into Europe increased to between 800 and 900 persons per year by 1470. Within a generation, the complexion of European slavery—an institution which re-emerged in the Mediterranean region in the twelfth and thirteenth centuries—changed from predominantly white to predominantly black.

Although an African presence became evident in some regions of Europe through the 1400s, the labor shortage caused by plagues and warfare in the late medieval period was being reversed and, as a result, the preconditions for a large-scale expansion of the institution of slavery did not exist. Rather, European contact with and colonization of the Americas initiated a sequence of historical events that would transform four continents—Africa, Europe, North and South America—and would increase the demand for and the flow of Africans into slavery in distant lands. The proximate causes of this transformation were greed, religious intolerance, the evolution of racism, warfare and disease. Its beneficiaries would be the European societies involved directly or indirectly with slave trade and colonization. Its victims would be the native peoples of both the Americas and Africa.

The largely inadvertent destruction of Native American civilizations would have far-reaching implications for the African Diaspora—and prove particularly problematic for the Spanish and Portuguese, virtually the only Europeans present in the New World for more than a century. While the Portuguese were limited to colonizing Brazil, as a result of the Treaty of Tordesillas (1494) which divided the world into Spanish and Portuguese "spheres" for exploration, conquest and colonization, most of two massive continents lay open to the Spanish. Having long been subject to enslavement themselves by their Muslim neighbors, the Spanish and Portuguese assumed that it was neither immoral or unethical to enslave people of other races and even of other European ethnic groups. Consequently, Native Americans were considered wholly suitable as a slave labor force for use in the extraction of mineral wealth or in agriculture. The Spanish attitude toward non-European and non-Christian people was exemplified by Christopher Columbus who wrote, following his initial contact with the Tainos of the Bahamas, the following chilling observations in his journal on October 12 and 18, 1492:

> They are well built, with very handsome bodies and very good faces; their hair coarse, almost like the silk of a horse's tail, and short ... they are the color of the Canary Islanders, neither black nor white ... It appeared to me that these people were very poor in everything ... they have no iron. They bear no arms, nor are they acquainted with them ... They ought to be good servants and of good intelligence ... I believe that they would easily be made Christians, because it seemed to me that they had no religion. Our Lord pleasing, I will carry off six of them at my departure to Your Highnesses, in order that they may learn to speak. [Sale, 1990]

This viewpoint, and the policies and practices it justified, are crucial to understanding the Spanish approach to colonization by force, "maximum exploitation" and slavery in the New World—a strategy that would become the prototype imitated and adapted by other nations. However, when this seemingly inexhaustible supply of enslaved or enserfed labor began to die off in staggering numbers, the Spanish confronted the dilemma of a burgeoning labor shortage. The perceived need to replace a dwindling Native American labor force caused the trickle of Africans flowing into Europe, the Mediterranean and the North Atlantic islands to become a flood of Africans surging across the Atlantic.

As early as 1501, Queen Isabella of Spain authorized the importation of Spanish-born enslaved Africans (ladinos) to the New World in an effort to relieve the Native American societies of the Caribbean of some of the burdens of slavery. By 1517, the Spanish crown inaugurated the practice of issuing licenses (the Asiento) to foreign traders who would contract to supply the Spanish colonies with enslaved Africans, since, based on a 1493 Papal Bull and the aforementioned Treaty of Tordesillas,

Africa was in the Portuguese "half" of the world and off-limits to Spain. Consequently, the African population in the New World increased as the Native American population declined and, by 1522, there were sufficient unhappy Africans in Hispaniola (the modern location of Haiti and the Dominican Republic) to stage the first recorded African slave insurrection in the Americas. By 1540, roughly 10,000 enslaved Africans were arriving in the New World each year. The demand for enslaved Africans remained steady as the Native American population diminished through the 1500s. This significant upsurge in the demand for slaves forced fundamental changes in the relations between Europe and Africa south of the Sahara Desert.

Most of the Africans enslaved and transported to Europe or the Americas were born in sub-Saharan West Africa, primarily in a region stretching from modern-day Senegal to modern-day Angola, up to several hundred miles inland. Before European contact, a succession of powerful kingdoms and empires (e.g., ancient Nok, medieval Ghana, Mali, and Songhay) had emerged in the Western Sudan, the inland savannah regions of West Africa. Large scale trading networks were established within sub-Saharan Africa and Muslim North Africa, and these empires grew wealthy, highly sophisticated, powerful and populous, as did the coastal trading cities and inland empires of East Africa. However, in the tropical forest regions along the coast of the Gulf of Guinea and to the south, hundreds of smaller and less powerful, but nonetheless highly structured and sophisticated societies, existed in comparative peace with one another and with their natural surroundings. They included Benin and the coalescing kingdoms of Bantu-speaking people in the Congo and Angola regions. As with the Native American empires in the New World, these large scale African social and political formations would ultimately be destabilized and destroyed by European contact — while the smaller scale societies would be exploited as sources of slaves.

As in most agricultural civilizations, various forms of servitude could be found throughout Africa. With few exceptions, these systems of servitude were more akin to serfdom than to slavery, and those who were debtors, war captives, et al., were most likely to find themselves subject to bondage. However, while servitude in Africa was benign in relative terms, servants were usually "outside" the kinship structures that lent cohesiveness and shared social identity to African societies. The servant might marry into this structure, making his or her offspring a part of it, but the servant would remain in a lower or marginal status. People so classified and situated were often deemed "less valuable" and often became "disposable." Such individuals were particularly vulnerable to kidnapping by or sale to the Europeans throughout the slave trade period.

The Portuguese developed, through trial and error in the 1400s, the practice of preying on the weaker African societies and conducting business with the leaders and merchants of the stronger African states. What could not be foreseen initially were the dramatic increase in the demand for slaves in the 1500s and the extent to which enslaved Africans would enrich and strengthen Europe and, correspondingly, the extent to which their loss would impoverish and weaken Africa. After the fall of Songhay (September 1591), there was no longer a strong, centralized empire in the Western Sudan, and African societies throughout West Africa became increasingly at risk with respect to the depredations of the Europeans. In this context, hundreds of fragmented, often quarrelsome societies—even with a total population in the tens of millions—were no match against one large state with a population only half as large.

In the mid–1550s, the Portuguese began experimenting with the cultivation of sugar cane in northeastern Brazil. Native Americans were used as slave labor, initially, but, after repeated epidemics struck in the 1560s and 1570s, large numbers of enslaved Africans were imported as the backbone of the Brazilian plantation labor-force. After 1600, sugar plantation colonies were established throughout the Caribbean, triggering another tremendous upsurge in the slave trade. By 1640, roughly 40,000 enslaved Africans were arriving in the Americas each year. By 1740, the annual rate of slave importation had risen to 100,000 — with most enslaved Africans bound for Brazil or the Caribbean. This "Atlantic

System" transformed the European political economy and created colonies that would evolve into the modern nations of the Americas. On the other hand, the vast regions of West Africa affected directly by slave trade of this magnitude were thrown into the chaos of war, depopulation and the ever more rigid structures of European influence and control that prefigured colonialism.

Estimates of the number of Africans who reached the Americas alive range from 9.5 million to over 20 million. Roughly 45 percent flowed into Brazil; 40 percent into the Caribbean. Another 10 to 12 percent were imported by the Spanish mainland colonies, with the remaining three to five percent reaching North America. For every African who reached some other part of the world alive, it has been estimated that between one and two other Africans died as victims of or in resisting enslavement in some way. Thus, allowing for high mortality rates in resisting enslavement in Africa and on the Middle Passage (the voyage to the Americas), at least 50 million Africans may have been affected by the slave trade between 1441 and the late 1800s.

Exact figures may never be known due to poor or lost records, smuggling, and historical bias. However, historians agree that approximately one-third of all enslaved Africans were victims of kidnapping (primarily women and children), another third were war captives (primarily adult men), and another third were victims of judicial, religious or simply business transactions.

As the Diaspora unfolded, Africans were delivered to two broad categories of American colonies. One, the "non-settler colony," was essentially an exploitative European economic enterprise in a non-European part of the world. The European population of non-settler colonies was usually small relative to the size of the indigenous or enslaved population. The classic examples of such "economic" colonies were the Caribbean islands whereon persons of African descent were usually 90 percent or more of the total population.

Conditions of enslavement were often brutal in such non-settler colonies. Heavy slave imports were needed to offset high slave mortality. Young adult males were the slaves of choice (usually two males to every one female were imported). Large scale revolts were frequent and, if a backcountry region existed, the formation of **maroon societies** was common. Furthermore, the small number of whites at times allowed for the emergence of an intermediate class of free blacks or mulattoes. In addition, "non-settler" colonies, given their economic purpose, were typically one-crop or one-commodity economies and, therefore, dependent on the "mother country" to a greater or lesser degree. Once again, the Caribbean example is useful in that, with so much land committed to sugar cultivation, there was insufficient arable land available on which food for colonists and slaves could be grown. As a result, the West Indian islands often depended on Europe or other New World colonies for food and other necessities of life. In the truest sense, these societies were fundamentally artificial.

In contrast, "settler" colonies represented efforts to establish permanent, more or less self-sufficient societies of transplanted Europeans outside the geographic boundaries of Europe. Settler colonies had to sustain themselves, which typically necessitated the cultivation of both staple crops for survival and commodity crops for profitable trade. As havens for followers of unpopular religions or political movements, or merely to adventurers and the displaced European poor, such colonies eventually attracted and retained enormous European populations. The conditions of enslavement in settler colonies were neither better nor milder than those prevailing in non-settler colonies, only different. Slave mortality was lower. Enslaved Africans were usually a minority in the population, e.g., there was a ratio of roughly one slave to two free or white persons. With no more than one third of the population enslaved, the number of slaves was sufficient to meet moderately heavy labor demands, without being too large to control effectively. Furthermore, a society in which the actual or potential slave-owning group represented two-thirds of the total population could also maintain its (European) racial and cultural identity.

Each type of colony served the interests of different groups of Europeans. None, in the long-term, served the interests of non-Europeans. The growth of such colonies dispossessed the Native Americans, promoted the enslavement of Africans and altered the natural ecological balance as well through such phenomena as deforestation, the introduction of new plants and animals, and diseases. However, non-settler colonies, because they existed to produce profit, were far more important to the European ruling and upper classes than were settler colonies. Of course, there were numerous mixed models and exceptions. For example, widespread racial mixing in Spanish America produced societies in which the majority population was neither white nor African nor Native American — and in which there were large free colored or mestizo groups. Brazil followed this pattern, but produced a large mulatto population, with harsh slavery in the sugar-growing northeast and, later, the coffee-growing south, but also with slaves and free people of color scattered literally throughout that vast country.

This tremendous diversity, both with respect to the many African societies affected by slave trade and the many different types of slave societies which evolved in the Americas meant that the African Diaspora was many distinct but related (and often inter-related) experiences, not merely one. However, in the broader sense, Africans of the Diaspora had much in common — a common point of origin, Africa, a common destination, the Americas, and a common condition, enslavement. *See also* Colonial Period (1607–1776).

FURTHER READING

Alexander, H. B. "Brazilian and United States Slavery Compared." *Journal of Negro History* 6(1922): 349–364.
Curtin, Philip D. *The Atlantic Slave trade: A Census.* Madison: University of Wisconsin Press, 1969.
Davidson, Basil. *Africa in History: Themes and Outlines.* New York: Collier Books, 1991.
_____. *The African Slave Trade.* New York: Little, Brown, 1980.
Davis, David B. *Slavery and Human Progress.* New York: Oxford University Press, 1984.
Diop, Cheik Anta. *Pre-colonial Black Africa: A Comparative Study of the Political and Social Systems of Europe and Black Africa, from Antiquity to the Formation of Modern States.* Westport, CT: L. Hall, 1987.
Inikori, J. E., ed. *Forced Migration: The Impact of the Export Slave Trade on African Societies.* New York: Africana, 1982.

Klein, Herbert S. *African Slavery in Latin America and the Caribbean.* New York: Oxford University Press, 1986.

Kolchin, Peter. *American Slavery: 1619–1877.* New York: Hill and Wang, 1993.

Mintz, Sidney. W. *Sweetness and Power: The Place of Sugar in Modern History.* New York: Viking Press, 1985.

Reynolds, Edward. *Stand the Storm: A History of the Atlantic Slave Trade.* London: W. H. Allen, 1985.

Rodney, Walter. *How Europe Underdeveloped Africa.* Washington: Howard University Press, 1974.

Rogozinski, J. *A Brief History of the Caribbean: From the Arawak and the Carib to the Present.* New York: Facts on File, 1992.

Sale, K. *The Conquest of Paradise: Christopher Columbus and the Columbian Legacy.* New York: Plume, 1990.

Sanders, R. *Lost Tribes and Promised Lands: The Origins of American Racism.* New York: Harper-Perennial, 1978.

Shillington, Kevin. *History of Africa.* New York: St. Martin's Press, 1989.

Thompson, Victor B. *The Making of the African Diaspora in the Americas, 1441–1900.* New York: Longman, 1987.

Williams, Eric. *From Columbus to Castro: The History of the Caribbean, 1492–1969.* London: Andre Deutsch, 1970.

Slavery

One cannot understand **fugitive slaves** — or the motivations of those who assisted some of them — unless one first understands the nature of the institution of slavery from which they fled, particularly in the United States.

British North America was primarily a collection of "settler" colonies (see **Slave Trade**) that expanded through the use of various forms of white bondage and African slavery — and ultimately displaced the indigenous Native American population. The evolution of these colonies into the United States occurred against the backdrop of the African Diaspora. Thus, as Ballagh (1972) noted: "For the institutional beginnings of the system of American Negro slavery we are to look, then, to the Bermudas and to Barbadoes rather than to North America itself."

After several unsuccessful attempts to establish colonies in North and South America in the late 1500s, James Fort (later renamed Jamestown) was founded on May 13, 1607 in the Chesapeake Bay region of Virginia. Conditions in the temperate woodland zone of North America were not conducive, initially, either to the development of large scale plantation agriculture (which drew millions of Africans to the Caribbean and Brazil) or even to the growth of major urban centers such as those of Spanish America — which depended to some extent on the labor of enslaved Africans and a growing class of **free people of color**. Still, labor was needed in North America to clear and cultivate land, build dwellings and other structures, and to defend and expand settlements. Because there were seldom enough settlers for this purpose, most early colonies sought desperately to find free, indentured or enslaved laborers.

In the summer of 1616, a ship owned by the Company for the Summers Islands, a London-based trading company, brought one African and some West Indian products from the Caribbean to Bermuda. This voyage was successful, in terms of profit, and was followed by several others. In April 1618, associates of the same company, who happened also to be members of the Virginia Company, sent the ship, *Treasurer,* to trade and prey on Spanish commerce in the Caribbean. In 1619, while the *Treasurer* was seeking plunder, a Dutch frigate with a predominantly English crew, also on a mission of piracy in the Caribbean, landed at Jamestown "about the last of August" and sold 20 Africans to the colonists. Shortly thereafter, in early September 1619, the *Treasurer* landed at Jamestown as well and sold an African woman before returning to Bermuda with 29 other Africans bound in its cargo hold. These Africans were the first introduced into a British North American colony and, with their arrival, the history of the African American branch of the Diaspora begins.

Considerable debate has been occasioned by the question of the precise legal status of these first Africans and those who would follow. The legal framework of slavery had been constructed in the Spanish and Portuguese colonies over a period of several generations, but the legal status of "slave" — as distinct from that of servant or serf — did not yet exist in the British colonies. American slavery in its fully-developed form would involve a

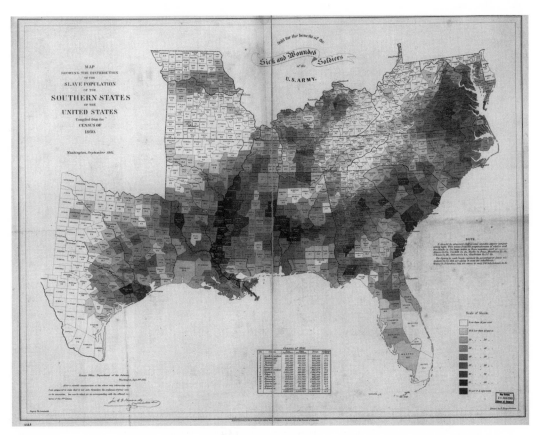

This 1861 map shows the distribution of the slave population in the South. The darker the shading, the more slaves in each county. (Library of Congress)

permanent and absolute loss of political and civil liberty for which there was no precedent. In other words, neither the Dutch nor English "privateers" had a legal right of ownership (under the laws of their home nations) with respect to Africans who were either captives or slaves of the Spanish, nor, by extension, the right to transfer ownership to others by sale. This right did not exist until 1623 in Bermuda and not until 1625 in Virginia, and the legal evolution of slavery would not be complete until around 1700. Consequently,

> ...the negroes were legally but colony servants, and a disposition to recognize them as such seems apparent ... they were put to work upon public lands to support the governor and other officers of the government; or ... they were put into the hands of representative planters closely connected with the government in order to separate them from one another ... Some of these negroes received wages and purchased their freedom, and the length of servitude seems to have

been dependent on the time of conversion to Christianity. [Ballagh, 1972.]

Despite the early arrival of Africans, the institution of slavery grew slowly in North America. Because of a labor surplus in Europe and wars throughout the seventeenth century, the initial labor needs of the fledgling North American and Caribbean British colonies were met more often through the importation of bound white laborers than through the enslavement of Africans or **Native Americans**. White indentured servants were plentiful and relatively cheap; indeed, through the 1680s, white servants—often children, debtors, criminals, or simply landless poor Europeans—constituted the bulk of the labor force in these colonies, particularly Virginia, Maryland and the Carolinas, as well as in the Caribbean. The Irish, for example, were quite prominent in the ranks of indentured servants in both Virginia and Barbados. In 1662, the

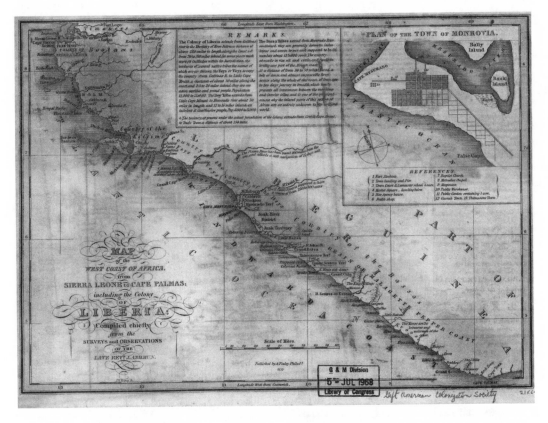

Liberia, 1830 (Library of Congress)

creation of the Royal African Company, headed by King Charles II and his brother, the Duke of York (the future King James II), followed by Bacon's Rebellion (1676) in Virginia simultaneously discouraged indentured servitude and promoted the growth of slavery. Other changes in royal policy also prompted the migration of Barbadian and other Caribbean planters and their slaves to North America, particularly to the newly chartered Carolina colony. As British Caribbean and North American settlements expanded, (e.g., Jamaica came under British control in 1655), the British also strengthened their position in West Africa. At the same time, the supply of white indentured servants dwindled after 1685 due to changing economic and political conditions in Europe. Thus, enslaved Africans came to represent an increasingly attractive, accessible and affordable source of bound labor.

Given the roles of white indentured servitude and fleeting experiments with en-

slaving Native Americans, African slavery was a marginal institution through most of the seventeenth century. With respect to numbers, the African American population in British North America grew very slowly. By 1625, there were only 23 Africans in Virginia, compared to 2,500 whites, and no Africans had been sold into the colony since 1623. As late as 1650, there were only 300 Africans in the entire colony, with white servants being vastly more numerous, and only 3,000 enslaved African Americans in all of British North America by 1660. However, the land and labor requirements of tobacco, as a cash crop, and the interests of Virginia tobacco growers in the Chesapeake Bay region, caused a fundamental transformation in the nature of the Virginia Colony and in the institution of slavery.

The Virginia Company, which founded Jamestown with the support of King James I, intended to create a non-settler colony that would seek gold and silver and produce useful and profitable goods for export to England. However, in 1612, John Rolfe (who later married the Powhatan princess, Pocahontas) planted the first crop of West Indian tobacco at Jamestown. The plants flourished and the quality of the product surpassed that of tobacco grown in the Spanish colonies. Despite the king's strong opposition to the "noxious" habit of smoking, tobacco became immensely profitable as an export crop and the Virginia colonists began committing more and more land to its cultivation, and pressing their Native American neighbors, the Powhatans, for additional land on which to expand tobacco production. By 1618, 20,000 pounds of tobacco were shipped to England. This amount grew to 60,000 pounds by 1622, then to 500,000 pounds by 1627 and 1,500,000 pounds by 1630.

Given the unscientific methods used to grow tobacco—the British colonists did not practice crop rotation as did Native Americans—fields became infertile after only a few years. This created tremendous pressure to acquire even more land, which led to bloody wars between the expanding colony and the Native Americans into whose domain the colony encroached. Since tobacco was a labor intensive crop, labor was as much a necessity as land and, while the success of tobacco cultivation drew increasing numbers of colonists to Virginia, identifying and controlling a suitable labor force became a prime concern of the early settlers. Because of this, the interests of the wealthier colonists who had acquired the most land and needed the most labor, and the interests of the poorer class, consisting of new colonists seeking their fortunes in the New World and former indentured servants, began to drift apart. This divergence erupted in Bacon's Rebellion in 1676, which was driven by class conflict and pressure to penetrate more deeply into Native American territory.

In the end, the life-long slavery of Africans took root in Virginia and the other southern colonies because it was to the interests of the planters to have a permanent labor force under its direct control. The resolution of this conflict also created a more-or-less permanent class of poor backcountry whites who would press for the opening of new western lands for settlement, which necessitated the removal of Native Americans from those lands. In both cases, these European colonists came to conceive of their future and that of their descendants as unfolding in North America as settlers, not as sojourners.

In 1659, the Virginia Assembly passed an act which give "head rights" (i.e., additional land) to colonists who imported slaves and servants, and the flow of Africans increased somewhat. By 1671, there were 2,000 Africans, but still 6,000 white servants in Virginia and, as late as 1683, there were roughly 2,700 Africans compared to 12,000 white servants. After the early 1680s, white indentured servants virtually disappeared from Virginia and large numbers of Africans were imported. As a result, by 1700, there were 12,000 blacks and 18,000 whites of all classes in Virginia, and a total of 28,000 in all British colonies. Virginia was fast becoming the prototypical North American "slave colony" and would establish most of the legal, cultural and behavioral precedents that would shape the institution of slavery in other North American colonies.

Significant black population growth continued and, by about 1760, there were 120,156 African Americans and 173,316 whites in the Virginia colony—and 325,000 African Americans in British North America. Thus, once the African population began to grow, growth was swift, alarming and explosive. Furthermore, along with huge importations of Africans, the African American population achieved natural population growth—more births than deaths—between 1730 and 1750, and was the only major African population in the Americas to do so, which triggered even more rapid and significant population expansion.

While the first Africans were "servants," a status they shared with many whites, this middle-ground between freedom and absolute subjection rested on the weak foundation of a legal technicality and soon became untenable. Thus, for whites, servitude became less common and freedom became an accepted and expected status. For Native Americans, servitude became less common, but because they were deemed too wild and uncivilized. For Africans, temporary servitude became less common as well, but was superseded by chattel slavery.

This change received statutory recognition generally between 1640 and 1700 using other slave societies as models, with the result being a clearly defined and fully developed institution of slavery. To illustrate, the Massachusetts Fundamental Acts sanctioned slavery in 1641. Connecticut followed in 1650. In March 1661, an act of the Virginia Assembly distinguished black from white servants by stating that "... negroes are incapable of making satisfaction by addition of time" (for the time lost in running away)— thus defining the enslavement of Africans as perpetual. Other colonies recognized slavery in rapid succession, depending largely on the timing of their creation: Maryland in 1663; New York and New Jersey in 1664 (after the British won these territories from the Dutch); South Carolina in 1682; **Pennsylvania** and Rhode Island in 1700; North Carolina (North and South Carolina became separate colonies in 1710) in 1715; and Georgia in 1755. Prior to these dates, whatever the popular prejudices and customary practices toward Africans, their legal status was that of servants with the same legal rights as white servants, although these rights were not always respected or protected.

The status of slavery was next extended across generations by declaring that children, one or both of whose parents (usually the mother) were enslaved, could be born into perpetual slavery. This elaboration was legalized as follows: 1662 in Virginia; 1663 in Maryland; 1698 in **Massachusetts**; 1704 in Connecticut and New Jersey; 1706 in New York and Pennsylvania; 1712 in South Carolina; 1728 in Rhode Island; and 1741 in North Carolina. These and other laws applied to Africans, persons of mixed race (mulattoes and racial hybrids referenced using a wide variety of terms), and, with the abolition of Native American slavery (by 1700 in most colonies), only to those of African birth or ancestry.

A host of complementary laws followed, relating principally to the status of slaves as "property" and the right and power of the "property owner" to dispose of and treat the property as the owner deemed fit. A well-known 1682 act of the Virginia Assembly also stipulated that conversion to Christianity could not bring freedom to any enslaved "... negroes,

mulattoes, hostile Moors and Turks ..." This law was designed, of course, to promote the proselytization of enslaved Africans whose owners objected to any efforts to bring Africans to Christianity if, by adopting the Christian religion, a slave would then become free. Finally, a related body of legal enactments, termed "Slave Codes" collectively, was developed to protect whites from the masses of Africans who were involuntarily enslaved and did not particularly relish slavery. These laws identified offenses and attendant punishments for violations by enslaved Africans, and gave the slave-owner, or the colony, the literal power of life and death over the slave.

Beyond legal enactments, most enslaved Africans were concentrated geographically in the south, where tobacco, rice and indigo were cash crops. This was a hemispheric rather than an American pattern and, simply put, as one moved toward the equator, both the number of Africans and their proportion in the total population of a particular colony increased. In the more northerly regions of North America, such as New England, slavery was not a significant institution. In the middle colonies, where plantation agriculture was not practiced, most slave-owners possessed fewer than 10 slaves. However, where commodity crops could be grown profitably through the use of intensive gang labor and plantation agriculture, land and slaves came to be concentrated in fewer and fewer hands. For example, only about 20 percent of all white families owned enslaved African Americans in the 1700s— and only 10 percent by 1860 — in contrast to slave-holding patterns in the Caribbean and Brazil. Consequently, through the colonial and ante-bellum periods, most white Americans did not own enslaved African Americans, and those who did owned comparatively few, but had power and wealth far out of proportion to their numbers.

Given this institutional and economic framework, the number of Africans in North America grew slowly before 1700 and rapidly thereafter. In 1625, there were only 23 Africans in Virginia, compared to 2,500 whites, and no Africans had been sold into the colony since 1623. As late as 1650, there were only 300 Africans in the entire colony, with white servants being vastly more numerous—

and only 3,000 enslaved African Americans in all of British North American by 1660. As noted previously in 1659, the Virginia Assembly passed an act which gave "head rights" (i.e., additional land) to colonists who imported slaves and servants, and the flow of Africans increased somewhat. By 1671, there were 2,000 Africans, but still 6,000 white servants in Virginia and, as late as 1683, there were roughly 2,700 Africans compared to 12,000 white servants. However, after the early 1680s, white indentured servants virtually disappeared from Virginia and large numbers of Africans were imported. As a result, by 1700, the bound population of Virginia and the other colonies had become predominantly black: There were 12,000 blacks and 18,000 whites of all classes in Virginia, and a total of roughly 28,000 blacks in the British North American colonies altogether.

African American Population, 1790 — 1860

	Enslaved		Free	
	N	%	N	%
1790	757,363	19.3	59,466	7.9
1800	1,001,436	18.9	108,395	10.8
1810	1,377,810	19.0	186,446	13.5
1820	1,776,194	18.4	238,156	13.4
1830	2,328,642	18.1	319,599	13.7
1840	2,873,758	16.8	386,303	13.4
1850	3,638,808	15.7	434,495	11.9
1860	4,441,830	14.1	488,070	11.0

U.S. Bureau of the Census. *Historical Statistics of the United States: Colonial Times to 1957.* Washington: Government Printing Office, 1960.

The evolution of "racial" slavery in the Americas was complicated tremendously by two loosely related factors common to other colonial slave societies: the ambiguous status of free people of color and persons of mixed African descent. In what were becoming "color-coded" societies, with rather definite statuses assigned to each racial or color group, persons of African ancestry who were not enslaved were a troublesome anomaly. By the late 1700s, sizeable free black and free colored populations could be found in Latin America. For example, 399,000 (28.5 percent) of the roughly 1,399,000 persons of African descent in Brazil were classified as "free colored." Even more significantly, 650,000 (or 70.5 percent) of the roughly 920,000 people of color in mainland Spanish America were so classified. Furthermore, somewhat smaller, but still significant, groups could be found in the Caribbean, e.g., 212,000 (or 15.9 percent) of more than 1,300,000 people of color in this region were free. In contrast, free persons of color were a small minority (32,000, or 5.3 percent, of 607,000) in British North America until after the **American Revolution** and the "First Emancipation," i.e., the gradual abolition of slavery in the North between 1780 and 1825. However, between 1800 and 1860, this segment of the African American population grew to represent 10 to 15 percent of all African Americans.

White Americans tended to view the presence of free people of color as a problem that required some sort of resolution. Most often, whites sought to subordinate and marginalize free people of color through discriminatory laws and outright mob violence, and even undertook to remove them from the United States through a variety of colonization schemes designed to protect slavery in the expanding **Cotton Kingdom** of the early 1800s. The perception of free people of color as a menacing and alien presence was epitomized in the goals of the American Colonization Society (founded 1816) and, even more graphically, in the creation of a U. S. colony in Africa (Liberia) in the 1820s to which free blacks could be "returned." However, the vast majority of free people of color rejected colonization and the aims of its supporters— and chose to engage in the struggle for abolition and full civil rights in the United States. Their role would be central to that struggle.

The other complicating factor was racial mixing and the rapid and virtually inevitable emergence of racially intermediate groups. Contrary to the pre-scientific notions of the early European colonists and slave traders, Africans and Native Americans were not distinct species and could not only "mate," but could produce fertile offspring (i.e., who were not the human equivalent of "mules," from which the term "mulatto" is derived in Portuguese). Since freedom and bondage were racially-constructed status classifications, the definition of what constituted membership in each racial group was of more than passing importance, and varied depending on how persons of mixed descent were viewed in each slave-holding society.

It is sufficient to note that different societies throughout the Diaspora addressed this phenomenon and the attendant "problem" of racial classification in radically different ways. Most societies developed both a "color line," with the most important distinctions being between those who were "white" and those who were not, and a "color spectrum" with one or more classifications between black and white (and "red"). By the time North America was being colonized, Latin America was becoming predominantly "brown" (i.e., Native American and European, with some African admixture) and the Caribbean was becoming predominantly, and Brazil significantly, "black"—with several intermediate categories. The English, having witnessed the proliferation of persons of color in neighboring colonies and hoping to maintain Anglo-Saxon "racial purity," labored diligently to prevent "miscegenation." Their efforts were unsuccessful since there were few European women among the early settlers and European men had power over enslaved African American and sometimes Native American women. Although miscegenation and the growth of mixed racial groups could not be prevented, the legal existence of these groups was seldom recognized, and persons of African ancestry (if their African-ness was detectable), to whatever degree, were all classified as black. Nevertheless, the question of "how African" one had to be to be so classified has been the subject of considerable debate as well. Ironically, for much of American history, persons with fractional African ancestry (one-fourth, one-eighth, one-sixteenth, one-thirty-second) were considered white in most states, depending on their appearance. In other words, in the United States, the system of racial classification was based on a "color line," not a "color spectrum," and how and where that line was drawn varied over time. Only since the early 1900s has the "rule of hypo-descent," or the "one drop rule," been applied consistently.

These factors—the presence of free persons of color and racially intermediate groups—often overlapped. Some white parents freed and provided in various ways for their African American offspring. Some African Americans of mixed parentage, while still held in bondage, were given the advantages of education or training in the trades—which often facilitated freedom through self-purchase. Consequently, while being racially mixed and being free were not highly correlated, it has been estimated that roughly half of the free persons of color in the United States (by the early 1800s) were of mixed racial ancestry.

In the end, three fundamental characteristics distinguished slavery in the Americas from earlier forms of human bondage:

(1) Those enslaved became *chattel*, i.e., property, not people, a degree of dehumanization or "social death" unknown in earlier historical periods;

(2) enslavement was *perpetual*, i.e., slave status was inherited from one's parents and could be bequeathed to one's children (one could be born and die a slave); and

(3) slavery was *racial*, i.e., slavery in the Americas was considered, by the 1700s, a status suitable only for Africans and persons of African descent.

Thus, the African Diaspora delivered Africans into the jaws of a type of slavery, as it evolved in its many New World incarnations, that would involve a permanent and absolute loss of political and civil liberty for which there was no historical precedent.

See also Colonial Period (1607–1776); Motivations for Escape.

FURTHER READING

Ballagh, J. C. "A History of Slavery in Virginia." In *Early Studies of Slavery by States*. Vol. 1. Northbrook, IL: Metro Books, 1972.

Baptist, Edward E. "'Cuffy,' 'Fancy Maids,' and 'One-Eyed Men': Rape, Commodification and the Domestic Slave Trade in the United States." *The American Historical Review* 106(2001): 1619–1650.

Bridenbaugh, Carl. *Jamestown, 1544–1699*. New York: Oxford University Press, 1980.

Cobley, Alan G., and Alvin Thompson. *The African-Caribbean Connection: Historical and Cultural Perspectives*. Bridgetown, Barbados: University of the West Indies, 1990.

Curry, Leonard P. *The Free Black in Urban America: The Shadow of the Dream*. Chicago: University of Chicago Press, 1991.

Davis, David B. *Slavery and Human Progress*. New York: Oxford University Press, 1984.

Davis, Frederick J. *Who is Black: One Nation's Definition*. University Park, PA: Pennsylvania State University, 1991.

Franklin, John Hope, and Alfred A. Moss, Jr. *From Slavery to Freedom: A History of African Americans.* 8th ed. New York: McGraw-Hill, 2000.

Freehling, William W. "The Founding Fathers and Slavery." *The American Historical Review* 77(1972): 81–93.

Horsman, Reginald. *Race and Manifest Destiny: The Origins of American Racial Anglo-Saxonism.* Cambridge: Harvard University Press, 1981.

Hudson, J. Blaine. "The African Diaspora and the 'Black Atlantic': An African American Perspective." *Negro History Bulletin* 60, no. 4(1997): 7–14.

Huggins, Nathan I. *Black Odyssey: The African American Ordeal in Slavery.* New York: Vintage Books, 1990.

Jordan, Winthrop D. *White over Black: American Attitudes toward the Negro, 1550-1812.* New York: W. W. Norton, 1968.

Klein, Herbert S. *African Slavery in Latin America and the Caribbean.* New York: Oxford University Press, 1986.

Kolchin, Peter. *American Slavery: 1619–1877.* New York: Hill and Wang, 1993.

Omi, Michael, and Howard Winant. *Racial Formation in the United States.* New York: Routledge, 1986.

Patterson, Orlando. *Slavery and Social Death.* Cambridge: Harvard University Press, 1982.

Rosenthal, Bernard. "Puritan Conscience and New England Slavery." *The New England Quarterly* 46(1973): 62–81.

Shriver, Phillip R. "Freedom's Proving Ground: The Heritage of the Northwest Ordinance." *Wisconsin Magazine of History* 72(1989): 126–131.

Thompson, Victor B. *The Making of the African Diaspora in the Americas, 1441–1900.* New York: Longman, 1987.

Thornton, John. "The African Experience of the '20 and Odd Negroes' Arriving in Virginia in 1619." *William and Mary Quarterly* 55(1998): 421–434.

Wiecek, William M. "Slavery and Abolition Before the United States Supreme Court, 1820–1860." *The Journal of American History* 65(1978): 34–59.

_____. "The Statutory Law of Slavery and Race in the Thirteen Mainland Colonies of British America." *William and Mary Quarterly* 34(1977): 258–280.

Williams, Eric. *From Columbus to Castro: The History of the Caribbean, 1492–1969.* London: Andre Deutsch, 1970.

Williams, George Washington. *History of the Negro Race in America.* 1883. Reprint, New York: Bergmann, 1968.

Woodson, Carter G. "The Beginnings of the Miscegenation of the Whites and Blacks." *Journal of Negro History* 2(1918): 335-353.

Slave's Room (Berrien County, Michigan)

Underground Railroad site. The "Slave's Room" is a cave hidden behind a waterfall on the St. Joseph River and is, perhaps, one of the most unusual of all hiding places for **fugitive slaves**. *See also* Underground Railroad, Sites of; and Appendixes 3 and 4.

Sloane, Rush R. (1828–1908)

A friend of the fugitive, Rush R. Sloan was born in 1828, the son of a jeweler who arrived in **Ohio** around 1815. Sloane studied law and was admitted to the bar in 1849. In 1854, he purchased a home in Sandusky, Ohio, and became active in the local antislavery movement and worked to assist **fugitive slaves**.

The defining moment in Sloane's antislavery career occurred in 1852, when seven fugitive slaves from **Kentucky** arrived in Sandusky on the Mad River & Lake Erie Railroad. The fugitives boarded a steamer bound across Lake Erie but were captured on board by three men from Kentucky who claimed to be the legal owners of the freedom seekers. Sloane acted as an attorney on behalf of the fugitive slaves and petitioned the mayor of Sandusky to investigate the evidence and questioned, on that basis, whether the arrest and imprisonment of the fugitive slaves were "legal." The judge concluded that there was no legal authority for their arrest and ordered that the fugitives be released immediately.

After the release of the fugitives, one of the Kentucky men was able to produce legal papers of ownership and filed charges against Sloane under the **Fugitive Slave Act of 1850**. Sloan was tried in the U.S. District Court in Columbus, Ohio, and fined $3,000, plus $1,330.30 in court and attorney fees. The local African American community, in appreciation of Sloane's efforts and his sacrifice, presented him with a silver-headed cane.

In 1855, Sloane became a probate judge in Erie County and, in 1861, was appointed an agent to the U.S. Post Office in Chicago where he prospered in real estate. He later returned to Ohio, became president of the Sandusky, Dayton, and Cincinnati Railroad in 1867, and was elected mayor of Sandusky in 1879. He died in 1908.

See also Rush R. Sloane House; and Appendixes 1 and 2.

Smallwood, Thomas

See Washington, D.C.

Smith, Charles

Friend of the fugitive in Oswego, New York. *See also* Buckout-Jones Building.

Smith, Gerrit (1797–1874)

New York philanthropist and friend of the fugitive. Gerrit Smith was born in Utica, New York, in March 1797, but for most of his life lived in the small community of Peterboro in Madison County, New York. Smith's father, Peter Smith, was a business partner of John Jacob Astor (fur trade and land speculation) and amassed immense wealth. The younger Smith attended Hamilton College, graduating in 1818. As an adult, Smith managed much of his family's landholdings, preserving his considerable wealth through the depression of the 1830s.

Smith's great fortune allowed him to become one of the leading philanthropists of the early nineteenth century and, in 1835, after a brief flirtation with and repudiation of colonization, the cause that claimed most of his attention was the crusade against **slavery**. In the 1840s, Smith became a key leader of the Liberty Party and its later incarnations, and was nominated to run for president of the United States in 1848, 1856, and 1860. Throughout the antebellum period, Smith's home in Peterboro was open to hundreds of fugitive slaves and **friends of the fugitive**— including Harriett **Tubman**.

Smith became increasingly radical in the 1850s and increasingly open to the idea of challenging slavery by violent means. He strongly opposed the **Fugitive Slave Act of 1850** and, in 1851, was involved in the "Jerry Rescue" in Syracuse, New York. After the passage of the Kansas-Nebraska Act in 1854, Smith gave roughly $16,000 to various free-state groups in Kansas— some of which was used to arm the settlers. Still, the most important influence on Smith's conversion to the use of violence was his friendship with John **Brown**.

Smith's relationship with Brown dated to 1846, when Smith sold Brown (for a dollar an acre) a 244-acre tract of land in Essex County, New York, where Brown proposed to live among and assist free African Americans. Brown himself lived on this land from 1849 to 1851 and, in 1855, left his wife and daughters there when he moved to Kansas to join the free-state struggle. Over the next few years, Smith loaned Brown money and, in February 1858, Brown visited Smith's home and outlined his plan to mount a direct and violent assault on slavery. This plan — which Smith helped to finance — led to Brown's failed raid on the federal arsenal at **Harpers Ferry** on October 16, 1859, which led to Brown's execution on December 2, 1859.

When Brown and his followers were captured, documents were found that implicated several abolitionists, among them Gerrit Smith and Frederick **Douglass**. More specifically, these documents included a letter from Smith to Brown written on June 4, 1859, and a canceled bank draft from Smith to Brown for $100, dated August 22, 1859. In addition, another letter from Brown to one of his sons described some of Smith's financial contributions and stated that "G. S." would cover

Gerrit Smith (Library of Congress)

one-fifth the costs of the planned slave insurrection to be incited by the raid on Harpers Ferry.

As suspicions grew, Smith, who had shown signs of instability in the past, panicked and destroyed all evidence tying him to Brown, and burned all letters in his possession related to the plot. Smith grew increasingly agitated and, on November 7, was committed to the state asylum at Utica. Smith, who would probably be considered bi-polar today, was under care for approximately eight weeks. He was released and returned to Peterboro on December 29, 1859.

For the remainder of his life, Smith adamantly denied any prior knowledge of or involvement in John Brown's raid on Harpers Ferry. Smith also denied that his suspicious mental collapse had been a "convenient" means of avoiding the furor and personal danger of the immediate aftermath of Brown's raid. *See also* Abolitionist Movement; Henry, William "Jerry"; Gerrit Smith Estate; and Appendixes 1 and 2.

FURTHER READING
Frothingham, Octavius Brooks. *Gerrit Smith: A Biography.* New York: Negro Universities Press, 1969.
McKivigan, John R., and Madeleine Leveille. "The 'Black Dream' of Gerrit Smith, New York Abolitionist." *Syracuse University Library Associates Courier* 20, no. 2(Fall 1985).
Sernett, Milton C. "Common Cause: The Antislavery Alliance of Gerrit Smith and Beriah Green." *Syracuse University Library Associates Courier* 21, no. 2(Fall 1986).

Smith, James Caesar Anthony

See Brown, Henry "Box"

Smith, Samuel A.

See Brown, Henry "Box"

Snowden, Benjamin

Fugitive slave. In the late 1830s, Benjamin Snowden escaped from **slavery** in Frederick County, Maryland, and reached New York with the assistance of Gerrit **Smith**, Lewis **Tappan,** and possibly Samuel R. **Ward.** Gerrit Smith, in particular, saw to Snowden's education and helped him find work, first with the railroad.

In 1847, Snowden met and married Violet, with whom he had five children. However, Violet suffered from a progressively worsening mental illness and Snowden was forced to shoulder most of the responsibility for raising his young family.

FURTHER READING
Frothingham, Octavius Brooks. *Gerrit Smith: A Biography.* New York: Negro Universities Press, 1969.
Harlow, Ralph Volney. "The Rise and Fall of the Kansas Aid Movement." *American Historical Review* 41, no. 1(1935): 1–25.

Somerset Case (1772)

In 1769, James Somerset (or Sommersett) was brought to England by his owner, Charles Stewart, a **Boston** customs official. After two years, Somerset escaped, but was apprehended on November 26, 1771, and placed forcibly on a ship bound for Jamaica. Through the auspices of Granville Sharpe, a leader of the early British antislavery movement, a writ of *habeus corpus* was obtained from Lord Mansfield, the lord chief justice of the Court of the King's Bench, that ordered Somerset brought before a court.

It was not uncommon for British subjects in the various slave colonies to bring their enslaved Africans as servants on their journeys to England. Their right to do so, while not protected by British law, was respected in practice. However, once in court, Somerset asserted his claim to freedom on the basis of British law itself: although **slavery** was legal in the British colonies, it simply did not exist under the law of England. In June 1772, Mansfield upheld Somerset's claim.

This decision was arguably the first significant legal victory in the long struggle to end human bondage. Apart from settling the question of whether slavery could exist in Great Britain, the ruling had two critically important consequences with respect to the struggle against slavery in North America.

First, the Somerset Case established the legal precedent that led eventually to the end of slavery in **Canada** by the early 1800s, which transformed Canada into a place of refuge for **fugitive slaves** from the United States. Second, the ruling would shape U.S. law regarding fugitive slaves. Specifically, with slavery ending in the northern states and outlawed in the Mid-west by the 1787 Northwest Ordinance, while still entrenched in the early South, the young United States faced the unique problem of becoming a nation in which slavery was legal in some regions and illegal in others. The Somerset Case complicated the question of the legal status of an enslaved African American who, for example, simply crossed the **Ohio River** from **Kentucky** (where slavery was legal) into **Indiana** Territory (where slavery was prohibited, technically) in 1787: Was the African American free or still enslaved? This was, of course, the fundamental question in the Dred Scott Case of 1857.

To address this question, a fugitive slave provision, Article IV, section 2, part 2, was included in the U. S. Constitution. *See also* Dred Scott v. Sandford; Fugitive Slave Act of 1793; Fugitive Slave Act of 1850.

FURTHER READING

David, C. W. A. "The Fugitive Slave Law of 1793 and Its Antecedents." *Journal of Negro History* 8, no. 1(1924): 18–25.

Nadelhaft, Jerome. "The Somersett Case and Slavery: Myth, Reality, and Repercussions." *Journal of Negro History* 51, no. 3(1966): 193–208.

Walvin, James. *Black and White: The Negro and English Society 1555–1945.* Aylesbury, 1973.

Songs

Music, particularly songs, played two important and sometimes related roles in the history of the slave escapes and the Underground Railroad. For **friends of the fugitive**, given the religious underpinnings of abolitionism, many antislavery songs were hymns or anthems that excoriated the evils of **slavery** and made powerful and inspiring emotional appeals to continue the struggle against that evil.

For freedom seekers themselves, songs were a special language adapted to a special purpose. Many of the West African societies from which the ancestors of African Americans were taken transmitted their history and culture through oral tradition, including songs and folklore. In North America, African Americans adapted this tradition and transformed songs, even Christian hymns and spirituals, into codes that conveyed information they wished to conceal from whites. Songs such as "Follow the Drinking Gourd" and "Swing Low, Sweet Chariot" were often used

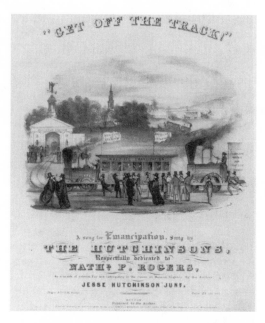

"Get Off the Track!" is a sheet music cover for an abolitionist song of 1844. (Library of Congress)

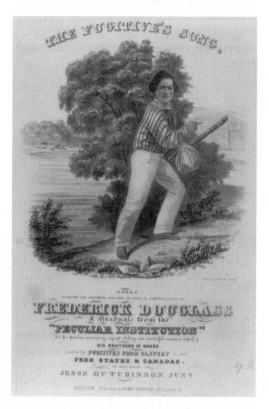

The cover of "The Fugitive's Song" sheet music from 1845 features a portrait of Frederick Douglass as a runaway slave. (Library of Congress)

as signals and information channels in slave escapes.

For the lyrics of a representative selection of antislavery songs, many collected by William Wells **Brown**, see Appendix 7.

FURTHER READING

Brown, William Wells. *The Anti-Slavery Harp: A Collection Songs for Anti-Slavery Meetings.* Boston: B. Marsh, 1849.

Fisher, Miles. *Negro Slave Songs in the United States.* Ithaca, NY: Cornell University Press, 1953.

Simpson, J. Mc. C. *The Emancipation Car, Being an Original Composition of Anti-slavery Ballads, Composed Exclusively for the Underground Railroad.* Miami, FL: Mnemosyne, 1969.

Southern, Eileen. *The Music of Black America: A History.* New York: W. W. Norton, 1971.

Work, John Wesley. *American Negro Songs and Spirituals.* Mineoloa, NY: Dover, 1940.

Sources for the Underground Railroad

See Underground Railroad, Historical Sources for

South Carolina Sea Islands

See Sea Islands; Underground Railroad, Sites of

Spradling, Washington, Sr. (1802–1868)

Washington Spradling, Sr., was born in **Louisville, Kentucky**, in 1802. He and his family were freed by the will of William Spradling and, as Spradling himself later stated, "I was born a slave ... My father bought me, and I bought my own children, five in number...." ("Testimony of Washington Spradling," 1863: 77.) Spradling was trained as a barber and used his inheritance to speculate in real estate. Significantly, his family soon became allied with another important family of **free people of color** when Shelton **Morris**, recently arrived from Virginia, married Evalina Spradling, Washington Spradling's younger sister, in 1828.

Spradling probably became the first African American in the state of **Kentucky** to amass significant wealth. His wealth was based largely on real estate speculation and appreciation of the value of his land holdings as Louisville grew into a major city and, by 1860, approached $100,000. Important beyond his obvious business acumen, however, was

how he used his wealth. For example, Spradling loaned enslaved African Americans funds with which to purchase their freedom, often purchasing and then freeing them himself. When interviewed in 1863 by the American Freedmen's Inquiry Commission, Spradling stated that he alone had bought and freed 33 enslaved African Americans. Some had repaid him, but most had not, and still owed him a total of $3,337.50 — which he remembered "to the penny."

Equally intriguing, although more difficult to document fully, is the strong probability that, apart from using this legal path to freedom, Spradling and other free African Americans in Louisville were deeply involved in the movement of enslaved African Americans along the illegal path as well. Spradling died in 1868, but, when Wilbur Siebert was researching his major study of the Underground Railroad in the 1890s, he found former fugitives who, a generation after Spradling's death, recalled that, "At Louisville, Kentucky, Wash Spradley, a shrewd negro, was instrumental in helping many of his-enslaved brethren out of bondage." (Siebert, 1898: 151.)

FURTHER READING

Gibson, William H., Sr. *Historical Sketches of the Progress of the Colored Race in Louisville, Kentucky.* Louisville: n. p., 1897.

Hudson, J. Blaine. "Crossing the Dark Line: Fugitive Slaves and The Underground Railroad in Louisville and North Central Kentucky." *The Filson History Quarterly* 75, no. 1(2001): 33–84.

Siebert, Wilbur H. *The Underground Railroad from Slavery to Freedom.* 1898. Reprint, New York: Russell and Russell, 1967.

"Testimony of Washington Spradling." American Freedmen's Inquiry Commission, November 26, 1863: 77.

Sprinkle, J.R.

Friend of the fugitive in **Louisville, Kentucky**. *See also* Appendixes 1 and 2.

Star Hill AME Church (Delaware)

Underground Railroad site. A small African American church that harbored **fugitive slaves** fleeing through rural Delaware. The church still stands and is located on Route 13, east of Country Road and Route 330. *See also* Harboring; Underground Railroad, Sites of; and Appendixes 3 and 4.

Starr Clark Tin Shop
(Mexico, New York)

Underground Railroad site recognized and documented by the National Park Service. *See also* Appendix 5.

Stations

See Underground Railroad, Stations on

Stevens, Thaddeus (1792–1868)

Congressman, friend of the fugitive, and antislavery leader. Thaddeus Stevens was born in Danville, Vermont, on April 4, 1792. His childhood was difficult and impoverished after his alcoholic father abandoned his family. Despite these obstacles, Stevens graduated from Dartmouth College in 1814, taught school and later practiced law in **Pennsylvania**. As a staunch opponent of **slavery**, he employed his legal skills to defend **fugitive slaves**.

Stevens served the Pennsylvania legislature from 1833 to 1841 and served in the U. S. Congress from 1849 to 1853 as an antislavery Whig, opposing the **Fugitive Slave Act of 1850** and the **Compromise of 1850**. In 1859, he was re-elected to the House of Representatives as a leader of the new Republican Party and, under President Abraham Lincoln, became a key congressional powerbroker as chair of the House Ways and Means Committee.

During the **Civil War**, Stevens led the Radical Republicans in the House of Representatives and was a strong proponent of emancipation and the full enfranchisement of freed African Americans. During Reconstruction, unlike other Radical Republicans, Stevens opposed leniency toward the defeated South and argued that the southern states should be treated as "conquered provinces" and that southern plantations should be confiscated and the land redistributed to the freedmen. Not surprisingly, he opposed President Andrew Johnson's approach to Reconstruction, helped draft the Fourteenth Amendment and was a leader in the effort to impeach Johnson in 1868.

Stevens' health failed during the impeachment struggle and he died August 11, 1868. At his own request, he was buried in an African American cemetery in Lancaster, Pennsylvania, and his tombstone bears the following inscription:

> I repose in this quiet and secluded spot, not from any natural preference for solitude; but finding other cemeteries limited as to race, by charter rules, I have chosen this that I might illustrate in my death the principles which I advocated through a long life, equality of man before the Creator.

See also Appendixes 1 and 2.

FURTHER READING
Korngold, Ralph. Thaddeus *Stevens: A Being Darkly Wise and Rudely Great*. New York: Harcourt, Brace, 1955.
McCall, Samuel W. *Thaddeus Stevens*. New York: Houghton, Mifflin, 1899.
Miller, Alphonse B. *Thaddeus Stevens*. New York: Harper & Brothers, 1939.

Steward, Austin (1793–1865)

Fugitive slave and friend of the fugitive. Austin Steward was born enslaved in Prince William County, Virginia, in 1793 to Robert and Susan Steward. When Steward was about nine years old, his owner, Captain William Helm, moved to New York, where **slavery** was still legal, with his human and other property. After being hired out and treated badly, Steward escaped to Canandaigua in 1813, where he found work with a local farmer and began attending school.

In 1817, Steward moved to Rochester, New York, and, during the 1820s, opened a successful grocery business and began teaching in a Sabbath school. After being chosen by Rochester blacks to deliver an oration at their July 5, 1827, ceremonies celebrating slave emancipation in New York State, Steward became increasingly involved in the antislavery movement and served as Rochester subscription agent for *Freedom's Journal* and the *Rights of All*. As an indication of his growing stature, Steward was chosen vice-president of the first black national convention in 1830.

In 1831, Steward joined the free African American colony in **Wilberforce, Canada**—established after the 1829 mob violence against blacks in **Cincinnati**, which also precipitated the call for the 1830 Convention of Free People of Color—at the urging of a group of settlers. He organized and directed the settlement for several years. He returned to Rochester in 1837 and, after fire destroyed his business, moved back to Canandaigua in 1842 to work as a teacher. In both cities, Steward's home was an important station for **fugitive slaves**.

Despite his business reverses, Steward presided over New York's African American conventions in 1840, 1841, and 1845, and developed an approach to antislavery work that was increasingly evangelical. In later years, Steward served as Canandaigua's subscription agent for the *National Anti-Slavery Standard* and was an outspoken opponent of the **Fugitive Slave Act of 1850**. He published his autobiography, *Twenty-Two Years a Slave, and Forty Years a Freeman*, in 1857; it is still considered one of the best slave narratives. Steward died in Rochester in 1865. *See also* Free People of Color; and Appendixes 1 and 2.

FURTHER READING
Steward, Austin. *Twenty-two Years a Slave, and Forty Years a Freeman; Embracing a Correspondence of Several Years, While President of Wilberforce Colony, London, Canada West.* 1857. Reprint, New York: Negro Universities Press, 1968.

Steward, James

Friend of the fugitive in **Madison, Indiana**. *See also* Appendixes 1 and 2.

Still, William (1821–1902)

Friend of the fugitive. William Still was born free in Burlington County, New Jersey, in 1821. His father, Levin Steel, purchased his freedom and changed his name to "Still" to protect the identity of his wife, Sidney — who also changed her name to "Charity." The couple had 17 children; two of the older boys, Peter and Levin, were kidnapped as children and taken into **slavery**.

Still received some formal education as a child and left home in 1841, eventually reaching **Philadelphia** in 1844. In 1847, he married Letitia George, with whom he had four children. Also in 1847, Still was hired by the **Pennsylvania** Society for the Abolition of Slavery initially as a janitor and clerk, and eventually achieved a measure of financial stability after establishing a successful coal business.

Not content to serve as a mere employee, Still soon began assisting **fugitive slaves** directly, often harboring them in his own home. According to his own records, he and his family alone assisted 649 freedom seekers. After the passage of the **Fugitive Slave Act of 1850**, Philadelphia abolitionists organized a vigilance committee to assist the growing number of fugitives flowing through the region — and to protect them from the designs of the growing number of slave-catchers in pursuit. Still was named chairman or secretary and became responsible for one of the largest and best organized Underground Railroad operations in the nation. Ironically, one of the fugitives aided by Still proved to be his long-lost older brother, Peter, kidnapped before Still's birth.

In 1855, Still visited **Canada** to assess the conditions of the African American refugees living primarily in Ontario. His report countered criticism that the fugitive slaves were destitute and making little progress, and his records were cited as examples that emancipation in the United States could "work."

Still kept detailed records of the fugitive slaves assisted by the vigilance committee and used these personal records and first-hand accounts as the source material for his seminal book, *The Underground Railroad*, published in 1872. Still's book was one of the few contemporary accounts written by an African American author and remains an indispensable source for the study of fugitive slaves and friends of the fugitives in the "east." Equally important, Still, from his first-hand experience, knew and stated that the fugitives themselves, not the African Americans and whites who assisted them, were the true heroes and heroines of the Underground Railroad drama.

After emancipation, Still championed the cause of black civil rights in many arenas. He crusaded for equal treatment on Philadelphia streetcars and railways between 1861 and 1867. In the 1870s, he founded a Mission School in north Philadelphia and organized one of the nation's first YMCAs for African Americans in 1880. Additionally, he later founded an orphanage for the children of deceased black soldiers and sailors. Still died in Philadelphia on July 14, 1902. *See also* Vigilance Committees; William Still House; and Appendixes 1 and 2.

FURTHER READING

Kashatus, William C. "Two Stationmasters on the Underground Railroad: A Tale of Black and White." *Pennsylvania Heritage* 27(2001): 4–11.

Siebert, Wilbur H. *The Underground Railroad from Slavery to Freedom*. 1898. Reprint, New York: Russell and Russell, 1967.

Simmons, William J. *Men of Mark: Eminent, Progressive and Rising*. Cleveland, OH: George M. Rewell, 1887.

Still, William. *The Underground Railroad*. 1872. Reprint, Chicago: Johnson, 1970.

Toplin, Robert B. "Peter Still versus the Peculiar Institution." *Civil War History* 13, no. 4(1967): 340–349.

Stowe, Harriet Beecher (1811–1896)

Author, abolitionist and friend of the fugitive. Harriet Beecher Stowe was one of the most popular American writers of the nineteenth century and author of **Uncle Tom's Cabin**, the most powerful literary indictment of **slavery** published in the antebellum period.

Harriet Beecher was born on June 14, 1811 in Litchfield, Connecticut. Her father, Lyman Beecher, was a Congregational minister well-known for his fiery evangelical sermons and zeal for moral reform, including strong opposition to slavery. Her mother, Roxana Foote

Harriett Beecher Stowe, circa 1880 (Library of Congress)

Beecher, died when Stowe was four years of age, leaving Stowe's oldest sister, Catharine, to serve as her surrogate mother well into adulthood.

Stowe received an unusually rich education for a girl and was influenced strongly by the pioneering spirit of her sister Catharine, who was active in the women's movement and opened a school for girls in Hartford, Connecticut. Stowe studied and later taught at her sister's seminary. At age 13, she experienced a religious conversion after one of her father's sermons and religion would remain a powerful force throughout her life.

In 1832, Lyman Beecher was appointed president of Lane Theological Seminary in **Cincinnati**, and both sisters moved with the family to Cincinnati, **Ohio**. There, she met and married Calvin Stowe, a professor and theologian, in 1836. Within the first four years of her marriage, Stowe gave birth to four of her seven children.

Stowe's antislavery ideals derived from her father's belief in human equality, but achieved greater depth and concreteness in Cincinnati. She witnessed the violence and brutality of slavery while residing briefly in Washington, **Kentucky** (near Maysville). She also became acquainted with famous **friends of the fugitive** such as Levi **Coffin**, and gained first-hand knowledge of some of the most legendary slave escapes from Kentucky, and points south, into Ohio and points north. Despite her strong abhorrence of slavery, Stowe nevertheless accepted many of the common racial stereotypes of enslaved African Americans, and believed that slave-owners too were victims who could be saved from the evil of their own peculiar institution only by the peaceful abolition of slavery. These views figured prominently in her work.

Stowe published her first story, "Uncle Lot," in the *Western Monthly Magazine* in 1834 and, after her marriage, began writing to supplement the income of her poor and growing family. In the 1840s, she contributed to the prestigious women's magazine, *Godey's Lady's Book*. In 1843, she published *The Mayflower,* a collection of her short stories, and began writing *Uncle Tom's Cabin.* The novel first appeared in installments for the *National Era* in 1851; Stowe published the novel in its entirety in 1852.

Many of the most memorable characters were stereotypical caricatures, such as the humble and long-suffering Uncle Tom, the evil Simon Legree, and the impish Topsy. Still others were based however loosely on real historical figures such as Eliza **Harris** and Levi Coffin. In later years, fugitive slave and friend of the fugitive Josiah **Henson** claimed to be the inspiration for Uncle Tom himself.

The book became an instant best-seller. In response to the venomous proslavery criticism elicited by the book, Stowe wrote the factual *Key to Uncle Tom's Cabin*. In describing her motivation, Stowe wrote in a letter to Lord Denman, January 20, 1853:

> I wrote what I did because as a woman, as a mother I was oppressed and broken-hearted, with the sorrows and injustice I saw, because as a Christian I felt the dishonor to Christianity — because as a lover of my country I trembled at the coming day of wrath. It is no merit in the sorrowful that they weep, or to the oppressed and smothering that they gasp and struggle, not to me, that I must speak for the oppressed — who cannot speak for themselves.

Uncle Tom's Cabin portrayed slavery and slave-owners in a decidedly unflattering light and, from the standpoint of the South, was a public relations disaster that flatly contradicted the southern image of slavery as a benign and paternalistic system. In a larger context, the book exerted a powerful influence on northern public opinion and even public opinion in other countries in the tumultuous years preceding the **Civil War**, when blocking the further extension of slavery into the western territories and opposition to the **Fugitive Slave Act of 1850** divided the nation. Recognizing the importance of this literary bombshell, Abraham Lincoln, upon meeting Stowe during the Civil War, was reported to have stated: "So you're the little lady who started this big war."

The sudden and ultimately international popularity of *Uncle Tom's Cabin* ensured the success of her subsequent works. Among the most praised are *Dred: A Tale of the Dismal Swamp* (1856); *The Minister's Wooing* (1859); *The Pearl of Orr's Island* (1862); *Agnes of Sorrento* (1862); *Palmetto Leaves* (1873); and *Poganuc People* (1878). Stowe also wrote fiction for the *Atlantic Monthly* from 1857

through the remainder of her career. In 1889, she collaborated with her youngest child, Charles, in publishing her first official biography.

Stowe died of brain congestion on July 1, 1896 in Hartford, Connecticut. *See also* Abolitionist Movement; Harriet Beecher Stowe House (Brunswick, Maine); Harriet Beecher Stowe House (Cincinnati, Ohio); and Appendixes 1 and 2.

FURTHER READING

Duvall, Severn. "*Uncle Tom's Cabin:* The Sinister Side of the Patriarchy." *The New England Quarterly* 36(1963): 3–22.

Gerson, Noel B. *Harriet Beecher Stowe: A Biography.* New York, 1976.

Hedrick, Joan D. 1994. *Harriet Beecher Stowe: A Life.* New York: Oxford University Press, 1994.

Young, Elizabeth. *Disarming the Nation: Women's Writing and the American Civil War.* Chicago: University of Chicago Press, 1999.

Strategies for Escape

Each slave escape was an event with its own history, much as each fugitive slave or friend of the fugitive was a protagonist with a unique and very personal role in that history. There were, however, common challenges confronting all fugitives that can be generalized broadly across the statistical universe of slave escapes.

A successful escape required information, planning, timing, resources (if possible), courage and good fortune. At one extreme, an enslaved African American could act on impulse or out of desperation — with little preparation and little knowledge beyond a vague sense of where "North" or some temporary haven might be found. Such escapes were likely to fail unless fugitives had a very steep "learning curve" and were very lucky. At the other extreme, an escape could be planned carefully over time.

Accurate information was critically important to planning a successful escape; few successful slave escapes were completely unaided even if the aid was rendered passively or inadvertently. Nevertheless, with good information and preparation, the freedom seeker would then proceed on his or her own, usually having obtained some food, clothing, sometimes some money, perhaps a weapon of some kind — and hope to elude capture en route to or in a free state. If successful, the fugitive would ultimately cross the U.S.-Canadian or U. S.-Mexican border, or live "passing for free" in some northern or Western community.

Several escape strategies evolved through trial and error over time. For example, because not all African Americans were enslaved, a fugitive slave could not be identified by color alone and pretending to be free or abroad on legitimate business was often an effective ruse. Among the more common stratagems was the use of forged passes or certificates of emancipation (free papers) that enabled **fugitive slaves** to pose as free persons. Deceptions and disguises that enabled very fair-complexioned African Americans to pass as white Americans were sometimes employed. In general, the simplest and most straightforward strategies were the most effective, and there was virtually no limit to the inventiveness — and often the desperation — of the fugitives who conceived and executed such strategies.

Allowing enslaved African Americans some relative freedom of movement often allowed them the opportunity to escape. Obtaining money or goods that could be exchanged for money to finance an escape was a recurrent theme before the **Civil War**. Sometimes, simple opportunism was sufficient.

Mailing oneself to freedom was yet another daring strategy and one made famous by Henry "Box" **Brown**, a rather diminutive fugitive, who escaped from bondage by having himself shipped in a crate to William **Still** in **Philadelphia**.

Timing was a critical factor as well. Slave escapes usually occurred at night and fugitives usually traveled by night unless in disguise or when using roads, railroads or rivers by subterfuge. However, some nights were far more promising than others. Enslaved African Americans were often allowed to tend their own gardens or the slave provision grounds on Saturdays and Sundays (which lowered the cost to slaveholders). As a result, enslaved African Americans were seldom supervised closely between Saturday evenings and Monday mornings, and fugitives took advantage of this work routine and often fled on Satur-

day or Sunday nights — giving themselves a head-start of a day or more.

Beyond time of the day and week, time of year was another crucial variable related both to the vagaries of regional climate and to changes in the local politics of **slavery**. Before 1850, fugitive slaves seemed to prefer the warmer months. However, after 1850, with patrols and slave-catchers better able to operate in good weather, slave escapes occurred more often in the cooler months.

Traveling on foot, fugitive slaves could seldom cover more than 10 to 15 miles per night, and the longer they were on the road, the more vulnerable they were to hunger, the whims of the climate, and the snares of patrols and slave-catchers. Consequently, transportation was yet another critical factor. Although most escapes in the 1700s and early 1800s involved relatively young men, the increasing proportion of fugitive slave women and children after 1830 made the use of horses and carriages, drays and wagons more common. Somewhat later, access to the actual "steel" railroad in the **1850s** became an important factor in free territory.

Large numbers of both free and enslaved African Americans worked on ocean-going and coastal vessels, and on the many steamboats that plied the major rivers and lakes of the ante-bellum United States. These vessels were important means of inter-regional communication and sometimes offered convenient and rapid means of escape. The importance of traveling swiftly, particularly from the southern interior, should not be underestimated since it greatly enhanced the probability of reaching free territory. The problem was how to travel fast and, at the same time, avoid detection. Despite the risks, such escapes occurred frequently.

As early as 1840, escapes by steamboat became so common that the editor of the *St. Louis Gazette* recommended "the disuse, on board steamboats navigating the western waters, of all free negroes ... as they cause excitement and discontent among slaves of the states through which they pass, many of whom they induce to run away." The editor of *The Colored American* responded that, if free people of color were banned, "what would they then have to do — take slaves? How glad they (the slaves) would be to get to Cincinnati, to Steubenville, to Wellsville, and to Pittsburgh. The boats would certainly have to get new help to go back with."

Both the use of steamboats as means of escape and the propensity of African Americans with familiarity with the river to become fugitives remained common in the 1850s. The opportunity to hide, travel in disguise, pass for white or as a free person of color — with a bit of money — was often sufficient for a successful escape by river.

By the 1850s, the steel railroad enabled fugitives to travel with unparalleled speed. As with steamboats, the advantages of rapid flight often outweighed the heightened risk of capture and enslaved African Americans attempted escapes by rail quite often.

To summarize, the simpler the strategy, the less likely it would unravel with the first delay or unforeseen event. The fewer people aware of the "plan," the lower the probability of inadvertent or intentional betrayal. The better one's directions, the more rapidly and efficiently one could travel. The better provisioned, the longer one could hide or journey without risking exposure through hunting, asking for or stealing food. If one had money or guile, the more likely one could travel faster and in greater comfort, if not greater safety, aboard a steamboat, stagecoach or train.

Fugitives and **friends of the fugitive** agreed that, if there was an Underground Railroad network in slave territory, it existed only in the extended **Borderland**. Most fugitives, until they reached the border region, were largely on their own and devised and executed their escape strategies accordingly. *See also* Canada; Mexico; Motivations for Escape; Routes of Escape.

FURTHER READING
Hudson, J. Blaine. *Fugitive Slaves and the Underground Railroad in the Kentucky Borderland.* Jefferson, NC: McFarland, 2002.
Siebert, Wilbur H. *The Underground Railroad from Slavery to Freedom.* 1898. Reprint, New York: Russell and Russell, 1967.

Strauther, Samuel

Friend of the fugitive in Battle Creek, Michigan. *See also* Hussey, Erastus; and Appendixes 1 and 2.

Sumner, Charles (1811–1874)

Senator, friend of the fugitive, and antislavery leader. Charles Sumner was born in **Boston, Massachusetts**, on January 6, 1811. The son of an attorney, he attended Harvard University and, in 1833, was admitted to the bar. Sumner became active in the antislavery movement, helping to organize the Free Soil Party in 1848. In 1849, he challenged segregated schools in Boston, unsuccessfully, in the Roberts case — which was later cited as a precedent in the 1896 *Plessy v. Ferguson* decision that gave constitutional sanction to racial segregation.

In 1851, Sumner was elected to the U. S. Senate and became the Senate's leading opponent of **slavery**. In 1856, he delivered his famous "Crime Against Kansas" speech against proslavery groups in the territory and, soon thereafter, was beaten unconscious by Preston Brooks, a congressman from South Carolina who felt that Sumner had insulted his uncle. His injuries were so serious that he was unable to return to the Senate for three years.

During the **Civil War**, Sumner led the Radical Republicans in the Senate. He argued strongly in favor of repealing the **Fugitive Slave Act of 1850**, the use of African American troops in the Union Army, the complete emancipation and enfranchisement of all African Americans, and land redistribution to and education for the formerly enslaved. Despite being more radical than President Abraham Lincoln, the two were fast friends, and Lincoln once remarked to Sumner that "the only difference between you and me is a difference of a month or six weeks in time." (Grimke, 1892: 338.)

Sumner supported Lincoln's plan for Reconstruction and became a leading opponent of President Andrew Johnson. He was instrumental in securing the passage of the 1866 Civil Rights Act, legislation to extend the life of the Freedmen's Bureau, and the Reconstruction Acts of 1867 and 1868. Between March and May 1868, Sumner led the Republicans in the impeachment trial of Andrew Johnson and declared that:

This is one of the last great battles with slavery. Driven from the legislative chambers, driven from the field of war, this monstrous power has found a refuge in the executive mansion, where, in utter disregard of the Constitution and laws, it seeks to exercise its ancient, far-reaching sway. All this is very plain. Nobody can question it. Andrew Johnson is the impersonation of the tyrannical slave power. In him it lives again. He is the lineal successor of John C. Calhoun and Jefferson Davis; and he gathers about him the same supporters. [Dewitt, 1967: 584–585.]

The Senate failed to impeach Johnson by one vote. Sumner later supported, but eventually became disillusioned with, the embattled administration of President Ulysses S. Grant. Sumner died of a heart attack on March 11, 1874. *See also* Appendixes 1 and 2.

FURTHER READING
Dewitt, David Miller. *The Impeachment and Trial of Andrew Johnson, seventeenth President of the United States: A History.* 1903. Reprint, New York: Russell and Russell, 1968.
Donald, David H. *Charles Sumner and the Coming of the Civil War.* New York: Knopf, 1960.
Grimke, Archibald H. *Charles Sumner: The Scholar in Politics.* New York: Funk & Wagnalls, 1892.
Ledbetter, Bill. "Charles Sumner: Political Activist for the New England Transcendentalists." *The Historian* 44(1982): 347–363.
Storey, Moorfield. *Charles Sumner.* New York: Houghton-Mifflin, 1900.

Sunnyside
(Kimberton, Pennsylvania)

Underground Railroad site. Sunnyside was the home and farm of Graceanna, Mariann and Elizabeth Lewis, three Quaker sisters who played a major role in the Underground Railroad in Pennsylvania. The Lewis sisters harbored **fugitive slaves** at Sunnyside and, in 1851, gave sanctuary to William Parker while he was being pursued by the authorities for his involvement in the Christiana Massacre. *See also* Christiana Resistance or Christiana Massacre; Harboring; Quakers; and Appendixes 1–4.

FURTHER READING
Blockson, Charles L. *Hippocrene Guide to the Underground Railroad.* New York: Hippocrene Books, 1994.
Forbes, Ella. "By My Own Right Arm: Redemptive Violence and the 1851 Christiana, Pennsylvania Resistance." *Journal of Negro History* 83, no. 3(1998): 159–167.

Swisshelm, Jane C. (1815–1884)

Friend of the fugitive. Jane Grey Cannon was born in Pittsburgh, **Pennsylvania**, on December 6, 1815. Her father died when she was eight years old and she helped support her family, first by lacemaking and, at age 14, by becoming a teacher.

In 1836, she married James Swisshelm and the couple moved to **Louisville, Kentucky**. Direct exposure to **slavery** made her a committed abolitionist and friend of the fugitive. Returning to Pittsburgh, Swisshelm founded her own antislavery newspaper in 1848, the *Pittsburgh Saturday Visitor,* and became a correspondent for Horace Greeley's *New York Tribune.* While she lived in Pittsburgh, her home was also a refuge for **fugitive slaves**.

She then moved to Minnesota and founded the *St. Cloud Visitor* and, in 1853, published a collection of her columns as a book, *Letters to Country Girls.* In reaction to her strong antislavery commentary, Swisshelm's newspaper office was attacked by a proslavery mob and her printing press was destroyed. She proceeded to purchase another press and establish another antislavery journal, the *St. Cloud Democrat.* During the **Civil War**, Swisshelm sold her newspaper and worked as a nurse. She retired to Swissvale, Pennsylvania, wrote her autobiography, *Half a Century* (1880), and died there July 22, 1884. *See also* Appendixes 1 and 2.

FURTHER READING
Blockson, Charles L. *Hippocrene Guide to the Underground Railroad.* New York: Hippocrene Books, 1994.
Swisshelm, Jane Grey Cannon. *Half a Century.* Chicago: Jansen, McClurg and Company, 1880.

Tallman, William M.

Friend of the fugitive in Janesville, Wisconsin. *See also* Tallman House; and Appendixes 1 and 2.

Tallman House
(Janesville, Wisconsin)

Underground Railroad site. William M. Tallman operated an Underground Railroad station in New York. In 1855, he migrated to Janesville, Wisconsin, and began constructing a 20-room house that served as an important sanctuary for **fugitive slaves**. Freedom seekers were concealed in servants' rooms in the rear of the house and, if in danger of recapture, could exit the house using a hidden staircase in the maid's closet. *See also* Underground Railroad, Sites of; and Appendixes 3 and 4.

Tappan, Arthur (1786–1865)

Friend of the fugitive and philanthropist. Arthur Tappan was born in Northampton, **Massachusetts**, on May 22, 1786. Tappan moved to **Boston** at the age of 15, and by 1807 established his own dry goods business in Portland, Maine. His business interests multiplied and diversified, and his wealth grew steadily. His silk-importing business based in New York was unusually successful and with his brother, Lewis **Tappan**, he established America's first commercial credit-rating service.

Arthur Tappan (Library of Congress)

Tappan helped fund several antislavery groups and, in 1831, again with his brother, helped establish the New York Anti-Slavery Society. In 1839, Tappan was instrumental in the legal proceedings that resulted in the release of the *Amistad* captives. Tappan, given his conservative religious convictions, broke ranks with many of the more liberal abolitionists by opposing the active role of women in the movement and, in 1839, forming the American and Foreign Anti-Slavery Society. He and his brother also supported the Liberty Party. However, after the passage of the **Fugitive Slave Act of 1850**, Lewis and his brother opposed the law and helped fund the Underground Railroad. Arthur Tappan died July 23, 1865 in New Haven, Connecticut. *See also* **Amistad** Affair; and Appendixes 1 and 2.

FURTHER READING
Feller, Daniel. "A Brother in Arms: Benjamin Tappan and the Antislavery Democracy." *The Journal of American History* 88(2001): 48–74.
Wyatt-Brown, Bertram. *Lewis Tappan and the Evangelical War Against Slavery.* Cleveland: Press of Case Western Reserve University, 1969.

Tappan, Lewis (1788–1873)

Friend of the fugitive and philanthropist. Lewis Tappan was born in Northampton, **Massachusetts**, in 1788. In 1828, he joined his brother, Arthur **Tappan**, in the silk trade in New York and later, with his brother, founded the nation's first commercial credit-rating service, the Mercantile Agency.

Tappan helped fund several antislavery groups and, in 1831, again with his brother, helped establish the New York Anti-Slavery Society. In 1839, Tappan was instrumental in the legal proceedings that resulted in the release of the *Amistad* captives and was involved in founding the **American Missionary Association**. Tappan, given his conservative religious convictions, broke ranks with many of the more liberal abolitionists by opposing the active role of women in the movement. However, after the passage of the **Fugitive Slave Act of 1850**, Lewis and his brother opposed the law and helped fund the Underground Railroad. Lewis Tappan died in Brooklyn Heights in 1873. *See also* **Amistad** Affair; and Appendixes 1 and 2.

FURTHER READING

Feller, Daniel. "A Brother in Arms: Benjamin Tappan and the Antislavery Democracy." *The Journal of American History* 88(2001): 48–74.

Still, William. *The Underground Railroad.* 1872. Reprint, Chicago: Johnson, 1970.

Wyatt-Brown, Bertram. *Lewis Tappan and the Evangelical War Against Slavery.* Cleveland: Press of Case Western Reserve University, 1969.

Tappan-Philbrick House (Brookline, Massachusetts)

Underground Railroad site recognized and documented by the National Park Service. *See also* Appendix 5.

Tatum, William (aka John Jones)

Friend of the fugitive in **Louisville, Kentucky.** *See also* Appendixes 1 and 2.

Temporary Escapes

Distance was a significant variable in slave escapes and, unless a fugitive slave could "travel fast" (e.g., by horse, stage coach, boat or railroad), the farther from free territory, the lower the probability of escaping successfully. This variable was especially problematic for African Americans enslaved in the deep southern interior, the heart of the **Cotton Kingdom,** where the numbers and population density of enslaved African Americans were greatest. Some defied the odds, but most in the deep South did not, unless they sought freedom in remote areas (see **Maroon Societies**) or in southern cities and towns. Slave escapes in these regions were still common, but many belonged to a different category.

Not all runaways were freedom seekers and some who sought freedom did so in slave territory — and, often, only for a limited time. Temporary escapes could involve "lying out" (escaping for a few days or even weeks to visit a loved one); taking a "holiday"; avoiding punishment; or as an act of protest or defiance. Many historians have cited this widespread phenomenon as evidence of the complex human dynamics that existed between African Americans and those who held them in bondage. "Lying out," of course, was an exercise in brinksmanship on the part of an enslaved African American, requiring an astute understanding of the slaveholder and a careful calculation of what one might gain from a temporary absence relative to the penalty one would pay. Serious miscalculation could result in brutal punishment, sale and separation from loved ones, or even death. *See also* Motivations for Escape.

FURTHER READING

Franklin, John H., and Loren Schweninger. *Runaway Slaves: Rebels on the Plantation.* New York: McGraw-Hill, 1999.

Tennessee

Tennessee had about 20,000 more residents than did **Kentucky.** Kentucky's white and free black populations were slightly larger than those of Tennessee, while Tennessee's enslaved black population was somewhat larger than that of Kentucky. African Americans were concentrated in the western and central regions of Tennessee, with some scattered areas of concentration in the eastern valleys. Central Tennessee formed the northern border of Alabama, and western Tennessee bore the same relation to northern **Mississippi.** Consequently, fugitives escaping overland from these cotton-growing states were funneled through central and western Tennessee, then through Kentucky, to free territory.

Nashville and its surrounding Davidson County dominated the central region of the state. As an urban center in the upper South, the African American population of Nashville bore some similarities to those of both Lexington and **Louisville**— with a number of **free people of color** and enslaved African Americans hired out in the town. For example, in 1830, 1,987 African Americans lived in Nashville, representing 35.7 percent of the town population. Free people of color represented 9.0 percent (179 of 1,987) of that number. By 1850, the African American population had increased slightly to 2,539, of whom 20.1 percent (511 of 2,539) were free. However, the white population had grown disproportionately and the African American percentage of population had dropped to 24.9 percent.

Tennessee's free black population, although small, was concentrated in pockets in the eastern valleys and in the north central sections of the state, generally along the course of the Cumberland River. Still, free people of color in Tennessee and the deep southern interior had far less freedom to assist fugitives and even the potential advantages of their presence in and around Nashville may have been offset by the sheer distance between northern Tennessee and free territory, by any route.

After 1840, the relative status of urban slaves and free people of color deteriorated as European immigrants and non-slaveholding whites pressed for severe restrictions on African Americans to limit competition for jobs and living space. Furthermore, Tennessee became a net exporter of slave property by 1850 and, as a result, "Negro stealing" and "Negro trading" became lucrative businesses. Running away was one response. *See also* Routes of Escape; Underground Railroad, Sites of; and Appendixes 3 and 4.

FURTHER READING
England, J. Merton. "The Free Negro in Ante-Bellum Tennessee." *Journal of Southern History* 9, no. 1(1943): 35–58.
Hudson, J. Blaine. *Fugitive Slaves and the Underground Railroad in the Kentucky Borderland.* Jefferson, NC: McFarland, 2002.
Lamon, Lester C. *Blacks in Tennessee, 1791–1970.* Knoxville: University of Tennessee Press, 1981.

Texas

In 1821, the Mexican government allowed American (or "Anglo") colonization of Texas, and early U.S. colonization efforts were led first by Moses Austin and later by his son, Stephen F. Austin. Nearly all of the settlers who accompanied Austin came from slave-holding states; many owned at least small numbers of African Americans. Not surprisingly, the "Texas Revolution," which wrested Texans from **Mexico**, and the subsequent Constitution of the Republic of Texas, guaranteed that the right to own slave property would be protected.

Abolitionism was never a strong presence in Texas. Public criticism could bring swift vigilante retribution. For example, in 1860, a proslavery gang hanged the Reverend Anthony Bewly because of his outspoken abolitionism. During the **Civil War**, Unionists were often associated with abolitionists and suffered a similar fate. During the Great Hanging at Gainsville, 41 suspected Unionists were hanged over a 13-day period.

In some urban areas of Texas, African Americans were allowed to live separately from owners, and to hire out their own time. One newspaper attributed slave escapes and other forms of resistance "to the unusual liberties which slaves in Texas seem to exercise in our towns, when out of the control of their masters." African Americans enslaved in Texas did not view the conditions of bondage so favorably, and often responded by fleeing to Mexico or other free lands. Texas newspaper editor John S. Ford stated that 4,000 African Americans left Texas in 1855 alone, although this estimate cannot be substantiated. *See also* Abolitionist Movement; Callahan Expedition; Routes of Escape.

FURTHER READING
Addington, Wendell G. "Slave Insurrections in Texas." *Journal of Negro History* 35, no. 4(1950): 408–434.
Barker, Eugene C. "The Influence of Slavery in the Colonization of Texas." *Mississippi Valley Historical Review* 11, no. 1(1924): 3–36.
Nash, A. E. Keir. "The Texas Supreme Court and the Trial Rights of Black, 1845–1860." *The Journal of American History* 58 (1971): 622–642.

Thomas, Nathan (1803–1887)

Friend of the fugitive. In 1803, Nathan Thomas was born in **Mount Pleasant, Ohio**, a "Quaker town" with strong antislavery sympathies. He became a physician and settled in Schoolcraft, Michigan, in 1833, becoming the first physician in Kalamazoo County. In 1838, he married Pamela Brown and the two operated an Underground Railroad station in their home, which also served as a medical office.

In her memoirs (1892), Pamela Brown Thomas wrote that her husband's "antislavery views were so well known, that, while he was a bachelor boarding at the hotel, fugitives from **slavery** had called on him for assistance and protection." Further, she estimated that between 1840 and 1860, she and her husband assisted between 1,000 to 1,500 **fugitive slaves**— forwarding them to Erastus **Hussey** in Battle Creek, en route to **Detroit** and then **Canada**.

Thomas practiced both medicine and politics. In 1837, he led local residents in a petition campaign against the annexation of

Texas. In 1839, he helped found an antislavery newspaper and, in 1845, ran unsuccessfully for lieutenant governor on the Liberty Party ticket. In 1854, he participated in the convention in Jackson, Michigan, at which the Republican Party was founded. *See also* Nathan Thomas House; Appendixes 1 and 2.

Thomas Lightfoote Inn (Williamsport, Pennsylvania)

Underground Railroad site. In Williamsport, **Pennsylvania**, a Quaker friend of the fugitive, Thomas Updegraff, and his family assisted freedom seekers at Thomas Lightfoote Inn. The inn was constructed in the late 1700s and served as a refuge for **fugitive slaves** arriving on packet boats on the Pennsylvania Canal. *See also* Quakers; Underground Railroad, Sites of; and Appendixes 1–4.

Thomas Root House (New York)

Underground Railroad station. In the 1850s, friend of the fugitive Thomas Root built his home near the U.S.-Canadian border. Considered the proverbial "last stop" on the Underground Railroad in that section of New York, Root sheltered **fugitive slaves** in his cellar and barn, then transported them by wagon to the border, with the fugitives hidden under produce and other goods. *See also* Canada; and Appendixes 3 and 4.

Thome, Arthur (1769–1855)

Abolitionist and friend of the fugitive in Augusta, **Kentucky**. *See also* White Hall; and Appendixes 1 and 2.

Thome, James (1813–1873)

Abolitionist and friend of the fugitive in Augusta, **Kentucky**. *See also* White Hall; and Appendixes 1 and 2.

Thompson, William Eberle (1835–1940)

Friend of the fugitive in Bethel, **Ohio**. *See also* **William Eberle Thompson Homesite (Bethel, Ohio)**.

Thoreau, Henry David (1817–1862)

Philosopher, abolitionist and friend of the fugitive. Henry David Thoreau was one of the most influential thinkers in American history; his writings on civil disobedience shaped the social philosophy of men such as Dr. Martin Luther King, Jr.

Thoreau eloquently opposed the government for waging the Mexican war (to extend **slavery**) in "Resistance to Civil Government." He lectured against slavery in "Slavery in Massachusetts." He defended John **Brown**'s efforts to end slavery after meeting him in **Concord** in "A Plea for Captain John Brown" (October 30, 1859), which began:

> I trust that you will pardon me for being here. I do not wish to force my thoughts upon you, but I feel forced myself. Little as I know of Captain Brown, I would fain do my part to correct the tone and the statements of the newspapers, and of my countrymen generally, respecting his character and actions. It costs us nothing to be just. (Salt, 1890: 51.)

Thoreau died of tuberculosis in 1862, at the age of 44. *See also* Appendixes 1 and 2.

FURTHER READING

Derleth, August William. *Concord Rebel: A Life of Henry David Thoreau.* Philadelphia: Chilton Co., 1962.

Salt, H. S., ed. *Anti-Slavery and Reform Papers by Henry David Thoreau.* London: Swan Sonnenschein, 1890.

Schneider, Richard J., ed. *Henry David Thoreau: A Documentary Volume.* Detroit: Gale, 2004.

Thurman, Fountain

Friend of the fugitive in Bethel, **Ohio**. *See also* Madison, Indiana; and Appendixes 1 and 2.

Tide Mill Farm (Mannington, New Jersey)

Underground Railroad station. Quaker George Abbot built his home near Mannington, New Jersey, in 1845. **Fugitive slaves** were concealed there and, in 1985, a secret room was discovered under one of the rooms of the home. *See also* Underground Railroad, Sites of; and Appendixes 3 and 4.

Timbuktu (Westhampton Township, New Jersey)

Ante-bellum African American community. Timbuktu, named for the legendary political and cultural center in West Africa, was established by **free people of color** in the 1820s, roughly two miles from Mount Holly in Westhampton Township, New Jersey. The town became a sanctuary for free blacks and **fugitive slaves** alike, particularly those crossing from or passing through Delaware. In 1860, residents of the town fought off **slave catchers** pursuing several fugitive slaves in the Battle of Pine Swamp. *See also* Underground Railroad, Sites of; and Appendixes 3 and 4.

Todd, John

Friend of the fugitive in **Madison, Indiana**. *See also* Appendixes 1 and 2.

Todd House (Tabor, Iowa)

Underground Railroad site. In 1853, the Reverend John Todd, a Congregational minister, built a home that became a refuge for **fugitive slaves** in Tabor, **Iowa**. The house was equipped with hidden room, roughly the size of a large closet. *See also* Underground Railroad, Sites of; and Appendixes 3 and 4.

Torrey, Charles (1813–1846)

Abolitionist and friend of the fugitive. Charles Torrey was born into "a distinguished if not wealthy New England family." (Harrold, 2000: 276.) His parents died of tuberculosis when he was very young and he was raised by his maternal grandparents. Torrey attended Phillips Academy and later graduated from Yale College in 1833. He was ordained a minister in 1836, but quit the ministry to work for the abolitionist cause, helping to organize the **Massachusetts** Abolition Society in 1839 and the Liberty Party in 1840.

In December 1841, Torrey went to **Washington, D.C.**, as a newspaper correspondent and, in January 1842 was jailed briefly for making antislavery remarks at a slaveholders' convention in Annapolis, Maryland. Returning to Washington, Torrey, unlike many white abolitionists, actively sought collaborators in the African American community and, having developed an effective escape network, aided nearly 400 runaways in a relatively short time.

Torrey moved to Baltimore in May 1844 and established a base of operations from which to assist freedom seekers fleeing bondage in Maryland, Virginia, and the District of Columbia. On June 24, 1844, he was arrested in Baltimore for assisting fugitive slaves, tried, convicted and sentenced to six years at hard labor. Unable to withstand the rigors of imprisonment, Torrey died at the Maryland Penitentiary on May 9, 1846 of pulmonary disease and became a martyr to the antislavery cause. *See also* Appendixes 1 and 2.

FURTHER READING
Harrold, Stanley. "On the Borders of Slavery and Race: Charles T. Torrey and the Underground Railroad." *Journal of the Early Republic* 20(2000).

Trueblood, James ("Little Jimmy")

See Portland Crossing Point

Trueblood, Thomas

See Portland Crossing Point

Truth, Sojourner (c. 1797–1883)

Fugitive slave, African American abolitionist, and women's rights activist. Although Sojourner Truth was not directly involved in the Underground Railroad, she contributed to the movement significantly as a fiery orator, committed abolitionist, women's and poor people's rights activist, preacher and singer.

Truth, known originally as Isabella, was born enslaved in 1797 in Ulster County, New York, and grew from childhood to adulthood during the decades during which **slavery** gradually ended in New York. She was the second youngest child in a family of 10, all of whom were owned by James and Elizabeth Baumfree. She was sold and resold several times, and was married at 14 years of age to another enslaved African American, an older man named Thomas. In 1826, only one year before the formal end of slavery in New York, she escaped and, with the assistance of the Von Wagener family, sued successfully for the return of her son, Peter, who had been sold illegally into bondage in Alabama.

Isabella moved to **New York City** and found work as a servant to support her son and herself. A woman with deep spiritual convictions, she became affiliated in the next decade with a succession of churches and spiritually oriented reform movements. In 1843, influenced by the Millerite belief that the end of the world was at hand, she changed her name to Sojourner Truth and became an itinerant evangelist who sang and spoke to those who would listen. Because Dutch was her first language, her unusual patterns of speech and her tall imposing figure made her an especially powerful and memorable presence.

Abolitionism was a central tenet of the liberal religious reform movements of the time, and Truth soon developed relationships with leading figures of the antislavery movement such as Frederick **Douglass** and William Lloyd **Garrison.** Garrison persuaded Truth, who was illiterate, to dictate her autobiography — *The Narrative of Sojourner Truth* — published in 1850. Now increasingly well-known, Truth became a popular speaker for abolition and women's rights. She moved **Washington, D.C.**, in 1863 to work with African American troops and freedmen, and even visited President Abraham Lincoln. After the Civil War, Truth led a petition campaign that failed to win congressional approval for the distribution of western lands to formerly enslaved African Americans. Further, in 1870, in the bitter controversy over voting rights for African Americans, she was a strong and often solitary voice arguing for the enfranchisement of African American women as well as men.

Sojourner Truth died in 1883, in Battle Creek, Michigan. *See also* Abolitionist Movement; Quakers; and Appendixes 1 and 2.

FURTHER READING

Bernard, Jacqueline. *Journey Toward Freedom: The Story of Sojourner Truth*. New York: W. W. Norton, 1990.

Engle, Diana P. "A Never-Ending Sojourn." *Michigan History Magazine* 84, no.1(2000): 29–39.

Mabee, Carleton. "Sojourner Truth, Bold Prophet: Why Did She Never Learn to Read?" *New York History* 69, no. 1(1988): 55–77.

Painter, Nell Irvin. "Representing Truth: Sojourner Truth's Knowing and Becoming Known." *Journal of American History* 81, no. 2(1994): 461–492.

Painter, Nell Irvin. "Truth, Sojourner." In *Black Women in America: An Historical Encyclopedia*. Volume II, edited by Darlene Clark Hine, Elsa Barkley Brown and Rosalyn Terborg-Penn. Bloomington and Indianapolis: Indiana University Press, 1993.

Ortiz, Victoria. *Sojourner Truth: A Self-Made Woman*. New York: Lippincott, 1974.

Sojourner Truth, 1864 (Library of Congress)

Tubman, Harriet (c. 1820–1913)

Fugitive and friend of the fugitive. Harriet Tubman was born enslaved as Araminta Ross in Dorchester County, Maryland, in about 1820, one of 11 children of Harriet Greene and Benjamin Ross. As a child, she worked as a maid and nurse, and was sent to labor as a field hand at age 12. At 13, her owner struck her in the head with a heavy weight, inflicting permanent neurological damage that caused her to suffer occasional blackouts for the remainder of her life.

In 1844, she married John Tubman, a free man of color. However, when her owner died in 1849, Harriet feared being sold south and fled north to **Pennsylvania.** Her husband refused to accompany her and, when she returned for him in 1851, he had remarried.

Tubman joined the antislavery cause and, given her knowledge of the Maryland countryside, began a series of clandestine expeditions into slave territory to organize slave escapes and lead other fugitives to freedom. On these forays, she carried sleeping powder to quiet restless infants and was known to carry a revolver in case any fugitive grew faint of heart and, because of his or her own fears, threatened to endanger the others.

In the next decade, operating from a base in St. Catherine, **Canada** West, Tubman made 19 journeys into Maryland and, working closely with William **Still** of **Philadelphia** and Thomas **Garrett** of Wilmington, Delaware, assisted over 300 fugitive slaves to freedom. In 1850, she returned and rescued her sister and her sister's two children. In 1851, she rescued her brother and, in 1857, her aged parents.

As her reputation grew, ever larger rewards were offered for her capture, but Tubman was both determined and clever. For example, she employed disguises, often dressing as an old man or woman. She changed her route and strategy repeatedly and took pride in never losing a passenger. John **Brown** dubbed her "General Tubman"— and others simply called her "Moses."

By the late **1850s**, due to New York's

Harriet Tubman, circa 1860–1875 (Library of Congress)

strong personal liberty law, Tubman felt safe to purchase land in Auburn, New York, for her parents and herself. In this region, Tubman also played a central role in the 1860 rescue of Charles **Nalle**, a fugitive slave detained in Troy, New York. During the **Civil War**, Tubman employed her well-honed skills and served as a spy, scout and nurse for the Union Army in South Carolina — and even cooked for the famous 54th **Massachusetts** as they prepared for battle.

In 1869, she married Nelson Davis, a Civil War veteran and, although illiterate, published her autobiography, *Scenes from the Life of Harriet Tubman,* with the assistance of her friend, Sarah Bradford. She became active in the women's rights movement and was instrumental in founding the black women's club movement. Eventually, she converted her home into a care facility for elderly African Americans and died there herself in 1913. *See also* Fugitive Slaves; Harriet Tubman Home; Personal Liberty Laws; Underground Railroad; and Appendixes 1 and 2.

FURTHER READING

Bradford, Sarah H. *Harriet Tubman: The Moses of Her People.* Bedford, MA: Applewood Books, 1993.

Siebert, Wilbur H. *The Underground Railroad from Slavery to Freedom.* 1898. Reprint, New York: Russell and Russell, 1967.

Still, William. *The Underground Railroad.* 1872. Reprint, Chicago: Johnson, 1970.

Twelfth Street Baptist Church (Boston, Massachusetts)

See Grimes, Leonard A.; Underground Railroad, Sites of; and Appendixes 3 and 4.

Twelve Knights of Tabor

See Dickson, Moses

Tyron's Folly (New York)

Underground Railroad station. Built in the 1820s overlooking the Niagara River, the home of the Rev. Amos Tyron was known as "Tyron's Folly" because of "its extravagant antiquarian design typical of the romanticism of the late eighteenth and early nineteenth centuries." (Blockson, 1994: 60–61.) This eccentric home, with its four underground cellars, was also an important Underground

Railroad station. *See also* Underground Railroad, Sites of; Underground Railroad, Stations on; and Appendixes 3 and 4.

FURTHER READING
Blockson, Charles. *Hippocrene Guide to the Underground Railroad.* New York: Hippocrene Books, 1994.

Uncle Tom's Cabin

Uncle Tom's Cabin, published by Harriet Beecher **Stowe** in 1852, was one of the most devastating and effective blows against **slavery** in the decades preceding the **Civil War**. The characters are numerous, but the plot is melodramatic and comparatively simple. Both characters and plot lines were drawn from Stowe's exposure to slavery while living near

An 1882 poster for *Uncle Tom's Cabin.* (Library of Congress)

Maysville, **Kentucky**, and then at **Cincinnati, Ohio**.

To summarize, Tom is the religious and kind-hearted slave manager of a Kentucky plantation owned by Mr. Shelby. Shelby suffers financial reverses and is compelled to sell two of his enslaved African Americans to a slave trader. Uncle Tom is one, and must leave his wife and children. The other is a four-year-old child, Harry, whose father has already fled bondage. His mother, Eliza, flees with Harry across the icy **Ohio River** when she learns of his impending sale. Eliza, of course, is based on the actual escape of Eliza **Harris**.

Tom is "sold down the river," deeper into the maw of slavery. En route, he saves Evangeline St. Clare, little Eva, from drowning, and is purchased by her grateful father, Augustine St. Clare. Life in the St. Clare household is idyllic until Eva becomes ill and dies. Soon after, St. Clare is killed accidentally and Tom is sold again, this time to the "evil" and sadistic Simon Legree. Tom helps an enslaved mother and daughter, Cassy and Emmeline, escape from the lascivious Legree and is savagely beaten for refusing to divulge their whereabouts. Tom dies as a result of his injuries.

The book is filled with memorable characters, the most popular of which is usually Topsy, the bright, strong-willed and rather amoral slave girl in the St. Clare household — who, after gaining her freedom, becomes a missionary. However, attitudes toward Tom himself have had a history of their own. As the "good and long-suffering slave," Tom was viewed quite favorably in the 1800s, and black Abolitionist Josiah **Henson** became famous for claiming the distinction, deserved or not, of being the original Uncle Tom. In later years, of course, the term "Uncle Tom" would be applied derisively to African Americans who were overly accommodating to whites.

In the end, although critics have long questioned the literary merits of the book, its greatest impact was in the political arena. *Uncle Tom's Cabin* dramatized the evils of slavery and was read widely in the United States and Europe, bringing the raw reality of slavery alive to non-southern readers and countering virtually every key contention of the southern defense of slavery as a "positive good." The **Abolitionist Movement** gained thousands of new supporters and antislavery sympathizers and public opinion began shifting strongly against the South, provoking southern outrage and causing a public relations disaster from which the South never recovered entirely.

FURTHER READING

Donovan, Josephine. *Uncle Tom's Cabin: Evil Affliction, and Redemptive Love.* Boston: Twayne, 1991.

Duvall, Severn. "*Uncle Tom's Cabin:* The Sinister Side of the Patriarchy." *The New England Quarterly* 36, no. 1(1963): 3–22.

King, Wilma. *Toward the Promised Land: From Uncle Tom's Cabin to the Onset of the Civil War (1851–1861).* New York: Chelsea House, 1995.

Stowe, Harriet Beecher. *The Key to Uncle Tom's Cabin.* 1854. Reprint, Salem, NH: Ayer Company, 1987.

_____. *Uncle Tom's Cabin.* 1852. Reprint, New York: Modern Library, 1996.

Underground Railroad, Historical Sources for

Fugitive slaves and the Underground Railroad belong, objectively, to the American past. Consequently, if history is the factual record of the human past, reconstructing and sharing the interlocking histories of those who fled **slavery** and those who sometimes assisted them requires factual evidence. Such evidence falls into two broad categories or types: *primary sources,* i.e., documents and other records dating essentially to the period under study; and *secondary sources,* i.e., documents and other records produced at a later time using primary or other secondary sources. The nature, quality and quantity of evidence available to support the study of fugitive slaves and the Underground Railroad are (and have long been) problematic and hotly contested.

The primary source record concerning fugitive slaves and the Underground Railroad can best be described as many "pools" of information — deep, but neither wide nor always connected. For example, there was no binding legal requirement that slave escapes be documented and, consequently, unlike tax records, wills and court actions, slave escapes did not produce a specific body of records maintained in and retrievable from some predictable place or places. Furthermore, few slaveholders or **friends of the fugitive** had the education or the leisure to produce collections of personal or family papers in which slave escapes might be mentioned. Even fewer African Americans had the opportunity to produce documents that captured their perspective as historical actors in or observers of this history.

Several sources have much to offer despite their many limitations. Among the most useful primary sources are antebellum newspapers. However, these sources have two inescapable limitations — one quite obvious and the other less so. First, many antebellum newspapers were not preserved, certainly not as complete sets. Second, not all slave escapes were reported and there is no reliable formula for determining what percentage of slave escapes left any record at all. As a result, even a complete newspaper record, if such existed, could not be construed as a comprehensive record of slave escapes.

Fugitive slave advertisements, news articles and court records can be used to estimate the actual number, frequency and patterns of slave escapes. For example, an enslaved African American who escaped successfully represented a substantial property loss to the owner — a loss to which a dollar value could be attached. This loss could not be recovered from the fugitive, but slave-owners often sued for compensation from individuals or businesses that may have unintentionally facilitated or consciously abetted the escape. Many of these cases were adjudicated in local, state and, occasionally, federal courts.

Other individuals suspected of aiding fugitives in some way were often arrested and tried in city or county courts. Once again, these criminal case records — as reported in the press or maintained as court documents — often provide important information concerning the identity and strategies of fugitives and their friends. Of course, court records of this kind, much like prison records, involved only the individuals who "got caught" — who were arrested and possibly convicted of violating a specific law — and, as such, represent only a fraction of the friends of the fugitive in a given region.

Professor Wilbur H. Siebert, in researching the Underground Railroad in the 1890s, contacted hundreds of individuals thought to have been involved in or to have some knowledge of the Underground Railroad. Many letters and related documents were cited in Siebert's seminal work, *The Underground Railroad from Slavery to Freedom* (1898). However, much original material was not included and much new material was added to the collection after Siebert became an acknowledged authority in his field, some by graduate students who conducted dissertation research on the Underground Railroad under Siebert's supervision. Interestingly, while Siebert's book tends to emphasize the role of whites in assisting fugitives, the role of African Americans looms much larger in the Siebert Papers.

Finally, beyond these traditional sources, what constitutes legitimate evidence in this field of historical research is subject at times to intense and bitter debate. The nature of American slavery created formidable barriers to the creation of primary source records by African Americans themselves. This is not to imply that antebellum African Americans left no "paper trail," only that the quantity of such evidence is disproportionately small compared to that produced by white Americans. Not surprisingly, much of this evidence is also considered subjective and suspect according to standards created by traditional historians that privilege certain types of evidence. However, what was preserved or can be reconstructed is invaluable—for example, oral traditions, family and community legends, the findings of archaeologists, slave narratives, the black and antislavery press, and post-**Civil War** interviews with and memoirs of former slaves. This body of evidence is extremely valuable and permits these men and women of the ever-receding past, black and white, to speak in their own voices.

To summarize, these other key sources of evidence (and their limitations) for the study of fugitive slaves and the Underground Railroad are:

• Myths, i.e., tales that explain the origin of things, set in a distant, even timeless era, and often with supernatural beings. Generally speaking, myths have great symbolic value, but rarely withstand close scrutiny.

• Legends, i.e., tales of events that took place in a familiar time and place. Unlike myths, legends are often based on the actual exploits of real people, though exaggeration and mystification may limit their accuracy.

• Personal or family accounts and anecdotes told as true stories that took place in a known time. Personal and family accounts are the most easily tested, and the most likely to be accurate.

In studying fugitive slaves and the Underground Railroad, both scholars and the general public should consider and weigh these non-traditional sources, but should also be aware of their strengths and weaknesses as historical evidence. *See also* Underground Railroad, Sites of; Underground Railroad, Stations on; and Appendixes 3 and 4.

FURTHER READING
Hudson, J. Blaine. *Fugitive Slaves and the Underground Railroad in the Kentucky Borderland.* Jefferson, NC: McFarland, 2002.
Siebert, Wilbur H. *The Underground Railroad from Slavery to Freedom.* 1898. Reprint, New York: Russell and Russell, 1967.

The Underground Railroad, by Charles T. Webber, 1893. (Library of Congress)

"Underground Railroad in Reverse"

See Cannon, Lucretia Hanley (Patty); and Crenshaw, John

Underground Railroad, Sites of

Every ante-bellum state or territory in the United States, particularly those east of the Mississippi River, has at least one existing site that was associated with **fugitive slaves** or the Underground Railroad. It is important to note that these sites describe neither the actual routes followed by fugitive slaves nor the full extent of the Underground Railroad network in any given region of the country. They reflect instead what is known of these journeys and the physical structures that have survived a century and a half after the last fugitive slave made his or her desperate break for freedom. What is best known relates more to those fugitives fortunate enough to tell or have their stories told — and the physical structures most likely to survive the ravages of time, e.g., church buildings in northern free black communities and the residences of white **friends of the fugitive**, particularly those with sufficient wealth that they could "build to last."

Some of the classic works on the history of the Underground Railroad identify numerous sites. More recently, Charles Blockson added immeasurably to public awareness of fugitive slaves and the Underground Railroad with his *Hippocrene Guide to the Underground Railroad* (1994). Readers should assume that site entries in the present encyclopedia without other specific references are documented in Blockson's *Hippocrene Guide,* or by the National Park Service. *See also* Underground Railroad, Historical Sources for; Underground Railroad, Stations on. Brief entries describing Underground Railroad sites are scattered alphabetically throughout this encyclopedia, and are grouped together in Appendixes 3, 4 and 5.

Underground Railroad, Stations on

The term "station" in Underground Railroad parlance has one of two meanings. The first, and better known, refers to a specific site such as a house or church, where fugitives could find sanctuary and from which they would often be "conducted" to the next "station." This type of station was usually associated with a particular individual, more often than not a free person of color or a white antislavery activist.

Although most stations were temporary stops on the Underground Railroad, free African American communities such as those in Syracuse, **Philadelphia, Boston, New Bedford, Detroit, Louisville,** and **Cincinnati** afforded fugitives the rare opportunity to "hide in plain view" — to blend in, at least for a while, with free African Americans who were usually faceless and invisible to whites. Thus, the free African American community itself was a "station" or junction of sorts — in essence, a nest or cluster of individual stations — where many people were capable of making various arrangements for the short- or long-term concealment of fugitives. *See also* Fugitive Slaves; Underground Railroad, Historical Sources for; Underground Railroad, Sites of; and Appendixes 3 and 4.

FURTHER READING

Hudson, J. Blaine. *Fugitive Slaves and the Underground Railroad in the Kentucky Borderland.* Jefferson, NC: McFarland, 2002.

Siebert, Wilbur H. *The Underground Railroad from Slavery to Freedom.* 1898. Reprint, New York: Russell and Russell, 1967.

Union Literary Institute

Friend of the fugitive. *See also* Joseph and Sophia Clemens Farmstead; and Appendixes 1 and 2.

United Church-on-the-Green (New Haven, Connecticut)

Underground Railroad site. Located in New Haven near Yale University, the United Church-on-the Green was pastored by the Reverends Simeon S. Jocelyn and Samuel W. Dutton in the antebellum period, both antislavery activists and **friends of the fugitive**. The Reverend Dutton, in particular, harbored **fugitive slaves** in his home. *See also* Harboring; Underground Railroad, Sites of; and Appendixes 3 and 4.

Utah

In Utah, permanent African American settlement began with the 1847 arrival of Mormon leader Brigham Young's advance party.

However, men of African descent, such James Beckworth and Jacob Dodson, were fur trappers and members of expeditions who traversed Utah's mountains and deserts decades before Mormon colonization. Numbers of enslaved African Americans were never high, and by 1850 there were approximately 60 Africans living in the Utah territory. No organized Underground Railroad system is known to have existed, although a few **fugitive slaves** joined the wagon trains moving westward through the Utah territory. *See also* Underground Railroad, Sites of; and Appendixes 3 and 4.

FURTHER READING
Bringhurst, Newell G. "The Mormons and Slavery — A Closer Look." *Pacific Historical Review* 50(1981): 329–338.
Savage, W. Sherman. "The Negro in the Westward Movement." *Journal of Negro History* 25, no. 4(1940): 531–539.

Vickers, John

Friend of the fugitive in Lionville, **Pennsylvania**. *See also* Vickers' Tavern.

Vickers' Tavern (Lionville, Pennsylvania)

Underground Railroad site. John Vickers, known as "the Quaker Abolitionist," harbored **fugitive slaves** in his Chester County, **Pennsylvania**, home. Typically, fugitives were forwarded to the next station with a personal letter from Vickers. *See also* Abolitionist Movement; Quakers; Underground Railroad, Sites of; and Appendixes 3 and 4.

Vigilance Committees

Deepening divisions over **slavery** in the late 1840s and through the **1850s** formed the catalyst that wove isolated local efforts into a larger Underground Railroad network characterized by significant local and regional coordination of the work of **friends of the fugitive**. The establishment of vigilance committees was, perhaps, the most concrete expression of and vehicle for such coordination.

The first vigilance committees formed in the 1830s, most notably the New York Committee of Vigilance in 1835 ably led by David **Ruggles** as secretary and general agent, and the **Philadelphia** Vigilance Committee in 1838 under the leadership of Robert **Purvis** and Daniel **Payne**. In 1846, a vigilance committee was established in **Boston** and came, ultimately, under the leadership of Lewis **Hayden**. In 1847, the New York State Vigilance Committee was organized under the leadership of wealthy white abolitionist Gerrit **Smith**. In the 1840s and **1850s**, similar groups formed in Cleveland, **Detroit**, **Cincinnati** and Syracuse. An antislavery league was organized in south central **Indiana** and the Knights of Liberty in St. Louis performed similar functions.

In the decade before the **Civil War**, the Vigilance Committee of Cincinnati, headed by Levi **Coffin**, and the reorganized and renamed General Vigilance Committee of Philadelphia, headed by William **Still**, and the Vigilance Committee in Boston were the best known and most effective instrumentalities of the Underground Railroad. *See also* Appendixes 1 and 2.

FURTHER READING
Perlman, Daniel. "Organizations of the Free Negro in New York City, 1800–186." *Journal of Negro History* 56, no. 3(1971): 181–197.
Siebert, Wilbur H. *The Underground Railroad from Slavery to Freedom.* 1898. Reprint, New York: Russell and Russell, 1967.
Smedley, R. C. *History of the Underground Railroad.* 1883. Reprint, New York: Arno Press, 1969.
Still, William. *The Underground Railroad.* 1872. Reprint, Chicago: Johnson, 1970.

Wadsworth, Timothy

Friend of the fugitive in Vassalboro, Maine. *See also* Farmington, Connecticut; and Appendixes 1 and 2.

Wagner, Jacob

Friend of the fugitive in **Madison, Indiana**. *See also* Appendixes 1 and 2.

Walker, Jonathan (1799–1878)

Friend of the fugitive. Jonathan Walker was born on Cape Cod, **Massachusetts**, in 1799. In his young adulthood, he captained a fishing vessel, but migrated to Florida in 1840, where he became a railroad-contractor.

Committed to the antislavery cause, in 1844, Walker aided several **fugitive slaves**

A U.S. marshal brands a hand of Jonathan Walker with the initials "SS," for slave stealer, in this 1845 engraving. (Library of Congress)

attempting to escape from Florida to the Bahamas in an open boat. However, Walker became ill and he and the freedom seekers were captured by a wrecking-sloop that bore them to Key West. Walker was sent in irons to Pensacola and imprisoned there under horrendous conditions—chained to the floor and deprived of light and proper food. When finally tried, he was convicted of aiding fugitive slaves and was fined, pilloried, and branded on his right hand with the letters "S. S." for "slave-stealer."

For the next five years, Walker lectured on the antislavery circuit and, in 1850, moved to Michigan. Walker became a famous symbol of the antislavery movement as the subject of John Greenleaf **Whittier**'s poem, "The Man with the Branded Hand"—and stated the "S.S" signified, not "slave stealer," but "Slave Savior." Walker died near Muskegon, Michigan, on May 1, 1878. *See also* Appendixes 1 and 2.

FURTHER READING
McCann, Dennis. "Abolitionist Wore His Brand with Honor." *Milwaukee Journal Sentinel,* March 21, 2000.
Walker, Jonathan. *The Branded Hand; Trial and Imprisonment of Jonathan Walker.* 1845. Reprint, New York: Arno Press, 1969.

Walls, John Freeman

Friend of the fugitive in Ontario, Canada. *See also* John Freeman Walls Cabin; and Appendixes 1 and 2.

Ward, Samuel Ringgold (1817–1866)

Fugitive slave and friend of the fugitive. Samuel Ringgold Ward was born enslaved in 1817 on Maryland's eastern shore. His father, who claimed descent from an African prince, and his mother had three children, all boys, the second of which was Ward.

In 1820, Ward escaped with his family to New Jersey and, in 1826, the family settled in New York. As a boy, Ward attended the African Free School in **New York City** and, in 1833, became a clerk of Thomas L. Jennings, an African American attorney. In 1838, Ward married Emily E. Reynolds, with whom he had four children. In 1839, he was granted his license to preach from the New York Congregational Association and, over the years, pastored several congregations, some of them entirely composed of white Americans.

Between 1838 and 1850, Ward worked for the American and New York State Anti-Slavery societies. He was a gifted orator and skilled educator, but also involved himself in antislavery politics. He joined the Liberty Party in 1840 and helped organize the Free Soil Party in 1848. He was even nominated as Liberty Party candidate for vice president of the United States. Although he was sometimes called "the Black Daniel Webster," he criticized the actual Daniel Webster sharply for supporting the **Fugitive Slave Act of 1850**.

Ward himself became involved in the rescue of a fugitive slave in 1851, after which he and his family were forced to flee to Ontario, **Canada**, to avoid arrest. While there, Ward maintained his ties to the American Anti-Slavery Society and established himself with the Anti-Slavery Society of Canada, taking a fundraising journey to Great Britain on behalf of the society in 1853. In 1855, Ward published the *Autobiography of a Fugitive Negro*, settled in Kingston, Jamaica, and served as pastor in a small Baptist church until 1860. Ward died in Jamaica in 1866. *See also* Appendixes 1 and 2.

FURTHER READING
Ward, Samuel Ringgold. *Autobiography of a Fugitive Negro: His Anti-Slavery Labours in the United States, Canada, & England*. London: John Snow, 1855.

Washington, D.C.

Washington, D. C., had one of the largest free African American populations in the nation and, although surrounded by slave states and home to some of the most successful U.S. slave traders, the District of Columbia was a promising location for the development of Underground Railroad operations. The free states, particularly **Pennsylvania**, were nearby and could be reached by a variety of modes of transportation, including railroad, road and, especially, by rivers, canals and Chesapeake Bay.

Among the more notable **friends of the fugitive** in the Washington area was Leonard Grimes, a free person of color, who worked as a hack driver and used his wagons to transport **fugitive slaves** from the city in the 1840s. Anthony Bowen, a free man of color, met fugitive slaves arriving at the District of Columbia wharf and harbored them in his home. Thomas Smallwood, formerly enslaved in Prince George's County, and the Reverend

Charles **Torrey**, a white abolitionist from Massachusetts, collaborated to assist fugitives between 1842 and 1844. In 1844, however, Torrey was arrested and jailed for assisting runaways and became a martyr to the antislavery cause after he died in prison in 1846.

William Chapman succeeded Torrey as the key Underground Railroad agent in Washington, D. C., until 1850, when he was arrested after a gun battle related to the escape of enslaved African Americans belonging to members of the U.S. Congress. Chapman's sympathizers raised $19,000 to post his bond and, once released from jail, he fled farther north to avoid future imprisonment and became a popular antislavery speaker. Further, in the **1850s**, Jacob Bigelow, an elderly white attorney, worked closely with members of the local free black community and with the **Philadelphia** Vigilance Committee to assist fugitive slaves.

Among the most important Underground Railroad stations were the **Metropolitan AME Church**, the **Mount Zion United AME Church**, and the Union Wesley Church, under the Reverend J.W. Anderson. *See also* Underground Railroad, Sites of; Vigilance Committees; and Appendixes 3 and 4.

Watkins, William

Friend of the fugitive in Baltimore, Maryland. *See also* Harper, Frances Ellen Watkins; Orchard Street Church; and Appendixes 1 and 2.

The Wayside
(Concord, Massachusetts)

Underground Railroad site recognized and documented by the National Park Service. *See also* Appendix 5.

Webb, William

Friend of the fugitive in **Detroit, Michigan**. *See also* Finney House; William Webb House; and Appendixes 1 and 2.

Webster, Delia (1817–1904)

Friend of the fugitive. Delia Webster was born in Vermont in 1817, studied briefly at **Oberlin College**, a center for antislavery activists in northern **Ohio**, and migrated to

Kentucky in 1842. By 1844, she headed the Lexington Academy, an exclusive school for young women.

In early September 1844, the Reverend Calvin **Fairbank** sought Webster's assistance after depleting his limited funds in an attempt to rescue the family of Gilson Berry, a fugitive with whom he became acquainted at Oberlin. Webster introduced Fairbank to Lewis **Hayden**, an enslaved waiter at the Phoenix Hotel who wished to escape with his wife and child.

On Saturday, September 28, 1844, Fairbank called for Webster in a hired carriage, then continued north, picking up Hayden, his wife Harriet and their son, Jo. The party then drove north along the Lexington-Maysville road and reached Washington in Mason County by four o'clock in the morning of September 29, 1844. Later that day, they drove the four additional miles to Maysville. James Helm ferried them across the **Ohio River** and they were delivered to the Reverend John **Rankin** and his famous hilltop Underground Railroad station in Ripley, Ohio. The Hayden family was then spirited north.

By the time Webster and Fairbank returned to Kentucky, news of the slave escape had already spread as far as Maysville. Suspicion soon fell on the two northerners and both were arrested en route to Lexington. The two were indicted in the Fayette Circuit Court for the crime of "aiding and enticing slaves to leave their owners"—and news of the incident and its principal figures spread across the nation. The two were tried separately and both were found guilty. Webster was sentenced to two years imprisonment, but outrage over jailing a woman outweighed outrage over "Negro stealing" and the "petticoat abolitionist" was pardoned by Governor Owsley on February 24, 1845.

Webster returned to New England after her release in 1845, but soon found her way back to Kentucky. Although stating that her "delicate and sensitive nature recoils at being thought an intruder," she purchased a 600-acre farm in Trimble County in February 1854, across from **Madison** and its long active Underground Railroad network. (*Louisville Courier*, December 27, 1851 in Hudson, 2002: 135.) Enslaved African Americans began disappearing "in considerable numbers, and in less than six weeks Miss Webster was waited upon by fifty enraged slave owners who ordered her to abandon her project and leave the State." Webster was unmoved, but was soon arrested and jailed for several weeks. She was then released, then subsequently indicted in Trimble County in June 1854, but managed to escape across the river to Madison, hotly pursued by a "posse of bloody hirelings." (Coleman, 1943: 138–139.) In the aftermath, Delia Webster's every move was monitored carefully as she traveled periodically to the North—and spoke often of "her sufferings in Kentucky." (*Louisville Courier*, October 22, 1855 in Hudson, 2002: 135.) She continued to operate her farm in Trimble County, although "from the safety of Madison and through the agency of tenants" until 1868. (Runyon, 1996: 203–204.) Although she was thought to have died in Jeffersonville, **Indiana**, in 1876, Webster actually relocated to **Iowa** and died at the home of her niece in 1904. *See also* Appendixes 1 and 2.

FURTHER READING

Coleman, J. Winston, Jr. "Delia Webster and Calvin Fairbank—Underground Railroad Agents." *Filson Club History Quarterly* 17(1943): 129–142

Hudson, J. Blaine. *Fugitive Slaves and the Underground Railroad in the Kentucky Borderland.* Jefferson, NC: McFarland, 2002.

Runyon, Randolph. *Delia Webster and the Underground Railroad.* Lexington: University Press of Kentucky, 1996.

Weeks, Israel

Friend of the fugitive. *See also* Farwell Mansion; and Appendixes 1 and 2.

Weems, Ann Maria

Fugitive slave. Ann Maria Weems was enslaved in Montgomery County, Maryland. Other members of her family gained freedom after being purchased with the help of abolitionists. Weems' owner, however, refused to sell her and, in 1855, she disguised herself as a boy, calling herself Joe Wright, and was smuggled by a friend of the fugitive to **Washington, D.C.** There, she met another traveling companion in front of the White House. Now playing the part of a servant to a professor, she traveled safely to **Philadelphia**. With the assistance William **Still** and his fellow **friends of the fugitive**, she was then spirited to New York, aided by Charles B. **Ray**, and eventually to **Canada**.

FURTHER READING
Horton, James O. *Free People of Color: Inside the African American Community*. Washington, D.C.: Smithsonian Institution Press, 1993.

Weld, Theodore Dwight (1803–1895)

Abolitionist and friend of the fugitive. Theodore Dwight Weld was born in Hampton, Connecticut, in 1803. In 1825, he entered Hamilton College in New York and was there converted to the antislavery cause. Weld studied for the ministry at Oneida Institute, and, after 1830, worked closely with Arthur and Lewis **Tappan** in the American Anti-Slavery Society.

Weld moved to Lane Seminary in **Cincinnati, Ohio**, and, in 1834, organized the famous antislavery debates that led to his dismissal. From 1836 to 1840, he worked in New York as editor of the society's publication, the *Emancipator,* and contributed antislavery articles to newspapers and periodicals. In 1838, Weld married Angelina Grimké, herself a significant figure in antislavery and other progressive reform efforts. In 1839, Weld published anonymously *American Slavery As It Is,* which influenced Harriet Beecher **Stowe** and is considered nearly as important as *Uncle Tom's Cabin* (1852).

Weld withdrew from public involvement in the antislavery struggle in the mid–1840s and established a school near Raritan, New Jersey. He returned to public affairs briefly during the **Civil War** to support the Union cause. Many historians regard Weld as the most important figure in the abolitionist movement, surpassing even Garrison, but his passion for anonymity long made him an unknown figure in American history. Weld died in 1895. *See also* Abolitionist Movement; and Appendixes 1 and 2.

FURTHER READING
Abzug, Robert H. *Passionate Liberator: Theodore Dwight Weld and the Dilemma of Reform*. New York: Oxford University Press, 1980.
Volpe, Vernon L. "Theodore Dwight Weld's Antislavery Mission in Ohio." *Ohio History* 100(1991): 5–18.

Wheeling House Hotel (Wheeling, West Virginia)

Underground Railroad site. Located at 10th and Main Streets in Wheeling, the Wheeling House Hotel harbored **fugitive slaves** escaping through the Appalachians. *See also* Harboring; Underground Railroad, Sites of; and Appendixes 3 and 4.

Whipper, William (1804–1876)

Friend of the fugitive. William Whipper was born free in Lancaster, **Pennsylvania**, in 1804. Later moving between Columbia and **Philadelphia**, Whipper amassed a sizable fortune through joint ventures with his business partner Stephen Smith. Their extensive investments included land holdings in Pennsylvania and **Canada**, lumberyards, railroad cars, and even a steam ship on Lake Erie. Many of these assets were employed directly in aiding **fugitive slaves** fleeing bondage in the South.

For several decades, Whipper also operated an active station of the Underground Railroad in Columbia. As he stated in an 1871 letter to William Still:

> I will say in conclusion that it would have been fortunate for us if Columbia, being a port of entry for flying fugitives, had been also the seat of great capitalists and freedom-loving inhabitants; but such was not the case. There was but little Anti-slavery sentiment among the whites, yet there were many strong and valiant friends among them who contributed freely; the colored population were too poor to render much aid, except in feeding and secreting strangers. I was doing a prosperous business at that time and felt it my duty to contribute liberally out of my earnings. Much as I loved Anti-slavery meetings I did not feel that I could afford to attend them, as my immediate duty was to the flying fugitive. [Still, 1872: 767.]

Between 1850 and 1855, Whipper organized and sponsored migrations from Columbia to Canada and even entertained personal plans for resettlement in Canada West. After the outbreak of the **Civil War**, he chose to remain in the United States. Whipper died in 1876. *See also* Appendixes 1 and 2.

FURTHER READING
Blockson, Charles L. *Hippocrene Guide to the Underground Railroad*. New York: Hippocrene Books, 1994.

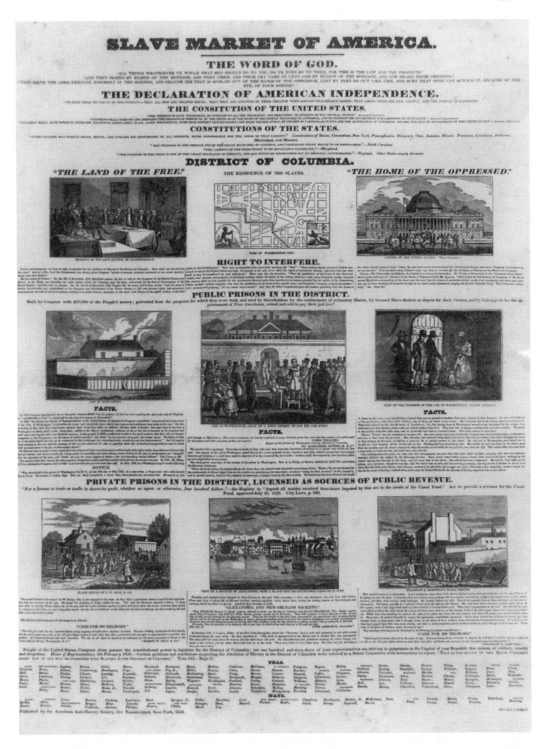

An 1836 broadside condemns the sale of slaves in Washington, D.C., and was issued by moderate abolitionists led by Theodore Dwight Weld. (Library of Congress)

Simmons, William J. *Men of Mark: Eminent, Progressive and Rising.* Cleveland, OH: George M. Rewell, 1887.

Still, William. *The Underground Railroad.* 1872. Reprint, Chicago: Johnson, 1970.

White, Addison

Fugitive slave. Addison White escaped from bondage in **Kentucky** in 1857 and was harbored near Mechanicsburg, **Ohio**, by a white friend of the fugitive, Udney H. Hyde, for several months. On May 21, 1857, White's owner, Daniel G. White — who had discovered the fugitive's hiding place through letters to his wife, a free woman of color still living in Kentucky — five Kentuckians, and Deputy U.S. Marshals B. P. Churchill and John C. Elliott, attempted to arrest Addison White under the provisions of the **Fugitive Slave Act of 1850.**

White saw the party of **slave catchers** approaching and concealed himself in the loft of Hyde's home. Marshall Elliott caught a glimpse of White climbing the ladder to the loft and followed. White was armed, fired at Elliott, and might have killed him had the bullet not ricocheted off the barrel of his shotgun. At this point, Elliott wisely retreated, leaving White in the loft.

In the midst of these events, Hyde sent his daughter to Mechanicsburg for assistance and as many as 30 heavily-armed **friends of the fugitive** soon gathered near Hyde's home to protect White. After long angry exchanges of threats, the slave-owner and the marshals left Hyde's property. Addison White was spirited to another place of refuge and a complicated and fascinating chain of events unfolded.

Having violated the Fugitive Slave Act, Hyde also went into hiding and, on May 27 the marshals returned to Mechanicsburg with a posse in search of both the fugitive and Hyde. Hyde's son, Russell, and a few of his associates confronted the officers and were arrested on the charge of obstructing justice and harboring White. When the Clark County, Ohio, Sheriff, John E. Layton, appeared with a writ for the release of Hyde and the others, Churchill and Elliott attacked and injured him. In response to this violence, Justice of the Peace J. A. Houston then ordered the arrest of the marshals on the charge of assault and battery with intent to kill, precipitating a conflict between the state and federal courts.

Churchill and Elliott were tried and released in **Cincinnati** on June 9 since, in the opinion of the presiding judge, they were acting within the provisions of the Fugitive Slave Act of 1850. The U.S. district attorney, as a demonstration of federal power, then moved to arrest and prosecute literally everyone who had aided White. At this point, Ohio Governor Salmon P. Chase brokered a compromise: $1,000 was raised by private subscription to compensate White's owner for his loss; and all parties who sought to protect White were released from jail. In the end, the Fugitive Slave Act was enforced, but Addison White remained free.

FURTHER READING

Campbell, Stanley W. *The Slave Catchers: Enforcement of the Fugitive Slave Law, 1850–1860.* Chapel Hill: University of North Carolina Press, 1968.

Prince, Benjamin Franklin. "The Rescue Case of 1857." *Ohio Archaeological and Historical Publications* no. 16 (January 1907): 293–306.

White Hall (Augusta, Kentucky)

Underground Railroad site. White Hall was the home of abolitionists and **friends of the fugitive**, Arthur Thome (1769–1855), and his son, James Armstrong Thome (1813–1873). Augusta was a central **Ohio River** border town and Arthur Thome was a slaveholder who converted to the antislavery cause and became a vocal opponent of **slavery**. As such, Thome used his home as an Underground Railroad station in slave territory — thus making White Hall one of the few Underground Railroad stations in the South.

In the 1830s, the Thome family emancipated their 15 enslaved African Americans and argued for an immediate end to slavery. For this act of conscience, they were driven from White Hall at gunpoint and forced to abandon their business interests in **Kentucky**. The Thomes moved to Athens, Missouri, and again used their home as a sanctuary for **fugitive slaves**.

James eventually relocated to Lane Seminary in **Cincinnati**, Ohio, later became vice president of the National Anti-Slavery Society, and was once forced to flee **Ohio** for a year to avoid arrest for assisting another fugitive slave from Kentucky. James Thome, credited by abolitionist Theodore Dwight Weld as "abolitionizing Ohio" once wrote: "Oh! The slave kitchens of the South are the graveyards of the mind. Every countenance of their miserable inmates is the tombstone of a buried intellect, and the soulless eye is its dreadful epitaph!" (Miller, 2003: 2.)

See also Underground Railroad, Sites of; and Appendixes 3 and 4.

FURTHER READING
Miller, Caroline. "Historic Register Nomination: White Hall/Arthur Thome." June 21, 2003.

White Horse Farm (Schuylkill Township, Pennsylvania)

Underground Railroad site recognized and documented by the National Park Service. *See also* Appendix 5.

Whittier, John Greenleaf (1807–1892)

Poet and friend of the fugitive. John Greenleaf Whittier was born December 17, 1807, in Haverhill, **Massachusetts**. Although he had little formal schooling, he developed into a fine poet and, given his Quaker background, his poetic themes brought him to the attention of the antislavery movement by 1826.

Whittier's first book, *Legends of New England in Prose and Verse,* was published in 1831 and, for the next 30 years, he produced a stream of poetry and prose, much of which concerned abolition. In 1833, Whittier published *Justice and Expedience,* urging immediate abolition. In 1836, he moved to Amesbury, Massachusetts, to work for the American Anti-Slavery Society and was an active antislavery editor until 1840, when poor health forced him to retire to his home. From there, he continued to write antislavery poetry — e.g., "The Man with the Branded Hand" (see Jonathan **Walker**) — and essays, and was even a corresponding editor of the *National Era* from 1847 to 1859. After a long and productive career, Whittier died at Hampton Falls, New Hampshire, on September 7, 1892. *See also* Abolitionist Movement; John Greenleaf Whittier House; Quakers; and Appendixes 1 and 2.

FURTHER READING
Lewis, Georgina King Stoughton. *John Greenleaf Whittier: His Life and Work.* Port Washington, NY: Kennikat Press, 1972.

Wilberforce, Canada

Fugitive slave destination. Named for William Wilberforce, leader of the British struggle against **slavery** and the **slave trade**, the Wilberforce colony in Upper **Canada** was founded in 1829 by free African Americans fleeing mob violence in **Cincinnati, Ohio**. Led by James C. Brown, an estimated 1,400 of Cincinnati's nearly 2,300 African Americans left the city after efforts to banish blacks precipitated a series of riots in June 1829. Roughly 400 reached the London District and were able to purchase land from the Canada Company. The colony faced immediate difficulties but survived until the mid–1840s. *See also* Ohio; Underground Railroad, Sites of; and Appendixes 3 and 4.

FURTHER READING
Baily, Marilyn. "From Cincinnati, Ohio to Wilberforce, Canada: A Note on Antebellum Colonization." *Journal of Negro History* 58(1973): 427–440.

Wilberforce College (Ohio)

Underground Railroad site. Early in 1856, the Methodist Episcopal Church purchased property for a college for African Americans at Tawawa Springs, near **Xenia, Ohio**. The original Wilberforce closed in 1862 and, in March 1863, Bishop Daniel A. **Payne** of the African Methodist Episcopal Church negotiated to transfer the institution and its property to the AME Church. Named in honor of the great British abolitionist, William Wilberforce, the college was newly incorporated on July 10, 1863, becoming the first African American controlled college in the United States. In 1887, the state of Ohio established a normal and industrial department at the college that evolved into its sister institution, Central State University. In 1891, Wilberforce also spawned another institution, Payne Theological Seminary.

Under the early leadership of Bishop Payne and his family, the college became an important station on the Underground Railroad in the vicinity of Xenia, Ohio. For many fugitive slaves, the region was, in fact, a destination.

FURTHER READING
Blockson, Charles L. *Hippocrene Guide to the Underground Railroad*. New York: Hippocrene Books, 1994.
Brown, Hallie Q. *Pen Pictures of Pioneers of Wilberforce*. New York: G. K. Hall, 1997.

Wild Cat

Friend of the fugitive in Florida. *See also* Black Seminoles; and Appendixes 1 and 2.

Wild Cat Manor (Dover, Delaware)

Underground Railroad site. Owned by the Hunn family, Wild Cat Manor and **Great Geneva**, a short distance away, were places of refuge for **fugitive slaves**. There, John **Hunn** worked closely with Quaker associates Thomas **Garrett** and Daniel Corbet (see **Clearfield Farm**) in the 1840s and **1850s**. This Underground Railroad station was also used by Harriett **Tubman** as she conducted runaways from Maryland to free territory. *See also* Quakers; Underground Railroad, Sites of; and Appendixes 3 and 4.

FURTHER READING
Blockson, Charles L. *Hippocrene Guide to the Underground Railroad*. New York: Hippocrene Books, 1994.
Still, William. *The Underground Railroad*. 1872. Reprint, Chicago: Johnson, 1970.

William Eberle Thompson Homesite (Bethel, Ohio)

Underground Railroad site recognized and documented by the National Park Service. *See also* Appendix 5.

William Jackson Homestead (Newton, Massachusetts)

Underground Railroad site recognized and documented by the National Park Service. *See also* Appendix 5.

William Lloyd Garrison House (Boston, Massachusetts)

Underground Railroad site recognized and documented by the National Park Service. *See also* Appendix 5.

William Still House (Philadelphia, Pennsylvania)

Underground Railroad site. Home of William **Still**, African American friend of the fugitive, once located at 224 South 12th Street in **Philadelphia**, was a significant center of Underground Railroad activity. Still estimated that 95 percent of the **fugitive slaves** passing through Philadelphia were harbored in his home for some period, however long or short. *See also* Underground Railroad, Sites of; and Appendixes 3 and 4.

William Webb House (Detroit, Michigan)

Underground Railroad site. William Webb, an African American businessman, was an abolitionist leader and a friend of the fugitive in **Detroit, Michigan**. His home served as a center of antislavery activity and as a station on the Underground Railroad. There, on March 12, 1859, Frederick **Douglass** and John **Brown** met with members of Detroit's African American community to discuss ways and means of ending **slavery**. *See also* Abolitionist Movement; Fugitive Slaves; Underground Railroad, Sites of; Underground Railroad, Stations on; and Appendixes 3 and 4.

Williams, Austin F. (1805–1885)

A friend of the fugitive, Austin F. Williams (1805–1885) was considered the leading abolitionist of Farmington, Connecticut, a major Underground Railroad junction. Williams worked as an Underground Railroad conductor and used his home as a refuge for freedom seekers. Beginning in 1839, Williams also played a central role in the *Amistad* **Affair**, and collaborated with Lewis **Tappan** of the **American Missionary Association** to arrange legal representation for the African captives. After the U. S. Supreme Court ruled, on March 9, 1841, that the Africans had been detained illegally, Williams constructed a building on his property in which many of the Africans lived until they set sail to return to Africa on November 27, 1841.

After the **Civil War**, Williams was appointed director of the Freedman's Bureau of New England and New York, and found housing and job opportunities for freed African Americans. He died in 1885.

See also Austin F. Williams House; Underground Railroad, Sites of; and Appendixes 3 and 4.

Williams House (Augusta, Maine)

The Williams family of Augusta was committed to the antislavery. From their 14-room home, located near the Kennebec River, they and their neighbors assisted **fugitive slaves** seeking to reach and board vessels bound for eastern **Canada**. *See also* Underground Railroad, Sites of; and Appendixes 3 and 4.

Wilson Bruce Evans House (Oberlin, Ohio)

Underground Railroad site recognized and documented by the National Park Service. *See also* Appendix 5.

Wing, Asa (1815–1854)

Friend of the fugitive in Parish, New York. *See also* Asa Wing House.

Woodruff, Charles

Fugitive slave. *See also* Bell-Wright Affair.

Wright, Oswell

Friend of the fugitive in Corydon, **Indiana**. *See also* Bell-Wright Affair; and Appendixes 1 and 2.

Wright, William

Friend of the fugitive in Lancaster County, **Pennsylvania**. *See also* Wright's Ferry Mansion; and Appendixes 1 and 2.

Wright's Ferry Mansion (Lancaster County, Pennsylvania)

Underground Railroad site. Beginning in 1804, William Wright played a major role in assisting **fugitive slaves** through Lancaster County, **Pennsylvania**. Wright worked closely with his sister, Hannah Gibbons, and her husband, Daniel. He also coordinated his efforts with neighboring African American **friends of the fugitive**, such as Stephen Smith and William **Whipper**. Wright harbored fugitives in his home, Wright's Ferry Mansion, built in 1738. *See also* Harboring; Underground Railroad, Sites of; and Appendixes 3 and 4.

FURTHER READING

Blockson, Charles L. *Hippocrene Guide to the Underground Railroad.* New York: Hippocrene Books, 1994.

Still, William. *The Underground Railroad.* 1872. Reprint, Chicago: Johnson, 1970.

Xenia, Ohio

Important Underground Railroad center in central **Ohio**. One of the most famous Underground Railroad routes in central Ohio followed an Indian trail known as the Bullskin Trace — extending from the **Ohio River** to Lake Erie — passing near Xenia and **Wilberforce College**. Antislavery sentiment was strong in this section of south central Ohio and numerous Xenia residents used their homes, farmsteads and nearby caves as Underground Railroad stations. Before the passage of the **Fugitive Slave Act of 1850**, freedom seekers not only found assistance in these Ohio communities, but often settled there themselves. *See also* Underground Railroad, Sites of; and Appendixes 3 and 4.

FURTHER READING

Blockson, Charles L. *Hippocrene Guide to the Underground Railroad.* New York: Hippocrene Books, 1994.

Siebert, Wilbur H. *The Underground Railroad from Slavery to Freedom.* 1898. Reprint, New York: Russell and Russell, 1967.

York

Explorer and possible fugitive slave. York accompanied William Clark, the younger brother of George Rogers Clark, on the Lewis and Clark Expedition (1804–1806) to explore the northwestern reaches of the Louisiana Purchase. As the only African American member of this historic adventure, York became one of the most famous African Americans in early American history.

Because York was William Clark's "body servant" and Clark referred to their being childhood playmates, it is highly probable that York was born between 1770, when Clark was born, and 1775. When Clark's family moved from Virginia to Jefferson County (surrounding **Louisville**), **Kentucky** in 1784, they brought their enslaved African Americans, including York, his parents and his sister. When Clark's parents died in 1799, he inherited a

"Negro man named York," along with York's parents and sister, Juba.

In late 1802 or early 1803, Clark moved to Clarksville and there, in July 1803, received his invitation from Meriwether Lewis to share leadership of the proposed expedition to the West. Because of his size and strength (York was described as being "big and black as a bear"), Clark decided to include York in the party. (Betts, 1985: 102–103.) The group left Louisville on October 26, 1803 and reached the Wood River (in modern-day **Illinois**) on December 12, recruiting additional volunteers en route. After constructing and then wintering at Camp Wood, the party started up the Missouri River on May 14, 1804. By this time, if not before, York no longer functioned solely as Clark's (and, probably, Lewis's) "body servant," but had begun to share the same status and responsibilities assigned to other members of the expedition.

As the expedition moved into the Great Plains, vast herds of buffalo became an awesome spectacle and a welcome source of food, and York was one of the men regularly deputized to hunt, which meant that he was allowed to bear and use arms. He performed physical labor, was present at meetings with the Native Americans of the Lower Missouri (who had seen African Americans before) and, in general, became a center of attention when the party reached the Dakotas. There, to the **Native Americans** who had never beheld a black man, York was called "the big medicine" and the Native Americans "... all flocked around him and examined him from top to toe." (Thwaites, 1904) York, for his part, joked with them and performed feats of strength and even danced — and it became readily apparent to Lewis and Clark that York was not only a servant and laborer, but an important asset in their dealings with the Native Americans of the Great Plains.

This and still another important indication of how the Native Americans perceived York were demonstrated on October 10, 1804 while visiting the Arikara Sioux:

York was a sensation. His size was impressive enough, but the Arikaras had never seen a black man and couldn't make out if he was man, beast or spirit being. York played with the children, roaring at them, chasing them between lodges.

One warrior invited York to his lodge, offered him his wife, and guarded the entrance during the act. [Ambrose, 1996: 180.]

When the expedition finally reached the Pacific Ocean in November 1805, York became the first person of African descent to cross the North American continent (north of **Mexico**). After returning to St. Louis in 1806, York was lionized along with his comrades. However, while Lewis and Clark received prestigious government appointments and each of the other men received double pay and a 320-acre land grant for his services, York (like the young Native American woman, Sacagewea, who left the expedition with her husband and child in the Dakotas) received nothing — not even his freedom.

In 1807, Lewis was appointed governor of the Territory of Upper Louisiana and Clark was appointed brigadier general of the Louisiana territorial militia and superintendent of Indian affairs. Clark's new responsibilities required that he relocate to St. Louis. Because Clark did not free York after the expedition, York accompanied him to St. Louis and managed his household for the next several years.

From letters that Clark wrote to his brother, Jonathan, it becomes clear that York pressed Clark for his freedom upon his return from the expedition — believing he had earned it and, possibly, believing that Clark had promised to emancipate him in recognition of his services. The fact that York had a "wife" who was enslaved in Louisville was also introduced in this correspondence. Although questions regarding whether York was "married" (since slaves could not marry legally) before or after the expedition, or whether he had any children, cannot be answered, it is likely that his marriage predated the journey and that he left children as well as his wife behind. Consequently, York not only wanted his freedom, but wanted his family as well. By 1808, York's persistent demands for freedom had caused a deep and bitter breach in his relationship with Clark. This breach remained and was noted in the last reference to York in 1811.

In 1832, the famous author Washington Irving asked Clark what happened to York and reported that Clark indicated that at some point between 1811 and about 1830, he emancipated

York and gave York the means with which to support himself as a drayman or teamster — presumably between Nashville, **Tennessee**, and Richmond, Kentucky. According to Clark, York failed due to his own "bad habits," returned to (domestic) service, ultimately found freedom distasteful and died of cholera attempting to return to Clark in St. Louis. Interestingly, there is no objective evidence to support Clark's statement: no record that Clark emancipated York and, if free when he died, no record of York's death.

An alternative account of York's fate was offered by Zenas Leonard, a fur-trapper who, in 1832, met an "old Negro" in a Crow village in northern Wyoming. Before departing, the "old Negro" told his story, stating that:

> ...he first came to this country with Lewis and Clark — with whom he also returned to the state of Missouri, and in a few years returned again with a Mr. Mackinney, a trader on the Missouri river, and has remained here ever since, which is about ten or twelve years ... He has rose to be quite a considerable character, or chief, in their village... [Evers, 1959: 41–42].

Leonard returned in 1834 and found the old black man still living with the Crows in "... perfect peace and satisfaction." No one knows the identity of this aged African American whose story is too eerily consistent with reasonably well-established facts of York's life after the Lewis and Clark expedition to be dismissed lightly.

York may have lived and died in his later years as Clark stated. However, in the absence of conclusive evidence to the contrary, it is plausible that he fled **slavery** after his breach with Clark — and probably after his wife was sold away or died — and that he returned to the only land in which he had ever known the taste of freedom.

FURTHER READING

Ambrose, Stephen E. *Undaunted Courage: Meriwether Lewis, Thomas Jefferson, and the Opening of the American West.* New York: Simon and Schuster, 1996.

Betts, Robert B. *In Search of York: The Slave Who Went to the Pacific with Lewis and Clark.* Boulder, CO: Colorado Associated University Press, 1985.

Curtis, K. D. "York, the Slave Explorer." *Negro Digest* (1962): 10–15.

Evers, J. C. *Adventures of Zenas Leonard, Fur Trader.* Norman, OK: University of Oklahoma Press, 1959.

Holmberg, James J. "'I Wish You to See and Know All': The Recently Discovered Letters of William Clark to Jonathan Clark." *We Proceeded On* 4(1992): 7–9.

Hudson, J. Blaine. "Slavery in Early Louisville and Jefferson County, Kentucky, 1780–1812." *Filson History Quarterly* 73, no. 3(1999): 249–283.

Polos, Nicholas C. "Explorer with Lewis and Clark." *Negro History Bulletin* 45(1982): 90–96.

Thwaites, R. G., ed. *Original Journals of the Lewis and Clark Expedition, 1804-1806.* 8 vols. New York: Dodd, Mead and Co., 1904–1905.

Young, Joshua (b. 1823)

Friend of the fugitive. Born in 1823, the Reverend Joshua Young was a graduate of Bowdoin College and, while living in **Boston**, harbored **fugitive slaves**. When he moved to Burlington, Vermont, he maintained his ties to the Underground Railroad, giving freedom seekers refuge in his barn.

In December 1859, Young preached the sermon at the funeral of John **Brown** at North Elba, New York, stating simply:

> Almighty and most merciful God! We lift our souls unto thee, and bow our hearts to the unutterable emotions of his impressive hour. O God, Thou alone art our sufficient help. Open Thou our lips and our mouth shall show forth thy praise. Thou art speaking unto us; in those grand and majestic scenes of nature, so in the great and solemn circumstances which have brought us together. Our souls are filled with awe and are subdued to silence, as we think of the great, reverential, heroic soul, whose mortal remains we are now to commit to the earth, "dust to dust," while his spirit dwells with God who gave it, and his memory is enshrined in every pure and holy heart. At his open grave, as standing by the altar of Christ, the divinest friend and Savior of Man, may we consecrate ourselves anew to the work of Truth, Righteousness and Love, forevermore to sympathize with the outcast and the oppressed, with the humble and the least of our suffering fellow-men.
>
> We pray for these afflicted ones — this sadly bereaved and afflicted family. O! God, cause the oppressed to go free; break any yoke and prostrate the pride and prejudice that dare to lift themselves up; and O! hasten on the day when no more wrong or injustice shall be done in the earth; when all men shall love one another with pure hearts, fervently, and love with all their

strength; which we ask in the name and as the disciples of Jesus Christ. Amen. [*New York Daily Tribune*, December 12, 1859.]

See also Harboring; and Appendixes 1 and 2.

FURTHER READING
Blockson, Charles L. *Hippocrene Guide to the Underground Railroad.* New York: Hippocrene Books, 1994.
"Spontaneous Prayer of the Reverend Young." *New York Daily Tribune*, December 12, 1859.

Zebulon Thomas House (Downington, Pennsylvania)

Underground Railroad site. Constructed in 1800, the home of Zebulon Thomas was a sanctuary for **fugitive slaves**. Freedom seekers were concealed by moving them through a tunnel that connected the house to a nearby structure also owned by Thomas. *See also* Underground Railroad, Sites of; and Appendixes 3 and 4.

Zion Baptist Church (Sandusky, Ohio)

Underground Railroad site. African Americans in Sandusky, **Ohio** had held reli-gious meetings for several years before, in 1849 — coincident with the repeal of the Ohio Black Laws — they were able to organize a formal church. The Zion Baptist Church was founded and supported largely by **fugitive slaves** living in Sandusky. Renamed the First Regular Anti-Slavery Baptist Church, the congregation harbored fugitive slaves and assisted them in arranging passage across Lake Erie to **Canada** West. Since the 1920s, the church has been known as the Second Baptist Church. *See also* Harboring; Underground Railroad, Sites of; and Appendixes 3 and 4.

Zion Baptist Missionary Church (Springfield, Illinois)

Underground Railroad site. The Zion Baptist Missionary Church was a station on the Underground Railroad. Among its most noteworthy members was Thomas Jefferson **Houston**, one of the African American founders of the church and himself a conductor on the Underground Railroad. *See also* Underground Railroad, Sites of; and Appendixes 3 and 4.

Appendix 1:
Selected Friends of the Fugitive
by Last Name

(Almost all of the individuals listed below have entries under their names in the encyclopedia's alphabetical section.)

Name, Location

Allen, Richard*, Philadelphia, PA
Alston, John, Odessa, DE
Anderson, Elijah, Madison, IN
Anderson, William J., Hanover County, VA
Anthony, Susan B., Rochester, NY
Ashley, James M. , Greenupsburg, KY
Barker, David, Niagara Falls, NY
Barker, Vania, Niagara Falls, NY
Baxter, James, Madison, IN
Beckley, Guy , Ann Arbor, MI
Beecher, Henry Ward, Brooklyn, NY
Bell, Charles, Brandenburg, KY
Bell, David, Brandenburg, KY
Benedict, Reuben, Marengo, OH
Bibb, Henry, Canada
Bigelow, Jacob, Washington, D.C.
Booth, Griffith, Madison, IN
Booth, Sherman, Wisconsin
Boulwar, John, Nebraska City, NE
Bowditch, William Ingersoll, Brookline, MA
Bowen, Anthony, Washington, D.C.
Brown, James, Wilberforce (Canada)
Brown, John, New York
Brown, Moses, Providence, RI
Brown, Thomas, Kentucky
Brown, William Wells, Boston, MA
Buckout, Abram , Oswego, NY
Burleigh, C. C., Florence, MA
Burris, Samuel , Philadelphia, PA
Bushnell, Simeon, Oberlin, OH
Butler, Benjamin F., Massachusetts

Name, Location

Cain, John, Louisville, KY
Carr, John, Madison, IN
Carter, John, Madison, IN
Cary, Mary Ann Shadd, Delaware; Canada
Chace, Elizabeth Buffum, Central Falls, RI
Chapman, William, Washington, D.C.
Cheney, Moses, Peterborough, NH
Cheney, Oren Burbank, Peterborough, NH
Chester, Thomas Morris, Harrisburg, PA
Clark, Starr , Mexico, NY
Clarke, Edwin , Oswego, NY
Clemens, James, Greenville, OH
Clemens, Joseph and Sophia , Greenville, OH
Coffin, Levi, Fountain City, IN; Cincinnati, OH
Coffin, Vestal, Guilford, NC
Corbet, Daniel, Smyrna, DE
Cowles, Horace, Farmington, CT
Crosby, William, Madison, IN
Cunningham, James, Louisville, KY
DeBaptiste, George, Madison, IN; Detroit, MI
Delany, Martin Robinson, Pittsburgh, PA
Dickson, Moses, Cincinnati, OH; St. Louis, MO
Ditcher (Dicher), James (Jack), Lawrence County, OH
Douglas, H. Ford, Cleveland, OH
Douglass, Frederick Augustus Bailey, Rochester, NY; Washington, D.C.
Downing, George T., Newport, RI
Doyle, Edward James "Patrick", Lexington, KY

Name, Location

Drayton, Daniel, Cumberland County, NJ
Dutton, Samuel W., New Haven, CT
Dyer, Edward Galusha, Wisconsin
Edwards, John B. , Oswego, NY
Eells, Richard, Quincy, IL
Emerson, Ralph Waldo, Concord, MA
Evans, George, Madison, IN
Evans, Henry, Oberlin, OH
Evans, Wilson Bruce, Oberlin, OH
Fairbank, The Reverend Calvin, New York
Fee, John Gregg, Berea, KY
Ferguson, Joseph, Detroit, MI
Finney, Seymour, Detroit, MI
Fitch, The Reverend James A., Oberlin, OH
Ford, Barney Launcelot , Chicago, IL
Foster, Abigail Kelley, Worcester, MA
Foster, Amanda, Tarrytown, NY
Foster, Stephen Symonds, Worcester, MA
Garnet, Henry Highland, Washington, D.C.
Garrett, Thomas, Delaware County, PA
Garrison, William Lloyd, Boston, MA
Gibbons, Daniel, Lancaster County, PA
Gibbons, Hannah, Lancaster County, PA
Gibbs, Mifflin Wistar, Philadelphia, PA
Giddings, Joshua Reed, Ashtabula County, OH
Goodnow, Lyman, Wisconsin
Goodrich, Joseph, Wisconsin
Goodridge, William C., York, PA; Minneapolis, MN
Goodwin, Abigail and Elizabeth, Salem, NJ
Grant, Tudor, Oswego, NY
Grimes, Jonathan, Mountain Lakes, NJ
Grimes, Leonard A., Washington, D.C.; Boston, MA
Grinnell, Josiah Bushnell, Grinnell, IA
Haines, Jonathan Ridgeway, Alliance. OH
Hanby, Benjamin R., Westerville, OH
Hanby, William, Westerville, OH
Hanover, John T. , Indiana
Harper, Frances Ellen Watkins, Philadelphia, PA; Ohio
Harris, Catherine, Jamestown, NY
Harris, Chapman, Madison, IN
Haviland, Laura S., Raisin, MI; Canada
Hayden, Lewis, Lexington, KY
Hayes, William, Randolph County, IL
Haynes, James, New Albany, IN
Henderson, Richard, Meadville, PA
Henson, Josiah, Canada
Higginson, The Reverend Thomas, Boston, MA
Hillyer, Elisha, Louisville, KY
Hise, Daniel Howell, Salem, OH
Hitchcock, George B., Lewis, IA
Hopper, Isaac T., Philadelphia, PA; New York, NY

Name, Location

Horse, John, Florida
Hossack, John, Ottawa, IL
Houston, Thomas Jefferson, Springfield, IL
Hoyt, Benjamin, Madison, IN
Hubbard, William, Ashtabula, OH
Huber, Charles B. "Boss", Williamsburg, OH
Hudson, John W., Sardinia, OH
Hunn, John, Odessa, DE
Hunn, Jonathan, Dover, DE
Hurlburt, Lyman, Farmington, CT
Hussey, Erastus, Battle Creek, MI
Hyde, Udney, Mechanicsburg, OH
Jackson, Francis, Newton, MA
Jackson, William, Newton, MA
James, The Reverend Thomas, Rochester, NY; Louisville, KY
Jeter, William, Louisville, KY
Johnson, Elizabeth, Philadelphia, PA
Johnson, Ellwood, Philadelphia, PA
Johnson, Israel, Philadelphia, PA
Johnson, Nathan and Mary, New Bedford, MA
Johnson, Rowland, Philadelphia, PA
Johnson, Sarah, Philadelphia, PA
Johnson, William H., Richmond, VA
Jones, John, Chicago, IL
Jordan, James Cunningham, West Des Moines, IA
King, The Reverend William, Buxton, Ontario, Canada
Knight, John, Louisville, KY
Lambert, William, Detroit, MI
Lane, Lunsford, Massachusetts
Langley, Loudon S., Hinesburg, VT
Langston, John Mercer, Oberlin and Cincinnati, OH
LeMoyne, Francis Julius, Washington, PA
Lewelling, Henderson, Salem, IA
Lewis, Elijah, Farmington, CT
Lewis, Elizabeth, Kimberton, PA
Lewis, Graceanna, Kimberton, PA
Lewis, Mariann, Kimberton, PA
Loguen, Jermain W., Syracuse, NY
Long, John C., Louisville, KY
Lott, John, Madison, IN
Lovejoy, Elijah P., Alton, IL
Lovejoy, Owen, Princeton, IL
Lovell, Lucy Buffum, Rhode Island
Lundy, Benjamin, Pennsylvania; various
Lusk, Dr. Mary, Salem, IN
Marks, Matthias, Salem, IN
Mattauer, John, Richmond, VA
May, Samuel J., Syracuse, NY
McClew, Charles and Libby, Burt, NY
McKim, James Miller, Philadelphia, PA
Meachum, Mary, St. Louis, MO

Name, Location

Miller, Jonathan P. , Montpelier, VT
Monroe, William, Detroit, MI
Morris, Shelton, Louisville, KY; Cincinnati, OH
Mott, Peter, Lawnside, NJ
Murray, Samuel, Reading, PA
Nell, William Cooper, Boston, MA
O'Neil, Joseph, Madison, IN
Osceola, Florida
Painter, H. F., Clarksville, TN
Palm, Margaret "Mag" (Maggie Bluecoat), Gettysburg, PA
Parker, John, Ripley, OH
Parker, William, Christiana, PA
Paxton, James, Washington, KY
Payne, Daniel Alexander, Wilberforce, OH
Pearson, Benjamin, Keosauqua, IA
Pease, Leavitt Thaxter, Williamsburg, OH
Peck, The Reverend Henry, Oberlin, OH
Pennington, James W. C., New York, NY
Pennock, Abraham L., Upper Darby Township, PA
Pennypacker, Elijah, Schuylkill Township, PA
Perry, Charles, Westerly, RI
Philbrick, Samuel, Brookline, MA
Phillips, Wendell, Boston, MA
Pinkerton, Alan, Chicago, IL
Pleasant, Mary, San Francisco, CA
Purvis, Robert, Philadelphia, PA
Quinn, William Paul, Richmond, IN
Rankin, The Reverend John, Ripley, OH
Ray, Charles B., New York, NY
Reed, Isaiah, Salem, IN
Remond, Charles Lenox, Boston, MA
Revels, Hiram Rhoades, Mississippi
Rice, Isaac, Newport, RI
Richards, John, Detroit, MI
Robinson, Rowland Thomas, Ferrisburg, VT
Roots, B. G., Tamaroa, Illinois
Ross, Alexander M., Detroit, MI; Canada
Ross, Jacob, Reading, PA
Ruggles, David, New York, NY
Rutter, Thomas, Pine Forge, PA
Ryker, Will, Madison, IN
Sanderson, J. B., San Francisco, CA
Sawyer, Moses, Weare, NH
Sering, John, Madison, IN
Sims, Marcus, Williamsburg, OH
Sloane, Rush R., Sandusky, OH
Smallwood, Thomas, Washington, D.C.

Name, Location

Smith, Charles, Oswego, NY
Smith, Gerrit, Peterboro, NY
Smith, James Caesar Anthony, Richmond, VA
Smith, Samuel A. , Richmond, VA
Spradling, Washington, Sr., Louisville, KY
Sprinkle, J. R., Louisville, KY
Stevens, Thaddeus, Lancaster, PA
Steward, Austin, Rochester, NY; Canada
Steward, James, Madison, IN
Still, William, Philadelphia, PA
Stowe, Harriet Beecher, Ohio; Maine, Connecticut
Strauther, Samuel, Battle Creek, MI
Sumner, Charles, Boston, MA
Swisshelm, Jane C., Pennsylvania; Minnesota
Tallman, William M., Janesville, WI
Tappan, Arthur, New York, NY
Tappan, Lewis, New York, NY
Tatum, William (aka John Jones), Louisville, KY
Thomas, Nathan, Mt. Pleasant, OH
Thome, Arthur, Augusta, KY
Thome, James, Augusta, KY
Thompson, William Eberle, Bethel, Ohio
Thoreau, Henry David, Concord, MA
Thurman, Fountain, Madison, IN
Todd, John, Madison, IN
Torrey, Charles, Washington, D.C.
Trueblood, James ("Little Jimmy"), Salem, IN
Trueblood, Thomas, Salem, IN
Truth, Sojourner, Washington, D.C.; Michigan
Tubman, Harriet, Auburn, NY
Vickers, John, Lionville, PA
Wadsworth, Timothy, Vassalboro, ME
Wagner, Jacob, Madison, IN
Walker, Jonathan, Massachusetts; Michigan
Walls, John Freeman, Ontario, Canada
Ward, Samuel Ringgold, New York
Watkins, William, Baltimore, MD
Webb, William, Detroit, MI
Webster, Delia, Kentucky; Indiana
Weld, Theodore Dwight, Raritan, NJ
Whipper, William, Philadelphia, PA
Whittier, John Greenleaf, Danver, MA
Wild Cat, Florida
Williams, Austin F., Farmington, CT
Wing, Asa , Parish, NY
Wright, Oswell, Corydon, IN
Wright, William, Lancaster County, PA
Young, Joshua, Burlington, VT

Appendix 2:
Selected Friends of the Fugitive
by State (and Canada)

(Almost all of the men and women listed here have entries under their names in the encyclopedia's alphabetical section.)

California
Mary Pleasant (San Francisco)
J.B. Sanderson (San Francisco)

Canada
Henry Bibb
James Brown (Wilberforce)
Mary Ann Shadd Cary
Laura S. Haviland
Josiah Henson
The Reverend William King (Buxton, Ontario)
Alexander M. Ross
Austin Steward
John Freeman Walls (Ontario)

Connecticut
Horace Cowles (Farmington)
Samuel W. Dutton (New Haven)
Lyman Hurlburt (Farmington)
Elijah Lewis (Farmington)
Harriet Beecher Stowe
Austin F. Williams (Farmington)

Delaware
John Alston (Odessa)
Mary Ann Shadd Cary
Daniel Corbet (Smyrna)
John Hunn (Odessa)
Jonathan Hunn (Dover)

District of Columbia
Jacob Bigelow (Washington)
Anthony Bowen (Washington)
William Chapman (Washington)
Frederick Augustus Bailey Douglass (Washington)

Henry Highland Garnet (Washington)
Leonard A. Grimes (Washington)
Thomas Smallwood (Washington)
Charles Torrey (Washington)
Sojourner Truth (Washington)

Florida
John Horse
Osceola
Wild Cat

Illinois
Richard Eells (Quincy)
Barney Launcelot Ford (Chicago)
William Hayes (Randolph County)
John Hossack (Ottawa)
Thomas Jefferson Houston (Springfield)
John Jones (Chicago)
Elijah P. Lovejoy (Alton)
Owen Lovejoy (Princeton)
Alan Pinkerton (Chicago)
B. G. Roots (Tamaroa)

Indiana
Elijah Anderson (Madison)
James Baxter (Madison)
Griffith Booth (Madison)
John Carr (Madison)
John Carter (Madison)
Levi Coffin (Fountain City)
William Crosby (Madison)
George DeBaptiste (Madison)
George Evans (Madison)
John T. Hanover
Chapman Harris (Madison)

James Haynes (New Albany)
Benjamin Hoyt (Madison)
Dr. Mary Lusk (Salem)
Matthias Marks (Salem)
Joseph O'Neil (Madison)
William Paul Quinn (Richmond)
Isaiah Reed (Salem)
Will Ryker (Madison)
John Sering (Madison)
James Steward (Madison)
Fountain Thurman (Madison)
John Todd (Madison)
James "Little Jimmy" Trueblood (Salem)
Thomas Trueblood (Salem)
Jacob Wagner (Madison)
Delia Webster
Oswell Wright (Corydon)

Iowa
Josiah Bushnell Grinnell (Grinnell)
George B. Hitchcock (Lewis)
James Cunningham Jordan (West Des Moines)
Henderson Lewelling (Salem)
Benjamin Pearson (Keosauqua)

Kentucky
James M. Ashley (Greenupsburg)
Charles Bell (Brandenburg)
David Bell (Brandenburg)
Thomas Brown
John Cain (Louisville)
James Cunningham (Louisville)
Edward James "Patrick" Doyle (Lexington)
John Gregg Fee (Berea)
Lewis Hayden (Lexington)
Elisha Hillyer (Louisville)
The Reverend Thomas James (Louisville)
William Jeter (Louisville)
John Knight (Louisville)
John C. Long (Louisville)
Shelton Morris (Louisville)
James Paxton (Washington)
Washington Spradling, Sr. (Louisville)
J.R. Sprinkle (Louisville)
William Tatum (aka John Jones) (Louisville)
Arthur Thome (Augusta)
James Thome (Augusta)
Delia Webster

Maine
Harriet Beecher Stowe
Timothy Wadsworth (Vassalboro)

Maryland
William Watkins (Baltimore)

Massachusetts
William Ingersoll Bowditch (Brookline)
William Wells Brown (Boston)

C.C. Burleigh (Florence)
Benjamin F. Butler
Ralph Waldo Emerson (Concord)
Abigail Kelley Foster
Stephen Symonds Foster (Worcester)
William Lloyd Garrison (Boston)
Leonard A. Grimes (Boston)
The Reverend Thomas Higginson (Boston)
Francis Jackson (Newton)
William Jackson (Newton)
Mary Johnson (New Bedford)
Nathan Johnson (New Bedford)
Lunsford Lane
William Cooper Nell (Boston)
Samuel Philbrick (Brookline)
Wendell Phillips (Boston)
Charles Lenox Remond (Boston)
Charles Sumner (Boston)
Henry David Thoreau (Concord)
Jonathan Walker
John Greenleaf Whittier (Danvers)

Michigan
Guy Beckley (Ann Arbor)
George DeBaptiste (Detroit)
Joseph Ferguson (Detroit)
Seymour Finney (Detroit)
Laura S. Haviland (Raisin)
Erastus Hussey (Battle Creek)
William Lambert (Detroit)
William Monroe (Detroit)
John Richards (Detroit)
Alexander M. Ross (Detroit)
Samuel Strauther (Battle Creek)
Sojourner Truth
Jonathan Walker
William Webb (Detroit)

Minnesota
William C. Goodridge (Minneapolis)
Jane C. Swisshelm

Mississippi
Hiram Rhoades Revels

Missouri
Moses Dickson (St. Louis)
Mary Meachum (St. Louis)

Nebraska
John Boulwar (Nebraska City)

New Hampshire
Moses Cheney (Peterborough)
Oren Burbank Cheney (Peterborough)
Moses Sawyer (Weare)

New Jersey
Daniel Drayton (Cumberland County)
Abigail Goodwin (Salem)

Elizabeth Goodwin (Salem)
John Grimes (Mountain Lake)
Peter Mott (Lawnside)
Theodore Dwight Weld (Raritan)

New York
Susan B. Anthony (Rochester)
David Barker (Niagara Falls)
Vania Barker (Niagara Falls)
Henry Ward Beecher (Brooklyn)
John Brown (New York City)
Abram Buckout (Oswego)
Starr Clark (Mexico, NY)
Edwin Clarke (Oswego)
Frederick Augustus Bailey Douglass
    (Rochester)
John B. Edwards (New York)
The Reverend Calvin Fairbank (New York City)
Amanda Foster (Tarrytown)
Catherine Harris (Jamestown)
Isaac T. Hopper (New York City)
The Reverend Thomas James (Rochester)
Jermain W. Loguen (Syracuse)
Samuel J. May (Syracuse)
Charles and Libby McClew (Burt)
James W.C. Pennington (New York City)
Charles B. Ray (New York City)
David Ruggles (New York City)
Charles Smith (Oswego)
Gerrit Smith (Peterboro)
Austin Steward (Rochester)
Arthur Tappan (New York City)
Lewis Tappan (New York City)
Harriet Tubman (Auburn)
Samuel Ringgold Ward (New York City)
Asa Wing (Parish)

North Carolina
Vestal Coffin (Guilford)

Ohio
Reuben Benedict (Marengo)
Simeon Bushnell (Oberlin)
James Clemens (Greenville)
Joseph Clemens (Greenville)
Sophia Clemens (Greenville)
Levi Coffin (Cincinnati)
Moses Dickson (Cincinnati)
James (Jack) Ditcher (Dicher) (Lawrence
    County)
H. Ford Douglas (Cleveland)
Henry Evans (Oberlin)
Wilson Bruce Evans (Oberlin)
The Reverend James A. Fitch (Oberlin)
Joshua Reed Giddings (Ashtabula County)
Jonathan Ridgeway Haines (Alliance)
Benjamin R. Hanby (Westerville)
William Hanby (Westerville)

Frances Ellen Watkins Harper
Daniel Howell Hise (Salem)
William Hubbard (Ashtabula)
Charles B. "Boss" Huber (Williamsburg)
John W. Hudson (Sardinia)
Udney Hyde (Mechanicburg)
John Mercer Langston (Cincinnati, Oberlin)
Shelton Morris (Cincinnati)
John Parker (Ripley)
Daniel Alexander Payne (Wilberforce)
Dr. Leavitt Thaxter Pease (Williamsburg)
The Reverend Henry Peck (Oberlin)
The Reverend John Rankin (Ripley)
Marcus Sims (Williamsburg)
Rush R. Sloane (Sandusky)
Harriet Beecher Stowe
Nathan Thomas (Mt. Pleasant)
William Eberle Thompson (Bethel)

Pennsylvania
Richard Allen (Philadelphia)
Samuel Burris (Philadelphia)
Thomas Morris Chester (Harrisburg)
Martin Robinson Delany (Pittsburgh)
Thomas Garrett (Delaware County)
Daniel Gibbons (Lancaster County)
Hannah Gibbons (Lancaster County)
Mifflin Wistar Gibbs (Philadelphia)
William C. Goodridge (York)
Frances Ellen Watkins Harper (Philadelphia)
Richard Henderson (Meadville)
Isaac T. Hopper (Philadelphia)
Elizabeth Johnson (Philadelphia)
Ellwood Johnson (Philadelphia)
Israel Johnson (Philadelphia)
Rowland Johnson (Philadelphia)
Sarah Johnson (Philadelphia)
Francis Julius LeMoyne (Washington)
Elizabeth Lewis (Kimberton)
Graceanna Lewis (Kimberton)
Mariann Lewis (Kimberton)
Benjamin Lundy
James Miller McKim (Philadelphia)
Peter Mott (Philadelphia)
Samuel Murray (Reading)
Margaret "Mag" (Maggie Bluecoat) Palm
    (Gettysburg)
William Parker (Christiana)
Abraham L. Pennock (Upper Darby Township)
Elijah Pennypacker (Schuylkill Township)
Robert Purvis (Philadelphia)
Jacob Ross (Reading)
Thomas Rutter (Pine Forge)
Thaddeus Stevens (Lancaster)
William Still (Philadelphia)
Jane C. Swisshelm
John Vickers (Lionville)

William Whipper (Philadelphia)
William Wright (Lancaster County)

Rhode Island
Moses Brown (Providence)
Elizabeth Buffum Chace (Central Falls)
George T. Downing (Newport)
Lucy Buffum Lovell
Charles Perry (Westerly)
Isaac Rice (Newport)

Tennessee
H.F. Painter (Clarksville)

Vermont
Loudon S. Langley (Hinesburg)
Jonathan P. Miller (Montpelier)

Rowland Thomas Robinson (Ferrisburg)
Joshua Young (Burlington)

Virginia
William J. Anderson (Hanover County)
William H. Johnson (Richmond)
John Mattauer (Richmond)
James Caesar Anthony Smith (Richmond)
Samuel A. Smith (Richmond)

Wisconsin
Sherman Booth
Edward Galusha Dyer
Lyman Goodnow
Joseph Goodrich
William M. Tallman (Janesville)

Appendix 3:
Selected Underground Railroad Sites by Site Name

(Sites marked with asterisks are described in detail in Appendix 5. Sites marked with daggers have more complete entries in the encyclopedia's main alphabetical section.)

Name, Location

The African Episcopal Church†, Edgar, Canada
African Meeting House†, Boston, MA
African Meeting House†, Nantucket, MA
African Union Methodist Church†, Oxford, PA
Allen B. Mayhew Cabin†, Nebraska City, NE
Appoquinimink Friends Meeting House*, Odessa, DE
Asa Wing House*, Parish, New York
Austin F. Williams House*, Farmington, CT
Barney L. Ford Building*, Denver, CO
Berea College†, Berea, KY
Bethel AME Church*, Greenwich Township, NJ
Bethel AME Church*, Indianapolis, IN
Bethel AME Church†, Providence, RI
Bethel AME Church*, Reading, Pennsylvania
Boston African American National Historic Site*, Boston, MA
Bowditch House*, Brookline, Massachusetts
Bridge Street AME Wesleyan Church†, Brooklyn, NY
Bristol Hill Church*, Fulton, New York
British Fort*, St. John's County, FL
British Methodist Episcopal Church†, St. Catherine, Canada
Buckout-Jones Building*, Oswego, New York
Camp Nelson†, Camp Nelson, Kentucky
Camp Warren Levis†, Godfrey, Illinois
Campbell African Methodist Episcopal Church†, Philadelphia, PA
Carleton House†, Littleton, NH

Name, Location

Carneal House (or Rothier House)†, Covington, KY
Cartland Homestead†, Lee, NH
Chamberlain Farm†, Canterbury, NH
Charles B. Huber Homesite†, Williamsburg, Ohio
Charles Perry House†, Westerly, RI
Cheney House†, Peterborough, NH
Clearfield Farm†, Smyrna, DE
Colonel William Hubbard House*, Ashtabula, OH
Daniel Howell Hise House†, Salem, OH
David Barker's House, Niagara, NY
Edgewater†, Haddonfield, NJ
Edgewood Farm†, Kennett Square, PA
Edwin W. Clarke House*, Oswego, New York
Eleutherian College*, Lancaster, IN
Episcopal Parish House†, Gardiner, ME
Fanueil Hall†, Boston, MA
Farwell Mansion†, Vassalboro Township, ME
Felicity Wesleyan Church*, Felicity, Ohio
The Finney House†, Detroit, MI
First African Baptist Church†, Savannah, GA
First Baptist Church†, Chatham, Ontario, Canada
First Congregational Church†, Detroit, MI
Forks of the Road Slave Market Terminus*, Natchez, MS
Fort Donelson National Battlefield*, Dover, Tennessee
Fort Mose*, St. John's County, Florida

Name, Location

Fort Pulaski*, Georgia

Foster Memorial AME Zion Church*, Tarrytown, NY

Frederick Douglass National Historic Site*, Washington, D.C.

Free Presbyterian Church†, Darlington, Pennsylvania

Free State Capitol†, Topeka, Kansas

Furber-Harris House†, Canaan, NH

Geneva College†, Northwood, OH

George B. Hitchcock House*, Lewis, IA

Gerrit Smith Estate†, Peterboro, NY

Grau Mill†, Illinois

Great Geneva†, Dover, DE

Grimes Homestead*, Mountain Lakes, NJ

Guy Beckley House*, Ann Arbor, Michigan

Hamilton and Rhoda Littlefield House*, Oswego, New York

Hanby House, Westerville, OH

Harpers Ferry*, Harpers Ferry, WV

Harriet Beecher Stowe House*, Brunswick, ME

Harriet Beecher Stowe House*, Cincinnati, OH

Harriet Tubman Home*, Auburn, NY

Honeycomb AME Church†, Lima, PA

House of Many Stairs†, Pennsdale, PA

James and Sophia Clemens Farmstead*, Greenville, Ohio

John B. and Lydia Edwards House*, Oswego, New York

John Brown, Jr.'s House†, Ashtabula County, OH

John Brown's Cabin*, Osawatomie, Kansas

John Brown's Cave, Nebraska

John Brown's Farm and Gravesite*, Lake Placid, New York

John Brown's Headquarters*, Samples Manor, MD

John Freeman Walls Cabin†, Ontario, Canada

John Greenleaf Whittier House†, Danvers, MA

John Hossack House*, Ottawa, IL

John Parker House*, Ripley, OH

John Rankin House*, Ripley, OH

Johnson House*, Philadelphia, PA

Jonathan Ridgeway Haines House†, Alliance, Ohio

Jordan House*, West Des Moines, IA

Joshua Giddings' Law Office†, Jefferson, OH

Kimzey Crossing/Locust Hill, Tamaroa, Illinois

Leavitt Thaxter Pease Homesite*, Williamsburg, Ohio

LeMoyne House*, Washington, PA

Levi Coffin House*, Fountain City, IN

Lewelling House*, Salem, IA

Liberty Farm*, Worcester, MA

Name, Location

Linn House†, Bellefonte, PA

Little Africa†, Mercersburg, PA

Mary Ann Shadd Cary House*, Washington, D.C.

Mary Meachum Freedom Crossing*, St. Louis, Missouri

Maulsby House†, Plymouth Meeting, PA

Metropolitan AME Church†, Washington, D.C.

Michigan Avenue Baptist Church†, Buffalo, NY

Milton House*, Milton, WI

Moses Sawyer House†, Weare, NH

Mother African Union Protestant Church†, Wilmington, DE

Mother Zion AME Church†, New York, NY

Mount Gilead AME Church, †, Buckingham Mountain, PA

Mount Pisgah AME Church†, Camden County, NJ

Mount Pleasant, Ohio*, Mount Pleasant, Ohio

Mount Zion AME*, Woolwich Township, NJ

Mt. Zion United AME Church†, Washington, D.C.

Murphy Orchards*, Burt, New York

Nason House†, Augusta, ME

Nathan and Mary Johnson House*, New Bedford, MA

Nathan Thomas House†, Schoolcraft, MI

Nemacolin Castle†, Brownsville, PA

Niagara Frontier Bible Church†, Lewiston, NY

Oakdale*, Chadds Ford, PA

Orchard Street Church†, Baltimore, MD

Oswego Market House*, Oswego, New York

Owen Lovejoy House*, Princeton, IL

Paxton Inn†, Washington, KY

Pearson House†, Keosauqua, IA

Peter Mott House*, Lawnside, NJ

Pine Forge†, Pine Forge, PA

Plymouth Church of the Pilgrims†, Brooklyn, NY

Polly Brandish House†, West Upton, MA

Portland Crossing Point†, Louisville, KY

President Street Station/Baltimore Civil War Museum†, Baltimore, MD

Quindaro†, Quindaro, KS

Quinn Chapel AME Church†, Louisville, KY

Robert Purvis House†, Philadelphia, PA

Rokeby*, Ferrisburg, VT

Rush R. Sloane House*, Sandusky, OH

St. James AME Church*, Ithaca, NY

St. John's AME Church†, Niagara Falls, NY

Samuel and Sally Wilson House*, Cincinnati, OH

Sandwich First Baptist Church†, Amherstburg, Canada

Name, Location

Schuylkill Friends Meetinghouse†, Phoenixville, PA

Second Baptist Church†, Detroit, MI

Slave's Room†, Berrien County, MI

Star Hill AME†, Delaware

Starr Clark Tin Shop*, Mexico, New York

Sunnyside†, Kimberton, PA

Tallman House†, Janesville, WI

Tappan-Philbrick House*, Brookline, Massachusetts

Thomas Lightfoote Inn†, Williamsport, PA

Thomas Root House†, New York

Tide Mill Farm†, Mannington, NJ

Timbuktu†, Westhampton Township, NJ

Todd House†, Tabor, IA

Twelfth Street Baptist Church, Boston, MA

Tyron's Folly†, New York

Union Literary Institute, Greenville, OH

United Church-on-the Green†, New Haven, CT

Vickers' Tavern†, Lionville, PA

Name, Location

The Wayside*, Concord, Massachusetts

Wheeling House Hote†, Wheeling, WV

White Hall†, Augusta, KY

White Horse Farm*, Schuylkill Township, PA

Wild Cat Manor†, Dover, DE

William Eberle Thompson Homesite*, Bethel, OH

William Jackson Homestead*, Newton, MA

William Lloyd Garrison House*, Boston, MA

William Still House†, Philadelphia, PA

William Webb House†, Detroit, MI

Williams House†, Augusta, ME

Wilson Bruce Evans House*, Oberlin, OH

Wright's Ferry Mansion†, Lancaster County, PA

Zebulon Thomas House†, Downingtown, PA

Zion Baptist Church†, Sandusky, OH

Zion Baptist Missionary Church†, Springfield, IL

Appendix 4:
Selected Underground Railroad Sites by State (and Canada)

(Sites marked with asterisks are described in detail in Appendix 5. Sites marked with daggers have more complete entries in the encyclopedia's main alphabetical section.)

Canada
African Episcopal Church (Edgar)†
British Methodist Episcopal Church (St. Catherine)†
First Baptist Church (Chatham, Ontario)†
John Freeman Walls Cabin (Ontario)†
Sandwich First Baptist Church (Amherstburg)†

Colorado
Barney L. Ford Building (Denver)*

Connecticut
Austin F. Williams House (Farmington)*
United Church-on-the-Green (New Haven)†

Delaware
Appoquinimink Friends Meeting House (Odessa)*
Clearfield Farm (Smyrna)†
Great Geneva (Dover)†
Mother African Union Protestant Church (Wilmington)†
Star Hill AME Church†
Wild Cat Manor (Dover)†

District of Columbia
Frederick Douglass National Historic Site (Washington)*
Mary Ann Shadd Cary House (Washington)*
Metropolitan AME Church (Washington)†
Mount Zion United AME Church (Washington)†

Florida
British Fort (Franklin County)*
Fort Mose (St. John's County)*

Georgia
First African Baptist Church (Savannah)
Fort Pulaski*

Illinois
Camp Warren Levis (Godfrey)†
Grau Mill†
John Hossack House (Ottawa)*
Kimzey Crossing/Locust Hill (Tamaroa)*
Owen Lovejoy House (Princeton)*
Zion Baptist Missionary Church (Springfield)†

Indiana
Bethel AME Church (Indianapolis)*
Eleutherian College (Lancaster)*
Levi Coffin House (Fountain City)*

Iowa
George B. Hitchcock House (Lewis)*
Jordan House (West Des Moines)*
Lewelling House (Salem)*
Pearson House (Keosauqua)†
Todd House (Tabor)†

Kansas
Free State Capitol (Topeka)†
John Brown's Cabin (Osawatomie)*
Quindaro (Quindaro)†

Kentucky
Berea College (Berea)†
Camp Nelson (Camp Nelson)†
Carneal House (or Rothier House) (Covington)†
Paxton Inn (Washington)†
Portland Crossing Point (Louisville)†

Quinn Chapel AME Church (Louisville)[†]
White Hall (Augusta)[†]

Maine
Episcopal Parish House (Gardiner)[†]
Farwell Mansion (Vassalboro Township)[†]
Harriet Beecher Stowe House (Brunswick)*
Nason House (Augusta)[†]
Williams House (Augusta)[†]

Maryland
Orchard Street Church (Baltimore)[†]
President Street Station/Baltimore Civil War
  Museum (Baltimore)[†]

Massachusetts
African Meeting House (Boston)[†]
African Meeting House (Nantucket)[†]
Boston African American National Historic
  Site*
Bowditch House (Brookline)*
Fanueil Hall (Boston)[†]
Jackson Homestead (Newton)*
John Greenleaf Whittier House (Danvers)[†]
Liberty Farm (Worcester)*
Nathan and Mary Johnson House (New Bed-
  ford)*
Polly Brandish House (West Upton)[†]
Tappan-Philbrick House (Brookline)*
Twelfth Street Baptist Church (Boston)
The Wayside (Concord)*
William Lloyd Garrison House (Boston)*

Michigan
Finney House (Detroit)[†]
First Congregational Church (Detroit)[†]
Guy Beckley House (Ann Arbor)*
Nathan Thomas House (Schoolcraft)[†]
Second Baptist Church (Detroit)[†]
Slave's Room (Berrien County)[†]
William Webb House (Detroit)[†]

Mississippi
Forks of the Road Slave Market Terminus
  (Natchez)*

Nebraska
Allen B. Mayhew Cabin (Nebraska City)[†]
John Brown's Cave

New Hampshire
Carleton House (Littleton)[†]
Cartland Homestead (Lee)[†]
Chamberlain Farm (Canterbury)[†]
Cheney House (Peterborough)[†]
Furber-Harris House (Canaan)[†]
Moses Sawyer House (Weare)[†]

New Jersey
Bethel AME Church (Greenwich Township)*
Edgewater (Haddonfield)[†]

Grimes Homestead (Mountain Lakes)*
Mount Pisgah AME Church (Camden County)[†]
Mount Zion AME Church (Woolwich Town-
  ship)*
Peter Mott House (Lawnside)*
Tide Mill Farm (Mannington)[†]
Timbuktu (Westhampton Township)[†]

New York
Bridge Street AME Wesleyan Church (Brook-
  lyn)[†]
Bristol Hill Church (Fulton)*
Buckout-Jones Building (Oswego)*
David Barker's House (Niagara)
Edwin W. Clarke House (Oswego, New York)*
Foster Memorial AME Zion Church (Tarry-
  town)*
Gerrit Smith Estate (Peterboro)[†]
Hamilton and Rhoda Littlefield House (Os-
  wego)*
Harriet Tubman Home (Auburn)*
John B. and Lydia Edwards House (Oswego)*
John Brown's Farm and Gravesite (Lake Placid)*
Michigan Avenue Baptist Church (Buffalo)[†]
Mother Zion AME Church (New York City)[†]
Murphy Orchards (Burt)*
Niagara Frontier Bible Church (Lewiston)[†]
Oswego Market House (Oswego)*
Plymouth Church of the Pilgrims (Brooklyn)[†]
St. James AME Church (Ithaca)*
St. John's AME Church (Niagara Falls)[†]
Starr Clark Tin Shop (Mexico)*
Thomas Root House (New York City)[†]
Tyron's Folly (New York City)[†]

Ohio
Asa Wing House (Parish)*
Charles B. Huber Homesite (Williamsburg)[†]
Colonel William Hubbard House (Ashtabula)*
Daniel Howell Hise House (Salem)[†]
Felicity Wesleyan Church (Felicity)*
Geneva College (Northwood)[†]
Hanby House (Westerville)
Harriet Beecher Stowe House (Cincinnati)*
James and Sophia Clemens Farmstead
  (Greenville)*
John Brown, Jr.'s House (Ashtabula)[†]
John Parker House (Ripley)*
John Rankin House (Ripley)*
Jonathan Ridgeway Haines House (Alliance,
  Ohio)[†]
Joshua Giddings' Law Office (Jefferson)[†]
Leavitt Thaxter Pease Homesite (Williamsburg)*
Mount Pleasant, Ohio*
Plymouth Church of the Pilgrims (Brooklyn)[†]
Rush R. Sloane House (Sandusky)*
Samuel and Sally Wilson House (Cincinnati)*

Union Literary Institute (Greenville)
William Eberle Thompson Homesite (Bethel)*
Wilson Bruce Evans House (Oberlin)*
Zion Baptist Church (Sandusky)†

Pennsylvania
African Union Methodist Church (Oxford)†
Bethel AME Church (Reading)*
Campbell African Methodist Episcopal Church (Philadelphia)†
Edgewood Farm (Kennett Square)†
Free Presbyterian Church (Darlington)†
Honeycomb AME Church (Lima)†
House of Many Stairs (Pennsdale)†
Johnson House (Philadelphia)*
LeMoyne House (Washington)*
Linn House (Bellefonte)†
Little Africa (Mercersburg)†
Maulsby House (Plymouth Meeting)†
Mount Gilead AME Church (Buckingham Mountain)†
Nemacolin Castle (Brownsville)†
Oakdale (Chadd's Ford)*
Pine Forge (Pine Forge)†
Robert Purvis House (Philadelphia)†

Schuylkill Friends Meetinghouse (Phoenixville)†
Sunnyside (Kimberton)†
Thomas Lightfoote Inn (Williamsport)†
Vickers' Tavern (Lionville)†
White Horse Farm (Schuylkill Township)*
William Still House (Philadelphia)†
Wright's Ferry Mansion (Lancaster County)†
Zebulon Thomas House (Downingtown)†

Rhode Island
Bethel AME Church (Providence)†
Charles Perry House (Westerly)†

Tennessee
Fort Donelson National Battlefield (Dover, Tennessee)*

Vermont
Rokeby (Ferrisburg)*

West Virginia
Harpers Ferry*
Wheeling House Hotel (Wheeling)†

Wisconsin
Milton House (Milton)*
Tallman House (Janesville)†

Appendix 5: National Park Service Underground Railroad Sites

In 1998, the United States Congress passed the *National Underground Railroad Network to Freedom Act of 1998*. This legislation established, under the National Park Service, the National Underground Railroad Network to Freedom program, with the following stated purposes:

1. To recognize the importance of the Underground Railroad, the sacrifices made by those who used the Underground Railroad in search of freedom from tyranny and oppression, and the sacrifices made by the people who helped them.

2. To authorize the National Park Service to co-ordinate and facilitate Federal and non-Federal activities to commemorate, honor, and interpret the history of the Underground Railroad, its significance as a crucial element in the evolution of the national civil rights movement, and its relevance in fostering the spirit of racial harmony and national reconciliation.

Among its many provisions, the act also stipulated that all sites with a "verifiable connection to the Underground Railroad" were "eligible for inclusion on, the National Register of Historic Places." Congress authorized the appropriation of as much as $500,000 per year to support the activities authorized by the act.

The Network to Freedom program evolved thereafter, encompassing "all the sites, facilities, and programs that have each, in their own way, met the basic criteria of showing an association to the Underground Railroad." The network also includes those sites and facilities "devoted to preserving, commemorating, or educating the public about places and stories from the Underground Railroad."

The Network to Freedom and National Underground Railroad Travel Itinerary sites, as of the date of publication of this encyclopedia, are listed below, along with brief descriptions based on or drawn from National Park Service documentation. For further and more detailed information, readers should consult the *Underground Railroad Special Resource Study* (1995) and *Researching and Interpreting the Underground Railroad* (1999), both published by the National Park Service.

Appoquinimink Friends Meeting House (Odessa, Delaware)

The Appoquinimink Friends Meetings House was constructed in 1783 near Odessa, Delaware, a community in which a strong Quaker antislavery movement existed. The Meeting House served as a station on the Underground Railroad and is associated with John Hunn and John Alston, two "station masters" who were members of the congregation.

Appoquinimink Friends Meeting House is located on SR 299, west of U.S. 13 in Odessa, Delaware.

Asa Wing House (Parish, New York)

Asa Wing (1815–54) was an important antislavery lecturer and organizer in central New York. Wing's home on Route 69 in modern-day Parish, New York served as an Underground Railroad station. For example, on Christmas Eve, 1850, Wing recorded in his diary that "today a colored man, his wife and five small girls came to my house on their way to Canada to save their children from the kidnappers."

Wing died in 1854, bringing a premature end to his career as an orator, organizer, and Underground Railroad agent. His contributions were memorialized in a monument at his gravesite and a dedicatory speech by Frederick Douglass himself.

Austin F. Williams House (Farmington, Connecticut)

An Underground Railroad site and home of Austin F. Williams (1805–1885), a staunch abolitionist, in Farmington, Connecticut. In 1839, Williams became deeply involved in the *Amistad* Affair — as a strong advocate for the freedom of the captured Africans. After their release, Williams housed many of the Africans on his property. The building in which he did so is today the east section of the carriage house — the west section was added on after the Africans returned to their homeland in Sierra Leone.

Barney L. Ford Building (Denver, Colorado)

The building at 1514 Blake Street was one of the earliest commercial successes for Barney L. Ford (1822–1902), a fugitive slave, Underground Railroad worker in Chicago and later a key black leader in the early history of Colorado. Ford was a black pioneer, businessman, civic leader and politician who actively fought for African American civil rights in the state.

Bethel AME Church (Greenwich Township, New Jersey)

An important Underground Railroad site, Bethel AME Church traces its origins to the early 1800s when white and African American Methodist Episcopalians began worshipping together at the Methodist Episcopal churches in Greenwich Township. However, as slavery ended in New Jersey and the number of African Americans in the congregations grew, slaveholding Methodists pressed church leaders to treat their black fellow Methodists as less than equals or to exclude them altogether. Finding themselves increasingly unwelcome, blacks organized the African Society of Methodists and, by 1810, had purchased land and a small building for a church. By 1817, the congregation affiliated itself with the newly chartered African Methodist Episcopal Church, based in Philadelphia, becoming the Bethel AME Church. The first building was destroyed by fire in the 1830s and, by 1841, a new building had been constructed a mile away from the original site.

As a centerpiece of the African American community of Springtown in Greenwich Township, the church and its members afforded sanctuary and assistance to fugitive slaves from Maryland and Delaware. Algy Stanford, who lived next door to the church, was an important friend of the fugitive and local folklore holds that Harriet Tubman used this station frequently between 1849 and 1853 on her passage north through Delaware to Wilmington, one of her most famous routes.

The Bethel AME Church is located on Sheppards Mill Rd. in Greenwich Township, New Jersey.

Bethel AME Church (Indianapolis, Indiana)

An important Underground Railroad site, the Bethel African Methodist Episcopal Church was founded in 1836 by William Paul Quinn and Augustus Turner. The first AME church in Indianapolis, Bethel, first known as "Indianapolis Station," originated as a small congregation that met in Quinn's log cabin until a small house of worship was constructed in 1841. By 1848, the church had 100 members, played an active role in the antislavery movement and served as a station on the Underground Railroad.

After the Civil War, Bethel remained a force for constructive change in Indianapolis, pressing to open schools for African Americans throughout the city and even operating a kindergarten. In the twentieth century, the Indianapolis chapter of the NAACP and the Indiana State Federation of Colored Woman's Clubs were organized at Bethel as well.

Bethel AME Church is located in Indianapolis, Indiana at 414 West Vermont Street.

Bethel AME Church (Reading, Pennsylvania)

An Underground Railroad site, the Bethel African Methodist Episcopal Church of Reading, Pennsylvania, was founded in 1837 by Jacob Ross, George Dillen, Isaac Parker, and Samuel Murray, who was primarily responsible for the construction of the church edifice. In the decades before the Civil War, the congregation of Bethel was active in the Underground Railroad and members often harbored fugitive slaves.

Bethel AME remains an important place of worship and a referral, social, and cultural center in the Reading community. Bethel AME Church is located in Reading, Pennsylvania, at 119 North Tenth Street.

Boston African American National Historic Site

A key center of antislavery and Underground Railroad activity, the Boston African

American National Historic Site includes 15 pre-Civil War buildings central to the history of the free African American community of Boston, Massachusetts. Among the buildings included are the home of Lewis Hayden, the African Meeting House, the Abiel Smith School, and Augustus Saint-Gaudens' memorial to Robert Gould Shaw and the black Massachusetts 54th Regiment. The African Meetinghouse, built in 1806 and the oldest known extant black church in the United States, provided a forum for most prominent abolitionists such as Frederick Douglass, William Lloyd Garrison, and Charles Sumner. Established in 1834, the Abiel Smith School was the first primary and grammar school established for black children in Boston. All of the sites in the National Historic Site are linked by the 1.6-mile Black Heritage Trail.

The site was authorized by Congress October 10, 1980 and its headquarters are located at 14 Beacon Street.

Bowditch House (Brookline, Massachusetts)

Located at 9 Toxteth Street in Brookline, Massachusetts, the William Ingersoll Bowditch House was built in 1844 and was purchased by Bowditch in 1845, after which the house served as an Underground Railroad station until the Civil War.

Bristol Hill Church (Fulton, New York)

The Bristol Hill Congregational Church originated in the 1820s at Fulton, New York. The church building was completed in 1832 and dedicated in 1835. Unlike most ante-bellum American churches, Bristol Hill Congregational had both African Americans and whites in its congregation. Many church members were active abolitionists and signed at least one antislavery petition in 1837, passed an antislavery resolution in 1843, supported the Liberty Party in 1844 and worked to free William Chaplin, arrested in 1850 for assisting fugitive slaves in Washington, D.C.

Involvement with the Underground Railroad was another concrete expression of the antislavery convictions of the Bristol Hill congregation. Two families in particular — one white, Hiram and Lucy Gilbert, and one black, Amos and Hannah Mason — played important roles in assisting fugitive slaves.

British Fort (Franklin County, Florida)

In the summer and fall of 1814, British Major Edward Nicholls recruited Seminoles and African Americans living in Florida to assist the British against the United States in the last phase of the War of 1812. These recruits and British soldiers constructed an extensive octagonal earthwork fort, "British Post," fifteen miles from the mouth of the Apalachicola River on Prospect Bluff in modern-day Franklin County, Florida. When the British withdrew from the area in 1815, the Seminoles and African Americans remained and the fort, soon known as "Negro Fort," became both a settlement and a source of protection for other settlements and plantations that developed nearby — a "beacon of light to restless and rebellious slaves."

Although the National Park Services considers British Fort, like Fort Mose in St. John's County, Florida, a precursor site to the Underground Railroad, it is important to remember that Black Seminoles and African Americans in early Florida were usually fugitive slaves or the descendants thereof.

British Fort, or Fort Gadsden, is located in the Appalachiola National Forest and is a short distance from State Road 65, near Sumatra, Florida.

Buckout-Jones Building (Oswego, New York)

Abram Buckout (1813–1884) was an "ardent abolitionist" who owned the west half of the Buckout-Jones Building in Oswego, New York, from 1852 until 1868. Buckout's barn on West Fifth Street Road, bordering Lake Ontario in Oswego County, New York, was used as an Underground Railroad station for fugitive slaves en route to Canada. The barn is now gone, although the Buckout residence still stands.

Charles Smith and Tudor Grant, both barbers who had been enslaved in Baltimore, Maryland, were among the tenants of the Buckout-Jones Building in the 1850s. Both shared Buckout's antislavery convictions and also worked to assist fugitive slaves.

Colonel William Hubbard House (Ashatabula, Ohio)

William Hubbard (1787–1863) moved to Ashtabula, Ohio, from Holland Patent, New York, around 1834. There he worked with relatives who ran a successful lumber-yard and warehouse. Earlier, Hubbard was a captain in the War of 1812 in a New York regiment, and after the war served as a colonel of militia. He built this house in about 1840, and became involved in the local antislavery society and town politics. A strategic location for an Underground Railroad station, the house is near Lake Erie, and was often the last stop for fugitive slaves before they reached Canada.

Edwin W. Clarke House (Oswego, New York)

Edwin W. Clarke (1801–1884) and Charlotte Ambler Clarke were well-known abolitionists in Oswego, New York. The couple married in 1833 and, for the first 25 years of their marriage, rented various homes. However, they built a large brick home on the southwest corner of East Seventh and Mohawk Streets in the Oak Hill section of Oswego. The Clarke home served as an Underground Railroad station and boasted a hidden room or hiding place for fugitive slaves in the basement.

Eleutherian College (Lancaster, Indiana)

Eleutherian College was built between 1854 and 1856 at Lancaster, Indiana, along a well-traveled corridor for fugitive slaves en route from north central Kentucky and Madison, Indiana, to Indianapolis. With its name derived from the Greek, "Eleutheros"—meaning "freedom and equality"—the college reflected the antislavery views of its founders, some of whom were among the most active friends of the fugitive in the region. For example, Eleutherian was the first college in Indiana to admit students without regard to race or gender—and three of Eleutherian's trustees, Samuel Tibbetts, Lyman Hoyt, and James Nelson, were frequently mentioned in connection with the Underground Railroad and its efforts in the vicinity of Lancaster and Madison. In fact, James Nelson was arrested by a local sheriff under the Indiana Fugitive Slave Act of 1851 for "encouraging Negroes to come into the state."

Eleutherian operated as a private secondary school until the mid–1880s. In 1888, it was then purchased by Lancaster Township and used as a public school until 1938. Eleutherian College Classroom and Chapel Building, now vacant, is located on State Route 250, just east of Lancaster.

Felicity Wesleyan Church (Felicity, Ohio)

The Felicity Wesleyan Church of Felicity, Ohio, was founded in 1847. By 1858, more than 200 persons comprised the congregation and many were actively involved in the Underground Railroad.

Forks of the Road Slave Market Terminus (Natchez, Mississippi)

As the Cotton Kingdom expanded after the War of 1812, Natchez, Mississippi, became a convergence point for most of the major domestic slave trade routes in the trans-Appalachian west. Domestic slave traders from Virginia, Georgia, Florida, the Carolinas, Missouri, Tennessee, and Kentucky transported enslaved African Americans "down the river" to this destination for sale to the cotton plantations of the South and southwest.

Although not related directly to the Underground Railroad in the antebellum period, the Natchez slave market embodied one of the principal motivations for slave escapes, i.e., sale or the threat of sale. However, during the Civil War, this area was a destination for enslaved African Americans seeking refuge with the Union Army and also was the site of an encampment of the U.S. Colored Troops at Fort McPherson.

The Forks of the Road Slave Market Terminus is located at St. Catherine Street, Liberty Road, in Natchez, Mississippi.

Fort Donelson National Battlefield (Dover, Tennessee)

The Fort Donelson National Battlefield at Dover, Tennessee, was established by the Act of March 26, 1928 to commemorate the battle of Fort Donelson, February 13–16, 1862, the first significant Union victory in the Civil War. Once under Union control, Fort Donelson became a magnet and safe haven for large numbers of African Americans in the surrounding region who emancipated themselves during the war. At this site, fugitive slaves received assistance from Union soldiers and the freedmen's aid societies that developed as an extension of the antislavery movement. The fort also became a recruiting station for African American troops in 1863.

Fort Mose (St. John's County, Florida)

In 1738, Fort Mose (originally, Gracia Real de Santa Teresa de Mose) was established by the Spanish governor of Florida as an emplacement on the northern defense line for St. Augustine. Fort Mose was abandoned in 1740, but reestablished at a nearby site in 1752. The early inhabitants were principally fugitive slaves from the British colonies of South Carolina and Georgia, who began fleeing to Spanish Florida as early as 1687—who were willing to defend Spanish Florida against the British as a means of defending their own freedom. As such, Fort Mose was the earliest legally sanctioned free black community in the present United States.

Although the National Park Services considers Fort Mose, like British Fort, in Franklin County, Florida, a precursor site to the Underground Railroad, it is important to remember that Black Seminoles and African Americans in Florida were usually fugitive slaves or the descendants thereof.

Fort Mose is now a state conservation site in St. John's County, Florida.

Fort Pulaski (Georgia)

An important destination for fugitive slaves during the Civil War, Fort Pulaski was constructed between 1829 and 1847 as part of a national defense system designed to protect key cities on the east coast of the United States from foreign attack. As a step toward secession and Civil War, Georgia State troops took possession of the fort on January 3, 1861. However, on April 10, 1862, Major General David Hunter regained control of the fort for the Union.

On April 13, 1862, Hunter issued General Order No. 7, which stated that: "All persons of color lately held to involuntary service by enemies of the United States in Fort Pulaski and on Cockspur Island, Georgia, are hereby confiscated and declared free, in conformity with the law, and shall here after receive the fruits of their own labor." This order conformed to the provisions of the Confiscation Act of 1861 and was issued three months before Abraham Lincoln wrote the first draft of the Emancipation Proclamation.

Through the end of the Civil War, Fort Pulaski was a magnet for freedom seekers from the surrounding region and became a recruiting center for freedmen desirous of serving in the Union Army.

Foster Memorial AME Zion Church (Tarrytown, New York)

The Foster Memorial AME Zion Church was founded in 1860 by Amanda and Henry Foster, the Reverend Jacob Thomas and Hiram Jimerson. Amanda Foster, considered the "Mother of the Church," allowed the congregation to meet in her confectionery until 1865, when a permanent church structure was built using funds donated primarily by local Dutch Reformed and Methodist congregations.

During the Civil War, members of Foster AME assisted fugitive slaves seeking refuge in Tarrytown and others bent on escaping to Canada. After the war, Foster remained a religious and social center of the local African American community.

Foster AME Zion Church is located in Tarrytown, New York, at 90 Wildey Street.

Frederick Douglass National Historic Site (Washington, D.C.)

The great fugitive slave and abolitionist, Frederick Douglass (1817–1895), lived at 1411 W Street, SE in Washington, D. C., from 1877 until his death. After Douglass died in 1895, his widow, Helen Pitts Douglass, bequeathed the house to the Frederick Douglass Memorial and Historical Association. The association, in conjunction with the National Association of Colored Women's Clubs, opened the house to the public in 1916. In 1962, the house was added to the National Park system and was designated a National Historic Site in 1988.

George B. Hitchcock House (Lewis, Iowa)

The stone house of the Reverend George B. Hitchcock (1812–1872), a Congregational minister and passionate abolitionist who migrated to in Lewis, Iowa, in the mid–1850s, served as a refuge to fugitive slaves and abolitionists traveling through the state. The George B. Hitchcock House is located on State Road 44, just west of the town.

Grimes Homestead (Mountain Lakes, New Jersey)

The Grimes homestead in Mountain Lakes, New Jersey, was constructed in the late 18th century and was home to the Grimes family, a Quaker family active in the New Jersey antislavery movement. Dr. Jonathan Grimes (1802–1875), the best-known abolitionist in the family, was born in the house, lived there until 1828 and periodically thereafter. During these periods, the homestead served as an active Underground Railroad station.

Guy Beckley House (Ann Arbor, Michigan)

Guy Beckley, a Methodist minister with strong antislavery convictions, lectured for the American Anti-Slavery Society in New England, moved to Michigan in 1839 and continued his antislavery work there. Beckley published an abolitionist newspaper, *The Signal of Liberty,* that included both antislavery articles and a chronicle of the passage of fugitive slaves through Ann Arbor. For example, Beckley documents how he assisted Lyman Goodnow as Goodnow escorted fugitive slave Caroline Quarreles (or Quarles) from Wisconsin to Canada.

Beckley's house on Pontiac Trail in Lower Town, Ann Arbor, Michigan, was significant as an antislavery center and a station on the Underground Railroad from 1842, when Beckley first occupied the house, until his death in 1847.

Hamilton and Rhoda Littlefield House (Oswego, New York)

Hamilton B. Littlefield worked closely with Gerrit Smith and Smith's land agent, John B. Edwards. His home in Oswego, New York, as documented by letters between Smith and Edwards, was one of many active Underground Railroad stations in Oswego from which numerous fugitive slaves crossed Lake Ontario to reach safe haven in Canada.

Harpers Ferry, West Virginia

During the summer of 1859, John Brown (1800–1859) devised his final plan for seizing the federal arsenal at Harpers Ferry, Virginia (now West Virginia), then liberating and arming enslaved African Americans, and establishing a free black stronghold in the Appalachians. Brown chose to begin his insurrection by attacking Harpers Ferry due to the quantity of weapons available there and its proximity to the mountains.

Brown made final preparations for his attack while living secretly at the Kennedy Farm, located seven miles away in Maryland. After stockpiling weapons and organizing his supporters, Brown crossed the Potomac River on October 16, and seized the bridge and the armory watchmen. Brown cut telegraph wires, but committed a fateful tactical blunder by barricading himself and his followers in the armory.

By noon of October 17, the militia had arrived and secured the Potomac River Bridge. Brown and the other surviving raiders fled to engine house of the armory's musket factory, where they finally overwhelmed by a party of marines on the morning of October 18. Two men were bayoneted and the others were captured, including John Brown himself.

The Harpers Ferry National Historical Park is located at the confluence of the Potomac and Shenandoah Rivers in the states of West Virginia, Virginia, and Maryland, 65 miles northwest of Washington, D.C., and 20 miles southwest of Frederick, Maryland.

Harriet Beecher Stowe House (Brunswick, Maine)

Antislavery site and home of Harriet Beecher **Stowe** (1811–1896), author and abolitionist, during her stay in Brunswick, Maine, from 1850 to 1852. There, Stowe wrote her famous novel and classic indictment of American slavery, *Uncle Tom's Cabin.* Thus, although the home at which Stowe lived in Brunswick bears no direct connection to the Underground Railroad, the book she completed there draws significantly on Stowe's familiarity with fugitive slaves, their modes of flight and those who assisted them.

The Harriet Beecher Stowe House is located at 63 Federal Street in Brunswick, Maine.

Harriet Beecher Stowe House (Cincinnati, Ohio)

In 1832, Harriet Beecher (1811–1896) — in later years, the antislavery author who wrote *Uncle Tom's Cabin* — moved from Litchfield, Connecticut, to Cincinnati, Ohio, with her sister and father, a Congregationalist minister who accepted an offer to teach at the Lane Seminary. Their home soon became a meeting place for members of the local antislavery community and Stowe lived with her family until she married Calvin Ellis Stowe in 1835. After her marriage, she moved into a nearby home in the Walnut Hills area, but was a frequent visitor in her family home.

The Harriet Beecher Stowe House is located at 2950 Gilbert Avenue in Cincinnati, Ohio.

Harriet Tubman Home (Auburn, New York)

Harriet Tubman (1820/21?-1913), the redoubtable Underground Railroad conductor, contracted for seven acres of land and a house from Governor William H. Seward in Auburn, New York, in 1859. Tubman moved her parents, after their initial stay in Canada, to this property and they remained there while she worked with the Union Army during the Civil War. After the war she returned to Auburn and transformed her house into a "home" for aged and indigent African Americans. In 1896, Tubman purchased 25 adjoining acres and, in 1903, deeded the property to the AME Zion Church with the stipulation that the church would continue to operate the home.

The Harriet Tubman Home for the Aged is located at 180 South St.; her home is located at 182 South St., and the church is located at 33 Parker St. in Auburn, New York.

Henderson Lewelling House
(Salem, Iowa)

Henderson Lewelling (1809–1883), a Quaker from Indiana, moved to Salem, Iowa, in 1837. There, with his brother, Lewelling opened a general merchandise store and established a small commercial fruit nursery. Until he migrated to Oregon in 1847, Lewelling's home on West Main Street was a meeting place for Quaker abolitionists in the area and served as a station for freedom seekers fleeing bondage in nearby Missouri.

Jackson Homestead
(Newton, Massachusetts)

The Jackson Homestead was built in Newton, Massachusetts, by Timothy Jackson (1756–1814) in 1809, a veteran of the Revolutionary War. One of his sons, William Jackson (1783–1855), moved to the house in 1820 and used the home as a safe haven on the Underground Railroad while another, Francis Jackson, served as treasurer of the vigilance committee in Boston.

After William Jackson's death in 1855, his widow, Mary Bennett Jackson, and their three unmarried daughters were left in reduced circumstances, but continued to play a role in the life of the community. For example, in 1865, his daughter, Ellen, helped to found the Freedman's Aid Society in Newton and served as its president until her death in 1902.

James and Sophia Clemens Farmstead
(Greenville, Ohio)

The James and Sophia Clemens Farmstead is located at 467 Stingley Road near Greenville, Ohio. The farm was the home of James Clemens (1781–1870), a free African American, who moved to the area in 1818 and founded the African American "Longtown" settlement. His farm served as an important station on the Underground Railroad in Darke County.

In an August 13, 1898 interview, David Putman stated: "At the Greenville Negro settlement was another station. The Clemens' and the Alexander's were the leaders in the movement there. These were Negro families." The Union Literary Institute, a vocational school founded by residents of the settlement and antislavery Quakers in 1845, was also located near the settlement and was open to local African Americans.

John B. and Lydia Edwards House
(Oswego, New York)

John B. Edwards (1802–1895) was Gerrit Smith's friend and agent in the city of Oswego, New York. Edwards corresponded frequently with Smith and his letters contain many detailed references to helping fugitive slaves. In 1836, Edwards and his wife, Lydia (1806–1856) bought land on West Third Street in Oswego and harbored freedom seekers in the home built thereon.

John Brown's Cabin
(Osawatomie, Kansas)

The John Brown Cabin, located a mile west of Osawatomie, Kansas, was built in 1855 by Samuel Glenn. Glenn sold the cabin to Samuel Adair, John Brown's (1800–1859) brother-in-law and, after moving to Osawatomie to join the antislavery struggle in Kansas territory, Brown himself used the cabin occasionally as a headquarters for his abolitionist activities.

The cabin was dismantled and reassembled in its present location, John Brown Park, in 1912.

John Brown's Farm and Gravesite
(Lake Placid, New York)

In 1849, John Brown (1800–1859), the great antislavery crusader and Underground Railroad conductor, moved from Springfield, Massachusetts, to Lake Placid, New York, after learning about wealthy businessman Gerrit Smith's plan to give parcels of land in upstate New York to free African Americans. Brown purchased a lot from Smith and moved his family to the upstate wilderness area where he acted as a leader and teacher to the black families who were developing their own farms. The settlement proved marginally successful at best and some of the black settlers soon departed. In 1855, Brown departed as well for Kansas and, in the years thereafter, returned to his farm for only six brief visits to see his wife and some of his children.

After Brown's execution in 1859, he was buried at the farm at his request and his gravesite soon became a "pilgrimage" destination for free black and white abolitionists. Brown's family moved to California, but, in 1870, the John Brown Association was organized and purchased the site of the farm and grave. The property was transferred to the state of New York in 1896, but the John Brown Association remained actively involved in its use, e.g., the association raised funds for a statue of John Brown and a young African American boy in 1935.

John Brown considered this farm, a National Historic Landmark and New York State Historic Site, his home during the 10 years preceding the 1859 raid on Harpers Ferry for which he was executed. The John Brown Farm and

Gravesite are located on John Brown Road, just south of the intersection with Old Military Road in Lake Placid, New York.

John Brown's Headquarters (Samples Manor, Maryland)

In the summer of 1859, John Brown (1800–1859), militant abolitionist and friend of the fugitive, rented the two-story Kennedy farmhouse from the heirs of William Booth Kennedy. The house, located approximately seven miles from Harpers Ferry, served as his headquarters where he planned, and stockpiled weapons and tools for his ill-fated raid on the federal arsenal at Harpers Ferry on October 16, 1859.

The Kennedy Farmhouse, a National Historic Landmark, is located at 2406 Chestnut Road in Samples Manor, Maryland.

John Hossack House (Ottawa, Illinois)

An Underground Railroad site, the John Hossack House was built in 1854 for businessman John Hossack. A Scottish-born immigrant, Hossack came to Ottawa, Illinois, from Chicago, where he had done contract work on the Illinois and Michigan Canal. In Ottawa, Hossack was engaged in the lumber business and grain trade, and instrumental in the building of the first Illinois River Bridge. Overlooking this river, Hossack's mansion at 210 West Prospect Street was significant for its role as an Underground Railroad station.

John Parker House (Ripley, Ohio)

John Parker (1827–1900), a free African American, was one of the most determined and intrepid friends of the fugitive in the Kentucky borderland. Parker lived at 300 Front Street near the Ohio River in Ripley, Ohio, from about 1853 until his death. From this base of operations, he ventured across the river to assist fugitive slaves and deliver them to other local friends of the fugitive, most notably the Reverend John Rankin, who would spirit them northward.

John Rankin House (Ripley, Ohio)

The home of Presbyterian minister John Rankin in Ripley, Ohio, is one of the nation's most significant and memorable Underground Railroad sites. In the decades before the Civil War, Rankin was one of Ohio's first and most active "conductors" on the Underground Railroad. Rankin's home, located at 6152 Rankin Road atop a steep hill overlooking the Ohio River, was considered one of the first stations on the Underground Railroad corridor leading from central and eastern Kentucky into central Ohio. By keeping a candle burning in his window, Rankin and his family created a beacon that could be seen from across the river and followed to freedom. Working closely with friends of the fugitive such as John Parker, Rankin is believed to have assisted hundreds, if not thousands, of fugitive slaves.

Johnson House (Philadelphia, Pennsylvania)

The Johnson family lived on Germantown Avenue in Philadelphia, Pennsylvania, between 1770 and 1908. The generation that came of age in the late ante-bellum period — specifically, Rowland, Israel, Ellwood, Sarah, and Elizabeth Johnson, and their respective spouses— was actively involved with abolitionist groups such as the American Anti-Slavery Society and the Germantown Freedman's Aid Association. During this same period, the Johnson house and the homes of neighboring relatives became stations on the Underground Railroad.

Jordan House (West Des Moines, Iowa)

James Cunningham Jordan (b. 1813) was the first white settler in West Des Moines, Iowa. A state senator and cattle farmer, he was one of Iowa's most influential early citizens. Jordan was also a staunch abolitionist and his home, built in 1851, was an important Underground Railroad station — with hiding places for fugitive slaves in the basement. Jordan even assisted John Brown at this site on February 17, 1859 as Brown spirited 12 fugitive slaves out of Missouri.

Jordan's house also provides one of the rare documented examples of the use of quilts as an Underground Railroad signaling system. Specifically, if a quilt hanging outside the house had a small black square woven into the design, then it was safe for fugitives to seek refuge there. However, if the square was a different color, there was danger and the fugitive was warned thereby to seek refuge elsewhere.

Kimzey Crossing/Locust Hill (Tamaroa, Illinois)

The home of B. G. Roots is a massive 12-room mansion located south of the town of Tamaroa, in Perry County, Illinois, situated near Kimzey Crossing. The house served as an Underground Railroad station and boasted secret passages that led to upstairs quarters for fugitive slaves and to hiding places elsewhere on Roots' property.

In the 1850s, Roots was able to prevent the rendition of a fugitive slave, Jim, who had escaped from Missouri, by securing a writ of habeas corpus from the Illinois Supreme Court. After a stormy trial, Roots aided the freedom seeker in escaping to Chicago and eventually to Canada.

Leavitt Thaxter Pease Homesite (Williamsburg, Ohio)

The home of Dr. Leavitt Thaxter Pease was an Underground Railroad station in Williamsburg, Ohio. Pease, who worked with Charles B. Huber as the assistant Underground Railroad "stationmaster" of Williamsburg, assumed the role of "stationmaster" in 1854 when Huber died. Pease was assisted ably by his wife, Nancy Fee — whose father and brother were also active friends of the fugitive.

LeMoyne House (Washington, Pennsylvania)

Dr. F. Julius LeMoyne (1798–1879), his wife, Madelaine, and his children were all active Underground Railroad agents. Their home, built in 1812, was a focal point of the antislavery movement in southwestern Pennsylvania from the 1830s through the end of the antebellum period.

Levi Coffin House (Fountain City, Indiana)

Levi Coffin (1789–1877), the famous Quaker abolitionist, lived in this house at 115 Main Street in Fountain City, Indiana, between 1827 and 1847, after which he moved to Cincinnati, Ohio. Coffin, often termed "president" of the Underground Railroad, and his wife, Catherine, assisted more than two thousand fugitive slaves while based at Fountain City — including the famous Eliza Harris, immortalized in *Uncle Tom's Cabin.*

Lewelling House (Salem, Iowa)

Henderson Lewelling (1809–1883), a Quaker from Indiana, moved to Salem, Iowa, in 1837 with his brother and opened a general merchandise store and established a small commercial fruit nursery. Lewelling's home was a meeting place for Quaker abolitionists in the area and served as an Underground Railroad station for freedom seekers fleeing bondage in nearby Missouri until he migrated to Oregon in 1847.

Liberty Farm (Worcester, Massachusetts)

Liberty Farm in Worcester, Massachusetts, was the home of Abigail "Abby" Kelley Foster, outspoken abolitionist and early suffragist, and her husband, Stephen Symonds Foster, from 1847 until 1881. In 1847, the couple purchased the farm and used their home as an Underground Railroad station. After the Civil War, Kelley Foster's attention shifted to equal rights and the enfranchisement of women.

Mary Ann Shadd Cary House (Washington, D.C.)

An Underground Railroad and antislavery commemorative site, this brick row house was the home of Mary Ann Shadd Cary, the noted abolitionist and editor, from 1881 to 1885. The Mary Ann Shadd Cary House is located at 1421 W Street, NW in Washington, D.C.

Mary Meachum Freedom Crossing (St. Louis, Missouri)

The Mary Meachum Freedom Crossing marks the site where, on May 21, 1855, eight or nine enslaved African Americans boarded a skiff north of St. Louis, Missouri, and rowed across the Mississippi River in hopes of reaching free soil in Illinois. Their escape had been organized and coordinated with free people of color in Illinois, some of whom were waiting to receive the freedom seekers. Unfortunately, police officers and slave-owners were waiting as well.

In the struggle and confusion that ensued, several of the fugitive slaves, including three owned by Missouri Botanical Garden founder Henry Shaw, were caught. Freeman, one of the black organizers on the Illinois side, was wounded and later died. Another organizer on the Missouri side, Mary Meachum, widow of the pastor of the First African Baptist Church of St. Louis, was arrested and charged with assisting the fugitive slaves. The final disposition of her case remains unknown.

Milton House (Milton, Wisconsin)

The Milton House was constructed in 1844 by Underground Railroad conductor and Wisconsin pioneer Joseph Goodrich (1800–1867). Located at 18 South Janesville Street in Milton, the house, with its unusual hexagonal three-story tower, served as a local inn and the Goodrich family residence — and a hiding place for fugitive slaves.

Freedom seekers could enter a log cabin located approximately 40 feet south of the Milton House. Once inside the cabin, they could enter a tunnel through a trap door — that, in turn, led to the basement of the inn. Once in the basement, the fugitives were protected and fed by Goodrich.

Perhaps the most remarkable feature of the Milton House is the tunnel. Although there are many rumors and legends regarding other tunnels, the Milton House tunnel may be the only completely verifiable branch of the Underground Railroad that was truly "underground."

Mount Pleasant, Ohio

Mount Pleasant, Ohio, was founded in 1803 by Robert Carothers, an Irishman from Virginia, and Jesse Thomas, a Quaker from North Carolina. Incorporated in 1814, the town became a center for pork packing, milling and shipping. With its strong Quaker influence, Mt. Pleasant also played an important role in both the antislavery movement and boasted a network of Underground Railroad stations.

Mount Zion AME Church (Woolwich Township, New Jersey)

Mount Zion African Methodist Episcopal (AME) Church was built in 1834 in Small Gloucester, New Jersey. Located at 172 Garwin Road, Mount Zion AME was an important Underground Railroad station on one of the more active fugitive slave escape routes in the east, a key link in a chain of communities between Springtown and Jersey City. For example, Harriet Tubman used this route for more than a decade.

One of the unusual and defining features of this site is a secret, three-by-four-foot trap door in the floor of the church vestibule which provided access to a hiding place in the crawlspace below. Once secure in their refuge, fugitive slaves were fed and tended by members of the Mt. Zion AME church, most notably Pompey Lewis and Jubilee Sharper.

Murphy Orchards (Newfane, New York)

The Murphy Orchards farmstead in Newfane, New York, was purchased in 1850 by Charles and Libby McClew. The McClew family harbored fugitive slaves on their farm — probably using a chamber under their barn (probably built as a cistern) as a hiding place for freedom seekers.

Nathan and Mary (Polly) Johnson House (New Bedford, Massachusetts)

Nathan (d. 1880) and Mary Johnson (d. 1871) were free African Americans who, in the mid–1820s, purchased land in New Bedford, Massachusetts, on which their home and other business stood. The Johnsons prospered, since New Bedford was enjoying a veritable Golden Age due to its tremendously profitable whaling industry. Some of the Johnsons' businesses were run from their home at 21 Seventh Street, including a bakery, an apartment building, a confectionary shop and even a school for African American children. At times, Nathan Johnson also owned a restaurant, a bathhouse and rental property.

The 21 Seventh Street property served as an Underground Railroad station, most notably as a refuge for Frederick Douglass in 1838, and is the only one of Douglass' three homes in New Bedford that survives. The Nathan and Mary Johnson Properties are located at 17–19 and 21 Seventh Street in New Bedford, Massachusetts.

Oakdale (Chadds Ford, Pennsylvania)

The home of Isaac and Dinah Mendenhall, important Quaker abolitionists, was built in 1840 at Oakdale, near Chadds Ford, Pennsylvania. Because of its location, Oakdale became the first stop on the Underground Railroad north of the Delaware state line, and the Mendenhalls were called upon often to provide food and temporary shelter for fugitive slaves on their northward journey.

One of Oakdale's most distinctive features is a concealed square room, built between a walk-in fireplace and the west wall of the carriage house and entered through a loft.

Oswego Market House (Oswego, New York)

An antislavery and Underground Railroad site located on the west side of the Oswego River, the Oswego Market House is a massive brick and stone Federal-styled building formerly used as a market place and seat of village and city government. In 1850, the annual convention of the Liberty Party met in the building. At this convention, Gerrit Smith was nominated for the presidency of the United States and Samuel Ringgold Ward, a fugitive slave, was nominated for the vice-presidency — the first African American ever nominated by any party for one of the highest national political offices.

Although the site itself was not related directly to the Underground Railroad, Oswego was a significant Underground Railroad center, and both Smith and Ward were important friends of the fugitive.

Owen Lovejoy House (Princeton, Illinois)

The home of Owen Lovejoy (1811–1864) in Princeton, Illinois, was used in the 1840s and 1850s to harbor fugitive slaves. So active was Lovejoy that freedom seekers passing through Princeton were described as riding the "Lovejoy Line." Lovejoy did not conceal his role with the Underground Railroad and often faced harassment and even legal prosecution.

Peter Mott House (Lawnside, New Jersey)

The Peter Mott House was built in Lawnside, New Jersey, around 1844 by Peter Mott (c. 1810–1881), an African American farmer who resided there until 1879. Mott and his family settled in a free black community known as Snow Hill that later merged with a neighboring settlement called Free Haven. In 1907, Snow Hill and Free Haven were renamed Lawnside, the only incorporated African American municipality in the northern United States, dating to the Colonial period as a settlement of people of color. Mott became a minister, influential local leader and Underground Railroad conductor.

Reuben Benedict House (Peru Township, Ohio)

The home of Reuben Benedict in Peru Township near Marengo, Ohio, was a station on the Underground Railroad and played a key role in the rescue of Bill Anderson in 1839. The Benedicts moved from New York to Marion County, Ohio, in 1812 and were the first white family on the still largely unsettled Ohio frontier.

Rokeby (Ferrisburg, Vermont)

Rokeby was built in 1793 by Thomas (1761–1851) and Jemima (1761–1846) Robinson, both Quakers and active members of the Vermont and Ferrisburg Anti-Slavery Societies. Rokeby was home to four generations of the Robinson family and, during the life of Rowland Thomas Robinson (1796–1879), played a significant role as a station on the Underground Railroad.

Now a museum, Rokeby is significant as repository of historical documents and artifacts. Visitors may examine Robinson's detailed records and the personal correspondence related to his work as a friend of the fugitive and the use of his home as a refuge for freedom seekers. The house is also fully furnished with Robinson family belongings, including furniture, clothing, dishes, books, art and other artifacts.

Rush R. Sloane House (Sandusky, Ohio)

Rush R. Sloane (1828–1908) was a Sandusky, Ohio, attorney, abolitionist and Underground Railroad activist who sacrificed his fortune and reputation by assisting fugitive slaves in the decade before the Civil War. His home at 403 East Adams Street in Sandusky, Ohio, was built in the early 1850s and served as an Underground Railroad station.

St. James AME Church (Ithaca, New York)

The St. James AME Zion Church was built in 1836 and is believed to be the oldest church in Ithaca, New York, and one of the first of the AME Zion churches in the country. Ithaca was located on an important corridor for fugitive slaves, and St. James AME Zion became an important Underground Railroad station. Further, along with assisting fugitive slaves escaping through New York en route to Canada, St. James embraced those who chose to settle in Ithaca, many of whom constructed homes near the church itself. Led by the Reverend Thomas James, who himself assisted fugitive slaves, St. James, located at 116–118 Cleveland Avenue, became a center of black antislavery activism and was visited at times by both Harriet Tubman and Frederick Douglass.

Samuel and Sally Wilson House (Cincinnati, Ohio)

Samuel and Sally Wilson, Presbyterians with strong antislavery convictions, moved to Cincinnati, Ohio, from Reading, Pennsylvania, in 1849 and built a Greek Revival home at 1502 Aster Place that operated as a station on the Underground Railroad until at least 1852. Fugitive slaves were hidden in the cellar and, as late as the early 1900s, groups of elderly African American men returned as visitors to the site at which they had once found sanctuary. In an 1892 letter, Harriet Wilson described some of her parents' efforts, noting that, on one occasion when slave-catchers were searching the area for fugitive slaves: "The women being 'entertained' by our family were terribly frightened declaring 'that they would die rather than be taken and carried back.' Though quite large in size they were ready and willing to crawl through a small aperture into a dark cellar where they would be safe."

As an adult, Harriet worked as a teacher in Cincinnati and returned to College Hill on the weekends. Prior to her trip home on Friday evenings, she was given the number of fugitive slaves en route to College Hill so the "station" would be prepared for their arrival. She recalled that "frequently, when at home on Saturday and asking for some article of clothing, I would receive the reply, 'Gone to Canada.'"

Starr Clark Tin Shop (Mexico, New York)

The home of Starr Clark (1793–1866) was an important Underground Railroad station in Mexico, New York. Clark, a major figure in the antislavery movement, operated the station in both his tin shop and his home on Main Street from the early 1830s until the Civil War. According to Clark's granddaughter, Cora Plumley Denton, a tunnel ran from the basement of the shop to the house next door.

Tappan-Philbrick House (Brookline, Massachusetts)

Samuel Philbrick, who was one of the first and most active abolitionists in Brookline, Massachusetts, was also the treasurer of the Massachusetts Anti-Slavery Society. According to one source, "Samuel Philbrick alone kept the spark of antislavery feeling alive in that very conservative community." He was also a friend and financial backer of William Lloyd Garrison and *The Liberator.*

Philbrick's house at 182 Walnut Street, known as the Tappan-Philbrick House, stood atop a hill in Brookline and was the site of many abolitionist meetings and a station on the Underground Railroad. The abolitionist Grimke sisters, Angelina and Sarah, spent the winter of 1837 there, and William and Ellen Craft hid with the Philbrick family after their freedom was threatened following the passage of the Fugitive Slave Act of 1850.

The Wayside (Concord, Massachusetts)

The Wayside in Concord, Massachusetts, was home to two of nineteenth century America's most influential literary figures, Louisa May Alcott and Nathaniel Hawthorne, each of whom had ties to the antislavery movement. The Way-side, then known as "Hillside," was one the childhood homes of Louisa May Alcott, author of the 1868 classic *Little Women.* Alcott lived there with her parents and three sisters from April 1845 to November 1848 during her early teenage years and documented that the home served as refuge for a fugitive slave in early 1847. Mrs. Alcott's family included Judge Samuel Sewall, who wrote an early antislavery tract, "The Selling of Joseph," in 1700, and her brother, Samuel J. May, one of the founders of The American Anti-Slavery Society and an Underground Railroad conductor.

Nathaniel Hawthorne, author of *The Scarlet Letter, The House of the Seven Gables,* and *Twice-Told Tales,* lived there from 1852 until 1870, and is responsible for the name by which it is still known. The Wayside was the only home Hawthorne ever owned and the place where he wrote his last works.

White Horse Farm (Schuylkill Township, Pennsylvania)

White Horse Farm was built around 1770 in Schuylkill Township, Pennsylvania, and was the lifetime home of politician and prominent abolitionist Elijah Pennypacker (1802–1888). In 1840, Pennypacker became a Quaker and used this home on Whitehorse Road as a major stop on the Underground Railroad. In the next decades, hundreds of fugitive slaves found sanctuary there and assistance in moving to stations farther north.

William Eberle Thompson Homesite (Bethel, Ohio)

In his adolescence, Dr. William E. Thompson (1835–1940) was a conductor on the Underground Railroad — escorting fugitive slaves from Bethel, Ohio, to the Elklick area of Clermont County near Williamsburg, Ohio. His former home and office are located 137 Main Street in Bethel, Ohio.

William Jackson Homestead (Newton, Massachusetts)

The Jackson Homestead was build by Timothy Jackson (1756–1814) in 1809 after he served in the Revolutionary War and returned to Newton to farm his family's land. The homestead at 527 Washington St., in Newton served as an Underground Railroad station for several decades.

William Lloyd Garrison House
(Boston, Massachusetts)

William Lloyd Garrison (1805–1879) was one of the most outspoken and effective leaders of the American antislavery movement. After the Civil War, Garrison went into semi-retirement, but maintained his interest and involvement in the crusades for prohibition and women's rights. After Garrison's death, his house at 125 Highland Street in the Roxbury section of Boston, Massachusetts, was purchased by the Rockledge Association, an organization of African Americans formed to preserve the building. In 1904, the house was acquired by the Episcopal Sisters of the Society of St. Margaret and remains in their possession.

Although not directly associated with the Underground Railroad, the William Lloyd Garrison House stands as a monument to a man whose zeal and moral authority were driving forces in the struggle against slavery.

Wilson Bruce Evans House
(Oberlin, Ohio)

Wilson Bruce Evans (1824–1898) and his brother Henry Evans were born free in Fayetteville, North Carolina, and learned the trade of cabinetmaking and carpentry as young men. In 1854, they moved with their respective families to Oberlin, Ohio, a college community known for its antislavery sentiments and its openness to free people of color, and established a cabinetmaking and carpentry business. Although not active abolitionists, the Evans brothers were key participants in the 1858 Oberlin-Wellington Rescue and risked imprisonment to oppose the operations of the Fugitive Slave Act.

The Wilson Bruce Evans House is located at 33 East Vine Street in Oberlin.

Appendix 6: Bibliography of Slave Autobiographies

Aaron. *The Light and Truth of Slavery. Aaron's History.* Worcester, MA: Privately printed, 1845.

Adams, John Quincy [b. 1845]. *Narrative of the Life of John Quincy Adams, When in Slavery, and Now as a Freeman.* Harrisburg, PA: Sieg, 1872.

Aga, Selim. *Incidents Connected with the Life of Selim Aga, a Native of Central Africa.* Aberdeen, UK: W. Bennett, 1846.

Albert, Octavia V. Rogers (Octavia Victoria Rogers) [1853–1889]. *The House of Bondage, or, Charlotte Brooks and Other Slaves, Original and Life Like, As They Appeared in Their Old Plantation and City Slave Life; Together with Pen-Pictures of the Peculiar Institution, with Sights and Insights into Their New Relations as Freedmen, Freemen, and Citizens.* New York: Hunt and Eaton, 1890.

Aleckson, Sam [1852–1914]. *Before the War, and After the Union: An Autobiography.* Boston: Gold Mind, 1929.

Allen, Richard [1760–1831]. *The Life, Experience and Gospel Labors of the Rt. Rev. Richard Allen to Which Is Annexed the Rise and Progress of the African Methodist Church in the United States of America: Containing a Narrative of the Yellow Fever in the Year of Our Lord, 1793, with an Address to the People of Color in the United States.* Philadelphia: Martin and Boden, 1833.

Anderson, Robert [1843–1930]. *From Slavery to Affluence; Memoirs of Robert Anderson, Ex-slave.* Edited by Daisy Anderson. Hemingford, NE: Hemingford Ledger, 1927.

Anderson, Robert [b. 1819]. *The Anderson Surpriser. Written After He was 75 Years of Age.* Macon, GA: Privately printed, 1895.

_____. *The Life of Rev. Robert Anderson: Born the 22d of February, in the Year of Our Lord 1819, and Joined the Methodist Episcopal Church in 1839. This Book Shall Be Called The Young Men's Guide, or, The Brother in White.* Macon, GA: J. W. Burke, 1892.

Anderson, Thomas [b. 1775]. *Interesting Account of Thomas Anderson, a Slave, Taken from His Own Lips.* Edited by J.P. Clark. Virginia, 1854?.

Anderson, William J. [b. 1811]. *Life and Narrative of William J. Anderson, Twenty-four Years a Slave; Sold Eight Times! In Jail Sixty Times!! Whipped Three Hundred Times!!! or The Dark Deeds of American Slavery Revealed. Containing Scriptural Views of the Origin of the Black and of the White Man. Also, a Simple and Easy Plan to Abolish Slavery in the United States. Together with an Account of the Services of Colored Men in the Revolutionary War — Day and Date, and Interesting Facts.* Chicago: Daily Tribune, 1857.

Arter, Jared Maurice [b. 1850]. *Echoes from a Pioneer Life.* Atlanta: A. B. Caldwell, 1922.

Arthur [1747–1768]. *The Life, and Dying Speech of Arthur, a Negro Man, Who Was Executed at Worcester, October 20th 1768. For a Rape Committed on the Body of one Deborah Metca.* Boston, 1768.

Ball, Charles. *Fifty Years in Chains; or, The Life of an American Slave.* Edited by Isaac Fisher. New York: H. Dayton, 1859.

_____. *Slavery in the United States: A Narrative of the Life and Adventures of Charles Ball, a Black Man, Who Lived Forty Years in Maryland, South Carolina and Georgia as a Slave.* Edited by Isaac Fisher. New York: John S. Taylor, 1837.

Baquaqua, Mahommah Gardo. *Biography of Mahommah G. Baquaqua, a Native Zoogoo, in* the Interior of Africa (a Convert to Christianity): with a Description of that Part of the World, Including the Manners and Customs of the Inhabitants, Written and Revised from His Own Words by Samuel Moore. Mahommah's Early Life, His Education, His Capture and Slavery in Western Africa and Brazil, His Escape to the United States, from Thence to Hayti (the City of Port au Prince): His Reception by the Baptist Missionary there, the Rev. W. L. Judd: His Conversion to Christianity, Baptism, and return to this Country, His Views, Objects and Aim. Edited by Samuel Moore. Detroit: George E. Pomeroy, 1854.

Bayley, Solomon. A Narrative of Some Remarkable Incidents, in the Life of Solomon Bayley, Formerly a Slave, in the State of Delaware, North America: Written by Himself. London: Harvey and Darton, 1825.

Bibb, Henry [1815–1854]. Narrative of the Life and Adventures of Henry Bibb, an American Slave, Written by Himself. New York: Privately printed, 1849.

Black, Leonard. The Life and Sufferings of Leonard Black, a Fugitive from Slavery. Written by Himself. New Bedford, MA: Benjamin Lindsey, 1847.

Blair, Norvel. Book for the People! To be Read by all Voters, Black and White, with Thrilling Events of the Life of Norvel Blair, of Grundy County, State of Illinois. Written and Published by Him, and with the Money He Earned by His Own Labor, and is Sent Out with the Sincere Hope that if Carefully Read, it will Tend to Put a Stop to Northern Bull-Dozing and will Give to all a Free Ballot, without Fear, Favor or Affection and Respect. Joliet, IL: Joliet Daily Record, 1880.

Branham, Levi [b. 1852]. My Life and Travels. Dalton, GA: A.J. Showalter, 1929.

Brinch, Boyrereau [fl. 1758–1810]. The Blind African Slave, or Memoirs of Boyrereau Brinch, Nick-named Jeffrey Brace. Containing an Account of the Kingdom of Pow-Woo, in the Interior of Africa; with the Climate and Natural Productions, Laws, and Customs Peculiar to That Place. With an Account of His Captivity, Sufferings, Sales, Travels, Emancipation, Conversion to the Christian Religion, Knowledge of the Scriptures, &c. Interspersed with Strictures on Slavery, Speculative Observations on the Qualities of Human Nature, with Quotation from Scripture. Edited by Benjamin F. Prentiss. St. Albans, VT: Harry Whitney, 1810.

Bristol. The Dying Speech of Bristol. Boston: Edes and Gill, 1763.

Brown, Henry Box [b. 1815]. Narrative of Henry Box Brown, Who Escaped from Slavery Enclosed in a Box 3 Feet Long and 2 Wide. Written from a Statement of Facts Made by Himself. With, Remarks Upon the Remedy for Slavery. Edited by Charles Stearns. Boston: Brown and Stearns, 1849.

Brown, John [fl. 1854]. Slave Life in Georgia: A Narrative of the Life, Sufferings, and Escape of John Brown, a Fugitive Slave, Now in England. Edited by Louis Alexis Chamerovzow. London: W. M. Watts, 1855.

Brown, Sterling Nelson [1858–1929]. My Own Life Story. Washington, D.C.: Hamilton, 1924.

Brown, William Wells [1814–1884]. The American Fugitive in Europe. Sketches of Places and People Abroad. With a Memoir of the Author. Boston: J. P. Jewett, 1855.

_____[1814–1884]. My Southern Home; or the South and Its People. Boston: A. G. Brown, 1880.

_____[1814–1884]. Narrative of William W. Brown, a Fugitive Slave, Written by Himself. Boston: American Anti-Slavery Society, 1847.

Bruce, Henry Clay [1836–1902]. The New Man. Twenty-nine Years a Slave. Twenty-nine Years a Free Man. Recollections of H. C. Bruce. York, PA: P. Anstadt, 1895.

Bruner, Peter [1845–1938]. A Slave's Adventures Toward Freedom; Not Fiction, But the True Story of a Struggle. Edited by Carrie Bruner. Oxford, OH, 1918.

Burton, Annie L. [b. 1858]. Memories of Childhood's Slavery Days. Boston: Ross, 1909.

Burton, Thomas William [1860–1939]. What Experience Has Taught Me. An Autobiography of Thomas William Burton. Cincinnati: Jennings and Graham, 1910.

Campbell, Israel. Bond and Free: or, Yearnings for Freedom, from My Green Briar House. Being the Story of My Life in Bondage, and My Life in Freedom. Philadelphia: Privately printed, 1861.

Charlton, Lewis. Sketch of the Life of Mr. Lewis Charlton, and Reminiscences of Slavery. Edited by Edward Everett Brown. Portland, ME: Daily Press, 1870?.

Chesney, Pharoah Jackson [1781?] and John Coram Webster [b. 1851]. Last of the Pioneers or Old Times in East Tenn., Being the Life and Reminiscences of Pharoah Jackson Chesney (Aged 120 Years). Knoxville, TN: S. B. Newman & Co., 1902.

Clarke, Lewis Garrard [1812–1897], and Milton Clarke [1817?-1901]. Narratives of the Sufferings of Lewis and Milton Clarke, Sons of a Soldier of the Revolution, During a Captivity of

More Than Twenty Years Among the Slaveholders of Kentucky, One of the So Called Christian States of North America. Dictated by Themselves. Edited by Joseph Cammet Lovejoy. Boston: Bela Marsh, 1846.

Clarke, Lewis Garrard [1812–1897]. *Narrative of the Sufferings of Lewis Clarke, during a Captivity of More Than Twenty-five Years, Among the Algerines of Kentucky; One of the So Called Christian States of North America. Dictated by Himself.* Edited by Joseph Cammet Lovejoy. Boston: D. H. Ela, 1845.

Clement, Samuel Spottford [b. 1861]. *Memoirs of Samuel Spottford Clement: Relating Interesting Experiences in Days of Slavery and Freedom.* Edited by Sara Ovington. Steubenville, OH: Herald, 1908.

Craft, William [1824–1900]. *Running a Thousand Miles for Freedom; or, The Escape of William and Ellen Craft from Slavery.* London: William Tweedie, 1860.

Cugoano, Ottobah [b. 1757?]. "Narrative of the Enslavement of Ottobah Cugoano, a Native of Africa; Published by Himself on the Year 1787." In Thomas Fisher. *The Negro's Memorial; or, Abolitionist's Catechism; by an Abolitionist.* London: Privately printed, 1825.

Davis, Noah [b. 1803 or 1804]. *A Narrative of the Life of Rev. Noah Davis, a Coloured Man. Written by Himself at 54.* Baltimore: J. F. Weishampel, Jr., 1859.

Delaney, Lucy Ann Berry. *From the Darkness Cometh the Light; or, Struggles for Freedom.* St. Louis: J. T. Smith, 1891.

Douglass, Frederick [1818–1895]. *Life and Times of Frederick Douglass Written by Himself. His Early Life as a Slave, His Escape from Bondage, and His Complete History to the Present Time.* Hartford, CT: Park, 1881.

_____. *Life and Times of Frederick Douglass Written by Himself. His Early Life as a Slave, His Escape from Bondage, and His Complete History to the Present Time.* Boston: De Wolfe & Fiske, 1892.

_____. *My Bondage and My Freedom.* New York: Miller, Orton and Mulligan, 1855.

_____. *Narrative of the Life of Frederick Douglass, an American Slave. Written by Himself.* Boston: American Anti-Slavery Society, 1845.

Drew, Benjamin, ed. [1812–1903]. *A North-Side View of Slavery. The Refugee: or, The Narratives of Fugitive Slaves in Canada. Related by Themselves. With an Account of the History and Condition of the Colored Population of Upper Canada.* Boston: J.P. Jewett, 1856.

Drumgoold, Kate. *A Slave Girl's Story. Being the Autobiography of Kate Drumgoold.* Brooklyn: Privately printed, 1898.

Elizabeth [1766–1866]. *Elizabeth, a Colored Minister of the Gospel Born in Slavery.* Philadelphia: Tract Assoc. of Friends, 1889.

_____. *Memoir of Old Elizabeth, a Coloured Woman.* Philadelphia: Collins, 1863.

Equiano, Olaudah [1745?-1797]. *The Interesting Narrative of the Life of Olaudah Equiano, or Gustavus Vassa, the African. Written by Himself. Sketches of the Life of Joseph Mountain, a Negro Who Was Executed at New-Haven, on the 20th Day of October, 1790, for a Rape, Committed on the 26th Day of May Last.* Edited by David Daggett. New Haven: T. and S. Green, 1790.

Fedric, Francis. *Slave Life in Virginia and Kentucky; or, Fifty Years of Slavery in the Southern States of America.* Edited by Rev. Charles Lee. London: Wertheim, Macintosh, and Hunt, 1863.

Ferebee, London R. [b. 1849]. *A Brief History of the Slave Life of Rev. L. R. Ferebee, and the Battles of Life, and Four Years of His Ministerial Life. Written from Memory, to 1882.* Raleigh, NC: Edwards, Broughton, 1882.

Flipper, Henry Ossian [1845–1940]. *The Colored Cadet at West Point; Autobiography of Lieut. Henry Ossian Flipper, U.S. A., First Graduate of Color from the U.S. Military Academy.* New York: H. Lee, 1878.

Fortis, Edmund [d. 1794]. *The Last Words and Dying Speech of Edmund Fortis, a Negro Man, Who Appeared to Be between Thirty and Forty Years of Age, but Very Ignorant. He Was Executed at Dresden, on Kennebeck River, on Thursday the Twenty-Fifth Day of September, 1794, for a Rape and Murder, Committed on the Body of Pamela Tilton, a Young Girl of about Fourteen Years of Age, Daughter of Mr. Tilton of Vassalborough, in the County of Lincoln.* Exeter, ME, 1795.

Fortune. *The Dying Confession and Declaration of Fortune, a Negro Man.* Boston: Fowle and Draper, 1762. No copy of this tract can now be located.

Frederick, Francis [b. 1809?]. *Autobiography of Rev. Francis Frederick, of Virginia.* Baltimore: J.W. Woods, 1869.

Garlick, Charles A. [b. 1827]. *Life Including His Escape and Struggle for Liberty of Charles A. Garlick, Born a Slave in Old Virginia.* Jefferson, OH: J. A. Howells, 1902.

Grandy, Moses [b. 1786]. *Narrative of the Life of Moses Grandy, Late a Slave in the United States of America.* London: Gilpin, 1843.

Green, Elisha Winfield. *Life of the Rev. Elisha W. Green, One of the Founders of the Kentucky Normal and Theological Institute — Now the State University of Louisville; Eleven Years Moderator of the Mt. Zion Baptist Association; Five Years Moderator of the Consolidated Baptist Educational Association and Over Thirty Years Pastor of the Colored Baptist Churches of Maysville and Paris.* Maysville, KY: Republican, 1888.

Green, Jacob D. [b. 1813]. *Narrative of the Life of J. D. Green, a Runaway Slave, from Kentucky, Containing an Account of His Three Escapes, in 1839, 1846, and 1848.* Huddersfield, England: Henry Fielding, 1864.

Green, William. *Narrative of Events in the Life of William Green, (Formerly a Slave.) Written by Himself.* Springfield, MA: L. M. Guernsey, 1853.

Grimes, William [b. 1784]. *Life of William Grimes, the Runaway Slave. Written by Himself.* New York: Privately printed, 1825.

_____. *Life of William Grimes, the Runaway Slave, Brought down to the Present Time. Written by Himself.* New Haven: Privately printed, 1855.

Gronniosaw, James Albert Ukawsaw [1712–1775]. *A Narrative of the Most Remarkable Particulars in the Life of James Albert Ukawsaw Gronniosaw, an African Prince.* Edited by Walter Shirley. Bath: S. Hazzard, 1770.

Hall, Samuel [b. 1818], and Orville Elder [b. 1866]. *Samuel Hall, 47 Years a Slave. A Brief Story of His Life Before and After Freedom Came to Him.* Washington, IA: Journal Print, 1912.

Hammon, Briton. *A Narrative of the Uncommon Sufferings, and Surprizing Deliverance of Briton Hammon, a Negro Man, — Servant to General Winslow, of Marshfield, in New-England; Who Returned to Boston, after Having Been Absent almost Thirteen Years. Containing an Account of the Many Hardships He Underwent from the Time He Left His Master's House, in the Year 1747, to the Time of His Return to Boston. — How He was Cast Away in the Capes of Florida;— The Horrid Cruelty and Inhuman Barbarity of the Indians in Murdering the Whole Ship's Crew;— The Manner of His Being Carry'd by Them Into Captivity. Also, an Account of His Being Confined Four Years and Seven Months in a Close Dungeon,— and the Remarkable Manner in which He Met with His Good Old Master in London; Who Returned to New-England, a Passenger in the Same Ship.* Boston: Green and Russell, 1760.

Hayden, William [b. 1785]. *Narrative of William Hayden, Containing a Faithful Account of His Travels for a Number of Years, Whilst a Slave, in the South. Written by Himself.* Cincinnati: Privately printed, 1846.

Heard, William Henry [1850–1937]. *From Slavery to the Bishopric in the AME Church: an Autobiography.* Philadelphia: AME Book Concern, 1924.

Henderson, Madison, et al. *Trials and Confessions of Madison Henderson, Alias Blanchard, Alfred Amos Warrick, James W. Seward, and Charles Brown, Murderers of Jesse Baker and Jacob Weaver, As Given by Themselves and Likeness of Each, Taken in Jail Shortly After Their Arrest.* St. Louis: Chambers and Knapp, 1841.

Henry, George [b. 1819]. *Life of George Henry. Together with a Brief History of the Colored People in America.* Providence: Privately printed, 1894.

Henry, Thomas W. [b. 1794]. *Autobiography of Thomas W. Henry of the AME Church.* Baltimore: Privately printed, 1872.

Henson, Josiah [1789–1883]. *The Life of Josiah Henson, Formerly a Slave, Now an Inhabitant of Canada, As Narrated by Himself.* Edited by Samuel A. Eliot. Boston: A.D. Phelps, 1849.

_____. *Truth Is Stranger Than Fiction. Father Henson's Story of His Own Life.* Edited by Samuel A. Eliot. Boston: J.P. Jewett, 1858.

Holley, James W. [b. 1848]. *Life History of J. W. Holley; the Old Faithful Servant. Born and Reared a Slave. After Freedom Became a Worker in the Master's Vineyard.* Columbus, OH: Privately printed, 1924.

Holsey, Lucius Henry [1842–1920]. *Autobiography, Sermons, Addresses, and Essays of Bishop L. H. Holsey.* Atlanta: Franklin, 1898.

Horton, George Moses [1797–1883]. *The Poetical Works of George M. Horton, the Colored Bard of North Carolina, to Which Is Prefixed the Life of the Author. Written by Himself.* Hillsborough, NC: Heartt, 1845.

Hughes, Louis [1832–1913]. *Thirty Years a Slave. From Bondage to Freedom. The Institution of Slavery As Seen on the Plantation and in the Home of the Planter. Autobiography of Louis Hughes.* Milwaukee: South Side, 1897.

Jackson, Andrew [b. 1814]. *Narrative and Writings of Andrew Jackson, of Kentucky; Containing an Account of His Birth, and Twenty-six Years of His Life While a Slave; His Escape; Five Years of Freedom, Together with Anecdotes Relating to Slavery; Journal of One Year's Travels. Sketches, etc.* Syracuse: Daily and Weekly Star, 1847.

Jackson, George Washington [1860?-1940]. *A Brief History of the Life and Works of G. W. Jackson; Forty-Five Years Principal of the G. W. Jackson High School, Corsicana, Texas.* Corsicana, TX: Privately printed, 1938.

Jackson, John Andrew. *The Experience of a Slave in South Carolina.* London: Passmore and Alabaster, 1862.

Jackson, Mattie Jane [1846]. *The Story of Mattie J. Jackson; Her Parentage — Experience of Eighteen Years in Slavery — Incidents during the War — Her Escape from Slavery. A True Story. Written and Arranged by Dr. L. S. Thompson, (Formerly Mrs. Schuyler,) as given by Mattie.* Lawrence, MA: Sentinel, 1866.

Jackson-Coppin, Fanny. *Reminiscences of School Life; and Hints on Teaching.* Philadelphia: AME Book Concern, 1913.

Jacobs, Harriet Ann [1813–1897]. *Incidents in the Life of a Slave Girl, Written by Herself.* Edited by Lydia Maria Child. Boston: Privately printed, 1861.

Jacobs, John S. [1815–1873]. "A True Tale of Slavery." *The Leisure Hour: A Family Journal of Instruction and Recreation.* February 7, 14, 21, and 28, 1861. London: Stevens and Co.

James, Thomas [1804–1891]. *Life of Rev. Thomas James, by Himself.* Rochester, NY: Post Express, 1886.

Jamison, Monroe Franklin [1848–1918]. *Autobiography and Work of Bishop M. F. Jamison, D. D. ("Uncle Joe") Editor, Publisher, and Church Extension Secretary; a Narration of His Whole Career from the Cradle to the Bishopric of the Colored M. E. Church in America.* Nashville, TN: Privately printed, 1912.

Jea, John [b. 1773]. *The Life, History, and Unparalleled Sufferings of John Jea, the African Preacher, Compiled and Written by Himself.* Portsea, England: Privately printed, 1811.

Jefferson, Isaac [b. 1775]. *Memoirs of a Monticello Slave, As Dictated to Charles Campbell in the 1840's by Isaac, One of Thomas Jefferson's Slaves.* Edited by Rayford W. Logan. Charlottesville: University of Virginia Press for the Tracy W. McGregor Library, 1951.

Jeffrey. *Declaration and Confession of Jeffrey, a Negro, Who Was Executed at Worcester, Oct. 17, 1745, for the Murder of Mrs. Tabitha Sandford, at Mendon, the 12th of September Preceding.* Boston: T. Fleet, 1745. No surviving copies.

Jeter, Henry Norval [1851–1938]. *Pastor Henry N. Jeter's Twenty-Five Years Experience with the Shiloh Baptist Church and Her History.* Providence: Remington, 1901.

Johnson, Isaac [1844–1905]. *Slavery Days in Old Kentucky. A True Story of a Father Who Sold His Wife and Four Children. By One of the Children.* Ogdensburg, NY: Republican and Journal, 1901.

Johnson, Thomas Lewis [b. 1836]. *Africa for Christ: Twenty-eight Years a Slave.* London: Alexander and Shepheard, 1892.

_____. *Twenty-eight Years a Slave: or, The Story of My Life in Three Continents.* Bournemouth, England: W. Mate, 1909.

Johnstone, Abraham [d. 1797]. *The Address of Abraham Johnstone, a Black Man, Who Was Hanged at Woodbury, in the County of Gloucester, and State of New Jersey ... the 8th Day of July Last; to the People of Colour. To Which Is Added His Dying Confession or Declaration, also, a Copy of a Letter to His Wife, Written the Day Previous to His Execution.* Philadelphia, 1797.

Jones, Friday [1810–1887]. *Days of Bondage. Autobiography of Friday Jones. Being a Brief Narrative of His Trials and Tribulations in Slavery.* Washington, D.C.: Privately printed, 1883.

Jones, Thomas H. *Experience and Personal Narrative of Uncle Tom Jones: Who Was for Forty Years a Slave; Also the Surprising Adventures of Wild Tom of the Island Retreat, a Fugitive Negro from South Carolina.* Boston: H. B. Skinner, 1854.

Jones, Thomas H. *The Experience of Rev. Thomas H. Jones, Who Was a Slave for Forty-Three Years. Written by a Friend, as Related to Him by Brother Jones.* New Bedford: E. Anthony & Sons, 1885.

_____. *The Experience of Thomas H. Jones, Who Was a Slave for Forty-three years. Written by a Friend, As Given to Him by Brother Jones.* Boston: Bazin and Chandler, 1862.

Jordan, Lewis Garnett [1854?-1939]. *On Two Hemispheres: Bits from the Life Story of Lewis G. Jordan, as Told by Himself.* 1935.

Joseph, John. *The Life and Sufferings of John Joseph, a Native of Ashantee, in West Africa Who Was Stolen from His Parents at the Age of 3 Years, and Sold to Mr. Johnston, a Cotton Planter in New Orleans, South America.* Wellington, New Zealand: Privately printed, 1848.

Joyce, John [ca. 1784–1808], and Peter Matthias [ca. 1782–1808]. *Confession of John Joyce, Alias, Davis, Who Was Executed on Monday, the 14th of March, 1808 for the Murder of Mrs. Sarah Cross: With an Address to the Public and People of Colour, Together with the Substance of the Trial, and the Address of Chief Justice Tilghman, On His Condemnation. Confession* of Peter Mathias, Alias Matthews, Who Was Executed on Monday, the 14th of March, 1808. For the Murder of Mrs. Sarah Cross; With an Address to the Public and People of Colour. Together with the Substance of the Trial, and the Address of Chief Justice Tilghman, on His Condemnation. Edited by Richard Allen. Philadelphia: Bethel Church, 1808.

Keckley, Elizabeth Hobbs [1818–1907]. Behind the Scenes, Or, Thirty Years a Slave and Four Years in the White House. New York: G. W. Carleton, 1868.

Kelley, Edmond [b. 1817]. A Family Redeemed from Bondage; Being Rev. Edmond Kelley, (the Author,) His Wife, and Four Children. New Bedford: Privately printed, 1851.

Knox, George L. [1841–1927]. Life as I Remember It — As a Slave and Freeman. Indianapolis Freeman, December 22, 1894 — December 21, 1895. Rpt. George L. Knox. Slave and Freeman: The Autobiography of George L. Knox. Edited by Willard B. Gatewood, Jr. Lexington: University Press of Kentucky, 1979.

Lane, Isaac [1834–1937]. Autobiography of Bishop Isaac Lane, L.L.D.: With a Short History of the C. M. E. Church in America and of Methodism. Nashville, TN: M. E. Church South, 1916.

Lane, Lunsford [b. 1803]. The Narrative of Lunsford Lane, Formerly of Raleigh, N.C., Embracing an Account of His Early Life, the Redemption by Purchase of Himself and Family from Slavery, and His Banishing from the Place of His Birth for the Crime of Wearing a Colored Skin. Boston: J. G. Torrey, 1842.

Latta, Morgan London [b. 1853]. The History of My Life and Work: Autobiography. Raleigh: Privately printed, 1903.

Lee, William Mack [b. 1835]. History of the Life of Rev. Wm. Mack Lee, Body Servant of General Robert E. Lee through the Civil War, Cook from 1861 to 1865; Still Living under the Protection of the Southern States. Norfolk, VA: Smith Printing, 1918.

Lewis, Joseph Vance. Out of the Ditch: A True Story of an Ex-slave. Houston: Rein, 1910.

Love, Nat [1854–1921]. The Life and Adventures of Nat Love, Better Known in the Cattle Country as "Deadwood Dick." By Himself. A True History of Slavery Days, Life on the Great Cattle Ranges and on the Plains of the "Wild and Wooly" West, Based on Facts, and Personal Experience of the Author. Los Angeles: Privately printed, 1907.

Lowery, Irving E. [b. 1850]. Life on the Old Plantation in Ante-bellum Days; or, A Story Based on Facts. Columbia, SC: Privately printed, 1911.

Lynch, John Roy [1847–1939]. Reminiscences of an Active Life; the Autobiography of John Roy Lynch. Edited by John Hope Franklin. Chicago: University of Chicago Press, 1970.

Mallory, William [b. 1826]. Old Plantation Days. Hamilton, Ontario: Privately printed, 1901–2?.

Manzano, Juan Francisco [1797–1854]. Poems by a Slave in the Island of Cuba, Recently Liberated, Translated from the Spanish by R. R. Madden, M.D., with the History of the Early Life of the Negro Poet, Written by Himself; to Which Are Prefixed Two Pieces Descriptive of Cuban Slavery. London: T. Ward, 1840.

Marrs, Elijah P. History of the Rev. Elijah P. Marrs. 1895.

Marrs, Elijah Preston [1840–1910]. Life and History of the Rev. Elijah P. Marrs. Louisville: Bradley and Gilbert, 1885.

Mars, James [b. 1790]. Life of James Mars, a Slave Born and Sold in Connecticut. Written by Himself. Hartford, CT: Case, Lockwood, 1864.

Mason, Isaac [1822-]. Life of Isaac Mason As a Slave. Worcester, MA: Privately printed, 1893.

McCline, John [1852–1948]. Slavery in the Clover Bottoms: John McCline's Narrative of His Life During Slavery and the Civil War. Edited by Jan Furman. Knoxville: University of Tennessee Press, 1998.

McPherson, Christopher [1817]. A Short History of the Life of Christopher McPherson, Alias Pherson, Son of Christ, King of Kings and Lord of Lords. Lynchburg, VA: Christopher McPherson Smith, 1855.

Meachum, John B. [b. 1789]. An Address to All the Colored Citizens of the United States. Philadelphia: Privately printed, 1846.

Mountain, Joseph [1758–1790]. Letters of the Late Ignatius Sancho, An African. In Two Volumes. To Which Are Prefixed, Memoirs of His Life. London: J. Nichols, 1782.

Northup, Solomon [b. 1808]. Twelve Years a Slave: Narrative of Solomon Northup, a Citizen of New-York, Kidnapped in Washington City in 1841, and Rescued in 1853, from a Cotton Plantation near the Red River, in Louisiana. Edited by David Wilson. Auburn, NY: Derby and Miller, 1853.

Offley, Greensbury Washington [1808–1859]. A Narrative of the Life and Labors of the Rev. G. W. Offley, a Colored Man, Local Preacher and Missionary; Who Lived Twenty-Seven Years at the South and Twenty-Three at the North; Who Never Went to School a Day in His Life, and Only Commenced to Learn His Letters When Nineteen Years and Eight Months Old; the Emancipation of His Mother and Her Three

Children; How He Learned to Read While Living in a Slave State, and Supported Himself from the Time He Was Nine Years Old Until He Was Twenty-One. Hartford, CT: Privately printed, 1859.

O'Neal, William. *Life and History of William O'Neal, or, The Man Who Sold His Wife.* St. Louis, MO: A. R. Fleming, 1896.

Parker, Allen [b. 1837]. *Recollections of Slavery Times.* Worcester, MA: Charles W. Burbank, 1895.

Parker, Henry [b. 1835]. *Autobiography of Henry Parker.* N.p.: Privately published, 186?.

Parker, John P. [1827–1900]. *His Promised Land: The Autobiography of John P. Parker, Former Slave and Conductor on the Underground Railroad.* Edited by Stuart Seely Sprague. New York: W.W. Norton, 1996.

Parker, William [b. 1822]. "The Freedman's Story." *Atlantic,* February 1866: 152–66; March 1866: 276–95.

Pennington, James W.C. [1807–1870]. *The Fugitive Blacksmith; or, Events in the History of James W. C. Pennington, Pastor of a Presbyterian Church, New York, Formerly a Slave in the State of Maryland, United States.* London: Charles Gilpin, 1849.

Peterson, Daniel H. [b. 1805?]. *The Looking Glass: Being a True Report and Narrative of the Life, Travels, and Labors of the Rev. Daniel H. Peterson, a Colored Clergyman; Embracing a Period of Time from the Year 1812 to 1854, and Including His Visit to Western Africa.* New York: Wright, 1854.

Picquet, Louisa [b. 1828]. *Louisa Picquet, the Octoroon: A Tale of Southern Slave Life,* Edited by Hiram Mattison. New York: H. Mattison, 1861.

Pomp. *Dying Confession of Pomp, a Negro Man Who Was Executed at Ipswich, on the 6th, August 1791 ... Taken from the Mouth of the Prisoner, by Jonathan Plummer.* Edited by Jonathan Plummer. Newburyport, MA: Jonathan Plummer, 1795.

Prince, Mary. *The History of Mary Prince, a West Indian Slave. Related by Herself. With a Supplement by the Editor. To Which Is Added, the Narrative of Asa-Asa, a Captured African.* London: F. Westley and A. H. Davis, 1831.

Randolph, Peter [1825–1897]. *From Slave Cabin to the Pulpit: The Autobiography of Rev. Peter Randolph: The Southern Question Illustrated and Sketches of Slave Life.* Boston: James H. Earle, 1893.

Randolph, Peter [1825–1897]. *Sketches of Slave Life: Or, Illustrations of the "Peculiar Institution."* Boston: Privately printed, 1855.

Ray, Emma J. Smith [b. 1859] and Lloyd P. Ray [b. 1860]. *Twice Sold, Twice Ransomed: Autobiography of Mr. and Mrs. L. P. Ray.* Chicago: Free Methodist, 1926.

Roberts, James [b. 1753]. *The Narrative of James Roberts, a Soldier under Gen. Washington in the Revolutionary War, and under Gen. Jackson at the Battle of New Orleans, in the War of 1812: "A Battle Which Cost Me a Limb, Some Blood, and Almost My Life."* Chicago: Privately printed, 1858.

Robinson, William H. [b.1848]. *From Log Cabin to the Pulpit: Or Fifteen Years in Slavery.* Eau Claire, WI: Privately printed, 1913.

Roper, Moses. *A Narrative of the Adventures and Escape of Moses Roper, from American Slavery.* Philadelphia: Merrihew and Gunn, 1838.

Sadler, Robert [b. 1911]. *The Emancipation of Robert Sadler.* Edited by Marie Chapian. Minneapolis, MN: Bethany Fellowship, 1975.

Said, Nicholas. *The Autobiography of Nicholas Said, a Native of Bornou, Eastern Soudan, Central Africa.* Memphis: Shotwell, 1873.

Said, Omar ibn [b. 1770?-1863 or 1864]. "Autobiography of Omar ibn Said, Slave in North Carolina, 1831." Edited by John Franklin Jameson. *The American Historical Review* 30 (1925): 787–95.

Sancho, Ignatius [1729–1780]. *Ignatius Sancho: An Early African Composer in England.* 2 vols. London: Privately printed, 1789. Edited by Josephine R. B. Wright. New York: Garland, 1981.

Singleton, William Henry [b. 1835]. *Recollections of My Slavery Days.* Peekskill, NY: Highland Democrat, 1922.

Smallwood, Thomas [b. 1801]. *A Narrative of Thomas Smallwood, Coloured Man: Giving an Account of His Birth — The Period He Was Held in Slavery — His Release — And Removal to Canada, etc. Together with an Account of the Underground Railroad. Written by Himself.* Toronto: Privately printed, 1851.

Smith, Amanda [1837–1915]. *An Autobiography: The Story of the Lord's Dealings with Mrs. Amanda Smith, the Colored Evangelist. Containing an Account of Her Life Work of Faith, and Her Travels in America, England, Ireland, Scotland, India, and Africa, as an Independent Missionary.* Chicago: Meyer, 1893.

Smith, David [b. 1784]. *Biography of Rev. David Smith of the AME Church; Being a Complete History, Embracing over Sixty Years' Labor in the Advancement of the Redeemer's Kingdom on Earth.* Xenia, OH: Xenia Gazette Office, 1881.

Smith, Harry [b. 1815]. *Fifty Years of Slavery in*

the United States of America. Grand Rapids, MI: West Michigan, 1891.

Smith, James Lindsay. *Autobiography of James L. Smith, Including, Also, Reminiscences of Slave Life, Recollections of the War, Education of Freedmen, Causes of the Exodus, etc.* Norwich, CT: The Bulletin, 1881.

Smith, Stephen [1769?-1797]. *Life, Last Words and Dying Speech of Stephen Smith, a Black Man, Who Was Executed at Boston This Day Being Thursday, October 12, 1797 for Burglary.* Boston: Privately printed, 1797.

Smith, Venture [1729-1805]. *A Narrative of the Life and Adventures of Venture, a Native of Africa: But Resident above Sixty Years in the United States of America. Related by Himself.* New London, CT: C. Holt, 1798.

_____. *A Narrative of the Life and Adventures of Venture, a Native of Africa, but Resident Above Sixty Years in the United States of America. Related by Himself. New London: Printed in 1798. Reprinted A. D. 1835, and Published by a Descendant of Venture. Revised and Republished with Traditions by H. M. Selden, Haddam, Conn., 1896.* Middletown, CT: J. S. Stewart, 1897.

Steward, Austin [1794-1860]. *Twenty-two Years a Slave and Forty Years a Freeman; Embracing a Correspondence of Several Years, While President of Wilberforce Colony, London, Canada West.* Rochester, NY: W. Alling, 1857.

Stroyer, Jacob [1849-1908]. *My Life in the South.* Salem, MA: Salem Observer Book and Job Print, 1885.

_____. *Sketches of My Life in the South. Part I.* Salem, MA: Salem Press, 1879.

Taylor, Susie King [b. 1848]. *Reminiscences of My Life in Camp with the 33d United States Colored Troops, Late 1st S. C. Volunteers.* Boston: Privately printed, 1902.

Teamoh, George [1818-1883?]. *God Made Man, Man Made the Slave.* Edited by F. N. Boney, Richard L. Hume, and Rafia Zafar. Macon, GA: Mercer University Press, 1990.

Thomas, James [1827-1913]. *From Tennessee Slave to St. Louis Entrepreneur: The Autobiography of James Thomas.* Edited by Loren Schweninger. Columbia: University of Missouri Press, 1984.

Thompson, Charles [b. 1833]. *Biography of a Slave; Being the Experiences of Rev. Charles Thompson, a Preacher of the United Brethren Church, While a Slave in the South.* Dayton, OH: United Brethren, 1875.

Thompson, John [b. 1812]. *The Life of John Thompson, a Fugitive Slave; Containing His History of 25 Years in Bondage, and His Prov-idential Escape. Written by Himself.* Worcester, MA: J. Thompson, 1856.

A Thrilling Narrative from the Lips of the Sufferers of the Late Detroit Riot, March 6, 1863. With the Hair Breadth Escapes of Men, Women and Children, and Destruction of Colored Men's Property, Not Less than $15,000.00 (Detroit: Privately printed, 1863).

Tilmon, Levin [1807-1863]. *A Brief Miscellaneous Narrative of the More Early Part of the Life of L. Tilmon, Pastor of a Colored Methodist Congregational Church in the City of New York. Written by Himself.* Jersey City, NJ: W. W. & L. A. Pratt, 1853.

Truth, Sojourner [1797(?)-1883]. *Fanaticism: Its Source and Influence, Illustrated by the Simple Narrative of Isabella, in the Case of Matthias, Mr. and Mrs. B. Folger, Mr. Pierson, Mr. Mills, Catherine, Isabella, &c. &c. A Reply to W. L. Stone, with the Descriptive Portraits of All the Parties, While at Sing-Sing and at Third Street. — Containing the Whole Truth — and Nothing but the Truth.* Edited by Gilbert Vale. New York: Gilbert Vale, 1835.

_____. *Narrative of Sojourner Truth, a Northern Slave, Emancipated from Bodily Servitude by the State of New York, in 1828.* Edited by Olive Gilbert. Boston: Privately printed, 1850.

Tubbee, Okah [b. 1810 or 1811]. *A Sketch of the Life of Okah Tubbee, (Called) William Chubbee, Son of the Head Chief, Mosholeh Tubbee, of the Choctaw Nation of Indians. By Laah Ceil Manatoi Elaah Tubbee, His Wife.* Toronto: Privately printed, 1852.

Tubbee, Okah [b. 1810 or 1811]. *A Thrilling Sketch of the Life of the Distinguished Chief Okah Tubbee Alias, Wm. Chubbee, Son of the Head Chief, Mosholeh Tubbee, of the Choctaw Nation of Indians.* Edited by Lewis Leonidas Allen. New York: L. L. Allen, 1848.

Turner, Nat [1800-1831]. *The Confessions of Nat Turner, the Leader of the Late Insurrection in Southampton, Va. as Fully and Voluntarily Made to Thomas R. Gray, in the Prison Where He Was Confined, and Acknowledged by Him to Be Such When Read before the Court of Southampton.* Edited by Thomas R. Gray. Baltimore: T. R. Gray, 1831.

Veney, Bethany [b. 1815]. *The Narrative of Bethany Veney, a Slave Woman.* Edited by M. W. G. Worcester, MA: George H. Ellis, 1889.

Voorhis, Robert [b.1770?]. *Life and Adventures of Robert, the Hermit of Massachusetts, Who Has Lived 14 Years in a Cave, Secluded from Human Society. Comprising, an Account of His Birth, Parentage, Sufferings, and Providential Escape from Unjust and Cruel Bondage in Early Life and His Reasons for Becoming a Recluse: Taken from His Own Mouth, and Published for His Benefit.* Edited by Henry Trumbull. Providence, RI: H. Trumbull, 1829.

Walker, Thomas Calhoun [1862–1953]. *The Honey-Pod Tree: The Life Story of Thomas Calhoun Walker.* Edited by Florence L. Lattimore. New York: John Day, 1958.

Walker, William [b. 1819?] *Buried Alive (Behind Prison Walls) for a Quarter of a Century: Life of William Walker.* Edited by Thomas S. Gaines. Saginaw, MI: Friedman and Hynan, 1892.

Walters, Alexander [1858–1917]. *My Life and Work.* New York: Fleming H. Revell, 1917.

Ward, Samuel Ringgold [b. 1817]. *Autobiography of a Fugitive Negro: His Anti-slavery Labours in the United States, Canada and England.* London: John Snow, 1855.

Warner, Ashton [d. 1831]. *Negro Slavery Described by a Negro: Being the Narrative of Ashton Warner, a Native of St. Vincent's: With an Appendix Containing the Testimony of Four Christian Ministers Recently Returned from the Colonies on the System of Slavery as it Now Exist*s. Edited by Simon Strickland. London: S. Maunder, 1831.

Washington, Booker Taliaferro [1856–1915]. *My Larger Education; Being Chapters from My Experience.* Garden City, NY: Doubleday, Page, 1911.

_____. *Up from Slavery.* Garden City, NY: Doubleday, Page, 1901.

Watkins, James [b. 1821]. *Narrative of the Life of James Watkins, formerly a "Chattel" in Maryland, U.S. Containing an Account of His Escape from Slavery, Together with an Appeal on Behalf of Three Millions of Such "Pieces of Property," Still Held Under the Standard of the Eagle.* Bolton, Eng: Kenyon and Abbatt, 1852.

_____. *Struggles for Freedom: Or the Life of James Watkins, Formerly a Slave in Maryland, U.S.; in which is Detailed a Graphic Account of His Extraordinary Escape from Slavery, Notices of the Fugitive Slave Law, the Sentiments of American Divines on the Subject of Slavery, etc., etc.* Manchester, England: Privately printed, 1860.

Watson, Henry. *Narrative of Henry Watson, a Fugitive Slave. Written by Himself.* Boston: Bela Marsh, 1848.

Webb, William [b. 1836]. *The History of William Webb, Composed by Himself.* Detroit: Egbert Hoekstra, 1873.

Wells-Barnett, Ida B. *Crusade for Justice; the Autobiography of Ida B. Wells.* Edited by Alfreda M. Duster. Chicago: University of Chicago Press, 1970.

Wheeler, Peter [b. 1789]. *Chains and Freedom: Or, The Life and Adventures of Peter Wheeler, a Colored Man Yet Living. A Slave in Chains, a Sailor on the Deep, and a Sinner at the Cross.* Edited by Charles E. Lester. New York: E. S. Arnold, 1839.

White, George [b. 1764]. *A Brief Account of the Life, Experience, Travels, and Gospel Labours of George White, an African: Written by Himself, and Revised by a Friend.* New York: John C. Totten, 1810.

Wilkerson, James. *Wilkerson's History of His Travels & Labors, in the United States, As a Missionary, in Particular, That of the Union Seminary, Located in Franklin Co., Ohio, Since He Purchased His Liberty in New Orleans, La., &c.* Columbus, OH, 1861.

Williams, Isaac D. [1821–1898]. *Sunshine and Shadow of Slave Life: Reminiscences As Told by Isaac D. Williams to "Tege."* Edited by William Ferguson Goldie. East Saginaw, MI: Evening News, 1885.

Williams, James [b. 1805]. *Narrative of James Williams, an American Slave, Who Was for Several Years a Driver on a Cotton Plantation in Alabama.* New York: American Anti-Slavery Society, 1838.

Williams, James [b. 1819]. *A Narrative of Events Since the First of August, 1834, by James Williams, an Apprenticed Labourer in Jamaica.* London: W. Ball, 1837.

Williams, James [b. 1825]. *Life and Adventures of James Williams, a Fugitive Slave, with a Full Description of the Underground Railroad.* San Francisco: Women's Union, 1873.

Appendix 7: Selected Antislavery and Underground Railroad Songs

1. Am I Not a Man and Brother?

Am I not a man and brother?
Ought I not, then, to be free?
Sell me not one to another,
Take not thus my liberty.
Christ our Saviour, Christ our Saviour,
Died for me as well as thee.

Am I not a man and brother?
Have I not a soul to save?
Oh, do not my spirit smother,
Making me a wretched slave;
God of mercy, God of mercy,
Let me Fill a freeman's grave

Yes, thou art a man and brother,
Though thou long hast groaned a slave,
Bound with cruel cords and tether
From the cradle to the grave!
Yet the Saviour, yet the Saviour,
Bled and died all: souls to save.

Yes, thou art a man and brother,
Though we long have told thee nay;
And are bound to aid each other,
All along our pilgrim way.
Come and welcome, come and welcome,
Join with us to praise and pray!

2. Amazing Grace

Text by John Newton

Amazing grace! How sweet the sound
that saved a wretch like me!
I once was lost, but now am found;
was blind, but now I see.

'Twas grace that taught my heart to fear,
and grace my fears relieved;
how precious did that grace appear
the hour I first believed.

Through many dangers, toils, and snares,
I have already come;
'tis grace hath brought me safe thus far,
and grace will lead me home.

The Lord has promised good to me,
his word my hope secures;
he will my shield and portion be,
as long as life endures.

Yea, when this flesh and heart shall fail,
and mortal life shall cease,
I shall possess, within the veil,
a life of joy and peace.

When we've been there ten thousand years,
bright shining as the sun,
we've no less days to sing God's praise
than when we first begun.

3. Be Free, O Man, Be Free

The storm-winds wildly blowing,
The bursting billow mock,
As with their foam-crest glowing,
They dash the sea-girt rock;
Amid the wild commotion,
The revel of the sea,
A voice is on the ocean,
Be free, O man, be free.

Behold the sea-brine leaping
High in the murky air;
List to the tempest sweeping
In chainless fury there.
What moves the mighty torrent,
And bids it flow abroad?
Or turns the rapid current?
What, but the voice of God?

Then, answer, is the spirit
Less noble or less free?

From whom does it inherit
The doom of slavery?
When man can bind the waters,
That they no longer roll,
Then let him forge the fetters
To clog the human soul.

Till then a voice is stealing
From earth and sea and sky,
And to the soul revealing
Its immortality.
The swift wind chants the number.
Careering o'er the sea,
And earth, aroused from slumbers,
Re-echoes, Man, be free.

4. The Bereaved Mother

O, deep was the anguish of the slave mother's
heart,
When called from her darling for ever to part;
So grieved that lone mother, that heart broken
mother,
      In sorrow and woe.
The lash of the master her deep sorrows mock,
While the child of her bosom is sold on the
block;
Yet loud shrieked that mother, poor heart bro-
ken mother
      In sorrow and woe.
The babe in return, for its fond mother cries,
While the sound of their wailings, together arise;
They shriek for each other, the child and the
mother,
      In sorrow and woe.
The harsh auctioneer, o sympathy cold,
Tears the babe from its mother and sells it for
gold;
While the infant and mother, loud shriek for
each other,
      In sorrow and woe.
At last came the parting of mother and child,
Her brain reeled with madness, that mother was
wild;
Then the lash could not smother the shrieks of
that mother
      Of sorrow and woe.
The child was borne off to a far distant clime,
While the mother was left in anguish to pine;
But reason departed, and she sank broken
hearted,
      In sorrow and woe.
That poor mourning mother, of reason bereft,
Soon ended her sorrows and sank cold in death;
Thus died that slave mother, poor heart broken
mother,
      In sorrow and woe.

O, list ye kind mothers to the cries of the slave;
The parents and children implore you to save;
Go! rescue the mothers, the sisters and brothers,
      From sorrow and woe.

5. The Blind Slave Boy

Come back to me, mother! why linger away
From thy poor little blind boy, the long weary day!
I mark every footstep, I list to each tone,
And wonder my mother should leave me alone!
But there's no one to joy or to sorrow with me;
For each hath of pleasure and trouble his share,
And none for the poor little blind boy will care.

My mother, come back to me! close to thy breast
Once more let thy poor little blind one be pressed;
Once more let me feel thy warm breath on my
   cheek,
And hear thee in accents of tenderness speak!
O mother! I've no one to love me — no heart
Can bear like thine own in my sorrows a part;
No hand is so gentle, no voice is so kind,
O! none like a mother can cherish the blind!

Poor blind one! No mother thy wailing can hear,
No mother can hasten to banish thy fear;
And for one paltry dollar hath sold thee, poor
   child!
Ah! who can in language of mortals reveal
The anguish that none but a mother can feel,
When man in his vile lust of mammon hath trod
On her child, who is stricken and smitten of
   God!

Blind, helpless, forsaken, with strangers alone,
She hears in her anguish his piteous moan,
As he eagerly listens— but listens in vain,
To catch the loved tones of his mother again!
The curse of the broken in spirit shall fall
On the wretch who hath mingled this worm-
   wood and gall,
And his gain like a mildew shall blight and destroy,
Who hath torn from his mother the little blind
   boy!

6. The Chase

Quick, fly to the covert, thou hunted of men!
For the bloodhounds are buying o'er mountain
   and glen;
The riders are mounted, the loose rein is given,
And curses of wrath are ascending to heaven.
O, speed to thy footsteps! for ruin and death,
Like the hurricane's rage gather thick round thy
   path;
And the deep muttered curses grow loud and
   more loud,
As horse after horse swells the thundering crowd.

Speed, speed to thy footsteps! thy track has been
  found;
Now, sport for the rider, and blood for the hound!
Through brake and through forest the man-prey
  is driven;
O, help for the hopeless, thou merciful Heaven!
On! on to the mountain! they're baffled again,
And hope for the woo-stricken still may remain;
The fast flagging steeds arc all white with their
  foam,
The bloodhounds have turned from the chase to
  their home.

Joy! joy to the wronged one! the haven he gains,
Escaped from his thraldom, and freed from his
  chains!
The heaven-stamped image — the God-given
  soul —
No more shall the spoiler at pleasure control.
O, shame to Columbia, that on her bright plains,
Man pines in his fetters, and curses his chains!
Shame! shame! that her star — spangled banner
  should wave
Where the lush is made red in the blood of the
  slave.

Sons of old Pilgrim Fathers! and are ye thus dumb?
Shall tyranny triumph, and freedom succumb?
While mothers are torn from their children apart,
And agony sunders the cords of the heart?
Shall the sons of those sires that once spurned
  the chain,
Turn bloodhounds to hunt and make captive
  again?
O, shame to your honor, and shame to your pride,
And shame on your memory ever abide!

Will not your old sires start up from the ground,
At the crack of the whip, and bay of the hound,
And shaking their skeleton hands in your face,
Curse the germs that produced such a miscreant
  race?

O, rouse ye for freedom, before on your path
Heaven without mixture the vials of wrath!
Loose every hard burden — break off every
  chain —
Restore to the bondman his freedom again.

7. Colonization Song

To the Free Colored People.

Will you, will you be colonized?
Will you, will you be colonized?

  'Tis a land that with honey
    And milk doth abound,
  Where the lash is not heard,
    And the scourge is not found.
      Chorus, Will you, &c.

If you stay in this land
Where the white man has rule,
You will starve by his hand,
In both body and soul.
    Chorus.
For a nuisance you are,
In this land of your birth,
Held down by his hand,
And crushed to the earth.
    Chorus.
My religion is pure,
And came from above,
But I cannot consent
The black negro to love.
    Chorus.
It is true there is judgment
That hangs o'er the land,
But 't will all turn aside,
When you follow the plan.
    Chorus.
You're ignorant I know.
In this land of your birth,
And religion though pure,
Cannot move the curse.
    Chorus.
But only consent
Though extorted by force,
What a blessing you'll prove,
Oh the African coast.
    Chorus.

8. Darlin' Nellie Gray

There's a low, green, valley on the old Kentucky
  shore
Where I've whiled many happy hours away,
Just a sitting and a singing by the little cottage
  door
Where lived my darling Nellie Gray

When the moon had climbed the mountain, and
  the stars were shining too
Then I'd take my darling Nellie Gray
And we'd go floatin' down the river in my little
  red canoe
While my banjo sweetly I would play

One night I went to see her, but she's gone the
  neighbors say
And the white man had bound her with his chain
They have taken her to Georgia for to wear her
  life away
As she toils in the cotton and the cane

Oh, my poor Nellie Gray, they have taken you away
And I'll never see my darling, anymore
I'm sitting by the river and a weeping all the day
For you've gone from the old Kentucky shore

Now my canoe is under water, and my banjo is
    unstrung
I am tired of living, anymore
My eyes shall be cast downward, and my songs
    will be unsung
While I stay on the old Kentucky shore

Now I'm getting old and feeble, and I cannot see
    my way
I can hear someone knocking on my door
I can hear the angels singing, and I see my Nel-
    lie Gray
So farewell to the old Kentucky shore

Oh, my darling Nellie Gray, up in heaven, so
    they say
And they'll never take you from me, anymore
I'm coming, coming, coming, as the angels clear
    the way
So farewell to the old Kentucky shore

9. Deep River
(traditional black spiritual)
CHORUS
Deep River, my home is over Jordan,
Deep River, Lord I want to cross over into camp-
    ground.
Oh, don't you want to go to that gospel feast
That promised land where all is peace?
Oh, don't you want to go to that promised land
    where all is peace?
Deep River, Lord I want to cross over into camp-
    ground.

CHORUS
I'll go up to Heaven and take my seat
And cast my crown at Jesus' feet
I'll go up to Heaven and cast my crown at Jesus'
    feet
Deep River, Lord I want to cross over into camp-
    ground.

CHORUS
Oh, when I get to Heaven I'll walk about
There's nobody there to turn me out
When I get to heaven there's no one there to turn
    me out.
Deep River, Lord I want to cross over into camp-
    ground.

CHORUS

10. Emancipation Hymn of the West
Indian Negroes
For the First of August Celebrations

Praise we the Lord! let songs resound
    To earth's remotest shore!
Songs of thanksgiving, songs of praise —
    For we are slaves no more.

Praise we the Lord! His power hath rent
    The chains that held us long!
His voice is mighty, as of old,
    And still His arm is strong.

Praise we the Lord! His wrath arose,
    His arm our fetters broke;
The tyrant dropped the lash, and we
    To liberty awoke!

Praise we the Lord! let holy songs
    Rise from these happy isles!—
O! let us not unworthy prove,
    On whom His bounty smiles.
And cease we not the fight of faith

    Till all mankind be free;
Till mercy o'er the earth shall flow,
    As waters o'er the sea.

Then shall indeed Messiah's reign
    Through nil the world extend;
Then swords to ploughshares shall be turned,
    And Heaven with earth shall blend.

11. Flight of the Bondman
Dedicated to William W. Brown

From the crack of the rifle and baying of hound,
Takes the poor panting bondman his flight;
His couch through the day is the cold damp
    ground,
But northward he runs through the night.
            Chorus.
O, God speed the flight of the desolate slave,
Let his heart never yield to despair;
There is room ' mong our hills for the true and
    the brave
Let his lungs breathe our free northern air!
O, sweet to the storm-driven sailor the light,
Streaming far o'er the dark swelling wave;
But sweeter by far 'mong the lights of the night,
Is the star of the north to the slave.
            O, God speed, &c.

Cold and bleak are our mountains and chilling
    our winds,
But warm us the soft southern gales
Be the hands and the hearts which the hunted
    one finds,
'Mong our hills and our own winter vales.
            O, God speed, &c.
Then list to the 'plaint of the heart-broken
    thrall,
Ye blood-hounds, go back to your lair;
May a free northern soil soon give freedom to
    all,
Who shall breathe in its pure mountain sir.
            O, God speed, &c.

12. Fling Out the Anti-Slavery Flag

Fling out the Anti-slavery flag
On every swelling breeze;
And let its folds wave o'er the land,
And o'er the raging sea,

Till all beneath the standard sheet,
With new allegiance bow;
And pledge them to onward bear
The emblem of their vow.

Fling out the Anti-Slavery flag,
And let it onward wave
Till it shall float o'er every clime,
And liberate the slave;
Till, like a meteor flashing far,
It bursts with glorious light,
And with its Heaven-born rays dispels
The gloom of sorrow's night.

Fling out the Anti-Slavery flag,
And let it not be furled,
Till like a planet of the skies,
It sweeps around the world.
And when each poor degraded slave
Is gathered near and far;
O, fix it on the azure arch,
As hope's eternal star.

Fling out the Anti-Slavery flag,
Forever let it be
The emblem to a holy cause,
The banner of the free.
And never from its guardian
Let it by man be driven,
But let it float forever there,
Beneath the smiles of heaven.

13. Follow the Drinking Gourd

When the sun comes back and the first quail calls
Follow the Drinking Gourd.
For the old man is waiting for to carry you to
   freedom,
If you follow the Drinking Gourd.
The river bank makes a very good road,
The dead trees show you the way,
Left foot, peg foot, traveling on
Follow the Drinking Gourd.
The river ends between two hills,
Follow the Drinking Gourd.
There's another river on the other side,
Follow the Drinking Gourd.
Where the great big river meets the little river,
Follow the Drinking Gourd.
For the old man is awaiting to carry you to free-
   dom if you
follow the Drinking Gourd.

14. Freedom's Star

As I strayed from my cot at the close of the day,
I turned my fond gaze to the sky;
I beheld all the stars as so sweetly they lay,
And but one fixed my heart or my eye.
Shine on, northern star, thou'rt beautiful and
   bright
To the slave on his journey afar;
For he speeds from his foes in the darkness of
   night,
Guided on by thy light, freedom's star.

On thee he depends when he threads the dark
   woods
Ere the bloodhounds have hunted him back;
Thou leadest him on over mountains and floods,
With thy beams shining full on his track.
Shine on, &c.

Unwelcome to him is the bright orb of day,
As it glides o'er the earth and the sea;
He seeks then to hide like a wild beast of prey,
But with hope, rests his heart upon thee.
Shine on, &c.

May never a cloud overshadow thy face,
While the slave flies before his pursuer;
Gleam steadily on to the end of his race,
Till his body and soul are secure.
Shine on, &c.

15. Fugitive Slave to the Christian

The fetters galled my weary soul —
A soul that seemed but thrown away;
I spurned the tyrant's base control,
Resolved at last the man to play: —
The hounds are baying on my track;
O Christian! will you send me back?

I felt the stripes, the lash I saw,
Red, dripping with a father gore;
And worst of all their lawless law,
The insults that my mother bore!
The hounds are baying on my track,
O Christian! will you send me back?

Where human law o'errules Divine,
Beneath the sheriffs hammer fell
My wife and babes— I call them mine —
And where they suffer, who can tell?
The hounds are baying on my track,
O Christian! will you send me back?

I seek a home where man is man,
If such there be upon this earth,
To draw my kindred, if I can,
Around its free, though humble hearth.
The hounds are baying on my track,
O Christian! will you send me back?

16. Get Off the Track

Ho! the car Emancipation
Rides majestic thro' our nation,
Bearing on its train the story,
Liberty! a nation's glory.
Roll it along, thro' the nation,
Freedom's car, Emancipation!

First of all the train, and greater
Speeds the dauntless Liberator,
Onward cheered amid hosannas,
And the waving of free banners.
Roll it along! spread your banners,
While the people shout hosannas.

Men of various predilections
Frightened, run in alt directions;
Merchants, editors, physicians,
Lawyers, priests, and politicians.
Get out of the way! every station!
Clear the track of 'mancipation!

Let the ministers and churches
Leave behind sectarian lurches;
Jump on board the car of Freedom,
Ere it be too late to need them.
Sound the alarm! Pulpits thunder!
Ere too late you see your blunder!

Politicians gazed, astounded,
When, at first, our bell resounded;
Freight trains are coming, tell these foxes,
With our votes and ballot boxes.
Jump for your lives! politicians,
From your dangerous, false positions.

All true friends of Emancipation,
Haste to Freedom's railroad station;
Quick into the cars get seated,
All is ready and completed.
Put on the steam! all are crying,
And the liberty flags are flying.

Now again the bell is tolling,
Soon you'll see the car-wheels rolling;
Hinder not their destination,
Chartered for Emancipation.
Wood up the fire! keep it flashing,
While the train goes onward dashing.

Hear the mighty car-wheels humming!
Now look out! the Engine 's coming!
Church and statesmen! hear the thunder!
Clear the track or you'll fall under.
Get off the track! all are singing,
While the Liberty bell is ringing.

On, triumphant see them bearing,
Through sectarian rubbish tearing;
The bell and whistle and the steaming,
Startle thousands from their dreaming.

Look out for the cars while the bell rings!
Ere the sound your funeral knell rings.

See the people run to meet us;
At the depots thousands greet us;
All take seats with exultation,
In the Car Emancipation.
Huzza! Huzza!! Emancipation
Soon will bless our happy nation,
Huzza! Huzza! Huzza!!!

17. Get On Board

Hm, hm,
The Gospel train's a-comin,'
I hear it just at hand,
I hear the car wheel rumblin'
And rollin' through the land.

CHORUS

Git on board little children,
Git on board little children,
Git on board little children,
There's room for many more.

I hear the train's a-comin,'
She's comin' round the curve,
She's loosened all her steam and
Brakes and strainin' every nerve.

CHORUS

The fare is cheap and all can go,
The rich and poor are there,
No second class aboard this train,
No difference in the fare.

CHORUS

18. Go Down, Moses

(words and music traditional)

When Israel was in Egypt land,
(let my people go)
Oppressed so hard,
They could not stand,
(let my people go)

(chorus)
Go down, Moses,
Way Down to Egypt land!
Gonna tell old Pharoah,
He's gotta let my people go!

Let them not in bondage toil ,
(let my people go)
Instead, emerge, with Egypt's spoil!,
(let my people go)

(chorus)

We need not always weep and mourn,
(let my people go)
Or wear these slavery chains forlorn,

(*let my people go*)

(*chorus*)

So let us all from slavery flee,
(*let my people go*)
And soon may all the earth be free,
(*let my people go*)

(*chorus*)

19. I Am an Abolitionist

I am an Abolitionist!
I glory in the name:
Though now by Slavery's minions hiss'd
And covered o'er with shame,
It is a spell of light and power —
The watchword of the free: —
Who spurns it in the trial-hour,
A craven soul is he!

I am an Abolitionist!
Then urge me not to pause;
For joyfully do I enlist
In Freedom's sacred cause:
A nobler strife the world ne'er saw,
Th' enslaved to disenthral;
I am a soldier for the war,
Whatever may befall!

I am an Abolitionist!
Oppression's deadly foe;
In God's great strength will I resist,
And lay the monster low;
In God's great name do I demand,
To all be freedom given,
That peace and joy may fill the land,
And songs go up to heaven!

I am an Abolitionist!
No threats shall awe my soul,
No perils cause me to desist,
No bribes my acts control;
A freeman will I live and die,
In sunshine and in shade,
And raise my voice for liberty,
Of nought on earth afraid.

20. Jefferson's Daughter

Can the blood that, at Lexington, poured o'er
the plain,
When the sons warred with tyrants their rights
to uphold,
Can the tide of Niagara wipe out the stain?
No! Jefferson's child has be bartered for gold!

Do you boast of your freedom? Peace, bab-
blers— bestill;
Prate not of the goddess who scarce deigns to hear;
Have ye power to unbind? Are ye wanting in will?

Must the groans of your bondman still torture
the ear?
The daughter of Jefferson sold for a slave!
The child of freeman for dollars and francs!
The roar of applause, when your orators rave,
Is lost in the sound of her chain, as it clanks.

Peace, then, ye blasphemers of Liberty's name!
Though red was the blood by your forefathers
spilt,
Still redder your cheeks should be mantled with
shame,
Till the spirit of freedom shall cancel the guilt.
But the brand of the slave is the tint of his skin,

Though his heart may beat loyal and true under-
neath;
While the soul of the tyrant is rotten within,
And his white the mere cloak to the blackness of
death.

Are ye deal to the plaints that each moment arise?
Is it thus ye forget the mild precepts of Penn —
Unheeding the clamor that "maddens the skies,"
As ye trample the rights— of your dark fellow-
men?

When the incense that glows before Liberty's
shrine,
Is unmixed with the blood of the galled and oppressed,
O, then, and then only, the boast may be thine,
That the stripes and stars wave o'er a land of the
blest.

21. Jubilee Song

Our grateful carts with joy o'erflow,
Hurra, Hurra, Hurra,
We hail the Despot's overthrow,
Hurra, Hurra, Hurra,
No more he'll raise the gory lash,
And sink it deep in human flesh,
Hurra, Hurra, Hurra, Hurra,
Hurra, Hurra, Hurra.
We raise the song in Freedom's name,
Hurra, Hurra, Hurra,
Her glorious triumph we proclaim,
Hurra, Hurra, Hurra,
Beneath her feet lie Slavery's chains,
Their power to curse no more remains,
Hurra, Hurra, Hurra
Hurra, Hurra, Hurra.
With joy we'll make the air resound,
Hurra, Hurra, Hurra,
That all may hear the gladsome sound,
Hurra, Hurra, Hurra,
We glory at Oppression's fall,
The Slave has burst his deadly thrall,
Hurra, Hurra, Hurra, Hurra

Hurra, Hurra, Hurra.
In mirthful glee we'll dance and sing,
Hurra, Hurra, Hurra,
With shouts we'll make the welkin ring,
Hurra, Hurra, Hurra,
Shout! shout aloud! the bondsman's free
This, this is Freedom's jubilee
Hurra, Hurra, Hurra, Hurra,
Hurra, Hurra, Hurra.

22. The Liberty Ball

Come all ye true friends of the nation,
Attend to humanity's call;
Come aid the poor slave's liberation,
And roll on the liberty ball —
And roll on the liberty ball —
Come aid the poor slave's liberation,
And roll on the liberty ball.
The Liberty hosts are advancing —
For freedom to all they declare;
The down-trodden millions are sighing —
Come, break up our gloom of despair.
Come break up our gloom of despair, &c.
Ye Democrats, come to the rescue,
And aid on the liberty cause,
And millions will rise up and bless you,
With heart-cheering songs of applause,
With heart-cheering songs, &c
Ye Whigs, forsake slavery's minions,
And boldly step into our ranks;
'We care not for party opinions,
But invite all the friends of the banks, —
And invite all the friends of the banks, &c.
And when we have formed the blest union
We'll firmly march on, one and all —
We'll sing when we meet in communion,
And *roll on* the liberty bill,
And roll on the liberty ball, &c.

23. The Man for Me

O, he is not the man for me,
Who buys or sells a slave,
Nor he who will not set him free,
But sends him to his grave;

But he whose noble heart beats warm
For all men's life and liberty;
Who loves alike each human form,
O, that's the man for me.

He's not at all the man for me,
Who sells a man for gain,
Who bends the pliant servile knee,
To Slavery's god of shame!
But he whose God-like form erect
Proclaim all alike are free
To think, and speak, and vote, and act,

O, that's the man for me.

He sure is not the man for me
Whose spirit will succumb,
When men endowed with Liberty
Lie bleeding, bound and dumb;
But he whose faithful words of might
Ring through the land from shore to sea
For man's eternal equal right,
O, that's the man for me.

No, no, he's not the man for me
Whose voice o'er hill and plain,
Breaks forth for glorious liberty,
But binds himself, the chain!
The mightiest of the noble band
Who prays and toils the world to free,
With head, and heart, and voice, and vote,
O, that's the man for me.

24. On to Victory

Children of the glorious dead,
Who for freedom fought and bled,
With her banner o'er you spread,
On to victory.
Not for stern ambition's prize,
Do our hopes and wishes rise;
Lo, our leader from the skies,
Bids us do or die.
Ours is not the tented field —
We no earthly weapons wield —
Light and love, our sword and shield,
Truth our panoply.
This is proud oppression's hour;
Storms are round us; shall we cower?
While beneath a despot's power
Groans the suffering slave?

While on every southern gale,
Comes the helpless captive's tale,
And the voice of woman's wail,
And of man's despair?
While our homes and rights are dear,
Guarded still with watchful fear,
Shall we coldly turn our ear
From the suppliant's prayer?
Never ! by our Country's shame —
Never! by a Saviour's claim,
To the men of every name,
Whom he died to save.
Onward, then, ye fearless band —
Heart to heart, and hand to hand;
Yours shall be the patriot's stand,
Or the martyr's graves.

25. Over the Mountain

Over the mountain, and over the moor,
Hungry and weary I wander forlorn

My father is dead, and my mother is poor,
And she grieves for the days that will never re-
turn;
Give me some food for my mother in charity;
Give me some food and then I will be gone.
Pity, kind gentlemen, friends of humanity,
Cold blows the wind and the night's coming on.

Call me not indolent beggar and bold enough,
Fain would I learn both to knit and to sow;
I've two little brothers at home, when they're old
enough,
They will work hard for the gifts you bestow;
Pity, kind gentlemen, friends of humanity.
Cold blows the wind and the night's coming on;
Give me some food for my mother in charity,
Give me some food, and then I will begone.

26. Pity the Slave Mother

I pity the slave mother, careworn and weary,
Who sighs as she presses her babe to her breast;
I lament her sad fate, all so hopeless and dreary,
I lament for her woes, and her wrongs unre-
dressed.
O who can imagine her heart's deep emotion,
As she thinks of her children about to be sold;
You may picture the bounds of the rock-girdled
ocean,
But the grief of that mother can never known.

The mildew of slavery has blighted each blossom,
That ever has bloomed in her path-way below;
It has froze every fountain that gushed in her
bosom,
And chilled her heart's verdure with pitiless woe;
Her parents, her kindred, all crushed by oppres-
sion;
Her husband stilt doomed in its desert to stay;
No arm to protect from the tyrant's aggression —
She must weep as she treads on her desolate way.

O, slave mother, hope! see — the nation is shaking!
The arm of the Lord is awake to thy wrong!
The slave-! heart now with terror is quaking,
Salvation and Mercy to Heaven belong!
Rejoice, O rejoice! for the child thou art rearing,
May one day lift tip its unmanacled form,
While hope, to thy heart, like the rain-bow so
cheering,
Is born, like the rain-bow, 'mid tempest and
storm.

27. The Promised Land
Samuel Stennett, 1787

On Jordan's stormy banks I stand,
    And cast a wishful eye
To Canaan's fair and happy land,
    Where my possessions lie.

Refrain:
I am bound for the promised land,
I am bound for the promised land;
Oh who will come and go with me?
I am bound for the promised land.

O the transporting, rapturous scene,
    That rises to my sight!
Sweet fields arrayed in living green,
    And rivers of delight!

Refrain

There generous fruits that never fail,
    On trees immortal grow;
There rocks and hills, and brooks and vales,
    With milk and honey flow.

Refrain

O'er all those wide extended plains
    Shines one eternal day;
There God the Son forever reigns,
    And scatters night away.

Refrain

No chilling winds or poisonous breath
    Can reach that healthful shore;
Sickness and sorrow, pain and death,
    Are felt and feared no more.

Refrain

When I shall reach that happy place,
    I'll be forever blest,
For I shall see my Father's face,
    And in His bosom rest.

Refrain

Filled with delight my raptured soul
    Would here no longer stay;
Though Jordan's waves around me roll,
    Fearless I'd launch away.

Refrain

28. Rescue the Slave!

Sadly the fugitive weeps in his cell,
Listen awhile to the story we tell;
Listen ye gentle ones, listen ye brave,
Lady fair! Lady fair! weep for the slave.

Praying for liberty, dearer than life,
Torn from his little one, torn from his wife,
Flying from slavery, hear him and save,
Christian men! Christian men! help the poor
slave.

Think of his agony, feel for his pain,
Should his hard master e'er hold him again;
Spirit of liberty, rise from your grave,
Make him free, make him free, rescue the slave

Freely the slave master goes where he will;
Freemen, stand ready, his wishes to fulfill,

Helping the tyrant, or honest or knave,
Thinking not, caring not, for the poor slave.

Talk not of liberty, liberty is dead;
See the slave master's whip over our head;
Stooping beneath it, we ask what he craves,
Boston boys! Boston boys! catch me my slaves.

Freemen, arouse ye, before it's too late;
Slavery is knocking, at every gate,
Make good the promise, your early days gave,
Boston boys! Boston boys! rescue the slave.

29. The Slave-Auction — A Fact

Why stands she near the auction stand,
    That girl so young and fair;
What brings her to this dismal place,
    Why stands she weeping there?

Why does she raise that bitter cry?
    Why hangs her head with shame,
As now the auctioneer's rough voice,
    So rudely calls her name?

But see! she grasps a manly hand,
    And in a voice so low,
As scarcely to be heard, she says,
    "My brother, must I go?"

A moment's pause: then midst a wail
    Of agonizing woe,
His answer falls upon the ear,
    "Yes, sister, you must go!

"No longer can my arm defend,
    No longer can I save
My sister from the horrid fate
    That waits her as a SLAVE!"

Ah! now I know why she is there, —
    She came there to be sold!
That lovely form, that noble mind,
    Must be exchanged for gold!

O God! my every heart-string ones,
    Dost thou these scenes behold
In this our boasted Christian land,
    And must the truth be told?

Blush, Christian, blush! for e'en the dark
    Untutored heathen see
Thy inconsistency, and lo!
    They scorn thy God, and thee!

30. The Slave-Holder's Address to the North Star

Star of the North! Thou art not bigger
    Than is the diamond in my ring;
Yet, every black, star-gazing nigger
    Looks at thee, as at some great thing!
    Yes, gazes at thee, till the lazy
    And thankless rascal is half crazy.

Some Abolitionist has told them,
    That, if they take their flight toward thee,
They'll get where " massa" cannot hold them,
    And therefore to the North they flee.
    Fools to be led off, where they can't earn
    Their living, by thy lying lantern.

We will to New England write,
    And tell them not to let thee shine
    (Excepting of a cloudy night)
    Anywhere south of Dixon's line;
    If beyond that thou shine an inch,
    We'll have thee up before Judge Lynch.

And when, thou Abolition star,
    Who preachest Freedom in all weathers,
    Thou hast got on thy coat of tar,
    And over that, a cloak of feathers,
    Thou art "fixed" none will deny,
    If there's a fixed star in the sky.

31. The Slave's Lamentation

Where are the friends that to me were so dear,
Long, long ago — long ago!
Where are the hopes that my heart used to cheer?
Long, long ago — long ago!
I am degraded, for man was my foe,
Friends that I loved in the grave are laid low,
All hope of freedom hath fled from me now,
Long, long ago — long, long ago!
Sadly my wife bowed her beautiful head–
Long, long ago — long ago!
She was my angel, my love and pride–
Vainly to save her from torture I tried,
Poor broken heart! She rejoiced as she died,
Long, long ago — long, long ago!
Let me look back on the days of my youth —
Long, long ago — long ago!
Master withheld from me knowledge and
    truth —
Long, long ago — long ago!
Crushed all the hopes of my earliest day,
Sent me from father and mother away —
Forbade me to read, nor allowed me to pray —
Long, long ago — long, long ago!

32. Song of the Coffle Gang

See these poor souls from Africa,
Transported to America:
We are stolen, and sold to Georgia, will you go
    along with me?
We are stolen and sold to Georgia, go sound the
    jubilee.

See wives und husbands sold apart,
The children's screams! — it breaks my heart;
There's a better day a coming, will you go along
    with me?

There's a better day a coming, go sound the jubilee

O, gracious Lord! when shall it be,
That we poor souls shall all be free?
Lord, break them Slavery powers — will you go
along with
                              Me?
Lord, break them Slavery powers, go sound the
jubilee.

Dear Lord! dear Lord! when Slavery'll cease,
Then we poor souls can have our peace;
There's a better day a coming, will you go along
with me?
There's a better day a coming, go sound the ju-
bilee.

33. Spirit of Freemen, Wake

Spirit of Freemen, wake;
No truce with Slavery make,
Thy deadly foe;
In fair disguises dressed,
Too long hast thou caress'd
The serpent in thy breast,
Now lay him low.
Must e'en the press be dumb?
Must truth itself succumb?
And thoughts be mute?
Shall law be set aside,
The right of prayer denied,
Nature and God decried,
And man called brute?
What lover of her fame
Feels not his country's shame,
In this dark hour?
Where are the patriots now,
Of honest heart and brow,
Who scorn the neck to bow
To Slavery's Power?
Sons of the Free! we call
On you, in field and hall,
To rise as one;
Your heaven-born rights maintain,
Nor let Oppression's chain
On human limbs remain; —
Speak! and 't is done.

34. Steal Away

Steal away, steal away, steal away to Jesus!
Steal away, steal away home,
I ain't got long to stay here.

My Lord, He calls me,
He calls me by the thunder;
The trumpet sounds within my soul,
I ain't got long to stay here.

Steal away, steal away, steal away to Jesus!
Steal away, steal away home,
I ain't got long to stay here.

Green trees are bending,
Poor sinners stand a-trembling;
The trumpet sounds within my soul,
I ain't got long to stay here.

Steal away, steal away, steal away to Jesus!
Steal away, steal away home,
I ain't got long to stay here.

My Lord, He calls me,
He calls me by the lightning;
The trumpet sounds within my soul,
I ain't got long to stay here.

35. The Sweets of Liberty

Is there a man that never sighed
To set the prisoner free?
Is there a man that never prized
The sweets of liberty?
Then let him, let him breathe — unseen,
Or in a dungeon live;
Nor never, never know the sweets
That liberty can give.

Is there a heart so cold in man,
Can galling fetters crave?
Is there a wretch so truly low,
Can stoop to be a slave?
O, let him, then, in chains be bound,
In chains and bondage live;
Nor never, never know the sweets
That liberty can give.
Is there a breast so chilled in life,
Can nurse the coward's sigh?
Is there a creature so debased,
Would not for freedom die?
O, let him then be doomed to crawl
Where only reptiles live;
Nor never, never know the sweets
That liberty can give.

36. Wade in the Water

Chorus
Wade in the water
Wade in the water children
Wade in the water
Don't you know that
God's gonna trouble the water
Don't you know that
God's gonna trouble the water

I stepped in water and the water is cold
Don't you know that
God's gonna trouble the water
Said it chilled my body but not my soul

Don't you know that
God's gonna trouble the water

Chorus

Well I went to the water one day to pray
Don't you know that
God's gonna trouble the water
And my soul got happy and I stayed all day
Don't you know that
God's gonna trouble the water

Chorus

There is love
(In the water)
In the water
(In the water)
There is joy yeah
(In the water)
In your water yeah
(In the water)
Your peace
(In the water)
Is in the water
(In the water)
Your deliverance
(In the water)
Is in the water yeah
(In the water)
Oh step in, step in
(In the water)
Joy is in the water
In the water yeah
(In the water)
Oh step in, step in
(In the water)
Love is in the water
(In the water)
Oh step in yeah
(In the water)
For deliverance
(In the water)
Everything
(In the water)
In the water yeah

God's gonna trouble the water
God's gonna trouble the water
(Yeah, yeah, yeah, yeah)
God's gonna trouble the water
(Ooh)
God's gonna trouble the water
Oh wade in the water

37. We're Coming! We're Coming!

We're coming, we're coming, the fearless and free,
Like the winds of the desert, the waves of the sea!
True Sons of brave sires who battled of yore,

When England's proud lion ran wild on our shore!
We're coming, we're coming, from mountain
and glen,
With hearts to do battle for freedom again;
Oppression is trembling as trembled before
The slavery which fled from our fathers of yore.
We're coming, we're coming, with banners un-
furled,
Our motto is FREEDOM, our country the world;
Our watchword is LIBERTY — tyrants beware
For the liberty army will bring you despair!

We're coming, we're coming, we'll come from afar.
Our standard we'll nail to humanity's car;
With shouting we'll raise it, in triumph to wave,
A trophy of conquest, or shroud for the brave.
Then arouse ye, brave hearts, to the rescue come
on!
The man-stealing army we'll surely put down;
They are crushing their millions, but soon they
must yield,
For freemen have risen and taken the field.

Then arouse ye! arouse ye ! the fearless and free,
Like the winds of the desert, the waves of the sea;
Let the north, west, and east, to the sea-beaten
shore,
Resound with a liberty triumph once more.

38. The Yankee Girl

She sings by her wheel at that low cottage door,
Which the long evening shadow is stretching be-
fore
With a music as sweet as the music which seems
Breathed softly and faintly in the car of our
dreams!

How brilliant and mirthful the light of her eye,
Like a star glancing out from the blue of the sky!
And lightly and freely her dark tresses play
O'er a brow and a bosom as lovely as they!
Who comes in his pride to that low cottage door —
The haughty and rich to the humble and poor?
'Tis the great Southern planter — the master who
waves
His whip of dominion o'er hundreds of slaves.

Nay, Ellen, for shame I Let those Yankee fools spin,
Who would pass for our slaves with a change of
their skin;
Let them toil as they will at the loom or the wheel
Too stupid for shame and too vulgar to feel!

But thou art too lovely and precious a gem
To be bound to their burdens and sullied by
them —
For shame, Ellen, shame!—cast thy bondage aside,
And away to the South, as my blessing and pride.

O, come where no winter thy footsteps can wrong,

But where flowers are blossoming all the year long,
Where the shade of the palm-tree is over my home,
And the lemon and orange are white in their
    bloom!

O, come to my home, where my servants shall all
Depart at thy bidding and come at thy call;
They shall heed thee as mistress with trembling
    and awe,
And each wish of thy heart shall be felt as a law.

O, could ye have seen her — that pride of our
    girls—
Arise and cast back the dark wealth of her curls,
With a scorn in her eye which gazer could feel
And a glance like the sunshine that flashes on
    steel:

"Go back, haughty Southron! thy treasures of gold
Are dim with the blood of the hearts thou hast sold
Thy home may be lovely, but round it I hear
The crack of the whip and the footsteps of fear!

And the sky of thy South may be brighter than
    ours,
And greener thy landscapes, and fairer thy flowers;
But, dearer the blast round our mountains
    which rave,
Than the sweet sunny zephyr which breathes
    over slaves!

Full low at thy bidding thy negroes may kneel,
With the iron of bondage on Spirit and heel;
Yet know that the Yankee girl soon would be
In fetters with them, than in freedom with thee

39. Ye Heralds of Freedom

Ye heralds of freedom, ye noble and brave,
Who dare to insist on the rights of the slave,
Go onward, go onward, your cause is of God,
And he will soon sever the oppressor's strong rod.

The finger of slander may now at you point,
That finger will soon lose the strength of its joint;
And those who now plead for the rights of the
    slave,
Will soon be acknowledged the good and the
    brave.

Though thrones and dominions and kingdoms
    and powers,
May now all oppose you, the victory is yours;
The banner of Jesus will soon be unfurled,
And he will give freedom and peace to the world.

Go under his standard and fight by his side,
O'er mountains and billows you'll then safely ride;
His gracious protection wilt be to you given,
And bright crowns of glory he'll give you in
    heaven.

40. Ye Spirits of the Free

Ye spirits of the free,
Can ye forever see
Your brother man
A yoked and scourged slave
Chains dragging to his grave,
And raise no hand to save?
Say if you can.
In pride and pomp to roll,
Shall tyrants from the soul
God's image tear,
And call the wreck their own —
While, from the eternal throne,
They shut the stifled groan
And bitter prayer?
Shall he a slave be bound,
Whom God hath doubly crowned
Creation's lord?
Shall men of Christian name,
Without a blush of shame
Profess their tyrant claim
From God's own word?
No! at the battle cry,
A host prepared to die,
Shall arm for fight —
But not with martial steel,
Grasped with a murderous zeal;
No arms their foes shall fell,
But love and light.
Firm on Jehovah's laws,
Strong in their righteous cause,
They march to save.
And vain the tyrant's mail,
Against their battle — hail,
Till cease the woe and wail
Of tortured slave!

41. Zaza — The Female Slave

O, my country, my country!
How long I for thee,
Far over the mountain,
Far over the sea.
Where the sweet Joliba,
Kisses the shore,
Say, shall I wander
By thee never more?
Where the sweet Joliba kisses the shore,
Say, shall I wander by thee never more.

Say, O fond Zurima,
Where dost thou stay?
Say, doth another
List to thy sweet lay?
Say, doth the orange still
Bloom near our cot?
Zurima, Zurima,

             Am I forgot?
O, my country, my country, how long I for thee,
  Far over the mountain, far over the seas.
        Under the baobab
        Oft have I slept,
     Fanned by sweet breezes
      That over me swept.
       Often in dreams
    Do my weary limbs lay
    'Neath the same baobab,
       Far, far away.
O, my country, my country, how long I for thee,

  Far over the mountain, far over the sea.
         O, for the breath
     Of our own waving palm,
      Here, as I languish;
      My spirit to calm —
      O, for a draught
  From our own cooling lake,
    Brought by sweet mother,
     My spirit to wake.
O, my country, my country, how long I for thee,
  Far over the mountain, far over the sea.

Bibliography

PRIMARY SOURCES

(See Appendix 6 for a list of slave autobiographies)

African American Newspapers

The African Methodist Episcopal Church Magazine (est. 1841, Albany, NY)
The Alienated American (est. 1852, Cleveland, Ohio)
The Anglo-American (est. 1859, New York City)
The Christian Herald (est. 1848, Philadelphia); continued as *Mirror of the Times* (1855, San Francisco)
The Christian Recorder (est. 1852, Philadelphia)
The Clarion (est. 1842, Troy, NY)
The Colored American (est. 1837, New York City)
The Colored Man's Journal (est. 1851, New York City)
The Elevator (est. 1842, Philadelphia)
Frederick Douglass Paper (est. 1851, when *The North Star* merged with the *Liberty Party Paper*)
Freedom's Journal (est. 1826, New York City)
The Herald of Freedom (est. 1855, Ohio)
The Imperial Citizen (est. 1848, Boston)
The Mystery (est. 1843, Pittsburgh)
The National Watchman (est. 1842, Troy, NY)
The North Star (est. 1847, Rochester, NY)
The Northern Star, later *The Genius of Freedom* (est. 1845, Philadelphia)
The Peoples Press (est. 1843, New York City)
The Provincial Freeman (est. 1853, Canada)
The Rams Horn (est. 1847, New York City)
Rights of All (est. 1828, New York City)
Voice of the Fugitive (est. 1851, Canada)
The Weekly Advocate (est. 1837, New York); continued as the *National Reformer* (1838, Philadelphia)

Government Documents

American Freedmen's Inquiry Commission Interviews. National Archives Microfilm, 1863, 1864.
National Underground Railroad Network to Freedom Act of 1998, Public Law 105–203.
U. S. Bureau of the Census. *Historical Statistics of the United States: Colonial Times to 1957.* Washington, D.C.: U.S. Government Printing Office, 1960.
U. S. Bureau of the Census. *Negro Population, 1790–1915.* Washington, D.C.: U.S. Government Printing Office, 1915.

Document Collections and Unpublished Documents

Anti-Slavery Collection, Boston Public Library.
Clarke, John Jackson. "Memories of the Anti-Slavery Movement and the Underground Railway." December 19, 1931. Clarke Papers. Oswego County Historical Society.
Cook, Iris L. "Underground Railroad in Southern Indiana." Federal Writers' Project, unpublished notes, ca. 1936. Presented to the author by Ms. Cook's grandniece, 1999.
Coon, Diane P. "Reconstructing the Underground Railroad Crossings at Madison, Indiana." Unpublished manuscript, 1998.
Da Silva, Janine. "Nathan and Mary (Polly) Johnson House 21 Seventh Street New Bedford, Massachusetts: Conservation Assessment." New Bedford, MA: New Bedford Historical Society, 1999.
Gionta, Mary Ann. "John B. Edwards." Papers. Special Collections, Penfield Library, Oswego, New York. Includes list of Edwards' correspondence with Gerrit Smith in Smith Papers, Syracuse University.
Lowder, Jerry E. "Benjamin Russell Hanby, Ohio Composer-Educator, 1833–1867: His Contributions to Early Music Education." PhD dissertation, The Ohio State University, 1987.
Pickard, John B., ed. *The Letters of John Greenleaf Whittier, Vol. III: 1861–1892.* Cambridge: Harvard University Press, 1975.
Pluchel, Erma Grant. Letter to Alliance Carnegie Library from Mrs. George Grant Pluchel, 1936, Rodman Public Library Collection, Alliance, Ohio.
Rawick, George P., Ed. *The American Slave: A Composite Autobiography.* 16 vols. Westport, CT: Greenwood, 1972.

Ripley, C. Peter, et al., eds. *The Black Abolitionist Papers.* Vol. 2, *Canada, 1830–1865.* Chapel Hill, NC: University of North Carolina Press, 1986.
_____. *The Black Abolitionist Papers.* Vol. 4, *The United States, 1847–1858.* Chapel Hill, NC: University of North Carolina Press, 1991.
Robinson Family Letters, Rokeby Collection, Sheldon Museum, Middlebury, Vermont.
Saulman, Earl O. "Blacks in Harrison County, Indiana." Unpublished manuscript, Corydon, Indiana, 1999.
Siebert, Wilbur H. *Papers.* Ohio Historical Society.

SECONDARY SOURCES

Articles

Addington, Wendell G. "Slave Insurrections in Texas." *Journal of Negro History* 35, no. 4(1950): 408–434.
Alexander, H. B. "Brazilian and United States Slavery Compared." *Journal of Negro History* 6(1922): 349–364.
Aptheker, Herbert. "Maroons within the present limits of the United States." *Journal of Negro History* 22(1939): 167–184.
Bacon, Margaret Hope. "The Double Curse of Sex and Color: Robert Purvis and Human Rights." *The Pennsylvania Magazine of History and Biography* 121(1997): 53–75.
_____. "One Great Bundle of Humanity: Frances Ellen Watkins Harper." *Pennsylvania Magazine of History and Biography* 113, no. 1(1989): 21–43.
Baily, Marilyn. "From Cincinnati, Ohio to Wilberforce, Canada: A Note on Antebellum Colonization." *Journal of Negro History* 58(1973): 427–440.
Ballagh, J. C. "A History of Slavery in Virginia." In *Early Studies of Slavery by States.* Vol. 1. Northbrook, IL: Metro Books, 1972.
Baptist, Edward E. "'Cuffy,' 'Fancy Maids,' and 'One-Eyed Men': Rape, Commodification and the Domestic Slave Trade in the United States." *The American Historical Review* 106(2001): 1619–1650.
Barker, Eugene C. "The Influence of Slavery in the Colonization of Texas." *Mississippi Valley Historical Review* 11, no. 1(1924): 3–36.
"Battle Creek Remembers the Underground Railroad." *Michigan History Magazine* 78(1994): 40–41.
Beasley, Delilah L. "Slavery in California." *Journal of Negro History* 3, no. 1(1918): 33–44.
Bell, Raymond M. "Washington County, Pennsylvania, in the Eighteenth Century Anti-Slavery Movement." *Western Pennsylvania Historical Magazine* 25(1942): 125–142.
Blackburn, George M., and Sherman L. Ricards.

"Unequal Opportunity on a Mining Frontier: The Role of Gender, Race and Birthplace." *Pacific Historical Review* 62(1993): 19–37.
Blight, David W. "Frederick Douglass and the American Apocalypse." *Civil War History* 31, no. 4(1985): 309–328.
Blue, Frederick J. "Oberlin's James Monroe: Forgotten Abolitionist." *Civil War History* 35(1989): 285–301.
Bolster, W. Jeffrey. "To Feel Like a Man: Black Seamen in the Northern States, 1800–1860." *Journal of American History* 76, no. 4(1990): 1173–1199.
Brewer, W. B. "Henry Highland Garnet." *Journal of Negro History* 13, no. 1(1928): 36–52.
Bringhurst, Newell G. "The Mormons and Slavery — A Closer Look." *Pacific Historical Review* 50(1981): 329–338.
Brooks, Elaine. "Massachusetts Anti-Slavery Society." *Journal of Negro History* 30(1945): 311–332.
Brown, Ira V. "An Anti-Slavery Agent: C. C. Burleigh in Pennsylvania, 1836–1837." *The Pennsylvania Magazine of History and Biography* 105, no. 1(1981): 66–84.
Butler, Dominique, "John Jones." *Illinois History* 1996.
Castel, Albert. "Civil War Kansas and the Negro." *Journal of Negro History* 51(1966): 125–138.
Chaplin, Joyce E. "Tidal Rice Cultivation and the Problem of Slavery in South Carolina and Georgia." *William and Mary Quarterly* 49(1992): 29–61.
Cheek, William F. "John Mercer Langston: Black Protest Leader and Abolitionist." *Civil War History* 16(1970): 101–120.
Coleman, Edward M. "William Wells Brown as an Historian." *Journal of Negro History* 31, no. 1(1946): 47–59.
Coleman, J. Winston, Jr. "Delia Webster and Calvin Fairbank — Underground Railroad Agents." *Filson Club History Quarterly* 17(1943): 129–142.
Collison, Gary L. "This Flagitious Offense: Daniel Webster and the Shadrach Rescue Cases, 1851–1852." *New England Quarterly* 68, no. 4(1995).
Cooper, Afua. "The Fluid Frontier: Blacks and the Detroit River Region, A Focus on Henry Bibb." *Canadian Review of American Studies* 30(2000): 129–149.
Cumbler, John T. "To Do Battle for Justice and the Oppressed." Unpublished manuscript. Department of History, University of Louisville, 2004.
Curtis, K. D., "York, the Slave Explorer." *Negro Digest* (1962): 10–15.
David, C. W. A. "The Fugitive Slave Law of 1793 and Its Antecedents." *Journal of Negro History* 8, no. 1(1924): 18–25.
Dean, Terry. "Present Owners of Crenshaw House Look to State for Funding." *Daily Egyptian* (Southern Illinois University at Carbondale), February 29, 2000.

Duvall, Severn. "*Uncle Tom's Cabin:* The Sinister Side of the Patriarchy." *The New England Quarterly* 36, no. 1(1963): 3–22.

England, J. Merton. "The Free Negro in Ante-Bellum Tennessee." *Journal of Southern History* 9, no. 1(1943): 35–58.

Engle, Diana P. "A Never-Ending Sojourn." *Michigan History Magazine* 84, no. 1(2000): 29–39.

Eslinger, Ellen. "The Shape of Slavery on the Kentucky Frontier, 1775–1800." *The Register of the Kentucky Historical Society* 92(1994): 1–23.

Farr, Joseph. "Joseph Farr Remembers the Underground Railroad in St. Paul." *Minnesota History* 57(2000): 123–129. Reprint of 1895 article in the *St. Paul Pioneer Press.*

Feller, Daniel. "A Brother in Arms: Benjamin Tappan and the Antislavery Democracy." *The Journal of American History* 88(2001): 48–74.

Finkelman, Paul. "The Kidnapping of John Davis and the Adoption of the Fugitive Slave Law of 1793." *Journal of Southern History* 56, no. 3(1990): 397–422.

_____. "Prigg v. Pennsylvania and the Northern State Courts: Anti-Slavery Use of a Pro-Slavery Decision." *Civil War History* 25, no. 1(1979): 5–35.

Finnie, Gordon E. "The Antislavery Movement in the Upper South Before 1840." *Journal of Southern History* 35, no. 3(1969): 319–342.

Fletcher, Robert S. "The Government of the Oberlin Colony." *The Mississippi Valley Historical Review* 20(1933): 179–190.

Forbes, Ella. "By My Own Right Arm: Redemptive Violence and the 1851 Christiana, Pennsylvania Resistance." *Journal of Negro History* 83, no. 3(1998): 159–167.

"Freedom Seekers: Underground Railroad Travelled through Valley." *Monongahela Valley Review* (February 1993): 8–9.

Freehling, William W. "The Founding Fathers and Slavery." *The American Historical Review* 77(1972): 81–93.

Galbreath, C. B. "Anti-Slavery Movement in Columbiana County." *Ohio State Archaeological and Historical Quarterly* 30: 389–91 (1921).

Gara, Larry. "The Fugitive Slave Law: A Double Paradox." *Civil War History* 10(1964): 229–240.

Geffert, Hannah N. "John Brown and His Black Allies: An Ignored Alliance." *The Pennsylvania Magazine of History and Biography* 126, no. 4(2002): 591–610.

Grant, John N. "Black Immigrants to Nova Scotia." *Journal of Negro History* 58(1973): 253–270.

Griffler, Keith. "Beyond the Quest for the 'Real Eliza Harris': Fugitive Slave Women in the Ohio Valley." *Ohio Valley History* 3(2003): 3–16.

Guy, Anita A. "The Maryland Abolition Society and the Promotion of the Ideals of the New Nation." *Maryland Historical Magazine* 84, no. 1(1989): 342–349.

Harlow, Ralph Volney. "The Rise and Fall of the Kansas Aid Movement." *American Historical Review* 41, no. 1(1935): 1–25.

Harris, Robert L., Jr. "H. Ford Douglas: Afro-American Antislavery Emigrationist." *Journal of Negro History* 62(1977): 217–234.

Harris, Theodore H. "The Carneal House and the Underground Railroad: A Covington Family Escapes from Slavery." *Northern Kentucky Heritage* 6(1999): 35–38.

Harrold, Stanley. "The Intersectional Relationship between Cassius M. Clay and the Garrisonian Abolitionists." *Civil War History* 35(1989): 101–119.

_____. "On the Borders of Slavery and Race: Charles T. Torrey and the Underground Railroad." *Journal of the Early Republic* 20(2000).

Hartgrove, W. B. "The Story of Josiah Henson." *Journal of Negro History* 3(1918): 1–21.

Hill, D. G. "The Negro as a Political and Social Issue in the Oregon Country." *Journal of Negro History* 33, no. 2(1948): 130–145.

Hill, James L. "Migration of Blacks to Iowa, 1820–1960." *Journal of Negro History* 66, no. 4(1982): 289–303.

Hodder, F. H. "Some Phases of the Dred Scott Case." *Mississippi Valley Historical Review* 16, no. 1(1929): 3–22.

Holmberg, James J. "'I Wish You to See and Know All': The Recently Discovered Letters of William Clark to Jonathan Clark." *We Proceeded On* 4(1992): 7–9.

Howard-Filler, Saralee R. "Detroit's Underground Railroad and the Museum of African American History." *Michigan History* 71(1987): 28–29.

Hudson, J. Blaine. "African American Religion in Antebellum Louisville, Kentucky." *The Griot: Journal of the Southern Conference on African American Studies* 17, no. 2(1998): 43–54.

_____. "The African Diaspora and the 'Black Atlantic': An African American Perspective." *Negro History Bulletin* 60, no. 4(1997): 7–14.

_____. "Crossing the Dark Line: Fugitive Slaves and the Underground Railroad in Louisville and North Central Kentucky." *Filson History Quarterly* 75, no. 1(2001): 33–84.

_____. "Frederick Douglass and W. E. B. DuBois: The Lessons of the Past." Lecture presented at the First Unitarian Church, Louisville, KY, February 24, 1991.

_____. "References to Slavery in the Public Records of Early Louisville and Jefferson County, Kentucky, 1780–1812." *The Filson History Quarterly* 73(1999): 325–354.

_____. "Slavery in Early Louisville and Jefferson County, 1780 — 1812." *The Filson History Quarterly* 73, no. 3(1997): 249–283.

Hudson, Lynn M. "A New Look, Or, 'I'm Not Mammy to Everybody in California': Mary Ellen

Pleasant, a Black Entrepreneur." *Journal of the West* 32(1993): 35–40.

"In Memoriam: John Hossack, Deceased November 8, 1891." *The Republican Times* (Ottawa, Illinois), 1892.

Jackson, Luther P. "Free Negroes of Petersburgh, Virginia." *Journal of Negro History* 41, no. 3(1927): 365–388.

Jacobs, Donald M. "William Lloyd Garrison's *Liberator* and Boston's Blacks, 1830–1865." *New England Quarterly* 44(1971): 259–277.

Jeltz, Wyatt F. "The Relations of Negroes and Choctaw and Chickasaw Indians." *Journal of Negro History* (1948): 24–37.

Jervey, Edward D., and C. Harold Huber. "The Creole Affair." *The Journal of Negro History* 65(1980): 196–209.

Johannsen, Robert W. "The Secession Crisis and the Frontier: Washington Territory, 1860–1861." *Mississippi Valley Historical Review* 39, no. 3(1952): 415–440.

Johnson, Michael P. "Runaway Slaves and the Slave Communities in South Carolina, 1799 to 1830." *William and Mary Quarterly* 38, no. 3(1981): 418–441.

Jones, Howard. "The Peculiar Institution and National Honor: The Case of the Creole Slave Revolt." *Civil War History* 21(1975): 28–50.

Kashatus, William C. "Two Stationmasters on the Underground Railroad: A Tale of Black and White." *Pennsylvania Heritage* 27(2001): 4–11.

Kay, Marvin L., and Lorin L. Cary. "Slave Runaways in Colonial North Carolina." *The North Carolina Historical Review* 63, no. 1(1981).

Kimmel, Janice M. "Break Your Chains and Fly for Freedom." *Michigan History Magazine* 80, no. 1(1996): 21–27.

Landers, Jane. "Gracia Real de Santa Teresa de Mose: A Free Black Town in Spanish Colonial Florida." *The American Historical Review* 95(1990): 9–30.

Landon, Fred. "Amherstburg, Terminus of the Underground Railroad." *Journal of Negro History* 10(1925).

_____. "The Anderson Fugitive Case." *Journal of Negro History* 7(1923): 233–242.

_____. "The Buxton Settlement in Canada." *Journal of Negro History* 3, no. 4(1918).

_____. "Canadian Negroes and the John Brown Raid." *Journal of Negro History* 6, no. 2(1921): 174–182.

Lapansky, Emma Jones. "Feminism, Freedom, and Community: Charlotte Forten and Women Activists in Nineteenth-Century Philadelphia." *Pennsylvania Magazine of History and Biography* 113, no. 1(1989): 3–19.

Lapp, Rudolph M. "The Negro in Gold Rush California." *Journal of Negro History* 49, no. 2(1964): 81–98.

Ledbetter, Bill. "Charles Sumner: Political Activist

for the New England Transcendentalists." *The Historian* 44(1982): 347–363.

Lee, R. Alton. "Slavery and the Oregon Territorial Issue: Prelude to the Compromise of 1850." *Pacific Northwest Quarterly* 64(1973): 112–119.

Levy, Leonard W. "Sims' Case: The Fugitive Slave Law in Boston in 1851." *Journal of Negro History* 35(1950): 39–74.

Lindsay, Arnett G. "Diplomatic Relations Between the United States and Great Britain Bearing on the Return of Negro Slaves, 1783–1828." *Journal of Negro History* 4(1920): 391–419.

Litwack, Leon F. "The Abolitionist Dilemma: The Anti-Slavery Movement and the Northern Negro." *New England Quarterly* 34(1961): 50–73.

Lockwood, C. R. "Africa." Interview with Catherine Harris, Jamestown *Evening Journal*, May 3, 1902.

Luckerman, Sharon. "Detroit Jews Broke the Law to Help Slaves Escape." *Detroit Jewish News On-line.*

Ludlum, Robert P. "Joshua R. Giddings, Radical." *The Mississippi Valley Historical Review* 23(1936): 49–60.

Mabee, Carleton. "Sojourner Truth, Bold Prophet: Why Did She Never Learn to Read?" *New York History* 69, no. 1(1988): 55–77.

Maginnes, David R. "The Case of the Court House Rioters in the Rendition of the Fugitive Slave Anthony Burns, 1854." *Journal of Negro History* 56, no. 1(1971): 31–42.

Mahoney, Olivia. "Black Abolitionists." *Chicago History* 20(1991): 22–37.

Marcus, Robert D. "Wendell Phillips and American Institutions." *Journal of American History* 56, no. 1(1969): 41–58.

McAfee, Ward M. "California's House Divided." *Civil War History* 33(1987): 115–130.

McCann, Dennis. "Abolitionist Wore His Brand with Honor." *Milwaukee Journal Sentinel*, March 21, 2000.

McGlone, Robert E. "Rescripting a Troubled Past: John Brown's Family and the Harpers Ferry Conspiracy." *Journal of American History* 75, no. 4(1989): 1179–1200.

McKibben, Davidson B. "Negro Slave Insurrections in Mississippi." *Journal of Negro History* 34, no. 1(1949): 73–94.

McKivigan, John R., and Madeleine Leveille. "The 'Black Dream' of Gerrit Smith, New York Abolitionist." *Syracuse University Library Associates Courier* 20, no. 2(Fall 1985).

Meadors, Daniel E. "South Carolina Fugitives as Viewed through Local Colonial Newspapers with Emphasis on Runaway Notices, 1732–1801." *Journal of Negro History* 59(1975): 288–319.

Middleton, Stephen. "The Fugitive Slave Crisis in Cincinnati, 1850–1860: Resistance, Enforcement, and Black Refugees." *Journal of Negro History* 72, no. 2(1987): 20–32.

Miller, Caroline. "Historic Register Nomination: White Hall/Arthur Thome." June 21, 2003.

Mullin, Gerald W. *Flight and Rebellion: Slave Resistance in Eighteenth Century Virginia.* New York: Oxford University Press, 1972.

Musgrave, Jon. "History Comes out of Hiding atop Hickory Hill." *Springhouse Magazine,* December 1996.

Nadelhaft, Jerome. "The Somersett Case and Slavery: Myth, Reality, and Repercussions." *Journal of Negro History* 51, no. 3(1966): 193–208.

Nash, A. E. Keir. "The Texas Supreme Court and the Trial Rights of Blacks, 1845–1860." *The Journal of American History* 58(1971): 622–642.

Nash, Gary B. "New Light on Richard Allen: The Early Years of Freedom." *William and Mary Quarterly* 46(1989): 332–340.

National Underground Railroad Freedom Center, Press Release, August 2004.

Nogee, Joseph. "The Prigg Case and Fugitive Slavery, 1842–1850." *The Journal of Negro History* 39, no. 3(1954): 185–205.

Oates, Stephen B. "John Brown and His Judges: A Critique of the Historical Literature." *Civil War History* 28, no. 1(1971): 5–24.

Olbey, Christian. "Unfolded Hands: Class Suicide and the Insurgent Intellectual Praxis of Mary Ann Shadd." *Canadian Review of American Studies* 30(2000): 151–174.

Painter, Nell Irvin. "Representing Truth: Sojourner Truth's Knowing and Becoming Known." *Journal of American History* 81, no. 2(1994): 461–492.

_____. "Truth, Sojourner." In *Black Women in America: An Historical Encyclopedia.* Vol. 2. Edited by Darlene Clark Hine, Elsa Barkley Brown and Rosalyn Terborg-Penn. Bloomington and Indianapolis: Indiana University Press, 1993.

Paynter, John N. "The Fugitives of the Pearl." *Journal of Negro History* 1, no. 3(1916): 243–264.

Pease, Jane H., and William H. Pease. "Ends, Means, and Attitudes: Black-White Conflict in the Antislavery Movement." *Civil War History* 18(1972): 117–128.

Peck, Douglas T. "Lucas Vasquez de Allyon's Doomed Colony of San Miguel de Gualdape." *Georgia Historical Quarterly* 85(2001): 183–198.

Perlman, Daniel. "Organizations of the Free Negro in New York City, 1800–1860." *Journal of Negro History* 56, no. 3(1971): 181–197.

Pirtle, Carol. "A Flight to Freedom: A True Story of the Underground Railroad in Illinois." *Ohio Valley History* 3(2003).

Polos, Nicholas C. "Explorer with Lewis and Clark." *Negro History Bulletin* 45(1982): 90–96.

Porter, Dorothy B. "David Ruggles: An Apostle of Human Rights." *Journal of Negro History* 38, no. 1(1943): 23–50.

Porter, K. W. "Relations between Negroes and Indians within the Present Limits of the United States." *Journal of Negro History* 16(1932): 287–367.

Porter, Kenneth Wiggins. "Negroes and the Seminole War, 1835–1842." *Journal of Southern History* 30(1964):427–450.

Preston, E. Delorus. "The Underground Railroad in Northwest Ohio." *Journal of Negro History* 17, no. 4(1932): 409–436.

Preston, Emmett D. "The Fugitive Slave Acts in Ohio." *Journal of Negro History* 28(1943): 422–477.

Prince, Benjamin Franklin. "The Rescue Case of 1857." *Ohio Archaeological and Historical Publications* no. 16 (January 1907): 293–306.

Pritchard, James M. "Into the Fiery Furnace: Anti-Slavery Prisoners in the Kentucky State Penitentiary, 1844–1870." Paper presented at the Kentucky Underground Railroad Symposium, June 1999, Maysville, Kentucky.

Quarles, Benjamin. "Sources of Abolitionist Income." *The Mississippi Valley Historical Review* 32(1945): 63–76.

Randall, James G. "Some Legal Aspects of the Confiscation Acts of the Civil War." *American Historical Review* 18, no. 1(1912): 79–96.

Ranney, Joseph A. "Suffering the Agonies of Their Righteousness: The Rise and Fall of the States Rights Movement in Wisconsin, 1854–1861." *Wisconsin Magazine of History* 75, no. 2(1992).

Roach, Monique P. "The Rescue of William 'Jerry' Henry: Antislavery and Racism in the Burned-over District." *New York History* 82, no. 3(2001): 135–154.

Robboy, Stanley J., and Anita W. Robboy. "Lewis Hayden: From Fugitive Slave to Statesman." *New England Quarterly* 46(1973): 591–613.

Rohrs, Richard C. "Antislavery Politics and the Pearl Incident of 1848." *The Historian* 56, no. 4(1994): 711–724.

Rosenberg, Norman L. "Personal Liberty Laws and Sectional Crisis: 1850–1861." *Civil War History* 18(1971): 25–44.

Rosenthal, Bernard. "Puritan Conscience and New England Slavery." *The New England Quarterly* 46(1973): 62–81.

Savage, W. Sherman. "The Influence of John Chavis and Lunsford Lane on the History of North Carolina." *Journal of Negro History* 25(1940): 20–24.

_____. "The Negro in the Westward Movement." *Journal of Negro History* 25, no. 4(1940): 531–539.

Schoonover, Thomas. "Misconstrued Mission: Expansionism and Black Colonization in Mexico and Central America during the Civil War." *Pacific Historical Review* 49(1980): 607–620.

Schor, Joel. "The Rivalry between Frederick Douglass and Henry Highland Garnet." *Journal of Negro History* 64, no. 1(1979): 30–38.

Schwartz, Harold. "Fugitive Slave Days in Boston." *New England Quarterly* 27, no. 2(1954): 191–212.

Sernett, Milton C. "Common Cause: The Antislavery Alliance of Gerrit Smith and Beriah Green." *Syracuse University Library Associates Courier* 21, no. 2(Fall 1986).

Sherwood, John C. "One Flame in the Inferno: The Legend of Marshall's Crosswhite Affair." *Michigan History* 73(1989): 41–47.

Shriver, Edward O. "Antislavery: The Free Soil and Free Democratic Parties in Maine, 1848–1855." *New England Quarterly* 42, no. 1(1969): 82–94.

Shriver, Phillip R. "Freedom's Proving Ground: The Heritage of the Northwest Ordinance." *Wisconsin Magazine of History* 72(1989): 126–131.

Siebert, Wilbur H. "The Underground Railroad in Massachusetts." *The New England Quarterly* 9(1936): 447–467.

Smardz, Karolyn E. "There We Were in Darkness, Here We Are in Light: Kentucky Slaves and the Promised Land." In *The Buzzel About Kentuck: Settling the Promised Land*, edited by Craig Thompson Friend, 243–248. Lexington: University Press of Kentucky, 1999.

Smith, Earl. "William Cooper Nell on the Fugitive Slave Act of 1850." *Journal of Negro History* 66(1981): 37–40.

Smith, Robert P. "William Cooper Nell, Crusading Black Abolitionist." *Journal of Negro History* 55(1970): 182–199.

"Spontaneous Prayer of Rev. Young." *New York Daily Tribune,* December 12, 1859.

Stampp, Kenneth M. "The Fate of the Southern Anti-Slavery Movement." *Journal of Negro History* 28(1943): 10–22.

Stewart, James B. "The Aims and Impact of Garrisonian Abolitionism, 1840–1860." *Civil War History* 15, no. 3(1969): 197–209.

Sumler-Lewis, Janice. "The Forten-Purvis Women of Philadelphia and the American Anti-Slavery Crusade." *Journal of Negro History* 66, no. 4(1982): 281–288.

Thornton, John. "The African Experience of the '20 and Odd Negroes' Arriving in Virginia in 1619." *William and Mary Quarterly* 55(1998): 421–434.

Toplin, Robert B. "Peter Still versus the Peculiar Institution." *Civil War History* 13, no. 4(1967): 340–349.

Towner, Lawrence W. "The Sewall-Saffin Dialogue on Slavery." *William and Mary Quarterly* 21(1964): 40–52.

Turner, Edward R. "The Abolition of Slavery in Pennsylvania." *Pennsylvania Magazine of History and Biography* 36 (1912): 129–142.

"The Two Autobiographical Fragments of George W. Latimer." *Journal of Afro-American Historical and Genealogical Society* No. 1(Summer 1980).

"The Underground Railroad." In the *Historical Encyclopedia of Illinois.* Chicago: Mansell Publishing Company, 1916.

Urwin, Gregory J. W. "'We Cannot Treat Negroes ... As Prisoners of War': Racial Atrocities and Reprisals in Civil War Arkansas." *Civil War History* 42(1996): 193–210.

Volpe, Vernon L. "Theodore Dwight Weld's Antislavery Mission in Ohio." *Ohio History* 100(1991): 5–18.

Waldstreicher, David. "Reading the Runaways: Self-Fashioning, Print Culture, and Confidence in Slavery in the Eighteenth Century Mid-Atlantic." *William and Mary Quarterly* 56(1999): 243–272.

Wax, Darold D. "'The Great Risque We Run': The Aftermath of Slave Rebellion at Stono, South Carolina, 1739–1745." *Journal of Negro History* 67(1982): 136–147.

Westwood, Howard C. "Benjamin Butler's Enlistment of Black Troops in New Orleans in 1862." *Louisiana History* 26(1985): 5–22.

White, Richard H. "The Spirit of Hate and Frederick Douglass." *Civil War History* 46, no. 1(2000): 41–49.

Wiecek, William M. "Slavery and Abolition Before the United States Supreme Court, 1820–1860." *The Journal of American History* 65(1978): 34–59.

_____. "The Statutory Law of Slavery and Race in the Thirteen Mainland Colonies of British America." *William and Mary Quarterly* 34(1977): 258–280.

Willis, William S. "Divide and Rule: Red, White, and Black in the Southeast." *Journal of Negro History* 48(1963): 157–176.

Winch, Julie. "Philadelphia and the Other Underground Railroad." *The Pennsylvania Magazine of History and Biography* 111, no. 1(1987): 3–25.

Wish, Harvey. "The Slave Insurrection Panic of 1856." *Journal of Southern History* 5(1939): 206–222.

Woodson, Carter G. "The Beginnings of the Miscegenation of the Whites and Blacks." *Journal of Negro History* 2(1918): 335–353.

_____. "The Negroes of Cincinnati Prior to the Civil War." *Journal of Negro History* 1(1916): 1–22.

Woolfolk, George R. "Turner's Safety Valve and Free Negro Westward Migration." *Pacific Northwest Quarterly* 56(1965): 125–130.

Work, M. N. "The Life of Charles B. Ray." *Journal of Negro History* 4(1919): 361–371.

Wright, Richard R., Jr. "Negro Rural Communities in the North." *The Southern Workman* 37(1908).

Yanuck, Julius. "The Garner Fugitive Slave Case." *Mississippi Valley Historical Review* 40, no. 1(1953): 47–66.

Zelinsky, Wilbur. "The Historical Geography of the Negro Population of Latin America." *Journal of Negro History* 34(1949): 153–221.

Zorn, Roman J. "The New England Anti-Slavery Society: Pioneer Abolition Organization." *Journal of Negro History* 43(1957): 157–176.

Books

Abdy, E. S. *Journal of a Residence and Tour in the United States of North America, from April 1833 to October 1834.* Vol. 2. London: John Murray, 1835.

Abzug, Robert H. *Passionate Liberator: Theodore Dwight Weld and the Dilemma of Reform.* New York: Oxford University Press, 1980.

Ambrose, Stephen E. *Undaunted Courage: Meriwether Lewis, Thomas Jefferson, and the Opening of the American West.* New York: Simon and Schuster, 1996.

Anderson, William L., ed. *The Oxford Frederick Douglass Reader.* New York: Oxford University Press, 1996.

Anti-Slavery History of Jefferson County. Madison, IN: Jefferson County Historical Society, 1998.

Aron, Stephen. *How the West was Lost: The Transformation of Kentucky from Daniel Boone to Henry Clay.* Baltimore: Johns Hopkins University Press, 1996.

Bailyn, Bernard. *The Ideological Origins of the American Revolution.* Cambridge, MA: Harvard University Press, 1967.

Barry, Kathleen. *Susan B. Anthony: A Biography of a Singular Feminist.* New York: New York University Press, 1988.

Beardon, Jim, and Linda Jean Butler. *Shadd: The Life and Times of Mary Shadd Cary.* Toronto: NC Press, 1977.

Bearse, Austin. *Reminiscences of Fugitive-Slave Law Days in Boston.* Boston: Warren Richardson, 1880.

Beasley, Delilah H. *The Negro Trailblazers of California.* 1919. Reprint, New York: Negro Universities Press, 1969.

Bennett, Lerone, Jr. *Before the Mayflower.* New York: Penguin, 1982.

Berlin, Ira. *Many Thousands Gone: The First Two Centuries of Slavery in North America.* Cambridge, MA: Harvard University Press, 1998.

_____, and Ronald Hoffman, eds. *Slavery and Freedom in the Age of Revolution.* Charlottesville: University Press of Virginia, 1983.

Bernard, Jacqueline. *Journey Toward Freedom: The Story of Sojourner Truth.* New York: W. W. Norton, 1990.

Bethel, Elizabeth R. *The Roots of African American Identity: Memory and History in Antebellum Free Communities.* New York: St. Martin's Press, 1997.

Betts, Robert B. *In Search of York: The Slave Who Went to the Pacific with Lewis and Clark.* Boulder, CO: Colorado Associated University Press, 1985.

Bial, Raymond. *The Underground Railroad.* Boston: Houghton Mifflin, 1995.

Billington, Monroe Lee, and Roger D. Hardaway. *African Americans on the Western Frontier.* Niwot, CO: University of Colorado Press, 1998.

Blackett, R. J. M., ed. *Thomas Morris Chester, Black Civil War Correspondent: His Dispatches from the Virginia Front.* New York: Da Capo, 1991.

Blasingame, John. *Slave Testimony: Two Centuries of Letters, Speeches, Interviews and Autobiographies.* Baton Rouge: Louisiana State University, 1977.

Blockson, Charles. *Hippocrene Guide to the Underground Railroad.* New York: Hippocrene Books, 1994.

_____. *The Underground Railroad.* New York: Prentice Hall, 1987.

Bode, Carl. *Ralph Waldo Emerson: A Profile.* New York: Hill and Wang, 1968.

Bolster, W. Jeffrey. *Black Jacks: African American Seamen in the Age of Sail.* Cambridge: Harvard University Press, 1997.

Boni, Margaret Bradford, ed. *The Fireside Book of Favorite American Songs.* New York: Simon and Schuster, 1952.

Bordewich, Fergus M. *Bound for Canaan: The Underground Railroad and the War for the Soul of America.* New York: Amistad, 2005.

The Boston Slave Riot, and Trial of Anthony Burns. Northbrooke, IL: Metro Books, 1972.

Botkin, B. A., ed. *Lay My Burden Down: A Folk History of Slavery.* Athens, GA: University of Georgia Press, 1945.

Bracey, John H., August Meier, and Elliott Rudwick. *Blacks in the Abolitionist Movement.* Belmont, CA: Wadsworth, 1971.

Bradford, Sarah H. *Harriet Tubman: The Moses of Her People.* Bedford, MA: Applewood Books, 1993.

Bragg, Reverend George F. *Men of Maryland.* Baltimore: Church Advocate Press, 1925.

Branch, Muriel Miller. *The Water Brought Us: The Story of the Gullah-Speaking People.* New York: Cobblehill Books/Dutton, 1995.

Bridenbaugh, Carl. *Jamestown, 1544–1699.* New York: Oxford University Press, 1980.

Brown, Hallie Q. *Homespun Heroines and Other Women of Distinction.* Xenia, OH: Aldine, 1926.

Brown, Hallie Q. *Pen Pictures of Pioneers of Wilberforce.* New York: G. K. Hall, 1997.

Brown, William Wells. *The Anti-Slavery Harp: A Collection Songs for Anti-Slavery Meetings.* Boston: B. Marsh, 1849.

Bruns, Roger, ed. *Am I Not a Man and a Brother: The Anti-Slavery Crusade of Revolutionary America, 1688–1788.* New York: R. R. Bowker, 1977.

Buckmaster, Henrietta. *Let My People Go: The Story of the Underground Railroad and the Growth of the Abolition Movement.* Boston: Beacon Press, 1941.

Butler, Benjamin F. *Autobiography and Personal Reminiscences of Major-General Benj. F. Butler; Butler's book. By Benj. F. Butler. A Review of His Legal, Political, and Military Career.* Boston: A. M. Thayer, 1892.

Cable, Mary. *Black Odyssey: The Case of the Slave Ship Amistad*. New York, Viking Press, 1971.

Campbell, Stanley W. *The Slave Catchers: Enforcement of the Fugitive Slave Law, 1850–1860*. Chapel Hill: University of North Carolina Press, 1968.

Camus, Albert. *The Rebel: An Essay on Man in Revolt*. New York: Vintage Books, 1956.

Catteral, Helen T., ed. *Judicial Cases concerning American Slavery and the Negro*. Vol. 1. Washington, D.C.: Carnegie Institution, 1926.

Chace, Elizabeth Buffum. *Two Quaker Sisters: From the Original Diaries of Elizabeth Buffum Chace and Lucy Buffum Lovell*. New York: Liveright Publishing Corporation, 1937.

Chadwick-Joshua, Jocelyn. *The Jim Dilemma: Reading Race in Huckleberry Finn*. Jackson, MS: University Press of Mississippi, 1998.

Cheek, William, and Aimee Lee Cheek. *John Mercer Langston and the Fight for Black Freedom 1829–1865*. Urbana: University of Illinois Press, 1989.

Clark, James I. *Wisconsin Defies the Fugitive Slave Law*. Madison, WI: State Historical Society of Wisconsin, 1955.

Cobley, Alan G., and Alvin Thompson. *The African-Caribbean Connection: Historical and Cultural Perspectives*. Bridgetown, Barbados: University of the West Indies, 1990.

Cockrum, Col. William M. *History of the Underground Railroad, As It Was Conducted by the Anti-Slavery League*. 1915. Reprint, New York: Negro Universities Press, 1969.

Coffin, Levi. *Reminiscences of Levi Coffin*. New York: Augustus M. Kelley, 1876.

Coleman, J. Winston, Jr. *Slavery Times in Kentucky*. Chapel Hill, NC: University of North Carolina Press, 1940.

Collison, Gary Lee. *Shadrach Minkins: From Fugitive Slave to Citizen*. Cambridge, MA: Harvard University Press, 1997.

Coon, Diane P. *Southeastern Indiana's Underground Railroad Routes and Operations*. Indianapolis: Indiana Department of Natural Resources, 2001.

Cord, Xenia E. *Underground Railroad Quilts — Another View*. American Quilt Study Group, 2004.

Crenshaw, Gwendolyn J. *Bury Me in a Free Land: The Abolitionist Movement in Indiana, 1816–1865*. Indianapolis: Indiana Historical Bureau, 1993.

Crum, Mason. *Gullah: Negro Life in the Carolina Sea Islands*. New York: Negro Universities Press, 1968.

Curry, Leonard P. *The Free Black in Urban America, 1800–1850*. Chicago: University of Chicago Press, 1981.

Curtin, Philip D. *The Atlantic Slave Trade: A Census*. Madison, WI: University of Wisconsin Press, 1969.

Davidson, Basil. *Africa in History: Themes and Outlines*. New York: Collier Books, 1991.

_____. *The African Slave Trade*. New York: Little, Brown, 1980.

Davis, David B. *Slavery and Human Progress*. New York: Oxford University Press, 1984.

Davis, Frederick J. *Who is Black: One Nation's Definition*. University Park, PA: Pennsylvania State University, 1991.

Deagan, Kathleen A., and Darcie MacMahon. *Fort Mose: Colonial America's Black Fortress of Freedom*. Gainesville: University Press of Florida, 1995.

Delany, Martin Robison. *The Condition, Elevation, Emigration and Destiny of the Colored People of the United States, Politically Considered*. Philadelphia: Martin R. Delany, 1852.

Derleth, August William. *Concord Rebel: A Life of Henry David Thoreau*. Philadelphia: Chilton, 1962.

Dewitt, David Miller. *The Impeachment and Trial of Andrew Johnson, seventeenth President of the United States: A History*. 1903. Reprint, New York: Russell and Russell, 1968.

Dillon, Merton L. *Benjamin Lundy and the Struggle for Negro Freedom*. Urbana: University of Illinois Press, 1966.

Dillon, Merton-Lynn. *Elijah P. Lovejoy, Abolitionist Editor*. Westport, CT: Greenwood Press, 1961.

Diop, Cheik Anta. *Pre-colonial Black Africa: A Comparative Study of the Political and Social Systems of Europe and Black Africa, from Antiquity to the Formation of Modern States*. Westport, CT: L. Hall, 1987.

Donald, David H. *Charles Sumner and the Coming of the Civil War*. New York: Knopf, 1960.

Donovan, Josephine. *Uncle Tom's Cabin: Evil Affliction, and Redemptive Love*. Boston: Twayne, 1991.

Douglass, Frederick. *The Life and Times of Frederick Douglass*. 1892. Reprint, New York: Macmillan, 1962.

Drayton, Daniel. *Personal Memoir of Daniel Drayton, for Four Years and Four Months a Prisoner (for charity's sake) in Washington Jail, Including a Narrative of the Voyage and Capture of the Schooner Pearl*. Boston: B. Marsh, 1854.

Drew, Benjamin. *The Refugee: Or the Narratives of Fugitive Slaves in Canada*. Boston: John P. Jewett, 1856.

DuBois, W. E. B. *Black Reconstruction in America, 1860–1880*. 1935. Reprint, New York: Macmillan, 1992.

_____. *John Brown*. 1909. Reprint, New York: International Publications, 1962.

Dunaway, Wayland Fuller. *A History of Pennsylvania*. Englewood Cliffs, NJ: Prentice-Hall, 1948.

Dykstra, Robert R. *Bright Radical Star: Black Freedom and White Supremacy on the Hawkeye Frontier*. Cambridge, MA: Harvard University, 1993.

Egerton, Douglas R. *Gabriel's Rebellion: The Virginia Slave Conspiracies of 1800 and 1802*. Chapel Hill: University of North Carolina Press, 1993.

Ellison, Ralph. *Shadow and Act*. New York: Random House, 1964.

Evers, J. C. *Adventures of Zenas Leonard, Fur Trader.* Norman, OK: University of Oklahoma Press, 1959.

Fairbank, Calvin. *Rev. Calvin Fairbank during Slavery Times.* Chicago: Patriotic, 1890.

Fehrenbacher, Don E. *The Dred Scott Case: Its Significance in American Law and Politics.* New York: Oxford University Press, 2001.

_____. *The South and the Three Sectional Crises.* Baton Rouge, LA: Louisiana State University Press, 1980.

Fields, Peter S. *Ralph Waldo Emerson: The Making of a Democratic Intellectual.* Lanham, MD: Rowman and Littlefield, 2002.

Fisher, Miles. *Negro Slave Songs in the United States.* Ithaca, NY: Cornell University Press, 1953.

Fishkin, Shelley Fisher. *Was Huck Black? Mark Twain and African American Voices.* New York: Oxford University Press, 1993.

Fletcher, Robert S. *A History of Oberlin College from Its Foundation through the Civil War.* Oberlin, OH: Oberlin College, 1943.

Fogel, Robert W. *Without Consent or Contract: The Rise and Fall of American Slavery.* New York: W. W. Norton, 1989.

Forbes, J. D. *Africans and Native Americans: The Language of Race and the Evolution of Red-Black Peoples.* Urbana: University of Illinois Press, 1993.

Fouche, Rayvon. *Black Inventors in the Age of Segregation: Granville T. Woods, Lewis H. Latimer and Shelby J. Davidson.* Baltimore: Johns Hopkins University Press, 2003.

Fox, Early Lee. *The American Colonization Society, 1817–1840.* Baltimore: Johns Hopkins Press, 1919.

Franklin, John H., and Loren Schweninger. *Runaway Slaves: Rebels on the Plantation.* New York: McGraw-Hill, 1999.

Franklin, John Hope, and Alfred A. Moss, Jr. *From Slavery to Freedom: A History of African Americans.* 8th ed. New York: McGraw-Hill, 2000.

Freehling, William W. *The Road to Disunion: Secessionists at Bay, 1776–1854.* New York: Oxford University Press, 1990.

Frothingham, Octavius Brooks. *Gerrit Smith: A Biography.* New York: Negro Universities Press, 1969.

Gara, Larry. *The Liberty Line: The Legend of the Underground Railroad.* Lexington: University Press of Kentucky, 1961.

Garrison, William Lloyd. *Thoughts on African Colonization.* 1832. Reprint, New York: Arno Press, 1968.

George, Carol V. R. *Segregated Sabbaths: Richard Allen and the Emergence of Independent Black Churches, 1760–1840.* New York: Oxford University Press, 1973.

Gerson, Noel B. *Harriet Beecher Stowe: A Biography.* New York, 1976.

Gibbs, Mifflin Wistar. *Shadow and Light: An Autobiography.* (1902).

Gibson, William H., Sr. *Historical Sketches of the Progress of the Colored Race in Louisville, Kentucky.* Louisville: n. p., 1897.

Gill, John. *Tide without Turning: Elijah P. Lovejoy and Freedom of the Press.* Boston: Starr-King Press, 1958.

Goodwine, Margaretta L., ed. *The Legacy of Ibo Landing: Gullah Roots of African American Culture.* Atlanta: Clarity Press, 1998.

Gordon-Reed, Annette, ed. *Race on Trial: Law and Justice in American History.* New York: Oxford University Press, 2002.

Graham, Ruth Morris. *The Saga of the Morris Family.* Columbus, GA: Brentwood Christian Communications, 1984.

Griffler, Keith P. *Front Line of Freedom: African Americans and the Forging of the Underground Railroad in the Ohio Valley.* Lexington, KY: University Press of Kentucky, 2004.

Grimke, Archibald H. *Charles Sumner: The Scholar in Politics.* New York: Funk & Wagnalls, 1892.

Grover, Kathryn. *The Fugitive's Gibraltar: Escaping Slaves and Abolitionism in New Bedford, Massachusetts.* Amherst: University of Massachusetts Press, 2001.

Gutman, Herbert G. *The Black Family in Slavery and Freedom.* New York: Random House, 1976.

Hagedorn, Anne. *Beyond the River: The Untold Story of the Heroes of the Underground Railroad.* New York: Simon and Schuster, 2002.

Harris, N. Dwight. *The History of Negro Servitude in Illinois and of the Slavery Agitation in that State 1719 to 1864.* Chicago: A. C. McClurg, 1904.

Hart, Albert Bushnell. *Commonwealth History of Massachusetts.* 1927. Reprint, New York: Russell & Russell, 1966.

Haviland, Laura S. *A Woman's Life Work.* Cincinnati: Walden and Stowe, 1882.

Hearn, Chester G. *When the Devil Came Down to Dixie: Ben Butler in New Orleans.* Baton Rouge: Louisiana State University Press, 1997.

Hedrick, Joan D. 1994. *Harriet Beecher Stowe: A Life.* New York. Oxford University Press, 1994.

Hendrick, George, and Willene Hendrick, eds. *Fleeing for Freedom: Stories of the Underground Railroad/As Told by Levi Coffin and William Still.* Chicago: Ivan R. Dee, c.2004.

Hill, Daniel G. *The Freedom-seekers: Blacks in Early Canada.* Agincourt: Book Society of Canada, 1981.

Horsman, Reginald. *Race and Manifest Destiny: The Origins of American Racial Anglo-Saxonism.* Cambridge: Harvard University Press, 1981.

Horton, James O. *Free People of Color: Inside the African American Community.* Washington, D.C.: Smithsonian Institution Press, 1993.

Horton, James, and Lois E. Horton. *Black Bostonians: Family Life and Struggle in the Antebellum North.* New York: Holmes & Meier, 1999.

Horton, Colonel John Benjamin. *Old War Horse of

Kentucky: The Life and Achievements of Albert Ernest Meyzeek. Louisville: J. Benjamin Horton and Associates, 1986.

Howard, Victor B. *Black Liberation in Kentucky: Emancipation and Freedom, 1862–1864.* Lexington: University Press of Kentucky, 1983.

_____. *The Evangelical War against Slavery and Caste: The Life and Times of John G. Fee.* Selinsgrove, PA: Susquehanna University Press, 1996.

Howard-Filler, Saralee R. "Detroit's Underground Railroad and the Museum of African American History." *Michigan History* 71(1987): 28–29.

Hudson, J. Blaine. *Fugitive Slaves and the Underground Railroad in the Kentucky Borderland.* Jefferson, NC: McFarland, 2002.

Huggins, Nathan I. *Black Odyssey: The African American Ordeal in Slavery.* New York: Vintage Books, 1990.

Inikori, J. E., ed. *Forced Migration: The Impact of the Export Slave Trade on African Societies.* New York: Africana, 1982.

Jacobs, Donald M., ed. *Courage and Conscience: Black and White Abolitionists in Boston.* Indianapolis, IN: Indiana University Press, 1993.

Jones, Howard. *Mutiny on the Amistad: The Saga of a Slave Revolt and its Impact on American Abolition, Law, and Diplomacy.* New York: Oxford University Press, 1987.

Jordan, Winthrop D. *The White Man's Burden: Historical Origins of Racism in the United States.* New York: Oxford University Press, 1974.

_____. *White over Black: American Attitudes toward the Negro, 1550-1812.* New York: W. W. Norton, 1968.

Katz, William Loren. *Black Indians: A Hidden Heritage.* New York: Atheneum, 1986.

_____. *Black Women of the Old West.* New York: Atheneum, 1995.

King, Wilma. *Toward the Promised Land: From Uncle Tom's Cabin to the Onset of the Civil War (1851–1861).* New York: Chelsea House, 1995.

Klein, Herbert. *African Slavery in Latin America and the Caribbean.* New York: Oxford University Press, 1986.

Klein, Philip Shriver. *A History of Pennsylvania.* University Park, PA: Pennsylvania State University Press, 1980.

Knoblock, Glenn A. *"Strong and Brave Fellows": New Hampshire's Black Soldiers and Sailors of the American Revolution, 1775–1784.* Jefferson, NC: McFarland, 2003.

Kolchin, Peter. *American Slavery: 1619 — 1877.* New York: Hill and Wang, 1993.

Korngold, Ralph. Thaddeus *Stevens: A Being Darkly Wise and Rudely Great.* New York: Harcourt, Brace, 1955.

Kutler, Stanley I., ed. *The Supreme Court and the Constitution: Readings in American Constitutional History.* New York: W. W. Norton, 1989.

Lamon, Lester C. *Blacks in Tennessee, 1791–1970.* Knoxville: University of Tennessee Press, 1981.

Langston, John Mercer. *From the Virginia plantation to the national capitol, or, The first and only Negro representative in Congress from the Old Dominion.* Hartford, CT: American, 1894.

Leaming, Hugo P. *Hidden Americans: Maroons of Virginia and the Carolinas.* New York: Garland, 1995.

Levine, Robert S. *Martin Delany, Frederick Douglass, and the Politics of Representative Identity.* Chapel Hill, NC: University of North Carolina Press, 1997.

Levy, Leonard W. *The Law of the Commonwealth and Chief Justice Shaw.* Cambridge: Harvard University Press, 1957.

Lewis, Georgina King Stoughton. *John Greenleaf Whittier: His Life and Work.* Port Washington, NY: Kennikat Press, 1972.

Lovett, Bobby L. *The African American History of Nashville, Tennessee, 1780–1930.* Fayettsville, AR: University of Arkansas Press, 1999.

Lucas, Ernestine G. *Wider Windows to the Past: African American History from a Family Perspective.* Decorah, IA: Anundsen, 1995.

Lucas, Marion B. *A History of Blacks in Kentucky.* Vol. 1 of *From Slavery to Segregation, 1760–1891.* Frankfort: Kentucky Historical Society, 1992.

Malone, Dumas. *Jefferson and His Time, Volume Six: The Sage of Monticello.* Boston: Little, Brown, 1981.

May, Samuel J. *The Fugitive Slave Law and Its Victims.* New York: American Anti-Slavery Society, 1861.

_____. *Some Recollections of Our Anti-Slavery Conflict.* 1869. Reprint, New York: Arno Press, 1968.

McCall, Samuel W. *Thaddeus Stevens.* New York: Houghton, Mifflin, 1899.

McCulloch, Margaret C. *Fearless Advocate of the Right: The Life of Francis Julius LeMoyne, M.D., 1798–1879.* Boston: Christopher Publishing House, 1941.

McDougall, Marion G. *Fugitive Slaves, 1619–1865.* 1891. Reprint, New York, Bergman, 1967.

McPherson, James M. *The Negro's Civil War.* New York: Ballantine Books, 1965.

Miller, Alphonse B. *Thaddeus Stevens.* New York: Harper & Brothers, 1939.

Mintz, Sidney. W. *Sweetness and Power: The Place of Sugar in Modern History.* New York: Viking Press, 1985.

Mitchell, William M. *The Under-Ground Railroad.* London, 1860.

Mooney, Chase C. *Slavery in Tennessee* (Westport, CT: Universities Press, 1971 (first published in 1957).

Moore, William F., and Jane A., Moore, eds. *His Brother's Blood: Speeches and Writings, 1838–64, of Owen Lovejoy.* Urbana, IL: University of Illinois Press, 2004.

Moses, Wilson Jeremiah. *The Golden Age of Black Nationalism, 1850–1925.* New York: Oxford University Press, 1978.

Mullin, Gerald W. *Flight and Rebellion: Slave Resistance in Eighteenth Century Virginia.* New York: Oxford University Press, 1972.

Nash, Gary B. *First City: Philadelphia and the Forging of Historical Memory.* Philadelphia: University of Pennsylvania Press, 2002.

_____. *Forging Freedom: The Formation of Philadelphia's Black Community, 1720–1840.* Cambridge, MA: Harvard University Press, 1988.

_____. *Race, Class, and Politics: Essays on American Colonial and Revolutionary Society.* Urbana, IL: University of Illinois Press, 1986.

National Historic Landmarks Survey. *Underground Railroad Resources in the United States.* Washington, D.C.: U. S. Department of the Interior, 1998.

National Park Service. *Researching and Interpreting the Underground Railroad.* Washington, D.C.: U.S. Government Printing Office, 1999.

_____. *Underground Railroad: Special Resource Study.* Washington, D.C.: U.S. Government Printing Office, 1995.

Nichols, Charles H., ed. *Black Men in Chains: Narratives by Escaped Slaves.* New York: L. Hill, 1972.

Oates, Stephen B. *The Fires of Jubilee: Nat Tuner's Fierce Rebellion.* New York: Mentor Books, 1975.

Omi, Michael, and Howard Winant. *Racial Formation in the United States.* New York: Routledge, 1986.

Ortiz, Victoria. *Sojourner Truth: A Self-Made Woman.* New York: Lippincott, 1974.

Osagie, Iyunolu F. *The Amistad Revolt: Memory, Slavery, and the Politics of Identity in the United States and Sierra Leone.* Athens, GA: University of Georgia Press, 2000.

Owen, William A. *Black Mutiny: The Revolt on the Schooner Amistad.* Baltimore, MD: Black Classic Press, 1997.

Patterson, Orlando. *Slavery and Social Death.* Cambridge: Harvard University Press, 1982.

Payne, Charles E. *Josiah Bushnell Grinnell.* Iowa City: State Historical Society of Iowa, 1938.

Payne, Daniel A. *History of the African Methodist Episcopal Church.* Nashville, TN: Publishing House of the AME Sunday School Union, 1891.

_____. *Recollections of Seventy Years.* Nashville, TN: Publishing House of the AME Sunday School Union, 1888.

Peck, Elisabeth S. *Berea's First Century, 1855–1955.* Lexington: University of Kentucky Press, 1955.

Pelton, Louise. *A Brief History of Berea College.* Berea, KY: N.p., 1963.

Peters, Pamela R. *The Underground Railroad in Floyd County, Indiana.* Jefferson, NC: McFarland, 2001.

Pettit, Eber M. *Sketches in the History of the Underground Railroad.* 1879. Reprint, Freeport, NY: Books for Libraries Press, 1971.

Philbrik, Francis S., ed. *The Laws of Indiana Territory, 1801–1809.* Illinois Historical Collections, Vol. 21. Reprinted by the Indiana Historical Society, 1931.

Phillips, Ullrich B. "The Slave Economy of the Old South," in Eugene D. Genovese, ed., *Selected Essays in Economic and Social History.* Baton Rouge: Louisiana State University Press, 1968.

Postell, William D. *The Health of Slaves on Southern Plantations.* Baton Rouge: Louisiana State University Press, 1951.

Price, Richard, ed. *Maroon Societies: Rebel Slave Communities in the Americas.* Baltimore, MD: Johns Hopkins University Press, 1996.

Quarles, Benjamin. *Black Abolitionists.* New York: Oxford University Press, 1969.

_____. *The Negro in the American Revolution.* Chapel Hill, NC: University of North Carolina Press, 1961.

Reid, Robert L., ed. *Always a River: The Ohio River and the American Experience.* Bloomington, IN: Indiana University Press, 1991.

Reynolds, David S. *John Brown, Abolitionist.* New York: Knopf, 2005.

Reynolds, Edward. *Stand the Storm: A History of the Atlantic Slave Trade.* London: W. H. Allen, 1985.

Rhodes, Jane. *Mary Ann Shadd Cary: The Black Press and Protest in the Nineteenth Century.* Bloomington, IN: Indiana University Press, 1998.

Robertson, David. *Denmark Vesey.* New York: Alfred A. Knopf, 1999.

Rodney, Walter. *How Europe Underdeveloped Africa.* Washington: Howard University Press, 1974.

Rogozinski, J. *A Brief History of the Caribbean: From the Arawak and the Carib to the Present.* New York: Facts on File, 1992.

Ross, Alexander M. *Recollections and Experiences of an Abolitionist; From 1855 to 1865.* Toronto: Rowsell & Hutchinson, 1875.

Runyon, Randolph. *Delia Webster and the Underground Railroad.* Lexington: University Press of Kentucky, 1996.

Sale, K. *The Conquest of Paradise: Christopher Columbus and the Columbian Legacy.* New York: Plume, 1990.

Salt, H. S., ed. *Anti-Slavery and Reform Papers by Henry David Thoreau.* London: Swan Sonnenschein, 1890.

Sanders, R. *Lost Tribes and Promised Lands: The Origins of American Racism.* New York: HarperPerennial, 1978.

Scharf, J. Thomas, and Thompson Westcott. *History of Philadelphia, 1609–1884.* Philadelphia: L.H. Everts, 1884.

Schneider, Richard J., ed. *Henry David Thoreau: A Documentary Volume*. Detroit: Gale, 2004.

Schor, Joel. *Henry Highland Garnet: A Voice of Black Radicalism in the Nineteenth Century*. Westport, CT.: Greenwood Press, 1977.

Sears, Richard D. *Camp Nelson, Kentucky: A Civil War History*. Lexington, KY: University Press of Kentucky, 2002.

_____. *A Utopian Experiment in Kentucky: Integration and Social Equality at Berea, 1866–1904*. Westport, CT: Greenwood Press, 1996.

Shillington, Kevin. *History of Africa*. New York: St. Martin's Press, 1989.

Siebert, Wilbur H. *The Mysteries of Ohio's Underground Railroads*. Columbus, Ohio: Ohio State University, 1951.

_____. *The Underground Railroad from Slavery to Freedom*. 1898. Reprint, New York: Russell and Russell, 1967.

_____. *Vermont's Anti-Slavery and Underground Railroad Record*. New York, Negro Universities Press, 1937.

Silverman, Jason H. *Unwelcome Guests: Canada West's Response to American Fugitive Slaves, 1800–1865*. Port Washington, NY: Associated Faculty Press, 1985.

Simmons, William J. *Men of Mark: Eminent, Progressive and Rising*. Cleveland, OH: George M. Rewell, 1887.

Simpson, J. Mc. C. *The Emancipation Car, Being an Original Composition of Anti-slavery Ballads, Composed Exclusively for the Underground Railroad*. Miami, FL: Mnemosyne, 1969.

Slaughter, Thomas P. *Bloody Dawn: The Christiana Riot and Racial Violence in the Antebellum North*. New York: Oxford University Press, 1991.

Smedley, R. C. *History of the Underground Railroad*. 1883. Reprint, New York: Arno Press, 1969.

Southern, Eileen. *The Music of Black America: A History*. New York: W. W. Norton, 1971.

Sprague, Stuart S., ed. *His Promised Land: The Autobiography of John P. Parker, former Slave and Conductor on the Underground Railroad*. New York: W. W. Norton, 1996.

Stanley, Jerry. *Hurry Freedom: African Americans in Gold Rush California*. New York: Crown, 2000.

Starling, Marion W. *The Slave Narrative: Its Place in American History*. Washington: Howard University Press, 1988.

Stevens, Charles Emery. *Anthony Burns: A History*. 1856. Reprint, New York: Arno Press, 1969.

Stevens, Elizabeth C. *Elizabeth Buffum Chace and Lillie Chace Wyman: A Century of Abolitionist, Suffragist and Workers' Rights Activism*. Jefferson, NC: McFarland, 2003.

Stevenson, Brenda E. *Life in Black and White: Family and Community in the Slave South*. New York: Oxford University Press, 1996.

Stewart, James B. *Joshua R. Giddings and the Tac-tics of Radical Politics*. Cleveland: Press of Case Western Reserve University, 1970.

_____. *Wendell Phillips, Liberty's Hero*. Baton Rouge: Louisiana State University Press, 1986.

Still, William. *The Underground Railroad*. 1872. Reprint, Chicago: Johnson, 1970.

Storey, Moorfield. *Charles Sumner*. New York: Houghton-Mifflin, 1900.

Stowe, Harriet Beecher. *The Key to Uncle Tom's Cabin*. 1854. Reprint, Salem, NH: Ayer, 1987.

_____. *Uncle Tom's Cabin*. 1852. Reprint, New York: Modern Library, 1996.

Strangis, Joel. *Lewis Hayden and the War Against Slavery*. North Haven, CT: Linnet Books, 1999.

Strother, Horatio T. *The Underground railroad in Connecticut*. Middletown, CT: Wesleyan University Press, 1962.

Swisshelm, Jane Grey Cannon. *Half a Century*. Chicago: Jansen, McClurg, 1880.

Switala, William J. *Underground Railroad in Delaware, Maryland, and West Virginia*. Mechanicsburg, PA: Stackpole Books, 2004.

_____. *Underground Railroad in Pennsylvania*. Mechanicsburg, PA: Stackpole Books, 2001.

Thomas, Alexander, and Samuel Sillen. *Racism and Psychiatry*. New York: Citadel Press, 1972.

Thompson, Julius Eric. *Hiram R. Revels, 1827–1901: A Biography*. New York: Arno Press, 1982.

Thompson, Victor B. *The Making of the African Diaspora in the Americas, 1441–1900*. New York: Longman, 1987.

Thornbrough, Emma L. *The Negro in Indiana before 1900*. Bloomington: Indiana University Press, 1957.

Thwaites, R. G., ed. *Original Journals of the Lewis and Clark Expedition, 1804-1806*, 8 vols. New York: Dodd, Mead, 1904–1905.

Tobin, Jacqueline L., and Raymond G. Dobard. *Hidden in Plain View: A Secret Story of Quilts and the Underground Railroad*. New York: Doubleday, 1999.

Trotter, Joe W. Jr. *River Jordan: African American Urban Life in the Ohio Valley*. Lexington: University Press of Kentucky, 1998.

Twyman, Bruce E. *The Black Seminole Legacy and North American Politics, 1693–1845*. Washington, D.C.: Howard University Press, 1999.

Ullman, Victor. *Martin R. Delany: The Beginnings of Black Nationalism*. Boston: Beacon Press, 1971.

Villard, Oswald Garrison. *John Brown 1800–1859: A Biography Fifty Years After*. 1910. Reprint, Gloucester, MA: Peter Smith, 1965.

Voss, Frederick, and James Barber. *We Never Sleep: The First Fifty Years of the Pinkertons*. Washington, D.C.: Smithsonian Institution Press, 1981.

Voss, Frederick, and Barber, James. *We Never Sleep: The First Fifty Years of the Pinkertons* (Washington, D.C.: Smithsonian Institution Press, 1981).

Wade, Richard C. *Slavery in the Cities: The South,*

1820–1860. New York: Oxford University Press, 1969.

Waldstreicher, David. *Runaway America: Benjamin Franklin, Slavery, and the American Revolution.* New York: Hill and Wang, 2004.

Walker, Jonathan. *The Branded Hand; Trial and Imprisonment of Jonathan Walker.* 1845. Reprint, New York: Arno Press, 1969.

Walther, Rudolph. *Happenings in ye Olde Philadelphia 1680–1900.* Philadelphia: Walther Printing House, 1825.

Walvin, James. *Black and White: The Negro and English Society 1555–1945.* London: Allan Lane the Penguin Press, 1973.

Ward, Samuel Ringgold. *Autobiography of a Fugitive Negro: His Anti-Slavery Labours in the United States, Canada, & England.* London: John Snow, 1855.

Weeden, Henry C. *Weeden's History of the Colored People of Louisville.* Louisville: H. C. Weeden, 1897.

Weisenburger, Steven. *Modern Medea: A Family Story of Slavery and Child-Murder from the Old South.* New York: Hill and Wang, 1998.

Wellman, Judith. *Grass Roots Reform in the Burned-Over District in Upstate New York: Religion, Abolitionism, and Democracy.* New York: Garland, 2000.

Wilhelm, Paul, Duke of Wurttemburg. *Travels in North America, 1822–1824.* 1824. Reprint, Norman, OK: University of Oklahoma, 1973.

Williams, Eric. *From Columbus to Castro: The History of the Caribbean, 1492–1969.* London: Andre Deutsch, 1970.

Williams, George Washington. *History of the Negro Race in America.* 1883. Reprint, New York: Bergmann, 1968.

Wilson, Henry. *History of the Anti-Slavery Measures of the Thirty-Seventh and Thirty-Eighth Congresses, 1861–64.* 1864. Reprint, New York: Negro Universities Press, 1964.

Winant, Howard. *Racial Conditions.* Minneapolis: University of Minnesota Press, 1994.

Winks, Robin W. *Blacks in Canada: A History.* New Haven, CT: 1971.

Winsor, Justin, ed. *The Memorial History of Boston, including Suffolk County, Massachusetts, 1630–1880.* Boston: N.p., 1880.

Wolseley, Roland E. *The Black Press, U. S. A.* Ames, IA: Iowa State University Press, 1991.

Work, John Wesley. *American Negro Songs and Spirituals.* Mineoloa, NY: Dover, 1940.

Wright, Donald R. *African Americans in the Colonial Era: From African Origins through the American Revolution.* Arlington Heights, IL: Harlan Davidson, 1990.

Wright, J. Leitch, Jr. *Creeks and Seminoles: The Destruction and Regeneration of the Muscolgulge People.* Lincoln, NE: University of Nebraska Press, 1986.

Wyatt-Brown, Bertram. *Lewis Tappan and the Evangelical War Against Slavery.* Cleveland: Press of Case Western Reserve University, 1969.

Yacovone, Donald. *Samuel Joseph May and the Dilemmas of the Liberal Persuasion, 1797–1871.* Philadelphia: Temple University Press, 1991.

Young, Elizabeth. *Disarming the Nation: Women's Writing and the American Civil War.* Chicago: University of Chicago Press, 1999.

Youngken, Richard C. *African Americans in Newport: An Introduction to the Heritage of African Americans in Newport; Rhode Island 1700–1945.* Providence: Rhode Island Historical Preservation & Heritage Commission, Rhode Island Black Heritage Society, 1995.

Zirblis, Raymond Paul. *Friends of Freedom: The Vermont Underground Railroad Survey Report.* Montpelier: Vermont Department of State Buildings, Vermont Division for Historic Preservation, 1996.

Index